Anthony Blunt

His Lives

WITHDRAWN

'The book is good and renders superfluous all others on the subject. These Miss Carter has tested against reason, probability and
her own enquiries, enlisted their material when she has found it
sound, dismissed it when not, setting the fact against the innuendo,
woven it all together with admirable clarity and produced 500
pages that almost make a ripping yarn. The curt chapter headings
– Son, Schoolboy, Undergraduate, Fellow Traveller, Recruit –
indicate something of her orderly thought and style, and rarely are
there longueurs to hasten the turning of the page.'
Brian Sewell, *Evening Standard*

'Finely researched . . . the scruple, the clarity of Carter's narrative of
Communist enlistments at Cambridge would be hard to better . . .
thoughtful and thorough.' George Steiner, *TLS*

'An enthralling work . . . written with a dry sense of humour and
a sure grasp of a wide range of material'
Richard Gott, *New Statesman*

'Impressively researched . . . an awesomely confident debut'
Paul Bailey, *Daily Telegraph*

Miranda Carter, whose first book this is, has written a shrewd,
informed and stylish life of a complex and enigmatic figure. She is
diligent, through, generous in detail, and scrupulously fair in her
judgments.' John Banville, *Irish Times*

For John and Finn

Anthony Blunt

His Lives

MIRANDA CARTER

Pan Books

First published 2001 by Macmillan

This edition published 2002 by Pan Books
an imprint of Pan Macmillan
20 New Wharf Road, London N1 9RR
Associated companies throughout the world
www.panmacmillan.com

ISBN 978-0-330-36766-0

Copyright © Miranda Carter 2001

The right of Mirander Carter to be identified as the
author of this work has been asserted by her in accordance
with the Copyright, Designs and Patents Act 1988.

11

A CIP catalogue record for this book is available from
the British Library.

Typeset by SetSystems Ltd, Saffron Walden, Essex
Printed and bound by CPI Group (UK) Ltd, Croydon, CR0 4YY

Visit www.panmacmillan.com to read more about all our books and to buy
them. You will also find features, author interviews and news of any author
events, and you can sign up for e-newsletters so that you're always first to hear
about our new releases.

Acknowledgements

I would particularly like to thank Blunt's executor, John Golding. This book could not have been written without his help.

I would also like to thank all the people whom I interviewed during my research. Their testimonies, of which I have made profuse and unashamed use, are the marrow of this book. Professor Christopher Andrew, Lord Annan, Jack Baer, Olivier and Quentin Bell, Sir Isaiah Berlin, David Bindman, John Blamey, Tom Bower, Sir Alan Bowness, Helen Braham, Desmond Bristow, Anita Brookner, Howard Capes, Robin Chancellor, Lord Charteris, Monique Chatenet, Professor Andrew Ciechanowiecki, Thomas Cocke, Rosalys Coope, Professor Joseph Connors, John Craxton, Norah David, His Grace the Duke of Devonshire, The Dowager Lady Egremont, Caroline Elam, Charles Elwell, Gavin Ewart, Denis Farr, John Fleming, Sibylla Jane Flower, Sir Edward Ford, Kenneth Garlick, Sir Ernst Gombrich, St John Gore, Michael Grant, Rosamund Griffin, Sir Stuart Hampshire, Jenifer Hart, Francis Haskell, Elizabeth Haslock, Alethea Hayter, Eric Hebborn, Jack Hewit, Derek Hill, Baronness Hilton, Michael Hirst, Clive Hislop, Hugh Honour, Lord Hunt, Sidney Hutchinson, Michael Jaffe, Stephen Rees Jones, Martha Kelleher, Francis King, Dick Kingzett, Raymond Klibansky, Richard Krautheimer, Michel Laclotte, Alastair Laing, James Lees-Milne, Sir Michael Levey, Lesley Lewis, Andrew Lownie, Alastair Macdonald, Neil MacGregor, Polly Maguire, Charles Madge, Sir Denis Mahon, Hugh Massingberd, Anne Marie Meyer, Leonard Miall, Erica O'Donnell, Edward Penning-Rowsell, Nicholas Penny, Sir Edward Playfair, Peter Pollock, Barbara Proctor, Kathleen Raine, John Richardson, Barbara Robertson, Pierre Rosenberg, Mark Roskill,

Acknowledgements

Miriam Rothschild, Tess Rothschild, Michael Rubinstein, John Russell, Charles Rycroft, Dadie Rylands, John Shearman, Peter Smith, Lindsay Stainton, Jon Stallworthy, John Steer, Michael Straight, Michael Parke-Taylor, Roddy Thesiger, David Thomson, Giles Waterfield, John White, Mary Whiteley, Sarah Whitfield, Frank Whitford, Simon Wilson, Margaret Wind, Christopher Wright, Richard Wollheim, Dikker Worcester, George Zarnecki, and a number of others who prefer to go unnamed. I owe further thanks to everyone who wrote to me, especially the former Courtauld students who sent me their recollections of Blunt, and also George Curry, Alan Berends, Lord Dacre and Sir Michael Levey. Any errors of fact or interpretation are of course, all mine.

I owe special a debt of gratitude to Peter Kidson, Brian Simon, Richard Verdi, and the late Michael Kitson. Barrie Penrose, who as a *Sunday Times* journalist broke many of the spy stories of the early 1980s and then, with Simon Freeman, wrote the first proper account of Blunt's spying, generously gave me his interview transcripts – allowing me, among other things, to read interviews with people who had long since died. Rupert Allason, aka Nigel West, answered many of my queries and passed me his copies of documents from the Russian Intelligence Archives. Thanks to Peter Parker, Nick Jenkins, Kate Bucknell, Edward Mendelson, Tom Henry, Jeremy Lewis, Alexandra Chaldecott, Adam Sisman. Thanks to my agent Bill Hamilton, for all his help, and especially to my excellent and long-suffering editor Georgina Morley, who has stuck with me cheerfully through the years.

I would like to thank Marlborough College and its former archivist David West; King's College Cambridge; and the Courtauld Institute. At the Courtauld, Professor Eric Fernie, Jane Ferguson, and most of all its former archivist Susan Scott, all went beyond the call of duty in helping me.

Extracts from Anthony Blunt's writings, his papers at the Courtauld Institute, the Lee papers and the Courtauld registry papers are reprinted by permission of the Courtauld Institute and Blunt's literary executor, John Golding. Extracts from the archives of the Colonial and Continental Church Society, Guildhall Ms,

Acknowledgements

are reprinted by permission of the Guildhall Library, Corporation of London. Extracts from the Isaiah Berlin Papers, Bodleian Library, Oxford, are reprinted by permission of the Isaiah Berlin Literary Trust. Extracts from W. H. Auden's *Collected Poems* are reprinted by permission of Faber and Faber. Extracts from W. H. Auden's unpublished writings, copyright The Estate of W. H. Auden, are reprinted by permission of Edward Mendelson. Extracts from *Letters from Iceland* by W. H. Auden and Louis MacNeice are reprinted by permission of Faber and Faber and David Higham Associates. Extracts from Louis MacNeice's *The Strings Are False* and *Collected Poems* are reprinted by permission of Faber and Faber and David Higham Associates. Extracts from Louis MacNeice's unpublished letters, copyright the Estate of Louis MacNeice, are reprinted by permission of David Higham Associates. Extracts from *Summoned by Bells* by John Betjeman are reprinted by permission of John Murray (Publishers) Ltd. Letters from Ezra Pound to Anthony Blunt, copyright © 2001 Mary De Rachewiltz and Omar S. Pound, are used by permission of New Directions Publishing Corporation. Papers from the Royal Archives are used by gracious permission of Her Majesty the Queen. Lord Crawford's unpublished article is used by permission of the NACF. Extracts from the diary of Ben Nicolson are printed by permission of Vanessa Nicolson. Extracts from the Bell and Charleston papers at King's College Library, Cambridge, are reprinted by permission of the Society of Authors. Extracts from the Rudi Wittkower papers are reprinted by permission of Columbia University and Joseph Connors. Extracts from the Edgar Wind papers are reprinted by permission of Margaret Wind and the Bodleian Library, Oxford. Extracts from Margot Wittkower's interview in the Getty Research Institute's *Interviews with Art Historians* are reprinted by permission of the Library, Getty Research Institute, Los Angeles, 94109. Extracts from *A Chapter of Accidents* by Goronwy Rees published by Chatto & Windus are reprinted by permission of David Higham Associates. Extracts from *Married to a Single Life* by Wilfrid Blunt published by Michael Russell are quoted by permission of the Estate of Wilfrid

Acknowledgements

Blunt. Extracts from *Conspiracy of Silence* by Barrie Penrose and Simon Freeman are reprinted by permission of HarperCollins. Extracts from the unpublished writings of J. M. Keynes, copyright © 2001 The Provost and Scholars of King's College, Cambridge. Extracts from the letters of Denis Mahon are reprinted by kind permission of the author. Extracts from letters and papers of Anthony Blunt, Fritz Saxl and Rudolph Wittkower in the Archives of the Warburg Institute, London, are reprinted by permission of the Warburg Institute. Extracts from the Blunt file at the BBC Written Archives Centre come by kind permission of the BBC. Extracts from Cecil Gould's memoir of Anthony Blunt copyright © 2001 The Estate of Cecil Gould, reprinted by kind permission of Sir Michael Levey on behalf of the Estate.

Every effort has been made to contact all copyright holders of material in this book. If any have been inadvertently overlooked, the publishers will be pleased to make the necessary arrangement at the first opportunity.

Contents

Contents

List of Illustrations

Section One

1. Blunt's house photograph of 1926. (*Marlborough College Archives*)
2. Blunt c. 1926. (*John Hilton*)
3. Clifford Canning. (*King's College Library, Cambridge*)
4. The 'enchanting' Michael Robertson. (*King's College Library, Cambridge*)
5. Blunt and MacNeice's study at Marlborough, c. 1925. (*King's College Library, Cambridge*)
6. Louis MacNeice in Oxford, c. 1926. (*King's College Library, Cambridge*)
7. The Marlborough *Heretick* (1924) and the Cambridge *Venture* (1928). (*Marlborough College Archives and The Courtauld Institute*)
8. Blunt in drag, June 1929. (*By permission of the Syndics of Cambridge University Library*)
9. Dadie Rylands. (*King's College Library, Cambridge*)
10. Blunt with second-generation Cambridge Bloomsbury. (*Courtesy of Frances Partridge*)
11. The younger members of the Apostles, c. early 1932. (*Peter Lofts*)
12–15. Blunt's Cambridge contemporaries: Michael Straight, Tess Mayor, John Cornford, Guy Burgess. (*Peter Lofts*)
16. Donald Maclean. (*Copyright © Hulton Deutsch*)
17. Kim Philby. (*Copyright © Bettman/CORBIS*)
18. Arthur Marshall. (*Peter Lofts*)
19. Victor Rothschild. (*Peter Lofts*)
20. Picasso's *Guernica*. (*Copyright © Succession Picasso/DACS 2001; Burstein Collection/Corbis*)

Prologue

From the moment of his exposure as a former Russian spy by the Prime Minister, Margaret Thatcher, in November 1979, Anthony Blunt became a man about whom anything could be said.

He was described as 'the spy with no shame'. He was 'an arrogant evil poseur'. He was a 'treacherous Communist poof'. It was rumoured that at Cambridge he had seduced and blackmailed impressionable undergraduates into serving his nefarious schemes. He had been responsible for the deaths of forty-nine wartime Dutch Special Operations agents behind enemy lines; he might, indeed, have been responsible for any number of deaths. He had been involved in devious conspiracies with Louis Mountbatten – possibly to put Mountbatten's relatives on the thrones of Europe after the Second World War. He had salted away a fortune abroad. He had brought about the suicide of one of his students, Virginia Lee. He had been a predatory homosexual, or even a paedophile with links to the Kincora children's home scandal in Northern Ireland; he had blackmailed the Establishment into granting him immunity from prosecution by threatening to reveal proof that the Duke of Windsor had been plotting with the Nazis during the Second World War; he had been an authenticator of forgeries, and had connived with the French picture dealer Georges Wildenstein to sell a fake Georges de la Tour to the Metropolitan Museum of Art in New York; he had stolen the credit for a book on Picasso from a pupil and colleague, Phoebe Pool; he had borrowed money from his friend Victor Rothschild to buy a Poussin, and never repaid it; he had cheated the elderly Duncan Grant out of a Poussin he had owned, subsequently using his influence to get an export licence to sell the picture at a hugely inflated price to a gallery in Canada; he had engineered the Courtauld Institute's move to Somerset House in the Strand in order to deprive the country of a Turner museum, as part of a fiendish plot to 'relegate British art to a secondary position'.*

After his exposure, Blunt became a kind of screen on which fiction and fantasy were projected. There was little he could do about this. After the publication of one of the more extravagant stories he asked his lawyer, Michael Rubinstein, if he had any legal recourse, and was told that he did not: he had lost his good name, and it would therefore be impossible to sue for libel. He had in effect so defamed himself that no further defamation was possible.

That was one of the main factors which helped to obscure the truth about Blunt after his downfall. Another was his sheer usefulness as a hate figure. At the time of his exposure the Cold War had led to a polarization of intellectual and political life so absolute that it was entirely taken for granted by all participants. For the Right in Britain, invigorated by Mrs Thatcher's victory in the general election of May 1979, Blunt was the apotheosis of a particular species of privileged, ungrateful, over-educated, unpatriotic, left-wing intellectual – and homosexual to boot. He embodied the hypocrisy of a liberal class which gave thanks for its inherited freedoms by betraying them. The press harped on about the naturally lax, relativistic morals of intellectuals and their automatic assumption that they were better than anyone else; these were the obvious reasons for Blunt's misdeeds. 'Less intellectual people have simpler ideas and more direct instincts,' one Thatcherite intellectual wrote. Blunt became defined as a caricature of his class (privileged, therefore overindulged), his calling (academic, therefore elitist and snobbish) and his sexual orientation (homosexual, therefore predatory and wedded to

* Most recently, in her autobiography, *The Truth at Last*, Christine Keeler has claimed, most improbably, that her sometime 'protector' Stephen Ward, who committed suicide in the midst of the Profumo scandal in which they were both deeply involved, was Blunt's controller.

secrets). Sometimes the results were unintentionally hilarious: *Mask of Treachery*, a prurient, feverishly homophobic, wildly fantastical (if interminable – at 761 pages) spy biography by the late journalist-turned-'contemporary historian' John Costello was subtitled in the USA 'Lies, Spies, Buggery and Betrayal'. The caricature continues to this day: 'Pampered with an upper class education and a comfortable lifestyle,' runs one entry for Blunt in a recent internet history of espionage, 'Anthony Blunt embraced espionage as easily as he would later accept the honours of the country he betrayed. An arrogant intellectual Blunt put himself and his ideas above his loyalty to England. Like most of his class, he felt himself superior to the concept of nations.'

There were other things that could have been said about Blunt; at the time, his friends were reluctant to say them. Many of these friends were in a dilemma. They had no wish to join the rush to public condemnation, but at the same time they were not keen to speak up on Blunt's behalf. For one thing, the torrent of public abuse was so overwhelming that any countervailing voices were drowned out: the publication of one former student's letter of support in *The Times* led to his denunciation for 'moral blindness', and death threats. For another thing, many of Blunt's friends felt personally betrayed by him. He had lied to them, systematically and without any apparent compunction, for as long as he had known them. Even for those who were by no stretch of the imagination Cold Warriors, the fact that he had passed secrets to the Soviet Union at a time when it was allied with Nazi Germany created no strong wish to enter the lists publicly on his behalf.

The fact that Blunt had been a spy, of course, muddied the waters from the start. Espionage seems naturally to attract conspiracy theorists and fantasists; but even serious would-be chroniclers have for the most part been forced to rely – in the absence of reliable information from British Intelligence – on the fallible, sometimes deliberately misleading, and often entirely self-serving memories of former Intelligence officers. In the last few years the Russian Intelligence Archives have made available more information about Blunt and his fellow spies, but they have kept the publication of material under careful control, making their information available only to those whom they choose – notably former KGB officers, the relatives of former KGB officers and former Cold Warrior spy writers. (It is a peculiar irony that, since the end of the Cold War, these spy writers and former KGB officers have found they have more in common with each other than with anyone else.) They have also given no indication of how complete their disclosures are. In this field, no one with information gives it without a strong reason, and the first question to ask of any revelation is always, *cui bono*?

The factor which most persistently kept Blunt a mystery, however, was his own fundamental mysteriousness, the fact that even to his friends he was an enigma. They were well aware that there were many things they did not know about him. 'I worked with him for thirty years, but I never felt I really knew him,' his deputy director at the Courtauld Institute of Art, George Zarnecki, said later. There were plenty of others who felt the same way. This was no accident. Blunt had spent much of his life in flight from being known and understood. He was a habitual compartmentalizer and withdrawer from the world. In contrast to the volumes of emotional autobiographical memoir left by the Bloomsbury Group – whom he knew and by whom he was fascinated in his early youth – Blunt left extraordinarily few permanent personal traces of himself. It was as if he had spent years trying to excise himself from the record. His letters were almost always undated and almost always empty of personal detail; his 'official' communications to his staff at the Courtauld were as ephemeral as it was possible to be, scribbled in the lightest pencil on torn scraps of paper. His prose style was as cool and impersonal as he could make it. His few attempts at memoir were exasperatingly pedestrian and clumsy, as if the effort of examining and explaining himself was both alien and discomfiting. Even in the face of total condemnation and loss of reputation, he resisted the urge to explain. After his exposure he gave one press conference, in which his evasions – some real, some apparent – merely fed the media's appetite for a monster. He seldom spoke about the matter again, and virtually never appeared in public.

Twenty-two years after Blunt's exposure, much has changed. Perhaps the most important of all these changes has been the end of the Cold War. The ideological polarizations which divided almost all political and intellectual life, in Britain as elsewhere, have eased. Blunt's history can be seen in its particularity, rather than as an exemplary (to many, exemplarily hateful) general case. From this new perspective, his life vividly illustrates certain key moments and themes of twentieth-century Britain: intellectual, political, sexual and social. Blunt was a public-school rebel of a near-textbook type; in the 1920s he became a follower of Bloomsbury; in the 1930s a left-wing intellectual; in the 1950s and '60s an impeccably camouflaged man of the Establishment. He turned the Courtauld Institute into a famous centre for research into art history. He was a great teacher who trained a generation of world-class curators and academics. He played a central role in restoring the reputation of the French painter Nicolas Poussin; he wrote several ground-breaking books on French art and architecture and baroque art, and was for decades the most powerful and influential man in British art history. He was homosexual in a world where homosexuality was against the law, and a traitor at a time when the penalty for the crime was death.

Three other factors have made a biography of Blunt possible. One of them is that his friends and colleagues – for the most part – came to forgive or to comprehend or to put in context his spying, and became willing to talk about their memories of him. It would not have been possible to write this book without these testimonies, which I make no apology for stressing throughout my account of Blunt. Another, linked, help in writing this book has been a gradual evolution in attitudes to homosexuality, which has caused friends and lovers of Blunt to speak much more openly about these sides of his life than would once have been possible. A last crucial factor has been the avalanche of material about spying which has been let loose by the end of the Cold War. As I have said, the sources need to be approached with scepticism, but a good deal is now known about Blunt's career as a spy, particularly through the recent publication of information from the Russian Intelligence Archives. I did not want to write a spy book, and hope that I have not done so, but a calmer synopsis of the primary material has become possible, and it is that which I have set out to provide, in the belief that the facts about Blunt are as interesting as any of the fantasies.

It is remarkable that Blunt, in addition to appearing as at least three characters in Louis MacNeice's work, and providing the inspiration for the central figure in Brigid Brophy's novel *The Finishing Touch*, has been the inspiration for two, very different, masterpieces: Alan Bennett's allegory of identity and personality *A Question of Attribution* and John Banville's novel *The Untouchable*, which gives a subtle and compelling voice to Blunt's wilful silence. Non-fiction has, for the most part, served him less well. That, in the end, has been my main reason for writing this book. Blunt said of Kim Philby that 'he only ever had one ambition in life – to be a spy'. While the other Cambridge spies subordinated their lives and careers to espionage, Blunt had a separate life as an art historian quite as, if not more, important to him than his work for the Soviets. I have tried to tell the story of the spying, of the art history, of the self-deception, and other stories besides – not least that of Blunt as a particular type of Englishman in whom almost all emotional effort was diverted into the denial of feeling. The closest thing to an intellectual biography he ever wrote was his academic writing, which traces a retreat from passionately committed Communist politics to a disillusioned embrace of the formal and private. It also sets out – especially in his writing on Poussin – his admiration for the Stoic philosophy which he was to have an opportunity to put into practice in the terrible days after his exposure. 'He lived only for his art and for the company of a very restricted circle of friends who really understood it,' Blunt wrote of his great hero. 'In his old age he cared nothing for what the world thought.' It is one of Blunt's many paradoxes that both his friends and his enemies could with justice regard those words as being utterly typical.

1. Son

'A ceaseless war against drunkenness and cruelty and vice'

For a man whose posthumous reputation would be mired in myths and rumours, Anthony Frederick Blunt had prosaically conventional beginnings. He was born on 26 September 1907, the third of three boys, in Bournemouth. The town's reputation was much the same then as it is now. In 1914, after attending a service at Holy Trinity church – where Blunt's father had formerly been vicar – Rupert Brooke wrote to a friend, 'I have been in this quiet place of invalids and gentlemanly sunsets for about 100 years, ever since yesterday week.' Blunt's father, Stanley, came from a family of impecunious but respectable and devout churchmen on the evangelical wing of the Anglican Church; his mother, Hilda, was from a well-to-do family of civil servants in the Indian Colonial Service. The Blunts were pious, austere, fiercely teetotal, anti-gambling and keen on charitable works. They had no money, but they did have good connections, both inside and outside the Church. They were a junior branch of the Blunts of Crabbet Park, landed gentry with a large estate near Horsham in Sussex, whose incumbent at Anthony's birth was the infamous poet and anti-imperialist Wilfrid Scawen Blunt.

Stanley Blunt was one of nine children, three of whom had died in infancy. Born in 1870, he had grown up in the shadow of his father, Frederick – whose biography (a 'sacred privilege') he had later written – and of his elder brother Walter. Frederick Blunt was a hard-working and successful career churchman who, after being made a canon of York Minster, had risen to become

Suffragan Bishop of Hull in 1891,* having turned down an invitation to become Archbishop of Melbourne, Australia. He had no money – he had scrimped and saved to send his two sons to public school – but he had a talent for making a good impression (a useful quality in a Church in which patrons were still very important) and for public speaking. He was made a chaplain to Queen Victoria in 1881 – an honour given in recognition of impressive preaching skills rather than intimacy with the royal family. 'One of his greatest friends' was Lady Sitwell (aunt of Edith), who travelled round Italy with him in the 1890s; a 'doting German Princess' followed him round the catacombs in Rome. When Stanley was born, Frederick selected a couple of influential Anglican churchmen – Dean Vaughan, a one-time headmaster of Harrow, and Dean Stanley, author of the *Life of Dr Arnold* and champion of the Broad Church movement – as godfathers. At home, however, his children 'saw but little of him except at midday dinner', and on Sundays at teatime, when he spent an hour grilling his children with Bible questions, a practice Stanley continued with his own sons. When the Bishop was home, he was lavished with attention by Stanley's four 'adoring' unmarried sisters and mother, who spent much of the rest of their time in charity work.

According to Stanley, his brother Walter, seven years his senior, 'was acknowledged to have a remarkable personality and brilliant gifts'. The Bishop 'had formed the highest hopes' of his career. As a student at King's College, Cambridge, he had been taken up as a protégé by one of the university's most famous and influential dons, Oscar Browning. (Walter was rather less flattering about Stanley; writing in 1890 to Browning about his undergraduate brother after he had committed some petty misdemeanour, 'He always seemed to me not deeply attached to work or thought but with a right appreciation of what is manly and Christian.') In 1898 Walter died suddenly of scarlet fever, 'the greatest sorrow'

---

* A suffragan bishop is a sort of sub-bishop, appointed to help out in a large diocese, in this case York.

their father 'had ever known'. Stanley, who had followed his father and sibling into the Church, slipped into his brother's shoes once again, taking over the parish of Ham, near Richmond in Surrey, where Walter had previously been vicar. Perhaps it wasn't entirely accidental that, as a child, Anthony's brother Wilfrid confused family photographs of Walter with pictures of Jesus.

Stanley was a 'good mixer' who liked company, an enthusiastic sportsman, and not uncultured: he was an avid concert-goer, and had inherited from his father a taste for history, art and travel. He was 'an effective preacher' with a line in Browning quotations, and he enjoyed performing. He was liked by his parishioners, and when he left Ham he was presented with a rather sugary portrait of his two eldest sons by the painter James Byam Shaw. He was kind to small children, and a soft touch. His eldest son, Wilfrid, felt he had the classic Blunt characteristics: he was 'emotional, sentimental, gullible'. At the same time, all his life Stanley held to the stiff Victorian values that had been instilled in him, and there was little evidence of the liberal thinker he believed himself to be. (Even in the 1920s he regarded the delicate verses of the nineteenth-century aesthete Ernest Dowson as 'degenerate'.) In Stanley's world there was no moral ambiguity. He was sure, as his son Wilfrid recalled, 'that right was right and wrong was wrong, that he knew them apart, and that the twain could never meet'.

In October 1900, at the age of thirty and within two years of becoming vicar of Ham, Stanley married Hilda Master, the twenty-year-old youngest daughter of John Master, a retired magistrate from the Indian Civil Service. Master had returned to England in 1877 with his formidable wife, Gertrude, and his family lived in a large and elegant late-seventeenth-century William-and-Mary mansion, Montrose House, in the next-door village of Petersham.

The Masters were certainly richer and, in the wearisomely precise class stratifications of England in the nineteenth and early twentieth centuries, slightly grander than the Blunts. Scottish by origin, they could trace themselves back to sixteenth-century gentry, the Masters of Barrow Green. Hilda was, moreover,

second cousin to the Earl of Strathmore, the father of the future
Queen Elizabeth, the Queen Mother. (There was also a distant
link with the Mosleys, whose youngest scion, Sir Oswald, would
head the fascist Right in the 1930s.) They were quietly proud
of their friendship with their near-neighbours the grand, but
appallingly spendthrift, Duke and Duchess of Teck. Mary
Adelaide, Duchess of Teck, a first cousin of Queen Victoria,
was the famously ungainly daughter of the Duke of Cambridge,
the youngest son of George III; her husband, Franz, Duke of
Teck, was an underemployed German princeling, a member
through a morganatic marriage of the royal house of Württem-
berg. Their daughter May, through her marriage to George,
Duke of York, the future George V, would become Queen Mary.
The Tecks had moved into White Lodge in Richmond, just up
the road from John and Gertrude Master, in 1870. The families
became friends and John Master taught Princess May how to
skate. Throughout her life Queen Mary remained on familiar
terms with all the Master daughters. The great secret of the
family was that the Queen passed her cast-off dresses on to
the Master women, who altered them and wore them with suppressed pride.

In the opinion of her eldest son, Wilfrid, who wrote two
volumes of witty and candid autobiography, Hilda Master had
had an unhappy childhood. Born in 1880, she was the youngest
of four daughters and had been dominated by her mother,
Gertrude, and bullied by her two eldest sisters, Mabel and Millie.
(She was once discovered chalking 'Millie is a bully' on the walls
of a summer house in Richmond public gardens.) Wilfrid thought
Gertrude a bit of a monster: 'of a domineering disposition, my
grandmother had been glad enough to leave home to marry a
man whom she could dominate to go to live in a country where
there were plenty of natives to bully'. As a memsahib in the
Indian famine 1876–8 she had poked the bellies of starving
children to check if they might be sucking them in to fake
starvation. As a grandmother she forced her grandchildren to

ingest every last vile piece of gristle on their plates: 'If you had seen what I have seen, you would never waste food again.' Her husband, John, a kindly, mild-mannered man who stuffed Harrogate toffees into his grandchildren's hot little hands and took them out boating, was banished to the smallest, darkest room in the house and coerced into giving up the solitary bottle of beer he drank at lunch because she thought it would corrupt the staff. If her friend the Duchess of Teck failed to answer her letters by return, she would send a servant to White Lodge with a pencil and paper. The two women shared 'the same brand of evangelical piety and the same sense of social duty', and together engaged in a perpetual stream of philanthropic projects. 'Together they bludgeoned the shopkeepers of Richmond into providing stools for their employees ... together they waged a ceaseless war against drunkenness and cruelty and vice.' This did not stop Gertrude renaming her own servants if she thought their real names too pretentious. She spent the last thirty-three years of her life lame because after a fall in 1891 she refused to let a doctor near her coccyx.

Hilda had been a sickly child, educated at home by a second-rate governess and then at boarding school in Margate, where she had been forced to drop out of school activities and had been miserable. A bungled operation left her completely deaf in one ear. This, along with a feeling that she had missed out on a decent education, contributed to a sense of isolation, and what Wilfrid divined was an 'inferiority complex'.

Socially, Hilda's marriage to Stanley might have been construed as a step down. Though he was utterly respectable, her sisters had all married richer, better-connected men. The union seems to have been happy, however. Despite the ten-year age gap, the couple had a great deal in common. Both had taken on the religious beliefs, puritan attitudes, and near-obsession with performing charitable works manifested by both their families; in a quiet way, both had had sad childhoods. This had left both of them with a streak of melancholy and implicit or potential rebellion, a feeling that life did not have to be quite as uninteresting as it seemed. Hilda, moreover, was not merely dutiful, she worshipped Stanley: she 'interested herself in his interests, supported him in everything, did the work of two unpaid curates and towards the end of his life, waited on him hand and foot'. They honeymooned in Venice, and on her return Hilda defeated her older sister Mabel's attempt to foist her taste on the marital home. Mabel – generally held in the family to be the 'artistic' one, on the grounds that she had heard of William Morris – came in one day when Hilda was out and rearranged the furniture. Partly against his better judgement, Stanley sided with his wife. It was a story she repeated to her children.

Anthony's oldest brother Wilfrid was born at Ham almost exactly nine months after the wedding, in July 1901. The name 'Wilfrid' was in some respects a startling choice, and showed in Stanley and Hilda a streak of romanticism and a usually hidden dash of contrariness. It was a reference to Wilfrid Scawen Blunt – Stanley's most famous, exotic and embarrassing relative. He was then aged sixty-one, and notorious as an atheist, libertine, Lothario, anti-imperialist, adventurer, and not a bad poet. During the 1860s he had seduced his way across Europe, before destroying a budding diplomatic career by running off with the most celebrated prostitute in Paris (Catherine Walters, aka 'Skittles'). He had married Byron's granddaughter, to whom he was systematically and publicly unfaithful. During his travels he had become militantly anti-imperialist and virulently anti-British. He encouraged dissent among the natives in Egypt, and stood in Ireland as a Home Ruler, going to prison in 1889 for inciting Irish tenants to resist eviction. In 1906, the year before Anthony's birth, he published *Atrocities of Justice under British Rule in Egypt*. He called the First World War 'The White Man's Suicide', and corresponded with Roger Casement as he awaited execution as a traitor in 1916. Casement was stripped of his knighthood; the next man to suffer the same indignity, sixty-three years later, was Anthony Blunt.

The Blunts' second son, Christopher, was born at home in July 1904. Two years later, in 1906, the family moved to Bournemouth where Stanley had been appointed vicar of Holy Trinity, the second most important, but perhaps the most fashionable, church in the town. Anthony was born here in 1907.

The first traces of his existence are to be found in photographs of the Bournemouth rectory, a large, ugly, red-brick building next door to a home for dying consumptives. Hilda and Stanley took many photographs of the rectory garden, and the pictures have an idyllic, prosperous, Edwardian feel. As babies, the Blunt boys sit swaddled in lace; then as boys they stand unselfconsciously in sailor suits, surrounded by toys and pets, in the rectory's flower-filled garden, with its roses and artichoke grove planted and tended by Hilda, who was an enthusiastic horticulturalist. Nurse Delling, a large lady in a wide-brimmed hat and little round glasses, watches benevolently, and a large Samoyed dog called Ivan, whom nobody liked – he was a wedding present – cavorts.

There are no pictures of the rectory's interior. Inside, the Blunt home was a spartan place. Hilda had inherited her mother's frugality. Anthony's schoolfriend Tom Mynors vividly remembered the Blunts' home in Paddington, where they moved in the 1920s, as 'bleak and cheerless', and after he left home Wilfrid found his mother's domestic habits infuriatingly dismal. Hilda nursed a maddening obsession for 'economizing': gas fires barely glimmered, light bulbs were of the lowest wattage, and chairs and mattresses were rock hard. 'You mustn't get soft, dear,' she would say when it was suggested the heating might be turned up. Though able to afford the basics of middle-class life – domestic help, for example, was comparatively cheap – the Blunts lived modestly. Church incomes, like congregations, had been dropping since the 1880s, and, in comparison with those of equivalent professionals such as doctors and solicitors, vicars' earnings were declining sharply. Holy Trinity, a newly endowed parish in a wealthy part of town, yielded an adequate but far from lavish living of £150 a year, plus the same again or more in pew rents;

the rectory came too. To this was added Hilda's small private income. 'Never marry for money, but there is no harm where there happens to be a little,' Stanley would say.

One respectable outlet for Stanley and Hilda's appetite for a little adventure was travel. Stanley had inherited his father's passion for it – the Bishop had journeyed as far as Russia in the 1870s; after her engagement, Hilda had intrepidly gone to Bad Nauheim for the waters and to Oberammergau for the Passion play. Together they had visited the Holy Land. Stanley paid for family trips by taking holiday chaplaincies at Lake Como or in the South of France, ministering to British travellers.

In 1912, when Anthony was four years old, his parents' love of travel would bear professional fruit. One morning in April, Wilfrid later recalled, as he was 'putting his spoonful of Sanatogen into a tumbler full of cold water', Stanley announced that the family were moving to Paris. In January he had been chosen from a shortlist of three as chaplain to St Michael's, the British Embassy church in Paris – though 'with some hesitancy' according to the relevant minutes of the Colonial and Continental Church Society (CCCS), in whose gift the position was. Stanley accepted the post, 'deeply sensible of the honour that had been conferred'. The Blunts moved to Paris a few months later.

It was a flattering appointment: the previous incumbent had been a bishop. Notionally at least, the chaplaincy's sphere of control spread over the whole of central and northern France – though there were twenty full-time chaplains in that area. (Anglican parishes abroad are often disconcertingly large: when the Bishop of Gibraltar described the extent of his diocese to Pope Pius VI, His Holiness observed, 'Then I'm a parishioner.') To the Blunts, as for most of the Edwardian English middle class, Paris was exotic, exciting, the centre of all creative things: where artists went to learn how to paint, where books, plays, fashion and music originated. But it was also a place of worrying moral laxity. Stanley told the CCCS that one of his main tasks would be to keep 'young Englishmen in Paris' on the straight and narrow. 'Up to the present it had been very difficult to get into touch with them, but we hope that now we shall be able to welcome them on week-nights, and by personal intercourse with them, to keep them from the temptations which all great cities provide.'

To welcome the new incumbent, the CCCS agreed to buy an enormous house on the rue Jouffroy in the seventeenth arrondissement. The house had a ballroom that could take 500 people for church gatherings, and Stanley received over £1,000 – an enormous sum – to renovate and redecorate it. The Blunts' new residence was officially opened by the British ambassador, Lord Bertie of Thame, in 1913. Relations with the Embassy were cordial, but the Blunts were not really Lord Bertie's kind of people, and vice versa. Bertie was generally viewed at the Foreign Office as completely ineffectual, though he was much appreciated by the French for his fancy wardrobe. He spent his time in the Faubourg Saint-Germain, among the grander echelons of French society, and his main interests were dirty stories (he owned a huge collection of pornographic prints) and society. His wife, Fedorewna – 'a dear old thing, very ugly' – was a keen poker player. Not an exact match with Stanley and Hilda Blunt, but over the years the Embassy was responsible for providing a number of holiday jobs for the Blunt boys. Embassy contacts got Wilfrid the post of secretary to the elderly Comtesse Greffuhle, one of several titled ladies said to have been Proust's inspiration for the Duchesse de Guermantes; he was to work on a doomed project to put into a *livre d'or* the signature of everyone in France and England who had done anything important during the war. Another introduction led to Anthony spending a summer as tutor to the children of the art dealer René Gimpel. However, the family's best friend was a rich American spinster, Miss Vandervoort, who adored Stanley and bought the Blunts lavish cream teas – of which Hilda disapproved – at Pré Catalan, and gave Wilfrid his first taste of Château d'Yquem.

For Anthony the move to France was 'an event which I think undoubtably coloured the whole of my later development . . . I spent the next ten years there, almost entirely living in Paris, and therefore developed a very strong French leaning which has coloured my whole attitude towards things ever since.' Paris was the place where he began to love art. It seems particularly apposite that the streets around the Parc Monceau where he played are all named after painters: Rue Rembrandt, Rue Murillo, Avenue Ruysdaël. His introduction to art came not so much from his father, but from Wilfrid, 'who was six years older and was becoming a painter by the time I was growing up, and had far closer contacts, naturally, with the artistic world'. Wilfrid, eleven years old when they arrived in Paris, took Anthony on expeditions to explore the city, wheeling him round on the handlebars of his bicycle. 'I was the guide and my brother Anthony the eager pupil; roles that were subsequently to be reversed.' Wilfrid and Anthony went to Versailles, Saint-Cloud, Saint-Germain and Malmaison, and wandered around the Marais and the Latin Quarter. Underneath the Place Denfert-Rochereau they visited the catacombs filled with skulls; another time they travelled on a barge on one of the huge underground sewers that criss-cross Paris, passing underneath the Place de la Madeleine.

'My earliest recollection connected with works of art,' Anthony wrote, 'is that I can just remember going to Louvre before the 1914–18 war. I cannot remember any of the pictures, I can merely remember the fact.' When the war started and the Louvre closed, 'one was automatically compelled to look at architecture and it was perhaps for that reason that I developed an interest in architecture which I have never lost'. He later winced at his conventional early enthusiasms, which he connected with his father's taste. Walking through Paris in 1960, he told Michael Levey, a future director of the National Gallery, that as a child he had been very fond of the Pont Alexandre-III, one of the most extravagantly ornate of the Seine bridges. He spoke, Levey remembered, 'as though admitting a heinous sin. More than a mock shudder went through him when I asked if his childhood taste had been so mistaken.' The Blunts were, like most of the Embassy staff, entirely oblivious of the Parisian avant-garde and its achievements in those last two years of the *belle époque*: Matisse painting *La danse* and *La musique*, Picasso finishing his greatest experiments in Cubism, Duchamp's *Nude Descending a Staircase* being mocked at the Armory show. They had not even heard of the Impressionists, recalled Wilfrid. They would, in any case, have entirely disapproved of them. In later years Hilda would complain that her youngest son had been taken in by that 'charlatan' Picasso.

Anthony was an appealing, well behaved, bright, skinny little boy. Wilfrid wrote, 'Anthony was so obviously brilliant and successful and attractive.' The older brother – open, good-humoured and something of an innocent – would always be impressed and slightly bemused by his youngest sibling. Anthony was his mother's favourite, her 'Benjamin'. Years later she would tell people how as a very small boy he had been solicitous of her, always trying to carry her heavy luggage, and performing other small feats of gallantry. She coddled him. 'My mother was very close to Anthony,' Christopher Blunt later told an interviewer. 'He was slightly delicate as a child but my mother exaggerated this and would give him tonics all the time.' Christopher was left out of the Paris jaunts. Maybe he and Wilfrid were too close in age, or perhaps Wilfrid sensed in some way that Anthony and he – both homosexual – were similar and Christopher different. 'I think both Anthony and I thought him a shade pompous,' Wilfrid later mused. 'We had our own little private jokes about him.'

With the outbreak of the First World War on 1 August 1914, Stanley and Hilda's industry and good works came into their own. When the Germans advanced on Paris and the Embassy staff evacuated to Bordeaux in September, they sent the children to stay with Hilda's favourite sister, Winifred, in Warwickshire, and remained behind to help stranded English tourists get home. They arranged for coal and food to be delivered to the 200–300 poor English families stranded in Paris, and visited the wounded. Hilda, otherwise a model of composed industry, hid the silver in the attic of the Rue Jouffroy and saw German spies everywhere.

Once the war was under way, and the German invasion threat had abated, life returned to a semblance of normality. The children came back to Paris – Wilfrid and Christopher just for the school holidays. Hilda retrieved the silver from the attic, and Stanley signed on as an army chaplain. His reports back to the CCCS were cheerful, high-minded and patriotic. Hilda started a series of sewing circles: 'Mrs. Blunt . . . reports that in the first year, 4,289 articles were made,' ran the CCCS's 1914–15 annual report. In 1917 Stanley and a glamorous English actress called Decima Moore started a club for British soldiers on leave in Paris. At the huge hall at the Rue Jouffroy they held 'patriotic concerts', and even a recruiting meeting. According to Wilfrid, the club's main purpose was to distract soldiers from the 'traditional pleasures of the French capital'. In fact it was probably one of the most practically useful things Stanley ever did. The club produced 40,000 meals a month and was, according to another eyewitness, 'a tremendous success', banking the soldiers' money, writing letters for them, and providing billiards, records, books and city tours – some conducted by the Blunt children. In 1917 the CCCS reported, gratifyingly, that 'the chaplaincy is at all times the most important on the continent and its value had never been more evident than since the war began'.

For the Blunt children the war had exciting unreality. Over Christmas 1914 Stanley took the boys on a day trip to Senlis, within earshot of the Western Front. He and Wilfrid were shown a bloodstained wall against which prisoners had apparently been shot. During Zeppelin raids the family hid in the cellar with their neighbours, and in 1916 the guns on the Somme could be heard in Paris on still nights. They even took three holidays in France between 1914 and 1918: one in Normandy (where the family are pictured on the beach with spades and fishing nets), one in the Auvergne, and one in Fontainebleau. Some things were less fun. The winter of 1916–17 was bitterly cold and fuel was scarce, and a shell shattered the windows of the house in the Rue Jouffroy. Rationing meant that sugar, flour, butter and meat were in short supply. Money was tight. Stanley had written to the CCCS in October 1914 explaining that he and the church were seriously short of funds. Church collections had fallen from 700F to 160F and he had had no income since June; 4000F was owed on the

Rue Jouffroy, and he had hundreds of 'English poor' to feed. The CCCS sent him £40 a month until the end of the war.

The war served as a partial excuse for Hilda to keep Anthony with her in Paris instead of sending him off to prep school in England like his brothers. Instead he was educated by a governess and then attended the École Villiers, a rather uninspiring local school, where Anthony's brother Christopher remembered they did little but recite nursery rhymes and read La Fontaine. It was a solitary life for him: his father was often travelling, his brothers came home only for the holidays. In the family album for 1916–17 – inscribed, 'To dear Mummy with best wishes from Tony, Xmas 1916' – Anthony is usually pictured on his own, a rather solemn, grown-up looking boy, occasionally joined by his brothers. In the latter, Wilfrid often has his arm protectively over his brother's shoulder.

At moments of particular danger Anthony and his brothers were sent back to England to stay with Hilda's sisters. For Wilfrid, at least, the experience was a constant reminder that the Blunts were not quite members of the club. An Easter at Baschurch in Shropshire with the domineering Aunt Mabel and her husband, Uncle Charlie, a retired soldier who had lost one of his three soldier sons in the war, left him with a sense 'that the three Blunt boys had been correctly marked down as not of the stuff of which heroes are made'. Christmas 1916 was spent at Downham Hall in Lancashire with Aunt Mildred and her husband Sir Ralph Assheton (whose brother, Will, was married to Hilda's sister Winifred). Downham was a grand country house with a butler and footmen. Aunt Mildred had once berated Stanley Blunt for asking his wife to 'chuck' him a piece of toast: 'We don't chuck – at Downham,' she told him. There was a family pew in the local church, talk of Eton, dressing for dinner, and a family tree going all the way back to Adam, explained at great length by cousin Ralph (pronounced 'Rafe'), who struck the Blunt boys as 'so poised, so clever, so self-assured, so man-of the world'. The Blunts – 'or at least I', said Wilfrid – felt like poor relations, 'inferior, ungrateful and even rebellious ... Anyone familiar with L. P.

Hartley's *The Go-Between* will understand how I felt.' He locked Ralph – the future Lord Clitheroe and Financial Secretary to the Treasury – in his bedroom and threw away the key.

In November 1918, the month the Armistice was signed, Stanley was awarded an OBE in recognition of his work with the troops. For Anthony, who was just eleven, the most memorable consequence of the end of the war was the reopening of the Louvre. He began to collect coloured postcards of paintings – particularly, as befitted the good son of devout parents, of religious subjects such as Botticelli madonnas. Hilda also consented to send him to prep school in England – St Peter's in Seaford, Sussex – but he seems to have spent only a short time there before returning to France, where in 1920, despite what appears to have been a fairly limited formal education, he won a scholarship, as both his brothers had done, to Marlborough College in Wiltshire, to start in January 1921.

Despite his reputation as an easy-going man, Stanley's sons did not warm to him. Wilfrid, in his memoirs, struggled to give him his due: 'he was a good father to us, but I could never get close to him. His heartiness continued to jar and his views were alien to me.' The very adjectives Wilfrid used were dismissive in their faint praise: he was 'mildly intellectual', 'efficient' in his church work, 'a very normal person'. Wilfrid found his father narrow, and resented Stanley's attempts to make a man of him by making him take more exercise and cold baths. As for Anthony, he never spoke of his father, and his schoolfriends found Stanley noteworthily aloof. Tom Mynors, who stayed with the Blunts in the early 1920s, said of him, 'I didn't like him at all, I found him vain and rather pompous, and in fact he paid very little attention to either of us. I felt he had a bit of *folie de grandeur*, he'd met a lot of high-flying types, and his latest parish was a bit of a come down.' Another friend spoke of Anthony's 'silent father'.

But Stanley did pass on to his sons his love of travel, history, music and art. It was a sign of his influence that Wilfrid became an artist and art teacher, Christopher an expert on Anglo-Saxon coinage, Anthony an art historian. Anthony later wrote, 'I was brought up from an early age, really almost unconsciously, to look at works of art and to regard them as of importance.' Stanley's tastes were conventional. He was 'a strict Ruskinian' – not Ruskin the radical thinker, the one-time critic of Victorian greed, exploitation and industrialism, but Ruskin the devout evangelical-Protestant champion of the Gothic, the hectoring voice of Victorian sanctimoniousness, who tied beauty and nature to morality. 'I was not encouraged to look at anything later than medieval architecture, but that I did look at with great enthusiasm,' Anthony added; and Wilfrid remembered that on a holiday to Belgium in 1925 he was 'rapped over the knuckles for enticing Anthony away from the Gothic, which alone it was respectable to admire'.

Hilda, Wilfrid felt, was 'a far more remarkable person' than her husband. 'Most mothers help us, wittingly or not, to see through our fathers,' he added. Unlike her husband, she was extremely shy, but she had her mother's toughness and puritanism. She strove always to do the right thing, especially when it was painful to her. She persevered in the constant social round of being a vicar's wife, even though her shyness and deafness made it excruciating for her. Wilfrid remembered her reproving him for trying to avoid children's parties: ' "You mustn't become a hermit, dear boy," my mother would say ... Perhaps the very fact that [parties] were distasteful meant that they were good for one.' She also possessed an 'aggressive truthfulness', which seemed almost physically to impel her to speak her mind. She once told a woman behind her in the Embassy church in Paris to sing more quietly. The woman replied that the Psalms encouraged one ' "to make a joyful noise unto the God of Jacob!" "Yours," replied my mother, "is not a joyful noise." ' Her forthrightness was accompanied by a profound dislike of losing any argument: 'her sharp little cry of triumph at having outwitted her opponent betrayed how much the victory meant to her'.

The Blunt boys adored her – 'a woman of infinite goodness and almost puritanical simplicity, incapable of the whitest of lies'

– and, as they grew up, were infuriated by her. Wilfrid found himself exasperated by her conservatism and crankiness: her manic frugality, her neurotic fear of non-existent burglars, her disapproval of all physical comforts. All these traits may have been a manifestation of a deeper disquiet. After her death in 1969 her sons discovered a series of poems that she had written in the 1920s, at a time when the family was still all together, and ostensibly all was well. They expressed a deep pessimism about the world as a place of irreparable iniquity and misery.

She certainly never knew that two of her three sons, Wilfrid and Anthony, were homosexual. According to Wilfrid, she realized that Anthony was agnostic only in the early 1960s, when she read the autobiography of his old schoolfriend Louis Mac-Neice. Both sons knew that their parents' views would make any acceptance of their sexuality impossible. In his memoirs, Wilfrid jibed at his parents' unquestioning certainty of their own rightness in all things, and the narrow strip of opinion that their world view occupied: those stricter than they were 'sadly narrow'; those more 'advanced' were to be 'regretted'. He relished the occasions when their naivety and stiffness prevented them from seeing the world as it really was. He particularly enjoys telling the reader that a Medici print of a Vermeer 'girl in a yellow bodice', sent to him along with devotional works by his Blunt aunts, in fact portrayed a prostitute receiving payment, and that his father's favourite godfather, Dean Vaughan, had been quietly removed from Harrow for paedophilia.

How ambiguous, how complicated was the impact on Anthony of his childhood's constricting respectability, narrow morality and physical austerity is evident in just a few examples. By the time he was a teenager he had developed a loathing for all sport as strong as his father's love for it, as well as a deep and lifelong antipathy to the works of John Ruskin. However, he remained an absolutely dutiful son to his mother. He was in thrall to her – as an adult he visited her at least once a week, invited her without fail to his lectures and exhibition openings, and never complained about his obligations towards her as Wilfrid did – and at the same time longed to escape from her. Outside her company he drank and smoked and was fiercely anti-religious, actively homosexual and opposed to her morality and values. But when his spying was threatened with exposure he contemplated suicide rather than subject her to the shame of his disgrace. He never shook off the spartan habits of his parents, never developing a taste for physical comfort, let alone luxury. At least one friend was convinced of the connection between his austere childhood and his later Marxism. 'Anthony and his brothers had been brought up in an atmosphere which combined strictness with a strong missionary urge,' wrote Cecil Gould. 'He himself was always zealous in supporting what he considered good causes.'

2. Schoolboy

'Upon Philistia Will I Triumph'

Almost without exception, every one of Blunt's generation of public-schoolboy writers, artists and intellectuals hated their places of education. Despite or perhaps because of this, public school played a profound and permanent role in shaping their characters. Too much so, perhaps: more than any other group of intellectuals in any other society, they remained preoccupied by what had happened to them at school. Cyril Connolly's 1938 *Enemies of Promise* and the collection of essays *The Old School Tie* edited in 1934 by Graham Greene were only the most explicit treatments of a subject which also appeared in the work of W. H. Auden, Louis MacNeice, John Betjeman, Christopher Isherwood, Evelyn Waugh, Anthony Powell and Henry Green. Blunt was as marked by his school years as were these others. It was at Marlborough College, where he arrived in January 1921, aged thirteen, that Blunt invented himself, deciding on the artistic preoccupations that would dominate his intellectual career, and making decisions about the kind of person he thought he was and how the world worked which he would never reconsider. He was quite aware of this: 'the people I came to know there ... the intellectual influences I underwent there coloured the whole of my later development'.

Blunt's first two years at Marlborough were pretty awful. He was useless at games – a prerequisite, for younger boys at least, for school success – treated as a freak, viewed as a loner. The school was on the site of an eighteenth-century coaching inn on the outskirts of the eponymous market town by the Wiltshire Downs: 'Deserted by the coaches, poorly served/ By railway', as John Betjeman wrote. It was also, as Blunt well knew – for both his older brothers had hated it – 'a notoriously tough school'. In his autobiographical poem *Summoned by Bells*, Betjeman, who was a year ahead of Blunt, summed up its awfulness in the phrase 'Doom! Shivering Doom!'. A contemporary of Betjeman's, the writer and critic T. C. Worsley, wrote of its 'hostile, friendless, solitary anonymity . . . Marlborough prided itself on its toughness. The amenities of life were non-existent: life was lived on the barest of bare boards, at the smallest and hardest of desks, in the coldest of cold classrooms, in a total absence of any possible privacy. One was always cold, usually hungry.'

'It was', Blunt's friend Tom Mynors recalled, 'only three years after the end of the war and Marlborough had had a pretty thin time. Food had been scarce during the war, nothing had been built, nothing developed. It was constantly freezing, and there was no hot water.' School food was either bland or disgusting, and there was never enough of it: one hot meal a day at lunchtime, plus bread, margarine and tea at breakfast and teatime. This was supplemented by buns bought from two women who arrived at the school gates each day from the local tea shops. For his first two years the poet Louis MacNeice, who would become Blunt's closest friend, wrote home almost exclusively about food and rugby. The lavatories were unbelievably insanitary: 'a double row of doorless compartments . . . substantially flushed down a common drain. About every twenty minutes, rafts of burning paper were floated down to singe the bottoms of other occupants.' In addition the previous headmaster, Dr Wynne Willson, had bequeathed a particularly unpleasant prefectorial regime, giving power to the boys as a way of shrugging off his own responsibilities. After two weeks at the school MacNeice wrote home, 'I have been beaten three times in dormitory for inefficiency in water fagging and time fagging.'

Marlborough had been founded in 1843 for the sons of the clergy. Links with the Church were still strong. There were reduced fees for vicars' sons, who were also entitled to sit for special foundation scholarships. All three Blunt boys won their scholarships. During his Marlborough career, Blunt won eight. The school was regarded as a place for the sons of the impecunious, respectable middle-class rather than the truly rich and grand. 'There were a few rich boys. You noticed the pinstripe of their trousers was somehow different – a nicer material,' remembered Tom Mynors. Another contemporary remembered a boy who was 'very poor and would stand in his clothes under a shower for people who thought it was funny watching him get wet, and they'd give him something for it afterwards. He was noticeably shabby.' The school did have a growing reputation for academic success, encouraged by its new and austere headmaster, Cyril Norwood – known as 'The Boot' – a former grammar-school head whom the boys professed to regard as 'not quite quite', since wearing boots was not 'quite quite'. Norwood went on to become headmaster of Harrow. His reforms had not succeeded, however, in counteracting the deep-seated institutionalized suspicion of intellectualism that was common to all the public schools, a seemingly inevitable corollary of the dominance of games, which were compulsory and permeated every area of school life. At Marlborough the senior prefects were always sportsmen. The triumph of sport was personified in the figure of 'the hearty'. The term denoted someone muscular, sporty, loud and stupid, and with a 'sneering contempt for "cleverness"'.

Blunt spent his first five terms in 'A' House, a dreary 1840s block where thirteen- and fourteen-year-olds lived while studying for their General Certificate, before they went on to senior houses. 'A' House was repeatedly described by its more imaginative inmates as a prison. Louis MacNeice saw it as 'a great square building of ugly brick, with a huge well down the centre surrounded by railed-in landings; you could look up from the basement, see the prisoners listlessly parading on every floor'. It was a great shock to the new boys, with its endlessly clanging bells, freezing dormitories, and total lack of privacy. Their first lesson was that they must learn the numerous arcane and pointless

Schoolboy

rules as quickly as possible, and that ignorance of them would not be excused. On his first day Wilfrid Blunt received a beating for hanging his mackintosh over 'A' House railings in contravention of a sign he hadn't seen. MacNeice didn't go to the lavatory for his first three days because he was too frightened to ask where they were. If younger boys broke the rules older boys could mete out punishments such as 'basements', which involved running up and down the sixty or seventy steps at the bottom of 'A' House at least ten times. A typical rule was that concerning the 'kish', the regulation bag of books, which boys were apparently obliged to hold under their left arms with only a quarter of it sticking out in front.

For a sensitive, physically weedy boy, whose distinguishing feature was that he spoke perfect French, it cannot have been fun. Blunt was terrible at sport and by his own admission 'hated compulsory Games and the [Officers' Training] Corps' (the compulsory exercises in basic soldiery every public schoolboy had to undergo). 'In fact', Tom Mynors recalled, 'he rarely played, he was so totally unsuited, his knees went in all directions.' He could do the long distance runs over the Downs – 'sweats' – but he was slow, and those who came in last were statutorily punished with a beating. Games players got precedence even in the showers, and so enjoyed the hot water before it ran out. It is quite likely that Blunt did not have a hot bath for five years; in adulthood he would have two a day. At school he was often forced to use a 'tolly' – a footbath – instead of the real bath. At the end of the wash the tolly user was expected to upend his footbath over his head. The sight of the water dripping down his long, pale, stick-thin body reminded somebody of a candle. Blunt became known as 'the Taper'.

'I did not mind "A" House,' Blunt later insisted, and it did at least provide a little shelter from the bullying of older boys. On the other hand, what it mainly substituted was boredom and isolation. Most of the teaching was by rote. Classics, the basis of public school education since the early nineteenth century and the subject in which most boys specialized, was unutterably dull. The

21

writer Beverley Nichols wrote that Greek was taught at Marlborough 'as though it were not merely dead but as though it had never lived at all'. Blunt chose to specialize in mathematics and was luckier than most. In his efforts to improve standards, Norwood had brought in talented and imaginative teachers like his maths master, Alec Robson. Blunt was also, from the start, effortlessly academically successful, winning prize after prize, routinely in the top three or four of every class.

In mid-1922 Blunt moved into his senior house, C3, the same house to which his brother Wilfrid had belonged. 'My first year in Senior House was awful,' he told an interviewer in the 1960s. 'My life was made misery for me for two terms by the bullying of one boy.' This was the only complaint he ever made about Marlborough's conditions, maintaining – characteristically and not quite convincingly – that it was the 'intellectual discomforts' that mattered most. In Wilfrid's time, 'C' House's housemaster had been Clifford Canning, who had held concerts and debates in his rooms, and encouraged Wilfrid's desire to be an artist. But Canning had recently got married (to the headmaster's daughter), and married men could not be housemasters. His replacement was Hugh Guillebaud, an Old Marlburian who had fought in the war and had emerged with a terribly scarred arm. He was an awkward man, devoted to the school ethos in its purest form and to Norwood, on whose speeches he made notes. He believed in short haircuts and obedience, and he distrusted his charges – particularly the more literate and unsporty ones. His confirmation classes deeply bored his pupils, and the sex education he was supposed to administer to each pupil never took place. (Perhaps this was just as well. T. C. Worsley's housemaster told him, 'You might find some white matter exuding from your private parts. Don't worry about it. It's only a sort of disease like measles.') Blunt disliked him intensely.

'C' House brought the additional trials of fagging, large dormitories and Upper School, the central fixture of John Betjeman's canon of Marlburian horrors. Upper School was a huge former warehouse where 200 boys between the ages of fourteen and seventeen spent their time when not eating, sleeping, playing games or being taught. It was heated – that being a relative term – by a fire at each end. 'Big Fire' was also the name given to the four prefects and their dozen or so best friends who presided over the place and got one whole fire to themselves. The rest huddled over 'Little Fire'. Every evening the youngest boys were required to pick up the detritus of the school day and put it into huge bins. Their fingers were permanently stuck with splinters. Big Fire monitored the other boys, and could cane miscreants more or less at will. The ultimate punishment they could inflict, however, was basketing.

'It was a perfectly bestial place. We all lived in fear that one day we too might be "basketed",' said Blunt later. Betjeman mythologized it in *Summoned by Bells*:

> They surrounded him,
> Pulled off his coat and trousers, socks and shoes
> And, wretched in his shirt, they hoisted him
> Into the huge waste-paper basket; then
> Poured ink and treacle on his head. With ropes
> They strung the basket up among the beams . . .

Basketing was a much-brandished threat, and Betjeman seems genuinely to have been scared of it, but it seems never to have actually happened during his and Blunt's time. The main occupation of the prefects seems to have been playing endless practical jokes on each other for the entertainment of their audience. 'If I were a captain I'd get tired of saucepans and things falling down on me,' remarks a little boy in Louis MacNeice's autobiographical 1954 radio play, *Return to a School*.

Blunt, to his relief, made a quick escape from Upper School. Norwood had established a classroom called the Bradleian for boys 'who were too clever to be kept in what they speedily regarded as the "barbarous" atmosphere of Upper School'. Louis MacNeice wrote home in October 1923 that, in Upper School, Big Fire had spent the entire term on an extended attempt to manufacture a horrible smell, whereas in the Bradleian there was 'a much more luscious life and there are no beatings'.

Up to and including most of his first year in C3, Blunt was regarded at best with a kind of condescending benevolence: 'The house's trophies were set out on our table at midday lunch,' remembered T. D. F. Money, who was also in C3, 'and we had the Bell trophy, the only one for academic work, and this was largely to do with Blunt. He was always spoken of quite kindly.' Tom Mynors saw it differently: 'I don't think he was physically beaten up, but certainly he was made to feel a misfit, a pansy and so on.' Nor did he make friends in those early years. 'He had no school chums from prep school, because his father had been in Paris. He was isolated and not used to school life – the rough and tumble. He wasn't tactful, and he would ruffle feathers, even with the masters.' From his mother he had inherited the habit of hating to lose an argument. 'He was always supremely conscious he was right. It was impossible to argue with him – he disliked being defeated in arguments.' This drew antipathy, for one of the chief sins at Marlborough – especially in younger boys – was be too free with one's knowledge and opinions: too 'coxy'. In that first year in C3, in the spring of 1923, John Hilton, who later became a good friend, wrote home about 'that terrible boy Blunt' arriving at a house tea and monopolizing the conversation.

It was towards the end of his third year, 1923–4, that Blunt's life seems to have changed. He began to make friends. 'What really dominated my life at Marlborough was the extraordinary luck I had in the people who were my contemporaries,' he later wrote. He first approached Tom Mynors, a bright classicist whom he knew a little.

Blunt was very keen to share a study with me. I was slightly reluctant: I didn't understand his aesthetic views. But we were both loners; I was younger than most, and was squashed and made to fetch the coal and that kind of thing. I agreed *faute de mieux*. We shared the same dormitory, and in the mornings we broke the ice together on the washbasins and gradually I got to know and like him – though I still found him a bit odd. I liked taking exercise, and he got out of it whenever he could. He was slightly on the extreme side, and I was on the more normal.

Blunt began to move with a small group of bright, like-minded boys in the year above, who were now senior enough to be able to manifest their dissatisfaction with the regime. 'The generation before mine had started a sort of revolt against the toughs, against the absolute dominance of games. They had a pretty rough time of it . . . They started the affirmation of liberty for the intellectuals and one must also, I think, use the word *aesthetes*, for we were extremely precious.'

The monolithic culture of the public schools had to have its dissenters, and there was a completely ritualized, perfectly understood mode of opposition. It had been in action since the 1850s. This was to become an 'aesthete', one of the bright boys who were often precociously intellectual, especially once they realized that intellectualism could be construed as revolt. Their trajectory as aesthetes was also formalized: downtrodden, bullied, ridiculed, subject to pointless rules in their first two or three years, they developed an antipathy to the prevailing culture, and began to go out of their way to oppose it, emerging in their final year sporting a shocking green waistcoat or its metaphorical equivalent, editing arty magazines, and actually having quite a good time. They were usually vociferously opposed to games and to the Officers' Training Corps. They ridiculed school orthodoxy, wore their hair long, and had feuds with their housemasters. They weren't automatically fey, but, having been teased as 'pansies', many of them deliberately assumed feyness as a way of annoying the enemy, and of standing out against a background of sweaty, muscular blandness. Marlborough, for all its heartiness, also had a 'highbrow tradition', as MacNeice noted: 'there was always a group among the older boys that was openly against the government, that mocked the sacred code and opposed to it an aesthetic dilettantism'.

The irony was that the public-school system, designed to be a factory for gentlemen, also offered an excellent training in dissidence. It inadvertently fostered a questioning and subversive attitude and a profound distrust of authority, necessary for any intellectual class and vital to the manufacture of an artist, writer or spy. At the same time, most of these rebels – Blunt included – accepted without question the schools' training in sexual guilt, the inevitability of class division, and the habit of emotional reticence.

Among these aesthetes whom Blunt now joined was John Betjeman, who was already able to deflect antipathy through humour – 'when the toughs tried to be bloody, he simply laughed in their face', Blunt recalled. Others were Ellis Waterhouse – self-styled anti-Establishmentarian and an art historian-to-be, several years older and destined to be Blunt's most long-standing school friend – and the grumpy future Oxford historian John Bowle. They cultivated their differentness. 'We went out of our way to be irritatingly provocative,' Blunt wrote. 'We used to walk down the aisle of Chapel flaunting our silk handkerchiefs – I used to wear mine from the strap of my wristwatch . . . And on Saturday evenings we used to go upfield where other boys were playing rounders, and infuriate them by playing catch with a large brightly-coloured ball right across their game.' They wore their hair 'long' (just over their collars), and pursued feuds with masters – Betjeman with his classics teacher, Alan Gidney; Blunt with Guillebaud and the art master, Christopher Hughes. Hughes 'believed that all art stopped dead at the Pre-Raphaelites, and this of course absolutely infuriated me. I was championing the cause of Cézanne and the Impressionists.' By coincidence, or perhaps not, Hughes also ran the Officers' Training Corps. Blunt and Betjeman made a joke of the OTC, dropping their rifles and turning everything into farce (as Isherwood at Repton and Evelyn Waugh at Lancing had done before them), and they shared an open contempt for games. 'I remember Betjeman and he were once watching the first eleven play a match, and one said to the other, "Men fighting," and there was a good deal of laughing.

They obviously didn't think that athleticism was a key to position, whereas in fact it was,' recalled one Old Marlburian sniffily.

There were masters who were sympathetic to the aesthetes' hunger for knowledge. One was George Sergeaunt, the 'very learned and Olympian Classics master, who was an expert on the Renaissance'. He had a print of the Botticelli Venus in his room, and knew about Greek sculpture and El Greco, an enthusiasm he passed on to Blunt. Another was Clifford Canning, Wilfrid's ex-housemaster, known as 'Foxy Ferdy': 'a man full of enthusiasm for everything,' Blunt later wrote, 'a sort of natural rebel, or at any rate, a natural encourager of rebels – which we all, of course, at that time were – who protected us.' Blunt remained close to Canning long after he had left Marlborough, and became god-father to one of his children.

In C3, Blunt was well known for being passionate about art. 'What the Louvre was to Anthony Blunt,' John Betjeman, who had fallen in love with a local manor house, wrote later, 'Rams-bury manor was to me.' At night in the dormitories, 'In the time between going to bed and the prefects coming up to turn the lights out,' remembered T. D. F. Money, who occupied the adjacent dormitory bed, 'Blunt would talk to me about the French Impressionists, and bring out postcards to show. And he would talk about Clive Bell and Significant Form.'

Louis MacNeice wrote that Blunt's enthusiasms were passion-ate but often fickle. In *Return to a School*, the Blunt character, Pinky, takes part in the following exchange:

'Botticelli? Leonardo? Second-rate artists, both of them.'
'But you admired them a year ago.'
'I never did any such thing. And, while we're on aesthetic questions, I see you still wear coloured socks.'

It would have been surprising if a schoolboy did not have fads; what is much more remarkable about the young Blunt is the extent to which his adult interests were already fixed. By now he already had two aesthetic constants, both of which were to last his whole life. The first of them was modern art, and in particular

Picasso, whom he had just discovered through Wilfrid. 'Modern art in 1923', Blunt wrote later, 'meant Cézanne first and the other Post-Impressionists, who were still regarded in this country as dangerous revolutionaries.'

It was Wilfrid who introduced his brother to Cézanne. In early 1921, after less than a year at Oxford, he had decided he wanted to be an artist and had persuaded his parents to let him return to Paris to study painting. There, walking down the Rue de la Boétie, he finally discovered modernism in the dealers' windows. His proximity to the avant-garde was to be short-lived, however. A few months after Anthony began Marlborough, in April 1921, Stanley, now fifty, moved the family back to England. He had accepted the post of vicar of St John the Evangelist, a small but prosperous parish in Paddington in west London, a triangle of large white stucco houses bounded by Southwick Crescent, Sussex Gardens and Cambridge Square, on the north side of Hyde Park.

In London, Blunt fuelled his passion at Zwemmer's, the new art bookshop which opened in 1921 in Charing Cross Road. It was the first place in London where it was possible to see colour prints, and the only place that sold *Cahiers d'art*, the bible of French modernism, as well as Wyndham Lewis's *Blast*. There he found everything that had been published on Picasso and the Cubists: on the proceeds of his school prizes he bought a small book by Maurice Raynal, a pamphlet by Jean Cocteau in French, two small books in German, and the theoretical writings of Albert Gleizes. He became friendly with the Zwemmer family, who allowed him to borrow prints to take back to Marlborough.

Blunt's other great, constant love was for the seventeenth-century French painter Nicolas Poussin. Where the fascination came from is hard to gauge. Poussin was then by no means what he is now – and what Blunt's efforts played no small part in making him – an unquestioned master in the central canon of Western painting. The artist had been out of fashion for years. The prevailing view of him was that he was a lifeless academic formalist. Only the first flickerings of a revival had begun to manifest themselves. One of Cézanne's gnomic utterances – that he had wanted 'to remake Poussin over again according to nature' – had attracted the attention of modern critics; Roger Fry had recently become the first Englishman to write about the earlier artist for a century. This very obscurity attracted Blunt, who was developing a taste for neglected artistic underdogs. Tom Mynors remembered half-complaining to his mother that Blunt had returned after the holidays with a pile of books for him to study. 'He gave me a book on Poussin which I think was the only book published at the time on him, and then he went on and on, so I had to learn every single detail. He was mad about Poussin, and he wanted others to be too.' In later life Blunt told a story that one night he, Ellis Waterhouse and John Betjeman had decided that they would resurrect great neglected parts of art. Betjeman said he would take on neo-Gothic; Waterhouse said he would do the Carracci brothers and the baroque; Blunt chose Poussin – 'the most difficult'.

In early 1924 Betjeman and his friends vented their disapproval of the school in a magazine, *The Heretick*. It 'was planned', Blunt wrote, 'to express our disapproval of the Establishment generally, of the more out of date and pedantic masters, of all forms of organized sport, of the Officers Training Corps and of all the other features that we hated in school life, not so much the physical discomforts – they were almost taken for granted – but, as you might say, the intellectual discomforts of the school'.

The first issue contained Blunt's first printed article – an energetic, opinionated, almost prim defence of modern art and its move towards abstraction, which began:

It is rather dangerous to defend modern art, as the general public have already decided that all artists are mad who are not photographically accurate, but dare to distort their subjects and to attempt – the worst crime of all – to create works of art. They are all classed under the term 'Cubist' and are consequently treated as a joke. This is partly due to ignorance and partly to an inability to realise the aim of art.

'It wasn't very good or very original,' Blunt reflected, 'but I was only sixteen.'

His account of the public response to modern art may not have been wrong, but he is noticeably willing to describe the public as stupid, and to celebrate the superior perception of an elite. The world is firmly divided into the ignorant Them and the insightful Us – a tendency in Blunt's character which Marlborough did nothing to dilute. *The Heretick* made the hitherto small set famous throughout the school. It was Blunt's first experience of belonging to a gang, and his first of public rebellion. The excited rumour was that the editors of the magazine would be beaten up by hearties at the end of term. Norwood warned in his end of term sermon that the magazine's motto 'Upon Philistia Will I Triumph' was fine as long as it meant 'overcoming the Philistine in all of us'.

The second issue of *The Heretick* came out in summer 1924, edited by Betjeman and Blunt. 'We had a great discussion about the frontispiece – a stone dropped into a pool, leaving ripples. We thought we were dropping the pebble into the middle of this pond of complacency and ignorance. We thought that was really going to change the world,' remembered Tom Mynors. 'The point is', announced the editorial, which countered public-school self-sacrifice with a hint of hedonistic atheism, 'that you must have as pleasant a time as you can while you are on earth.' Blunt contributed an article, 'Art and Morality'.

'There is no such thing as an immoral or moral book. Books are well or badly written. That is all.' So says Oscar Wilde of literature, and the same applies to all branches of art . . . Moral effects only come into consideration when the painting is no longer regarded as a work of art . . . To say that a painting is immoral merely shows a lamentable incapacity for appreciation.

The article was 'provoked by a row with my housemaster who thought that the reproductions of Matisse and Rouault which I had in my study were indecent'.

It caused a furore, and 'was apparently regarded as so shocking that one parent threatened to remove his boy from the school', Blunt claimed. The paper was closed down. The invocation of Oscar Wilde – at the instigation of Betjeman, much more of a Wildean than Blunt – was the fatal provocation.* The row was more entertaining than the magazine. 'The second issue was already duller than the first,' Blunt later admitted, 'and it did not sell nearly so well. I remember that we were almost scraping together our pocket-money to pay our debts for the thing.' His favourite teacher, Canning, published a sympathetic review of *The Heretick* in the school's official organ, the *Marlburian*, in July that year, congratulating the editors on their attempts to change the school's attitudes. He singled out Blunt, and offered him a piece of advice that he would not take: 'Fire always burns if one approaches too close – however much one insists that it doesn't.'

Perhaps the most important consequence of *The Heretick*'s short life was that it started Blunt on his career as a commentator on art. 'We were inspired', he wrote (characteristically hiding himself in a 'we'), 'by the writing of Roger Fry and Clive Bell, and believed without any qualification in Pure Form. In fact it was really the only thing in art that we did believe in.'

Fry and Bell were the two leading art critics of Bloomsbury, the loosely knit group of painters, artists and thinkers which included Vanessa Bell, Virginia Woolf and John Maynard Keynes and which was the closest England had to an artistic and moral avant-garde. Blunt had become an enthusiastic disciple of the Bloomsbury line on art by the winter term of 1924. A year before, Wilfrid had managed to engineer an introduction to Roger Fry via one of his four unmarried, charity-working, paternal aunts, Edith, who knew Fry's sister Margery through her prison-visiting. It was at Fry's that Wilfrid first saw 'a room with walls of

---

* 'I discovered that Oscar Wilde was someone whom one ought not to mention; so naturally he had a great attraction for me,' said Betjeman.

different colours'. In September 1924 Anthony was allocated a study with Tom Mynors and painted it red and green in homage to Fry.

In his first article in *The Heretick* earlier that year, Blunt had explained Fry and Bell's theoretical justification for modern art – 'Pure Form' or 'Significant Form' – which was to remain central to his aesthetics until 1933. The ultimate aim of art was not imitation: 'if imitation were the end of art then would the photographer be the greatest of artists'. The 'fundamental quality of art' was its 'pictorial' or abstract qualities: the play of lines, colour, harmonies, the balance of space and design. These were the things that aroused 'aesthetic emotion' in the viewer. 'Since all works of art arouse the same emotion, there must be some quality common to all of them which causes these emotions.' This quality was called 'Significant Form'. The argument implied that no importance could be attached to subject matter. So a Titian, a Persian carpet and an abstract painting could all be judged by the same criteria and were potentially of the same worth.

Significant Form, however, was far from all that Fry and Bell had to offer. Bloomsbury represented a glamorous, exciting, rebellious alternative to the world in which Blunt had grown up. In Clive Bell's writing, in particular, he found an overheatedly passionate approach to art and an attack on English philistinism and conservatism, couched in the kind of pseudo-scientific terms guaranteed to thrill a logically minded schoolboy rebel. In his 1914 book *Art*, Bell denounced the tastes and values of 'teetotallers, anti-gamblers, and public benefactors' – Blunt's parents to a T – before announcing that 'art is good because it exalts to a state of ecstasy far better than anything a benighted moralist can even guess at'. It sounded dangerous, as it was supposed to. Bell said that art represented the 'general ferment and the inspiration of a young, violent and fierce generation'. He dismissed real politics, which most of Bloomsbury regarded as a distraction: 'To call an artist ... a democrat is to call him something irrelevant or insulting.' Blunt followed: 'He considered it very low to talk politics', recalled John Hilton, and insisted 'that he preferred

Things to People.' (Hilton felt this to be a pose, which 'certainly didn't prevent him entering keenly – often, it seemed agonizingly – into the lives of quite a number of people. Perhaps the slogan voiced an aversion not to individuals but to people in the abstract.')

By 1924 Blunt was also ripe for Bell's message that art was a superior alternative to religion. As with his elder brother before him, Marlborough's twice-daily chapel and his father's piety had bored the religion out of him. According to Clive Bell, art was 'a religion without a priesthood' – a claim often made during the modernist period. What religion had provided in earlier days – the individual's sense of 'the emotional significance of the universe', 'the conviction that some things are universal', 'an inspiration for the whole of life' – art now did better, and with less baggage. The new religion came with a set of 'scientific' aesthetic absolutes by which all art could be judged and explained. In the religion-shaped hole he had, Blunt now put Bloomsbury's intense theology of art, just as he was later to do with Marxism.

He was also now 'the dominant intellectual' in 'C' House, with 'a precocious knowledge of art and a habitual contempt for conservative authorities'. He had started his own arts society (like Harold Acton and Anthony Powell at Eton and Evelyn Waugh at Lancing) in 'counter-attack' to the art master, Christopher Hughes, the year before.* Blunt asked his favourite master, Canning, to be president, but Hughes insisted that if there was going to be an art society at Marlborough then he would be president. Rather than accept the art master, Blunt renamed his art club the Anonymous Society, in hindsight a peculiarly appropriate name for a Bluntian project. He asked another sympathetic teacher, George Turner, to be president, and inaugurated the society in November 1923 with a paper on Titian – 'astonishingly

* The founding of the Anonymous Society has usually been dated to 1924, but Blunt's first paper, a 'highly respectable' one on Titian, in the Courtauld Institute archives, is dated November 1923. It was followed by John Betjeman's first paper on Victorian art.

dull', in his later recollection. (Canning later quietly took over, and meetings took place at his house.) By 1924 Blunt was delivering precocious defences of Picasso and Cubism, 'the logical end to which painting must tend', and praising Cézanne as 'the greatest innovator in art that there has been for centuries'.

By the beginning of his fourth year at Marlborough Blunt had metamorphosed into a charismatic figure. His gangliness had turned into a kind of loose elegance. 'He was very tall and very thin and drooping,' MacNeice wrote,

> with deadly sharp elbows and the ribs of a famished saint; he had cold blue eyes, a cutaway mouth and a wave of soft brown hair falling over his forehead. His features were far from classical but he had at times a pre-Raphaelite beauty; when he was annoyed he pouted and stuck out his lip, his good looks vanished and sulkiness was all.

John Hilton, a fellow mathematician, who was then outgrowing a sporty background and a hesitating manner, found he liked Blunt's irresistibly infectious enthusiasm, his 'fervour' for paint, his 'dedicated, unswerving intensity ... assurance and incandescent spirit'. Under Blunt's languidly elegant frame was a bundle of tireless, organizing energy. He seemed to know exactly what he wanted to do with his life, and what he was interested in. His disciplined, channelled enthusiasms were exhilarating, and bore no relation to anything in the curriculum.

He had read all the latest literary totems: Eliot, the Sitwells, Virginia Woolf, Forster, Huxley. Tom Mynors recalled that Blunt somehow got the two of them an entrée to the private art collection of Sir Philip Sassoon, a socially prominent art-loving bachelor and friend of Joseph Duveen, London's most famous and influential art dealer. Blunt wrote long papers for the Anonymous Society and borrowed prints from Zwemmer's and put up exhibitions of them in the gym, greatly to Hughes's irritation. 'We traipsed along eagerly with him as well in his more special domains of passion for Blake, Brueghel, El Greco, Poussin, Thomas Hardy, Beckford,' wrote John Hilton.

Schoolboy

From the age of sixteen, Blunt went to Paris every spring to see the new pictures in the Rue de la Boétie, where 'there would almost certainly be the latest works of Picasso at Paul Rosenberg'. One year he took Tom Mynors with him. 'We went on the cheapest route, via Newhaven, and stayed in some very grotty hotel. I'd never been to Paris before, and it was part of my enlightenment. I remember his burning enthusiasm: we rushed from one place to another.' Blunt loved these trips to France. He came back from them 'possessed, rather surprisingly, I think, looking back, with a great desire to proselytize ... we were determined to put the good news about, so to speak, partly to exasperate the other boys and masters at school, but partly genuinely'. Here in his reminiscence of the trips, as often in Blunt's autobiographical writing, there is a striking clumsiness. It is as if the effort of writing about himself is so great that his control over his normally limpid prose breaks down.

Apart from his discovery of modern art and Poussin, the most important event of Blunt's time at Marlborough was his friendship with the poet-to-be Louis MacNeice. MacNeice was, like Blunt, a vicar's son; his father would go on to become a bishop. He was an Ulsterman. He had grown up in a strict Protestant household in Carrickfergus, County Down, ten miles from Belfast. He had been a troubled, lonely child, plagued by nightmares. After years of illness, his mother had died when he was seven, and his father had withdrawn into himself. It was an isolated upbringing, more so even than Blunt's: 'so many human contacts in my father's Ulster parish were taboo. The Catholics were obviously taboo; the working classes were given to drink, bad language and the throwing of rotten eggs; and many of the "gentry" were ruled out because they were "fast", which meant little more than that they kept a decanter of whisky on the the sideboard.' (The MacNeice household was teetotal.) MacNeice the schoolboy combined a brooding, introverted side with being a brilliant, apparently extroverted, imaginative talker. His Irishness, which could have been a serious problem at Marlborough, was alleviated by an enthusiasm (though not much of a talent) for rugby. His first close friend at the school was Graham Shepard, son of Ernest Shepard, the illustrator of *Winnie the Pooh*. Already making up poems and saturated in Norse sagas, Shelley, Keats, Sidney and *Le Morte D'Arthur*, MacNeice was 'itching to write.'

In the autumn term of 1924 MacNeice, who was also in C3, began to attend Anonymous Society meetings and to borrow art books and prints from Blunt. At weekends they went on long walks together across the downs overlooking Marlborough. 'As Blunt says,' MacNeice wrote home, 'this is really the most beautiful country in the world.' Blunt began to be always present in MacNeice's letters home. He credited Blunt with turning him from a 'shy little boy' to a rebel 'trailing my coat'. Blunt wrote that MacNeice, 'by far my closest friend', was 'the strongest and most important figure in the school . . . he was already a person of extraordinary vitality, imaginative force, brilliance and charm'. John Hilton, who became the third member of the triumvirate, called MacNeice 'the Irish genius'.

To their contemporaries, Blunt and MacNeice seemed very unalike. John Hilton described Blunt as 'an austere hedonist living for disciplined gratification of the senses, with an eye for social esteem and seeking anchorage in system and scholarly detail'. (Hilton perceptively noticed Blunt's emerging taste for social acceptance at a point when ostensibly he rejected convention.) MacNeice was 'a ribald seer, an anarchic and mocking seeker after the deep springs of action or faith . . . often ludicrous, sometimes brave and occasionally tender'. His acute perception of the visual world, which was to prove so characteristic of his poetry, provided the territory on which he and Blunt made friends. Blunt spoke of MacNeice's 'astonishing visual sensibility, both to paintings but also simply to things seen, colours of the most curious kinds'. Before long MacNeice was devouring books on Van Gogh and – to use the contemporary term – Negro art. The early letters that MacNeice sent to Blunt just after they finished school in September 1926 were filled with long, vivid descriptions of the Irish landscape and weather, because, he told Blunt, he'd truly looked at it and was 'afflicted' by it. He also described paintings: an El Greco 'all slate blues with white streaks splashed with yellow and framed very suitably in darker slate blue and very tarnished gilt' and 'A bit off an altar by Fra Angelico with two saints standing on a biscuit surrounded by a ring of fire like red strings of seaweed or an anemone or starfish.' The main currents of feeling in the letters are about paintings and books. 'Thanks awfully for introducing me to Art. The saints send you what you want.'

Blunt was sixteen when he made friends with MacNeice. At that age, an important part of friendship is the process of self-definition: of defining who one is and isn't. Blunt's character was thrown into relief by his relationship with MacNeice. He was attracted by MacNeice's wit and chatter and penchant for non-sense and 'pure feeling', but he felt that he himself was different: cool, logical, reticent, mathematical. Their friendship encouraged Blunt to emphasize those qualities. It was as if he consciously decided to be Reason to MacNeice's Chaos, and deliberately set out to train himself into that mould. Hilton wrote to his parents that Blunt 'stands for "sense", while MacNeice stands for "non-sense"'. Sense and nonsense were topics that often came up in their discussions, and it was typical that MacNeice should give a talk at the Anonymous Society on 'The Mailed Fist of Common Sense and How to Avoid It'. He said that 'pure feeling' was not 'a matter of reason, it must therefore be described not rationally, but emotionally.' Blunt did not agree then, and probably never would agree, but he was fascinated by MacNeice's fascination with feeling. He would continue to be intrigued by excessive, emotional people, and would adopt MacNeice's favourite poet, William Blake, the artist of anti-rationalism, as one of his long-lasting passions. And it would take him a great deal longer than it would MacNeice to grow out of this simplistic division of the world into black and white, thought and feeling, rational and irrational.

Another trait that became clearer through Blunt's friendship with MacNeice was his fundamentally unaccommodating attitude to the forces he was rebelling against. Most of the Marlborough aesthetes were essentially playing games with – teasing – the school authorities. MacNeice, *au fond*, thought Marlborough was a joke. Blunt did not: his dislike of the institution had an edge to it that his contemporaries' attitudes lacked. It was one of the ways in which he led the others. MacNeice, by his own admission, saw himself as 'emulating Blunt's antagonism to the generation of our parents'. John Hilton noted of Blunt, 'Parents he already rejected rhetorically', and that his dismissal of religion was far deeper and stronger than MacNeice's. In fact dismissal was one of Blunt's specialities: 'Blunt had a flair for bigotry. Every day he blackballed another musician; he despised Tennyson, Shakespeare, the Italian High Renaissance.' His grounds were that they were too 'establishment'. 'The difficulty with Blunt', John Hilton wrote to his parents, 'is that when you suddenly find out that he's very narrowminded or something else which makes you feel thoroughly superior, and mention the fact in a tactful manner, you find that he's been perfectly aware of the fact for years and proud of it more than otherwise. He's infinitely more intelligent than MacNeice, but not nearly such a genius I should think.'

Tom Mynors felt that during his years at Marlborough he observed in Blunt 'a growing antagonism to school which made him slightly bitter. He was a very cerebral sort of person, very intense, he focused his brain very narrowly. I think this was possibly because of his disappointment that there were so few people who were interested, and that made him contemptuous of people who were so much less clever than he was.' In later years John Betjeman wrote of Blunt, 'He always makes me feel trivial and shallow.' From Marlborough on, Blunt gave a good many people that impression – though they tended to be people who thought highly of their own intellectual abilities, and were piqued by the possibility that Blunt did not. (Betjeman was not wrong in feeling that Blunt disapproved of him. According to Wilfrid, Blunt felt that the grown-up Betjeman had chosen to 'prostitute his talents by popularising what he could have directed into serious study'.) John Bowle, a fellow aesthete and famously irascible himself, speaking after Blunt's exposure, told an interviewer that Blunt was a 'colossal bore. Spelled BORE. Enormously conceited, contemptuous of other people.' He didn't like MacNeice either: 'MacNeice was physically repulsive to me. Never taken with him at all. He was a wit, a real Irish wit.'

'Blunt and I made hay in our last year,' wrote MacNeice. The two arranged to share a tiny study from September 1925, after Mynors and Betjeman had left for Oxford. Blunt painted the walls with white distemper, and the picture rail black. He provided two lustreware vases in which they placed bunches of chrysanthemums, and a constant stream of shilling prints, including Brueghel's *Hunters in the Snow*, a Picasso still life, and a Cézanne Mont Sainte-Victoire. It all seemed, observed Hilton, 'very daring amid the encircling gloom of grease-stained wallpapers'.

Part of what made the last months at school enjoyable was the traditional pastime of finding a younger boy to admire. The object of MacNeice's affections was a certain 'C.I.'; Blunt's were directed towards an 'Edward'. 'I wish you dreams of Edward's eyes,' MacNeice wrote in September 1926. In October that year, as they set off for university, he informed Blunt that he'd told his old friend Shepard of his crush. 'I expect he was shocked by my revelations about C.I. I hope you saw Edward. He is so responsive.'

Most of this was just talk. Blunt's sexual experiences at school were limited. 'There was not much "quick practical sex" at Marlborough,' he said in 1977, 'but there were many romantic friendships. John [Betjeman] was wildly in love at one stage with a boy in my house and once asked me to deliver a note to him, but I annoyed him considerably by delivering it too *publicly*.' Blunt's contemporaries were remarkably uninformed about sex, though there was a general sense among the authorities that the boys, collectively and individually, would abandon themselves to vice at the slightest opportunity. Even Norwood, not especially obsessed with sex by the standards of his time and *métier*, shared this view. On a walk through the Savernake Forest in the autumn of 1920, a young master observed to the headmaster how beautiful the autumn leaves looked. 'Yes, beautiful, beautiful outside,' murmured 'The Boot', 'but corrupt within, like the boys.'

In truth, throughout the system there was less sex than the authorities feared in their more fevered imaginings. Some schools – like Wellington in the 1930s – went through periods in which 'the vice was sensational, with young boys being virtually raped', but they were the exception. At Marlborough, as at most schools, the boys approached sex in an embarrassed, inarticulate atmosphere where the 'the convention of the crush', in which the older boy conceived a passion for a passive, usually younger, boy, was the rule. As for their information on sex, that mainly consisted of dirty jokes and the half-informed chatter of other boys. Wilfrid was told by a boy who had had 'the talk' that sex was like 'a cup and saucer'. Neither could work out who was the cup and who the saucer. There was also the not quite explicit sexuality of dormitory rough and tumble. A favourite dormitory game at Marlborough was 'hot potting': a lighted match was placed inside two cups to make a vacuum; a boy would stick the cups on to his bare buttocks and parade naked up and down the room.

Mynors felt that Blunt was was even less interested in sex than in politics. (With the exception of one school debate on the subject, the General Strike, which took place in that final year. passed Marlborough by. The boys decided that the workers were wrong to have broken their contracts.) 'He was sexless. He was so intellectual it didn't mean anything to him. There was the usual stuff of people having crushes on pretty boys, but the big excitement in our house was when a boy was expelled because he was found in bed with a barmaid from the town.'

But during his last year Blunt did have a more serious crush on a boy his own age – one of the new members of the Anonymous Society. In old age he described Michael Robertson as 'enchanting, highly intellectual and good at games'. The tall, square-jawed Robertson was the captain of school and therefore editor of the *Marlburian*, into which MacNeice was able to infiltrate poems and for which Blunt wrote more pieces on modern art. The attraction was 'quite unconsummated and not reciprocated', recalled Alastair MacDonald, another new recruit to the aesthetes:

Robertson had a girlfriend. They were great friends, but so unalike. It was a strange relationship. Blunt was primarily a homosexual, but it didn't go very far at Marlborough, and it didn't impinge on our friendship. He was friendly with a boy called Basil Barr [later referred to by MacNeice in letters to Blunt as 'beautiful Basil'], who was very homosexual, but I don't think he had a crush on him.

Blunt's final year saw the fruition of Norwood's academic reforms. In the autumn term Marlborough won twenty university scholarships, among them one for MacNeice to Merton College, Oxford, to study Classics, and one for Blunt to Trinity College, Cambridge – not King's, his father's college – to study mathematics. MacNeice told his parents that a newspaper had reported that 'Marlborough is not a public school, it is miracle. I should not say so myself, yet I think it is less cruel to people with minds than any other school.' Norwood left that year for Harrow. The new head was George Turner, first president of the Anonymous Society, who took over in January. Blunt was made a prefect, which as far as MacNeice was concerned represented a triumph for the aesthetes.

Despite this, Blunt's feud with Hughes, the art master, rumbled on. When Blunt planned to stage an exhibition of borrowed posters and modern prints, Hughes responded with an exhibition of dull pictures by Old Marlburians and deliberately excluded a painting of a mackerel by Wilfrid, saying it was 'worthy of a pavement artist'. Blunt read a paper to the Anonymous Society denouncing all art between the Renaissance and Cézanne, with a few exceptions – Brueghel and El Greco – and put Hughes into a rage. 'We are afraid Blunt is breaking his [Hughes's] heart,' MacNeice wrote home in November 1925. 'He was so roused by Blunt's last paper at Mr Canning's that he is going to produce an answering paper, which will be rather tragic as he has no power of logic.' When Hughes delivered his paper at the next meeting, Blunt came down with an unstoppable attack of church giggles. Hughes stumbled on, ignoring the effect he was having. Blunt remembered, 'With tears in his eyes he said, "You've hurt me many times, and now I'm hurting you."'

Blunt and MacNeice were by now genuinely enjoying themselves. Over-literally adopting Clive Bell's recommendation that everyone should 'make himself an amateur', they took up painting and declared themselves Marlborough's equivalent of Bloomsbury. 'If the artist is completely sincere,' the seventeen-year-old Blunt announced, 'he will produce a great painting whatever his subject or his lack of technical skill.' Perhaps luckily, none of the pictures survive. Under MacNeice's encouragement Blunt tried his hand at a little poetry, producing an attempt at modern pastoral. This, unfortunately, does survive:

> The harsh green outline of the downs
> Tight as a bow string
> Strikes a discord on the sky.
>
> This edge of the abyss
> Is fixed, immutable
> Beyond the power of time
> Or God.
> Beyond it lies a land of spirits
> Continually striving to break it
> Drag it down
> And trample it under their feet

They spent hours practising the kind of conversations they imagined they would have at university. From their study an endless gabble of ideas, rhymes and nonsense emerged. MacNeice quoted bits of Pope, Latin, Norse saga, advertising slogans and hymn parodies, 'every little blasphemy a blow for the Better Life'. Blunt read Sacheverell Sitwell's *Southern Baroque Art* (1924), and they went round praising what they liked as 'too *devastatingly* baroque'. 'One sometimes got the impression that the closing scene of the Mad Hatter's tea party was being performed, with Louis in the role of the dormouse being stuffed into the teapot,' thought Hilton. The dialect of their friendship is apparent in MacNeice's letters home, the 'curious mixture of seriousness and slightly wilful whimsy' that Blunt observed, and a fey, Sitwellian, note absent before. 'I am indeed wicked. We have been painting our study with white distemper, and my sense of duty was washed away in the flood.'

The Anonymous Society had become fashionable. 'I believe there was some competition to get in – well, the meetings were so delightful,' Blunt recalled. He gave papers on Picasso and in defence of the much-abused baroque style. Hilton derived enormous pleasure from a Marlborough version of a popular song, 'Yes, we are collegiate', which went 'Yes, we are aesthetic', with the chorus 'Blunt, MacNeice and Hilton'.

The summer term of 1926 – their last – 'was an idyll'. Blunt and MacNeice went for runs and walks over the Downs, Blunt 'wearing a blue silk handkerchief floating from the strap of his wrist watch, and we would come back with our arms full of stolen azaleas'. They walked to nearby Martinsell Hill to get apple blossom, 'And we would spend whole afternoons lying naked on the grassy banks of the bathing place, eating strawberries and cherries.' Blunt set up an easel at the bathing pool, and the bathing master tried to chase him away thinking he wanted to paint naked boys, when he was only interested in the corrugated-iron shed nearby. It was a kind of love affair. Half a century later, Blunt told MacNeice's biographer, teasingly, that Louis had been 'beautiful', but 'irredeemably heterosexual'. Sex was rarely at the heart of his closest relationships, and thus it was with MacNeice.

Fifty years later Blunt summed up his Marlborough experience:

We lived in this little self-contained world of art and literature, with no awareness of what was taking place in the outside world at all. Politics was simply a subject never discussed at all, and what happened to be going on at that

43

time in Europe was no concern of ours. Inflation in Germany merely meant that one could get an incredibly cheap holiday! ... We lived this extraordinarily protected existence, very contented but absolutely unreal. You might think that this was because we were terribly rich or something; not at all, we were not any of us well off, but our family system and the school system provided a sort of shell into which we could retreat and where we were extremely happy.

On speech day, Turner made special mention of Blunt and his

persistent efforts to interest an incurably sentimental society in modern aims in art and literature. I confess the world to which he would introduce us seems to me a very odd one, a world of angles and dissonances and mis-shapen objects, but it is a world in which many people are trying nowadays to find, if not beauty, at least truth. Blunt and some others may go image-breaking, but that is no bad thing so long as the hammer is swung fair and square, and at the image and not at the heads of rival worshippers (laughter).

Like Canning, another teacher well disposed to Blunt, Turner had combined his encomium with a note of warning: he spoke of swinging hammers, where Canning had spoken of fire. Both seemed to sense a potential for trouble in Blunt's future.

For now, the enemy was confounded. MacNeice wrote to his parents, 'Guillebaud was enraged. He has been rampant lately – looking forward, however, to next term when he shall have no more "long-haired aesthetes" and "intellectual snobbery".' He and Blunt threw a final tea party in their study, and at the end of it they dropped the tea set out of the window piece by piece, watching the pot spew its brown fountain of tea as it fell and smashed. ' "Ruins of Carthage," we said, and washed our hands of Marlborough.'

3. Undergraduate

'the young Alcibiades'

Blunt's first year at Cambridge was not at all what he had expected – a fact he later conveniently forgot. 'He had a rather miserable time,' said Tom Mynors, who was then in his second year at Oxford. 'Being a rather isolated figure didn't endear him to life generally.' Trinity College, where he arrived in October 1926, was by far the largest college at the university and not noted for its friendliness. Even buoyed up with a scholarship and the privilege of a room in college – in Bishop's Hostel, an undistinguished Queen Anne building behind New Court – Blunt found the place intimidating and alienating, as did many new students. 'There was in general a stifling atmosphere of closed windows, drawn blinds, expiring candles,' wrote the historian V. G. Kiernan, who came up to the college in the mid-1930s. The master of Trinity, J. J. Thomson – whose mode of dress led to him being frequently and famously mistaken for a tramp – 'used to drift through the College courts with a bowler hat perched on his abundant white hair, and undergraduates were not encouraged to greet him'.

Blunt confided his anxieties to MacNeice – or 'Louis', as he now was; since their last term at Marlborough the two were on first-name terms. MacNeice was at first encouraging. 'I'm sure you'll bear Cambridge all right', he wrote.* 'I imagine you could bear most things like Atlas.' But after a few weeks he was

---

* Blunt and MacNeice began an eleven-year correspondence in the summer after they left Marlborough. Blunt kept MacNeice's letters and gave them to King's College, Cambridge, between 1968 and 1972. Blunt's letters do not survive.

reproving. 'You must not become an hypochondriac,' he told Blunt. 'Universities are really rather amusing.' Blunt's misanthropy, however, was stimulated by his shyness, and he continued to insist he preferred things to people. 'If one keeps seeing through things one never sees into them,' MacNeice warned him.

Trinity's unwelcoming *froideur* was not Blunt's only burden. He had fallen in love with 'John', a younger boy at Marlborough. It was to MacNeice that he went for advice. Others also knew he was prey to ups and downs in his emotional life: 'He was always going through a crisis for his friends,' John Hilton said wearily. 'I don't know what kind of crises they were, but he was always going through one.' This was Blunt's first experience of not a schoolboy crush but real unrequited love, and he took it hard. 'He didn't talk about his emotional life,' remembered his schoolfriend Alastair MacDonald, 'but I do remember him not being very happy in his first year. I don't know why.'

In November, halfway through his first term, Blunt made the long and tiresome trip from Cambridge to Marlborough, no longer a prison but, as MacNeice wrote, a haven of 'lots of solacing and suitable O.M.'s [Old Marlburians] to support one'. There he vented his full loathing of Trinity to his old teacher Canning, who, MacNeice later reported, 'was very worried about your hatred of Cambridge and couldn't believe me when I told him it was somewhat exaggerated'. That weekend Blunt declared himself to the object of his affections, and was summarily rejected. On the way back to Cambridge, in a bad state, he decided to drop in on MacNeice at Oxford. His unannounced visit to Merton College took his friend quite by surprise. 'I'm sorry to have been rather stupid the other night,' MacNeice wrote shortly afterwards. 'I was dazed by your appearance. I'm afraid Mynors, too, was rather silly. I hope you did not go away enraged with us. But your appearance was so meteoric.' Feeling he had not been sufficiently attentive to Blunt and his difficulties, MacNeice tried to make up for it in his letter, the most explicit he ever wrote about Blunt's emotional life. Uncoincidentally, Blunt put a lifelong moratorium on any quotation from it.

I'm sorry John was unresponsive but (not to be an emotional pander) I will say that I think he is quite hopeless – and secondly that I don't think him worth hoping for. And I don't see anything but mutual loss in the continuation of this affection – except a little emotion which might be called Platonic. Edward is far superior in every way and Michael, I should say, is superior to Edward. I think the only satisfactory end for a violent affection is a break ... I am afraid this is a brutal letter, especially considering C.I. But I think he would be better off not to be subjected to this admiration. (I still believe in the ideal mutual affection but I have never yet seen two people capable of it.) ... I'm sorry to be a didactic and moralising pig.

Blunt remained depressed and depressing despite the attempts of his old Marlborough friends Alastair MacDonald and Michael Robertson, both now up at Cambridge, to cheer him up with visits to concerts and musical salons run by a group of middle-aged ladies who kept open house for new undergraduates. (Blunt's was called Mrs Gordon, and flirtatiously called the trio of boys who turned up on her doorstep her 'Marlborough Musketeers.') MacNeice, still in his 'didactic and moralising pig' mode, was exasperated. He was enjoying Oxford – not least because he had discovered alcohol.

Just because you yourself are 'affecting to seem unaffected' why on earth shouldn't I continue to wear a red tie which I like rather than a grey tie ... which is all that my artificiality and my poses and affectations and my aberration and my egotisticalities and all the rest of it amounts to. I should have thought your position would be more distressing to an intelligent observer – seeing that you keep kicking against imaginary pricks and blaming actualities, while I am at least contented with my circumstances.

But things began to pick up, and when John Hilton went to visit him in Cambridge in March 1927 he saw the energetic old

Blunt. 'I had tea with Blunt and Co. and lunch the next day. His chief asset is an extraordinary vitality; he is a perfect conductor for the life-force.'

Nevertheless, Cambridge had nothing as intense and as exciting to offer him as his friendship and correspondence with MacNeice. And it was not so different for Louis: 'As I had no religion and no exciting personal relationships, my approach to ideas was very emotional.' He makes this sound like a phase, which for him perhaps it was; but the investment of ideas with intense – often displaced – emotion was to be characteristic of Blunt throughout his life. The two put enormous energy and feeling into their reading. MacNeice wrote to Blunt breathlessly about Hardy, Milton, Roger Fry, *The Waste Land*, Webster, Yeats, Gertrude Stein, Lawrence, Joyce ('Shepard has got hold of a copy of *Ulysses* which I am about to read'), Dostoevsky and Nietzsche. They pored over Wyndham Lewis's 'onslaught on the moderns'. Blunt and his appetite for the new made MacNeice feel like 'the precious little boy . . . who . . . picks up fag ends of a dozen latest ideas and says "Look at me smoking!"' Their squabbles over ideas were like lovers' tiffs: 'I don't believe in pure form. I don't believe in pure anything. Anything pure is an abstraction. All concretes are adulterated.'

Not that all the letters were at quite this intellectual pitch. An unmistakable camp thread ran through MacNeice's missives: 'I shall give you a peony to wear,' he wrote when Blunt announced that he was coming to an Oxford ball – 'if you're good.' They'd invented girl's names for each other: MacNeice was 'Susie', Blunt was 'Antonia'. 'Get yr hair washed Antonia (in gypsum),' Mac-Neice ordered in his next letter; it was signed 'Yr meticulous aunt Susie'.

The year ended with another setback, and Blunt's first experience of unhappy love was followed by his first taste of – by his standards – academic failure. He took a second in his mathematics part ones.* For a Trinity mathematics scholar, and one who had

---

* Cambridge degrees are divided into two parts, with part ones taken at the end

always passed near or at the top of his class, this was a considerable blow to the self-esteem.

Mathematics was considered the most difficult subject at Cambridge – not least by the mathematics faculty. At Trinity it was taught by G. H. Hardy, a pure mathematician of world stature (and author of the best book ever written about the appeal of his subject, *A Mathematician's Apology*), and it enjoyed some of the glamour radiating from Cambridge science, then in arguably its greatest period. During the 1910s and '20s the university had been the site of a series of crucial discoveries, including those of J. B. S. Haldane in the study of enzymes, Joseph Needham in the development of the fertilized egg, and J. D. Bernal (who was also a founder of the study of molecular biology) in X-ray crystallography. In 1906 J. J. Thomson, master of Trinity, had won a Nobel Prize for discovering the electron, and in 1919 his pupil Ernest Rutherford, head of the Cavendish Laboratory and another Nobel laureate, had split the atom. These and other breakthroughs not only were momentous in themselves, but also encouraged ambitions to emulate scientific methodology in other areas. The results were often mixed. Clive Bell's theory of Significant Form, a self-styled attempt at a 'science of aesthetics', produced a dreadfully limited and simplistic analysis of anything that wasn't modernism, and a pretty limited one of anything that was. More successfully, I. A. Richards, the energetic English don at Magdalene College, was inventing 'Practical Criticism' as an attempt to show how literary effects could be analysed, taken apart, and explained. This intellectual climate had a strong effect on Blunt, even – or perhaps especially – after he had abandoned mathematics. As an undergraduate, he often treated art as if it were a scientific hypothesis or a mathematical problem in need of a solution: Picasso was 'the logical explanation and development' from Cézanne and had acquired 'complete mastery over the problem of form' by becoming a Cubist. The scientific ideals of

---

of the first year or second year, and part twos – finals – at the end of three or four years.

clarity and demonstrability, more subtly applied, would continue to be especially important throughout Blunt's career as an art historian. At Cambridge, however, his adherence to Clive Bell's theories led him to disregard the meaning and significance of most art, from the ritualistic importance of 'Negro' art to the religious intensity – 'very distasteful' – of El Greco. 'We were, I think,' he admitted later, 'unaware of the degree to which we totally misunderstood these artists.'

There may also have been a darker and less foreseeable consequence to his apprenticeship. The sense of intellectual momentum generated by Cambridge science during this remarkable period encouraged Blunt and others to believe that similar progress and similar certainties were available in other areas of human activity – such as the great social 'experiment' in the Soviet Union.

Following his second in Maths, Blunt took refuge abroad. On the recommendation of the British Embassy in Paris, he had been offered a summer job as tutor to the three young sons of M. and Mme René Gimpel. Gimpel was a well-known French picture dealer; his wife was the daughter of the dealer Joseph Duveen. They were spending the summer on Lake Como. 'What fun selling your soul to those millionaires in Italy,' MacNeice wrote. Unfortunately Mme Gimpel just wanted a glorified nanny to take her sons swimming. He was treated as a servant by the status-conscious Gimpels, who required him to eat on his own while the family dined in full evening dress next door. Back in London he complained to MacNeice and others about his 'Italian purgatory'. 'He had put it about that we had behaved naughtily,' Jean and Peter Gimpel, the two youngest boys, remembered. It was Blunt's last excursion into teaching small boys for a very long time.*

In October 1927, the beginning of a new academic year, Blunt changed his course from mathematics to modern languages and began his Cambridge career again. In one sense the move must

* In the 1970s Blunt began to give art talks at the National Gallery to the under-eights.

have felt like a defeat, an exile from Cambridge's intellectual peaks where he had hoped he belonged. Languages were certainly easier than mathematics, especially as he already spoke fluent French, but they had less intellectual cachet. However, the change gave Blunt the opportunity to study French literature and culture, and thus to approach obliquely the subject which interested him more than any other: art history. Whereas on the Continent art history was a respected discipline, it did not exist at Cambridge, or at any other English educational institution. In England it was mainly a rich man's occupation. The art historians Kenneth Clark and John Pope-Hennessy, for example, spent a couple of years working unsalaried for the American connoisseur Bernard Berenson at his villa I Tatti, in Tuscany, then wrote their first books. For Blunt, obviously, this was not possible. He would have to earn his living.

There were advantages to Blunt's situation. His new tutor H. F. Stewart – known as 'Creeping Jesus' because of the way he padded round Trinity in a black gown with his head bowed – was probably the best language teacher at Cambridge and a world expert on Pascal. He was very taken with Blunt. 'He certainly saw him as a special pupil,' remembered Frida, one of Stewart's four daughters, who met Blunt when he was brought home for tea. Another, Jean, was said to have fallen wildly for Blunt, even to the extent of following him round Cambridge. She was the first in a line of female admirers Blunt would attract throughout his life.

The new year also brought Blunt his first real love affair. Peter Montgomery, freshly arrived in Cambridge, was a quiet boy from a wealthy landowning Northern Irish family. His uncle was Field Marshal Sir Archibald Montgomery-Massingberd, Chief of the Imperial General Staff in the 1930s. Peter Montgomery was, in the words of the King's College don George Rylands, 'a dear sweet poetical boy'. He was not an intellectual – some considered him dim, others charmingly vague – but he had a passion for the arts, a real talent for music, and film-star looks. Among their friends, the story went that he and Blunt had been each other's respective deflowerers – one reason why, though Montgomery was not especially academic, they remained deeply affectionate throughout their lives, always regarding each other generously through the eyes of youth. 'They were simpatico together,' Montgomery's nephew Hugh Montgomery Massingberd recalled; 'they laughed a lot. Blunt shared with Peter a weakness for bad schoolboy puns and finding most people utterly absurd, beginning and ending very much with oneself. Neither of them were pompous, and Peter didn't take himself at all seriously.'

Montgomery was an Old Wellingtonian with grand friends, the most exotic of whom was the extremely rich and more than slightly preposterous Prince Chula Chakrabongse, half-Russian scion of the Thai royal family. Chula painted his rooms peacock blue, went to parties in London attended by Tallulah Bankhead, and rarely got up before noon. He was impressed by Blunt, whom he called 'one of the bright stars of the intellectual firmament'.

Blunt's relative poverty – he had no dinner jacket, for example, and wore his grey flannel bags to every engagement – seems not to have barred his entry to the smart set at Cambridge. Conspicuous consumption played a more central role in creating exclusivity at Oxford. At the fashionable don Maurice Bowra's Oxford parties the drink was champagne; in Cambridge it was (warm) gin and tonic. At Oxford, Blunt's old roommate Tom Mynors was dropped by John Betjeman, who was in expensive pursuit of the grand and wealthy. 'After a term or two I realized he was living in a circle that was quite above anything that I could afford. At Cambridge, Anthony was moving in a different kind of circle. It was more intellectual, not so class superior.'

Blunt's most important new social introduction had come at the end of his first year, when he had been introduced by Guy Barton, a former pupil of his brother Wilfrid, who was now teaching art at Haileybury, to George Rylands. 'Dadie' Rylands, as he was known, gave him his entrée to Cambridge Bloomsbury. He was a well-connected, cosmopolitan young English don about five years older than Blunt, famously handsome – 'the most beautiful blond at King's' – passionate about the theatre, and a great taker-up of promising undergraduates. 'The people who taught me were uniformly uninspiring,' remembered one protégé. 'You were educated by your contemporaries, and Dadie, of course.' Rylands's best friend was Rosamond Lehmann, newly famous since the success of her novel *Dusty Answer*, and he was an intimate of Lytton Strachey – who called him his 'sweet canary Don' – and a former employee of Virginia and Leonard Woolf at the Hogarth Press.

Rylands took to Blunt – or 'Ant' as he called him – 'not as a pupil, as a friend'.

He was taller than the usual undergraduate, rather more lean, reserved, remote, not talkative. He was mad keen about painting, and I was entirely devoted to acting, directing, and the theatre. Anthony never went in for that, but he was a great encourager. He was a hard worker at painting, and was frightfully keen on Picasso and Blake. I knew very little about painting, but his passion affected me a lot. He always had a particularly dry sense of humour, and could be sardonic and satirical and could mock people. Always one felt he was an intellectual, and when we got on to serious things, such as painting, he was serious. Otherwise, as regards people and behaviour, he was always amused by it. He was not at all prudish, he was rather high-minded, but not priggish.

King's was the Cambridge outpost of Bloomsbury, which was in the late 1920s – to use Blunt's own description – the 'dominant force' in the university, and then at the zenith of its fame and powers. Many members of the group – Roger Fry, Lytton Strachey, E. M. Forster – were King's alumni. John Maynard Keynes was the college's bursar; G. E. Moore, philosopher and author of the *Principia Ethica*, was a don there. Dadie Rylands incarnated the King's ethos, which much of the rest of the university regarded as dangerously informal (a relative term, since everyone still wore gowns, undergraduates had to be in by midnight, and the arrival of women at the college was still forty-four years away). King's, according to E. M. Forster, had a tradition 'of easy intercourse between old and young'. The general *on dit* was against public schools, muscular Christianity and Tory imperialism, and, according to Forster, for 'personal relations, philosophic discussion and aesthetic appreciation'. In short, 'it was not sufficient glory to be a Blue there, nor an additional glory to get drunk.'

A large part of the special atmosphere of King's involved being aware of the special atmosphere of King's. 'For the halcyon period of my undergraduate days,' gushed L. P. Wilkinson, a student there in the 1920s, and author of the official college history, 'we felt free (more free no doubt than our special circumstances should have allowed us to be) to enjoy the individualistic pleasures of literature, art, scientific discovery and personal relationships.' In his first years at Cambridge Blunt preferred King's to his own, more chilly, college.

Rylands's rooms, the site of many parties, were where grown-up Bloomsbury met undergraduate Cambridge. At Marlborough, Blunt had been inspired by Bloomsbury and its theories. Now he met its creators. He later wrote as if the sequence was automatic, insisting that Cambridge was 'to an extraordinary extent for me an extension of life at Marlborough. The ideas that we had been absorbing about art and literature were really already based on Bloomsbury and although these figures were remote to me ... their ideas were very firmly implanted in all of us.' But at the time it must have felt more like the fulfilment of an impossible fantasy.

In his diaries of the 1980s, Anthony Powell mused on the feats of social climbing performed by a group of his friends and contemporaries. Evelyn Waugh, Cecil Beaton, John Betjeman, Cyril Connolly, the writer Peter Quennell and the painter Adrian Daintry had all been born 'middle class', rather than 'out of the top drawer' and had worked hard to climb into the beau monde. Powell thought that Betjeman was the most interesting case among the social-climbing intellectuals. He had been the most socially successful, while 'at the same time avoiding almost all opprobrium for being snobbish'. A very English aspect to this game was the importance attached to succeeding without visible expense of effort. Blunt was arguably even better at this than Betjeman. His ability to move into the 'right' set, and later to fit into the heart of the British Establishment, always appeared effortless; in the words of Quentin Bell, brother to Blunt's new friend Julian, and son of the art critic Clive, 'Blunt didn't have the same thing as Betjeman at all. Betjeman was much more frantic.' A measure of Blunt's success is that no one perceived him as a climber – though they did sometimes think of him as a snob. Below the surface, however, there was a powerful desire for inclusion.

Through Rylands, Blunt met the young Michael Redgrave, an actor from Magdalene College, and Arthur Marshall, an undergraduate who specialized in delivering comic monologues while dressed up as an Angela Brazil-type schoolgirl. He also met the children of the Cambridge and Bloomsbury intelligentsia, among them Clive and Vanessa Bell's son Julian, who had just arrived at King's, and the painter Julian Trevelyan, who wrote that Blunt was 'one of the most amusing people at Cambridge'. Eddie Playfair, another of Rylands's young friends, thought Blunt was 'delightful. The things people blamed Anthony for later hadn't really shown up at that stage. A very good companion, really good company, witty always.'

Blunt was soon a fully fledged Bloomsbury protégé. Along with Julian Bell and Michael Redgrave, in January 1928 he went for lunch with John Maynard Keynes, who later confided to Vanessa Bell, apropos the occasion, that he found the young 'rather hard work'. He visited Ham Spray, the house where Lytton Strachey lived in a complicated *ménage à trois* with Dora Carrington (who loved him) and Ralph Partridge (whom he loved). Frances Partridge (Frances Marshall as she then was; she married Ralph Partridge in the mid-1930s) met Blunt at Ham Spray. 'I think he was a bit shy,' she remembered, 'and he asked me to go for a walk with him. We walked up the downs in front of the house and at the side. Quite a long walk and a good intimate talk . . . He was one of the current Cambridge young men Lytton took an interest in and used to visit.'

Rylands's set – Blunt included – seemed to the poet Kathleen Raine, then studying at Girton, 'incredibly glamorous'. 'They were all immensely good looking, and knew it. They walked with the look of the young Alcibiades. Anthony was this tall, elegant, distinguished figure, the quintessential Athenian aristocrat in the Platonic sense.' Nor was she the only one to note the glamour and faintly homoerotic qualities of this group. The February 1928 issue of the Cambridge magazine *Granta* described a party of Rylands's as a 'bacchanalian revel at which the more brilliant Adonidiae of Cambridge were present'.

To Blunt, part of the appeal of the circles around Keynes and Rylands was that they did not regard homosexuality with disgust or embarrassment. In the early years of the century Keynes and his friend Lytton Strachey had half-seriously tried to rationalize and theorize their situation, calling it 'the higher sodomy'. The idea was that homosexuality might be a way of life superior to heterosexual love. By the late 1920s L. P. Wilkinson noticed that at King's homosexuality was 'the constant topic of serious discussion and of gossip. By now it had ceased to have any moral overtones. In the general absence of women in the 'twenties homosexual affairs were natural and common, and passionate relationships were accepted and sympathetically regarded by the friends of those concerned . . . in the end most of the participants got married.'

One of the consequences of this was that 'we *all* talked about our love affairs *all* the time', as Rylands recalled. 'Our conversation was extremely frank and randy,' wrote John Lehmann, another homosexual Trinity undergraduate who found his way to King's, 'and our amours were talked about quite openly. It was definitely considered bad form, in fact ridiculous, to show embarrassment or guilt about them, whether they were concerned with males or females.' However, there was a great deal more talk than action.

Though homosexuality was treated sympathetically at King's, it provided no obvious model of happy or guilt-free love. When the Trinity economics don Dennis Robertson fell deeply and unsuccessfully in love with Dadie Rylands, he was so tortured with guilt that he went to visit Freud in Vienna. Rylands, so apparently at ease with himself, was extremely reticent about his own passions. It was rumoured that he had to be completely drunk in order to have sex, and was afterwards agonized with guilt. Many young men in the Bloomsbury circle remained sexually inexperienced throughout university. John Lehmann had one fumbled and embarrassing sexual experience at Cambridge. He could find no one to tell him what to do: 'Physically we lacked a down-to-earth well-wisher to teach us how to cope with the sexual side of our relationship.' In the end, 'the higher sodomy' seemed to mainly be about acquiring grace and wisdom through suffering the pangs of unrequited love. 'The homosexual temperament must, I think, be regarded as a misfortune, though it is possible, with that temperament, to have a better, more passionate and more noble life than most men of normal temperament achieve,' wrote the King's don Goldsworthy Lowes Dickinson, who spent his entire life in a series of unrequited passions for straight men, and who had by the 1920s become to his circle the embodiment of noble, disappointed homosexual love.

Still, these surroundings were more positive for Blunt than most settings would have been. His brother Wilfrid's wretched experience of acknowledging his homosexuality was closer to the norm. A virgin at the age of twenty-eight, he went to see a Harley Street doctor, who explained that his feelings for men were a disability, 'like being blind or deaf. Or, he added – rather charmingly, and as if in afterthought – a Jew (he was clearly one himself).' He suggested Wilfrid sleep with a woman and see if that might do the trick. It didn't. That Anthony was also homosexual was something Wilfrid 'did not know for certain, though of course I had guessed it, until some time after the War, when we exchanged confidences – curiously enough at a reception at Windsor Castle'.

Although the atmosphere of Rylands's circle was liberating, Blunt was not open about his affairs. His main confidant was still MacNeice, whose letters continued to make occasional reference to Blunt's proclivities and love objects: 'Please don't have me [to stay] if you are busy or in love or in any other elevated and nonsociable situation,' he wrote in the spring of 1928; 'My love to Michael and Alastair and Basil and Adonis and Attis and Orsino and Hyacinthus and Prometheus and Ganymede.' Blunt was known as an easy conversationalist with a taste for the absurd and a liking for jokes and puns, but he rarely revealed either his camp or his emotional side in public. (In later life he hated the thought that he might be regarded as 'pansyish' or limp-wristed, though a later boyfriend thought he had 'a strong girlish streak', and a habit of flicking his forelock back and stroking it on to his hair which was 'a dead giveaway'.) One exception to this is recorded in the June issue of *Granta* in 1929. Michael Redgrave and a few others had written a parody of Virginia Woolf's just published *Orlando*, about a character called Verandah who changed sex so often 'no one was quite certain of what turn his sexual arrangement might take at any minute'. The article was illustrated by a picture of Blunt, dressed as a woman, reclining fragrantly on a couch while wearing a long dress and sporting an elaborate and luxuriant wig.

Already he kept his life in different boxes. 'I never think of Blunt in love: he was rather remote about it,' said Rylands, who could recall only one young man apart from Peter Montgomery who took Blunt's fancy in all his time at Cambridge. 'He was rather fond of Claude Phillimore, a very good-looking Trinity boy, an architect. He was a rather large fellow, gentle, like some nice dog.' But Rylands's recollection is a reflection of Blunt's reticence as much as anything. There were other affairs, but he tended to keep them secret.

When John Hilton came to Cambridge in that spring of 1928 he found Blunt once more at the centre of things. 'Julian Bell, John Lehmann, George Rylands, Michael Redgrave and others seemed more three-dimensional, less odd and at the same time more exciting than most of what we could find among students or dons.' Hilton was even more impressed the following year, when E. M. Forster attended a tea party for a hockey game played by two teams of hopeless Oxbridge aesthetes, captained by Blunt and Stephen Spender. Blunt won, by the underhand expedient of smuggling in a rugby blue. Spender scored an own goal.

During the academic year of 1927–8 Rylands made another important introduction for Blunt, this time to the Trinity Classics don and art collector Andrew Gow. Gow had taught and befriended Rylands at Eton (another of his favourite pupils had been Eric Blair – the young George Orwell). At Cambridge they played bridge. Gow had a collection of Degas drawings, as well as an encyclopedic knowledge of the Italian Renaissance and French, Dutch and Flemish painting. 'His rooms were the one place where one could find a library of books about the Italian Renaissance, a fine collection of photographs of paintings and above all stimulating conversation about the arts in general,' Blunt later recalled. Gow had a reputation for being dry, withdrawn, bad-tempered, sardonic, and was, it was assumed, a non-practising homosexual – in other words, a Cambridge don of a recognizable type, very much in the vein of his friend A. E. Housman. A poem by W. H. Auden about a Cambridge don who 'kept tears like dirty postcards in a drawer', usually taken to be about Housman, could also be a description of Gow. 'He had an unwelcoming manner and very often an acid tongue,' remembered Alan Hodgkin, the Nobel-prizewinning scientist, who as an undergraduate met him in the 1930s. However, with a small group of students in whom he took an interest – women as well as men – he would take tremendous pains. Even with them he would often sit in total silence. 'He is', Hodgkin wrote home to his parents, 'about the most difficult person to talk with.'

'Gow became extremely fond of Anthony,' remembered Eddie Playfair. 'I don't think they had a homosexual relationship, because I don't think Gow did that sort of thing. One was usually invited to come and see him at 10 p.m., but Blunt was more privileged.' The admiration was mutual. Through his insistence on accuracy and high scholarly standards, Gow was to be an important mentor for Blunt. 'If I have any standards of scholarship,' Blunt wrote, 'they are based on what I learnt from him.'

Hilton remembered that 'Blunt always mentioned him in tones of reverence, as though he was the embodiment of all wisdom.' 'He was certainly a very impressive man,' said Ernst Gombrich, who encountered Gow in his capacity as a *grand homme* of British art, on the numerous art committees on which he served. 'He was like a nineteenth-century aesthete. An interesting figure, not at all involved on the political side. I really think Blunt felt he was his disciple.'

Hilda Blunt – who met Gow through her assiduous efforts to keep up with her son's career – was less impressed. According to Wilfrid, she 'viewed him with some mistrust and took a particular dislike ... to two outcrops of scrub ... that he cultivated on his cheekbones'. Although Blunt never grew the facial hair, his post-war persona as director of the Courtauld owed something to the crusty/kindly, distant/helpful, dried out/ enthusiastic manner of the Cambridge don embodied by Gow. Blunt remained loyal and close to him for half a century, visiting him regularly until his death in 1978, when he was elderly, ill and increasingly sour.

In the Easter holidays of 1928 Blunt went to Vienna with John Hilton to assuage his latest aesthetic passion, German rococo and Austrian baroque architecture – an appetite quite out of keeping with his taste for the austere intellectualism of Poussin. It had been inspired by a trip to Munich with his brother Wilfrid the previous summer. With his old schoolboy enthusiasm, Blunt persuaded Hilton to walk everywhere, though the weather was unseasonably cold and they had not brought enough warm clothes. 'I was wound round with an excessively dark muffler of my mother's,' Hilton remembered:

I must have looked a caricature anarchist. Plain-clothes police followed us back to the train and demanded papers ... We spent a couple of days with rucksacks looking at the monasteries on or near the stretch of Danube called the Wachau. The fitting climax was the fabulous Melk, whose photographs we had pored over in the close confines of our studies in Marlborough.

'I couldn't have asked for a better companion during those weeks. He was intensely alive, amusing and considerate,' Hilton said later, adding that Blunt, whose austere tastes sometimes bordered on the punishing, tried to get him to sleep in ditches.

The following term, in May 1928, the last of his second academic year, Blunt received a definitive token of his position as a protégé of Cambridge Bloomsbury. He was elected to or 'born into' the Apostles, or 'the Society', as its members called it – the secret debating society still presided over by Keynes, of which almost all the key male figures of Bloomsbury had been members.

From the Society's records it is impossible to know for sure who inducted Blunt into the Apostles. Although new members were 'fathered' by existing Apostles, new recruits (or 'embryos', in the tedious pregnancy metaphor employed by the Society) were usually suggested by several people and had to be vetted by older members like Keynes. Dadie Rylands was already a member, but the two most recent recruits to the Society were also friends of Blunt's, and it seems probable that they put him up for election. Alister Watson, a King's mathematician-turned-physicist, was one: he was probably also the only undergraduate Blunt knew at this time who was a Marxist.* Watson was the most active Apostle of his generation, giving nineteen papers to the Society, all but two as an undergraduate. The other was Dennis Proctor, an economist a year older than Blunt, who was the last great unrequited passion of Goldie Lowes Dickinson.

The existence of the Apostles was supposed to be a secret. This was ostensibly to discourage would-be members from canvassing for election, and to ensure that in debates members would say exactly what they felt and thought, without fear of censure – the

---

* According to Peter Wright, Blunt told him that 'I learnt my Marxist theory at Alister's feet.' However, Watson is not mentioned at all in Blunt's 1943 memoir for Soviet Intelligence, in which he described his conversion.

implication being that they would openly discuss taboo subjects. (In the early years of the century, when homosexual acts were criminal offences – they would remain so until 1967 – 'the higher sodomy' had been a favourite Apostolic topic.) Of course, the secrecy and intellectual snobbery did nothing to reduce the Society's cachet. The main obligation of Apostles in discussion was to be as frank and honest as possible, even at the risk of hurting feelings. For the Apostles of Keynes's generation, the experience of such intellectual and verbal freedom had apparently been intoxicating. Bertrand Russell, who had been an active member in the early years of the century, along with Lytton Strachey, Roger Fry, the social historian G. M. Trevelyan, Ludwig Wittgenstein and G. E. Moore, wrote, 'It was a principle in discussion that there were no taboos, no limitations, no barrier to absolute speculation.'

By the 1920s the Apostles' heroic period was over. 'I think that in my generation the importance [of the Apostles] had become less great,' Blunt later wrote. 'If one heard people like Forster and Strachey and particularly [Goldie Lowes] Dickinson talking about it, it was clear that the Saturday evening meeting of the Apostles was the centre of their life, and that everything was regulated according to this, and everything that was non-Apostolic was in some way inferior.' By 1928 the secret was much less secret, and plenty of non-members seemed to know about it. Membership seems to have become an acknowledgement of intellectual standing and clubbability, rather than anything else. Julian Bell wrote that his election was 'the most important event of my Cambridge life', because it meant that he had 'reached the pinnacles of Cambridge intellectualism'. Eddie Playfair, who was put up for election by Bell, was blackballed by Blunt 'for being intellectually inadequate' – or so Leonard Woolf thoughtfully told him. All the Society's members were from King's or Trinity and were already part of the extended circle of Bloomsbury and its protégés. In the mid-1930s – when the society was supposed to have been dominated by Marxists – a new member was told by J. T. Sheppard, the ageing and exceptionally camp provost of

King's, that the main criteria for membership were that 'one must be *very* brilliant and *extremely* nice'. In some more lurid accounts, the Apostles has been portrayed as a kind of knocking shop for predatory homosexuals, among them Blunt. This vastly overstates the case. While it seems that a few young men were elected for their beauty rather than their brains, this was far from the norm and of Blunt's friends Bell, Proctor and Watson were all clubbable, clever and heterosexual, as were two more young men he would induct into the Society, Victor Rothschild and Hugh Sykes Davies.

For the Apostles of Keynes's generation the Society had been especially significant because 'their view of life was very largely formulated in the discussions there, under the distant influence of [G. E.] Moore'. At Apostles meetings thirty years before, Moore had refined the arguments that he set out in his 1903 book *Principia Ethica*, which had become a sacred text to certain members of Bloomsbury. Moore wrote that the greatest good was to be found in 'personal affections and aesthetic enjoyments'. These emotions or rather 'states of consciousness' as Moore called them – love and friendship, the contemplation of beauty – were the only things valuable in themselves and the only justifiable ends of human acts. On its publication, Keynes, Strachey and E. M. Forster had hailed *Principia Ethica* as a work of genius. It chimed perfectly with Bloomsbury's instinctive antipathy to Victorian morality and its near-obsession with its own feelings and emotions. In addition, Moore offered the members of Bloomsbury a seemingly 'objective' justification for dispensing with conventional sexual morality. Keynes wrote later, 'We repudiated entirely customary morals, conventions and traditional wisdom.' Another way of putting it was to say, as Beatrice Webb wrote tartly, that the *Principia* mainly provided Bloomsbury with a justification for 'doing whatever they liked'.

The Apostles did not record the titles of papers delivered at meetings, but did note the motion the Society voted on after each talk. By 1928 the prevailing atmosphere was, according to Julian Bell, 'Bloomsbury un peu passé' – an allegation that the list of motions does nothing to refute. The Society discussed 'a classic, post-impressionist view of the arts' and 'anarchism in the mode of Blake and Dostoevksy'. The subjects were aesthetic, abstract, ethical. Among the votes following Blunt's papers of the late 1920s were 'Must art come from the heart?' (Blunt voted no); 'Is an opera because a string quartet' (*sic*) (Blunt voted no); 'Smooth or Hairy?' (smooth); 'Great + Sublime equals Good' (yes); 'Does England have the Academy it deserves?' (yes). In classic Bloomsbury style, practical politics were of little interest. 'States of mind were the only things that mattered,' Blunt recorded, 'and direct action was of quite secondary importance.'*

At the time, this was the generally held belief among Blunt's set. 'In the Cambridge I first knew in 1929 and 1930,' Julian Bell wrote in 1933, 'the central subject of ordinary intelligent conversation was poetry. As far as I remember we hardly ever talked or thought about politics.' This was true of Blunt too, who still claimed that politics were not worthy of attention. For Bell – a would-be poet who followed the gospel of I. A. Richards – it was literature, not politics, that promised to provide answers to the big questions. Literature, Richards wrote – especially poetry, 'the supremely civilising pursuit' – 'is capable of saving us; it is a perfectly possible means of overcoming chaos'.

Perhaps the two biggest lessons Blunt learned from the Apostles were that sexual and emotional honesty was vital – so, though he did not broadcast news of his affairs or his homosexuality, he did not lie about them – and that all forms of orthodoxy should be questioned. But, though membership was extremely gratifying, the greater part of his intellectual interests were not addressed by the Society. 'The Apostles were never primarily interested in the arts,' he wrote later, 'and on the whole my own activities lay very largely outside [the Society].' This seems to have been true. Quentin Bell, who had decided to skip university and become a painter, regarded Blunt as 'practically the only person at Cam-

---

* Not all Bloomsbury was politically apathetic. Leonard Woolf was an active socialist, and Lowes Dickinson a supporter of the League of Nations.

bridge who took an interest in painting', the only person who 'actually went to the Fitzwilliam'.

It was to create an outlet for these interests that, in the summer of 1928, Blunt and two friends co-founded a literary magazine called the *Venture*. His accomplices were Michael Redgrave and Romilly, known as Robin, Fedden. Blunt, 'who was already establishing a reputation for himself at Cambridge as a formidable and disputatious art critic', planned to write about art in it and approached John Lehmann to be a contributor. 'From that moment till I went down it occupied a central place in my interests,' Lehmann wrote. This was not least because a rival magazine, *Experiment*, had been started simultaneously by William Empson, a brilliant and fervent admirer of I. A. Richards from Magdalene, with two friends, Jacob Bronowski and Hugh Sykes Davies. 'For the next two years a furious battle raged (in our minds at any rate) between the protagonists of the two magazines,' according to Lehmann.*

Kathleen Raine, who was published by *Experiment* but played snakes and ladders on the lawns of Trinity with Blunt, felt the two magazines had distinct identities: Empson and Bronowski were 'brilliant' and 'rather scruffy' and distinctly heterosexual. (Empson was sent down from Cambridge for having contraceptives in his room.) The *Venture* editors, however, were 'a natural part of the apolitical, aristocratic, cultured, learned elite of Cambridge'. They were 'all homosexuals. We all knew they were. Nobody talked about it, but we all knew that in the Society it was rather a mark of distinction. We had all read Plato, and in Plato it was the done thing.'

When the two magazines came out in the winter term of 1928, *Experiment* was immediately cast as the more radical publication.

---

* In reality the polarization was much less exaggerated. Several *Experiment* writers, including Humphrey Jennings and Basil Wright, happily wrote for *The Venture* (though Julian Bell called them 'mercenaries'). Michael Redgrave used many of *Experiment*'s writers when he later became editor of the *Cambridge Review*, and in 1932 Blunt brought Hugh Sykes Davies into the Apostles.

It was hospitable to Surrealist and Imagist poetry; it published work by Boris Pasternak, Conrad Aiken and Empson himself. John Lehmann described the magazine, rather exaggeratedly, as belonging to 'the extreme left'. Though William Empson was a Wykehamist and hardly a stranger to privilege, Bronowski was a scholarship boy from a poor Jewish family.* In Humphrey Jennings, the future documentary-maker and co-founder of Mass Observation, *Experiment* had an art critic who was as familiar with contemporary art as Blunt, and more straightforwardly supportive of its strivings for newness. Exposed to Jennings's real enthusiasm for the modern, Blunt revealed himself in comparison as a closet conservative.

The *Venture*, which had set out to publish new poetry and writing, began by defining itself in contrast to *Experiment*'s modernity. In its first issue in November 1928, Blunt wrote 'Self-Consciousness in Modern Art', a Bloomsbury-inspired criticism of modern artists for over-intellectualizing their work. It was a Bloomsbury tenet that painting should be instinctive and anti-intellectual. 'Theories are dangerous for the artist,' Roger Fry had written. 'It is much better to know nothing about them.' Blunt argued that the dangers of the opposite course were apparent in 'the epidemic of Surrealisme' (*sic*), a movement of which he was profoundly suspicious. In the *Venture*'s last issue Julian Bell attacked T. S. Eliot and the increasing obscurity of modern poetry.

Experiment, Blunt concluded in retrospect, was 'much the more positive and creative journal of the two'. The *Venture* 'was really as Louis MacNeice remarked in his review of it at the time when it first appeared, dangerously safe and Georgian and respectable'. Blunt was rather hard on himself. Although not at the modernist cutting edge, his articles for the *Venture* covered subjects as diverse as the still unfashionable Brueghel, Cubism and Surreal-

* According to his daughter, Lisa Jardine, Bronowski was told that, despite getting a starred first at Jesus College, as a Jew he had as much chance of getting a fellowship as of becoming archbishop.

ism, the Italian Renaissance and his erstwhile hero Sacheverell Sitwell (an attack written under a pseudonym), as well as including what was probably the first article in English on Johann Michael Fischer, the unsung genius of German rococo architecture.

In fact Blunt *was* working in the cause of modern poetry. In an early example of his later talent for fixing, he did all he could to get Louis MacNeice's poems published by the Hogarth Press. He gave them to Dadie Rylands to read, and set up a meeting in Cambridge between the poet and Leonard Woolf in November 1928. In one of the misadventures in which MacNeice seemed increasingly to find himself – fires, car crashes, chaotic drinking bouts – he crashed his car into a tree on the way to Cambridge. By the time he arrived Woolf had left. His first collection, *Blind Fireworks*, was published the following year by Victor Gollancz.

Blunt's love affair with Bloomsbury continued throughout his undergraduate years. During 1928–9 he became increasingly close to the contemporary most directly connected to Bloomsbury, Julian Bell, whose election to the Apostles he almost certainly secured, three months after his own. It was entirely in character that at the same time he should have been engaged in a half-serious battle with the elders of his adoptive philosophy. He was joined in this by Bell, who, according to his biographers, 'loved and admired Bloomsbury, and respected it and even believed in it; yet at the same time, although rarely explicitly and openly, he was in rebellion against it'. In the autumn of 1928 Bell wrote to his mother, Vanessa, 'I sent Blunt a long list of everyone's opinions about Maynard, which ought to encourage him. I think we shall have a fine to do next term. With any luck we ought to be able to set everyone on to Maynard, whilst appearing to be most magnanimous and forgiving ourselves.'

There was real antagonism with another older member. After sixteen years away – during which time he had written *Tractatus Logico-Philosophicus* – Ludwig Wittgenstein returned to

Cambridge in January 1929. (Keynes had written to Vanessa Bell, 'Well, God has arrived. I met him on the 5.15 train.') The deeply unclubbable, but now revered, Wittgenstein had been 'excommunicated' from the Apostles in 1912, for feuding with two other members. He returned for Blunt's first paper at the Apostles in February 1929, when the Society was asked to vote on the question 'Must art come from the heart?' Blunt voted no; Wittgenstein yes. It appears that Wittgenstein took his opposition rather further than a mere vote; or that Blunt felt he had. Wittgenstein was inclined to be aggressive in argument; Julian Bell later wrote, 'In every company he shouts us down, / And stops our sentence stuttering his own'. After the meeting, Keynes wrote to Blunt that he had heard that he was 'upset by what you think happened when Wittgenstein returned to the Society. But the facts are not as you suppose'; he invited him and Julian Bell to lunch to talk about it. Wittgenstein quickly became, John Hilton noted, one of Blunt's 'not rare, *bêtes noires*'. The philosopher was irascible and anti-social, and his rigorous asceticism was quite at odds with Bloomsbury's gossipy self-absorption. He hated Cambridge academic life, and felt a fully reciprocated dislike of the younger Apostles, whom he called collectively 'the Julian Bells'.* The lines quoted below are from a satirical poem Julian Bell himself was moved to write, pointing out that the great advocate of the meaninglessness of qualitative judgements failed to follow his own precepts:

> But who, on any issue, ever saw
> Ludwig refrain from laying down the law?

* Wittgenstein's closest friends and allies among the younger Apostles were the brilliant young mathematician Frank Ramsey and George Thompson, a Marxist classicist who, from the 1930s, was one of the best known hard-line Stalinists in British academia. He married one of the four daughters of Blunt's tutor, H. F. Stewart. 'George was very strange unless you were a pure Marxist, he was really hard to talk to. Blunt certainly wasn't part of his set,' recalled his sister-in-law, Frida Knight.

For he talks nonsense, numerous statements makes,
Forever his own vow of silence breaks:
Ethics, aesthetics, talks of day and night,
And calls all things good or bad, and wrong or right.

Despite these ructions, Blunt still very much wanted to be part of Bloomsbury. A few months later, in the spring of 1929, his wish was fulfilled, and he was actually accused of *being* Clive Bell. A sharp exchange of letters in the *Cambridge Review* prompted an intervention by Geoffrey Rossetti, an occasional contributor to *Experiment*. (Earlier in the correspondence, Blunt had criticized Humphrey Jennings for claiming that a Brueghel painting was 'put to shame by the average Dutch power station'.) Rossetti claimed that Blunt's most recent piece in the *Venture*, on William Beckford's Fonthill Abbey, merely parroted Bell's most recent publication, *The Gothic Revival*. Perhaps they were the same person. It was supposed, of course, to be a slur, but one can almost feel Blunt's frisson of belonging. His reply to his critics – Rossetti was not the only one – was almost too apologetic. 'Bad temper and bad manners, as these gentleman acutely discern, are the weapons upon which I principally rely, and I stand disarmed before such excesses of urbanity.'

There were other, more self-interested, reasons for his abasement: one of Blunt's targets earlier in the correspondence had been J. W. Goodison, a curator at the Fitzwilliam Museum. Blunt had just applied for a curatorial job at the Fitzwilliam, and needed to do some energetic backtracking after he had described Jennings and Goodison as 'fairly complete examples of all that is to be avoided in art criticism . . . both unintelligible and nonsensical'. He didn't get the job.

Julian Bell, however, leaped to his friend's, and his father's, defence. He attacked Rossetti for his 'rude' letter, coyly adding, 'May I assure you, Sir, from personal, and I may venture to add, intimate acquaintance with both, that there are numerous and profound differences in their characters.'

Bell was a few months younger than Blunt, a socialist, and

ambitious to be a poet. 'He was a great, untidy, sprawling figure of a young man,' wrote John Lehmann, 'awkward in manner and dressed always in dishevelled clothes with buttons rarely meeting button-holes at the neck and wrists. He imposed, nevertheless, by charm of expression on the smiling, intelligent face under the curling tangled hair, by natural force of temperament and by an obstinate persistence of intellectual curiosity.' He had been a tough little boy, who once punched his governess in the face, and had been fascinated, since boyhood, with military history. This was much disliked by his pacifist parents. His brother Quentin was certain that this fascination was one of the things which would later take him to the Spanish Civil War. Blunt was very attracted by untidy, rumbustious masculinity.

During the spring months of 1929, Bell's letters to his brother Quentin, who was living in Paris, constantly mentioned Blunt. In March he wrote, 'I shan't dare to send my friend Anthony Blunt, who is going to Paris, to see you. You are both far too pretty to be good, whereas I am unfortunately far too good to be pretty.' And three weeks later, 'I have had a letter from Anthony Blunt, he says he is going to call on you. I dare say he has already done so. Do let me know what you make of him, and any indiscreet remarks he may make about Cambridge.' And shortly after that, 'I hope Anthony Blunt has been to see you. If he has, do present him to Roger [Fry], who I know he wants to see. They have met vaguely at Cambridge, I think.'

Blunt was looking for a new confidant; relations were strained between him and MacNeice, who had got himself engaged on almost no acquaintance to the stepdaughter of an Oxford Classics don. Mary Ezra was very young, beautiful, and determinedly anti-intellectual. Blunt did not like her and thought the marriage a bad idea. 'Yes, Mary Ezra,' MacNeice had written to him in March 1929. 'She doesn't like you and I gather you don't like her. Which is very bad taste on both sides.'

In early May, Blunt and Bell became lovers – rather surprisingly, as Bell was, hitherto and afterwards, resolutely heterosexual. He wrote to his mother Vanessa:

I have so much to tell you I shall have the greatest difficulty in getting everything down … my great news is about Anthony. I feel certain you won't be upset or shaked by my telling you that we sleep together – to use the Cambridge euphemism. It's a great mercy, thinking that you aren't a moral and disapproving parent. Still, don't let it go any further, or it may get round to Virginia, and then one might as well put a notice in *The Times*. As his parents are strict and proper clergymen of the church of England and a number of his friends highly shockable athletes we have to take precautions. So now I am feeling that life, though crowded and distracting enough in all conscience, is a very pleasant business on the whole.

Bell had apparently been the pursuer, but for Blunt it was the literal consummation of his affair with Bloomsbury. The reaction of their friends was mixed. 'It was very strange,' remembered Eddie Playfair. 'Julian was the passive one, and yet it was he who made the going. I don't think Blunt was really interested in Julian sexually. I may have been the only one who knew about it while it was going on, though Julian was a great one for talking about his affairs … I regarded it as a bit of fashion more than anything else.' According to Quentin Bell, 'the story as I had it from Julian himself was that he had one night with Blunt, which involved scaling the walls of Trinity, and he said it really wasn't worth the climb. That sort of thing was really not for him, but he was quite devoted to him.'

As for the older generation, Keynes liked Bell but wasn't so sure about Blunt. He wrote to Vanessa:

Lytton (who is here staying with Dadie) thinks that the young lack blood and it would be better if they cared more about politics and less about aesthetics; however we all agree that Julian is miles the best of the younger generation; the magazines are plastered with his poems – some not at all bad; whether Anthony Blunt (with whom he is hopelessly infatuated) is quite all that Julian thinks him may be found doubtful in the future – but that doesn't matter at present.

Roger Fry, however, liked Blunt. 'I had a charming evening with Julian and Anthony Blunt who is a very nice boy,' he wrote to Vanessa Bell after Julian introduced them in May. Blunt had admired Fry since his schooldays. There was something appropriately Bloomsbury about the fact that, when they finally met, Fry was his boyfriend's mother's ex-lover.

While Keynes and Strachey's attitudes to homosexuality had influenced Blunt's private life, Fry had a comparable effect on his intellectual development. Fry's writing had introduced Blunt to El Greco, Italian baroque painting, so-called 'Primitive art', Blake, Seurat and Poussin. Fry had also shucked off some of Bloomsbury's insularity: he was less inward-looking and a more subtle and less dogmatic critic than Clive Bell; he no longer regarded Significant Form as a universal doctrine. Blunt would come to disagree with many of Fry's opinions, and the scholarly approach he was learning from Gow was quite at odds with Fry's instinctive art appreciation. Nor did they become close friends. But Blunt liked and admired Fry, and found in him a role model complementary to Gow – especially in his treatment of the young. 'He would always listen to the ideas of others however young and however arrogant', he wrote of Fry in 1965, no doubt recalling his own youthful presumption. It was a quality people later noticed in Blunt's teaching.

During the summer, Blunt went to stay at Charleston, the Sussex farmhouse rented by Vanessa Bell and Duncan Grant, already famous for its interior decoration, though not yet for its interesting sleeping arrangements.* Virginia Woolf had met Blunt

* Bell and Blunt had talked of going to Pontigny in France for '*l'entretiens d'été*', the annual discussion group organized by Paul Desjardins, a literature professor at the École Nationale and a friend of Lytton Strachey and André Maurois, but it appears they did not go.

on one of her occasional visits to Rylands' salons – the model for the convivial male college occasion described in *A Room of One's Own*. 'Lytton and Anthony Blunt and Peter [F. L. Lucas] are all at Charleston,' she wrote in her diary for 21 September 1929. 'Please God I say these delightful and divine people don't come and make me concentrate again.' The young men of King's were slightly frightened of the formidable and serious Vanessa Bell, but found Virginia, in Rylands's words, 'delightful. A frivolous butterfly in comparison.'

Only a couple of weeks before this visit, Stanley Blunt, now fifty-nine and still vicar of St John's, Paddington, had been taken seriously ill. A preliminary operation diagnosed cancer. Another one promised a cure, but Stanley relapsed. According to Wilfrid, who was living in Munich at the time, Hilda kept her children away from the sickbed. 'It was characteristically understanding of my mother,' he wrote, 'that, when she knew (but he did not) that he was dying, she begged me not to come. I had, she said, been with him when I could be of help; now there was nothing that I could do and my return would only alarm him. I obeyed her command, thereby (I learned later) causing offence in certain quarters.' Queen Mary wrote to Hilda, 'What a loss he will be. Why should he have been taken, who was doing such good work on earth when such useless, evil people are allowed to live? However, this we shall never understand.' He died in November. Hilda moved to a small Edwardian house in Ham, near her childhood home. She lived there until her death in 1969, keeping up with her sons' brilliant careers and becoming more and more eccentrically ascetic.

Blunt made no public recognition of the loss of his father, then or later. Neither MacNeice nor Bell, his closest confidants, mentioned it in their letters of the period. Blunt appears not to have mentioned Stanley's initial illness to MacNeice, and after October the two had a serious falling out over MacNeice's deepening relationship with Mary Ezra. MacNeice felt that Blunt had sided with Mary Ezra's mother against him. He sent only one short telegram to Blunt between October 1929 and July 1930. By November 1929 the relationship with Julian Bell was petering out. Bell wrote to his mother that his love affairs were 'at present in rather a gloomy position Blunt and I being about equally bored with each other', and he quickly fell into a relationship with a girl at Girton. For both men the relationship established the pattern of many of their future affairs. For Bell, 'intense involvement followed by withdrawal'; and for Blunt involvement with a 'masculine' bisexual or mainly heterosexual man.

By now, however, the failure of such a relationship could not distress him in the way that it would have done three years before. Life continued, and in his final year as an undergraduate a first-class degree beckoned, and a new – platonic – friendship was made. Victor Rothschild, heir to the English branch of the banking family, arrived at Trinity in October 1929 to study natural sciences. He was quickly co-opted into Dadie Rylands's set. Rothschild was energetic, tough, funny (not always intentionally), almost handsome though tending to plumpness, easily bored, and an accomplished jazz pianist. He was also extremely rich, a fact he enjoyed – he drove a Bugatti, took his friends to Monte Carlo, collected paintings, English silver and rare books and gave extravagant presents. However, he liked to play down his wealth, preferring to stress his academic ambitions. A certain bullishness was perhaps the result of having overcome a difficult childhood: his father had committed suicide when Victor was twelve, and he had spent his childhood surrounded by women at home, or being bullied at a series of boarding schools where he was ragged for being a 'dirty little Jew'. As an adult, he considered himself an expert in 'putting people at their ease', but he would also provoke in his quest to entertain himself. 'He was alarming, a person of great whims, but his mind was very superior,' thought his friend, the Cambridge academic and future provost of King's, Noel Annan.

'Like many others,' Rothschild wrote in his 1983 book *Random Variables*,

I was immediately impressed by [Blunt's] outstanding abilities, both artistic and mathematical, and by what, for want of a better phrase, I must call his high moral or ethical principles. I knew or suspected he was a homosexual, but I saw no reason why this characteristic should conflict with the others mentioned above ... Blunt seemed to me a somewhat cold and ascetic figure but with a sense of humour ... he was an excellent conversationalist and habitual party goer.

When Rothschild wrote this, in the early 1980s, he was still furious and bitter at his recently exposed former friend, as well as keen to distance himself from a famous traitor. Dadie Rylands remembered that in 1929 Victor had become 'one of Anthony's closest friends'.

Blunt was now a well-known figure both at Trinity and among the wider self-consciously literary set, for his rivalry with the *Experiment* editors and for his hopeless aestheticism. In February 1930 the *Trinity College Magazine* described him at a private view of Julian Trevelyan's paintings: 'Anthony Blunt was seen, magnificently plastic, with the inimitable Hawk's smile, the Footlights frown.' (This was a Cambridge attempt at a joke; Blunt was of course, pointedly, neither a 'Hawk', a blue – a Cambridge sporting hero, nor an actor.) Another observer of the event noted how he and Bronowski still behaved like 'rivals' pouring out 'remarks endlessly'. In that month's *Experiment* Bronowski had obliquely attacked the *Venture*'s aesthetes and their political passivity: 'It would be a pity ... if the arts or aesthetics were to obscure the very deep unrest among the "Younger Generation".' A few months later, in June, an article in the *Cambridge Review* held up Blunt as an illustration of the deficiencies of a non-political outlook. The piece, by one of the few Communist dons at Cambridge, Roy Pascal, claimed that Blunt's views on art, particularly Significant Form, exposed 'the falseness of considering any art unhistorically'. He also denounced Cubism, which

Blunt had praised in an article in the *Venture*, as 'one of the most barren and abstract of all theories of painting, like constructivism in architecture'.

That month Blunt sat his finals and was awarded a first. His career as an academic seemed assured. He was granted a further two years at Trinity in which to produce a fellowship dissertation, the first stage on the road to becoming a Cambridge don.

On 21 June, after getting news of *his* first, in Classics, Louis MacNeice married Mary Ezra in Oxford. Neither his nor her parents were present. Nor was his best friend. 'I hear you were much pained by my treatment of you,' MacNeice told Blunt when he finally wrote in July. '[Mary's mother] (I gather) regards me as a friend forsaker – the sort of man, in fact, who lets everyone down in the long run.' He realized he had upset Blunt by his 'non confidence' and 'general negligence', but he had not wanted to 'publish private squalors'. 'Mary is quite different from what you think and is not to be totted up and analysed and prescribed for like any creature off the streets or tennis-courts. I write this because I don't want you to dislike me. I am tired, however, of talking apologies.' The ties of their friendship had been fatally weakened, and their lives were diverging. MacNeice was now a married man, and had a job at Birmingham University teaching Classics. Blunt had elected for the life of a bachelor don. By the time relations had improved, MacNeice's place in Blunt's life had been taken by someone else.

4. Angry Young Man

'You always were so handy with the intellectual spanner'

There are two resonant images of Guy Burgess: the endearing, homesick victim of his mistakes as portrayed in Alan Bennett's play *An Englishman Abroad*, and the dirty, drunken predator of conventional spy literature. In reality – and especially in middle age – Burgess was both. But in October 1930, when he arrived at Trinity from Eton to study history, he was a fresh, entertaining eighteen-year-old with the look of a slightly overripe cherub, and seemed destined for great things. A characteristic remarked on by everyone who met him was how much, and how well, he talked. 'He was marvellously irreverent, amusing, quick and clever,' remembered a Cambridge contemporary. He seemed remarkably fully formed and precocious, with an opinion on everything. He had a passion for Victorian literature, a soft spot for Victorian politicians, and an obsession with fast cars: he had 'missed hardly one issue of *The Autocar* since he was nine years old', wrote his biographer thirty years later.

The other thing everyone noticed about Burgess was that he was openly homosexual and recklessly promiscuous. He never missed an opportunity to repeat his own explanation for his homosexuality: he claimed that his father, a naval commander who had died when he was thirteen, had expired in flagrante on top of his mother; he had walked in on the scene, and the sight had put him off sex with women for ever. He also told everyone that his stepfather, whom he hated, was a professional gambler. In fact his stepfather was a perfectly respectable retired army officer. His mother, Mrs Bassett, adored, indulged and endlessly forgave her eldest son, and blamed everything that went wrong in his life on something else – usually the malign influence of his boyfriends. Apart, that is, from Blunt, of whom she approved.

Even as an undergraduate Burgess was a man of great appetites: 'He was immensely energetic, a great talker, reader, boaster, walker, who swam like an otter and drank, not like a feckless undergraduate, as Donald [Maclean] was apt to do, but like some rabelaisian bottle-swiper whose thirst was unquenchable,' wrote Cyril Connolly. He managed, at the same time, to charm and impress people as a young *homme sérieux*. Noel Annan noted 'how many serious people thought Guy Burgess the youth one of the most brilliant, compelling, promising human beings they had ever met'. Among them were two eminent Trinity historians: G. M. Trevelyan, who through the 1930s recommended Burgess for various jobs, and Steven Runciman, who recalled nostalgically, 'I always rather liked him. When sober he was very good company.'

At Cambridge Burgess swiftly introduced himself into Dadie Rylands's fashionable circle and soon he was at the heart of it. 'We were a little band, partly Trinity, partly King's, of *great friends,*' Rylands remembered. At the heart of the group were himself, Blunt, Victor Rothschild, Arthur Marshall – who was still doing his schoolgirl turn at the Footlights – and Burgess. Life was easy and hedonistic. 'Our sheltered existence went on through the twenties and the first years of the thirties,' Blunt wrote later, 'and we continued to live in this kind of dream world spinning our little intellectual webs.' According to Rylands, 'We were jokers. We played charades with all kinds of acting and absurdities.' There was much emphasis on practical jokes. One involved smuggling Mary St-Clare Erskine, a famously gamine debutante Blunt took out a few times, into one of Steven Runciman's all-male parties, cutting her hair and stuffing her into a dinner jacket. It was not a joke the famously misogynistic Runciman appreciated.

There were those who disliked Burgess, who found his stories repetitive, his name-dropping tedious. Stuart Hampshire, the Oxford philosopher, found him 'amusing and clever but fundamentally really destructive'. Miriam Rothschild, sister of Victor, who quickly succumbed to Burgess's energetic friendliness, recognized his 'infinite, eager charm' but likened him to

the Vicar of Bray – anything that suited his coat. He phoned me up one day and said, 'You're a scientist: can you tell me something? I went to Pruniers and they served fish and it was covered in maggots, and now I've got a tapeworm. Can I sue them?' I told him there was no connection between the tapeworm and the maggots. He said, 'Oh, how disappointing! Well, I'll sue them all the same!'

Nevertheless, in 1930, among Dadie's circle, it was felt that the lively, good-humoured Burgess would be a positive influence on the reticent Blunt. Their friendship was encouraged. In the 1970s Blunt wrote of Burgess:

at this time he was not only one of the most intellectually stimulating people I have ever known but also had great charm and tremendous vivacity; and those people who now write saying they felt physically sick in his presence are very often simply not speaking the truth ... He was a terrific intellectual stimulus. He was interested in everything, and although he was perverse in many ways, there was no subject which one could discuss with him without his expressing some interesting and lively and worthwhile views.

Burgess in part filled the gap in Blunt's life left by MacNeice. He was Blunt's antithesis – hot, wild, emotional – and in a more insistent way than MacNeice had he dragged Blunt from burying himself entirely in work. He made him laugh. 'Guy could never stop chattering,' Rylands said. 'He was wonderful company – full of jokes and ideas and stories and scandal and all that. Whereas Blunt wasn't. I thought Guy had a good effect on Blunt: he brought him out. He broke through Blunt's reserve through jokes.' He also encouraged him to shed some of his sexual inhibitions.

The Welsh writer and journalist Goronwy Rees, who became a close friend of Burgess's in the 1930s, believed that Burgess played the role of 'father confessor and pimp' to his friends in Cambridge. Most them were 'homosexual but a good deal more timid than Guy, a good deal more frustrated and a good deal less successful in their sexual adventures'.

> At one time or another he went to bed with most of these friends, as he did with anyone who was willing and was not positively repulsive, and in doing so he released them from many of their frustrations and inhibitions. He was a kind of public schoolboy's guide to the mysteries of sex and he fulfilled his function almost with a sense of public service. Such affairs did not last for long; but Guy had the faculty of retaining the affection of those he went to bed with, and also, in some curious way, of maintaining a kind of permanent domination over them ... he continued to assist his friends in their sexual lives, which were often troubled and unsatisfactory, to listen to their emotional difficulties and when necessary find suitable partners for them.

Rees had Blunt in mind when he wrote this. It was widely assumed among their friends that it was Burgess who introduced Blunt to the rough trade – the sailors and working-class men – he pursued in later life. Burgess himself, Rees wrote, was 'gross and even brutal in his treatment of his lovers'. There is reason to believe that Rees was actually referring to the fact that Burgess liked a little S and M (with him administering the S). The painter John Craxton remembered that in the 1940s Burgess tried and failed to pick him up at the Gargoyle club with the line 'I'd love to beat you; I'm sure you'd enjoy it.' Another much-told story about Burgess concerned his taking home an art student who would later become a well-known interior decorator, and proposing, to the art student's increasing unease, that they undertake various athletic and extremely uncomfortable activities with coat hangers.

Burgess's tendency to seek dangerous extremes was a quality

to which Blunt, quiet and famously courteous, would be attracted all his life. 'How could you not be enthused by Guy?' asked Dadie Rylands. 'He was so amusing and lively, and such a bad hat. Anthony wasn't at all strait-laced, but he liked being melted and tempted.' Blunt's own rebellions had so far been confined to the printed page. Burgess acted. He was constantly getting away with things, pushing the boundaries of what was acceptable, voicing outrageous views, planning wild escapades, getting falling down drunk, passing out in front of important people. Burgess needed to dominate in a way that Blunt did not, and beneath his chatter was a formidable will. 'He was the most persistent person in achieving his own ends that I have ever known,' wrote Rees. Blunt, who seemed so self-sufficient and so controlled, had a lifelong susceptibility to powerful, persuasive characters. It sprang from an intimation that at heart he was not quite as sure of himself or what he was, as he liked to let on. He was often unexpectedly swayable. Despite his attempts to escape his home, he had, in his own way, the classic family traits: 'emotional, sentimental, gullible'.

Goronwy Rees claimed that Blunt's bond with, and loyalty to, Burgess was due to the fact that he was sexually obsessed with him. Though they probably did have a brief sexual affair, neither of them cited it as the crucial fact of their friendship. Others who knew the two, including Burgess's lovers Jackie Hewit and Peter Pollock, insisted that the relationship was not sexual and that there were many other aspects of Burgess which appealed to Blunt. Nevertheless, the relationship may have had its romantic side for Blunt. 'He was secretly in love with the Greek ideal of male love and companionship,' remembered a lover of the 1940s. 'He seemed to want it all to be, oh, the classical world, Plato, all that sort of thing: dignified, honourable.' The feelings Blunt had for Burgess were intense, but sex was not – or he did not allow it to be – a prime motivator in his life. Nor did he share Burgess's reputation for promiscuity. Indeed, some thought he was under-sexed – 'unlike Guy Burgess,' recalled Charles Rycroft, a Trinity undergraduate of the mid-1930s. 'People did contrast the two of them. They were each other's best friends, but it was quite all right to dislike one and like the other.'

By the time Burgess was established at Cambridge, Blunt was himself beginning to acquire a reputation as 'a marvellous figure of great glamour', remembered Stuart Hampshire, who met him in the mid-1930s. He had new friends beyond the King's/Bloomsbury set, such as the Irish landowner Milo Talbot, the gentleman architect Claude Phillimore (with whom he had an affair), and the *Times* journalist Ian Morrison, whose love affair with Han Suyin became the basis for her novel *A Many Splendoured Thing*. Burgess's brother, Nigel, preferred Blunt to his own sibling: 'he was amusing and highly intelligent. I feel a lot of highly intelligent people make me feel stupid. He did not.' As for his own flesh and blood, 'I don't think I ever said anything he found interesting.'

There was one part of Blunt's life into which Burgess only made occasional interventions: his work. From 1930, still in his old lodgings in Bishop's Hostel, with a scholarship worth about £250 a year – just about enough to pay his bills – Blunt worked on his postgraduate thesis. This was supposed to be on a French literary theme, and Blunt had persuaded his tutor H. F. Stewart to let him work on Poussin and the (often literary) sources of his theories on painting. In artistic terms this was a subject ripe for study. An unfashionable painter, condemned as unemotional and esoteric, Poussin had been the subject of very little scholarly work since the early nineteenth century. Some biographical accounts and letters survived, however, and in them the artist had set down his ideas about painting – ideas which had had an enormous influence on French art in the 150 years after his death, and had won him the title of '*peintre-philosophe*'.

However, Blunt soon discovered that Poussin was by no means an original thinker. One of the painter's most famous statements, that different subjects required different 'modes' or styles to express them, turned out to be an almost verbatim quotation from a treatise on music, the *Instituzione Harmoniche*, by a sixteenth-century Italian writer, Gioseffo Zarlino. Other statements derived from Italian Renaissance writers on art. Blunt's findings were incorporated into an article by Paul Alfassa, a French art historian, in 1933. It was Blunt's first academic contribution. The discovery prompted him to turn his attention to the Renaissance theories that had influenced Poussin – research that, ten years later, would eventually become his first book.

By 1932, as Blunt put the finishing touches to his fellowship dissertation, new opportunities beyond Cambridge began to offer themselves. During the summer, his tutor, H. F. Stewart, gave him an introduction to an old friend, Owen Morshead, the Royal Librarian at Windsor, where there was a huge collection of Poussin drawings. 'He is an extremely serious student and a very agreeable young man,' Stewart wrote to Morshead. In the autumn, Stewart introduced him to another friend, W. G. Constable, the director of the new Courtauld Institute of Art.

At Stewart's request, Constable read Blunt's fellowship dissertation. He was ecstatic. 'This is a remarkable piece of work,' he wrote.

Mr Blunt has done what has never been systematically or satisfactorily done before – traced the process by which French art, both in theory and practice, became heir to the art of the Italian Renaissance, and perpetuated the classic tradition in Europe . . . It is difficult to speak too highly of the care, judgment and perception which have brought this part of the work to so successful a conclusion . . . I should have no hesitation in recommending the thesis for immediate publication. I hope it is not irrelevant to add that I have been so impressed with Mr Blunt's work, that on my recommendation, Mr Blunt has been invited to lecture on the subject of his thesis at the Courtauld Institute of Art.

As a result of the success of his dissertation, Trinity granted him a four-year research fellowship to allow him to extend his dissertation. His new subject was 'artistic theory in France and Italy during the Renaissance and the 17th century'. That autumn, at the Royal Academy's winter exhibition on French art which he had curated (and which Blunt reviewed for the *Cambridge*

Review), Constable did Blunt another service. He introduced him to the world expert on Poussin, Walter Friedlaender. Friedlaender was the author of a 1914 monograph on the artist: *Poussin: Die Entwicklung Seiner Kunst*. Then in his sixties, he was a genial and talkative German Jew who spoke execrable English. He and Blunt got on brilliantly. 'Friedlaender loved him and thought he was a wonderful boy,' recalled another German art historian, Margot Wittkower. Blunt was an eager pupil. Friedlaender was his first encounter with German art history, then arguably the most admired school of art history in the world and known for its rigorous empirical research and high standards of scholarship. In fact Friedlaender was a rather idiosyncratic representative of the German school: he was full of brilliant ideas, but distinctly chaotic. Blunt was, nevertheless, deeply impressed. Friedlaender's book – in particular its suggestion that Poussin had been inspired by Stoic philosophy – would greatly influence the younger man's work on the artist, a debt he freely admitted; and Friedlaender's preoccupation with the symbiotic relationship between classicism and romanticism would also become a preoccupation of Blunt's.

There was yet another exciting advance from beyond Cambridge that autumn, when Derek Verschoyle, literary editor of the *Spectator*, who had seen Blunt's acerbic pieces in the *Cambridge Review*, asked him to write a weekly art review for the magazine. He accepted.

It was perhaps as a result of these widening horizons that Blunt decided, at the end of 1932, to 'take wings' and cease to be an active member of the Apostles. Coincidentally, it was at the same meeting, on 12 November, that Guy Burgess and Victor Rothschild were elected to the Society. According to Andrew Boyle's *The Climate of Treason*, the book that exposed him as a spy, Blunt 'secured' Burgess's election to the Society. But, while Blunt encouraged the election of his friends, it took more than one person to get a would-be Apostle into the Society, and Burgess had plenty of other supporters. It has been suggested that the two of them subsequently dominated the Society, using it as a recruiting ground for their spying, and possibly even for homosexual seduction. 'There can be no question but that Blunt was an increasingly powerful influence within the Society from his joining it until almost a quarter of a century afterwards,' an author of a history of the Apostles (and also, not coincidentally, of a voluminous collection of spy and conspiracy-theory books) has written. There is no evidence to support this assertion. Following his promotion to 'angel', as older members were known, the records suggest that Blunt ceased to take much interest in the Society. He attended only two meetings in the following year and a half: in March 1933, when Bertrand Russell gave a paper, and in June 1933, when he gave his last ever paper, on aesthetic appreciation. In contrast, other angels, like Keynes and the middle-aged philosophy don Richard Braithwaite, often came to meetings. By 1935, according to Alan Hodgkin, one of the Society's undergraduate members, 'Anthony Blunt, whom I had met in Trinity, and liked, had ceased to be active and rarely came to meetings when I was a member.' Plenty of his friends, however, including Rothschild, were still regulars.

It was not until the following spring of 1933 that Blunt made his debut as a lecturer at the Courtauld Institute of Art in London. The Institute, the first of its kind in Britain, had opened the previous October. It was the brainchild of Lord Lee of Fareham, an arts grandee who wanted to set up a centre for the professional study of art to rival similar institutions in Europe and America. Arthur Lee was a self-made man – or rather he was the combination of his own determination and his wife's money. An orphan who had gone to America to make his fortune, he had returned with a rich and devoted wife and influential friends, among them Theodore Roosevelt. Energetic but chippy, he had failed to make the mark he would have liked in politics, and, though he became a Tory minister during the 1914–18 war and left Chequers to the nation, he had decided that the art world would provide a better stage for his ambitions. He had bought a great deal of art from

Joseph Duveen (a quantity of which turned out later to be fake), and sat on every relevant committee and board – though he was dropped as a trustee of the National Gallery for throwing himself on the floor and screaming until he got his own way. He was, wrote Kenneth Clark, who as director of the National Gallery benefited a great deal from his patronage, 'the most detested figure of the museum world'.

Lacking funds for his project, Lee had brought in a distinguished art collector, Sir Robert Witt, who offered his drawings to the new institute, and Samuel Courtauld, a textile millionaire and England's foremost collector of Impressionist and Post-Impressionist paintings, who agreed to give £100,000. Lee also solicited £20,000 from Joseph Duveen. When Courtauld's wife died suddenly, in 1931, he left the Institute his own home at 20 Portman Square, a large Adam house built for the Countess of Home in 1772, famed for its grand double staircase and glass domed roof. Over the years it had accumulated an Oliver Messel bathroom and many paintings – including a Van Gogh self-portrait with a bandaged ear and Renoir's *La Loge* – all of which Courtauld passed to the new institute. The place remained the Courtauld's impressive but quite inappropriate premises for the next fifty years.

The Institute had a full-time staff of three. The aim was to teach art and a little archaeology from 'the pyramids to Picasso', at all levels – from basic art appreciation, through preparation for museum and gallery work, to postgraduate research. It was a tall order for such a small place. However, one thing Constable did have at his disposal as director was an impressive collection of occasional lecturers: Roger Fry, Kenneth Clark, Herbert Read and, as the 1930s progressed, an increasing number of eminent foreign art historians in flight from fascist regimes. They included Erwin Panofsky, en route to America, and Nikolaus Pevsner, who emigrated to England in 1933.

Fifty years later Blunt could still remember his first lecture. 'I was absolutely terrified. I couldn't find my way to the lecture room, and no one seemed to know what I was supposed to be doing. I was terrified. It's the only lecture I've ever read completely from a full text. I was so frightened I thought I'd better have a full text. I gave, I think, six, and in the second I ad libbed.' He was, he discovered, a natural on the podium: confident, intimate, passionate, as he so often was not with one person. One of the Courtauld's first students, Ruth Harwood, remembered his lectures well. From her lecture seat she could see Lautrec's *Jane Avril at the Moulin Rouge* and a sketch for Manet's *Dejeuner sur l'herbe*. 'Probably our most compulsive lecturer was Anthony Blunt – listening to his lecture on aesthetic theory meant intense concentration and it was hard to keep up but from the beginning to the end he never once lost his line. I think he and Maurice Bowra were the best lecturers I ever heard.' Also in the audience was the young art historian Denis Mahon, with whom Blunt would feud furiously over Poussin thirty years later.

A month or so later Blunt's love affair with Poussin was consummated with a purchase. At Duit's in Jermyn Street, behind Piccadily, he spotted a seventeenth-century painting of a biblical scene, *Rebecca and Eliezer at the Well*. It was attributed to Poussin. Since the artist was unfashionable and the painting quite damaged and of uncertain provenance, the price – £100 – was cheap. (Duit's had bought it at Christie's for £46 in 1929.) Blunt had developed an eye for bargains. He had begun to build a collection of rare architectural books, bought for a few shillings in London and Paris, which at his death would be worth nearly £100,000. (MacNeice commissioned him to look for eighteenth-century editions of Latin texts, if his 'impeccable eye happens to light on such while you are digging down to the Folios'.) Unfortunately he did not have £100. He asked Victor Rothschild if he could lend him the money. Rothschild bought the painting for him instead, sending Burgess to pick it up. 'My father told me,' he later wrote – 'or my mother said my father believed – that if humanly possible, one should never lend people money as it almost invariably made them hate you. You should give them money if you could, and if it could be done without embarrassment.' Rothschild's generosity was legendary: he gave Leonard

Woolf a marmoset and presented Dadie Rylands with a Shake-speare Second Folio, and the story went that at one of his parties the men received a bottle of champagne and women a flask of perfume as they left.

By 1933 Blunt had settled into his new role as the *Spectator*'s art critic, making regular trips to London to see the latest exhibitions. He had quickly made a name for himself as opinion-ated and controversial, and a staunch adherent of the Bloomsbury line. As such, he was a broadly progressive, though not always heartfelt, supporter of modern art, with particular blind spots. He now criticized Matisse for having become too decorative, rather than the 'serious' innovative artist he had once been. Abstraction made him uneasy, in particular the deliberate lack of meaning of Ben Nicholson's and Barbara Hepworth's work. He wrote that he found their work 'limited' and not 'serious' – 'when you have seen one you have seen them all'. Nor did he warm to Surrealism: he disliked its negation of reason, its encouragement of chaos. 'It denies to reason the right of any control in the creation of a work of art,' he had written in 1929; '. . . it asserts the absolute power of the imagination . . . it is, in fact, a sort of mysticism, based on an implicit belief in the value of whatever comes from the subconscious . . . The result is complete chaos and they produce works without significance or coherence.' An objection to Sur-realism which today seems more cogent is that it was a formulaic way of producing art. Blunt's response shows how vividly he feared unreason, 'the subconscious', and loss of control. (He had also noted, perceptively, that William Blake – who had claimed he received inspiration for his art in visions – had done it all 150 years before, and better.)

In the context of 1930s London, however, Blunt was rabidly modern. It was a hard time for modern art in Britain. The public galleries took almost no interest in it – and they were in any event desperately short of money. The only collection of Cézannes in the country was owned by Samuel Courtauld, and the only places to see modern art were the commercial galleries round Cork

Street in London, who found sales hard to come by. When the Leicester Galleries showed the most lyrical and domestic of the Post-Impressionists, Berthe Morisot, they could not sell a single work; Knoedler's sold original Epstein drawings for £30. Americans came to London to buy modern art cheap. In this culturally stagnant landscape, Blunt stood out as an advocate of important work. When, in 1933, amid great denunciation, the Tate Gallery contemplated buying its first Picasso, Blunt wrote in support of the purchase both in his column and in a letter to the *Listener*. He argued that Picasso, as 'the greatest living painter', and an artist who belonged to the great traditions of Western art, should be represented at the Tate. He wrote seriously about Leger and Braque, African sculpture ('curious and captivating') and Man Ray ('the best achievement of modern photography'). In the same year that the allegedly liberal *New Statesman* described Henry Moore's work as 'positively shocking – ferocious objects such as might serve a despot to cow a conquered population, symbols fit for a Hitler or a Stalin', Blunt called Moore 'a sculptor of genius'. He was also scathing about the kind of art with which most of his *Spectator* readers were most familiar, regularly attacking the Royal Academy – 'I found almost as little skill as soul,' he wrote in 1933 – most of whose members' work looked as if Post-Impressionism had never happened, and denouncing the society portraitist Philip de Laszlo for showing 'the disastrous result of serving mammon'.

Blunt was not a great critic. Sometimes he wasn't even a good one. He lacked the vision, taste and enthusiasm for the modern of, say, Herbert Read. His writing could be exceptionally stodgy and dull: reviewing the painter Mark Gertler, Blunt wrote that he lacked in 'inventiveness . . . and perhaps life', but at least his work was 'restrained by a certain taste'. Blunt was too frequently locked into his dogma of the moment, too keen to make snap judgements about contemporary art, and his early articles betrayed a clunky, oversimplified view of art as a lurch from one art style to another, the latest being the natural outcome of the

last. Thus the Irish painter Jack Yeats's works were 'the outcome
of impressionism'.

He was, however, noticeably more measured and less prescriptive about the art of the past. He was also more readable when
he was stirred and angry – which he often was – though he was
careful to express himself in a careless tone that would provoke,
rather than reveal how provoked he himself was. He was a young
man in a hurry, but he was also motivated by exasperation with
the soggy, genteel laxity in the way art, and books about art,
were treated in England – a laxity born of not really minding.
Blunt minded. He believed that England lagged behind the rest of
Europe in both its receptiveness to modern trends and its treatment of art. He felt, with justification, that English art books,
compared to their European counterparts, were often amateurish,
unresearched, badly produced, full of mistakes and lazily edited.
He had determined to aim for professionalism and scholarship in
his own work, inspired by the obsessive accuracy of Andrew Gow
and his first encounter with German scholarship. 'Purely scholarly
analysis of art which is always regarded as aesthetically the most
barren very often leads to the discovery of beauties of actual
execution', he wrote in his review of the Royal Academy French
art exhibition where he had met Walter Friedlaender. In a particularly pedantic mood he would list mistakes in the books he
reviewed. 'You always were so handy with the intellectual spanner,' Louis MacNeice wrote to him. This was not what was
necessarily expected in the cosy world of English letters. After one
of his pieces, one reader wrote to the *Spectator*: 'I cannot remember ever having read a review which had such a spiteful tone,'
and suggested that, if Blunt had nothing nice to say, he shouldn't
say anything at all. Underneath Blunt's righteous anger, art had
once again become for him a vent for stronger feelings.

By the end of 1932 he had already provoked the popular art
critic R. H. Wilenski to paroxysms of fury, and had again turned
on his former hero Sacheverell Sitwell, whose *Southern Baroque
Art* and aesthetic mannerisms he had so enthusiastically adopted
at school. Wilenski was a prolific writer and supporter of modern

art, though much of his writing was terrible and incomprehensible – he combined a propensity for cod psychology and scientific jargon with conspiracy theories and even algebraic equations. Blunt had written three devastating pieces on his books in the *Cambridge Review* by the end of 1932, concluding in one, 'Mr Wilenski has clearly attempted the impossible. But he need not have failed so grossly.' The last straw came when he noted in an aside in his *Spectator* column that modern sculpture had fallen into disrepute 'owing to the recent defences of Mr Wilenski' – who had written a long apologia for it. Wilenski wrote furious, pompous letters to the magazine.

'This is to say to you', went his letter to Blunt, '. . . If you make a series of misrepresentations of this kind in the *Spectator* I shall have to expose them in a further letter which would bore me even if I could spare the time which I cannot . . . I am, as you know, not a newcomer in the world of letters or Fleet Street.' He rebuked Blunt for misrepresenting him, and told him that if he continued, 'You will cause me a lot of unnecessary trouble and only look silly yourself at the end. For the rest you can damn the book in any way and all ways you like.'

As for Sitwell, Blunt had first written critically about his writings on baroque art under the pseudonym of George Oglethorpe in the *Venture* in 1929. 'He is not a great art critic,' he had written. 'A visit to the Church of Santa Chiara in Naples, followed by a reading of *Southern Baroque Art*, makes one wonder whether he is even a good one.' In 1932 he renewed the attack under his own name in a long critical piece in the *Cambridge Review*. While acknowledging that Sitwell had produced the best introduction to the baroque, Blunt attacked his books for having no indexes and no pictures, and listed hundreds of mistakes, many of which, he suggested, might have been avoided by a careful reading of Baedeker.

Sitwell replied that, since he rarely sold more than 100 copies of each book and 'I receive practically no payment whatever for my labours', he did the best job he could. 'I cannot help, whilst being flattered by any attention to the subject, being struck by the petulant note in your review as though you knew more about it than anyone else, and could express yourself much better. If this is so, why have you not appeared in print before upon the subject?'

Occasionally Blunt seems to have regretted his intemperance. In 1933 he praised a Wilenski book on Ruskin as 'an admirable introduction', and he apologized in print the following year for writing a 'petulant' review. 'Petulance' was a significant word. He rarely described his own emotions in print, and, while it did describe his tendency to occasional sulkiness, the word also suggested – as had his earlier apology for 'bad temper and bad manners' in his attack on Humphrey Jennings – a belittling of the feelings which had generated the writing, and a belief that such feelings – that strong feelings – were wrong.

The bloody-mindedness of Blunt's writing on art found an echo in the irritations and indignation expressed by many other contemporary young writers. There was an almost tangible Oedipal fury in the air among the aspiring writers and artists of his generation, an anger and resentment at the anachronisms of orthodoxy and authority of complacent Middle England. The same aggression could be found in the work of the young W. H. Auden – born within a year of Blunt – well before he discovered Marx in 1932. His early poems were full of apocalyptic warnings to the marshals of the status quo. In 'Consider this and in our time', written in 1930, Auden told his cast of villains, 'The game is up for you and for the others.' 'It is time for the destruction of error,' Auden announced; he prophesied the 'Death of the old gang'. The poet's minatory tone exactly caught his generation's aggressive exasperation with what had gone before.

There were many sources for the general sense of dissatisfaction among the young. One was the rigid out-of-date values of their parents, who mostly still held to the belief that the Great War had been a righteous one. The war had come to be a barrier between the younger generation and their seniors. George Orwell, a few years older than Blunt, later wrote:

by 1918 everyone under the age of forty was in a bad temper with his elders, and the mood of anti-militarism which followed naturally upon the fighting was extended into a general revolt against orthodoxy and authority. At that time, there was among the young, a curious hatred of 'old men'. The dominance of 'old men' was held to be responsible for every evil known to humanity.

The anachronisms and brutalities of public school were another common bond among the young. For some, including Blunt, the experience later fed into left-wing commitment. In *The Old School Tie*, a 1934 anthology of essays on public schools, Graham Greene predicted the institution's imminent demise, and Auden, Rex Warner, and others drew a connection between their political radicalism and their school rebellion. In the same year the economist John Strachey half-laughingly attributed his Communism to having been left out of the Eton cricket eleven. In *The Strings Are False* Louis MacNeice wrote of himself and Blunt, 'I honestly believe that, though we were fresh from school, we had absorbed that sense of futility, of belonging to a society without values, which the ebbing of World War I had left behind it.' There was also a feeling that England was a country in decay. The pre-Marxist Auden wrote of it as a place of 'silted harbours, derelict works' and 'strangled orchards'; the young Cyril Connolly that 'Everybody is so weak and knock-kneed, a race of little ferrets and blindworms. England is a problem: parts of it are so beautiful, a few people so intelligent, yet never can I manage to fit it . . . There is no place in England for a serious rebel.' From such fertile ground the young British Marxist intelligentsia of the 1930s sprang. Louis MacNeice later wrote that though, unlike many of his fellow writers and friends, he never became a Communist, 'I joined them . . . in their hatred of the *status quo*'.

Despite his new London life, Cambridge remained Blunt's intellectual and social base. Though he frequented the West End galleries where most of the exhibitions were held, he was not attracted by bohemian London, and its base in Hampstead, where Hepworth, Nicholson, Herbert Read, Elias Canetti and newly arrived European artist refugees such as Lázló Moholy-Nagy were beginning to settle. This was perhaps a deliberate assertion that he belonged not to the artistic, literary milieu but to academia. Nevertheless, he did make two new friends in the London art world.

The first was Tomás Harris, whom Blunt probably met through Harris's sister Enriqueta, who was doing postgraduate work on Spanish baroque art at the Courtauld. Harris was a dealer specializing in Spanish art and owned a gallery in Bruton Street. In December 1932 Blunt devoted one of his more temperate reviews to an exhibition at Harris's gallery on the differences between Northern and Italian schools of drawing.

Harris was half-Spanish, and almost exactly the same age as Blunt. He was energetic, clever and always immaculately turned out – though in a distinctly un-English way, with a neatly trimmed beard. He smoked hand-rolled yellow cigarettes filled with black tobacco. He was a famously generous host and friend, but possessed (and cultivated) an enigmatic air. Blunt liked him enormously: 'The first thing that struck one about Tomás Harris, was the total and disinterested enthusiasm with which he threw himself into any enterprise on which he embarked . . . at that particular moment all his energies and all his imaginative force went into that one objective . . . Tomás was one of the most complete human beings I have ever known.'

Harris had what the art business calls 'a good eye', and possessed an acknowledged talent for finding great things in unexpected places – a fifteenth-century panel once in the National Gallery at a country sale; various other lost masterpieces languishing in the crumbling stately homes of the English aristocracy, who often had no idea what they owned. His status as a dealer was offset in the non-commercial art world by the fact that he was also an acknowledged and scholarly expert on El Greco and Goya, whose drawings he collected. Blunt admired his artistic judgement, which he came to value, and on occasion to rely on.

In the late 1930s and the 1940s he wrote in learned journals about three Poussins that Harris had rediscovered – a risky thing for an art historian to do, since it might suggest an overly close relationship with the trade. After Blunt's exposure, there were suggestions that he might have allowed himself to get too close to Harris.

Blunt was also attracted by the fact that Harris was an outsider in the art world, and didn't care. In a market where respectability and class often counted for more than talent and expertise, he was regarded in some quarters as slightly raffish, too casual, not quite 'Establishment'. It was never clear whether this slight resistance to him was due to envy at his success mixed with old-fashioned conservatism and xenophobia, or to the fact that he was a secretive and charismatic character who might not be absolutely honest. 'Tomy was a very very strong personality,' recalled Dick Kingzett, a member of Agnew's – traditional purveyors of old masters to the English middle and upper classes. 'He was a very persuasive person. If you looked at a picture with him you found at the end of twenty minutes you were thinking the same as him.'

Blunt's other new acquaintance also demonstrated the attraction he felt to outsiders. Douglas Cooper was a twenty-two-year-old, rich, outspoken, homosexual art collector, then in the process of building what would become probably the best private modern art collection in the country. He opened the Mayor Gallery in Cork Street in April 1933 with twenty-six-year-old Freddie Mayor, the son of a Cambridge family with connections with Bloomsbury. With its clean, white, functionalist premises and pictures by artists hitherto unseen in London – Joan Miró and Paul Klee among them – it quickly became perhaps the most influential modern gallery in London. Miró was the subject of Blunt's first, and rather leaden, piece about Cooper's new venture in August 1933: he was 'not one of the great artists of Surrealisme [sic] – if any there be, for it seems to be a style ill-suited to real greatness for which a high level of intellect is required', Blunt wrote. He did however allow that Miró had 'many of the less serious qualities which make painting both enjoyable and profitable'.

Cooper, like Guy Burgess, was a completely unmediated personality – witty, envious, splenetic and, as John Pope-Hennessy said, 'embarrassingly unpredictable'. 'An unholy alliance between Mae West and the Baron de Charlus' was how the curator Bryan Robertson described him. His family's money had originally come from Australia, where they shipped gold and owned the Woollahra section of Sydney – though Cooper's great-grandfather had moved back to England. Such was his touchiness on his origins that he could be moved to hysteria and great venom if it was suggested (as his enemies liked to do) that he was descended from convicts and that his money came from sheep dip. He felt, and frequently articulated, a deep-seated Anglophobia and was equally ready to denounce 'ghastly English philistinism' and 'those awful prissy Bloomsberries'. He had inherited a £100,000 trust fund in 1931 and had set out to spend it on Cubist paintings. It was rumoured that he egged Blunt on to his most outspoken attacks in his art columns, particularly on Ben Nicholson and Barbara Hepworth, for Cooper regarded abstraction as a fallacious dead end for modern art.

Not everyone welcomed Blunt's entrenchment at Cambridge. Visiting his now 'palpably academic' friend there, Louis MacNeice was depressed by his circle and their incessant parlour games – though he liked Guy Burgess: 'quite the nicest of your pals by a long way'. 'A charade', he observed, 'was good if it was risqué or blasphemous, and I felt I was back at Marlborough. The same private gossip and tittering, the same disregard for everybody not ourselves.' Marriage and life in Birmingham had intensified MacNeice's dislike of the claustrophobic, pernickety Oxbridge world. His wife, Mary, also had a strong aversion to it. Things were not helped by the mutual coolness between her and Blunt, who later told MacNeice's biographer that he had clearer memories of MacNeice's borzoi Betsy than of Mary. Moreover, living in Birmingham exposed MacNeice for the first time to the realities of life for the less fortunate. While he scraped to make a living himself – Blunt got him reviewing work at the *Spectator* to supplement his income – many of his students, especially the local ones, were much worse off: shabbily dressed, ill-prepared for their courses, even underfed. Until now, according to John Hilton, the rest of the world had barely existed for MacNeice. 'Even his close friends – speaking for myself – felt at times as though they only existed as part of this king's, or that jester's, dream. The break-through to full awareness of humanity, common or uncommon, and its obstinate way of continuing to be when not thought about . . . proceeded rapidly among the practicalities of life in Birmingham.' In contrast, Blunt's world seemed trivial and narrow.

In October 1932 MacNeice published his first novel, *Roundabout Way*, under the pseudonym Louis Malone. It was a lightweight piece which he disowned almost immediately, later describing it as 'basically dishonest'; but it was obviously autobiographical and contained a lethal portrait of Blunt in Cyril Hogley, a bitchy Oxford don who had Blunt's 'cold blue eyes', sulky lower lip and taste for the baroque. MacNeice told Blunt that Hogley was 'spiced up with my idea of what might be if you were two-dimensional and lived in Oxford (I have made him a little more unpleasant, of course, but just for fun)'. Hogley was snakelike – 'head poised like a Cobra' – a thoroughly unappealing creation, and the most vivid character in the book. He lapped up scandal and dirty stories – Blunt had a taste for both. He was an intellectual snob 'who keeps apes in order to gloat at the chapel of his reason over their flat skulls'. He was a misogynist: 'Women, according to the ancient tradition, had no souls, that was why Hogley disliked them – or why he said he did.' And he was creepily predatory: 'Devlin saw the ominous, rather sickly, light in Hogley's eyes: with persons like Hogley that meant pawing.' Most of all, he was a passive observer of life, a critic on the way to desiccation. Once he had been a bright young man, fresh and free, who loved 'the space and wealth of high gradual contours', but the academic world of 'snakes and drunkards' had subsumed him.

MacNeice had written the book two years before, when he had first married Mary it had been intended as a way of making money and as an expression of loyalty and love to her. She featured as a girl 'who picked violets' with whom the hero ran off, thus escaping the dead hand of academia. There is no record of Blunt's reaction to *Roundabout Way*. MacNeice was, perhaps not surprisingly, sheepish when he sent him a copy: 'Herewith my unhappy novel . . . a negative experiment.' Blunt had every reason to be surprised. In January that year MacNeice had asked him to comment on a novel about public school – perhaps one he had been writing in the late 1920s in which his friend featured as the handsome cricket-playing hero. Blunt either forgave him or never referred to *Roundabout Way*; a month after he sent the book, MacNeice invited Blunt to Birmingham after Christmas and thanked him for the work from the *Spectator*, and their friendship seemed to pick up where it had left off.

MacNeice meant some of what he wrote: in his posthumously published memoir, *The Strings are False*, he criticized Blunt's academicism and the claustrophobic world of Cambridge, though never with the all-out condemnation of *Roundabout Way*. The portrait in the book was both a mark of the strong reservations that MacNeice now had about Blunt and a warning, a prophecy of what he thought Blunt threatened to become. It followed on from the advice and criticism he so often handed out to his friend in his letters: 'If one keeps seeing through things one never sees into them,' he had told Blunt in 1928. Already Blunt was capable of great coldness and self-absorption, and, just as there were those who admired, even glamorized him, there were those who intensely disliked him. Some took against him simply because he was homosexual and not ashamed of it. Geoffrey Agnew, a Trinity contemporary who was a member of the Bond Street art-gallery family, took against him for this reason. When Blunt had an affair with a mutual friend, a history undergraduate and a keen mountaineer, Agnew apparently made it his mission to break up the relationship and get his friend married. The marriage took place, and the friend and his wife remained lifelong friends of Blunt's; Blunt and Agnew quietly detested each for the rest of their lives.

In another category were those whose *amour-propre* was irritated by a feeling that Blunt somehow did not sufficiently acknowledge them. These were often his academic peers; later in his life they were the ones who tended to accuse him of intellectual snobbery – not an accusation often heard from his students, or those younger than him. The history don Steven Runciman, who was three or four years older than Blunt and with whom he had friends in common – Peter Montgomery and Guy Burgess – 'never frightfully liked Anthony. He was always very supercilious and I rather disliked being patronized when I was a young don . . . He was always, I think, rather pleased with himself.' In turn, Runciman, a Firbankian dandy who wore heavy rings and cut his hair in an Italianate fringe, and was himself not free of intellectual and social snobbery, was not Blunt's type at all. Observers suggested there was a tinge of rivalry to their relationship, particularly over Burgess. 'Youngish dons would regard their undergraduate friends as their property, and they wouldn't let each other lay their hands on them.'

Then there were those who simply found Blunt chilly and condescending. Often these were the wives of his friends – among them Mary Ezra and Victor Rothschild's first wife, Barbara Hutchinson. Victor's sister, Miriam, remembered, 'When Victor asked me why I didn't like him, I said, "I don't like people with iced coffee in their veins instead of blood."' Blunt's attitude to women was confused. He was in part jealous of his friends' new wives. He had also absorbed much of the automatic misogyny of public school, and he knew few women. Even so, he was not universally dismissive: in 1931 he had gone to some lengths to get a woman friend a teaching job at Birmingham University; and Burgess, who liked women, gradually relieved him of some of his unthinking chauvinism.

But, if he had been in any doubt on the point, *Roundabout Way* forcefully told Blunt that some people saw him as an observer: cold, detached and voyeuristic. It was an aspect of his own personality about which he was ambivalent: he did not mind being disliked, but he did not want to be an observer for ever. An increasingly strong desire to avoid this fate would lead him to take crucial steps to become an active participant in the world.

5. Don

'the most amusing man in Cambridge'

In January 1933, the month that Adolf Hitler became Chancellor of Germany, Louis MacNeice wrote to Blunt, who had just been to stay with him in Birmingham, 'Auden turned up again after all and talked a deal of communism. So I dare say you were well out of him. You wouldn't have liked his ears either.* He is really a good man though.' Wystan Auden was the same age and of similar background to Blunt and MacNeice (his uncle was a vicar), and was already making a reputation for himself as a poet with an uncanny ability to speak for his generation's preoccupations. MacNeice had met him at Oxford. Auden had recently read Marx, and also Edmund Wilson's *Devil Take the Hindmost*, an account of the slump and its human cost in America. He had come to believe that Marxism offered both an analysis of, and an answer to, mass unemployment and the rise of fascism.

Blunt as yet had no interest in politics. 'I do not think anything in my career is of interest before 1934, when I first came in contact with Party members,' he wrote in a memoir for the NKVD, as Soviet Intelligence then called itself,† in 1943. 'Up till

---

* Auden's ears resembled large teapot handles.
† In its first thirty-seven years (1917–1954), the Soviet Intelligence service and its various branches underwent many name changes. Strictly, it was known as the NKVD (*Narodny Komitet Vnutrennih Del* – People's Commissariat for Internal Affairs) only between 1934 and 1941, undergoing many organizational and name changes up to its renaming in 1954 as the KGB. However, for the purposes of this book I have decided to keep things simple, and use 'NKVD' to denote Soviet Intelligence in all its guises until 1954.

then I had been an ordinary Cambridge intellectual – an art for art's sake type, with no interest in politics at all and even an active [dis]belief that the arts – in which I was genuinely interested – had any connection with active life or politics at all.'

But by 1933, though he did not yet know it, Blunt was ready for a new intellectual creed. His faith in Bloomsbury was waning. Fry and Bell's emphasis on instinctive appreciation seemed insipid when compared with the solidity of Walter Friedlaender's scholarship, and Bloomsbury's contrariness no longer seemed to him as outspokenly risqué as it had. In February 1933, in a *Spectator* review of Roger Fry's latest book on French art, Blunt praised Fry for his 'sympathy' with his subject, but pointed out that it was impossible fully to appreciate painters like Claude and Poussin without taking the subject matter of their work as seriously as its design and colour. The importance of Poussin's subject matter was central to Friedlaender's view of the artist. By the summer of 1933 Blunt had moved so far from Bloomsbury that he now allowed it the same weight as what he called a 'materialist' (or Marxist) approach. Bloomsbury divorced 'art from life', he wrote, whereas the materialist approach described art movements as the outcome of historical events. 'As usual,' he concluded, 'the truth usually lies halfway between the two views.'

By the time this article appeared, Blunt had left the country. He had been granted a year's sabbatical to work in Rome. Victor Rothschild drove him on the first leg of the journey, along with Burgess and Dadie Rylands – down to Monte Carlo in his Bugatti. The trip was in part a celebration of Burgess's finals – or rather his achievement in just about getting through them. He had been too busy being brilliant to do any work – though he had acquired a serious talent for drinking and creating mayhem – and on the eve of his exams he had collapsed. He had been awarded an aegrotat. He later claimed to have got a first, 'even though illness prevented him from completing his papers'. It wasn't clear whether this implosion was due to panic or to calculation. 'Guy thought all you had to do was work fourteen hours before the exam and have a lot of strong coffee,' one sceptic remembered.

'He cracked up on it.' Burgess had nevertheless persuaded his tutors to allow him to return in the following autumn term to begin work on a thesis on the 'intellectual background of the Puritan Revolution', making him perhaps the least-qualified post-graduate in the history of Trinity College.

From the South of France Blunt travelled on alone to the British School in Rome, in whose Lutyens-designed building in the Valle Guilia, ten minutes from the Pincio – one of Rome's most elegant public gardens – British artists, archaeologists and the occasional art historian came to study. His Old Marlburian friend Ellis Waterhouse had recently been appointed librarian there, and was writing a book on Italian baroque painting. Waterhouse, three years older than Blunt, had become a hard-working and occasionally pedantic art historian. He had recently resigned from a curator's job at the National Gallery, an institution with a well-earned reputation for being mediocre, back-biting and amateurish, and which he had hated, though the new director, Kenneth Clark, had recognized that he was the 'cleverest' member of staff.

Blunt fell in love with Rome and southern Italy. He had come to study the Italian baroque as background for his work on Poussin, who had spent most of his life there. 'I came to Rome', he wrote, 'thinking that I ought, rather as a matter of duty than of pleasure, to study the roots of the style in Italy. What I saw in Rome was a revelation to me, and though I have never given up my love for Johann Michael Fischer and Baltasar Neumann [the doyens of German baroque architecture], my perspective was changed.' Though Blunt was aware of Mussolini – 'Anyone living in Italy at the time was aware of the growing menace of Fascism, especially after the Nazis came to power in Germany in 1933, and as the Italian attack on Ethiopia gathered strength,' a member of the British School staff recalled – his time in Italy was an extremely happy one. With Waterhouse, he visited almost every baroque church and building in the city and discovered Bernini, Pietro da Cortona and the work of Francesco Borromini, the seventeenth-century architect who would become the great artistic preoccupation of his latter years. He and Waterhouse also took picnics out to the Campagna, and searched for the places which had inspired the paintings of Poussin and his followers. They resurrected an irritating schoolboy language of puns and bad jokes, which they found amazingly funny and which the British School's secretary exasperatedly christened 'Blunterhouse'. It would madden other secretaries and fellow academics, including Ernst Gombrich, for the next fifty years.

From the British School Blunt corresponded briefly with Ezra Pound over a *Spectator* review in which he had neglected to mention Pound's memoir of Henri Gaudier-Brzeska. 'Being a Goddamn Britson,' Pound sputtered, 'you probably didn't know that any book save Ede's mess [H. S. Ede's book *Savage Messiah* which had been published in 1931] was in existence. As you show ignorance of the Memoir pubd/ in 1916/ you are necessarily an English authority on Gaudier literature. Not that any engman [*sic*] ever wants to larn anything he dont know.'

'Complimenti,' Pound wrote three weeks later, after Blunt had apologized elegantly on a postcard showing the 400 martyrs of Otranto, a small baroque town in southern Italy, 'yr/ p/c izza lot funnier'n mine. Delighted to find there is still an Englander with traces of the speret ova man in him. /Any relation of the real Blunt, be chance?' By which he meant Wilfrid Scawen, for whom he had had a youthful admiration.

Otranto had been visited as part of a trip Blunt and Waterhouse made that autumn to Puglia, cycling on 'bikes of excruciating form', to visit the neglected baroque city of Lecce – 'the Florence of rococo art' as Osbert Sitwell called it. The only book on the subject, M. S. Briggs's *In the Heel of Italy*, was full of mistakes which they took great delight in correcting, and Waterhouse remembered years later that they read 'the sillier passages out loud to each other'.*

Blunt went on to Naples and, in an uncharacteristically senti-

---

* Blunt's copy is still among his papers at the Courtauld Institute.

mental mood, wrote an exceptionally purple piece about the ruins of the temple at Paestum for the *Spectator*:

> Then the rooks took possession of the temple, the hills turned blue and a cloud came up over Capri. And the sun shone gold on the temple as if to prove that it was really he who was responsible for its beauty – and won his case. But only for a moment for later, against a flamboyant sunset and then against a rapidly darkening sky, the temple reasserted its superiority as a work of Mind, and stood out, even in the half-darkness, as one of the greatest creations of Man.

Into this idyll crashed Guy Burgess. He was full, as ever, of impossible stories. 'He used to tell us about his adventures with politicians and young boys,' Waterhouse said later, 'and Blunt and I used to decide they were probably untrue. He was the biggest liar in the western hemisphere you know. But they were very funny.' Burgess, however, had more than gossip on his mind: he was in thrall to a new passion – Marxism. 'Blunt was politically naive,' Waterhouse continued. 'I don't think he had the slightest idea about politics. We never talked about politics at all. But that was all Guy wanted to discuss. He was exceedingly intelligent about politics and Blunt followed what he did.'

By his own account, Burgess had been a 'socialist' at school. When an old teacher visited his rooms at Trinity in 1931 he found Marxist books on his shelves. Burgess was, however, always very woolly about exactly when he had become a Communist, probably because his real involvement began comparatively late. Until 1933 he appeared to disapprove of those who took an active role in politics – an attitude common among Rylands's set. When Charles Madge, the poet and co-founder of Mass Observation, joined the tiny Cambridge Communist group in 1932, Burgess cut him dead in the street. 'He didn't approve of people who joined the Party. At the point I joined, neither Blunt nor Burgess was connected with Communism.'

Burgess's commitment to Communism seems to date from the autumn of 1933, the term when, according to Blunt, 'Marxism hit Cambridge.' 'I can date it precisely because I had sabbatical leave for that term, and when I came back I found that almost all my younger friends had become Marxists and joined the Communist Party.' Marxism had suddenly become fashionable. Blunt was not the only one to register the change. In December that year, Julian Bell wrote to the *New Statesman*, 'By the end of 1933 we have arrived at a situation in which almost the only subject of discussion is contemporary politics, and in which a very large majority of the more intelligent undergraduates are Communists.'

Before 1933 there had been very few Marxists at Cambridge. Most of them were at Trinity, where Blunt had encountered them. The best known was Maurice Dobb, the Trinity economics don, who from the 1920s held weekly political meetings at his home.* His faithful lieutenant was the Pembroke language fellow Roy Pascal, who had attacked an article by Blunt in the *Cambridge Review* in 1930. A number of science dons, such as J. B. S. Haldane and the charismatic 'Sage' Bernal, had become fascinated by the Soviet Union's claims that the country was making huge social and economic advances through the application of scientific methods, and had become Communists too. Among the Apostles, George Thomson, a Classics don three or four years older than Blunt, was a severe and unfriendly Stalinist, and Blunt's friend Alister Watson had been an avowed Marxist since arriving at the university – though his Marxism had thus far made almost no impact on his friends. In 1931 Watson had joined a tiny student Communist group which had been founded by David Haden Guest, a Trinity undergraduate who had returned from a year at Göttingen University in Germany – which had included two weeks in a Nazi jail cell for joining a Communist march – a confirmed Marxist. Early members included another Trinity undergraduate, Kim Philby, who was the group's treasurer, and Donald

* Several unconvincing attempts have been made to link Blunt with the group around Maurice Dobb in the 1920s, e.g. by Anthony Cave Brown and by John Costello. No interviewees or documents are cited in either case.

Maclean, a second-year modern-languages student at Trinity Hall. By 1932 the group had twenty-five members and was affiliated to the Communist Party of Great Britain (CPGB).

Though Communist recruits were thus far few, there were signs in the university, as at other universities, of a groundswell of opinion among the students towards the Left. In October 1931 at the Cambridge Union – one of the traditional bastions of Cambridge Conservatism – the Conservatives won the annual political debate as usual by a hefty majority of 257 votes to 83. A year later they won by only eight votes. That year Clement Attlee came to speak about child poverty in England, and his speech shocked many in his audience. In March 1933 the Union debated the abolition of the Means Test, 'which we felt bore heavily on the unemployed,' one young Union official remembered. 'It was a grim debate. The suffering and semi-starvation in the outside world was beginning to be realised in the Union. The vote was carried.' An article on Cambridge in the *Spectator* that month reported that 'politics and religion, so recently mere supers in the drama of discussion have achieved a startling come-back; Dr Buchman [founder of the 'Oxford Group', later Moral Rearmament] and Karl Marx bask in the warm limelight of interest from which so suddenly and so decisively they have elbowed Proust and Picasso ... much of the gay froth has gone.' The writer attributed this newfound enthusiasm to 'the external pressure of events', and noted that it was 'the intellectual side of undergraduate opinion' which had taken the bait. 'The need for able high Conservative propaganda is acute.'

One reason for this political shift was the deepening of the Depression in Britain and the seeming inability of the government to do anything about it. In January 1933 unemployment had reached a peak of nearly 3 million, or 23 per cent of all insured workers, and the newspapers and magazines were full of the sufferings of the poor: malnutrition in the inner cities, children with rickets, TB and diphtheria. The government – now a 'National' coalition led by Ramsay MacDonald since the collapse of the Labour government in 1931 – could not, or would not, do anything about the situation. It preached the old dogmas of balanced budgets and free trade to which the Conservatives had stuck fast throughout the 1920s; it cut unemployment benefit and introduced the hated Means Test. While the economy did improve during 1933 and 1934, large areas of Britain – the North-East and Wales in particular – remained in deep depression, and the plight of the poorest and the unemployed seemed to get worse and worse. 'Coffee and potatoes were being thrown into the sea to keep prices up,' Stuart Hampshire, who was then at Oxford, remembered. Disgust at the complacency of the government and his parents' generation in the face of such suffering – 'Poverty in the midst of plenty' was a popular slogan of the time – made Hampshire an eager fellow-traveller for three or four years in the mid-1930s. The Cambridge Communist James Klugmann recalled that the phrase 'seemed so simple and so ample a demonstration of the contradictions of capitalism amidst the hunger, which made even advanced capitalist countries – like Britain and France – countries of great poverty and malnutrition'. Even those not in the slightest bit sympathetic to the Left recognized social breakdown on an unprecedented scale. 'It had become evident that the structure of capitalist society in its old form had broken down, not only in Britain but all over Europe and even in the United States,' Harold Macmillan wrote later. 'The whole system had to be reassessed. Perhaps it could not survive at all; it certainly could not survive without radical change.'

Beyond England, events were equally unsettling: Japan had invaded Manchuria in 1931; Mussolini was running Italy; and in January 1933 Hitler became Chancellor of Germany. A month later came the mysterious burning of the Reichstag, which Hitler announced was the result of a Communist plot – he had been preaching a Jewish–Communist world conspiracy since the 1920s. He interned the leaders of the German Communist Party – the only serious political challenge to his authority – and won 44 per cent of the vote in the panic-ridden general elections held a few weeks later, immediately voting himself dictatorial powers for the next four years. In October that year he took Germany out of the League of Nations. The spectre of another war loomed.

The growing anxiety among students was not alleviated by a feeling that the British government seemed as unconcerned by Hitler as by unemployment. Even those as yet unaffiliated with the political Left believed this: the young A. J. P. Taylor, then a member of a Quaker peace group, wrote, 'In opposing the National Government, we were opposing Hitler's potential allies or so we thought . . . I believed that if Great Britain were involved in the war it would be on Hitler's side against Russia.' Isaiah Berlin, who was deeply opposed to Communism and had left Soviet Russia after the Revolution ('It was the worst government there's ever been, I can assure you of that,' he said in an interview in 1994), looked to Roosevelt's New Deal as the way forward. He could nevertheless see why so many of his contemporaries had such a suspicion of their government. 'The Chamberlain government clearly preferred Hitler to Stalin. It was a horrible regime. It was pro-Nazi – or at least not anti enough. Appeasement was not founded on the pursuit of peace, mainly fear of Russia. The thinking was Hitler was terrible, but he was a bulwark.'

While external events played their role in creating an appetite for left-wing politics at Cambridge, the reason why 'Marxism hit Cambridge' in the autumn of 1933 was largely because the small Communist group at the university was taken over by two determined and persuasive young men from Trinity: James Klugmann, a postgraduate, and John Cornford, a first-year undergraduate. In early November, collaborating with a Christian peace group, they organized a peace demonstration outside the Tivoli cinema, which was showing a recruitment film, *Our Fighting Navy*. A group of 'patriotic' students arrived, and there was a brawl. The event attracted publicity quite out of proportion to its scale. 'Quite a decent amount of fighting,' Blunt's former lover Julian Bell wrote to his brother Quentin excitedly – adding that he planned to 'ignore the party curse and lend a hand with the anti-war movement in Cambridge . . . It's all rather fun – I find it very difficult not to be carried away by my feelings and join the Communists – all my friends seem to have.' Within a week of the Tivoli fracas, and to capitalize on its impact, the Communists organized another peace march for 11 November, Armistice Day. The demonstration drew large crowds, including hundreds of students sympathetic to the cause of peace. Bell drove a car with mattresses strapped to its sides, for the purpose of dispersing, 'like a tank', the hearties and Conservatives who had come to hurl flour and eggs at the marchers. Guy Burgess, as excited by the energy of the Communists as was Bell, was his navigator. Thus the erstwhile literary aesthetes began to fall in love with the idea of themselves as men of action.

Another milestone in the growth of the Cambridge Left was the arrival of hunger marchers in the town the following February. These unemployed men, usually from the North East, embarked on a series of gruelling marches from their homes to London during the mid-1930s, to bring attention to their desperate situation – ultimately to no avail. Their poverty, their exhaustion and their hunger profoundly shocked many students, who had never encountered such deprivation before. 'The hunger marchers were older men and very fragile. Their faces had fallen in and they had ill-fitting boots,' remembered Margot Heinemann, who was later John Cornford's lover. 'After seeing them it was only a matter of time before I joined the Party.' She remained a lifelong member.

To many students who, like the poet Stephen Spender, felt 'hounded by external events', Communism offered answers and comfort. It seemed, irrefutably, to describe and diagnose the apocalyptic moment in which they were living. Capitalism seemed to be on the verge of collapse. In addition, the deliberately aggressive language of the Communist critique of bourgeois society fed the simmering exasperation that so many of the young felt towards the 'old men'. The Communists were openly critical of the government's policy on poverty and unemployment, and seemed far more concerned by this and the rise of fascism than anyone else, and for the first time in a decade the Communist

Party was beginning to welcome, or at least not to reject, the middle-class sympathizers whom it had hitherto branded as 'social fascists'. As if to illustrate the fact that Communism was right, the Soviet Union was proclaiming itself an economic miracle in apparent defiance of the depression that had engulfed the Western world. It had also set itself up as the natural and definitive opponent of fascism. Many British sympathizers, depressed by their own government's pusillanimity, justified and accepted the Soviet regime, which they themselves described as harsh and authoritarian, on the grounds that only a tough and ruthless power would be strong enough to take on the fascists.

Marxism played on two other qualities peculiar to the middle-class British students and intellectuals of the 1930s. It offered absolution from the guilt many of them felt about being part of the privileged ruling class. If one joined the Party and adhered to its strict demands, one was no longer part of the problem: one was helping to solve it. The philosopher Richard Wollheim believed that Blunt shared the 'great sense of shame about England and their class, the feeling that the upper classes of England had betrayed the world through their cowardice and greed'. Second, though the young would-be leftists deplored the notion of devoting, even sacrificing, oneself without question to one's country as a nonsense exposed by the First World War and part of the public schools' twisted value system, they had nevertheless subconsciously absorbed the idea of utter devotion to an ideal and now applied it to Marxism. 'The strongest appeal of the Communist Party was that it demanded sacrifice; you had to sink your ego,' wrote MacNeice. It offered 'self-fulfilment through self-abnegation'.

At Cambridge, Klugmann and Cornford began systematically and determinedly to target sympathetic non-Party members, engaging them in nights of 'discussion' until they succumbed to the 'logic' of joining 'the only organization that was doing anything about fascism and poverty', as one recruit put it. Charles Rycroft, later an eminent psychoanalyst, joined 'after a marathon series of indoctrination sessions lasting far into the night', run by a researcher who took more trouble to educate him – in Marxism – than any teacher or don ever had. Another recruit, Brian Simon, an educationalist who stayed in the Party until the 1970s, was inducted after nights and nights of conversation with James Klugmann.

However, not everyone who felt that Marxism correctly diagnosed the world situation wanted to join the Party. After the subject of Marxism was discussed at the Apostles in December 1933, Blunt's old friend Dennis Proctor, now a civil servant and an occasional visitor to the Society, wrote to Julian Bell:

> I like your visualisation of Marxism very much ... I've become a convert too since that meeting of the Society. Partly from the delayed action of the Society (which is usual with me), partly from reading Strachey's book* which I hadn't, but ought to have read before I read my paper. It is something to have come nearer to a conclusion, but I find it very upsetting to have come to that one, and I don't know what to do.

Like Proctor, Julian Bell believed that Marxism was right – 'It is not so much that we are all Socialists now as that we are all Marxists now,' he wrote – but he was depressed by its predictions of society's imminent collapse and repelled by the Party's demands. Nevertheless, he recognized the compulsion that many of his friends felt to join. 'There is a general feeling ... that we are personally and individually involved in the crisis, and that our business is rather to find the least evil course of action.'

Guy Burgess was intoxicated by Marxism and readily joined the Party. When Blunt returned briefly from Italy in January 1934

* *The Coming Struggle for Power*, by John Strachey, published in 1932, described the European crisis in Marxist terms and predicted another world war. It was credited with converting a lot of young intellectuals to Communism, though its author never joined the Party and later abjured his Communist sympathies.

to stay with his mother at Ham, and went up to Cambridge for
an exam, he

> found that the intellectuals whom I had known before I went
> away were all coming under the influence of Communism.
> Guy Burgess who had been almost my closest friend before I
> went away had joined . . . I was only in Cambridge a week
> or so at this time, and was not affected by what I saw
> beyond a vague surprise at finding so many intelligent people
> joining the Party.

Burgess was present at the reception organized for the hunger
marchers in February, sporting, rather inappropriately, his Pitt
Club tie (the Pitt Club named, of course, after the nineteenth-
century Tory Prime Minister, was a Cambridge dining club where
public schoolboys took their lunch). By October he was a stalwart
of the Trinity Communist cell and was giving talks on Marxist
interpretations of history at the Trinity History Society.

Though Blunt was not consciously touched by his friends' new
political discovery, politics did suddenly make a entrance into his
writing for the first time in the New Year of 1934. It seemed that
Italian Fascism had made some impact upon him after all. In his
first article of the year he contrasted Nazi Germany's policy on
'degenerate art', which involved removing from public view the
products of all 'advanced' schools of art from Cubism onwards,
with the way the Italian Fascists had co-opted Futurism as the
country's official art. The Nazis, Blunt noted, implicitly acknowledged the power of modern art, whereas the Italians had pulled
its teeth, making it 'nothing but a means of advertising the aims
and theories of fascism. As . . . a display of art it is valueless.' Art
as propaganda, he was saying, was not art at all. This was
something about which he would change his mind. In another
article, in March, he described the French expressionist Georges
Rouault, whose work – introduced to him by Roger Fry –
combined both social comment and religious belief, as 'perhaps
the only painter of his generation who has produced great works

of art out of violent feelings about social conditions, a good refutation of extreme theories of pure form'.

After spending March in Rome, Blunt travelled north to Germany, where he spent May in Bavaria. In Munich, where for the past four years Wilfrid had spent part of the year learning how to sing, Blunt received a letter from MacNeice announcing the birth of a son. 'There are quite a lot of interesting details but I don't include them in case you have got censorship or some other Nordic notion in those parts.' It was his time in Germany that awoke Blunt to what was happening in Europe. 'Events which took place in Germany had begun to penetrate even my intellectual isolation,' he wrote in his NKVD memoir, 'and I was becoming dimly aware that my own position wasn't quite satisfactory.'

It was impossible not to notice the changes that had taken place in Germany since Hitler had come to power. Blunt himself wrote, coolly, about the German academics he met who had become gushing proponents of the superiority of the Fatherland's culture. 'I would quote an ardent young National Socialist *Kunstforscher* who tried to prove to me that the good in Raphael derived from Germany. I forget his arguments.' Wilfrid now found himself making detours rather than give the Nazi salute to the insolent Brownshirts in the Munich streets. He had begun to take great care over what he said to German acquaintances, and worried about his anti-Nazi German friends. When Guy Burgess's friend Goronwy Rees went to Berlin in 1934, he found the streets uneasily silent. He was told that prominent cultural figures had simply vanished; the socialists who had opposed Hitler seemed shrunken and dispirited, or had simply disappeared. 'Here what seemed a nightmare in London is the sober everyday reality,' he wrote home. 'The betrayal and the death of every human virtue; no mercy, no pity, no peace; neither humanity nor decency nor kindness: only madness, shouted every day on the wireless and in the newspapers, spoken by ordinary people as if it were sober sanity.' Charles Rycroft and Brian Simon also saw the Nazis in action that year; both cited their experience as a milestone on their journeys to Communism. Simon was particularly shocked by the pressure schoolchildren were put under to join the Hitler Youth.

Blunt was in eastern Germany on 30 June 1934, the Night of the Long Knives, when Hitler disposed of all his closest rivals in one stroke, executing them without trial, and within a few days banned all other political parties. It was a scandal which took foreigners by surprise, even after the Reichstag fire. The most prominent of those murdered was Ernst Röhm, leader of the Nazi storm troopers and Commissar of Bavaria, whom Hitler now accused of 'homosexual depravity'. For many of Blunt's homosexual contemporaries – Auden, Christopher Isherwood, John Lehmann – the sexual freedom under Weimar had been one of Germany's most intoxicating attractions. Along with the destruction of Magnus Hirschfeld's Institute of Sexology in Berlin in 1933, the Röhm affair demonstrated the Nazis' determination to persecute sexual aberration. Blunt was never a devotee of the homosexual world of Weimar Berlin, but there are hints that he had found Germany a sexually liberating place. In the late 1920s he had travelled there with an Oxford friend of MacNeice's, the 'sexually bold' Moore Crossthwaite, who had spent time trawling the Berlin clubs with Isherwood. When John Hilton went to study architecture in Stuttgart in 1929, Blunt gave him an introduction to a publisher: 'This person took me to see part of a six-day bicycle race before trying to seduce me,' Hilton wrote. 'He said that Blunt was overrated.' MacNeice also seemed to think that Blunt had sexual links with Germany: in *Roundabout Way* the Blunt character bandies sexual gossip and innuendo with a German visitor; and when MacNeice wrote to Blunt in Germany in 1934 he urged him to 'Write and tell us all about the Young Men like Gods, not to mention the Kunst.'

It may be that Blunt's political awakening was, like that of his Trinity contemporary, John Lehmann, crucially tied to his sexual experiences. This was something he did not confide to his Soviet masters. What educated Lehmann to the effects of the Depression and the viciousness of the Austrian government were his relationships with the working-class Viennese boys he picked up when he was living in the city in the early 1930s: 'the keenness of my interest in what was happening to the people of Austria, and particularly of Vienna . . . [was] suffused by sexual desire', he wrote. In 1934 he returned to help the beleaguered left-wing parties in their last stand against Chancellor Dollfuss's imposition of a one-party state.

Blunt witnessed at first hand the persecution of Walter Friedlaender, whom he visited in Freiberg in June. Within a few weeks the sixty-one-year-old scholar was both honoured with a Festschrift for his achievements in art history and dismissed from his professorship for being a Jew. Friedlaender was stoic about his fate – Blunt later remembered that they had studied photographs of Poussin drawings and had drunk delicious wine in the Black Forest – but he left Germany two months later. By the autumn he was in London, reduced to giving the occasional lecture at the Courtauld. All of this shook Blunt. He had been planning, with MacNeice's encouragement, to apply for the post of professor of the new Barber Institute of Fine Arts at Birmingham, but he asked MacNeice whether, if he stood aside, there was any chance that Friedlaender might get the job. MacNeice, himself married to a Jew, was matter-of-fact: 'About your quandaries: No foreigners (especially a Jew) would have much of a chance here though it's just possible he might get it if all the other chaps were dumb or mad, or something. Dodd says you would be a fool to stand down for Friedlaender, or indeed for anyone.'

Apart from a brief trip to Berlin in 1962, Blunt would not return to Germany again for forty years.

Blunt was not looking forward to returning to Cambridge in October. 'Cambridge seems a little topsy turvy at the moment . . .' he wrote to Dadie Rylands in early October.

I'm afraid that my year away had not left me with that homesickness for the old University which I expected to feel . . . Apart from about half a dozen people whom I really want to see and the prospect of getting in to my new rooms (which are lovely) I can't see quite why I would want to go back at all. In fact I am doing my best to desert the place.

Blunt did apply – optimistically, given his lack of experience and publications – for the post of director of the Barber Institute. Louis MacNeice summoned him to come and 'exhibit your personal charm', suggesting that in order to impress the intellectually fashion-conscious vice-chancellor, Charles Grant Robertson, 'you should . . . be represented to him as slightly left-wing' and drop the names of dons from Oxford's intellectual Olympus, All Souls. Blunt's seriousness about the job may be judged by the fact that he went to Oxford almost immediately to see Isaiah Berlin, whom he had met that spring in Florence, writing to thank him from Birmingham the following week, where he was exhibiting his charms on MacNeice's orders. 'I feel that my knowledge of Oxford', he wrote, 'has been vastly increased by meeting all those distinguished members of your College, and I am delighted to be in a position now to make comparisons between the Common room life of Oxford & Cambridge – equally unkind to both.' MacNeice's house, he added, was 'A routine of dogs & babies with the occasional interspersion of profound remarks from Louis who is in vivacious form.' (Blunt was a multiple, but neglectful, godfather, and claimed to be bad with animals, which he liked more than he admitted.)

The Birmingham worthies, however, were not persuaded. MacNeice wrote in November, 'The bloody old sots are, I fear, not going to have you. It's all because of your youth; they can't see what a young man would do with all that money.' The job went instead to Thomas Bodkin, a dull and self-important middle-aged lecturer from London University. Had Blunt gone to Birmingham, his future might have been very different.

So Blunt was forced to stay at Cambridge. It was not turning out quite as badly as he had feared. His beautiful new rooms in Trinity's intimate Neville's Court were perfect for parties. MacNeice wrote that the sitting room was a 'coquettishly chaste room with white panelling and Annunciation lilies'; it was lined with enormous seventeenth- and eighteenth-century tomes on architecture and art theory. Blunt began to entertain regularly, bringing together the new crop of undergraduates and older friends, as Rylands did. 'He used to have a party every two weeks,' the poet Gavin Ewart, a first-year undergraduate, recalled; 'the gin and tonic flowed like water. I was introduced to Isaiah Berlin at one of Blunt's parties.' 'Blunt was handsome, agreeable, civilized, charming and distinguished. What more could you want?' Berlin said later. The atmosphere was by no means exclusively intellectual: another student remembered meeting Lady Penelope Dudley Ward, reputedly the illegitimate daughter of Edward VII and a minor film star.

A certain type of socially successful, academically ambitious undergraduate seemed naturally to gravitate to Blunt's rooms. 'When I went to up Cambridge in 1934,' remembered Ewart, 'I asked Stephen Spender, "How do you get to know the interesting people?" and Spender said, "You must try and meet Anthony Blunt – he's the most amusing man in Cambridge."' (In the 1980s, when Blunt was disgraced, Spender would claim that he had barely known him and had always disliked him.) Like Rylands, Blunt took it upon himself to watch over his undergraduate friends' interests. When Charles Rycroft confided that he found his tutor disappointingly dull, 'Blunt took an intelligent interest. He asked me to parties and lent me books. He liked taking people on.' 'He made jokes and was very sophisticated and slightly camp,' said Ewart. 'He always knew what you might call the important people. He was interested in poetry and novels. He was a cultured man.'

The following year, when he gave the cast party for Dadie Rylands's production of *Julius Caesar*, Blunt met Tess Mayor, a first-year at Newnham, whom Dadie had cast as Calpurnia and who had instantly become the most sighed-after girl at Cambridge. Her admirers included the American Michael Straight, Charles Madge's brother John and Brian Simon, and she would eventually marry Victor Rothschild. The party also brought an

introduction to another first-year, Noel Annan. Mayor's friendship with Blunt would outlast his disgrace; Annan's would founder through academic competitiveness and Blunt's own chilliness
in the 1950s.

Another event that vastly improved Cambridge was his meeting
with a handsome, dark-eyed first-year to whom he was deeply
attracted. The young man had never had a homosexual relationship – and never would again – but he admired and liked Blunt,
and was in awe of his sophistication and intelligence. In the autumn
term of 1934 they began an affair which lasted two years, until the
young man fell in love with a girl. Blunt's role in the relationship
was one that would become familiar to him: that of a mentor. 'He
was different from anyone I'd ever known – awfully easy to get on
with; very easy,' the young man remembered many decades later.
'He was a life-enhancer, extraordinarily vivacious, he had enormous energy, he liked to gossip: it was fun to be with him. He took
me to France to see Courbet and Daumier.' But Blunt was also
extremely careful with his feelings – kindly but always controlled,
and a little distant. 'He did keep his emotions to himself; he didn't
really express himself verbally very much. It felt like disinterested
affection. We didn't have long sessions on our own – we were
often at parties, and he was tremendously studious.' Publicly Blunt
was sceptical of romantic love, writing of James Thurber, whose
cartoons he admired, 'the most romantic scenes enacted by squalid
and repulsive figures, blow the gaff about many of the false values
attached to human activities'. The relationship was, if not secret,
not widely advertised. Blunt was usually regarded as rather under-
sexed and uninterested, though Gavin Ewart reckoned he once
showed him an engraving with a large erect penis in it 'as a test of
my persuasions'. Another student was shocked, and for a time ill-
disposed to Blunt, after 'I happened to be present when he was
having a conversation with Constant Lambert on how to persuade
people they were homosexual even when they weren't, as a prelude
to getting them into bed.'

Blunt's instinct that Cambridge was 'topsy turvy' was not
wrong. It was soon clear that the Marxism he had glimpsed early

in 1934 was no passing fad: it had become one of the major preoccupations in the circles in which he moved. 'The undergraduates and graduate students were swept away by it,' he later wrote, 'and during the next three or four years almost every intelligent undergraduate who came up to Cambridge joined the Communist party some time in his first year.' But obviously not every undergraduate was a Communist. Most of the colleges experienced nothing of the hothouse left-wing politics of Trinity and King's. Alan Berends, an undergraduate at Downing College at the time, did not remember anyone discussing Communism at his college. When there was a bus strike in Cambridge (a strike for which Guy Burgess later took the credit), students from his college turned out to break it, he remembered. However, within the circles in which Blunt moved, left-wing politics were the subjects of the day: at Trinity, the centre of student Communism; among the children of Bloomsbury; among the writers he met through Louis MacNeice; among some of the artists he reviewed; among German émigré academics he met at the Courtauld who had fled from Hitler; even among the young upper-class dilettanti, anti-fascism was a fashionable topic.*

The undergraduate Marxists initially thought Blunt just another hopeless aesthete with a congenital resistance to politics. Brian Simon remembered asking who the new don who gave parties was. 'He's an ineffectual homosexual,' was the withering answer. 'I found myself in constant contact with members of the Party whose whole outlook was totally different from mine,' Blunt remembered. He told the NKVD that his change of heart was due to three people: John Cornford, James Klugmann and, of course, Guy Burgess.

* The writer Julian Symons, who edited a small left-wing magazine in the 1930s, estimated that the total number of people sympathetic to left-wing politics during the 1930s was never more than 1 million in a total population of 40 million, i.e. 2.5 per cent; this figure encompassed everyone from W. H. Auden to the man or woman who bought books on the dangers of fascism from Victor Gollancz's Left Book Club. Even at its pre-war height in 1939, Communist Party membership reached only 18,000.

John Cornford's death in the Spanish Civil War in the last days of 1936, when he was not quite twenty-one, made him such a tragic and perfect martyr that it is hard to disengage his life from the myth that has surrounded him since his death. Blunt saw him as

> a glamorous figure, a romantic, fanatical character and a very remarkable speaker . . . a vehement orator who would carry an audience with him; he was also highly intelligent but his intelligence was much more imaginative than the cold, clear mind of Klugmann. It may sound a callous thing to say but it was in a way appropriate, though tragic, that he should have gone to Spain and been killed. He was the stuff martyrs are made of, and I do not at all know what would have happened to him if he had survived. He was a highly emotional character and I strongly suspect that he might have gone back on his Marxist doctrine, and if so I think he would have suffered very acutely.

Cornford was a Galahad figure: nineteen years old, a poet, single-minded, charismatic, a little humourless, and utterly devoted to building the Party. Steven Runciman, who disliked him – a 'strange and, I thought, very unattractive boy' – acknowledged that 'He was an extremely clever, forceful, merciless, rather inhuman boy.' He also felt that Blunt and Burgess were 'absolutely glamorised by him'. Cornford dressed in ragged trousers, when even the most committed student Communists stuck to their flannels – a mannerism that served only to show off his spare young beauty – lived publicly with a working-class girl called Ray, and numbered real working-class activists among his friends. (Rather less convincingly, his favourite words were apparently 'bloody' and 'bastard'.) Blunt was not close to Cornford, but he admired his conviction and commitment. He also read Cornford's poetry – some of which was good – and, according to Brian Simon, made editorial suggestions: he had, after all, been Mac-Neice's unofficial reader for years.

Blunt knew James Klugmann, 'who had been a brilliant student of mine and also a friend', far better. Klugmann was a different animal: Jewish, clever, affable, persuasive. He had been to Gresham's – the school in Norfolk which had produced Auden, Britten and the future spy Donald Maclean. Blunt regarded him as

> the pure intellectual of the Party. He was a very good scholar and also an extremely good political theorist. He was the person who worked out the theoretical problems and put them across. He ran the administration of the Party with great skill and energy and it was primarily he who decided what organisations in Cambridge were worth penetrating and what were not.

Under Klugmann's auspices the Party took over the Socialist Society and members were given clandestine tasks such as cultivating foreign students, or working to get firsts in order to get into the BBC or the Foreign Office.

Klugmann was fond of Blunt, and cited him as an intellectual mentor. 'He would say that through Blunt he was put in touch with the world of European culture, in these huge tomes that Blunt collected of engravings and drawings,' said Brian Simon. 'I was surprised by this, I thought of James as widely cultured when I met him.' Klugmann was known for preaching a moderate, literate, rather comforting-sounding Communism, while Cornford's politics were austere and painful. Cornford's converts tended to be either poker-faced grammar school boys or public-school boys trying to look like 'proletarians'. Klugmann, however, told his converts 'that Communism was the heir to all that was best in Liberalism, Socialism, Conservatism, Rationalism, Catholicism and Anglicanism. It was "Forward from Everything", and he encouraged his recruits to continue exactly as they had before their conversion.' Klugmann made Communism sound easy. Charles Rycroft, however, came to believe that Klugmann had soft views for some ears and harder ones for 'real' Communists.

Klugmann's 'moderate' Communism was very much in line

with the Soviet Union's new policy of encouraging the goodwill and support of foreign well-wishers who shared its antipathy to Germany. It had begun tacitly to endorse the idea of a 'Popular Front' against fascism, drawing together, under the aegis of the Western Communist parties, those who were concerned about fascism, feared another war, or wanted to do something about the depression. Many well-wishers and fellow-travellers who would previously have been spurned by the Party were now actively welcomed. They were those who had come to believe that the Communist Party offered the best hope against fascism and depression, and who had concluded that, for all the harsh rhetoric, Communism was really just a kind of up-to-date Liberalism – a characteristically English response to extreme political ideology. Klugmann did not dissuade them from this view which in hindsight seems so naive; to some extent he shared it himself. By 1935 those in King's and Trinity circles who professed to have liberal views found it hard to reject advances from the Communists. Tess Rothschild recalled, 'You felt that if you were approached to join the Party you'd have to say yes. One felt slightly ashamed if one refused. It meant one wasn't fighting for the people, one was just being selfish.' She was relieved when she was dismissed by Party recruiters as being 'too frivolous'. Even those who remained aloof from the Left, like the undergraduate Michael Grant, found 'There were Communists on all sides, and you couldn't help being friendly with them – you saw them every day. I had sympathy with people like John Cornford, who felt so strongly that they went and did something about it.'

As for Burgess, he was now known as one of the Party's great persuaders. 'Burgess was a great propagandist,' Gavin Ewart remembered. 'He would say, "If you want to know about dialectical materialism come to see me."' As his hopes for academic celebrity waned – due to his lack of application – Communism became increasingly important to him. It anchored his life and gave him some claim to authority. His greatest achievement of his last years at Cambridge was organizing a successful strike by the college waiters to protest at their employment as casual labour.

When he met him in 1934, Goronwy Rees was dazzled by how confidently articulate Burgess was on the subject of Marxism. Noel Annan described it as a kind of 'second skin' for Burgess, it seemed utterly natural to him. On a pilgrimage to the Soviet Union in summer 1934, Burgess claimed to have had a long discussion with Nikolai Bukharin, the former secretary of the Comintern, whom he later said recruited him – this turned out to be another Burgessian fantasy. It was also said that he had been found dead drunk in the Park of Rest and Culture in Moscow.

It was Klugmann's emphasis on intellectual Marxism and Burgess's determination that his friend would be convinced – along with his lectures on Marxist interpretations of history – which caught Blunt. Even so, Blunt was mulishly slow to catch on. 'At first I could see no arguments for their views,' he later told the NKVD,

> but gradually I came to feel that apart from their attitude towards politics – about which I still felt completely unable to form any opinion – their views on subjects which I understood such as history, and above all my own subject of history of art, were not only interesting, but even provided a real basis for understanding the subject correctly and in a scientific manner.

Klugmann 'held that culture was a weapon in the class struggle', Charles Rycroft recalled, 'and that even research into aesthetics was a legitimate form of revolutionary activity. Prolonged meditations on the foot of a Chippendale chair would, I once heard him say, bring a Marxist to a closer understanding of the class structure of eighteenth-century England.' Blunt would go further than this, writing a couple of years later, 'Painting being as important an expression of man as, say, political action, the history of a period or a race cannot be complete without the history of its painting.' Klugmann might have been writing about Blunt when he described the aesthetes of the 1920s as precursors of the Cambridge Communists of the 1930s: 'They were against the sexual customs, against institutional religion, against their

parents, against academic arts in the sense of the Royal Academy
. . . They were often known as aesthetes . . . they were angry, they
were rebellious.'

Marxism filled the gap left by Blunt's rejection of Bloomsbury's
theories. Its insistence on the importance of history and social
conditions as crucial to the development of artistic styles opened
up a new way of thinking about art. Its aggressive opposition to
current orthodoxy made it feel thrillingly active, of the world and
new. 'The intellectual is no longer afraid to own an interest in the
practical matters of the world,' Blunt wrote excitedly, 'and Communism is allowed to be a subject as interesting as Cubism.' As
Klugmann commented, 'Marxism made everything rich.' Its claim
to be precise, scientific and rational appealed to Blunt's weakness
for absolutes. It provided a new set of criteria by which to judge
and define art, and much more besides. It had explanations for
Blunt's ambivalent feelings about much modern art: a Marxist
would say that abstraction and Surrealism failed because they
were not sufficiently engaged with the world in which they had
been produced. Significant Form, which Blunt had once so passionately espoused, now seemed a poor thing indeed: it 'reduces
[painting] to something entirely cut off from the serious activities
of life', he wrote.

Blunt's first article which drew, albeit loosely, on Marxist
theory was published in November 1934. Great art, he wrote,
was 'made out of materials found in the outer world and is
directly connected with material reality'. Its antithesis, 'the arts of
escape' – the fairy tales of Lord Dunsany, for example – could be
lovely, magical even, but could not compare in seriousness with
the work of the great realists, like Balzac or Courbet. 'Serious'
artists reflected and described their social milieu. The Surrealists,
with their obsession with dream worlds, he added – unable to
resist a jibe – 'seem to be failing for the same sort of reason. They
use material objects in their paintings only as a means of expressing the fantasies with which their minds are obsessed.'

The need for art to portray the world as it was, was the central
tenet of contemporary Marxist art criticism. Social realism had

been adopted as the official art of the Soviet state in the summer of 1934 at the First All-Union Congress of Soviet Writers in Moscow. It had intellectual foundations in the writings of Marxist critics like G. V. Plekhanov and Georg Lukács. It was now popular with the Soviet government because it was easy to understand, potentially populist – certainly more so than the modernist avant-garde – and easy to put at the service of the state for propaganda purposes. The English Marxist art critic Francis Klingender, whom Blunt invited to lecture at Cambridge in the mid-1930s, liked to quote Lenin on this: 'Art belongs to the people. Its roots should penetrate deeply into the very thick of the masses of the people. It should be comprehensible to these masses and loved by them. It should unite the emotions, the thought and the will of these masses and raise them to a higher level.' For Blunt, with his covertly conservative tastes, realism seemed the answer to his concerns about the future of art.

His increasing knowledge of Marxist art theory during the winter of 1934–5 was, however, due not so much to Klugmann and Burgess as to his meeting with an older, more experienced and sophisticated Communist theorist. Friedrich (or Frigyes) Antal was a forty-seven-year-old Viennese art historian and Communist Party member who arrived in London – via Moscow – in 1933, having left Austria as the right-wing government began its brutal attempts to set up a one-party state. On his arrival, like many refugee art historians from central Europe, he found his way to the Courtauld, where W. G. Constable was trying to make use of the sudden influx of eminent foreign art historians as best he could.

Antal is now largely forgotten. He published only one major book in English during his lifetime, and he never occupied an elevated position in British academia, which was alienated by his extreme politics. Nevertheless, in the 1930s he impressed a number of young British art historians – including, rather surprisingly, the conservative John Pope-Hennessy. He was tall, dark, attractive, often irascible and given to extreme views; even his fellow émigrés thought of him as a loner. He had also been a real revolutionary. In Budapest, where he was born, he had as a young man attended the weekly salons of Georg Lukács, who had become his mentor. During Béla Kun's shortlived Hungarian Soviet Republic of 1919, Antal had been made Commissar for Arts and Museums by Lukács, who was Deputy People's Commissar of Education. He had been given the task of 'nationalizing' private art collections – i.e. relieving their owners of them, with a view to setting up a new public museum. Very little had actually been done before the Republic collapsed, when Antal left the country for Vienna. There he studied under the great art historian Max Dvořák. Antal combined the esoteric scholarship of the Viennese school with an unusually wide knowledge of art, and could write with equal confidence on seventeenth-century Mannerism and German expressionism.

Antal's Courtauld lectures on sixteenth- and seventeenth-century Italian painting and classicism and romanticism attracted Blunt's attention. The former's attempts to translate into English his recently finished *Meisterwerk* on Florentine art may also have brought him to Blunt, who later helped several émigré academics to translate their work. However they met, it quickly became apparent that, as the beady-eyed John Pope-Hennessy was quick to note, Blunt, had been 'captivated' by the Hungarian, with his passionately held views, his spikiness, and his impressive scholarship. Ernst Gombrich, a recent Austrian arrival who met Antal in the mid-1930s and knew of Blunt's admiration for him, reckoned that

> Of the Marxist art historians around, he was by far the most learned and sophisticated. He was very doctrinaire in his political views, but he had a good eye. I remember going with him to an exhibition and was struck by the freshness of his response. He was not a negligible person, and I can quite understand that Blunt was impressed by him.

Much of Antal's work centred on the historical see-sawing between classicism and romanticism, which he saw as the two key opposing art trends in Western art. This viewpoint had a ready appeal for Blunt, who had never thrown off his simplistic schoolboy habit of splitting the world into rational and emotional, black and white, Us and Them. As articulated by Antal, classicism was the tendency towards realism and 'rationalism'. Its great exponents – Poussin, David and the Dutch genre painters – had painted predominantly for what Antal called the 'progressive bourgeoisie', merchants and professional civil servants, the rising middle class, whose role since the Industrial Revolution had been taken over by the workers. Romanticism was the opposite, 'anti-rationalistic', tendency. It could be decorative, like rococo or chinoiserie (which Blunt described as an art 'of escape of an insecure aristocracy'), or distort reality, like Mannerism or Cubism, or shy away from reality, like Surrealism. It came to the fore at times when the inevitable rise of the bourgeoisie was momentarily halted by a revival of the monarchy or the aristocracy. This, however, merely formed the basis of Antal's work, rather than being a straitjacket into which he tried to fit his history, as other clumsily deterministic English-speaking Marxist art critics such as Arnold Hauser and Francis Klingender did. No doubt this was due to his early friendship with Lukács, the most sophisticated Marxist critic of his generation as well as a lifelong defender of realism. Lukács also passed on his passionate belief that the defence of art and culture must be at the forefront of socialism's crusade against fascism.*

It may have been Antal who encouraged Blunt to venture beyond theory and into politics in early 1935, when Virginia Woolf made a fleeting diary reference to him as a member of an anti-fascist committee. Blunt had come to see her after she had

* There is no direct evidence Blunt read Lukács, but in 1937 he reviewed a new collection of letters by Balzac, Lukács' favourite realist. He praised, just as Lukács did, the acuity of Balzac's observation of society, 'the banker against the aristocrat, the merchant against the banker, the peasant against the landlord'. A year later he wrote an enthusiastic article on Balzac's villains in the Warburg journal. The art historian Peter Kidson has ventured the alluring theory that Blunt might have met Lukács in Berlin in 1933–4. However, at the time Blunt was in Germany, Lukács was at the Moscow Academy of Sciences.

tried to get Clive Bell to join the organization; Bell had refused, arguing that it was Communist-dominated, and had written an angry letter to its chairman, Ivor Spencer Churchill.

By this time Blunt was beginning to draw regularly on Antal's theories. The first signs were that the older man's influence might be positive. In January 1935 he wrote probably the first piece in Britain on the Mexican muralist Diego Rivera, whose work could be seen only in imported art books. Rivera's massive, explicitly political murals seemed to be all that a contemporary realist's work should be, and Blunt devoted three articles to him in 1935. 'Rivera's frescoes are the *Kapital* of the Illiterate,' he wrote, and compared them to the monumental frescos of Giotto – 'he paints for the same reason, he has a particular kind of idea to convey to the world and his method of expression is developed for that purpose'. (When he finally saw Rivera's work *in situ*, in the late 1950s, Blunt found that he preferred the work of the artist's fellow muralist José Orozco.)

Three weeks after his first Rivera article, Blunt published an article on a much-explored theme of Antal's. It compared Mannerism and Cubism to show that both had developed in periods when society had been in chaos: in the sixteenth century Italy had been the battlefield of Europe; Cubism had developed in the years before the First World War. Both styles showed that artists had responded by fleeing from reality, 'to play . . . their own variations on their own formal themes'.

He seemed, however, a far from unquestioning devotee of intellectual Marxism. 'As a critic, I reserve the right to apply one theory when I discuss Bernini and the contradictory theory when I discuss Mr Moore', he wrote the week after his Mannerist article, describing Moore as 'a sculptor of genius' – 'genius' being a distinctly un-Marxist concept, and Moore being an artist who tended dangerously towards abstraction. At the time, the only other art writer taking Moore so seriously was Herbert Read, who had written a small pamphlet on him. Blunt also showed a distinctly un-Soviet taste for Picasso, whose Cubist still lifes he exempted from his assessment that Cubism had been a retreat from reality, and whom he claimed was making 'almost the only form of serious art that could be produced in the given circumstances'.* Read, who was editor of the *Burlington Magazine*, was impressed; he commissioned some reviews from Blunt, and recommended him to the *Listener*.

It is a sign of how closely Blunt's articles tracked his regularly fluctuating views and his emotional life that the Henry Moore piece, with its apparent retreat from Marxism, came out just after Burgess had left Cambridge in the early months of 1935, having failed to do any work on his postgraduate thesis, and Victor Rothschild's mother had brought him to London and put him on a retainer as a financial adviser. He produced a newsletter every few months giving investment advice and making financial forecasts – a task for which he was almost completely unqualified. Though Burgess later claimed that Mrs Rothschild relied on his advice, it seems more likely that she viewed her handouts as a dressed-up subsidy to her son's clever young friend while he found his feet and made the next move in the brilliant career that everyone still predicted for him – the Rothschilds liked to support their friends and money was something they had plenty of.

At Cambridge Blunt was still not considered a Communist. The general view was that, like Victor Rothschild, he was broadly but uncommittedly left-wing. Some of his friends were Party members, others, like Dadie Rylands and Arthur Marshall, were completely politically apathetic. 'I always thought of him as a fellow-traveller, never as a Party member,' recalled Charles Rycroft, who remembered him 'making extremely cynical remarks about Communism that went beyond the call of duty in suppressing the fact that he was one.'

---

* In March 1935 Blunt wrote a piece almost completely unmarked by theory explaining the accomplishments of the French painter Georges de la Tour, whose work was being rediscovered after 300 years in obscurity. It was almost certainly the first piece in English about the artist, and earned Blunt a place as a perceptive commentator on de la Tour.

6. Fellow-Traveller

'I was only a paper *Marxist'*

By the mid-1930s, visits to the Soviet Union by enthusiastic fellow-travellers had become almost commonplace. In August 1935 Blunt and his brother Wilfrid joined a party of Cambridge undergraduates on just such an Intourist trip. The Soviet Union had been wooing the West for several years. It had joined the League of Nations after Hitler's precipitous departure, and had invited famous foreign visitors such as George Bernard Shaw and Beatrice and Sidney Webb on carefully stage-managed tours to view its achievements. They came away dazzled and impressed by what they had been shown. The country's 'scientific' economic planning appeared to have been a huge success: its first Five Year Plan was reported to have been completed ahead of schedule, and industrial growth rates were said to be 20 per cent a year. For those who felt that Western governments were failing, the Soviet Union had taken on a mythic glow. As one Cambridge contemporary of Blunt's put it, Russia 'was terra incognita, land of mystery and, for some, infinite promise, where dreams would come true and the evils of contemporary society be corrected. If old men insisted that the dawn in the East was a false one, that made it all the more likely that young men would run to meet it.'

As far as Wilfrid was concerned, however, 'Anthony and I were making the journey in search of pictures and architecture, and gullible though I was in many ways, I was certainly never taken in by Communist propaganda.' His brother's existing notebooks show that he also spent most of the trip looking at buildings and studying paintings – the Hermitage had important Poussins – but he was more ready to be impressed by the Soviet Union's economic claims than Wilfrid.

The rest of the group Wilfrid called the 'left-wing pilgrims'. The organizer was John Madge, a Communist and younger brother of the poet Charles Madge. The others were Blunt's young friends Brian Simon and Charles Rycroft; a rich American left-wing firebrand called Michael Straight; Charles Fletcher-Cooke, later a Tory MP but then a socialist; and Michael Young, another sceptical young socialist who would become a well-known sociologist, a Labour peer and the founder of the Open University.

The group caught the Leningrad boat from London Bridge at the beginning of August. The heiress Nancy Cunard was also on board, along with her black lover, and so was a former pupil of Wilfrid's, Christopher Mayhew, a socialist undergraduate at Oxford, who would later become a Labour, then Liberal, MP. The Intourist boat was not an impressive introduction to the Soviet Union. Cabins that should have slept two 'in moderate discomfort' held eight. Wilfrid and Anthony's included 'a Chinese who each evening handed round dirty postcards before turning in'. The lavatories were unbelievably filthy – a first test of the pilgrims' faith. Christopher Mayhew, revolted by them, told himself that this was 'the kind of thing that would only be of interest to people from sheltered bourgeois homes such as ourselves'. When they arrived at Leningrad, Wilfrid recalled tartly, one of the eager young men cried 'Freedom at last', and fell over the notice forbidding him to walk on the grass.

It was a significant moment to be in Moscow. The seventh, and last, International Congress of the Comintern (which was by now the organ of Soviet control over international Communism) was in the process of adopting the policy of popular fronts. Ostensibly this involved making alliances with social-democratic parties across Europe in order to defeat fascism; tacitly it was viewed by Stalin and his advisers as a way of infiltrating non-Communist groups and gaining control of public opinion beyond the Soviet Union. The Moscow Metro, with its grandiose marbled and gilded stations, had just opened. It had been built (largely by forced labour) in a year, and heralded, according to Moscow City Council, 'a new and higher phase of Soviet architecture, which will be manifested in the reconstruction of Moscow'. New plans for the reconstruction of Moscow had just received Stalin's signature. Blunt noted later that the Metro, 'to which so much publicity has been given, is perfect in comfort and efficiency, but it has Parisian chic and one almost expects a top-hat to emerge from its doors'. The Metro did bear a more than passing resemblance to the neo-baroque movie palaces of 1930s Europe, and its function – to bring a little luxury into the lives of a people starved of any – was also not so different.

Intourist tours were carefully managed. It was hard for visitors to see anything other than what they were supposed to see. Guides painted a glowing picture of the Soviet Union. Unsupervised contact with ordinary Russians was actively discouraged – and in any case few visitors spoke the language. There were trips to new factories and collectivized farms, and a plethora of amazing statistics and stories. In fact the Soviet state had made an industry in itself out of publishing false statistics. Almost every government figure of the time, from famine and kulak deaths to economic development rates, was falsified. The USSR claimed, for example, to have accomplished a five-fold increase in production between 1929 and 1941. In the 1980s the Soviet government admitted that the true figure was more like one and a half times.

Most of the young men were suitably impressed. 'Some things we saw pleased us,' remembered Christopher Mayhew. 'These were the proofs that socialism worked. Other things we saw disappointed us; these showed that the vestiges of capitalism could not all be eradicated overnight.' 'We could see the primitivism,' remembered Brian Simon, 'but it was the middle of the five-year plans and we told ourselves the USSR had industrialized itself very fast. It reinforced our positive feelings.' Blunt himself wrote admiringly of Leningrad and its 'buildings heroic in simplicity and scale': 'Before the grandeur of the best Russian buildings Regent Street and London University must yield at once.'

'For our part, we knew nothing about the horrors of Stalinist oppression, which we assumed to be a fiction of capitalist propaganda,' Mayhew recalled. By 1935 there were rumours about forced collectivization, concentration camps and the Ukrainian famine, but the full extent of the famine was not known – and it was not until the 1980s that its real impact was understood. The authorities vigorously suppressed the truth. Journalists were not allowed to visit famine areas or camps. Records of deaths and arrests were simply not kept. What information there was, was conflicting – not least because those who could have found out, such as Western journalists in Moscow like the *New York Times*'s Walter Duranty, who suspected that millions had probably died, made a decision to write nothing. Among the Soviet Union's supporters abroad the desire for it to be, if not perfect, then at least a bulwark against Germany in which they could believe, was so intense that rumours were put down to the same old anti-Russian propaganda from the Right that had been around since the Crimean War. The truth was that the place was a long way away and, for the many on the Left whose main preoccupation was the hopelessness of the British government and fear of fascism, its function was as a symbol, not a reality. Those who knew more about Soviet conditions told themselves that the country could not be judged by Western criteria – after all, it had been so backward, so brutal before the revolution. 'I believe nobody can begin to understand Soviet Russia until he has discarded all attempts to make judgements about events in terms of an a priori scale of values,' wrote the Cambridge don Maurice Dobb. Trust to blind faith he was saying, and, like the religious believers to whom they have so often been likened, many foreign Communists and fellow-travellers allowed themselves to suspend their judgement and believe things they would never have swallowed at home. Blunt's old Trinity contemporary John Lehmann, writing for *Left Review* from Tiflis (Tbilisi) in Georgia in 1936, blithely told his readers that local writers had actually accepted censorship of their own writing voluntarily for the good of the nation. Christopher Mayhew later wrote, 'I feel genuinely ashamed about my obtuseness on this Russian visit. Our British system of society seemed so detestable that I simply could not believe that its exact antithesis could be even worse.'

It was far, far worse. Stalin's terror was in full flow. For six years the peasants had been forced into state collective farms – effective serfdom at gunpoint. An estimated 15 million people – a figure arrived at only in the 1980s, after Robert Conquest's relentless researches – died in the collectivizations, and agricultural production dropped by 30 per cent. From the early 1930s the gulags – state concentration camps – were expanded until by 1939 they contained 10 per cent of the population: they had become the biggest 'employer' in Europe. In December 1934 the purges had begun with the murder of Sergei Kirov, the head of the Communist Party in Leningrad, and second only to Stalin.

It was fairly easy to hide the camps and prisons, but not the poverty, the dirt and squalor. Nevertheless, most of the members of Blunt's party chose not to notice such conditions and returned to England with their faith for the time being intact. Years later, however, they remembered their circumstances vividly. Brian Simon recalled the day-and-a-half train journey to Kiev, fourth class, when the food went bad and it was impossible to buy more; Charles Rycroft the bleakness of Leningrad, where the neoclassical buildings were being allowed to fall apart. 'The guides said it would all be bombed in a few years anyway, and if you looked carefully you could see beggars, and that the churches were always full.' Blunt failed to mentioned the beggars and the decay in his articles, but years later he remembered the chilling atmosphere of Moscow. Christopher Mayhew remembered the dirt and the endless petty restrictions on foreigners. When he was forbidden to take photographs of the Kremlin, he took them from his hotel room, getting Blunt to hold his legs while he leaned perilously out of the window with his camera.

Anthony, like his brother, showed no interest in political

discussion and never gushed approval of the Soviet regime. He avoided the factory and farm tours – though he and Wilfrid did go on a trip to the second-largest shoe factory in the world. Wilfrid later wrote that he persuaded one of the 'innocents' that all the right feet were made in Moscow and all the left feet in Leningrad. When the undergraduates went on to Kiev and Kharkov the two brothers remained in Moscow, where they went to see Lady Muriel Paget, who was working to get the British-born out of Russia. 'I have never forgotten the atmosphere of conspiracy that prevailed in Lady Muriel's flat, with its clandestine coming and goings, with sinister figures half-glimpsed through swiftly closed doors,' Wilfrid wrote. Lady Muriel's husband got them to the medieval capital of Russia, Novgorod, which was not on the Intourist schedule. Having somehow procured a letter of introduction, Anthony took Wilfrid to dinner with the acting counsellor at the British Embassy, Noel Charles. Dinner was a slightly awkward affair, despite the appearance of a bucket of caviar. The butler was believed to be NKVD. The brothers had only 'conscientiously shabby clothes', and they eventually realized that their hostess had invited them under the mistaken impression that Wilfrid was his wicked uncle, the late Wilfrid Scawen Blunt – who would have been ninety-five.

Blunt's limited enthusiasm for the factory tours owed more to his lack of engagement in politics than to scepticism about what he saw. Where art was concerned he was as credulous as the students. He filled a notebook entitled 'Notes on paintings and drawings and buildings in Russia, August–September 1935'. The book is still in Blunt's papers at the Courtauld Institute, though on it in his hand is scrawled, tantalizingly, 'To be destroyed'. It is, predictably, filled with close-written notes on art – not a paean to the Soviet miracle in sight – starting with Poussin's *The Defeat of the Amonites* at the Hermitage, about which he wrote 'condition looks dangerous'. There were, however, a few enthusiastic phrases dedicated to Soviet aesthetics. In front of the Leningrad Museum of Russian Art, Blunt applied his Marxist methodology: 'Czarist and not Bourgeois, it retains the expense but loses the taste – hence extreme richness and vulgarity'; before the neo-classical Horse Guards, the former indoor riding school of the Russian Life Guards, he noted that the original ornaments on the pediments had been replaced by the hammer and sickle, which 'fits wonderfully well'. Back in England he wrote admiringly of the Hermitage's 'scientific' arrangement of its collection. Paintings were grouped according to the society in which they had been produced and their historical background, and the social group with which they had been associated.

He was, however, disappointed by the Soviet Union's new art and architecture. Where was the new vision he had expected? He felt that the plans for the reconstruction of Moscow showed a 'regrettable' return to 'the uninteresting use of classical orders' – it is certainly true that they owed more to Haussmann's Paris than to any contemporary ideas about planning. The Palace of Soviets 'threatens to look more like a giant Selfridge's Wedding Cake'. As for painting, 'In some cases the works produced now are considered less attractive than those of ten years ago.' Ten years before, the Russian Constructivists had been a force in Soviet art. Now almost the only art on public display was social realism by arch-conservative painters like Izaak Brodsky. Blunt tried to be optimistic. Soviet painters, he told his *Spectator* readers, 'are trying to absorb all that is useful in Western culture as a prelude to developing a real style appropriate to Soviet conditions'. Thus far, however, the results were 'not particularly attractive to Western minds'. In fact artists who showed traces of 'foreign influences' or 'cosmopolitanism' were already being denounced, even persecuted. Earlier in the year a number of avant-garde painters from the circle round Malevich, who had died in May, had been interrogated after the assassination of Kirov. One, Yermolayeva, was accused of putting coded criticism of the NKVD in her illustrations for a retelling of *Renard the Fox*, and was sent to a camp. A series of articles in *Pravda* denounced formalism in painting and the other arts as an enemy of the State.

*

Though Blunt had not been voluble in his admiration of the
Soviet Union, the visit seems to have reinforced for him, as it did
for many others, a sense that he was on the right side. Towards
the end of 1935 his articles began to take on an uncomfortably
prescriptive, orthodox left-wing tone. All modern art that wasn't
realist was damned, although he allowed that it might serve a
purpose in shaking up bourgeois conventions. In a review of an
exhibition by the 7 and 5 Society – the first exhibition of
completely abstract art in Britain, and since recognized as a
landmark in British modernism – he sneered at the artists for
shying away from reality, describing them as a 'bedful of dreamers' whose art touched 'the iciest heights of unreality'. 'Hepworth
snores à la Brancusi, Mr Piper "à la Picasso".'* At times he
showed a chilling naivety. He criticized a German refugee artist's
drawings of his persecution at the hands of the Nazis for being
too 'close' to the experiences that had produced it. 'When his
experiments are a little more remote [from his experiences] they
will be easier to systematize and objectivize, and his works may
lose their slightly nightmarish quality and become important
chunks of reality.' Elsewhere he argued lamely that in the Soviet
Union the 'dictatorship of the arts' was justified, while in
Germany it wasn't. This was because 'the function of abstract art
is to destroy bourgeois ideology' and in the USSR there was no
such ideology left to destroy, hence abstraction was 'wasteful',
unlike realism, and therefore should be banned.

In his NKVD memoir, Blunt wrote of this time in the curiously
leaden prose he specially reserved for writing about himself:

* Blunt's view of the 7 and the 5 and contemporary art was shared by several
non-Marxist critics, including Kenneth Clark, who wrote on the future of
painting in the same week as Blunt's review. Though he had no ideological axe
to grind, Clark's views on modernism were very similar to Blunt's. He felt that
Ben Nicholson's total abstraction, purged of all recognizable content, was a
barren alley; and he found little more in Surrealism's empty 'vamped up
emotional states'. As for the 'belated impressionists' of the School of Paris, he
wrote that the decorative canvases of Jean Marchand, André Derain etc. had
become as tired and unimaginative as those shown in the Royal Academy.

Naturally when I was becoming acquainted with the Marxist approach to different subjects, I also listened to various discussions on political topics of the contemporary situation and gradually became convinced that the Marxist point of view in the given matter made sense. I know this is already outdated but I am speaking about the way my personal consciousness changed. In spite of the fact that I still feel that politics is a difficult subject for me, my views changed entirely and I realised the importance of understanding politics not only for practical purposes but also as a necessity for my own specialist studies.

At Cambridge,

I was seeing almost entirely left-wing students . . . and came to be regarded as very close to them in sympathy. Many people in fact thought that I was a member of the Party . . . During my last years at Cambridge roughly from 1935 to 1937 I knew a great many of the Party members among the students . . . Brian Simon, Michael Straight, John Cairncross, Leo Long, Matthew Hodgart, Charles Rycroft, John Simmonds, John Madge, Peter Newmark, John Waterlow. And among dons, Maurice Dobb, Roy Pascal, George Thomson, Bernal, Waddington and his wife. My contacts with all these people were entirely in the general intellectual field rather than over strictly political issues. I used to attend and lecture to the various student societies . . . but always on literary or historical subjects.

By the Party members themselves, however, Blunt was still regarded as fundamentally frivolous. He told the NKVD, 'I was . . . commonly thought to be a sympathiser though I knew from things I heard later that the tougher Party members such as Klugmann thought I was hopeless and would never get any further.' His grasp of contemporary politics was far from profound: Charles Rycroft remembered being slightly taken aback when Blunt – who rarely talked about politics per se – declared that, if the revolution came, 'England would go back to being the most important country in the world. There would be a new British Empire.' Rycroft recognized this as a garbled version of an idea current in left-wing circles at the time – one that Burgess, with his passion for Victorian England and the Empire, had particularly espoused. Blunt's interest in manning the barricades was also severely limited: when he attended an anti-fascist rally at Trafalgar Square with Rycroft, they left early to have tea at the Reform Club.

What was pushing Blunt further to the Left was not politics but old family habits about belief. As for so many others, Marxism was for Blunt a substitute for religion. The only kind of belief that made sense to him was one that was radical and all-embracing. As the literary critic James Wood has written:

> The child of evangelicism, if he does not believe, inherits nevertheless a suspicion of indifference: he is always evangelical. He rejects the religion he grew up with, but rejects it religiously. He is perpetually rejecting it, just as the evangelical believer is perpetually believing. He has buried belief but he has not buried the evangelical choice, which seems to him the only important dilemma. He respects the logical claustrophobia of Christian commitment, the little cell of belief. This is the only kind of belief that makes sense, the revolutionary kind. Nominal belief is insufficiently serious; nominal unbelief seems almost a blasphemy against earnest atheism.

Blunt had a more temperate revelation of another kind through the offices of Walter Friedlaender. Still in London in 1935, Friedlaender took Blunt along to a Monday-evening salon given by another émigré German art historian, Rudolf Wittkower, and his wife, Margot. Wittkower was a huge, affable, bearlike German architectural historian in his mid-thirties. Margot remembered later that Blunt 'got on very well with my husband, who saw that this was a very intelligent young man'. The Wittkowers had started the salon in order to try to make contact with young English art enthusiasts and interest them in the activities of the Warburg Institute, which had decamped from Hamburg to London in 1933, and of which Rudi was deputy director.

The Warburg had been founded by the great Aby Warburg, a German Jewish art historian whose fascination with historical context, and the way that apparently universal symbols migrated and changed meaning through time, led him to start a library that challenged traditional subject boundaries, encouraging the study of all kinds of disciplines – from medieval astrology to Renaissance literature – which might elucidate the meanings of art. His successor, Fritz Saxl, a small, mercurial Viennese Jew, who had studied not only under Warburg, but also with the eminent art historians Heinrich Wölfflin and Max Dvořák, had recognized the threat the Nazis posed to this Jewish-dominated institution and had shipped 60,000 books to England. With him came the large and extrovert Wittkower – he and the neat and tiny Saxl made an eye-catching double act – and the Renaissance scholar Edgar Wind, who would go on to acquire an Oxford chair in art history, and impress and alienate the British academic community in equal measure. They were followed by a group of uprooted scholars associated with the Institute, most of whom had lost everything. One, Raymond Klibansky, abandoned seven years' work when he fled Heidelberg University under cover of night in 1933. Ernst Gombrich's friend and mentor the eminent art historian Otto Kurz had been hit over the head with a metal truncheon by right-wing thugs at Vienna University and had spent months in hospital.

Life in London was hard for them. Gombrich and Kurz lived in adjoining rooms in a boarding house for several years, cooking on their respective gas rings. Though it had taken a great act of generosity and organization to bring the Warburg's library to England – the move was organized and paid for by Lord Lee and Samuel Courtauld on the instigation of W. G. Constable* – the

* There has been much debate over who instigated the Warburg's move to

scholars were for several years either ignored, for no one was quite sure what they did, or viewed by the art world with suspicion. Their serious professionalism seemed so different to the British tradition of connoisseurship and amateurism. This was a polarization that would continue for many decades, caricatured in the feud between Nikolaus Pevsner, who arrived in Britain from Leipzig in 1933, and John Betjeman: humourless scholarship versus dashing, slipshod, populist amateurism. Blunt, from the first, sided with the foreigners and scholarship. Others were attracted too: John Pope-Hennessy saw the Warburg's arrival, rightly, as a turning point in the development of British art history, and said his own debt to Fritz Saxl was 'boundless'. John Summerson wrote, 'We found ourselves faced with a range and quality of scholarship we had never met before.' The appeal stemmed in part from the fact that in one crucial sense the Warburg was not at all alien to British culture. Its method was based on scrupulous empirical research. This made it enemies among some rich amateur English dilettanti, but found it allies within British academia.

Soon after Blunt met the Warburg scholars, Saxl went to hear him lecture at Cambridge. 'I am delighted that you enjoyed my lecture,' Blunt wrote to him, 'though I am afraid you must have found it very elementary indeed.' The Warburgers liked Blunt, and also saw him as a potential disciple. His fluency in French, German and Italian and his passion for France marked him out from the normal run of parochial Englishmen: 'He had inter-national feelings, bonds,' recalled Richard Krautheimer, another

London. Edgar Wind, who later fell out with the Institute, claimed that he took the first steps in spring 1933, when he met a member of the Academic Assistance Council, of which W. G. Constable was a member, set up to help 'displaced scholars'. Raymond Klibansky says that he took a night train to Hamburg on 1 April 1933 to warn Saxl he must get the library out. Arthur Lee also claimed the credit for making it happen. W. G. Constable certainly visited the Warburg in 1933, and he and Saxl (who actually did more than anyone) arranged the move. The story that Blunt was involved in the Warburg's move is without foundation.

German émigré, who remembered 'his warmth of personality, the immense kindness, the ease with which he carried his knowledge'. He seemed to identify with their outsider status, and was comfortable with their foreignness. (Unlike many of his British academic peers, foreigners rarely commented on Blunt's coldness.) As for their politics, having fled Hitler many of the Warburg scholars were very sympathetic to the Left, though none of them was a Communist: 'At that time everyone who we knew and who was interested in the slightest bit in politics was Left,' remembered Margot Wittkower. 'I don't think I ever met anyone who was an English Nazi . . . We didn't talk politics [with Anthony]; it was a given thing . . . I didn't know whether he was Communist or not a Communist, but even if I had known that he was a Communist it wouldn't have mattered.' In person Blunt rarely talked Marxism, and he was far less stridently political in his academic writing than in his journalism. Moreover, intellectual Marxism's emphasis on the social and political conditions in which an art work was created had much in common with the Warburg's stress on historical context.

Though they welcomed them, the Warburg scholars were quietly appalled by the amateurism and ignorance of their self-taught young fans. It was said at the Institute that Blunt had written half of his thesis without consulting Schlosser, the standard text on artist's theories. (Actually this wasn't true.) Saxl, Ernst Gombrich recalled, seeing 'the insularity of these people', was very keen to 'wean these young men from a certain amateurishness'. He also seems to have disapproved of Blunt's more extreme and deterministic pronouncements on art. He certainly thought that Blunt should give up his journalism. To begin with, however, he came up with a plan to give his new protégé a little education in German methods, and to rescue another project he'd initiated. He had recently persuaded Walter Friedlaender to turn an essay he'd been planning on Poussin's drawings into a catalogue raisonné in English. 'This was not Friedlaender's cup of tea at all,' Blunt later recalled. Richard Krautheimer said, 'It was hard to make [Friedlaender] sit down and write; he had a hard time concentrating. He liked to talk – he could talk endlessly in that horrible language of his.' Friedlaender's English was so awful, indeed, that the other émigrés had a special word for it: 'Friedlaenderish'. Saxl asked Blunt if he would translate Friedlaender's work. He was given a copy of the manuscript and photographs of the drawings. Almost immediately:

> It became perfectly clear (a) that Friedlaender's idea of spelling names, particularly non-German names, was nil; and also that he had simply accepted all the provisional attributions. And I remember translating the entries of the first twenty drawings and then looking at the photographs and thinking, 'But surely even in my state of ignorance these certainly can't be by the same hand.' So I then went to Saxl and we looked at it, and he said, 'This is impossible.'

Saxl asked Rudi Wittkower to help Blunt, 'and as Rudi's English was very imperfect at this stage . . . Rudi gave me lessons in art history, and I taught him English, and Margaret [*sic*] cooked the dinner.'

Blunt's collaboration with Friedlaender on the Poussin drawings would run to five volumes and last thirty years, though he would not get his name on the title page as co-author until the third volume, in 1953. It helped to make him, in time, Friedlaender's successor as the world expert on Poussin. It cemented a new and important friendship with Rudi Wittkower. But it came at a cost. By 1936, Friedlaender, who had taken a job as professor of art history at Pittsburgh in the USA, was already in his sweet way driving Blunt mad. 'Friedlaender has a habit of simply leaving out my corrections or copying them out wrongly,' he wrote exasperatedly to the Warburg editors in 1936, asking for a new set of proofs to incorporate the masses of corrections he made, and pleading that they 'must not be taken out by F.'. Thirteen years later he was having the same conversation: '[This] is contrary to our most rigid convention and your firmest promise, which is that . . . we were to proceed with the publication on the basis WITHOUT ANY ALTERATIONS . . . if we start altering again, you and I will unquestionably both die before anything gets into print . . . and then who will see it through the Press?'

In December 1935 Louis MacNeice wrote urgently asking Blunt to come to Birmingham. 'M. is not here but Daniel [MacNeice's baby son] will be. As a matter of fact I have much to tell you but think I had better not put it on paper . . . Don't mention to anyone I have had a family crisis (which is what it is).'

During the summer and autumn, MacNeice's life had fallen apart. While his latest volume, *Poems*, had been a success, it had been followed by a car crash – his third at least. Then his house had caught fire, and his wife had left him. All three disasters were arguably caused by his prodigious drinking. Mary had run off with a 'great big Rugger-playing American Russian Jew . . . not unlike Clark Gable in looks', leaving behind her and Louis's two-year-old son. A cook and a nurse had been hired to look after the boy, and MacNeice, who had felt that Blunt had been neglecting him – 'You needn't come if we have now fallen into the Basil Barr category and you find us good creatures but just too deadly tiresome,' he'd written, semi-jokingly in the summer – now appealed slightly desperately for support. For one last moment, their friendship's old intimacy was revived: 'I must stop now Auntie,' MacNeice signed off in early 1936. MacNeice's friend Graham Shepard reported to John Hilton, who now barely saw Blunt, that MacNeice was planning on 'going to Spain with Herr Professor Anton Strumpf [i.e. Blunt] quite soon and looking forward to it very much'. MacNeice was so short of money that Blunt paid for his ticket.

When he interviewed Blunt in 1982, MacNeice's biographer assumed he had gone to Spain for political reasons. 'Clearly you with your politics saw something happening in Spain, the start of a people's revolution?' he asked. Blunt 'looked at me as though I was mad and said "No, not at all! I went to see the pictures, dear boy! The Prado is Mecca for art historians." "Was that your only interest in going to Spain? I mean you were a Marxist art historian?" "Oh, I was only a *paper* Marxist!"'

Blunt and MacNeice set out in early March, taking a boat from London Docks to Gibraltar. Blunt was horribly seasick. Spain, as MacNeice wrote later in his long poem *Autumn Journal*, was 'ripe as an egg for revolt and ruin'. Over half the land was owned by 1 per cent of the population. It was dominated by the Catholic Church, which was not only deeply reactionary but a major landowner and business investor, and by an army overmanned by bored officers and under the sway of monarchism and ultramontanism. Most of the population were peasants living on starvation wages or tiny holdings. The small urban working class had been stricken by recession. A constitutional government elected in 1931 had introduced new laws to bring about land reform, establish state schools and make divorce legal, but the measures had not been enacted. However, in February the left-wing Frente Popular (Popular Front) – an alliance of republicans, socialists, Catalans and Communists – had won the general election, and later that year Spain was declared a republic. It seemed like a triumph for popular fronts all across Europe.

The weather – cold and drizzling – somehow set the tone. Blunt had organized an exhausting itinerary of towns, churches, museums and monuments. In the Andalusian hill town of Ronda he and MacNeice looked down into the deep gorge and saw eagles circling below. MacNeice described the moment in *Autumn Journal*:

> And a vulture hung in air
>   Below the cliffs of Ronda and below him
> His hook-winged shadow wavered like despair
>   Across the chequered vineyards.

They met a Cambridge Spanish don whom Blunt particularly disliked, escorting three or four undergraduates – 'a favourite occupation of his', Blunt told MacNeice's biographer tartly – who prophesied 'with an air / There's going to be trouble shortly in this country'. In Madrid, which they reached on an overnight train, sleeping on the hardest of wooden seats, they took shelter in the Prado, and looked at Goyas, El Grecos and Zurbarans – 'the three great artists', MacNeice wrote.

'The Hammer and Sickle was scrawled over Spain that Easter,' MacNeice observed. It was graffitied all over Madrid, where, in the rain, the two friends saw a political demonstration. In Seville for Easter week they watched bored-looking soldiers marching out of step, and saw a sloppy bullfight. In Algeciras, on the way back to Gibraltar to pick up their boat, 'We saw the mob in flower'; a ransacked church, its walls covered in red Communist slogans; and a man trying to fix a red flag in an altar niche – 'looking, Anthony said, like a figure in a Toller play'; and the local mayor being, as Blunt later told MacNeice's biographer, 'slightly stoned'. MacNeice, he said, 'treated the slogans and riots as a joke'.

Blunt, the paper Marxist, had hopes for Spain, but he expected a revolution from the Left: 'If Spain goes Communist, Anthony said, France is bound to follow,' MacNeice wrote later, 'and then Britain, and then there'll be jam for all. Which incidentally will mean new blood in the arts – in every parish a Diego Rivera. And easel-painting at last will admit it is dead and all the town-halls will bloom with murals and bas-reliefs in concrete. For concrete is the new medium, concrete is vital.' MacNeice disagreed. He understood the lure of Marxism's absolutes in return for giving up one's own will, but he would not – could not – suspend his disbelief.

> And the next day took the boat
>   For home, forgetting Spain, not realising
> That Spain would soon denote
>   Our grief, our aspirations;
> Not knowing that our blunt
>   Ideals would find their whetstone, that our spirit
> Would find its frontier on the Spanish front,
>   Its body in a rag-tag army.

At home MacNeice found that Mary had sent him divorce papers. He went to Cambridge a few weeks later at the end of

April. This time he was reminded of everything he disliked about Blunt's life. 'Cambridge was still full of Peter Pans but all the Peter Pans were now talking Marx.' In a bout of self-destructiveness he drank a bottle of Blunt's gin for breakfast and then tried to thrust a cigarette into the eye of a 'very elegant evergreen don' whom Blunt had asked to lunch, before passing out at the table. 'You see, I am really so much happier when drunk,' he wrote to Blunt. His excuse for the visit was that he had brought with him a semi-abstract Gaudier-Brzeska-like sculpture called *Cyclamen* by an impoverished Birmingham artist called Gordon Herrickx, which he hoped, vainly, Blunt might be able to sell to Victor Rothschild. 'Couldn't you get old V. R. to buy it to reduce his weight with if nothing else?' Rothschild, who was distinctly portly and now investing in the Post-Impressionists, was not interested. Blunt, a doctrinaire realist, wasn't either. On the way back to Birmingham, MacNeice gave a lift to Burgess and John Cornford, who was standing trial for obstruction. He had been caught distributing Communist leaflets in Birmingham town centre. 'I really must congratulate you and your university for producing this Cornford boy because obviously he is the one chap of the whole damn lot of you who is going to be a great man,' MacNeice told Blunt. Burgess, he added, 'thought all the young men in the streets of B'ham were queer. I daresay they are, lucky creatures.'

On his return from Spain, Blunt began to lecture for the Communist-organized Artists International Association,* and to write for *Left Review*, the Soviet-backed literary magazine – of which the critic Julian Symons wrote, only slightly unjustly, 'the chief criticism to be made of *Left Review* is that the effect of its conscious party line was to make its contributors write so uncom-

---

* The AIA as it was known, was run by Communists, and its publications of the 1930s were explicitly Marxist in tone. However, it spent most of its time making all kinds of contemporary art accessible to the general public and helping refugee artists from central Europe – two features which attracted to it a wide membership, including such figures as Kenneth Clark and Augustus John.

monly badly'. His first lecture for the AIA, announced in *Left Review* in April 1936, was entitled 'Is Art Propaganda?'. A year before he would have denounced the idea, but now his views had changed, as could be seen in his first article for *Left Review* which came out in July that year: 'A new art is beginning to arise, the product of the proletariat, which is again performing its true function, that of propaganda'. In his *Spectator* columns he began to champion a great new discovery, a sculptor who, he claimed, would rescue art from 'the dead end to which abstraction has brought painting'. His name was Peter Peri, and he was a Hungarian Marxist who had lived in Germany and who now produced lifesize human figures in concrete ('the new medium' Blunt had told MacNeice), showing the 'ordinary life of the people in the streets and parks of London'. Quentin Bell, who knew him from the AIA, remembered Peri as 'nice, admirable, dull and infuriating, without meaning to be. He drove us mad, he was very impressed by himself.' The work was terrible – grey, worthy, dull – but Blunt insisted it was the future. For the next three years he was Peri's most vociferous supporter.*

By now Blunt was at the centre of the furious squabbles and ideological divisions in London art circles about the relative merits of abstraction, Surrealism and realism, the key proponents of which, with the exception of Herbert Read, were all extremely hostile to each other. The leader of the abstract artists, Ben Nicholson, was utterly hostile to all forms of figurative art; his opponents attacked abstraction for its meaninglessness. The advocates of realism, of whom Blunt was now a leading light,

---

* Blunt was loyal to Peri to the end. When the artist died in obscurity and poverty in the late 1960s, *Arts Review* reported that Blunt, 'who had been instrumental in making Peri known in this country', had opened a small memorial exhibition at Swiss Cottage Library. Peri became a Quaker in later life: 'he was a lone figure displaced in time, conforming to the past image of the artist lacking recognition; in poverty, integrity and a black beret. Modern with-it youth was remarkably absent from his show.' I am told that Peri's sculptures can still be seen in various public spaces in Leicester.

accused the others of being inaccessible to a general audience and out of touch.

However, it was Surrealism – or Superrealism as Blunt now preferred to call it – that was Blunt's major target. In the summer of 1936 the first all-Surrealist exhibition opened at the New Burlington Galleries in June. Its exhibits – which included Meret Oppenheim's fur cup and saucer, and Joan Miró's bowler hat with a stuffed parrot on top and a dead fish on the brim – attracted crowds, mostly gawping and giggling, and acres of press attention. 'Take Blake's anti-rationalism,' Blunt wrote excitedly, 'add Lamartine's belief in the individual, stir in some of Coleridge's faith in inspiration, lard with Vigny's ivory tower doctrines, flavour with Rimbaud's nostalgia, cover whole with a thick Freudian sauce, serve cold, stone-cold (dead, stone-dead) and you will have before you roughly the Superrealist dish, varieties of which are now thrilling, horrifying, puzzling, scandalising or just boring London.'

Blunt spoke against Surrealism at an AIA debate on the subject at Conway Hall, arranged to coincide with the exhibition. He branded it not just an 'anti-rationalist' art produced by artists in flight from reality, but a sidetrack which failed to perform the primary function of art, to convey political ideas. He denounced it for being by its very nature unpolitical. Surrealism's supporters – Herbert Read spoke at the debate – insisted that it was a truly revolutionary art movement which undermined bourgeois ideology by attacking bourgeois values, and that it showed dialectical materialism in action, since a Surrealist painting was 'reality transformed by the imagination'. The 'debate' ended in stalemate, but the Surrealist exhibition was a success, and £200 worth of work by Salvador Dali was sold. In yet another article in the *Spectator*, the following month Blunt returned to the subject, insisting that this success only confirmed

the suspicions which I have long felt and recently tried to express, that the Superrealists are at least mistaken when they passionately claim to be revolutionaries . . . Their belief that they are the true repositories of the orthodox Marxist faith is perhaps shaken but certainly not destroyed by the fact that the Voice of Moscow constantly condemns them as heretical ... The Superrealists may be contributing to the break up of Capitalist ideology, but they are doing it as disgruntled members of Capitalist society, not as representatives of the proletariat.*

In hindsight, the most surprising aspect of the debate was the extent to which the Surrealists, while disagreeing with the Marxists on everything, seemed to feel so strongly the need for acknowledgement that theirs was a revolutionary movement. It was a manifestation of the way in which politics had come to dominate British art and culture.

The Surrealists were not the only ones who looked askance at Blunt's art criticism. John Pope-Hennessy called him 'jejeune', and thought his journalism 'more than a little naive'. To Isaiah Berlin, 'He was like a man in a straitjacket, and the articles were not very good. He was not really doctrinaire by nature. The amount he praised this Hungarian, Peri, was an absurdity. He kept returning to him: "What a wonderful man." Of course no one else thought he was wonderful.'

It may be that it was at this point that Roy Pascal invited Blunt to join the Party. 'I did not accept, giving as my excuse that there were still too many points about which I was not really clear and that I did not want to commit myself till I had thought them out.'

Blunt's last article on Surrealism appeared in the *Spectator* on 19 July 1936, the day after the Spanish Civil War broke out. It followed a series of depressing international events in the spring of that year which seemed to signal ever more obviously that fascism was gaining ground all over Europe. In March 1936, as

---

* Blunt attributed Surrealism's success in Britain, 'to the repressive education and way of living characteristic of the English. After all, the psychological confusions created in the average Englishman by public school education are such that he may well find in front of a Superrealist painting that kind of sexual liberty and excitement that suits him.'

Blunt and MacNeice travelled round Spain, Germany moved troops back into its demilitarized border zone with France. In May, Italy invaded Abyssinia. Then, after months of sloganeering and threats, General Franco, at the head of a group of disgruntled Spanish generals, left his post in the Canaries for Spain and announced that he would deliver the country from the Communists (who in fact had only 16 of the Popular Front government's 277 seats). Army garrisons across Spain declared for him, and the war began. Just as it was for the poets and writers of his generation, the Spanish Civil War would be the climax of Blunt's love affair with Communism. Its consequence for him, however, would be very different.

7. Recruit

'The new ills are real and can only be cured by real means'

In June 1934, while Blunt was taking his sabbatical in Germany, Kim Philby, a twenty-two-year-old Communist and graduate of Trinity College, met a man who called himself 'Otto' on a bench in Regent's Park. Otto, whose real name was Arnold Deutsch, was a Soviet 'illegal' – an agent of the Soviet Intelligence service, the NKVD, who assumed disguises and pseudonyms in order to operate clandestinely outside the Soviet Union. He encouraged Philby to fight fascism and invited him to join him in what the younger man later told his fellow recruit Donald Maclean was 'a very serious international anti-fascist organisation, which may be tied to Moscow'. 'You are a bourgeois by education, appearance and origin. You could have a bourgeois career in front of you – and we need people who could penetrate into the bourgeois institutions. Penetrate them for us!' said Otto. Philby consented.

Up to 1934, Soviet espionage in Britain had been limited, despite the fact that the NKVD believed Britain to be one of the Soviet Union's most important and threatening enemies. One incident in particular had provoked this anxiety: the 1918 'Lockhart Plot'. This was a shambolic plan hatched by Robert Bruce Lockhart – the acting consul-general in Moscow, famous for his energetic love life – and a group of Moscow-based, gung-ho 'casuals'. (Casuals were part-time British intelligence agents – usually travelling businessmen asked to keep an eye out for interesting foreign happenings.) They had planned to murder all the Bolshevik leaders on the same night, as a concerted Allied attack on the young Soviet state. Soviet Intelligence – then known as the Cheka – knew about the conspiracy from the start. Bruce Lockhart was arrested in August 1918 and later deported. But, according to the intelligence historian Christopher Andrew, instead of seeing the plot for what it was, the Soviet authorities convinced themselves it was evidence 'not of confusion or amateurism but of a deep-laid, labyrinthine plot by Western intelligence services'. Well into the 1980s KGB historians claimed its discovery as 'a triumph of epic proportions'.

In Britain, rumours of Russian spies and sabotage had been around since the Crimean War. They had been resuscitated in 1924 by the 'Zinoviev letter', which purported to be a secret missive from Grigori Zinoviev, then head of the Comitern, to covert supporters in the Labour Party. Though many thought it was a fake, as indeed it turned out to be, the letter frightened the electorate so much that Labour lost the general election they had expected to win. But in 1927 British Intelligence and the police did find evidence of Soviet spies in London when they raided ARCOS, the All-Russian Co-operative Society – the Soviet trade mission in London. The raid proved that the trade delegates were working for Soviet Intelligence, but it produced very little of value apart from the embarrassing fact that the Soviets now knew that Britain had broken its diplomatic codes. By the end of the 1920s a similar raid in Beijing, and revelations of Soviet espionage in six other countries, left the country's foreign-intelligence operations in ruins. One consequence of these events was to persuade Stalin that there was an imperialist plot against the Soviet Union and that its chief instigator was 'the English bourgeoisie and its fighting staff, the Conservative Party'. Within Russia, Stalin used this to attack his rival Trotsky and other Bolshevik 'dissidents'. Outside it, Soviet Intelligence switched from using legal residents, who could be traced back to trade delegations and embassies, to greater use of illegals, who couldn't be linked to embassies.

The illegals, who operated on their own and were not attached to any Soviet delegations, came into their own in the late 1920s. They were a long way from the textbook Russian agent. Political idealists and internationalists, moved by their own experiences and the suffering they had seen to try to change the world, they had been recruited by the NKVD because they were intelligent and deeply committed. They had gone underground because they had been persuaded that it was necessary for the survival of Communism and the USSR. They were, naturally, ruthless in its service. They were often not from the Soviet Union but were eastern European and Jewish, in exile from regions to which they could not return, or which had been transformed by the changing map of Europe. They were usually well educated and cosmopolitan, independent, and able to pass themselves off in many social situations. Under them, the Foreign Directorate of the NKVD,* recalled Nadezhda Mandelstam, wife of the great and persecuted Russian poet Osip, was 'distinguished by its sophisticated tastes and weakness for literature'. Arnold Deutsch's colleague in London, Theo Maly, was a perfect example. A Hungarian in his early forties, a former novice priest, he had converted to Marxism in a Russian POW camp in the First World War and joined the Cheka as a gesture of sacrifice for the revolution. All accounts describe him as cultivated, sincere, gentle, kind, resilient, with an attractive underlying vulnerability. He was multilingual and highly intelligent. He had witnessed massacres and great brutality, but through all this he had hung on to a shred of idealism and still believed in the revolution and that the Comintern should be an independent international organization and devote itself to fighting fascism, instead of being, as it now was, the grovelling servant of the Soviet government. These views would ultimately cost him his life.

Philby's 'Otto', Arnold Deutsch, was not one of the most senior illegals, but he was one of the most impressive. Born in 1904 in

---

* The Foreign Directorate of the NKVD, which ran all foreign intelligence, was also known as the First Chief Directorate. Within it there were myriad different departments. Operations against Britain, Ireland, Malta, Scandinavia and Australasia were run by the Third Department. Illegals were additionally run by Directorate S. For simplicity's sake, this book will use 'Foreign Directorate' as a catch-all title for Soviet foreign intelligence.

Vienna, the son of a poor, devout Czech Jew whom he hated, he won scholarships through school and on to university. In the space of five years at Vienna University he studied physics, chemistry, philosophy and psychology, and received a PhD with distinction in 1928. He spoke German, French and English fluently, and could read and write Italian and Spanish. Among his teachers had been members of the Vienna Circle, the group of philosophers, scientists and mathematicians who had promulgated and investigated the theory of logical positivism. On leaving university he joined the Austrian psychoanalyst Wilhelm Reich's Sexpol movement, running Reich's publisher, Munster Verlag. Reich – a former disciple of Freud who had fallen out violently with his mentor and was to have a variety of often highly eccentric ideas during his career – was at this point attempting a synthesis of psychoanalysis and Marxism, arguing that the abolition of the bourgeois family would eliminate the Oedipus complex, and that political and sexual repression were a recipe for fascism. Deutsch was already politically committed. At sixteen, he had joined a group of left-wing intellectuals calling themselves Clarté, after Henri Barbusse's literary journal. At twenty, he had joined the Communist Party, and in 1927 he got himself temporarily suspended from his studies for Communist activities. In 1928 he had become a part-time courier for the Comintern's 'International Liaison Department', its clandestine arm, and began to travel round Europe as an agent. The summons to Moscow had come in 1932, when he had joined the Foreign Directorate of the NKVD and trained as an illegal. In 1934 he had returned to Vienna and fought on the streets against the right-wing takeover: a plaque on his former home still records his work in the resistance. Following the defeat of the Left in Vienna, Deutsch came to London, enrolling in a course at London University. Russian Intelligence claims he recruited seventeen agents in Britain between 1934 and 1937.*

---

* Russian Intelligence has never named all the agents he apparently recruited, but the following have been attributed to him: Philby, Maclean, Burgess, Blunt,

When the illegals began to operate in England, the NKVD's successes were limited. Its first source was Ernest Oldham, a cipher clerk in the British Foreign Office communications department. In 1929, on a trade-delegation trip to Paris, he walked into the Soviet Embassy and offered to sell a diplomatic cipher – the code into which messages from British embassies round the world were translated – for $2,000. The offer was refused – it was assumed to be British provocation – but the document was photographed and turned out to be genuine. It took the Soviets a year to track Oldham down. They paid him and asked him to provide more material. He complied, but the strain proved too much and in September 1933 he committed suicide by gassing himself in his kitchen. The NKVD went on to pay another cipher clerk, John Herbert King, for similar information.

Kim Philby had been spotted not in Cambridge, but in Vienna, where he worked for the left-wing resistance in the spring of 1934. Philby was the son of a famous and controversial father, St John Philby, an Arabist and a friend of Ibn Saud, the founder of the state of Saudi Arabia. He had come to Cambridge to study history in 1929. He was never part of Blunt and Guy Burgess's set, but was introduced to Burgess, a fellow historian, by the Trinity economics don Dennis Robertson, and, according to Philby's biographer, was dominated by Burgess for the next thirty-five years. Philby's interest in socialism had started at school. In 1929 he had been shocked by what he had seen on a cycling holiday around the depressed areas of the Black Country with a confirmed Communist; the failures of the Labour government had filled him with disgust. He was one of the earliest members of Maurice Dobb's tiny Marxist caucus, and one of the first to join the Trinity Communist cell.

Philby later claimed that it wasn't until his final term at Cambridge, in the summer of 1933, that he shed all doubts about

John Cairncross, James Klugmann and Percy Glading, who ran a spy ring at Woolwich Arsenal and was arrested in 1937. It is possible, however, that Blunt, Cairncross and Klugmann may have been recruited by Theo Maly.

Communism. On the recommendation of Maurice Dobb, he went to Paris and presented himself at the Austrian Committee for Relief from German Fascism, and from there he was sent on to Vienna to help the beleaguered Communist underground. The depression in Austria and the Dollfuss government's attempts to create a one-party state further confirmed his political convictions, and he was inducted into the underground by his landlady's daughter, Litzi Friedman, and began to work as a courier for left-wing groups. In February 1934, after fighting in the streets between Dollfuss's troops and the Left, nine socialist leaders were hanged without trial, and a one-party state was announced. Philby helped to smuggle wanted leftists out of the country. Eric Gedye, the *Daily Telegraph* correspondent in Vienna, recalled that Philby told him, 'I've got six wounded friends in the sewers in danger of the gallows', and borrowed six suits to smuggle them into Czechoslovakia. His work was spotted by Austrian Communist Party members who were also working for Soviet Foreign Intelligence. Litzi, whom he took back to England in the spring of 1934 and married, had links with these people.

Back in London, where Philby tried to join the CPGB, he was informed that his application would take five weeks while he was vetted. The British Party was still wary of middle-class members. In those five weeks he was recruited to Soviet Intelligence. An acquaintance of Litzi's, Edith Tudor Hart, an Austrian Communist who had also escaped from Vienna (she married a sympathetic English doctor), invited him to tea. Philby's passion for the cause made a good impression, and Tudor Hart, who was a 'cultivation officer', reported favourably to Arnold Deutsch, who in turn took the matter to his chief, Ignace Reif, the NKVD *rezident*, or chief, in London.

According to the Russian Intelligence Archives, what had really grabbed the interest of the NKVD was Philby's father, St John Philby, his connections with Ibn Saud and the fact that he had introduced his son to the infamous Robert Bruce Lockart. As Philby's Russian biographer Genrikh Borovik records, 'The KGB took on Philby not through a brilliant, long-term plan to recruit

British university students who would one day hold positions of power, but simply because it believed – mistakenly – that his father, St John Philby, was in British intelligence.' Reif wrote to Moscow. 'I have decided to recruit the fellow without delay – not for the "organisation", it is too early for that, but for anti-fascist work.' This was standard procedure. 'Sincere' recruits were told they were working for the Comintern and international Communism, and were gradually acclimatized to the idea that they were reporting to Soviet Intelligence. 'The result', Reif reported on 22 June 1934, 'is his complete readiness to work. Sonny [sometimes Söhnchen – Philby's none-too-subtle code name] made an excellent impression on Arnold.' In turn Philby was full of admiration for 'Otto'. His first task was to spy on his father.

In his message reporting Philby's recruitment, Reif added a piece of information that Moscow appears not to have known: 'It turns out that Sonny's sympathy for the Party comes from the socialist club at Cambridge University, that the sons of many important Anglo-functionaries sympathise with the club and did work for it.' Meanwhile, Philby later told the KGB, Otto 'taught me the rules of conspiracy. He hammered them into my head; how to call the necessary person on the phone, how to check, how to recognise a tail in a crowd, and other basics.' Otto also told Philby that he must break off all connections with the Party, and asked him for a list of Cambridge Communists. Donald Maclean's name was at the top of the list, and Burgess's, according to one source, was on the bottom. Blunt's wasn't on it at all.

The decision to start recruiting a spy ring from Philby's fellow student Communists appears to have been taken by Alexander Orlov, Deutsch's new boss, who arrived in London in late 1934. Reif reported to Moscow in October 1934, 'The Swede [Orlov] and I decided that he [Philby] must work over all his friends from Cambridge who share his views, so that we could use some of them in our work.' Philby approached Donald Maclean first. Maclean was a serious-minded modern-languages student who was in his third year at Trinity Hall and had been an early member of the Cambridge Communist group. Philby probably made his proposal in the autumn term of 1934, when he returned to Cambridge to address the Socialist Society. Maclean appears to have met Ignace Reif in October or November 1934. He hesitated – wanting to discuss the offer with James Klugmann, which he was forbidden to do – but then accepted. He too was told that he must sever links with the Party. It is possible that other members of the Cambridge Communist Party were approached at this time, though thus far neither the Russian Intelligence Archives nor the papers in the so-called 'Mitrokhin archive' have revealed this.

As for Guy Burgess, Kim Philby later wrote, 'He must have been one of the very few people to have forced themselves into the Soviet special service.' Philby had been very wary of involving Burgess at all. Although he thought him clever, he doubted his ability to keep his mouth shut. Orlov, however, thought Burgess should be sounded out, particularly because he believed his homosexual contacts might be useful – he was convinced that all upper-class Englishmen were homosexual. He reported to Moscow that 'the majority of this country's most polished sons are pederasts'. He believed Burgess could exploit 'the mysterious laws of sex in this country'. Deutsch was hesitant. In the event Burgess's recruitment came about almost by accident, as a clumsy attempt at damage limitation.

Maclean and Philby's sudden resignations aroused Burgess's suspicions. He tried to talk them into staying in the Party, and became convinced that something was going on. Philby later wrote:

While we were talking, he was drawing conclusions and acting on them. He had convinced himself that Maclean and I had not undergone a sudden change of views, and that he was being excluded from something esoteric and exciting. So he started to badger us, and nobody could badger more effectively than Burgess. He went for Maclean and he went for me. Doubtless he went for others as well, for Theo and Otto became increasingly worried that, if he got nowhere, he might try some trick – perhaps talk about us to people outside our circle. He might well be more dangerous outside than inside. So the decision was taken to recruit him.

So Burgess, as ever, got his way. Orlov took the decision to recruit him sometime between December 1934 and February 1935, just as Burgess was leaving Cambridge for London. During these months communication between the London base, the *rezidentura*, and Moscow – which normally took place through microfilms sent via Copenhagen – had been interrupted. When Moscow found out about Burgess it was not pleased. His flagrant homosexuality offended the Soviets' puritanism. Eventually, however, permission was given, and in early 1935 Burgess was introduced to Otto, by whom he was tremendously impressed. Deutsch quickly recognized that he would be a valuable agent, in particular for 'his ability to get to know anyone'. In a psychological profile of Burgess, he later wrote that 'the party work was something of a salvation for him, especially its life and its purity', noting that Burgess was 'a very temperamental and emotional man and he is easily subject to mood swings. The party was for him a saviour. It gave him above all an opportunity to satisfy his intellectual needs.' Burgess was given the code name 'Mädchen' – the German for girl: the illegals had a sense of humour. To begin with he was allotted tasks such as making friends with people in the government and Civil Service, such as Tom Wylie, a former private secretary at the War Office who was now its resident clerk, which meant he lived there in order to attend to after-hours business. He was also given the task of making a list of potential contacts. Burgess's list was mad and enthusiastic. It was four pages long and included just about everyone he'd ever met, from G. M. Trevelyan and Maynard Keynes to London prostitutes.

It was to be another two years before Blunt was introduced to Arnold Deutsch and recruited for 'Comintern' work. In those two years Burgess, like Philby and Maclean, was told to distance himself from Communism. This he did in a spectacular manner.

After months of 'advising' Mrs Rothschild, he announced he had completely changed his mind about Communism and applied for a job in late 1935 with the Conservative Party's director of research, Major Joseph Ball, who passed him on to Captain Jack Macnamara, Conservative MP for Chelmsford, an extremely right-wing member of the Anglo-German Fellowship, who also happened to be homosexual. Together they went on several 'fact-finding missions' to Germany, which Burgess told his friend Goronwy Rees – whom he now lectured on why Communism wouldn't work in Britain – were mainly an opportunity to have lots of sex with boys. On one trip they were accompanied by J. H. Sharp, a senior member of the Church of England, and by Tom Wylie, who was also homosexual. It was almost certainly through Macnamara's contacts that Burgess met Édouard Pfeiffer, *chef de cabinet* of Édouard Daladier, the radical French politician who was Minister of War from June 1936 and Prime Minister from 1938, and a supporter of appeasement. Burgess's stock story about Pfeiffer was that he had once discovered him in Paris playing ping-pong in a tailcoat, with a naked young man draped across the table instead of a net. Pfeiffer, unabashed, told Burgess that the young man was a professional cyclist. 'There was', Rees wrote, 'the sense that the element of farce in Guy's life had become completely uncontrollable.' He assumed that Burgess had fallen prey to the seductions of capitalism.

The Russian Intelligence Archives have so far failed to produce a date for Burgess's first approach to Blunt. It may be that he told Blunt that he was working clandestinely in the cause of anti-fascism in early 1935 in order to reassure him about his apparent apostasy. On the other hand, the fact that it was only in the spring of 1936 that Blunt began to associate himself with Communist-backed organizations – organizations from which Burgess would have told him to distance himself – and that he told an interviewer that up to that spring he was only a '*paper* Marxist', suggests that the proposal came later. In his only public statement after his exposure, Blunt claimed, confusingly – and perhaps deliberately so – that he could date Burgess's approach only imprecisely, to 'late 1935, early 1936', adding that he thought it was just before the outbreak of the Spanish Civil War.

What Burgess said to Blunt we can guess at from the memories of others who heard his 'work for peace and anti-fascism' pitch. Noel Annan became a good friend of Burgess's during the period when he was supposed to have been right-wing – this stance appears to have become distinctly wobbly by the middle of 1936, when Burgess was about to leave the employ of Macnamara to join the BBC. He remembered that Burgess 'had this way of implying to those who were deeply on the Left, "You say you're an anti-fascist. What are you doing about it? You say you went on a demo. Don't be so silly – that has no effect at all!" He had a wonderful way of ridiculing them and making them feel small, and at the same time he could be so charming.' Burgess also made his pitch to the Oxford philosopher Stuart Hampshire.

> I suppose, in hindsight, it was a recruiting spiel. It went, 'Everybody needs some serious political purpose.' You couldn't just be a political dilettante: you had to size up the conditions of the world. It was about objectivity. You couldn't dally with different types of aesthetic interests, you had to make your life coherent ... It was that kind of speech: 'Be serious!' With the implication that I'd think it was a bit odd that someone like him would say that. In hindsight, I think Anthony was bullied by Guy into some moral position. He was persuaded that it was his duty to back the Communist side.

Without Burgess, Blunt would never have become a spy. He barely knew Philby and Maclean, and it is impossible to imagine who else would have considered him good recruitment material, who else would have so persevered to engage him, who else so successfully 'tempted and melted' him. 'It used to amuse me to observe Guy's power of manipulating his friends,' Goronwy Rees wrote, 'and it was clear to me that on the whole they were chosen precisely because they were willing victims for it.'

Why Burgess approached Blunt is another question. He was far from an obvious choice. He was not a committed Communist; he had no plans to join the BBC or the Foreign Office; nor did he have any contacts of particular interest to the NKVD. Nevertheless there was a clear rationale behind the approach. Deutsch wanted someone to exploit the left-wing commitment of the Cambridge undergraduates now that Burgess, Philby and Maclean had left. He needed a talent spotter. Blunt fitted the bill. He already had a reputation as a don who mixed with bright left-wing students. He had an ability, as John Hilton had recognized, for making himself 'the nucleus of a cloud of circling electrons'. He was not too closely identified with the cause, but he was interested in left-wing ideas. Burgess was also perceptive enough to realize that Blunt would make a very good spy. He was already well adapted for living a double life: he habitually compartmentalized; he was compulsively reticent; he suppressed his feelings; he was wary of emotional intimacy. There was a part of him which needed to have secrets. Eventually Blunt would find satisfaction in the game of keeping his lives separate.

That, however, was still to come. Meanwhile, it was the Spanish Civil War, which began in mid-July 1936, that was the catalyst for his decision to accept Burgess's offer in January 1937.

'To us the issue seemed as clear as anyone could possibly want,' wrote Blunt's old Marlborough contemporary T. C. Worsley, who had also found salvation in left-wing politics. 'The Spanish Popular Front Government had been elected by democratic government processes and was clearly entitled to receive every support. The Generals' rebellion was obviously Fascist-inspired. Here was the whole European issue at its most naked and pure. Democracy versus Fascism.' Many people felt that, if sufficient force was brought to bear in Spain on the democratic side to beat the fascists, the terrifying European conflict that had loomed since the early 1930s might be avoided. A victory in Spain might prevent a world war. Worsley's feelings were echoed by many, many writers and intellectuals of his generation. 'Never since', wrote the author of a study of the writers who went to Spain, 'has a cause so captured the moral and physical influence of so many makers and molders [*sic*] of the language, or created such relentless pressure upon so many members of the intellectual communities in the English-speaking world to take sides, to make a stand.'

The British government, along with the rest of the Western powers, failed to support the elected government. 'The Tory press justified the revolt on the grounds that the elections were not valid and that the Popular Front had not been able to establish order,' Worsley wrote. It was assumed that the French president Leon Blum, himself the head of a Popular Front government, would support the Republic and that the British would follow. But instead he set up a non-intervention committee, asking Hitler and Mussolini to join. They signed the treaty but did not abide by it: 'It was common knowledge, too, that Germany and Italy were sending arms, aircraft and troops to Spain in defiance of the Non-Intervention agreement. And though we marched, demonstrated and organised petitions day after day and week after week, they made (to our surprise and indignation – so innocent were we) not a scrap of difference.' It seemed as if the British government was trying to pacify Hitler, especially when, in January 1937, it was made illegal to volunteer to fight in Spain or to recruit volunteers or to arrange passage to Spain. Instead it was the Soviet Union who helped the Republican side. Stalin sent 648 aircraft and 407 tanks, along with 3,000 Soviet 'volunteers'. The war galvanized even the most apolitical. Cyril Connolly wrote that it was impossible 'to remain an intellectual and admire Fascism for that is to admire the intellect's destruction, nor can one remain careless and indifferent. To ignore the present is to condone the future.'

In his only public interview after his exposure in 1979, Blunt said, 'I was persuaded by Guy Burgess that I could best serve the cause of anti-fascism by joining in his work for the Russians', because 'the Communist Party and Russia constituted the only firm bulwark against fascism, since the Western democracies were taking an uncertain and compromising attitude towards Germany'.

The war made an enormous impact on Blunt. Having never

discussed contemporary politics with much enthusiasm, he began to talk about Spain. Even in later life, when he tried to forget his spying, Spain still haunted him. 'It is hard for anyone who was not grown-up at that time to realize the importance of the Spanish Civil War for intellectuals in Western Europe,' he wrote in the 1960s.

> There were many, particularly in England but also to a lesser degree in France, who could still delude themselves into believing that Communism was a matter which primarily concerned Russia, and that Fascism was an affair for Central Europe. The Spanish war raised the issue of Fascism versus Democracy to a different plane, it brought it to Western Europe, and it gave it the form of an armed conflict instead of the persecution of a minority. Even for the most ivory-tower intellectual it meant that the time of not taking sides was past; the conflict was too near and involved too many of one's personal friends.

From the 1950s Blunt gave an annual lecture on the Spanish Civil War and Picasso's *Guernica*. One of his audience recalled it as

> a polished and public statement, argued along the line of the opposition of Good and Evil – a classical theme in painting – and delivered with an intensity disturbing to those of us who as students were more accustomed to a manner which was both shy and aloof. With killing intensity he outlined the plunge into Fascism, the 'maenadic horror' as he called it. Each point was meticulously illustrated with slides. There was the 'obscenity of Franco' as portrayed in Picasso's cartoons and the figure of Truth lying in a field, derived from Goya; 'Will she ever rise,' he asked . . . It made even the least perceptive student reflect on what its impact must have been on the young men . . . in Cambridge.

Another student remembered, 'it gave me the chills. The lecture was brilliant but the iciness of the delivery frightened me.' The combination of intensity and control that Blunt brought to bear on it betrayed the lecture's importance to him. Not for nothing did MacNeice write in *Autumn Journal* that in Spain 'our blunt / Ideals would find their whetstone . . .'

It was, perhaps, no accident that at precisely this time Blunt should have found that his aesthetic and political beliefs were, to an extraordinary extent, shared by W. H. Auden, nominal leader of the writers and poets whose politics and consciences would take many of them to Spain. Auden had communicated his approval of Blunt's views through MacNeice in May 1936: 'Wystan is very pleased with your article on realism at the Academy,' he wrote to Blunt. The article had announced that 'The only hope for European painting at the present time is the development of a New Realism' which confronted the big issues of the age 'directly in terms of politics'. In June, as Blunt was launching his attack on Surrealism, Auden published a pseudonymous article deeply critical of Surrealism's methodological and revolutionary claims, in the literary journal *New Verse*. The two men probably met to discuss their aesthetic views, and perhaps their political ones, during this time. In August, MacNeice and Auden went to Iceland 'to do a book about it for Cape full of verse epistles'. They sent Blunt a postcard. 'Pity you didn't come here,' wrote MacNeice. 'We are just going round a glacier with horses and blondes [they were travelling with a group of school-boys]. There are some very fine baroque churches. Expect a letter in verse (we are writing a book you know). Remember that you are coming to a breakup party with me in September.' And underneath, in Auden's scrawled hand, 'A donor, who prefers to remain anonymous, is sending a very pretty piece to Kings [*sic*] this October. Impey's the name.'

Auden's own aesthetic trajectory had mirrored and preceded Blunt's. In the late 1920s his work was often wilfully obscure. 'The subject of a poem is a peg to hang the poem on,' he had told Stephen Spender. During the early 1930s, partly as a result of his discovery of Marx, he revised his ideas and had begun to reject the modernist orthodoxy of the 'formal autonomy of art'. He decided he wished to restore 'poetry to a didactic relationship with its audience' or, rather, make it more accessible to his readers. He began to use conventional forms like the sonnet, and to fill up his poems with 'things' – people, actions, events, politics. It was a kind of poetic realism. The arguments about what poetry should be that were advanced by Auden's more politicized followers, particularly the poet Cecil Day-Lewis, were very similar to Blunt's arguments about art and the need to do something. Day-Lewis wrote in 1932, 'I am for anything that will help to throw open the park to the public: it makes me despair to think that one is preserved for an aesthetic aristocracy'. He added, 'our writing is half propaganda . . . we can't help it . . . nobody else seems to be doing anything'.

Two poems Auden wrote in the summer of 1936, which appeared in *Letters from Iceland*, the book that came out of the Iceland trip, show the extent to which he shared Blunt's political and aesthetic views, and perhaps had been influenced by the latter. One poem, addressed to Auden's friend the painter William Coldstream, an artist who had embraced figurative painting and was beginning to call himself a realist, described how 'We'd scrapped Significant Form, and voted for Subject.' The other poem was 'Letter to Lord Byron', whose third section contained a statement of Auden's artistic credo of the time:

> To me Art's subject is the human clay,
>   And landscape but a background to a torso;
>   All Cézanne's apples I would give away
>   For one small Goya or a Daumier.

Goya and Daumier had both long been high on Blunt's list of favourite, 'progressive' painters. In the *Spectator* that June he had described Daumier as 'the most likeable and at the same time the grandest product of the revolution of 1830'.

In 'Letter to Lord Byron', Auden echoed an idea that Blunt repeated in many of his articles, that over the centuries artists and writers had lost contact with their audience by striving to become recognized as individualistic creators with no responsibility to their audience, rather than servants of their audience or patrons:

> A new class of creative artist set up,
> On whom the pressure of demand was let up:
> He sang and painted and drew dividends,
> But lost responsibilities and friends.

The worst offenders of this disengagement with audience, Auden noted, 'Belong to Painting not to Literature'. Blunt wrote of artists that 'though they once spent their energy in proving they were better than the ordinary worker, it is now their only hope to show that they are essentially workers'. And Auden pronounced:

> As long as art remains a parasite,
> On any class of persons it's alright;
> The only thing it must be is attendant,
> The only thing it mustn't, independent.

The difference was that, while Auden was willing to write that 'Those most affected were the very best' – those with the talent and the facility to plough their own furrow – he didn't, as Blunt did, damn great artists he had once admired, and set in their place second raters like Peri and the would-be Mexican muralist Lord Hastings.

There were other symmetries between Auden and Blunt – who were in so many other ways utterly different: the former so open to ideas, so comfortable with his emotions; the latter holding on so tightly to a few certainties, so wary of his emotions. Both came from the professional middle class, both were angry at orthodoxy and convention. Both had rebelled against 'the small smothered morality of their mothers' and were homosexual. Both were viewed at times – though Auden to a much lesser extent – as betrayers of their country: Auden's move to America 1939 was publicly condemned as an act of cowardice and betrayal. Auden understood the consuming desire felt by so many of his contemporaries – many of them homosexual – to rebel violently against the polite, circumscribed, stagnant world that had produced them, to try to reinvent themselves with the opposite qualities. When Burgess disappeared to Russia in 1951, Auden said, 'I know exactly why Burgess went to Moscow. It wasn't enough to be a queer and a drunk. He had to revolt still more, to break away from it all. That's just what I've done by becoming an American citizen.' Perhaps the strangest symmetry of all is the totemic figure of the spy, which reoccurred through Auden's poetry of the late 1920s and 1930s. Auden called his first verse play, written in 1928, 'Paid on Both Sides'. Another poem of 1928, sometimes known as 'The Secret Agent', starts strikingly, 'Control of the passes was, he saw, the key', and contains the line 'He, the trained spy, had walked into the trap'. These 'frontier' poems had many associations for Auden, but in them the spy was unambivalently the hero, the brave man fighting against the odds, a border war with the enemy: orthodoxy, 'society', convention. It was a fantasy of solitary, clandestine bravery against omniscient, immovable foes; and about holding on to one's true self when the enemy was everywhere. By 1937, while much about Auden's poems had changed, the spy was still there: in his 'Letter to Lord Byron', Auden claims that the artist, 'like a secret agent, must keep hidden / His passion for his shop'. And in his 'Letter to William Coldstream' he writes, 'An artist you said, is both perceiver and teller, the spy and the gossip.'

Auden came to stay with Blunt at Cambridge in mid-November 1936, ostensibly to hear him lecture, planning to ask for him at King's – presumably because he regarded Blunt as the quintessential liberal-minded King's don. It may have been on this visit that Auden told Blunt about William Coldstream, whose cool, remote portraits went on show in London for the first time that month. If so it was a fateful introduction. Blunt immediately heralded him as a new realist, writing a few weeks later, 'Mr Coldstream is one of the few artists at the London Group in whom sensitiveness does not seem to lead to a sapping of vitality or realism, and his portrait of Miss Anrep is one of the most hopeful works in the exhibition.' However, the weekend was memorable chiefly because Auden made an entirely inappropriate pass at Les Hum-

phries, a golden-haired, pink-cheeked undergraduate who set
elderly dons' hearts beating faster (and who might well, according
to his brother John, have been having an affair with Blunt), and
that, Gavin Ewart remembered, 'caused a bit of a kerfuffle'.
Humphries had been given the job of showing the great poet
around, and was apparently rather shocked. Nevertheless, Auden
enjoyed himself: 'Dear Blunt, just a pc to thank you for the
wonderful time you gave me. You can show this to H[umphries]
and say "Would you on this fair mountain leave to feed and
batten on the moor?". Love Wystan.' This was a misquotation of
Hamlet's speech to Gertrude comparing his father's portrait to
that of her new husband, Claudius – evidence, perhaps, that
Humphries had chosen Blunt over Auden.

Auden's biographer Humphrey Carpenter has speculated that
the weekend may have had another significance, and that Blunt,
who was about to make his own momentous decision, encouraged
Auden to go Spain. A few weeks later the poet wrote to Mac-
Neice's friend and mentor E. R. Dodds, 'I have decided to go out
in the new year as soon as the book [*Letters from Iceland*]
is finished, to join the International Brigade in Spain . . . here is
something I can do as a citizen and not as a writer, and as I have
no dependents, I feel I ought to go; but O I do hope there are not
too many Surrealists there.' The trip, in January 1937, the same
month as Blunt's recruitment, instigated Auden's disenchantment
with politics and destroyed his faith in 'action'.

To Blunt, joining the fight against fascism in a clandestine way
probably did not seem so very different from going off to fight in
the Spanish Civil War. When Goronwy Rees told Rosamond
Lehmann in 1937 that Burgess had asked him to work for anti-
fascism, she 'didn't think it was such a shocking announcement.
All the young men were going off to fight in Spain and I
[Lehmann] thought that this was just Guy's way of helping.' In
describing Burgess's approach to him, Goronwy Rees wrote:

It is perhaps not necessary to explain that the fact did not
shock me . . . in any case, it would take too long, as it would

entail writing the history of an entire generation, and also describing once again the appalling political tragedy of the thirties. I was indeed not shocked; rather, Guy's revelation seems to provide a genuine and solid basis for my liking and admiration of him, as one who had in the most real sense sacrificed his personal life for what he believed in.

Nor were Blunt's reasons for taking up Burgess's offer different from those that prompted writers and intellectuals to go to Spain. Both the NKVD and the Spanish Civil War provided the opportunity to be a man of action rather than just an observer, and to put one's ideals into practice. As Cecil Day-Lewis later wrote, 'What attracted me most, perhaps, in the Communist philosophy was the concept that we discover reality by acting on it, not thinking about it; to one whose grasp on reality seemed so insecure, and who at times craved for action like a drug, this concept felt like salvation'. 'The final test', wrote Stanley Weintraub of the writers who went to Spain, 'was action – to expose the body to danger and discomfort and to offer it, if necessary, in sacrifice. Only then would the ideals about which one wrote be put to the ultimate test of sincerity.' Blunt wrote again and again about artists who had 'lost contact with life', and in 1937 pronounced that 'The new ills are real and can only be cured by real means.' Like the writers, he was tantalized by the idea of being in a situation where hard moral choices had to be made. 'I could believe it permissible that one might have to do evil that good may come,' Day-Lewis wrote, and in his poem 'Spain, 1937', Auden proclaimed 'The conscious acceptance of guilt in the necessary murder' (a phrase he later regretted, describing his Marxist phase as in large part an overexcited pose). Blunt wrote in the *Spectator*, 'The forces of evil are not now those of mere decay and chaos; they are organised against the forces of progress on a far grander scale than then [the First World War] or fifteen years ago. In the face of Fascism it is no use just throwing up one's hands and crying horror; the only hope is to organise defence against the enemy.' He weighed up the morality of working clandestinely for an organization in conflict with his own government, and took his decision. Unlike the poets, his choice had consequences beyond his own life.

For many of the young intellectuals who went to Spain during 1936 and 1937, the consequence of their action was swift disenchantment. 'Nobody I know who went to Spain during the Civil War who was not a dyed-in-the-wool Stalinist came back with his illusions intact,' Auden wrote nearly twenty years later. The disillusionment had many causes: the infighting among the forces of the Left; the atrocities committed on both sides; the realization that idealism was not compatible with modern warfare, that force would not necessarily solve the problems of Spain, that war was chaotic, messy and boring, that physical action was not an ideological panacea. Blunt, however, experienced the idealism and the anger but never had to go through the disillusionment. His commitment, such as it was, was protected by the fact that he was *au fond* a fellow-traveller, a sympathizer who never joined the Party, never underwent the boredom of meetings, never sold the *Daily Worker* on wet streets to uninterested 'workers', never had to examine the contradictions of his position, never had to be disenchanted by the mundanity and orthodoxy of the Party. He never went to fight in Spain. He could choose the aspects of Communism he would adopt. He just had to listen to Burgess.

He had also to avert his eyes from the Soviet Union. Just as the Spanish Civil War seemed to make the European conflict so clear, just as Blunt was approaching his moment of commitment, the Moscow show trials began in August 1936. Senior members of the Soviet Communist Party – Zinoviev, Kamenev and others – were charged and tried with secretly plotting against Stalin, and being in league with the now exiled Trotsky. All but one of the defendants publicly confessed their guilt in court, and Zinoviev told the court that they had been conspiring with the Gestapo and international fascism. The charges were all invented, but the defendants had been both tortured and well rehearsed. They were found guilty and shot. The trials ran for the next five years, claiming the lives of all potential political challengers to Stalin and plenty of innocent bystanders. Those on trial admitted to extraordinary crimes, corroborating each other in great detail. The foreign Communist faithful swallowed their stories, as did many fellow-travellers. This was not just blindness: even people not sympathetic to the USSR were taken in – Bernard Pares, the anti-Soviet Russian expert, was convinced of Zinoviev's guilt. There were inconsistencies in the state's allegations, and these were pointed out by the American Dewey Commission which examined the evidence of the trials and published its findings, but once again scepticism was repressed. The thought that the trials might be a sham perpetrated by a dictator as monstrous as Hitler was too awful to contemplate. Spain seemed a more pressing cause. 'We were uneasy about the trials, but we thought it must be all right because the defendants had confessed,' remembers one Communist Party member. Sympathizers listened to D. N. Pritt, the fellow-travelling lawyer who wrote about the trials for the British media, and who argued that it wasn't possible that Stalin could invent such an enormous conspiracy; there was no way that the defendants could have come up with so much corroborating material if they weren't telling the truth; they looked too healthy to have been tortured. The French writer Louis Aragon wrote of the accused at the trials, 'To claim innocence for these men is to adopt the Hitlerian thesis on all points.'

One of Blunt's undergraduate friends, Michael Grant, a Trinity classicist who was an avowed liberal, remembers arguing with Blunt at this time: 'I used to say to Blunt, "How can you be a Communist when they're doing such awful things?" Blunt used to say, "The end justifies the means." He thought the Baldwin government was not doing all it should to counteract Nazism.' It may be that it was now that Blunt got his one invitation to join the Communist Party. It came from fellow don Roy Pascal. 'I did not accept, giving as my excuse that there were still too many points about which I was not really clear.'

One consequence of Blunt's response to the political situation was his further separation from MacNeice, who once again challenged

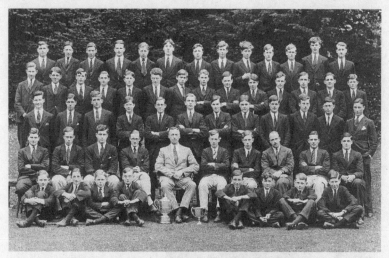

Blunt's house photograph of 1926. Blunt is seated, a perk of his prefect status, fourth from the right, next to his much-disliked housemaster Guillebaud. Louis MacNeice is in the back row, sixth from the left.

Blunt c. 1926: MacNeice wrote of him: 'he was very tall and very thin and drooping . . . he had at times a pre-Raphaelite beauty; when he was annoyed he pouted and stuck out his lip, his good looks vanished and sulkiness was all.'

Clifford Canning, aka 'Foxy Ferdy', Blunt's favourite master at Marlborough.

The 'enchanting' Michael Robertson (left), on whom Blunt had a crush, and John Hilton, c. 1926.

Blunt and MacNeice's study at Marlborough, c. 1925. John Hilton wrote that 'it always seemed to smell of distemper and dying chrysanthemums'. Blunt bought penny prints from Zwemmers' book shop to decorate it.

The 'beautiful but irredeemably heterosexual' Louis MacNeice in Oxford, c. 1926.

The Marlborough *Heretick* (1924) and the Cambridge *Venture* (1928), both of which were edited by Blunt. The former was planned, he wrote, 'to express our disapproval of the Establishment generally'.

"UPON PHILISTIA WILL I TRIUMPH"

THE VENTURE

EDITED BY
ANTHONY BLUNT, H. ROMILLY FEDDEN
AND MICHAEL REDGRAVE

NUMBER ONE, NOVEMBER
1928

CONTRIBUTORS:

J. R. ACKERLEY	GUY BARTON	J. C. BEAGLEHOLE
ANTHONY BLUNT	FRANK BIRCH	JOHN DRINKWATER
EDWARD CATTLE	SHELDON DICK	CLAUDE FLIGHT
CLEMENCE DANE	R. J. F. LEHMANN	RAYMOND McGRATH
C. M. MILLETT	E. B. PHARE	LOUIS MacNEICE
G. H. W. RYLANDS	J. C. THORNTON	MICHAEL REDGRAVE
F. McD. C. TURNER	HUMBERT WOLFE	ALISTAIR WATSON
	DOUGLAS DAVIDSON and BASIL WRIGHT	

PUBLISHED ONCE A TERM AT CAMBRIDGE. PRICE ONE AND SIXPENCE

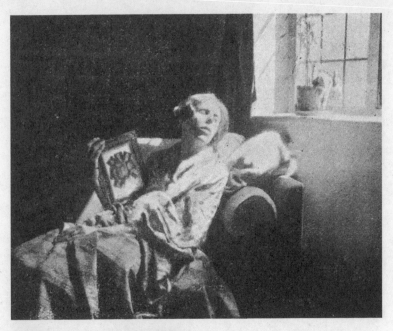

Blunt in drag, accompanying a pastiche of *Orlando* by Michael Redgrave, which appeared in *Granta*, June 1929. Forty years later the picture did the rounds of the ladies' loos at the Courtauld.

Dadie Rylands, the young Cambridge don known as 'the most beautiful blond at King's'.

Blunt with second-generation Cambridge Bloomsbury. From the left: Francis Warre-Cornish, Dickon Steele, Dadie Rylands and Eddie Playfair, c. 1928.

The younger members of the Apostles, c. early 1932. From the left: Richard Llewellyn Davies, Hugh Sykes-Davies, Alistair Watson, Blunt, Blunt's sometime lover Julian Bell and Andrew Cohen.

Michael Straight: a 'dynamic combination of playboy and Sir Galahad'.

Tess Mayor: the most sighed-after girl in Cambridge and Blunt's closest female friend.

John Cornford: poet and martyr to the Communist cause aged twenty-one.

Guy Burgess in the early 1930s: cherub, charmer and *homme sérieux*.

Donald Maclean in the early 1930s: as a history student at Trinity Hall and early member of the Cambridge communist group, Blunt barely knew him.

Kim Philby, taken in the 1950s. Philby, a history student at Trinity, and enthusiastic left-winger, was the founder of the Cambridge spy ring.

Arthur Marshall, seen here as the cross-dressing star of a Footlights revue. Marshall was at the heart of Dadie Rylands's social set in the late 1920s.

Victor Rothschild: energetic, tough, funny (not always intentionally), easily bored, clever, and extremely rich.

Picasso's *Guernica*. 'There is something pathetic in the sight of a talented artist struggling to cope with a problem entirely outside his powers,' Blunt wrote in 1937 of Picasso's response to the Spanish Civil War, and branded him 'a pygmy'. Fifteen years later he hailed the painting as a 'modern calvary', and 'the last great painting in the European tradition'.

– as always semi-jokingly – his friend's increasing extremism. In 'Hetty to Nancy' (hetero to nancy-boy, as one critic has glossed it), the epistle in *Letters from Iceland* which he addressed (tacitly) to Blunt, he wrote, 'you keep to the Arts, darling, though in Cambridge I suppose even the Arts are just a teeny bit marked with the beast – all this psychology and politics. The hammer and sickle are all right where they belong but they don't suit lady dons.' (The piece purported to be about a couple of schoolmarms taking a gaggle of schoolgirls on a camping trip round Iceland, and was extremely camp and very silly. Naturally everyone was referred to as a girl.) In *The Strings are False* he was blunter: 'the Marxist, who is only human, finds it such fun practising strategy – i.e. hypocrisy, lying, graft, political pimping, tergiversation, allegedly necessary murder – that he forgets the end in the means, the evil of the means drowns the good of the end, power corrupts, the living gospel withers, Siberia fills with ghosts. Fills with the victims of idealists trying to be pragmatic.' The chaotic schoolboy irrationalist was now revealed as more moderate, more sensible, more sceptical than the self-styled schoolboy rationalist.

Their friendship reached a symbolic turning point in the autumn of 1936, when MacNeice moved to Hampstead after taking up a new teaching post at Bedford College in London, and their correspondence came to an end. They were physically closer but they were less intimate. This was not, as some have suggested, a result of some sexual advance or impropriety on Blunt's part. MacNeice was quite at ease with Blunt's sexuality. Perhaps MacNeice's proximity made him harder to confide in; perhaps Blunt's closeness exposed those things about him that MacNeice liked least. Certainly their lives were taking them in different directions. MacNeice had move into the heartland of London's arty bohemia in Hampstead – a world Blunt studiedly avoided. Blunt had embraced Cambridge academia, which MacNeice found dispiriting and desiccated, even though he was an academic himself. In 'From Hetty to Nancy' MacNeice wrote, 'Not that personally I could breathe if I lived in Cambridge. All those coffee parties you have with people talking about Marx. *And the intrigues, darling, the intrigues.*' And then there was the politics. 'Synthesis is a bloody word, isn't it?' MacNeice wrote in one of his last letters. 'Like progress. Progress is a bloody word. Well, here ends the jeremiad.'

What, beyond the lure of politics and action, which appealed to so many of his contemporaries, made Blunt take the decision to go with Burgess – a decision that would blight his life? Blunt himself was never able, or willing, to dissect what it was that made him take that step beyond his contemporaries. At the time, in any case, he would probably not have admitted it was such a great step. Consciously, the idea of logic mattered deeply to him. He was able to persuade himself that his choice was the rational one. Marxism provided an absolute standard by which to judge art, by which to judge everything, on 'the only possible scientific basis, namely that of history'. Becoming a Communist was a logical act in the face of contemporary events. Accepting Burgess's offer to work for the Communist International – secretly of course – was the logical next move. In common with many academics, Blunt possessed a stubborn confidence in his own conclusions, despite a naive and limited understanding of politics. This was aided by his tendency to see the world in stark and obvious oppositions. Once his mind had been made up, the decision was screwed in place. All doubts were quashed. Noel Annan saw this and didn't like it: 'There was a very strong streak of dogmatism in Anthony – "I've told you this and this is how it is."' Once he had reached the point of commitment he was able to shut out what he didn't want to see or hear. To some extent the atmosphere of King's College and its promotion of Bloomsbury's values had fostered this. John Maynard Keynes wrote of his early years at King's among the Apostles, 'We entirely repudiated a personal responsibility on us to obey general rules ... We repudiated entirely customary morals, conventions and traditional wisdom.'

Subconsciously, there were many jostling reasons for his choice that Blunt himself never tried to identify. His desire to *épater les bourgeois*; his fury at the older established world; his conviction that the state could be, and often was, wrong; his fatal attraction to the dangerous; his desire to lose himself, to be persuaded – all were simply deeper, more literal, than those of his contemporaries. One manifestation of this was his deliberate perversity and contrariness. The same perversity made him denounce medieval Gothic, express boredom with the Renaissance, and champion poor, demonized, misunderstood baroque. The same suspicion of the universally loved made him dislike Florence and prefer Rome; made him in later life feud with the powerful and the established, and attracted him to the young, the difficult and the dangerous. It was born of both of a desire to escape the suffocating convention of his background, and a feeling of being always an outsider. He never felt he belonged, no matter how many doors were opened to him, and he always half-hated the worlds he so wanted to join. He was furious, though he would never have owned up to such a passionate emotion.

His homosexuality obviously played a large role in all this. The sympathetic atmosphere he had encountered at King's helped the homosexuals who lived within it to objectify the illegality of homosexuality, to reassure them that they themselves were not to blame for their persecution. For some, that fostered anger against the society that tried to change them and told them they were criminals. In his autobiographical novel *Christopher and his Kind*, Christopher Isherwood wrote that, once he got over his shame at his homosexuality, he found himself 'blindly furious' at what Society 'command[ed] me to desire. My mother . . . is silently, brutishly willing me to get married and breed grandchildren for her. Her will is the will of Nearly Everybody, and in their will is my death. *My* will is to live according to my nature, and to find a place where I can be what I am . . . But I'll admit this – even if my nature were like theirs, I should still have to fight them, in one way or another.'

Blunt's consciousness of the illegality of homosexuality, which meant that his very identity broke the law, may well have helped to make acceptance of Burgess's approach seem less of a big step. Many homosexuals hated being by their very nature in conflict with the state. This was in large part the reason for Isherwood's decision to live outside England. But for some respectable middle-class homosexuals breaking the law did not become merely an accepted part of life, but acquired a kind of nobility and appeal. Auden romanticized crime as a rebellion against the system, as a manifestation of life: 'Every criminal act is a revolt against death,' he wrote. 'Stealing is an attempt to perform a miracle.' On the subject of his homosexuality, he declared, with some relish, 'I am a criminal'. To make society angry was an added pleasure. Blunt certainly got a kick out of it. The boyfriends of J. R. Ackerley, the homosexual writer and critic, were usually petty burglars or servicemen on the run. Burgess also had a taste for petty thieves, as did his friend James Pope-Hennessy. After the war, Blunt too had a number of boyfriends who were small-time ex-cons. In 1937 he wrote an article about the character of the 'Criminal King' in nineteenth-century novels, writing of Vautrin in Balzac's *Père Goriot*, that he was 'the type of hundred-per-cent criminal whose powers are so vast that they appear superhuman'. He is the 'superhuman and subhuman' criminal 'in whom are mixed the god and the king as least as much as the brute'. Blunt noted that Balzac 'put the final touch to his picture of the perversity of society and the topsy-turvy state of the world, by allowing his hero in *La Dernière Incarnation de Vautrin*, to assume the most unexpected of all roles, and to become the highest agent of the secret police'.

When he tried to explain his spying in 1979, Blunt invoked as an explanation E. M. Forster's statement that, if he had ever to choose between betraying his friend and his country, he hoped he would have the guts to betray his country. 'Love and loyalty to an individual', Forster's article went on, 'can run counter to the claims of the State. When they do – down with the State, say I.' The statement had reverberated with Blunt for many years: according to Goronwy Rees, he used the same words to try to persuade him not to denounce Burgess to MI5 in 1951. Forster's maxim has often been condemned on the grounds that if you betray your country you betray your friends too (even though the condemners would no doubt have accepted it as an argument for acting against a totalitarian state such as the Soviet Union or Nazi Germany). One should remember, however, that for Blunt's generation of homosexual men, friends in innumerable ways provided a support network in a hostile world, and defended the individual against the state. They kept one's secrets. Against the vitality of love, of friendship, of honesty – qualities elevated at King's, where Blunt had learned about relationships – was opposed the dead hand of the state.

Burgess's timing was perfect. In early January 1937 he arranged for Blunt to meet his Soviet recruiter, who was almost certainly Deutsch.* Blunt, too, was invited to fight against fascism. 'We did not think of ourselves as working for Russia,' he said after his exposure. 'We were working for the Comintern' – though by now the Comintern, while making great public play of its independence, was just a tool for the furtherance of Soviet aims. Any lingering doubts that Blunt may have had about the cause were swept aside by the death, two days before the New Year, of John Cornford. He had gone out to fight for the Republic in August, and had been killed in a skirmish near Córdoba a few days before his twenty-first birthday. His death had an enormous impact on his contemporaries. Stephen Spender wrote of him, 'Cornford is immensely significant not merely because he is young and brave, but because he lived and died with the courage of a purpose which reaches far beyond himself and which effectively challenges the barbarism and defeatism of the age we live in.' As Blunt later wrote, 'the conflict was too near and involved too many of one's personal friends'.

Blunt was impressed by Deutsch. He accepted the offer to work

* According to Nigel West and Oleg Tsarev, authors of *The Crown Jewels*, precise details of Blunt's recruitment – Burgess's initial approach etc. – do not survive in his files in the Russian Intelligence Archives. They conclude that Deutsch, rather than Maly (as has occasionally been suggested), was Blunt's recruiter. This is likely, since Blunt told Peter Wright that his contact was called 'Otto'.

for the Soviets. He later told his MI5 interrogator Peter Wright that 'he doubted he would ever have joined had the approach come from a Russian', by which he meant the uninspired Russian apparatchiks who later became his controllers. 'To Blunt,' Wright wrote, 'the talented European controllers of the 1930s were artists.' Arnold Deutsch seemed to prove that the movement was not just an arm of Soviet Intelligence – though in fact that was exactly what it was. He was living proof that you could be an intellectual and a street fighter. His involvement in the Sexpol movement seemed to confirm that Communism and sexual toleration went hand in hand – which in fact they didn't. But this may explain why Burgess was always insistent that Stalin's views on homosexuality were much more enlightened than 'American propaganda' suggested.

The NKVD gave Blunt the code name 'Tony'. In his NKVD memoir he later summarized his instructions as being to 'combine the difficult task of not being thought left wing and at the same time being in the closest contact with all left-wing students in order to spot likely recruits for us'. Deutsch wrote of Blunt:

> Tony is a typical English intellectual. Speaks very high-flown English. Looks very feminine. A pederast. Mädchen says that with Tony it is congenital [which was rich coming from Burgess]. He is very educated and clever. Communism for him is based on theory. Has several works on Marxism in the history of art. Is considerably steadier and more rational than Mädchen. He is a simple person and without big pretensions. Can control himself, is cold and a little mannered. Is to a lesser degree connected to the Communist Party than Mädchen. He would hardly give up his career for the sake of our work. He understands well the tasks he is to do for us and is ready to help us. He has a large influence on students.

8. Talent Spotter

'We simply knew, *all of us, that the revolution was at hand'*

It is not at all clear that Blunt had any idea of what he was getting himself into. He almost certainly assumed that his talent spotting would be a temporary assignment. He knew it could only be a short-term activity at Cambridge, since he was due to leave the university at the end of the academic year, in June. His fellowship was up; he had thus far failed to turn his thesis into a book, and several attempts to stay in Cambridge – an application for a fellowship at King's and, more implausibly, for the directorship of the Fitzwilliam – had failed. ('It is of course a joke for me to apply,' he wrote to Fritz Saxl about the Fitzwilliam post, 'only I think it is in general a good thing to put in occasionally for this kind of job.') Moreover, the great conflict that would decide the future of Europe – even the world – was, his political mentors told him, imminent. 'We simply *knew*, all of us,' said James Klugmann in the 1970s, 'that the revolution was at hand. If anyone had suggested that it wouldn't happen in Britain for say thirty years, I'd have laughed myself sick.' Blunt seems to have seen himself as a revolutionary intellectual in the mould of Friedrich Antal. Within days of his meeting with Deutsch, he wrote in the *Spectator*, 'What a field day the Minister of Fine Arts will have, when, after the revolution, the State takes over all privately-owned paintings and collects the best in a central museum!' This was more or less the job that Antal had held under the Hungarian Soviet Republic.

Looking back on the period from 1937 to the beginning of the war, Blunt later told the NKVD, 'I can say that I did almost nothing.' His file in the Russian Intelligence Archives apparently bears this out. 'As you already know,' he added, 'the actual recruits I took were Michael Straight and Leo Long. John Caincross I was asked to contact and did so for Guy Burgess.'

The only account of Michael Straight's recruitment is the one given by Straight himself in his 1983 memoir *After Long Silence*. It suggests that he was manipulated and emotionally bullied by Blunt into agreeing to work for the Comintern, and that he was never really a Communist at all.

Straight was an American, a member of the rich and influential Whitney family and the son of the philanthropist and social reformer Dorothy Elmhirst. He had had an unconventional upbringing. In 1925, when he was nine, his mother had moved the family from New York to Devon, where she had set up a progressive school and utopian community at Dartington Hall. Sean O'Casey, the Huxleys and Bertrand Russell all came to stay; Michael Chekhov taught drama; and, as well as studying for their School Certificate, the children had their dreams analysed in class. The emphasis was on sexual and social freedom. Straight claimed that, of the ten pupils in his final-year class, seven went on to join the Communist Party. He was among them. After he arrived at Trinity in 1934, to study economics, he became involved with the Socialist society and eventually joined the Trinity Communist cell, because, he later said, he was deeply impressed by the charismatic John Cornford. 'I was an amateur Communist. I didn't take any of it seriously. I was a Keynesian, and economic Marxism was unintelligible to me. I didn't understand it and I didn't want to read it.' At meetings of the Trinity Communist cell, 'I sat leaning against the wall doing my homework while they discussed "C" contacts [people about to be recruited to the Party]. I couldn't care less.' In 1935, however, Cornford gave him the task of infiltrating the Cambridge Union for the Party. 'John said, "This is your arena. Go in there like a gladiator and hold forth", which to my own amazement, I was able to do.' He was duly elected secretary in 1936 and became president-elect in 1937.

Blunt and Straight were on the 1935 Intourist trip to Russia, and they had friends in common like Tess Major – 'a student of unearthly beauty', by whom Straight was 'stricken'. ('It was no use,' he wrote of his abortive pursuit, in characteristically dramatic tones. 'Tess needed as I did to love and to be loved. But there was a knot within her that I could not untie.') However, Straight did not notice Blunt until they were finally introduced at the end of 1935 by Klugmann and Burgess, who shared a passion for cars with Michael's racing-driver brother, Whitney. From then on, Straight believed, Blunt deliberately cultivated him and sought to make him 'emotionally dependent on him'. Straight came to think that this might have been at Klugmann's instigation. When Straight was nearly expelled by the Trinity authorities in connection with a petition organized by the Trinity Communist cell to protest at college servants' wages, Blunt helped to calm the waters. In actual fact, Straight later insisted, he had not been involved with the protest, which 'enraged' the college authorities, but someone had to take responsibility for it, and, 'being financially independent, I couldn't care less if I was expelled. Each evening, Anthony came by my rooms to assure me that the weight of opinion was shifting.' Blunt also advised him on his love life. 'Victor Rothschild's wife [Barbara Hutchinson] had fallen in love with me and was desperate to sleep with me. She needed desperately to have some affection. Victor was this totally cold repulsive human being. She tried very hard and nearly succeeded sleeping with me. Had she done so it would have been very dangerous.' She nearly had her way with him under a blanket one evening after a picnic by the Cam. 'Blunt took on the role of being an intermediary, encouraging me to see her. Victor had suspicions. He came back at midnight, and found his wife reading the love poems of John Donne.' Barbara Hutchinson had married Victor in the early 1930s, when he was still an undergraduate. Her serial infidelity was well known among the Rothschilds' friends. 'She was a bad girl,' recalled Dadie Rylands. 'She was a winner, a darling, but she kept going off.' She and Victor were eventually divorced in the 1940s. Straight was also seeing a German ballet dancer, and wooing his future wife, Belinda Compton. On Straight's behalf, Blunt consulted Compton's sister Catherine Walston (who would later become Graham Greene's lover), a regular guest at his parties: 'I would say, "I don't know if this girl is serious or not", and he would say, "Well let me find out. I'll talk to Catherine and see what she's found out."'

In turn, Straight claimed, a trifle exaggeratedly, that he was responsible for Blunt's discovery of intellectual Marxism:

> We never spoke of Communist principles ... On one occasion only, we wondered together what a Marxist theory of aesthetics might be. He was writing an article on art for a journal of opinion. In an effort to be helpful, I developed the preposterous notion that works of art might be considered in terms of their historical impact rather than their intrinsic worth. It was an indication of Anthony's own lack of political indoctrination that he incorporated my notion in his article.

Blunt was asked to approach Straight only a few weeks after he himself was recruited. He invited the younger man to his rooms in Neville's Court, and asked him what he wanted to do when he left Cambridge. Straight later said that he was close to breakdown at the time, what with the shock of Cornford's death and his own complicated love affairs. He began to talk, but before he could finish, Blunt cut in. 'Some of your friends ... have other ideas for you,' he said, and told Straight that he should consider returning to America to work in international banking so that he could provide 'economic appraisals of Wall Street's plans to dominate the world economy'.

> Our friends have given a great deal of thought to it. They have instructed me to tell you that this is what you must do.'
>
> 'Why do they tell me this now?'
>
> 'Because of John's death ... It will be necessary for you to cut all your political ties ...'
>
> 'I stage a break with all my friends,' I said, 'I leave my

home and my family. I go back to a country that I barely remember. I live a life of deceit—

'John gave up his life, remember that,' Blunt interrupted, and told Straight to go away and get some sleep.

The invitation, Straight claimed afterwards, was not at all welcome. He wanted to refuse, but 'my response was shaped substantially by Anthony's own personality'. 'Why didn't I take Anthony's scheme by the throat and fling it away?' he later asked: because he was in emotional turmoil after Cornford's death, and he 'lacked the will' to say no. This he put down to not being sufficiently 'self-centred, as most sensible people are'. Blunt had insinuated himself into his life as 'a wise and valued counsellor', and 'I had no resistance to very powerful resolute people'. He claimed he made three pleas through Blunt to be excused, the second of which 'would be considered in the highest circles in the Kremlin' – this meant 'Stalin, of course'. The requests were refused.

His last was in a letter sent from a boat he took to visit America in the spring holidays of 1937. 'I cited every argument I could think of for resisting his claims upon me. I even offered to turn over all the wealth that I had if I were released.' In 1983 Straight sent Blunt a copy of *After Long Silence*. In this copy, Blunt corrected the spelling mistakes and left a trail of question marks and exclamation marks down the margins. In response to Straight's claim about the letter, he wrote in the margin, 'If so the letter never reached me!' When asked what he thought of Blunt's claim not to have received his plea for release, Straight said in 1996, 'Really? Well, it wouldn't have made any difference anyway.' Whatever the truth, he agreed to be recruited.

Within months he had overcome his 'emotional crisis' and got himself a first – 'My name became an epithet among economics students for years to come' – and severed his connections with the Party, though apparently not very convincingly. 'Michael had been obviously very Communist, then suddenly pretended not to be,' remembered Brian Simon. 'We felt it was very much bound up with his mother. He used to write to her almost every day, and both he and Anthony were very taken up with what happened to Cornford. They both had a colossal admiration for John.' He told everyone he was going back to America – not, as Blunt had suggested, to work on Wall Street, but to 'a job in the Roosevelt administration'.

Straight's account of his recruitment is perhaps somewhat one-sided, particularly in its insistence on his lack of political commitment. There are compelling reasons for this. In the 1940s and '50s Straight became a public figure on the American Left, as the editor of *New Republic* (which was owned by his family) and a highly visible critic of McCarthyism. The revelation that he had been recruited as a Soviet spy would have caused incalculable damage to him, his family and the whole opposition to McCarthy. He had a strong motive for diminishing his own involvement and responsibility. At times he denied having been a member of the Party at Cambridge at all.

At Cambridge in the 1930s, however, Straight was known as the most glamorous figure of the far Left, and Blunt had reasons for supposing that he would be receptive to his invitation. He was not in the business of recruiting non-believers. When asked by an old Cambridge friend, Tom Brocklebank, why he had never tried to recruit him in the 1930s, Blunt answered, 'You never showed the slightest interest in Marxism.' Attractive and energetic, Straight was seen as a proselytizer and an activist, renowned for having converted a convinced Conservative, John Simmonds, to socialism. ('I made absolutely no effort to change Simmonds to left politics,' Straight later insisted. 'He simply came over himself. I would not take responsibility for bringing somebody into this organization, because I didn't really believe in it myself.') Gavin Ewart remembered him as someone with a distinct taste for cloak and dagger: 'He was very melodramatic. You felt he was in a deep conspiracy all the time. He wanted to be. He thought he was doing something important and remarkable. But he was likeable.' Charles Rycroft – one of those who made the trip to Russia with Straight – recalled, 'He was an attitudinizer. I remember him in a hotel in Moscow turning to me with some new clothes on and saying hopefully, "Do I look like a proletarian?" And I said, "No, you look like a millionaire pretending to be a proletarian." ' On the 1935 Russia trip, Straight was said to have 'stroked one of the mantelpieces murmuring reverently, Soviet timber. Soviet marble.' Perhaps less forgivably, he wrote and performed his own socially conscious jazz songs:

> Sing me a song of social significance
> There's nothing else that will do
> Sing me of bread lines, sing me of wars . . .

'And a lot of other things I secretly found very dreary,' one contemporary remembered.

> But so compelling was his personality that I was swept along in his wake. He was very left-wing. He was very wealthy. He was both English and American. He was handsome, gifted, versatile, precocious, virile. What on earth was he not? He played squash with one of the Sitwells . . . and he loved the masses. How could any of us resist this dynamic combination of playboy and Sir Galahad? The hunger-marchers were made to march through Cambridge and we were to entertain them. I can see now the shuffling column taking a wrong turning in the direction of Midsummer Common . . . and being headed off by our hero, leaping along with all the agility with which he had once danced the part of the Dominant Male Principle in the choreography of Sibelius's second symphony.

Straight's portrayal of Blunt as a dark manipulator may have some truth in it, though in terms of experience Blunt was as new to the NKVD as he was. While it is possible that Straight had been chosen as a prospective recruit several months before Blunt met Deutsch, the timing of Blunt's first interest in Straight – before Blunt and Klugmann had any connections with the NKVD – makes it questionable that he had cultivated Straight purely to recruit him. Blunt's interest in him was not out of character, and his sexual intriguing was in keeping with the obsessive gossiping and matchmaking which characterized Dadie Rylands's set. It demonstrated how perfectly fitted he was for his new job. In his memoir, Straight admitted that it was more than Blunt's bullying that made him agree to be recruited. 'I needed to sacrifice myself,' he wrote. Like Blunt, he felt a need to make a gesture. As a child, he had been told by his mother – who had both fascinated and neglected him – 'those who are privileged and conscious owe it to volunteer and be the one that dies'. He also claimed, despite his description of Blunt as Svengali-like, that he had not been over-bearing or didactic: 'He was on the contrary, compassionate.' He said he liked Blunt: 'he was a serious, conflicted, scholarly man, who was led into a fantasy world by a gypsy. He was fascinated and awed by Guy, and his comments about German agents infiltrating the British Conservative Party. He had nothing to balance that with.'

Blunt's second target, John Cairncross, was in hindsight even more critical of Blunt and no less keen to assert his own inno-cence. Cairncross could not have been more different from the rich and clubbable Straight. A twenty-three-year-old languages graduate from a lower-middle-class Glaswegian family, he had passed top of his year in the Civil Service exams of 1936, and now worked at the Foreign Office. When he arrived at Trinity in 1934, he already had a degree from the Sorbonne. His subject was seventeenth-century literature, Blunt's period – though he was emphatic that Blunt never taught him – an assertion contra-dicted by contemporaries. He got his degree in two years, having spent most of his time working.

But there was another side to Cairncross. He had held on to his left-wing politics, his broad Glaswegian accent and his sense of his differentness from the complacent upper-class boys by whom he was surrounded. He was often socially awkward and quick to take offence, which made him hard work. He was thought not to 'fit in' at the Foreign Office – not least because he couldn't stop himself criticizing Appeasement – and he was eventually moved to the Civil Service. 'One could not call him a gentleman,' wrote Burgess, who saw Cairncross as a man torn by his desire both to enjoy the good things for which he had worked so hard and to fight the system he despised. Arnold Deutsch liked him, describing him as 'lively and warmhearted', but noted, 'The Scots hate the English.' According to Stuart Hampshire, Cairncross had liked Blunt at Cambridge. 'I remember him talking with starry eyes about Blunt to me. He was an absurd and rather untidy scholar, very bright and academic. He was socially from the lower rather than the higher, very talkative, sort of chaotic.' Blunt gave him a glowing reference to the Foreign Office,* and he entered the Spanish section in October 1936.

In his 1993 autobiography, *The Enigma Spy*, Cairncross claimed that he had been trapped by Blunt and Burgess into a 'secretly stage managed' meeting with his Soviet control. He also displayed an intense dislike of Blunt, whom he accused of being 'the moving spirit and main strategist in the KGB's recruiting network at Cambridge'. He characterized Blunt – whom he had barely seen since 1937 – as a second-rater with a thirst for power who had built 'a powerful position of authority in the art world in which he was able to blight the careers of those daring to disagree with him, those unfortunate scholars who based their conclusions about art on actual details dated and controlled, whereas Blunt insisted that it was connoisseurship which counted'. (If anything, Blunt was on the side of the empiricists.) However, the accounts published which quote from the Russian Intelligence Archives contradict Cairncross's account of his own reluctance, and suggest that Blunt's role in his recruitment was minimal.

Blunt's task was to introduce Cairncross to Guy Burgess, which he did at the end of February 1937, several weeks after he had approached Straight. He invited Cairncross back to Trinity to meet Louis MacNeice for tea, and Burgess was there too. This

* It was Blunt's reference for Cairncross which alerted the journalists who tracked him down in 1979 to Cairncross's possible involvement with the NKVD. Ironically, the reference appears to have had nothing to do with Cairncross's subsequent recruitment.

was the extent of his involvement in Cairncross's recruitment, though he may also have been asked to provide an opinion on Cairncross's suitability as a recruit, although no documentary evidence has been produced to prove this. Thereafter, Blunt reported, he was never officially told whether Caincross had been taken, and Cairncross knew nothing about his activities. After the tea, Burgess took the train down to London with Cairncross, and they discussed politics. Later Cairncross turned up at Burgess's London flat to talk again. According to the Russian Intelligence Archives, he was introduced to Deutsch or his colleague Theo Maly three months later by James Klugmann (who himself had been reluctantly recruited only a few weeks before, specially for the job). Maly reported to Moscow, 'He was very glad that he could make contact with us and not feel himself cut off from the party.'

Cairncross became a very productive spy, passing great numbers of papers to the Soviets, including crucial strategic information which helped them to win the battle of Kursk, one of the turning points of the Second World War – and an act for which he was happy to take credit. He also saw himself as an idealist and sincere in his desire to help the Soviet Union. It may be that this made him particularly keen to emphasize, as much to himself as to anyone else, how different he was from Burgess and Blunt, those sinister plotters who had been so condemned for their actions, and who by association sullied his own activities. He may also have blamed Blunt for his precipitous departure from England and the end of his Civil Service career in 1951, after MI5 became suspicious of him in the wake of the Burgess and Maclean scandal. Thereafter Cairncross lived in self-imposed exile. He could hardly have been thrilled by Blunt's continued meteoric rise at home.

Blunt made one other recruit at Cambridge: Leo Long. Like Cairncross, Long was another bright left-wing modern linguist from a poor background. His father was a carpenter from Holloway in north London who – when he was in work – earned less than half Long's Trinity scholarship of £250 a year. Long had arrived at Trinity in 1935 already committed to Communism. 'I had a deep sense of the iniquity of society,' he said later. He remembered the hunger marchers coming through Cambridge: 'They couldn't eat the food we gave them, eggs and so on, because their stomachs had shrunk . . . We felt we were the only people who took the threat of Fascism seriously.' Blunt taught him and, though Long knew about Blunt's Marxism, he never felt he understood what its attraction was for Blunt: 'the world of politics meant nothing to him. It is hard to know what his motivation was for being a Communist. I think the conspiracy must have appealed to him.' As with Blunt, the Spanish Civil War was the catalyst for Long's political commitment: 'You have to remember we were desperately committed . . . We didn't trust the British government. It seemed to prefer links with the Nazis . . . What did we think would happen? I don't think there was much discussion about it. We just assumed there would be a war.' Unlike Cairncross, Long was clubbable and was eventually elected to the Apostles. Unlike Straight and Cairncross, he never accused Blunt of manipulation: 'Blunt never tried blackmailing or bullying me, because we shared a deep belief in the Communist cause.'

Blunt seems to have done very little else for the Soviets before the war. Michael Straight claimed that Blunt approached one other of his friends, who managed to avoid recruitment by pleading that he was 'not sufficiently strong to survive going underground'. This may have been Brian Simon, whom Blunt later wrote he contacted 'in order to remake contact with possible students'. When Blunt met him in 1938, Simon was working in London for the National Union of Students, preparing a book on universities. He recalled that Blunt announced rather grandly that he was working for the Communist International. 'The penny didn't drop,' said Simon. 'I thought the CI was a prestigious organization which stood up to the Nazis – Dimitrov, who stood up to Goering at the Reichstag Fire trials, was in the Communist International. It just seemed a rather good thing to be doing. I don't recall him making a big thing of asking to meet students.' Blunt did not pursue the matter, and apparently no students were put his way. He also held at least one meeting for clandestine student Communists – those who had applied to the Party but had been advised to become secret members so as not to blight their career prospects. Gavin Ewart remembered 'a meeting in Anthony's rooms, with a lot of people I knew quite well who I didn't think were members of the CP, and it transpired they were. It was organized by Anthony. One was Gerald Croasdell, president of the Union.'

Michael Straight also claimed that he was never told that Leo Long had been recruited by Blunt (it was Straight who later named Long to MI5) but he guessed that it must be so when Guy Burgess told him that Blunt had taken an interest in Long and brought him into Apostles. '*If Anthony has taken Leo under his wing, that can only mean one thing*,' Straight wrote (he added the italics too). But, according to Long, it was Straight himself who introduced him to the Society in 1937. Long was distinctly underwhelmed. 'It was all a bit of a racket really. They were not the brightest people at all. It was a King's–Trinity monopoly and you got in because you happened to know someone.' The Society has long been assumed to have been significant in the history of the Cambridge spies because of its traditions of secrecy and its sympathy towards homosexuality. But it seems unlikely that Blunt tried to use the Apostles as an incubator for spies, as has sometimes been suggested.* Though it is true that Blunt, Guy Burgess, Leo Long and Michael Straight were all members, Kim Philby, Donald Maclean, John Cairncross and James Klugmann were not. Blunt at this time barely took an interest in it. Noel Annan, a former member, has calculated that only 3 of the 44 members

---

* In *Mask of Treachery*, p. 272, John Costello cites as evidence of Blunt's control over the Society that he 'actively canvassed' for Leo Long's election with a young Apostle called John Astbury (who Costello named as a possible recruit of Blunt's, though the Russian Intelligence Archives have produced nothing about him and his name has not inspired any further speculation). But, according to Costello's own book, Astbury (who was in fact known as Peter) was elected to the Apostles after Long, and therefore could not have supported Long's election.

who joined the Apostles between the wars 'could be called lifelong homosexuals', and that of 31 members elected to the Society between 1927 and 1938, only 15 were Communist or could at a stretch have been called 'marxisant'.

In any case, by 1936 the Apostles had almost ground to a halt over a dispute about the significance of Communism. On one side were Keynes, other senior members and Julian Bell; on the other Alister Watson, Burgess, Hugh Sykes Davies and younger radical members. Bell wrote in 1937, 'I think the bitterest thing about the Communist hysteria at Cambridge has been the virtual death of the Society; my hope is that it is only a temporary coma.' By the time Straight was elected in 1936, there were only two active undergraduates left. He was asked to bring in new blood. Keynes had told him, 'We're going to kill it unless you want to revive it.' His first move was to bring in three fellow Communist Party members: John Waterlow, Gerald Croasdell and John Humphrey. 'I responded with the names of my friends who were radical but Apostolic,' he said later by way of justification. Leo Long was the next to join.

Though Blunt confidently announced the coming revolution, he was a great deal less confident about his own future. His four-year fellowship had finished in 1936, and

> To my *great* sorrow and regret, I was *not* put on the staff, not given a fellowship. And this, I was quite certain, was due to [his tutor, H. F.] Stewart, who knew perfectly well – I know he wanted me to succeed him – but he knew perfectly well that my heart was not in French grammar or indeed even in some parts of French literature, and so they gave me an extra year, '36 to '37, just to tidy up my thesis, which I was turning into a book.

Various subsequent attempts to get jobs had failed. His career was stuck, he had no books or research articles to his name, and in some art circles he was regarded as dangerously left-wing.

Despite glowing recommendations from W. G. Constable,

Walter Friedlaender and H. F. Stewart, he had been turned down for a Harris scholarship, a fellowship open to all applicants at King's. Stewart had described him as having 'a mind of great refinement and delicacy', while allowing that his primary allegiance was to art rather than French literature. It may be that Trinity and King's now regarded him as too Marxist; it is equally possible that it was felt that there was no room for an art scholar, which was, in effect, what Blunt had become.

The answer seemed to be a job in art history, and, despite their limited funds, both Fritz Saxl and W. G. Constable came up with positions for Blunt, at the Warburg and the Courtauld. Saxl, Blunt later recalled, 'in that marvellous way he did, decided he wanted to take me on. There was no money and no job, so he invented a job, which was in fact to look after the publications, which I'd absolutely no qualifications for, and there was no money so he went out and got it – I don't know where from.' The problem was that both jobs were part-time and poorly paid. Moreover, Lord Lee, head of the Courtauld management committee and one of the Warburg's main patrons, protested against Blunt's appointment because of his left-wing views. Money in particular preyed on Blunt's mind. In April 1937 he wrote to Gertrude Bing, Saxl's partner and colleague, that the Courtauld job would take up 'much more than half of one's time. It would be paid £400 a year to which I could add at least £200 by journalism. If I took up the Warburg work it would no doubt mean that I should have to give up this journalism.' On the other hand, he worried that journalism 'is probably such a bad thing for me that it would in any case be a good thing to give it up before I become a real and incurably superficial journalist'.

That resolution did not last long. 'I am trying to get the job of art critic to the *Sunday Times*,' he confessed sheepishly to Bing a few weeks later.

> I am doing this not because I want to go on doing this kind of journalistic stuff, but because it is a very well paid job which would give me a living wage or nearly a living wage

for very little work, so that I would have a great deal of freedom for my own work, and for such things as you suggest for the Warburg. I feel very doubtful whether I shall get it ... I know for certain of several serious candidates who are applying for it – serious I mean in the journalistic world, not of course as scholars!

He didn't get it. In May he applied for the Slade professorship at London University, a lectureship that usually went to figures of some renown, like Roger Fry: 'I don't think there is any more than a very faint chance of my getting it,' he wrote to Saxl, 'but I want at any rate to have a shot at it.' He asked Saxl for a testimonial which would emphasize how close he was to publishing his book, adding that he had discussed his 'Slade attack' with his other mentor, Andrew Gow. He also asked him whether 'perhaps a word could be said' to the vice-chancellor of London University. 'I still think it was a good thing to try for it,' Blunt reassured himself after this attempt also failed. 'But I am getting a little tired of failing to get jobs and then being told that it was only because I was too young.'

In *Letters from Iceland*, which came out that year, Auden and MacNeice wrote 'Last Will and Testament', an overextended joke in which they left appropriate presents to everyone they knew. MacNeice left 'to my old friend Anthony Blunt' a deliberately surreal combination of 'A copy of Marx and £1000 a year / And the picture of Love Locked Out by Holman Hunt'. A thousand pounds was what Blunt needed to finish his book and pursue his art history, though obviously the juxtaposition of a tidy private income and Marx was supposed to rile. As was the inclusion of a particularly prim Pre-Raphaelite painting, which these days Blunt's ideological stance obliged him to take seriously, though it was completely at odds with his personal taste. As for the painting's subject matter, it was probably a not especially discreet reference to Blunt's homosexuality, though MacNeice may also have intended it to refer to Blunt's own cloistered heart, suggesting that his old friend had chosen to lock love out.

Blunt was downcast by his attempts to turn his thesis into a book on Italian and French art theory. 'It is far too amateur a piece of work,' he complained to Gertrude Bing.

> The most fatal thing is that my whole treatment of the earlier part, dealing with the Italian Renaissance is faulty ... It is arguable that I ought not to publish it at all in its present form ... It may still be necessary from a careerist point of view to publish it in something like this form with the blatant mistakes taken out; this is the result of never having had any training in *Kunstgeschichte* at all and having like everyone else in England to plough through the whole thing from scratch without outside help.

These career worries dragged on. In June Blunt wrote excitedly to Saxl telling him that he'd been offered a year's work in America, in Pittsburgh, where Friedlaender was working. It is tempting to wonder what would have happened if Blunt had gone to America. The move would have put him beyond Burgess's reach, away from the Communist orbit of Cambridge. Saxl, for one, thought he would never come back and urged him not to go. He had other plans for Blunt.

> [The] collaboration between us would never take place. I should consider this undesirable not only from my point of view, but also from yours ... America ... is most stimulating and a very great experience, but an experience which I should rather wish you to have after having had a couple more years for your own work in art history. What you need most at the present moment is time and opportunity to go on and develop the work begun in the last years.

Blunt listened to Saxl and refused the offer. In the event, his indecision was final: he chose all three of his other options. At the end of June he finally committed himself to the Warburg, resolved to keep the journalism going, and offered himself as a tutor to the Courtauld.

As Blunt's last term at Cambridge came to an end, the Rothschilds organized a huge party at Merton Hall, their house opposite St John's College. The occasion coincided with the arrival of Haile Selassie at the Cambridge Union, which had given him an honorary membership to demonstrate its solidarity with beleaguered Abyssinia. There was champagne, caviar and fireworks. 'I don't remember a party ever like this,' recalled Leonard Miall, a contemporary of Michael Straight's at the Union. 'It was straight out of Evelyn Waugh, we were in tails and slightly drunk. Cab Calloway was playing duets with Victor Rothschild. It was a lovely, balmy night, there was a supper of caviar and vodka on the terrace.' Everyone got extremely drunk, including Blunt.

At the far end of the gardens, which stretched down to the Cam, Miall and his friend Charles Fletcher Cooke wandered past 'a raffia bower in which Anthony was lying deep in the embrace of a youth from Pembroke. Which was no surprise to anybody.' Except of course that Blunt was usually extremely discreet. Miall returned to the party for more caviar, and

> much later on, I wandered past again, and there was Anthony in exactly the same position, this time with the wife of a don at Jesus. Still later I was listening to Cab Calloway playing the piano, and in came Anthony looking for a drink. I said to him, 'Aren't you being a little fickle tonight?' He put his finger up against his nose and said 'Many a fickle makes a fuckle!'

The lady in question, with whom Blunt apparently decided to try out heterosexual sex, has usually been assumed to be Patricia Rawdon-Smith, still an undergraduate but by then the errant wife of a young science don. Patricia Parry, as she had been, was Tess Mayor's best friend, and, while Tess was famous for being the most beautiful girl at Cambridge, Patricia was known for being sexy, bright and politically radical. (She leaned more to socialism than to Communism, and later in life became a Labour peer.) Her marriage to Anthony Rawdon-Smith, an Apostle and don with a personal fortune, proved a rash move, and it collapsed soon after she left Cambridge the following year. 'She had lots of affairs, she liked to sleep with interesting men, and she was frightfully serious about her politics,' remembered Stuart Hampshire. As for Blunt's brief fling with her, it became widespread gossip among his set. Sixty years later octogenarian contemporaries were still dishing the dirt on this short-lived affair.

Before Michael Straight left for America he met Blunt in London on Oxford Street and they went to a 'Roadhouse' (a pub) on the Great West Road, where they met 'a stocky, dark-haired Russian', most likely Arnold Deutsch (who was Czech by birth and Austrian by upbringing). Straight pronounced himself unimpressed. Blunt tore an old postcard in half, giving one half to Straight and telling him the other half would be produced by his American contact. Straight returned to the States and got a job working for the government's economic adviser. In spring 1938, when working in the Department of State, he was contacted by a 'Russian' calling himself Michael Green. Though Straight insisted he never passed any secret documents, he did admit that he provided Green with four or five commentaries while he had a job at the US Department of the Interior, along with 'a plea to the Soviet government to give up its revolutionary ideology in the interests of world peace'. According to recent researches in the Soviet Intelligence Archives, Straight also recommended to Michael Green a rising star in the State department, whom he had noticed had 'progressive', pro-Communist views: Alger Hiss. Unbeknownst to Straight, Hiss was, of course, already working for the Soviets.

Blunt's work for the NKVD came to a stop not just because he had left Cambridge, but because in the summer of 1937 Stalin's purges reached Soviet Intelligence. The European illegals were recalled to Moscow one by one, and the London *rezidentura* was left virtually unmanned for nearly three years. In March 1937 the new head of the NKVD, Nikolai Yezhov, who had already deposed his former boss, Yenrik Yagoda, and imprisoned his department chiefs, announced to a group of senior intelligence officers that the NKVD had been penetrated by a Trotskyist conspiracy. Yezhov told them that their former boss had been recruited by the German secret service. The intelligence officers nervously applauded, and then lined up to save their skins by informing on each other. Under the new regime, illegals like Arnold Deutsch and Theo Maly – educated foreigners, independent of thought – were deeply suspect. 'We are international Communists,' the illegal Walter Krivitsky told his colleagues who had witnessed Yezhov's performance, 'our time is over. They will replace us with Soviet Communists . . . to whom the revolutionary movement means nothing.' Krivitsky fled to the United States, where he turned himself over to the American authorities and wrote a series of alarming articles about the purges. He was found dead in his hotel bedroom in 1941. Whether it was murder or suicide – he was profoundly depressed at the time – has never been established.* An illegal called Ignace Poretsky, Krivitsky's friend and colleague, fled the summons to Moscow and went to Switzerland with his family. He was assassinated in his car in September 1937. He had been rash enough to send an open letter to the Central Committee:

> I should have written the letter I am writing to you today a long time ago, on that day when the Sixteen were massacred in the cellars of the Lubianka on the orders of the 'Father of the People' . . . I bear a heavy responsibility . . . Up to this moment I marched alongside you. Now I will not take another step . . . the day when international socialism will judge the crimes committed in the past ten years is not far off.

Of those who had run the London *rezidentura*, Arnold Deutsch's first boss, Ignace Reif, was shot as a German and Polish Spy. Alexander Orlov escaped to America. He had been posted to Spain, where he managed Kim Philby and oversaw the shipping

---

* The not especially reliable former KGB agent Pavel Sudaplatov says in his memoirs that the NKVD didn't kill Krivitsky, and assumed he had killed himself. 'We were not sorry to see him go.'

of the Spanish Republic's gold to Moscow (whence it has never returned), and survived by writing directly to Stalin that, if he or any of his family were touched, a letter he had deposited in a Swiss bank would reveal various highly embarrassing operational details concerning Russian involvement in the Spanish war. He lived quietly in America until Stalin's death, after which he published two lurid books about Soviet Intelligence and Stalin's crimes. Among the things he did not reveal in them was his detailed knowledge of the Cambridge group. Theo Maly went back to Moscow in the early summer of 1937, knowing quite well what awaited him, 'They will kill me here and they will kill me there. Better to die there,' he told Ignace Poretsky's wife. And to Orlov, 'I have decided to go there so that nobody can say: "That priest might have been a real spy after all."' He was shot as a German spy in 1938. Arnold Deutsch returned to Moscow in autumn 1937, mainly because Special Branch was about to break the Woolwich Arsenal Ring. This group of British agents had been recruited by Deutsch, and was managed by Percy Glading who, in his capacity as a senior Communist Party member had persuaded the initially reluctant Klugmann that he must accept his recruitment by Deutsch. In Moscow, Deutsch somehow avoided execution and went on to work as a handwriting and forgeries expert. He was not permitted to go abroad until 1942. He is variously described as having been captured and shot by the Nazis after parachuting into Austria; or as having drowned en route to New York – where he was due to work with the NKVD's American recruits – when his ship was sunk by a U-boat.

The Cambridge spies never knew what happened to their first NKVD contacts, even though they had in some cases developed close, even filial, relationships with them. In the summer of 1937 Theo Maly appears to have gone to some lengths to absolve the young Philby of any blame for having failed to carry out a harebrained scheme initiated by Moscow to assassinate Franco. He openly criticized his bosses for coming up with tasks that were plainly impossible for his agents to perform.

*

After Blunt's uncharacteristically exhibitionist exit from Cambridge, he went to stay with his mother at Pond House in Ham. In July, Julian Bell, just back from a trip to China, was killed in Spain. There was a terrible irony in the fact that, in deference to his mother's fears and pacifist beliefs, he had gone as an ambulance man, rather than as a soldier as he would have preferred.* Blunt failed to write in commiseration to his ex-lover's mother for over a year. When Vanessa Bell finally wrote to ask if he had any correspondence to put into a memorial volume, his answer was polite, embarrassed, and distant:

> I hardly like even to ask to be forgiven for not answering your letter sooner. I am afraid it was very remiss of me, and can only plead that I have been hopelessly busy for the last weeks . . . I am afraid I have no letters of Julian's. I never had very many from him, and hardly ever keep letters at all. I will look again, but I feel fairly certain that I have nothing. I look forward very much to reading the book.

He reported that Guy Burgess had spoken to 'someone who had met Julian when he was at the front and had evidently seen a good deal of him. He spoke of him in the highest terms, particularly of the incredible energy which Julian showed in taking on all sorts of jobs which were not really part of his ordinary duty.'

If Bell's death did affect Blunt, the feelings were channelled into his writing. He had been told by his recruiters to distance

* The American writer Stephen Koch has claimed that it was 'Blunt and his people who guided Julian Bell towards Spain, where he was killed.' This is not true. Blunt saw Bell, who was in China for the eighteen months before he went to Spain, perhaps once during the short period between his return from China and his trip to Spain. They were no longer close friends. Bell's brother Quentin has said, 'Nobody forced Julian to go to Spain except himself. Most of his Communist friends tried to dissuade him – that's certainly true of Guy Burgess and Stephen Spender. Julian was interested in military history. He enjoyed it enormously for the short time he was there, as he knew he would.' His letters to his mother from China make it clear that 'There was no question but that Julian was coming home with a desire to fight.'

himself from Communism, and this he did by never explicitly discussing his politics. At the same time his journalism had never been more hard-line, as his essay in *The Mind in Chains*, a collection of earnest pro-Soviet articles on Marxism and culture, edited by Cecil Day-Lewis, demonstrated. *The Mind in Chains* was one of a flood of left-wing books about culture and politics that came out in 1937: among the others were the Marxist critic Philip Henderson's *The Novel Today*, Ralph Fox's *The Novel and the People*, Alick West's *Crisis and Criticism* and Christopher Caudwell's *Illusion and Reality*, as well as Stephen Spender's idiosyncratic *Forward from Liberalism*. Even the *Spectator* was caught up in the debate over audience and politics, devoting a whole issue to 'reaching the public'.

Blunt's essay, 'Art Under Capitalism and Socialism', repeated the orthodox line which equated artistic achievement with ideological purity. It also announced that Marxism's great strength was that it replaced the unscientific subjective judgements of personal taste with objective standards with which to judge a work of art. These standards were the (political) ideas the work aimed to represent, and how effectively it represented them. The essay had an extremism and doctrinaire note out of step with the other benevolent-sounding, idealistic contributions. 'In the present state of Capitalism, the position of the artist is hopeless,' Blunt wrote. 'Now that the class struggle has grown more acute and has become the dominating fact in the world situation, any artist who cuts himself off from his class is automatically excluded from the possibility of taking part in the most important movement of his time.' His vision of art's future under Communism was a combination of dogma, naivety, and woolliness: 'The culture of the revolution will be evolved by the proletariat to produce its own culture,' he stated – a sentence that sounded as if it had been badly translated from a Russian cultural commissar's rule book. Artists would be public servants in 'the right relation to the society' in which they lived – in 'efficient' contact, no less. What that was he was unable to say, though he thought that easel painting would decline, and everyone would have posters of great paintings in their homes – destroying the idea of value residing in the uniqueness of an art work. 'If an art is not contributing to the common good, it is bad art,' he concluded.

Cyril Connolly, newly returned from Spain, where he had lost his enthusiasm for the Left, reviewed the book in the *New Statesman*. He noted how reassuring, naive and utopian most of the pieces were, and described their authors – in a pithily dismissive quotation that has often been repeated since – as part of 'the typically English band of psychological revolutionaries, people who adopt left wing political formulas because they hate their fathers or were unhappy at their public schools or insulted at the Customs or lectured about sex'. On this count Blunt scored three out of four. (The following year, in *Enemies of Promise* Connolly would rank politics top of his list of barriers to achievement, the others being drink, journalism, sex – homosexuality chiefly – and domesticity. Blunt was guilty of all of them except the last. Perhaps that was why his career was in the doldrums.) However, Blunt's essay was different: 'I don't think any painter can read [it] without an apprehensive shudder, its conception of art under Communism not being very different in form from that obtaining under Fascism.' If nothing else, the article set the stamp on Blunt's reputation as an intellectual Stalinist.

Blunt was far from unaware that there was a gulf between what he thought he should think and what his personal preferences were. He had come to believe that he must simply discount the latter. It was not just his Marxism that seemed to dictate this: his academic study seemed to demand it too. 'It is still an effort to me to eliminate likes and dislikes from what I say,' he wrote to Fritz Saxl, describing how he disliked the High Renaissance art of 'the Vasari gang in Florence' while being obliged to acknowledge their importance. In the *Spectator* that April he had written of Picasso that his work appealed 'to those whose minds, like mine, are clogged in a love of the obscure and the unusual'. He went on, 'but it is doubtful whether it has much to contribute to the development of painting at the present time. It is the last refinement of a dead tradition . . . It is a lovely decay which will give pleasure to those who are themselves involved in the general decline of which it is the finest expression'. Speaking on modern art for the BBC in July the following year, he admitted:

> Now I had better say at once that, personally speaking, I do rather enjoy this kind of thing, particularly the abstract kind. On the other hand I think it is a very odd thing to like and I regard myself as rather odd for liking it. It seems to me a queer taste of a rather remote and not very valuable kind like, say, having a passion for higher mathematics.

Blunt's sacrifice of his own feelings about art would bring about another betrayal, in its way a paradigm of his recruitment. In August he went to the 1937 Paris Exhibition. Organized by Leon Blum's popular front government as a celebration of culture and civilization, the event was an extravaganza in the tradition of the Great Exhibitions and World Fairs of the Victorian and Edwardian era. It featured three enormous exhibitions of nine-teenth-century, contemporary French, and foreign avant-garde art, and a series of national pavilions celebrating cultural achieve-ments. In hindsight it is easy to see the event was ominously dominated by the German and Soviet pavilions, two mammoth monoliths which stood opposite each other on the right bank of the Seine and dwarfed everything around them. The Soviet pavil-ion, Boris Iofan's thrusting skyscraper-like pedestal, was topped by two giant workers who, holding aloft a giant hammer, strode towards the German pavilion where they were faced by a huge fearsome imperial eagle perched on Albert Speer's giant sarcoph-agus-like tower. Inside, both pavilions were filled with official state art. Blunt wrote nothing about either. Maybe he felt it judicious to keep clear of the Soviets; more likely he found the art undiscussably bad.

The true star of the exhibition was the small Spanish pavilion organized by the Republican side. The building had been designed by a pupil of Le Corbusier; inside, photomontages showed images of contemporary Spain. There were posters, paintings and sculp-ture by, among others, Miró, Alexander Calder and Picasso. At its heart was *Guernica*, Picasso's response to the firebombing of the Basque town.

'I was very much moved by it,' Blunt wrote of *Guernica* years later, 'but I was horrified by it from a theoretical point of view.' He mentioned it only briefly in his column, and chose to put political priorities before aesthetic and emotional ones. 'The painting is disillusioning. Fundamentally it is the same as Picasso's bull-fight scenes. It is not an act of public mourning, but the expression of a private brain-storm which gives no evidence that Picasso has realised the political significance of Guernica.' Two months later, as *Guernica* toured Britain to raise money for the Spanish cause, Blunt wrote again about Picasso. This time his subject was *The Dream and Lie of Franco*, the series of nine etchings and a short poem which Picasso had produced to raise money for the Republican side. It was obvious that the shadow of *Guernica* lay over the article, which was called 'Picasso Unfrocked'.

> There is something pathetic in the sight of a talented artist struggling to cope with a problem entirely outside his powers. This is the feeling aroused by Picasso as his contribution to the struggle in Spain. The *Sueno y Mentira de Franco* unquestionably expresses a genuine hatred for the Spanish rebels, and if it does nothing else it shows Picasso's heart is in the right place. But the questions remain: Where is his brain? and where are his eyes?

The etchings had 'the same nightmare atmosphere as the Guernica mural, and the conventions are in many ways the same as those which the artist has used for bull-fights and for all the private paintings of the last years. They are undoubtably terrifying . . . And this is Picasso's contribution to the Spanish civil war.' It was all wrong. Picasso had spent too much of his life in the 'Holy of Holies of Art'. He was no longer communicating with the people:

> for the initiate [his paintings] grew in significance, but for the world they became ever more remote and unreal. And

now the earthquake which is shaking the world has brought the artfully constructed temple toppling down and the inhabitants of it are thrown out into the open air and find themselves in a real world full of unpleasantness ... In his new etchings and poems Picasso seems to be aware of what is going on around him, but not of its real meaning. And, indeed, how could he be? For so many years he has been unaccustomed to looking anything in the face, that when he needs to do so he does not know how to set about it. What he does is to register horror – genuine, but useless horror. Useless, because all that these etchings will do is to make certain of the devotees feel that at last they have made contact with reality ... whereas they have not really stepped a yard outside their old circle. The etchings cannot reach more than the limited coterie of aesthetes, who have given their life so wholly to the cult of art that they have forgotten about everything else. The rest of the world will at most see and shudder and pass by.

Blunt knew what Picasso should have done, he should have 'seen more than the mere horror of the civil war ... he should have realised that it is only a tragic part of a great forward movement ... he should have expressed this optimism in a direct way and not with a circumlocution so abstruse ... In the religious half-light of the temple Picasso looked a giant. Now, in a harsher glare, and up against more exacting standards, he appears a pigmy.'

It was a far more vivid piece than Blunt's usual fare – a sure sign that strong feelings were involved. And indeed they were: Blunt hated *Guernica*, or rather what it stood for, because it showed that Picasso had chosen to do the opposite of what he had done – given up choice, judgement, art – and because he knew, deep down, that Picasso was right and he was wrong.

Herbert Read rushed to Picasso's defence. He believed that the painting was a masterpiece, a 'modern Calvary, the agony in the bomb-shattered ruins of human tenderness and faith' – an image that Blunt would later borrow. In his letter to the *Spectator* he pointed out that not only was Picasso actively linked to the Republican cause – he had accepted the honorary directorship of the Prado at its invitation – but that hundreds of thousands of postcards of the Franco cartoons had already been sold, showing that Picasso's work was accessible and popular. 'It is only too evident to anyone who knows the real facts that the particular form of opposition to modern art adopted by Mr Blunt comes from middle-class doctrinaires who wish to "use" art for the propagation of their dull ideas.' Moreover, Read added, Picasso and his supporters 'have had rather more experience of the actual horrors of war than Mr Blunt and other ideologists of his generation.'

Blunt replied, chastened and disingenuous, that he had never tried to 'use art for some end', nor had he ever said that Picasso was a bad artist – just that his was 'the last refinement of a private art' and 'therefore not easily applied to public problems'. Such art did not have 'the far-reaching importance which it seems to have for the specialists'.

When, in another article in that issue of the *Spectator*, Blunt wrote that what Picasso and other modern artists like him needed was 'a revitalisation of art by contact with life', Read wrote in again. This time it was to ridicule Blunt's universal panacea: 'I can only suspect that by "contact with life" your correspondent means something like "contact with a political party" or "contact with a particular section of the workers".' Blunt answered that 'contact with life' meant 'merely an awareness of what is taking place outside one's own room and studio'.

Then Picasso's friend Roland Penrose wrote in to take Blunt to task for suggesting that Picasso's response had been inappropriate – 'it would be of little use to disguise the suffering of the Spanish people with starry-eyed platitudes', Penrose wrote. He attacked Blunt for making a distinction between 'private' and 'public' art. It was, Penrose said, personal emotion in art that made it universal; it was impossible to separate 'private' from 'public' emotions. Blunt, who had done just that to himself, replied with another lengthy defence which concluded that personal emotion had its place, 'though I think its importance is constantly over-emphasised'. It is clear that he badly needed to believe this.

Beyond the columns of the *Spectator*, the debate 'was all carried out in the most friendly manner, because Read and I happened to be members of the same club', Blunt later wrote. He had joined the Reform Club in May, sponsored by his old friend Dennis Proctor. 'We used frequently to meet there by chance, and one would say to the other "I hope that you did not take my saying that you were stupid and wrong etc. in my last letter in any personal manner", and we would then go and have lunch together.' Read had encouraged Blunt's writing, and, though Blunt had frequently disagreed with him before, it was always on the most respectful terms. They also had a mutual friend in the capricious Douglas Cooper, who seems to have egged Blunt on to attack Read for his support of modernism.*

For Blunt, the gap between the two sides of himself – 'thought' and 'feeling' – had never been clearer. He regretted the damning article almost the minute it appeared. When he died in 1983 his executors found one of the special limited editions of *The Dream and Lie of Franco* he had so excoriated among his possessions. It seems he had bought it in 1937.

* After the war Blunt opened a Picasso retrospective at the Institute of Contemporary Arts, which had been founded by Penrose and Read.

9. Art Historian

'He was frightfully smart and absolutely enthralling'

In London, Blunt moved into a flat at 30 Palace Court, a mansion block in the Edwardian red-brick style he detested, on the north side of Hyde Park. It consisted of a large front room filled with books, and a smaller one at the back, also piled high with them, where the Poussin *Rebecca and Eliezer* hung alongside a Picasso he didn't own (probably something loaned to him by Douglas Cooper). He gave occasional parties there – the few occasions on which his new academic circle, his Cambridge friends, and an increasingly odd carnival of Burgess's acquaintances came together to mix. 'Anthony had a few peculiar friends whom I wouldn't have asked into my house,' Margot Wittkower remembered. 'He gave a lot of parties and there were sometimes very odd characters, but if that was the way he wanted his visitors, well, it was not a reason not to like him.' Another visitor, Edgar Wind, reported that Blunt's parties were full of 'young boys', though he also met Isaiah Berlin at one of them.

Thus settled, Blunt began in earnest to pursue a career in academic art history. His arrival at the Warburg on 13 September 1937, thirteen days short of his thirtieth birthday, was a crucial turning point in his career. With its scholarship and its almost metaphysical belief that art was a manifestation of the triumph of reason over chaos, the Warburg attracted him enormously. He felt at home there. 'He was utterly charming – wonderful manners – was very polite,' remembered one of his colleagues. The job that Fritz Saxl had created for him was as a general editor for the

Warburg's publications, which included new books by well-respected European scholars such as Jean Adhémar and Jean Seznec. Saxl wanted the books to feel more 'English' – a euphemism for the fact that, while the foreign scholars persevered in English, many were still dreadful at it. Blunt, the conscientious stickler for detail, was perfect for the job, and he showed extreme dedication. Even his holidays were spent in daily contact with the Institute.*

'I'd never had a day's training in art history,' he said later. 'There was no means of doing so in this country . . . Coming into this professional atmosphere was of enormous importance to me. In five minutes one learnt more from Saxl than in an hour from anyone else.' The art historian John Pope-Hennessy, paying a characteristically backhanded compliment, agreed. Saxl, he wrote, 'transformed Anthony Blunt from a jejeune Marxist journalist into one of the most accomplished art historians of his day'. Saxl helped him in particular with his book, which had become an albatross. Blunt realized now that the project had been overambitious, and he was embarrassed by its generalizations and mistakes. It was, however, his only prospect for a publication, and he needed something in print to get his career off the ground. The first half, on Renaissance art theories, was a rehash of published material (most of it in German) on famous artists like Michelangelo on whom he was far from expert; the second half was his own research on seventeenth-century French theories of art. Together they made an unwieldy whole. 'I am most grateful for all your suggestions,' he wrote to Saxl, 'I think I have put in almost everything that you proposed.'

It was the big, affable deputy director, Rudi Wittkower, however, who became Blunt's closest Warburg colleague, and from whom he later felt he had learned most. Blunt made a weekly pilgrimage to the Wittkowers' home, where Rudi lent him rare

* In August 1938, after nearly a letter a day had passed between them, Blunt's Warburg office contact wrote apologetically, 'Sorry to encroach so regularly on your "holiday".'

books and encouraged his interest in architectural history. He also made Blunt a co-editor of the new *Journal of the Warburg Institute* which he and Edgar Wind were putting together. 'You know how much I admired and loved him,' Blunt wrote to Margot Wittkower after her husband's death thirty-five years later,

> and I can truly say that I learnt more from him than from anyone. In fact he was really my only master – because though I was thirty when we met I had, as you will remember, no training at all, and it was my short period at the Warburg and – with him – the relationship during the War years, that gave me any idea of method that I may have.

Six years older than Blunt, Wittkower was warm, extrovert and very ambitious – he was the son of middle-class parents who had been financially ruined. He already had impressive publications to his credit, including a catalogue of drawings by Bernini and a ground-breaking article, 'Carlo Rainaldo and the Roman Architecture of the Full Baroque', the first account in English of the achievements of the seventeenth-century architect Francesco Borromini. Blunt was profoundly influenced by it, and profoundly grateful to Wittkower. He began to lecture on Borromini at the Courtauld. Looking back, another émigré, Richard Krautheimer, reflected that 'It seemed entirely appropriate that Wittkower should write about Bernini the extrovert, and Blunt about Borromini the introvert – an impossible, tortured man who never kept a deadline and was impossible with his patrons.'

It was Wittkower who supervised and published Blunt's first research articles. The first issue of the *Journal of the Warburg Institute*, which came out in 1938, was so embarrassingly short of contributions that Wittkower and Wind were forced to write most of it themselves, and Blunt was encouraged to contribute too. His first article was on Balzac's 'Criminal King' – a piece which obliquely, in its Lukácsian subject matter, showed the influence of Friedrich Antal, from whom Blunt was also receiving guidance on his book. The second article showed how the *Hypnerotomachia Poliphili*, a medieval romance with woodcuts published in 1499, had influenced seventeenth-century perceptions of antiquity. The research came from Blunt's thesis, but the treatment was Warburgian, and Blunt was heavily edited by Wittkower. 'I have absolutely no critical sense about things of this kind and am incapable of judging true from false and important from irrelevant,' Blunt wrote to him in 1937, adding a few weeks later that he had 'incorporated pretty well all that you and Wind suggested'.

Blunt's most important piece, however, was written almost as an afterthought – 'the results, incomplete though they are, seem worth publishing', he told Wittkower. It became his first article on Poussin, and reported the results of his research into the artist's collected philosophical observations about art: that every one had been derived from the earlier writers, mainly Tasso and Quintilian. It showed that Poussin might have lacked originality but that he had been extremely learned – a fact which became a linchpin of Blunt's vision of the artist as a painter-philosopher. Two further articles on Poussin came out in 1938. One demonstrated the artist's familiarity with Greek philosophy and how he used it in his early paintings. The other was Blunt's first published attribution: an *Augustus and Cleopatra* which he believed was a lost Poussin. It had been discovered, and was now owned, by his friend the dealer Tomás Harris. (In future years, Blunt was to tell his students not to publish anything about paintings that were already owned by dealers. It was good advice, but it was a view he had arrived at the hard way: this first attribution was wrong. To compound the error, in 1953 Blunt recommended that the National Gallery of Canada, which he was advising on art purchases, should buy the painting. *Augustus and Cleopatra* was de-attributed in the 1960s.)* Blunt's Poussiniste credentials were

* There have been suggestions that this incident provides evidence that Blunt was dishonest in his attributions and was 'in business' with Harris. This seems unlikely. Harris did not sell the picture until 1953, and when Blunt made the attribution in 1938 he was not yet known as a Poussin expert, and would have had nothing to gain – and a great deal to lose – if his first attribution had been discovered to be wrong.

impressively confirmed the following year, when he was cited as Friedlaender's collaborator on the first volume of his catalogue of Poussin's drawings.

The Warburg's influence on Blunt was many-faceted. The Institute's preoccupation with cultural context resonated with what he had learned from Marxist criticism, and remained in his work long after all traces of Marxist dogma had disappeared. Its stress on the idea that the meanings of images resided in their iconography would steer his lifelong work on Poussin. Its emphasis on ancient and Renaissance esoteric written sources would inform his study of William Blake, Poussin and Borromini. Most of all, the Warburg scholars' scholarship and their very survival despite the threat of Nazi persecution confirmed Blunt's belief that art history was a subject of vital importance to civilization and to human nature, and one which demanded an almost mystical depth of knowledge and devotion to accuracy.

Alongside his work at the Warburg, Blunt began to take a greater role at the Courtauld. He taught classes, which he had not done before, and was more often seen at Portman Square. His timing was fortuitous. The Institute was now desperate for energetic young teachers. By 1937 almost the entire staff, including Blunt's erstwhile patron W. G. Constable, its director, had left and the place had been threatened with closure. There had been problems since the Institute's beginning. It was chronically short-staffed and underfunded, and its aim to cover the whole of art history at every level had been overambitious. Nor had the art world been welcoming. In the pages of the *Sunday Times* the paper's art critic Frank Rutter had consistently attacked the Institute for favouring foreign art at the expense of British. At the *Architectural Review*, John Betjeman had accused it of making art 'the province of pedantry and donnishness' – an argument that fed the suspicions of the gentleman autodidacts and connoisseurs of the London galleries and dealerships. In fact there wasn't much that was professional about the early Courtauld. Neither Constable nor any of his tiny staff had any experience in teaching, and it showed. Foreign students in particular were appalled by the lack of structured courses and found the teaching alarmingly primitive. The story went that in the first year, in order to try out the exam papers, the staff had submitted their questions to Kenneth Clark, then Director of the National Gallery. If he couldn't answer a question, it was judged to be a bit too hard. When the students' papers were marked, it was discovered that no one had passed. Nor were Constable's eminent foreign lecturers always a great success. After the head of the Prado delivered the first of three lectures in English, the students petitioned for the rest to be given in Spanish because, although 'they didn't understand Spanish, they thought he would probably make more sense'. On another occasion, Walter Friedlaender read a lecture that Blunt had translated for him into English. After struggling awkwardly with the words for half an hour or so, Friedlaender gave up, flung down his papers, walked up to the projection screen, pointed at the painting, and said, 'Lovely picture – I like him!'

Most of all, the Institute couldn't seem to decide whether it wanted to be a place of serious academic learning or a finishing school for young ladies. An endless stream of girls from grand country houses, most of them arriving under the auspices of the frighteningly correct and eternally be-gloved librarian Rhoda Welsford, came for the one-year diploma course, which provided what Herbert Read slightingly described as 'a smattering of secondary school art history'. 'You do *close* during the season?' one of these girls had apparently asked at interview. Lord Lee – who interfered constantly (and who had protested at Blunt's appointment at the Warburg) – wanted the place to have a social cachet. Nor was the usually fearsomely serious Sir Robert Witt averse to the young ladies. It was delicately said that he took 'a great interest' in them. In fact he was a serial groper, and no woman who came within his orbit was safe. He was known as 'the massage king' – 'because he couldn't keep his hands off us', recalled Mrs Constable. Since Sir Robert was leaving his collection of drawings to the Institute, the women were encouraged to suffer in silence and went everywhere in pairs until arthritis confined Witt to a wheelchair and his own home.

Things came to a head in 1936, when London University, to which it was affiliated, complained that the Institute's standards were inadequate. Constable suggested they cut their losses and turn the Courtauld into a postgraduate research centre with public lectures. The Institute's founding fathers utterly disagreed. Samuel Courtauld, who was a self-taught enthusiast, was insistent that the Institute should not turn away those hungry to learn. Witt was critical of Constable. In a report on the Institute he concluded, 'The teaching staff complain, and with justice, that some students are neither adequately equipped nor serious. Some students complain, and perhaps with equal justice, that the system of teaching could be substantially improved.' Lee had a dislike of 'experts' and 'highbrows', and his resistance to change may have stemmed from a fear that he might lose control of the Institute to them. Irritated and frustrated, Constable resigned. The tantrum-throwing Lee flew into a temper and simultaneously tried to threaten and sweet-talk him into staying. He accused him of having coveted the job of director of the National Gallery as well as the Courtauld, and of being 'consumed by personal ambition' and 'insane jealousy' of Kenneth Clark – a story Clark, who had been Lee's protégé, repeated in his own memoirs years later, though no one else seemed to believe it. The art world accused Lee and Witt of hounding out Constable, and a petition to reinstate him was sent to Senate House. 'Lord Lee was very very nice to be with,' Mrs Constable recalled in 1980, 'as long as absolutely everything was done absolutely according to his wishes.'* Within six months the deputy and assistant directors, the registrar, the head of the science lab, and the photographic

* After Constable left, Lee tried to get him a job as art critic of the *Sunday Times* without telling him. When Constable discovered this he refused to apply for the job, writing to Lee that he had already 'wholeheartedly backed' another man – this might have been Blunt. Constable went to the USA to become curator of paintings at the Boston Museum of Fine Arts and enjoyed a long museum career.

and library assistants and typists – almost the entire permanent staff – had left. By mid-1937 the Institute was tottering, and Lee's appointment of Tom Boase, an Oxford don with no art-history background at all, was not reassuring.

Despite the Institute's troubles, Blunt decided that it was worth persevering with, if only because the lack of staff meant he might get a permanent post there. He discussed the matter with Saxl and Constable: 'I believe I shall be asked to be on the Board of Studies which is I imagine a useful body from the point of view of getting into the organisation of the Institute. So I shall accept if I get the offer.' From the moment he became a fixture Blunt made a big impact on the place and its inmates. Stephen Rees Jones, a lab technician, who eventually came to run the Courtauld's science department, soon decided that he was different from the other lecturers, most of whom 'weren't art historians, they were gentleman connoisseurs'. Blunt's association with the Warburg gave him, to some eyes at least, an extra cachet. Another new arrival, Margaret Whinney, conceived a hopeless devotion for him, paralleled by, or perhaps indivisible from, her devotion to the Institute. Whinney – hard-working, honourable, humourless and unmarried – was thirteen years older than Blunt, and was gradually edging her way from the slide library into teaching, through her indefatigable willingness to take on the dullest jobs. She was the first and the most faithful in a line of innocent, spinsterish ladies who would haunt the Institute throughout Blunt's time there and sigh for him in vain. 'Margaret was devoted to Anthony. Embarrassingly so,' recalled one student of the time. 'She adored him, but she knew it was hopeless,' said another.

Blunt's pupils remembered him as cutting quite a figure. He was tall and surprisingly well dressed, in a blue-and-white pinstripe suit, with a blue shirt and a scarlet tie – a dandyish mark of Communist sympathies. In an additional gesture of deliberate nonconformity he refused to wear a hat.

'He was frightfully smart and absolutely enthralling,' remembered Olivier Bell, one of Blunt's first students, whose father, A. E. Popham, ran the prints and drawings department at the

British Museum, and who later married Quentin Bell. 'He lectured to us on the history of aesthetics. Gripping stuff. We were spell-bound. He was an exciting teacher – one felt one was expanding one's world. I had tutorials with him, and had become under his influence a mad Poussiniste.' Another pupil, Cecil Gould, who went on to become Keeper of Paintings at the National Gallery, instantly conceived a bad case of hero worship. After Blunt's death he wrote to Wilfrid that Anthony had been 'glamour personified'. For a while Gould even dressed like Blunt. 'Though I was still in my 'teens when I first met him,' Gould later wrote,

> I recognised at once that he was the star among the Cour-
> tauld lecturers. You only needed to be with him for a few
> moments to be aware of this. Other people thought him
> handsome, and perhaps he himself did. But it was not a
> conventional kind of good looks. With his very long, thin
> and bony face and rather prominent front teeth he looked a
> little like the Mad Hatter. The great height and the exqui-
> sitely modulated and melodious speaking voice, combined
> with the mental alertness, which took in immediately what
> you were driving at and as immediately threw it back with
> a pertinent comment – these were more impressive than a
> consideration of his features.

At the time, Gould, in the grip of his youthful admiration, told other Courtauld students that Blunt conducted his tutorials, which he often taught at his flat, from the bath. They didn't believe him. 'Cecil was naive and given to great exaggerations,' one remembered. In a memoir he later wrote about Blunt, Gould did not mention the bath, while musing, a little Pooterishly, on Blunt's intentions:

> Very often my tutorials with him took place at his flat in
> Palace Court, Bayswater, sometimes in the evenings. On
> looking back in the light of later events I have sometimes
> wondered whether his initial idea in suggesting this venue

was one of possible seduction. Knowing what I did later of his habits I think it not impossible that he may have had some such idea. But he soon abandoned it. I had at that time no sexual experience of any kind and this possibility never occurred to me. I was regarded indeed, as I know, as being as immature in a worldly sense as I was precocious as a student. For his part, Anthony never made the slightest advance, and I was so keen to learn all I could from him that I can never have given him the smallest encouragement. It may well be that I do him an injustice . . .

Teaching a subject he cared about, Blunt discovered, suited him. He had an innate need to explain, even to proselytize, and he responded to the intense yet controlled relationship between the mentor and the pupil. For him such relationships had been some of the most fruitful and nurturing of his life. He also enjoyed the admiration he inspired. Not everyone was quite so admiring, however: he could be impatient and intimidating. 'I somehow knew he didn't really like young women, though I didn't know what homosexuality was,' remembered Erica O'Donnell, whom he first taught in 1937:

When I read my essays out Anthony would walk up and down impatiently, flexing his fingers, though he was very courteous. As a lecturer he could be maddening. He would lower his voice when he came to a proper name. We'd get 'Piero mumble mumble'. So we'd rush off to the library, where we'd find Piero della Francesca and Piero di Cosimo . . . but which one? He gave lectures on Picasso too, and would say, 'Of course, as you know . . .', and of course we didn't.

By 1937 even the Courtauld's town-house gentility had been stirred by politics. Stephen Rees Jones discovered that a member of the photographic department was using laboratory chemicals to make little bombs to throw at fascist marches. There were two Marxist students, Ewen Philips, who went on to run the Institute of Contemporary Arts in the 1950s, and Millicent Rose, who lived with the critic Francis Klingender. When Herbert Read gave lectures on aesthetic theory, Rose heckled him so severely that she 'made him retreat back to the wall, his heels apparently trying to climb up the wainscot'. There was at least one fist fight over politics between a White Russian student and a Dutchman, who had to be physically separated by the caretaker, Mr Winkle.

When a Greek student called Zidis painted a mural of the staff in the student common room in 1938, Blunt was portrayed holding a glass of wine and a copy of Marx. However, he confined his politics to intellectual matters. Cecil Gould remembered coming across a copy of a memorial book on John Cornford at Blunt's flat, but could recall nothing he ever said about current politics. 'Though the international situation in 1939 was becoming increasingly ominous he only once referred to it. When I made some remark alluding to a date some months ahead he said, "We shall be at war by then." ' Blunt's most overtly political act at the Courtauld was to identify himself closely with the Warburg scholars. It was felt among the students that some of the staff and the management – 'the snobs' – were not especially friendly towards the Warburg people for professional or even perhaps anti-Semitic reasons. Blunt was an anti-snob. In 1938 he went with a group from the Warburg to an anti-fascist meeting at the Albert Hall, where Paul Robeson appeared.

Blunt's gamble on the Courtauld turned out to be a good one. Though, as Herbert Read had pointed out, he was an unlikely choice, the new director was a great success. Tom Boase was a history don whose specialism was the medieval papacy, with a sideline in crusader castles. He loved the theatre, counting Peggy Ashcroft and John Gielgud among his friends, was thought to be a non-practising homosexual, wore a glass eye, and looked, it was said, a little like T. S. Eliot. Certain Oxford colleagues, like Isaiah Berlin and Stuart Hampshire, considered him 'perfectly bland and middlebrow'; others suggested he was rather beady-eyed and calculating. But in the eighteen months he spent at the Institute before the war he reorganized all the courses and quietly got rid of the infamous one-year diploma, while managing to keep the management committee happy. He was encouraging and attentive, and came to every lecture. Recognizing that such links would raise the Courtauld's intellectual currency, he invited Warburg scholars in to teach and lecture regularly – an act which made a huge impression on many of the Institute's students – and in 1939 he proposed a collaboration with the Warburg on its journal, henceforward the *Journal of the Warburg and Courtauld Institutes*, with Blunt as the Courtauld's co-editor.

To the 'astonishment and shock' of Isaiah Berlin, Boase got on extremely well with Blunt. This was despite the fact that he was extremely right-wing – an anti-Communist and an appeaser. The two men needed each other, which helped; but their friendship went beyond that. Even after Boase returned to Oxford in 1947, Blunt 'would go and have tea with him' when he visited the university, Berlin recalled. 'He never came to see me.'

Beyond academia, Blunt was increasingly becoming a public intellectual. Thanks to Guy Burgess, who described him as a 'reputable art critic', Blunt made his first BBC broadcast – his first address to a mass audience – in January 1938, giving a talk on the Royal Academy's big winter exhibition of Dutch art. A few weeks later he gave another, on Michelangelo beginning the Sistine Chapel, for Burgess's series on *Forgotten Anniversaries*. Burgess told his boss George Barnes, an old King's acquaintance, that he wanted his talks to cater to the 'technician' class, workers who went to evening classes and 'read Darwin'. According to the broadcasting historian W. J. West, the Michelangelo talk was 'certainly the first talk about such matters treated at the highest level over the air'. Barnes worried that Blunt would be too highbrow, and he was evidently encouraged to make connections – sometimes wince-makingly – with the audience's 'ordinary' lives. Speaking of Dutch interiors, he told his listeners, 'The many housewives listening will see familiar domestic scenes.' Even so, the talks were rather good: clear, informative and immediate, not overtly Marxist but broadly informed by Marxism – the Sistine

Chapel was a great work of art because 'It is the most complete and most profound expression of what people felt and thought about the world at that time'; Dutch genre paintings were 'an eye-witness account of the past'. In a reading redolent of John Berger's analysis of Dutch portraiture thirty years later in *Ways of Seeing*, he observed of Rubens's portrait of the Duke of Buckingham, 'Buckingham . . . gives the impression of not being quite sure of himself. We feel that the one thing he cared about was to make everyone know how important he was . . . In fact, it is the portrait of an upstart.' More commissions followed.

In the pages of the *Spectator*, Blunt was heralding a new school of British realism – what would come to be known as the Euston Road School, after the small establishment that William Coldstream founded in October 1937 with his fellow artists Claude Rogers and Victor Pasmore. Blunt had begun to write lavishly complimentary articles about Coldstream, declaring him if not the equal then perhaps even the superior of Picasso. For though Picasso was unsurpassed in sheer 'talent' – positively a bad word in Blunt's lexicon – 'In the heaven of painting there are many studios, and, though it is unlikely that he will have to share one with Picasso, he will be in company no less distinguished. And even now he has his consolation: the future belongs to him, but Picasso belongs to the past.' Coldstream had left his salaried job at the GPO Film Unit to paint, and Blunt tried to find ways to put a little money his way. He introduced Coldstream to his old teacher Clifford Canning, now headmaster of Canford School in Dorset, who made the artist a part-time adviser to the school's art department in April 1937.* He got Coldstream to fill in for him occasionally at the *Spectator*, and encouraged him to ask the literary editor, Derek Verschoyle, for work.

Coldstream was no Communist, but his conversion to realism had come about for similar reasons to Blunt's. In 'How I Paint', which he published in the *Spectator* in September 1937, he wrote that

* Coldstream painted Canning's portrait in the 1940s.

The slump made me aware of social problems and I became convinced that art ought to be directed to a wider public; whereas all the ideas which I had learned to regard as *artistically* revolutionary ran in the opposite direction. It seemed to me important that the broken communications between the artist and the public should be built up again and that this most probably implied a movement towards realism.

He wanted to produce what he called 'ordinary realistic painting' – a cool, almost documentary style of painting that showed life as 'realistically' as possible. (His touching belief in the possibility of showing things 'as they really were' was an authentic period touch.) Blunt dubbed his portrait of Wystan Auden a 'most striking ordinary painting'. Coldstream wrote to the *Spectator* in support of Blunt over the Picasso debacle. Their closeness was noted. When Geoffrey Grigson, chief literary curmudgeon, reproved Auden in the pages of *New Verse* for his praise of Coldstream's paintings – 'very feeble, very theoretical and very corn-flake paintings they have all been to date', he wrote – he added, 'before you can say knife, if things don't stop, we shall have Mr Auden, victimized by morality, crisis, and idea, bluntly proclaiming the pre-eminent magnificence of Rivera'. The weak pun was clear for all those who followed art-world politics. (Grigson also wrote 'A Coldstream exhibition is like a double number of *Left Review*'.)

There was more to Blunt's affinity with Coldstream's work than politics. It was no accident that, as David Sylvester has written, the mainspring of Coldstream's painting was a 'holding back, a positive self-effacement', a refusal to impose himself on his work, which under normal circumstances would have been a shortcoming, but which Coldstream forced to his advantage. Those exact qualities were becoming, and would be, the hallmark of Blunt's own work, his writing, and ultimately his identity. (Blunt never had his portrait painted, but a Coldstream Blunt would have been an intriguing portrait: the self-effacing by the self-effacing.) Sylvester has also attributed to Coldstream 'an element of snobbism in setting out to do something so unfashionable as to paint banal subjects greyly from nature: so dowdy an activity must have appealed to his particular kind of dandyism (he is the very type of the Baudelairean dandy, with his *"air froid qui vient de l'inébranlable résolution de ne pas être ému"*)'. That sentence could have been written about Blunt – especially the references to inverted dandyism and suppressed passion: the 'coldness that comes out of a burning resolution not to be moved'.

Although Blunt seemed to embrace his new status as a public intellectual, and his predictions of a new movement in British art seemed to be coming to pass, his career as a proselytizing populist was actually in its final phase. The great burst of artistic energy, idealism and ideology that had fired English writers and artists during the 1930s was everywhere beginning to ebb. The excitement over the possibilities of a marriage of art and politics was beginning to wear off. This was evident at the last of the AIA's public debates, again between the Surrealists and their opponents, at the Group Theatre headquarters in Great Newport Street in March 1938. It was chaired by the Group Theatre's Robert Medley – fashionable theatre designer and friend of Auden and Coldstream. Once again Blunt faced Herbert Read – this time as a defender of the realists, and was supported by Coldstream, the South African painter Graham Bell and the Marxist literary critic Alick West. Read was accompanied by Roland Penrose and by two of Surrealism's most vociferous supporters: Blunt's old Cambridge *Experiment* rival Humphrey Jennings, who ran Penrose's London Gallery, and the painter Julian Trevelyan.

The debate was heated. Jennings in particular was extremely aggressive, and afterwards wrote, 'Our English Realists are not the tough guys they ought to be, but the effete and bastard offspring of the Bloomsbury school of needlework.' The realists in turn accused the Surrealists of 'pseudo-philosophical, pseudo-psychological, pseudo-literary, pseudo-phraseology which has nothing to do with art'. Both sides claimed victory. But things had changed: the Surrealists were no longer looking for confirmation of their political credibility. They simply argued that their paintings were better, and that the realists produced dull and gloomy work. Coldstream – demonstrating how ideology was ebbing out of British art – acknowledged that the Picasso and the Miró that the Surrealists had brought along were better than anything the realists side had produced, and that realism had 'no artist comparable in quality to Picasso'. Even Blunt, extolling Coldstream, could not dispute that next to Picasso, the realists were awfully dull. Coldstream, he wrote, was good because he had 'honesty'. 'In art, as in morals, honesty is often unexciting at first sight. But the test comes not at the first but at the fiftieth view; and it is not obvious which will look duller then – a Picasso or a Coldstream.'

Blunt's journalism had run out of steam too. It was repetitive: the same message was endlessly reiterated, the same apocalypse endlessly predicted. 'In the present state of Capitalism, the position of the artist is hopeless', he had written in *The Mind in Chains*. It seemed truer that Blunt's position was hopeless. In his less prescriptive moments he must have realized that he was trying to hold back the sea, that the whole of modern art was moving in the opposite direction to himself. Even Coldstream and the realists, whose work Blunt responded to personally, did not share his stance. Olivier Bell remembered a lecture Blunt gave on Diego Rivera at the Conway Hall in the summer of 1938:

> He was absolutely spellbinding. He said how wonderful it was – art by the people for the people – and, as I went out of the door with my gang and we were all thrilled, I saw in the background Bill Coldstream and Graham Bell. Graham had been sitting with his head in his hands, and I said 'What did you think?' And Graham said, 'It was horrifying.' I was shocked to the core, because as far as I was concerned this was great and exciting. My memory is that Graham didn't approve of him. Coldstream didn't commit himself either way, but Graham would embarrass me by coming into the

Courtauld and saying, 'I'm the person this place is all about,' very loudly.*

The sticking point was Blunt's demand that the artist must accept the dictates of his audience – or the state.

Coldstream was more explicit when Blunt interviewed him in the last of a four-part series he did for the BBC in June and July 1938, called *How I Look at Modern Painting*. The series was an unambiguous statement of Blunt's position, and made many listeners furious, while also attracting a brilliant parody in the form of a letter to the *Listener*.† Amicable though the conversation was, Coldstream consistently and politely rejected Blunt's equally polite suggestions that the artist must prostrate himself before his audience. 'It's no good painting a certain way merely because you think you "ought" to, unless such a subject or such a treatment comes naturally to you. So I don't think an artist should make it his primary aim to be understandable as that so often ends in his misjudging the intelligence of his public and becoming dull.'

In hindsight it is not altogether surprising that, in August, Blunt quit the *Spectator* column. He signed off with a three-part article, 'Standards', which stated the old arguments as robustly as ever. It

---

* Graham Bell shared many of Blunt's opinions on contemporary art. He criticized Henry Moore, whose imaginative brilliance he admired, because he felt that Moore 'saw his new idiom as a kind of private game which could only interest a select few', and he wrote with regret that 'Art now has so little relation to society.' Like Blunt, he viewed British abstraction as a kind of escapism, which he described in an article called 'Escape from Escapism' in *Left Review* in December 1937.

† Dictating what artists should paint was a very good idea, this writer thought: 'little thatched cottages . . . that's the sort of thing artists ought to paint and everyone I know thinks the same, although my wife would rather they did nice little kittens – fluffy ones'. He ended by querying Blunt's praise for Diego Rivera: 'Besides isn't the man a Communist or something? As though a Communist could paint pictures! . . . But perhaps Mr Blunt is pulling our legs.' It had the air not just of spoof, but of having been written by someone all too familiar with Blunt's personal political views – MacNeice perhaps, or Betjeman.

has been suggested that his resignation was in response to orders from the Soviets. This seems unlikely, as it was a year since he had been in touch with them. It is more likely, as John Pope-Hennessy later suggested, that the impetus was given by Fritz Saxl, who warned him that his articles 'would impede his acceptance as a serious art historian'.

There had, in those last two dogmatic years, been moments of artistic insight. Blunt wrote perceptively about the modernity of Rodin's sketches, on de Chirico's early work, on *Die Brücke* and its links with the German tradition of Cranach and Grünewald, and on the genius of Walter Gropius. However, the end of the columns marked virtually the end of his involvement in contemporary art, as well as the end of his overt Marxism. It also, to a great extent, ended his attempts to address a wider mass audience. It is ironic that he had so often castigated artists for a similar kind of withdrawal. 'I had become more and more shut off from what was happening and more and more concerned with the art of the past,' he admitted many years later, 'and since the war that has been my main preoccupation and I have very much lost touch altogether with contemporary painting, and indeed cannot comprehend much of what has happened in the last twenty or thirty years.'

That closing down was part of a general tendency in his life. When John Hilton met him in November 1938, having not seen him for several years, he was disappointed by his old friend. Hilton was married and living in Bristol. Blunt was visiting to open an exhibition and deliver a lecture, and came for dinner. 'I'd scarcely seen him for years, but he seemed the same brilliant, enthusiastic and entertaining person.' He'd brought a present, a wooden Komodo dragon for Hilton's new baby daughter, Blunt's latest godchild, 'but according to my wife didn't look at her'. And Hilton found the lecture 'abysmally dry and pedantic, flatly delivered'. He couldn't help but contrast the man on the podium with the schoolboy he had known and 'the irresistibly infectious enthusiasm he radiated about whatever was his current fancy. When he gave his lecture, a flame seemed to have died. Anthony shocked me by appearing to be a different person from the one I had thought I knew.'

He also showed little interest in mixing with the new circle of writers, artists and poets – Auden, Spender, Robert Medley and the composer Michael Tippett among them – who were congregating round Coldstream and the Euston Road School, and who frequented the bars and restaurants round Charlotte Street. Louis MacNeice was part of the set: he was having an affair with Coldstream's wife, while Coldstream was having an affair with Sonia Brownell, later Sonia Orwell. Nor did Blunt show a taste for Burgess's late-night life of drinking at the Gargoyle club with fashionable bohemian London, or picking up men at Soho dives with his friend Brian Howard, the Old Etonian queen who had recently announced his conversion to Communism, and Gerald Hamilton, the confidence trickster on whom Christopher Isherwood had based his anti-hero Mr Norris.

It sometimes seemed as if Blunt wanted to suppress his old exuberance. One letter to Fritz Saxl from around March 1938 illustrates this. He reported on an errand he had undertaken to examine nine folios of Poussin sketches from a Poussin enthusiast in the artist's birthplace, Les Andelys:

> I must, I think, report at once on my amusing, exhausting, interesting and lunatic visit to Les Andelys to see the engravings of Contil. M. Contil himself is in many ways so much more remarkable than the collection that there is a great temptation to write only of him . . . he is 82, almost blind, four times as active as I am, has a wholly uncritical passion for Poussin, cultivates a small estate, hates M. Blum, Mussolini, Hitler, Stalin, Chamberlain, the mayor, sous-préfet, préfet, député, sénateur . . . etc. etc. of the neighbourhood . . . In fact the whole episode was very *Bouvard et Pécuchet* with an occasional Stendhalian touch.

Contil had talked continually, mostly of 'the outrages which had been perpetrated on the seven different statues of Poussin which M. Contil has erected in the locality'.

Then, after a page of breathless enthusiasm, Blunt suddenly apologized for his gush, and asked Saxl to ignore his first page, finishing 'please do not file this'. It was as if he was suddenly embarrassed by his unfettered amusement and liveliness, as if he felt such a demonstration was unseemly. At other times he seemed half-proud and half-regretful of the effect his manner had on other people: 'It was very good seeing [Stuart] Hampshire in Paris,' he wrote to Isaiah Berlin in 1937, after being introduced to the young philosopher. 'Though I hear he has been saying the most savage things about me ever since. But to that I am by now used.' 'I rather think I'm becoming an intellectual snob,' he wrote half-jokily to Dadie Rylands, shortly after the war began. 'And that, as I so constantly have rubbed into me, is not what we want in the army. Do you think I shall ever be a "good mixer"? So far I am always getting it in the neck for being "cliquey".'

There was one person Blunt did not keep at a distance: Guy Burgess. Their relationship was compulsive, intimate, almost incestuous. Most evenings the two could be found at the Reform Club, where Burgess's drink of choice – a double port – was known as a double Burgess and Blunt saw art-world acquaintances like Ben Nicolson, the art-historian son of Harold Nicolson and Vita Sackville-West, and old friends like Dennis Proctor.

Burgess's life was growing racketier by the day. His home was a flat at 8 Chester Square, in Belgravia, decorated in his favourite colours, red, white and blue. It was famous for its squalor, permanently 'submerged in the indescribable debris and confusion of the party which had evidently taken place the night before'. Next to his bed he kept a copy of *Middlemarch*, two unfinished bottles of red wine and, according to Goronwy Rees, 'a very large, very heavy iron saucepan filled to the brim with a kind of thick, grey gruel, compounded of kippers, bacon and garlic, onion, and anything else that may have been lying around', which formed his main nutritional intake. He was no longer the pretty plump cherub he had once been. 'He was fascinating just to look at,' remembered Leo Long. 'In a sense he was revolting, a sort of

Dylan Thomas figure, who was larger than life, always drunk. He was a creature from a different world. Loud and camp.'

His love life was frenetic. In 1937 he set up with a twenty-year-old chorus boy called Jackie Hewit. Hewit was a working-class youth from Gateshead who had run away to London at fifteen. 'I was steeped in sin by the time I was ten or eleven,' he liked later to tell interviewers. Hewit worked his way up from sleeping rough to occasional jobs in the chorus of musical revues and working in hotels. He met Burgess and Blunt in 1937 at a party at the War Office given by Tom Wylie, to which he had been brought by a man he had met in a pub. (The Russian Intelligence Archives suggest that Burgess had been drugging Wylie on the orders of Arnold Deutsch, so he could examine the contents of the War Office safe.) Burgess had extricated Hewit from the insistent attentions of Rudolf Katz, the German Jewish Communist with whom he had written his financial newsletter for Victor Rothschild's mother, and had taken him home. Hewit, who was then unemployed and broke, stayed and became house-keeper, lover and valet – though not to much effect, as Burgess always managed to look as if he had fallen into a rubbish tip two minutes after he had dressed. He gave Hewit Paine's *The Rights of Man*. 'I told him I couldn't afford to be a socialist,' Hewit said.

'Jackie was sweet and silly, but with more sense than you thought,' recalled Burgess's other boyfriend of the time, Peter Pollock. Pollock, who was from a wealthy family of gentlemen farmers, was said to be so beautiful that Burgess took him to see Lord Alfred Douglas just to show him that his new boyfriend was prettier than the legendarily golden youth Douglas had been. Pollock met Burgess and Blunt in Cannes where he was staying with his grandfather, at Christmas 1937. He was sixteen and had long known that he was homosexual. Burgess was 'fleeing from the law. He'd been picked up in a cottage or something,' Pollock recalled. Blunt and Burgess's mother, Mrs Bassett, had decided he had to get out of England for a while. 'He was blown away by me. So was Anthony – but Guy got there first.' Pollock was not bowled over by Burgess, but 'I adored all the people he could pour into my lap – all the people I'd read about: Ros Lehmann and E. M. Forster. And I was fascinated by his brain. He was the best conversationalist I ever knew apart from Francis Bacon.' Pollock was, Hewit said, the love of Burgess's life. Pollock agreed. Nevertheless Burgess continued to be systematically promiscuous – 'Promiscuity?' Hewit would say. 'He practically invented it: everything from seventeen to seventy-five'. Pollock didn't mind. He did not enjoy sex with Burgess, and he had his own affairs. Hewit continued to live intermittently with Burgess, who made sure that he was either in work or provided for.

Burgess and Blunt lived in each other's pockets, but, according to Pollock, 'Guy was in the spotlight and Anthony was always hanging around on the fringes.' Olivier Bell remembered a disrupted tutorial at Blunt's flat:

> In rushed this crumpled person called Guy Burgess, and he went into the back room and after a bit was rumbling around and came out and said, 'Haven't you got a decent tie?' And of course all Anthony's ties were brought out. I thought this was disgraceful, this familiarity with the great man whom I treated with utmost respect and deference.

Hewit liked Blunt. Pollock did not. Hewit found him kind and never patronizing, as some of Burgess's friends were; he was good at comforting Hewit when he rowed with Burgess, as he often did. 'He was good at that. You felt he had time for people. He made you think that perhaps you were important.' Pollock found Blunt 'horrifyingly cold. I never got to know him very well – I never wanted to. We had to be friends, because Guy was determined that Anthony would accept me as a friend. We were perfectly polite to each other, but I thought he was an intellectual snob; in any conversation you felt it was all very carefully prepared and calculated.' Both Pollock and Hewit insisted that the relationship between Blunt and Burgess was not sexual in any way. But it was a mark of its unspoken intensity that at different times both Hewit and Pollock went to bed with Blunt, at least partly to revenge themselves on Burgess. Hewit got so angry one night that he threw a concrete statue at Burgess and stormed out of the Chester Square flat. He ran across Hyde Park to Palace Court, where he rang the doorbell, shouting, 'I'll kill him, I'll kill him!' until Blunt answered. 'I stayed the night and was calmed down,' Hewit said later – adding coyly, 'Of course I went back to Guy the next morning.' (Hewit additionally put an affair he had with Christopher Isherwood in 1938 down to his jealousy over Pollock.) Pollock also went to Blunt after an argument with Burgess: 'I was so angry I went to bed with Anthony just to annoy Guy. There was a tremendous row. Everyone took sides.'

Just as Burgess drew Blunt into his sex life, he also kept him closely involved in his political intriguing. Though Burgess had had no contact with anyone from the NKVD since the summer of 1937 – the purges had brought foreign intelligence to a complete standstill – he was determined to keep up his secret work.* 'Burgess was the greatest intriguer you've ever met in your life,' Hewit recalled, 'often for no reason at all – just to make mischief.' He was determined that none of his recruits would fall by the wayside, and on his own initiative he got in touch with John Cairncross, explaining his role in his recruitment, because 'I was afraid that he might drop out altogether, feeling isolated.' With Blunt, he talked politics endlessly. 'I heard a great deal of political talk,' remembered Peter Pollock. 'It was what Guy's whole life was, talking about politics. He and Anthony talked incessantly about it. I was bored stiff.'

At the end of 1937, with no authority from Moscow, Burgess decided to recruit his friend Goronwy Rees. Rees, a bright Welsh grammar-school boy and the son of a Methodist preacher, had won a scholarship to Oxford and gone on to All Souls. In the mid-1930s, unable to settle in academic life, he had left Oxford

* Both Kim Philby, who had spent most of 1937 and 1938 in Spain, covering the Civil War for *The Times* from the Franco side, and Donald Maclean, who was working at the British Embassy in Paris, had more or less kept in touch with Moscow. A new control, Grigori Grapfen, came to London in 1938, but he appears to have met only Maclean, and in December was recalled to Moscow, where he was sentenced to five years in a labour camp.

and, after a spell in Vienna and Berlin, where 'I played at conspiracy with the decimated and demoralised remnants of the German Communists and Social Democrat parties', he had become an assistant editor at the *Spectator*. He had met Burgess in 1934, through the Oxford don Maurice Bowra, and had been bowled over by his eloquence and political commitment – then embarrassed by the pass which inevitably followed. Despite Burgess's attempt at seduction, Rees was fascinated by him and they became close friends. 'Charming he was, but innocent never,' recalled Isaiah Berlin of Rees. 'The charm was irresistible and he got things very easily. He was friendly, he was physically attractive, he had a beautiful voice and charming manners, and he always seduced girls with no difficulty.' The novelist Elizabeth Bowen, with whom he had an affair in the mid-1930s, and whom he then left for Rosamond Lehmann, portrayed him in her 1938 novel *The Death of the Heart* as Eddie, the twenty-three-year-old 'brilliant child of an obscure home': handsome, selfish, paranoid, desperate for favour, a 'vacuum inside him'. By 1938 Rees was preaching a very similar artistic credo to Blunt's. Louis MacNeice recorded him declaring at a public debate that writers and artists 'must not think for themselves, they were only there to take orders, orders from the only progressive class in society, orders from the Proletariat, no writer could do anything at all of value unless he laid down his personality, made himself a mouthpiece and nothing more than a mouthpiece'.

What actually happened when Burgess approached Rees has been heavily debated ever since. Rees wrote in his memoir *A Chapter of Accidents* that Burgess made his pitch one night at his flat after reading a piece he'd written on the deprived children of South Wales. 'I want to tell you', Burgess suddenly said, 'that I am a Comintern agent, and have been ever since I came down from Cambridge . . . They told me that before going underground I must break off all connection with the party as publicly and dramatically as possible.' He asked Rees to work with him. Rees was amazed, and told Burgess there was nothing useful he himself could do, though he admired Burgess for his commitment. They discussed the anguish Burgess had suffered in breaking off from, and being reviled by, the Party and his friends in it. When Rees woke up the next morning he couldn't believe what he had heard – Burgess was, after all, a famous teller of tall tales – so he did nothing about it and Burgess did not refer to it again.

The Russian Intelligence Archives suggest that what actually happened was that Rees voiced a desire to join the Communist Party and Burgess persuaded him he could do more outside it. Rees's job would be to pass on any political hearsay he might glean.

Rees also claimed that, in order to convince him to take on the task, Burgess named someone who was working with him – someone

> who could not have carried more weight with me. He was someone whom I both liked and respected greatly, and with whom I would gladly have joined in any enterprise. Nor was I alone in admiration; there was no one who did not praise his intelligence, his upright-ness, his integrity. Indeed, he quite conspicuously possessed all those virtues which Guy did not, all they had in common, except friendship, was that they were both homosexuals.

Rees did not dare to name Blunt – for that was who it was – in the book, which was published seven years before Blunt's disgrace, when he was still a highly respected figure. The description was, however, strange. The two had never been friends. They had almost certainly met through Burgess, though they had other people in common too: Louis MacNeice, and Rosamond Lehmann, a good friend of Dadie Rylands' and Burgess's. Rees's daughter wrote of this passage, 'I have always felt very doubtful about Rees's response on being told that Blunt was involved; he never liked him.' Blunt turned up, unnamed, in various guises throughout Rees's book, as if Rees wanted to leave a trail of clues about Burgess's collaborator – as indeed he did – but did not quite dare name him. In the years between Rees's recruitment and the writing of the memoir, Rees would come to hate Blunt for avoiding the disgrace which he felt had attached to him for his association with Burgess, and for reminding him of his own shame. Blunt's 1943 NKVD memoir suggests that Rees actually found out about him later, in 1939, 'when Guy Burgess thought we might all be scattered and should therefore be in a position to make direct contact if necessary'. Whichever version was true, Rees's discovery of Blunt's recruitment would have deeply destructive consequences for both of them.

Rees's recruitment was only the beginning for Burgess, who gradually wove his uncommissioned secret work into every part of his life. He collected gossip from his friends, among them Dennis Proctor, who was rising high in the Civil Service; Harold Nicolson, a respected member of the Tory government, with whom he probably had an affair in the mid-1930s; and Tom Wylie. He used his BBC work to cultivate people in whom Deutsch and Maly had expressed an interest. In early 1938 he got to know a man called David Footman, whom Donald Maclean had years before identified as an MI6 officer, by inviting him to give talks on the BBC on his specialism, the Balkans. Through his contact with the creepy Édouard Pfeiffer, *chef de cabinet* of the French Prime Minister Daladier, and the Conservative grandee Sir Joseph Ball, he somehow became involved in ferrying documents between Daladier and Chamberlain in 1937 – papers he apparently also managed to pass on to Footman and eventually to Soviet Intelligence. He got his lovers to do little tasks for him. Hewit, who was working as a hotel switchboard operator, was asked to listen in to the phone conversations of Konrad Henlein, leader of the Sudeten Germans, when he came to London in 1938. The information Hewit gleaned was passed to Footman. Later Hewit was asked to sleep with a German anti-Nazi aristocrat called Gans zu Putlitz, whom Burgess had begun to cultivate because Maly had once shown an interest in him. 'He was a sweet man, and he hated Hitler,' remembered Hewit, who rather liked the idea of himself as Mata Hari. 'Burgess never said, "You have to." I regarded it as comfort for the troops. If they wanted to, I thought, "What have I got to lose?"'

Not that it all ran smoothly. Often Burgess's life seemed like some Feydeau farce, always on the brink of chaos and discovery. Goronwy Rees claimed that amid all the debris of old bottles, food and clothes at the Chester Square flat he saw rolls of bank-notes half-stuffed into cupboards. Somehow Burgess managed to keep the right secrets from the right people.

Blunt had none of Burgess's enthusiasm for conspiracy just for the sake of it. 'Burgess would play people off against each other just for fun. I never saw Blunt do that,' remembered Jackie Hewit. He seems to have made a vague effort to meet Communist students in London through Brian Simon, but never followed it up. He also seems to have rather desultorily introduced Stuart Hampshire to James Klugmann in Paris in 1938, as a possible recruitment prospect. 'I was kind of leftish at the time,' Hampshire remembered, 'and I think I was sort of being sized up. I do remember that Anthony wasn't enthusiastic, and he wasn't the main participant in the meeting. I had the impression that I was being dangled as a possibility by Anthony in a not very enthusiastic way.' Being constantly in Burgess's company, however, ensured that Blunt was aware of all Burgess's projects. And when they went to France together for holidays in those last two years before the war, Burgess made several attempts to contact the NKVD in Paris to hand over his tribute. The first few times, however, he failed. The new Paris *resident*, moreover, had never heard of him or Philby, and when he did work out who Philby was he showed no inclination to develop the acquaintance, telling Moscow that this was the English agent whose co-workers were tarred with 'filthy homosexuality'.

Burgess was nothing if not persistent. In the late summer of 1938, when Blunt was looking at churches in Provence on the way to meeting him in Cannes,* he made another attempt to

* Blunt wrote to Saxl: 'my visit to Beziers has not been a great success as the concièrge of the museum went to Vichy for a cure last week with the keys of the museum. So that I shall never see the Stella and the Bourdon! I hope none of our publications (or authors) have exploded in my absence.'

contact the NKVD in Paris. There he managed to track down the Spanish *rezident* Leonid Eitingon – the man who later gave the order to assassinate Trotsky – who was temporarily in the city. Burgess gave Eitingon his hoard of information, asked him to confirm Goronwy Rees's recruitment, and offered to courier information from Cairncross, who had been transferred from the Foreign Office to the Treasury. But his pièce de résistance was the news that David Footman had asked him to join MI6, or SIS – the Special Intelligence Service – as it was usually known. Eitingon immediately forbade it, saying it was too risky. This was the era of 'sniff up, suck up, survive' in the NKVD. Its apparatchiks avoided initiatives outside the parameters of Stalin's diktats like the plague: Eitingon was probably made extremely nervous by Burgess's enthusiastic and daring proposals.

At the end of September came the national humiliation of Munich. Neville Chamberlain acceded to Hitler's demands that the Sudetenland be ceded to Germany. The following months the Germans marched across the Czech border to occupy it, leaving the rest of Czechoslovakia wide open to future attack.

In January 1939, through its contact in Paris, Moscow finally gave permission for Burgess to join SIS. His job was in Section D – for 'Destruction' – which operated out of the apparently above-board 'Joint Broadcasting Committee'. It was the dirty-tricks department of SIS, which put out anti-Hitler propaganda and came up with ideas for misinformation – a job highly appropriate for an ex-BBC producer, though perhaps not quite what Burgess had had in mind

On 19 January 1939, Wystan Auden and Christopher Isher-wood left England for America – an act which was to bring against them accusations of betrayal. In retrospect their decision to go does not seem so surprising. Both writers had spent most of the 1930s outside England; both found it easier to work outside the suffocating world of literary London. In his preface to Blunt's 1967 *Festschrift*, Ellis Waterhouse wrote of the occasion as if it had a special significance for Blunt. 'The curtain lines of this period', he wrote, 'were spoken, if my memory is correct, on platform 3 at Waterloo Station. Messrs Auden and Isherwood were being seen off to the United States, and a voice I never identified said, "I suppose everyone in England worth saving is here!"' Jackie Hewit – who had been living with Isherwood in Belgium during the winter – left the platform in tears and was taken home by Benjamin Britten and Peter Pears, 'who made a pass at me'. He had hoped that Isherwood might send for him. Eventually he went back to Burgess.

Auden's ship arrived in New York on 26 January – the same day that Barcelona fell to Franco. The Spanish Civil War limped to its depressing conclusion in March, when Franco's forces finally took Madrid. Though the Civil War had been lost as much by the horrible internal divisions among the Republicans, as the Communists tried to crush the Trotskyite POUM and Catalan anarchists, Franco's victory, aided by the Germans and Italians, magnified the fear of fascism across Europe. Almost simultaneously the Germans overran Czechoslovakia – an act that could in no way be justified on the grounds of defensive strategy. In April the Italians invaded Albania. It was clear to everyone in Britain that fascism was suddenly and unarguably a more immediate menace than Communism.

March was also the month in which Blunt was made deputy director of the Courtauld. The previous incumbent, Willy Gibson, had gone to be Keeper of Paintings at the National Gallery. It was clear that Blunt would replace him: Tom Boase asked him to apply, and Saxl was on the panel of interviewers. Indeed, one of his rivals, Philip Hendy – who would become director of the National Gallery in the late 1940s and another of Blunt's 'not rare, *bêtes noires*' – announced in front of all the other applicants, ' "Of course this is all a waste of time, because we all know they're going to appoint you." I'm afraid,' Blunt admitted, 'there was a certain amount of jobbery.' Even Lord Lee set aside his qualms about Blunt's politics: 'I am very glad to hear that Dr Anthony Blunt has been nominated . . . and I entirely concur in his appointment,' he wrote on 10 March 1939. Blunt did not have long to enjoy his promotion. 'I couldn't do very much. I planned a long course of lectures on French painting from 1500 to as far as one could go. But of course that was before the autumn term, and everything was put on ice . . . I was really just able to install myself, and then everything was reduced to an absolute minimum in September '39.'

Stalin and his admirers interpreted British and French passivity over the Czech invasion as proof that the West was trying to encourage Germany to push East. Litvinov, Stalin's Commissar for Foreign Affairs, who had been actively, or at least publicly, pursuing a negotiated security pact with the Western powers since 1935, told the Polish ambassador in January 1939 that he knew that Britain had given Germany assurances that it would not take issue over any attempts to push east into Poland and the Ukraine. Almost the sole task of the now much weakened and desperately toadying NKVD was to provide corroboration of Stalin's conviction that this was true. There are KGB men who still claim that Burgess was among those who provided proof that the British were secretly negotiating with Hitler against the Soviet Union, though no documentary evidence for this has ever been produced. Such reports fed Stalin's omnivorous paranoia and allowed him to justify the secret negotiations – conducted through the NKVD – he opened in April with Hitler. Simultaneously, Litvinov was requesting talks with Britain and France for a new defensive alliance against Germany.

Although Munich appeared to be proof that Britain and France would turn a blind eye to German aggression, it was actually the turning point for the British government. Having been outman-oeuvred and humiliated by Hitler, it determined this would not happen again. Rearmament had begun in 1937 – among its most enthusiastic supporters was Winston Churchill. When Germany invaded Czechoslovakia in March 1939 the British government gave an unsolicited assurance to Poland – obviously Hitler's next target – that it would guarantee its independence: in other words, that Britain would take whatever actions were necessary to defend

Poland from attack. In view of its inaction over Czechoslovakia, there were those who felt this might be an empty assurance; in reality it was this promise that would take Britain to war.

In August the first volume of *The Drawings of Poussin* was published and Blunt delivered *Artistic Theory in Italy* to the Clarendon Press for publication. He travelled with Burgess to Cannes for their annual Côte d'Azur holiday. En route, in Paris, he bumped into his former Courtauld pupil Alla Weaver. She had just got her parents out of Berlin, and they hoped to stay in France.

> It was clear there was going to be a war. We had Lithuanian passports, though we didn't speak Lithuanian. We were walking down the Champs-Elysées and I saw Blunt. I dashed up to him and said, 'I'm travelling with my parents, we have passports, will my visa be valid to get back into Britain if we wait?' And Anthony said, 'Certainly not. You MUST leave at once.' Then Mother looked him over – his flannels and tweed, and asked, 'And who is that *terribly* untidy man with him?' I said, 'I don't know, but he's an Etonian, it's the only tie I can recognise.'

A few days before, the new Soviet *rezident* in London, Anatoli Gorsky, had met Burgess probably for the first time. Burgess had passed on a request from Blunt for advice on whether, in the event of war, it would be more useful for him to apply for the Territorial Army or Military Intelligence. Moscow was hesitant, 'since there was no personal contact with Tony', but conceded that Military Intelligence would be preferable. In fact Blunt had already been turned down for the army reserves. He had applied mentioning the name of his brother Christopher, who was an active member of the Territorial Army. (When he disclosed this in an interview in 1980, he asked his interviewer not to reveal it until after his death, so as not to upset his brother.)

On 23 August the news broke that the two arch-enemies, the Soviets and the Nazis, had agreed a non-aggression pact. What was not reported (and was not revealed until the Nazi archives

came to light after the war) was that they had made a secret
agreement to split up Poland and the Baltic states between them.

A week later, on 1 September, the Germans invaded Poland;
on 3 September Britain and France declared war on Germany,
and two weeks later the Soviet Union marched into the Baltic
states and eastern Poland. In New York, W. H. Auden wrote his
famous poem condemning the decade which had raised his hopes
of peace, only to dash them:

> I sit in one of the dives
> On Fifty-Second Street
> Uncertain and afraid
> As the clever hopes expire
> Of a low dishonest decade . . .

10. Soldier

'the compartmentalization of the heart'

Blunt was always keen to emphasize that neither he nor Guy Burgess had a moment of doubt about the Nazi–Soviet Pact. They rushed back to London from their annual trip to Cannes, he later told Ellis Waterhouse, because 'Guy said instantly that various people like Goronwy would be upset and they would have to get back to reassure them.' 'Guy and I were not at all upset because it was just what we thought was going to happen,' he told Robert Cecil in 1980. 'We argued', he said at his 1979 press conference, affecting a confidence that was not at all current in 1939, 'that it was simply a tactical necessity for Russia to gain time, as indeed turned out to be the case; it gave them time to re-arm and to get stronger to resist what was clearly going to happen'. (By which he meant Germany's eventual invasion of the Soviet Union.)

According to Goronwy Rees and Rosamond Lehmann, however, Burgess was far from calm at the time. Lehmann thought him 'shattered', and remembered that in his desperation to get back to London he left his prize possession, his car, at Calais. Then he disappeared for a few days to 'think things over'. In his memoirs Goronwy Rees claimed that, when Burgess came to see him within days of the announcement of the Pact, he told Burgess, 'I never want to have anything to do with the Comintern for the rest of my life ... Or with you, if you really are one of their agents.' Burgess agreed that 'The best thing to do would be to forget the whole thing', and implied that he too had been disillusioned by the Pact. The Russian Intelligence Archives suggest that Burgess explicitly told Rees that he was going to stop his clandestine work. In 1943 Blunt reported, 'Goronwy thinks that I stopped working at the time of the Russo-German treaty at the same time as Guy Burgess.' Other members of the ring were equally shocked by the Pact. When Anatoli Gorsky, the NKVD's newly promoted London chief, met Kim Philby for the first time in September 1939, he reported that the Englishman plied him with 'puzzled questions such as, "Why is this necessary?", "What will happened to the single-front struggle against Fascism now?"' The following month Philby failed to turn up at the meeting they had planned. He had gone to France for *The Times*, following the British Expeditionary Force, and did not want to be found.

Within weeks, however, Burgess and Blunt had rationalized their reservations. In mid-September, two weeks after the war had begun, Burgess met Gorsky and pledged his loyalty. (The new generation of NKVD staff, incidentally, knew so little about Philby, Burgess, Blunt and the rest, that they were forced to ask Arnold Deutsch for detailed descriptions of them all.) Blunt – who had still not met Gorsky – applied for a job in Military Intelligence. His and Burgess's acceptance of the Pact mirrored that of the Communist parties across Europe, including the Communist Party of Great Britain (which had momentarily tried to support both Britain's declaration of war and the Soviets' signing of the Pact). Douglas Hyde – a prominent wartime member of the CPGB – later described how Party members convinced themselves that the Soviet Union had done right and insulated themselves from the obvious fact that it had betrayed its popular-front allies. The rationalization went like this:

> I am fighting for a better Britain and for the destruction of all that is rotten and decadent. In that fight I have the assistance of all who are operating on the same world front against Capitalism. My desire to make my country Communist therefore makes me an internationalist . . . At all costs, therefore Russia, bastion of Communism, must be defended . . . who attacks Russia attacks my hope of a Communist Britain.

When Cecil Gould saw Blunt at the Courtauld a few days after war had been declared, he found him 'much more cheerful' than Tom Boase, 'who was appropriately gloomy and said there was little or no hope'. The Institute was being closed down. A skeleton staff would keep the slide and book libraries open, with Blunt coming in once a week to look things over. He helped Margaret Whinney move to Guildford, where she continued to teach the last five or six students (including, Blunt remembered, 'an *enchanting* girl who later became a Mother Superior') at a room in the local technical college. Gould recalled that Blunt was 'engaged in carrying some of the pictures to the safe on the ground floor. I helped him do this and we had a jolly discussion about which of the pictures we would most like to see bombed ... When I asked Anthony if he were staying in London he replied, "I'm expecting to be called up. I'm going into a thing called Field Intelligence. It needs languages."'

Blunt received two replies to his application to join Military Intelligence. One rejected him, most likely on the grounds of his fellow-travelling past; the other asked him to report on 16 September to Minley Manor, near Aldershot in Hampshire, for a course in basic training and rudimentary intelligence. (The confusion seems to have been a consequence of the War Office's sudden inundation of applicants to join up.) Linguists were in great demand and short supply; that month the Field Security section of Military Intelligence took the unprecedented step of advertising on the BBC for language-speaking volunteers.

Ten days after he began at Minley, however, Blunt's past caught up with him. He was summoned to London – much to the horror of the course's officers, who had never known such a thing – for an interview with Brigadier Kevin Martin, deputy director of Military Intelligence. Blunt's anxiety can be gauged by the fact that he got Burgess to send a message to Gorsky, explaining the situation. He assumed that either his homosexuality or his political past had been discovered. His situation was more precarious than he realized. Alexander Orlov, the former London *rezident*, who knew all about the Cambridge spy ring, had recently sent a letter to Stalin threatening to reveal everything he knew to the Americans if he and his family were not left alone. MI5 had just arrested the NKVD's Foreign Office source, Captain John Herbert King, the successor to the unfortunate Ernest Oldham, on the testimony of the renegade illegal Walter Krivitsky. Krivitsky had also told the British authorities that the Soviets had recruited two young men of good family. But further investigation was hobbled by Krivitsky's confusion over certain details: he described one as a Scotsman (which Donald Maclean was), educated at Eton and Oxford (which he was not); the other as a journalist reporting on Spain. It had not occurred to MI5 to check journalists working on the fascist side, which was what Philby had done.

In the course of what Blunt described as 'a long and difficult conversation carried on under extreme strain', Brigadier Martin informed him that the War Office knew of his university Communism, his Marxist articles and his visit to the Soviet Union in 1935. Blunt tried to persuade him that the Marxism had been purely intellectual, though he admitted that it had 'given a great deal of offence to many people'. Silently he wondered if he had been denounced by someone like Lord Lee or Dennis Robertson, the Trinity economics don who had refused to give a reference to Kim Philby because he was too left-wing. One of the details of the conversation which Blunt later put in the account he wrote for the NKVD was a peculiarly Freudian reference to his father: 'I am sure', he reported the Brigadier as saying, 'he would turn in his grave if he thought you were doing subversive work.' Blunt's excuses were persuasive and were given weight by Dennis Proctor, who went to see the Brigadier the next day at Burgess's prompting. Proctor knew Martin and told him, 'All decent people have if not left wing views then at least left wing friends.' In Proctor's case his friends – and Burgess and Blunt regarded him as one of their best friends – were shamelessly using him. A week or so afterwards Proctor invited Blunt and Burgess to dinner. The writer Anthony Powell was also there. He found Blunt 'quite nice in a very Cambridge way'. Burgess turned up late. 'A BBC fairy of the fat go-getting sort,' Powell wrote in his diary. 'Absolutely nauseating.'

Four years later, Blunt looked himself up in the MI5 registry and found that his file consisted of a postcard from the Trinity don Maurice Dobb recommending him to the editors of *Left Review* and a note that he had visited the USSR.

Cleared by the Brigadier, Blunt returned to Minley in October. He completed the course, and another at Mytchett Camp in November. On each he made notes, compiling a list of the various departments of Military Intelligence from MI1 (intelligence in the field) to MI10 (artillery and gas), which he handed on to Burgess for the Soviets. By mid-December he was a captain on his way to Boulogne, in charge of Field Security Section 18, which consisted of ten lance corporals (most of them middle-class NCOs who spoke several languages), two sergeants, a sergeant-major and a batman. Their job was to oversee port security for the British Expeditionary Force in Boulogne – a distinctly dreary posting. Most of Blunt's fellow officers had got comfortable jobs in the War Office; an earlier posting at General Headquarters had been cancelled: it seemed that Blunt was, after all, being punished for his politics.

One of his lance corporals, George Curry, who later became a major and after the war an academic, remembered his first impression of Blunt at Folkestone:

We were all very curious about our new and quite unfamiliar officer – I saw him then as youthful, very thin and tall, slightly round-shouldered, professorial looking, with long brown hair showing under his flat uniform cap . . . he left our party to approach a Movement Officer, a red-faced Major, wearing tunic, breeches, puttees and well-shined brown boots. This gentleman was already staring, without enthusiasm, at our free-standing, chattering group when Blunt confronted him and asked – rather off-handedly it would appear – what were the arrangements for his section? The Major looked very fierce, drew himself up, and yelled out for all to hear, 'It is customary to salute when approaching a senior officer!!' Blunt was obviously taken aback but did manage a sort of salute and was given his instructions. We were greatly embarrassed for him, indignant that 'our' officer should receive such boorish treatment. At the same time the incident reinforced a general impression that our Commander (like ourselves, of course) was almost the complete amateur when it came to practical soldiering, a judgement which our subsequent service under him did little to change.

In France, where the phoney war was at its height, the Section's main task was to stop men going on leave from carrying home uncensored letters. All missives were supposed to be inspected by officers in case they gave away strategic information. It was an impossible job, and involved standing on the quayside between 4 a.m. and 8 a.m. each day – in one of the coldest winters of the century – asking embarking soldiers to hand over letters, with the threat of loss of leave should random searches produce anything. Other duties included infiltrating local units to plant dummy bombs to test security, and monitoring the local prostitutes and the licensed brothel, at 31 Rue de Saint-Pol, to check that no untoward approaches had been made – for military information by the women, rather than of a sexual nature by the men. All these tasks made them deeply unpopular.

As head of his unit, Blunt, was regarded as 'a pleasant, cultured, rather aloof man', very busy, often absent, with a particular talent for negotiating with the notoriously tricky French authorities – he described it to Fritz Saxl as 'getting to know the French from a purely Maupassant point of view'. 'Up to the imminent arrival of the Germans in May 1940 he was liked and respected by all,' thought another of his troop, Alan Berends, though George Curry found him rather distant. He gave no hint of his homosexuality. Occasionally he was moved to acts of unmilitary familiarity. When he discovered that Berends, who had been posted to Dunkirk in the French zone, had never had oysters, he took him out for lunch. Berends was surprised; in the British zone officers did not take the men out to lunch. The conversation turned to the French Impressionists. 'Suddenly the penny dropped. I looked closely at him and exclaimed: "You're *Tony* Blunt."' Berends – a graduate of Downing College who, like most of his college and acquaintances, had never been drawn into the politics and aesthetics of Blunt's circle – remembered he'd attended a lecture given by Blunt at the French Society. 'I was filled with indignation that the rather weedy aesthete I recalled had somehow been transformed into an officer despite having no more military background than the rest of us.'

It soon became clear that the Section's tasks were virtually pointless. In five months not a single case of genuine espionage was discovered. 'There were', Berends thought, 'surely easier for ways for the Germans to compile the British order-of-battle than by trying to question a million British housewives.' Morale began to fall, but Blunt seemed oblivious to this. He was, he told Dadie Rylands, shocked by 'how little I mind my present existence. It is perfectly comfortable', though he noted 'it means dealing with people, which is a completely novelty to me'. He wrote to Fritz Saxl:

> It is only tiresome that there is so little here to look at . . . driving around the countryside looking at minor gothic churches and good 18th century panelling makes the time pass – though I sleep and eat so much that I threaten to become pure vegetable. I think I shall have to find a good cathedral soon. There are none in my area, but I am getting quite clever at inventing reasons for going to distant places.

He corrected the proofs of *Artistic Theory in Italy*, and asked Saxl to send him the latest Warburg Journal to proofread: 'There have been moments when I wanted to get something (however irrelevant) to get my teeth into, and to produce even three lines for the Journal will give a little island of reality.'

As if to demonstrate how irrelevant the Section was, in April its revolvers were confiscated because there was a shortage of guns for the new allied campaign in Norway.

On 10 May 1940 a German bomber dropped its load on

Boulogne airfield, and the war finally came to Anthony Blunt. During the next ten days the town became clogged with refugees. On his way through Boulogne Kim Philby met Blunt, later claiming that the latter was organizing defences from the remnants of the troops. That wasn't how Blunt's section remembered it. They were virtually idle until some British Embassy staff arrived from Paris to see Blunt, when they were told to burn papers and disable the embassy cars. Then GHQ shipped out; but the Section – now depleted, as various members had been dispatched to other jobs – was never called together to discuss its own evacuation, 'and, in all honesty,' George Curry recalled, 'I do not believe it was even thought of. It was certainly never mentioned, either by Blunt or by our sergeant-major or among ourselves.' It seemed that FSS18 had been forgotten, and Blunt did nothing to remind anyone about it. He seemed struck by apathy, immobilized, withdrawing to his billet, 'apparently content to await the arrival of the Germans'.

On 25 May the Second Panzer Division captured Boulogne. Three days before, someone – it wasn't Blunt – managed to get a call through to army headquarters at Dover, where a duty officer ordered the Section to evacuate. (In fact an order had already been given for the evacuation of all 'useless mouths'. No one knows if Blunt was aware of this.) The Section rump picked up the stragglers, and sent Blunt's batman to rouse him from his billet and bring him down to the port. Curry recalled, 'The sight of the abandoned hospital trains, their doors still open, mattresses trailing down the steps, remains with me to this day.' A small cargo steamer agreed to take them back to Dover, but they had to wait for five hours, hungry and thirsty, till high tide. In the Channel they passed a bombed oil tanker burning up the sea; later they heard planes overhead and thought they would be sunk. At daylight they arrived at Hythe, where they were given breakfast and railway warrants to the military depot in Sheerness. 'I do not know what part Blunt played in the fight for washing facilities, replacement of clothing, etc., but I know C. S. M. Buss [the Company Sergeant-Major, a professional soldier] was active.'

Shortly afterwards Blunt disappeared for good. They were told he'd gone to London to be employed on other duties.

In the light of their later war experiences, Berends and Curry felt that Blunt's behaviour as their CO was deeply inadequate. 'Blunt always showed too little interest in us as individuals and far too little interest in our duties. His total lack of leadership at the end was unforgivable,' Berends concluded. Yet his subsequent actions never suggested a man who lacked nerve or organizational ability. It may be that his first encounter with physical danger terrified him. If, as some commentators have suggested, his aims were merely destructive, the loss of one small Field Security unit was hardly a significant blow to Britain. Perhaps he thought that capture would relieve him of the inevitable choice to be made back in England: to get further involved in Burgess's plans, to aid the Soviet Union during war at a time when that was also to aid the Nazis. It may be that for the first time his decision to spy for the Soviets seemed horribly real. Sitting out the war in a POW camp may have seemed almost tempting. Later in the war he seemed at pains to prove his courage: Wilfrid remembered accompanying him to a dealer's glass-roofed gallery, and how, throughout a flying-bomb attack, he sat studiously in front of a Flemish panel painting, as Wilfrid and the dealer cowered in the corner expecting the roof to cave in at any moment.

In June 1940, Blunt wrote in his NKVD memoir, 'he joined MI5'.

For Blunt's career in MI5, as in all writing about espionage, historians are dependent on a series of fundamentally unreliable sources. First there are the intelligence services – those, that is, who choose to provide information at all. They have their own agendas and their own idiosyncratic ideas of 'access'. The Russian Intelligence Archives, for example, have shed much light on what the spies actually did, but need to be treated with some scepticism. They are not open to the public. The several recent books on Soviet penetration of the West which claim to quote from these archives have all been written by either former KGB officers or their relatives: the Russian author of a biography of Kim Philby,

Genrikh Borovik, is the brother-in-law of a former director of the KGB. Despite promises to the the contrary, even documents extensively quoted from in these books have not subsequently been made available to the public. The other major source for intelligence is the all-too-fallible memories of former intelligence agents, who usually have their own reasons for telling their stories. *My Five Cambridge Friends*, written by the former KGB officer Yuri Modin, Blunt's last control, came out in 1994. The book is a model of self-serving inaccuracy, written with an often blithe lack of regard for the facts. At the same time it offers a few tantalizingly credible insights into the minds and motivations of the Cambridge spies during the period between 1948 and 1953, when Modin actually knew Blunt, Burgess and Cairncross. Then there are the secondary sources, books by espionage writers. Even conscientious writers have to make guesses about some things and to take others on trust; less conscientious ones – less sane ones even – have published all kinds of nonsense as fact. The sane and conscientious Nigel West, whose first books largely relied on former intelligence officers, and whose more recent ones have been written with direct access to the Russian Intelligence Archives, quotes Malcolm Muggeridge: 'Diplomats and intelligence agents, in my experience, are even bigger liars than journalists, and the historians who try to reconstruct the past out of their records are, for the most part, dealing with fantasy.'

The story of Blunt's entry into MI5 is a good example of the morass into which intelligence history can fall. In the 1980s Nigel West interviewed both Victor Rothschild and Anthony Blunt, and came up with the following account. In early June 1940 Rothschild invited Blunt to meet a 'Captain Black of the War Office'. The man was actually Guy Liddell, the newly promoted head of MI5's 'B' division, its most glamorous and secret department. Rothschild had been in MI5 for about six months when he suggested to Liddell that Blunt, just returned from France, might be a suitable recruit – whether this was on Blunt's own prompting is not known. During the course of the meeting it became clear that Liddell was impressed. He dropped his pseudonym, reintroduced himself, and invited Blunt to join MI5.

The new job was not all Blunt had hoped, however. In his NKVD memoir, he wrote that he assumed he would be working with Rothschild in counter-sabotage, but instead he was claimed by a Brigadier Allen who ran 'D' Division, which dealt with military security, and was put to work 'on the purely military side' for nine months. (Another reminder of the problems with research on intelligence is the fact that forty years later Blunt told Nigel West that he worked in 'D' Division for only two months.)

There have, however, been other versions of Blunt's recruitment. In the early 1980s the spy writer Chapman Pincher, whose main source was the embittered former MI5 officer Peter Wright, claimed that Blunt was brought into MI5 by his friend Tomás Harris, the art dealer (who actually joined MI5 after Blunt). Chapman Pincher suspected Harris of having been a co-conspirator of Blunt's. In 1985 Dick White, former director of both MI5 and MI6, announced that he wanted to set the record straight, and gave another version. White's deeply fudged account was designed to protect British Intelligence from charges of ineffectuality, and to exonerate his late colleague and friend Guy Liddell, who had been posthumously accused of both carelessness and conspiracy. In White's account, no one was responsible for letting in Blunt.

The way Blunt came into MI5 is quite simple. He was in the War Office in military intelligence of some sort and he was given the job of being a personnel assistant to someone called Brigadier Allen – War Office liaison officer with MI5. And he came over to MI5 with Brigadier Allen. Allen spent part of his time at the War Office and part of his time at MI5. Blunt was recommended to us as being a very able man which he certainly was and he got himself taken on. And I suppose it's perfectly true that Guy [Liddell] could

have stopped that ... but he didn't have any particular
reason for doing so.

White's version was disingenuous, not least because MI5 was
itself part of the War Office, and Allen was a paid-up member of
MI5.

Perhaps more surprising than the bare facts of Blunt's entry to
MI5 were the circumstances which gave rise to them. At the time
when he got into British Intelligence, the Cambridge spies were
once again out of contact with the NKVD and had been since
February, when the London *rezidentura* had been closed again in
a last burst of purge paranoia. It was not prodding from Moscow
that pushed Blunt into British Intelligence, but his own initiative,
and the encouragement of Burgess. At precisely the moment that
Blunt got into MI5, Burgess was also arranging to get Philby into
MI6/SIS. Burgess, who was still in SIS's Section D, introduced
Philby to a veteran SIS recruiter, Marjorie Maxse. Maxse liked
him, and he was sent to Brickendonbury Hall, a new school for
the training of SIS agents in subversion, an idea of Burgess's.
Burgess had also brought in Tomás Harris and his wife, Hilda,
who were famously lavish hosts, as housekeepers: a move which
suggests that he envisioned his brainchild as a luxury country-
house hotel for spies – one reason, perhaps, why it lasted only
two months. It was closed down when Section D was merged
with the Special Operations Executive (SOE), which had its own
training centre. Philby and Tomás Harris, both Spanish speakers,
were given new jobs on Spanish intelligence, but Burgess was
dumped. He returned to his job at the BBC and was never again
formally employed by British Intelligence.

The other extraordinary fact about Blunt's recruitment to MI5
is that, at precisely the moment at which he presented himself,
the Service – which a few months before would have looked at a
former left-wing academic with intense suspicion – was now actively
looking for recruits with precisely his academic background.
Before the war, MI5 had been largely made up of a small group
of upper-class gentlemen, somewhat past their best, recruited at

the bars of Boodle's and White's, with First World War opinions to match. In the nine months since war had declared it had transformed into a staff of 570. The early manifestations of MI5's metamorphosis were not impressive. The first wartime recruits were chosen according to the preferred methods of its founder and director, the sixty-seven-year-old Sir Vernon Kell. They came from the aristocracy or from the families of MI5 officers: 'young men who had never worked before', as an MI5 secretary, Joan Miller, observed. The burgeoning organization was moved to Wormwood Scrubs prison, where none of the cells had interior door handles, there were no electricity sockets, and there was nowhere to lock the registry where all the secret files were kept. The Bertie Wooster types and debs who got off the bus each morning at the Scrubs – a particularly down-at-heel part of west London – were extremely conspicuous.

Things were changing, however. Guy Liddell, one of Kell's most effective and intelligent officers, and his young colleague Dick White came up with a plan to bring in academic high-flyers. This was quite at odds with British Intelligence's long-established distrust of education and eggheads. Among the new recruits were the lawyer Martin Furnival-Jones, a future director-general of MI5, and academics like Herbert Hart, D. S. Masterman, Stuart Hampshire, Gilbert Ryle and Hugh Trevor-Roper. (The latter three were eventually moved into MI6.) Victor Rothschild had been brought in as a scientific adviser on industrial sabotage, and had become a good friend of Guy Liddell's. They rented a cottage together outside Tring, and shared a passionate love of music – Liddell was a talented amateur cellist. They were also both the victims of recently broken marriages: Barbara Hutchinson had finally left Victor; Liddell's wife, the exotic Calypso Baring, had run off to America with her stepbrother and Liddell's four children. (This, it was said, was a blow from which Liddell never recovered.) The new recruits were completed by a couple of former Special Branch policemen, William Skardon and Leonard Burt, noted both for their skills in interrogation and for the fact that they could 'talk to the working classes'. (This has been a perennial problem for the intelligence services. Anthony Duff, head of MI5 in 1984, was apparently particularly admired because 'he could talk to working-class people without fuss'.)

Liddell's recruitment policy was indirectly approved in June 1940 when Sir Vernon Kell and his deputy were dismissed by Churchill for being old-fashioned and Blimpish. Kell was replaced by Sir David Petrie, a sixty-one-year-old former colonial police officer. Liddell was made head of MI5's 'B' Division, which dealt with counter-espionage and subversion, and Dick White became his deputy. The recruitment policy was expanded. Blunt – who came with intelligence training, fluent French, German and Italian, and a recommendation from Rothschild – must have seemed perfect.

To Hugh Trevor-Roper and Stuart Hampshire, who had experience of both MI5 and MI6, MI5's reforms were a great success. The service was 'more efficient and better organised than MI6', Trevor-Roper has written. MI5's great wartime success, the 'Double-Cross' system, was largely manned and masterminded by the newcomers. It was a huge project which exploited Britain's success at breaking German codes, a success which had ensured that every enemy agent in Britain was captured – a remarkable feat in any circumstances. Many were subsequently persuaded to work for the British. More fictional agents were invented, and all were used to feed false information back to the Germans to Britain's great military advantage.

MI6, in comparison, was still run by clubbable gentlemen, or immensely conservative former members of the colonial Indian police force. 'Neither class had much use for ideas,' Trevor-Roper later wrote. 'The former had seldom heard of them; the latter regarded them as subversive.' There was also an abiding suspicion of 'university men'. 'This was not true of MI5.' Parts of MI6 were successful, but most of these tended to be run by newly recruited 'amateurs'. Between MI5 and MI6 there was a barely submerged animosity. 'A large part of the suspicion with which my section was regarded in MI6,' Trevor-Roper recalled, 'came from the fact that we were regarded as too intimate with MI5 (i.e. the "B"

Division).' Guy Liddell, in turn, could not stand his stuffy opposite numbers. Trevor-Roper felt the distinctions between the two organizations went even deeper. 'The essential difference in attitude was that MI5 (section "B") believed in intelligence as a means of formulating policy (e.g. deception) whereas MI6 regarded it solely as a means of protecting their own (often worthless) spies.'

Guy Liddell, the central figure in MI5's reinvention, was fifteen years older than Blunt, balding, slightly pudgy, a chain-smoker and a First World War hero (he had won the Military Cross). Stuart Hampshire found him

> a fascinating character, very unconventional, with an exceed-ingly conventional outside. He was always very beautifully dressed, with handmade shoes. He was immensely cultivated (though he hadn't been near university), intensely musical and very sensitive – an admirable character. He'd been in Special Branch, and that had left him with an utter contempt for the British police whom he knew – which most of us didn't – were riddled with corruption. He knew that every single Met officer was on the take. In the short time that he was married to Calypso Baring he acquired a real dislike of the British ruling class – at odds with his personality, which was much more like someone from a good cavalry regiment.

Some people found him vulnerable and shy, others saw this as a deliberately inscrutable blind. Desmond Bristow, an MI6 officer who liaised closely with MI5, recalled, 'I admit I was never sure with Liddell . . . I know he was married, but he had a sort of, he was a bit too "nice" to be completely "man".' Miriam Roths-child, Victor's sister, felt Liddell was in 'terrible distress because his wife had gone off. I had a feeling he was easily taken in, impressionable, an innocent. I wasn't close to him, though. He gave the impression of holding all his cards close to his chest. I thought, "That's nonsense – he's really an innocent."'

His lieutenant, and supporter, Dick White had been to Oxford and had entered MI5 in 1935, after a spell as a teacher. He harboured a secret desire to be a writer. His biographer Tom Bower could 'never decide whether White was just a very naive schoolmaster or very shrewd. I met him as an old man and so it's hard to assess him as a young one, and the problem is that all those [in British Intelligence] who spoke highly of him are themselves incredibly stupid.' Desmond Bristow thought White, who would come to run both MI5 and MI6, 'was never one of the boys, but he was smart'.

From the start White and Liddell had more in common with the new MI5 'amateurs' than with the conservative old guard and what Trevor-Roper described as the 'gung-ho colonels and paranoid policemen of MI6'. Blunt made a particularly strong impression on them both. Liddell not only admired Blunt's intelligence, he took his advice on aesthetic matters too – he would accompany Blunt on trips to the salerooms. 'Blunt definitely cultivated Liddell as a way of protecting himself,' Dick White later said. 'I think Guy Liddell was too trusting . . . I think he [Blunt] made a general assault on key figures to see they liked him and thought well of him.' White could not exempt himself from this. He later maintained that he disliked Blunt, but observers such as Hugh Trevor-Roper and Stuart Hampshire were of the opinion that he liked and admired him very much. White virtually admitted as much in an interview in 1985. 'I saw quite a lot of him. He frequently sat down next to me at the [canteen] table . . . he was very intelligent, very nice, very civilized. I'm interested in art and I talked with him – pictures and drawings. I was never conscious of being cross-examined by him.' It seems likely that White disavowed the friendship not merely for professional reasons, but because he felt Blunt's betrayal more personally and keenly than Philby's, whom he knew less well – though the latter was a more dedicated spy. 'I must say if I resent any particular member of that group more than another, it's Blunt,' White said later, 'because I think he went further than the others in ingratiating measures to get accepted and very successfully betrayed us all. This is something you can't imagine unless you've been through it.'

These friendships were cemented by frequent meetings at the Reform Club, of which White, Liddell, Blunt and Burgess were all members, and by regular visits to the house of Tomás Harris. Harris had been moved to MI5 to work on Double-Cross and ran one of its most successful agents of disinformation, Jean Pujol, known as Garbo. It was a job he enormously enjoyed. Throughout the war he and his wife kept open house for their friends in Intelligence and the art world at their home in Chesterfield Gardens in Mayfair. There seemed to be an endless supply of champagne and canapés. Liddell, his brother David, Dick White, Victor Rothschild and Blunt often went. Other guests included Burgess and MI6 officers with whom Harris liaised over Spanish matters, among them Desmond Bristow and Kim Philby, whom Harris was coming to number among his best friends. Harris's art-world friends included the illustrator Nicolas Bentley, Colin Agnew of Agnew's, the Establishment art dealers in Bond Street, Ralph Partridge and Peter Wilson, an auctioneer rising fast at Sotheby's who worked in MI5 on Bermudan security, and whom Blunt disliked. Blunt and Philby, Desmond Bristow remembered, were always late, and Blunt would stand 'in the corner with a group of four or five doting people'. Once, much to his disgust, he saw Blunt making an (unsuccessful) pass at a young man. Bristow, who liked Philby, observed that he seemed to have an 'inferiority complex about Blunt'. Blunt did not warm to Philby's slightly desperate, relentless need to charm.

Harris's closeness to Blunt and Philby has given rise to suspicions that he too might have been involved in the spy ring. Certainly, his immaculate presentation, his sophisticated tastes and the ever-present air of mystery made him far more of a James Bond figure than any of the Cambridge spies themselves. He has been accused of having been the Cambridge spies' 'paymaster' – a rumour which seems to have come from Malcolm Muggeridge, who never knew him well. So far, nothing about him, except as a bona-fide member of MI5, has come out of the Russian Intelligence Archives. Whatever the truth, his home certainly provided a setting in which it was easy for Blunt and Burgess to become personally friendly with White and Liddell.

Their approval and promotion of Blunt was in no way stalled by their knowledge that he was both a former left-winger and a homosexual. Dick White told his biographer that he didn't know about Blunt's Communist sympathies or his homosexuality. This was not true. Hugh Astor, a contemporary of Blunt's at MI5, remembered, 'It was quite well known that Blunt was left wing and that he was gay.' Indeed Blunt's later wartime work for MI5 exploited his homosexual contacts. As for his Communism, in his 1943 NKVD memoir Blunt actually described how he took

> the precaution to mention, privately and in a half-joking way to Liddell and White that 'C' Division had once recommended that I should not be employed. I did this partly because they both know all about my past contacts with the Party, and also because I want if ever challenged on the subject to be able to say that I had not concealed the fact that I had been turned down, but had on the contrary mentioned it to my bosses.

According to Stuart Hampshire, Liddell and White felt that left-wing views were an occupational hazard of the intellectuals and academics they wanted; they 'needed to have people who were pretty clever, and if they had a Communist background that didn't matter since we were all at war with the Germans. Lots of people had been interested in it at university. It wasn't taken very seriously.' (One recruit to MI6 with a Communist past had been told in 1936, 'Oh yes, we know about that. We've talked to your tutor and we think this is a form of undergraduate measles and not to be taken seriously.') Liddell 'always joked about Communism', Hampshire recalled, 'because we knew very well that there were a number of clandestine Communists in positions of authority and that to him was a bit of a joke'. This had not been the case before the war, when Liddell had led MI5's investigations into Communist subversion. In 1938 he had arrested the Woolwich Arsenal ring, who had been trying to steal naval plans for the Soviet Union. Dick White did not describe himself as left-wing, but he had some sympathy with left-wing views: he had joined MI5 because he felt that fascism was a 'monumental threat and that something catastrophic was going to take place'. Nor was he averse to having left-wingers in MI5: 'It was an orthodox position,' he said later, 'and everybody was on the right side in this war who was against the Germans . . . a security service when all is said and done, particularly a small one like ours, is just as much a part of the public's attitude as any other part of government . . . influenced by the general ethos at the time.'

Most of their colleagues agreed with Liddell and White, though there were pockets of severe anti-Communism in MI5, and more particularly in MI6. These tended to coincide with the more traditional and conservative parts of the organizations: 'the people you thought were stupid', as Stuart Hampshire bluntly put it. None of these people really understood the pull of Communism. As Trevor-Roper wrote, 'Our more conservative colleagues . . . saw communism as mere "subversion", the doctrine of subject class and peoples. They underestimated its power to convert English gentlemen . . . We thought that there were no Philbies; they insisted that all who tasted communism were Philbies – except Philby himself . . . We were all wrong.'

As for Blunt's homosexuality, White reluctantly admitted in an interview in 1985, 'I thought he was homosexual, yes. You know one has got to be careful about that if you don't have any evidence, but I suppose it did cross my mind that he was in love with Burgess.' He also claimed that he felt that Burgess had 'absolutely taken over Blunt's soul. How that had come about I don't know. Blunt seemed a man of some discrimination and civilized instincts. I couldn't understand how he could be so besotted by Burgess. This was always evident to me, that he was under the influence of Burgess.' Wartime practice on the subject of homosexuality, in Intelligence as in the military, was to turn a blind eye to such things: at least a quarter of a million homosexuals fought for Britain in the Second World War. In MI5 and MI6 at least two homosexuals had been recruited before the war. One, who in fact pretended to be a near-hysterical homophobe, was 'M', Maxwell Knight, the eccentric, rather sinister head of MI5's counter-espionage section, known as B5(b). Knight was also extremely right-wing, anti-Communist and anti-Semitic, and at one point was director of intelligence for the British Union of Fascists. The MI6 officer – who was also a former Communist – joined SIS in 1936 and spent his career there. He felt that his sexual and political orientation were politely ignored. 'They wanted me because I was a German specialist. In the 1930s and 1940s the intelligence services were largely recruiting against Hitler and so many people had left-wing sympathies.' Several homosexual wartime recruits went on to very successful careers in British Intelligence, among them Maurice Oldfield, who became head of MI6 in the 1960s, and Alex Kellar, a future head of 'F' Division, which monitored political parties. Kellar, a lawyer with a postgraduate degree in international law from Columbia University, New York, wore purple socks and purple silk ties, and at his dinner parties beefy young men waited at table in white tuxedos. They turned out to be off-duty members of the Household Cavalry. 'All too obviously a homosexual, he blissfully thought that no one was aware of this,' wrote his friend the novelist Francis King. 'We called him Liberace,' recalled his fellow MI5 officer Ann Glass. Kellar briefly shared an office with Blunt at Wormwood Scrubs, and latterly claimed he'd never trusted him.

'A.'s book is out with a most flattering reference to me in the foreword,' Burgess wrote to Peter Pollock in late 1940. *Artistic Theory in Italy* was finally published in August. In it, Blunt thanked Burgess for 'the stimulus of constant discussion and suggestions on all the more basic points at issue' – an acknowledgement which he never removed, even after Burgess's defection. He also paid tribute to Andrew Gow and to Friedrich Antal, to whom, he wrote, 'I am indebted for instruction in a method which has, I feel, been applied in an only too slipshod manner'. The book did have a Marxist slant. Blunt had linked the development of sophisticated theories of art to artists' attempts to raise their social position. He implied that the character of the theories owed much to the political atmosphere and wealth of the societies in which the artists practised. Thus the writings of the rationalist Alberti emerged from the liberal, relatively democratic, bourgeois republican Italian city states of the fifteenth century. Michelangelo's idealization of the human form reflected the peak of wealth and decadence in High Renaissance Rome before it was sacked in 1527, and his subsequent loss of interest in representing idealized physical beauty reflected the general sense of decline in Italy afterwards. These ideas, however, were implicit rather than stated, and Blunt kept his explorations of the theories clear of politics – in his chapter on Michelangelo's ideas about art he used the artist's love poems to reveal his thoughts about beauty. (Burgess recommended the poems to Pollock: 'there's a lot about his poetry which is a) important b) lovely c) sympathetic . . .'.) The influence of the Warburg – in the way Blunt used such literary sources to illuminate art works – was clear. The book marked his passage from disciple of Antal to devotee of the Warburg, where, he wrote in the preface, 'I have had the inestimable advantage of seeing a really scientific method consistently applied'. Antal's widow later commented that the relationship between the two men was closest during the writing of *Artistic Theory in Italy*, 'and it markedly cooled afterwards'. That Blunt was moving on from intellectual Marxism at the point at which he was committing himself most unequivocally to the Soviet Union, suggests a continuing conflict within him about his actions – one, however, which he did nothing to resolve.

The book was praised for its 'thoroughness' and 'clarity', but it did not set the world on fire. The one reviewer to mention the book's Marxism was the up-and coming John Pope-Hennessy, who was now making a name for himself as an expert on Sienese and Florentine art. He suggested that Blunt's 'milk-and-water Marxism' had brought about 'errors of emphasis'. He also compared the book unflatteringly to the encyclopedic German tome by Julius von Schlosser which had inspired it, and declared it dull. His criticism had some justice, but it was informed by an intense competitiveness that had grown up between the two men. As a former protégé of the arch-connoisseur Bernard Berenson, moreover, Pope-Hennessy's approach to art history was at odds with Blunt's emphasis on written sources and social background. Truth to tell, Blunt himself was far from enthusiastic about his first published effort. 'I now hate the sight of every word of the book', he told Saxl in early 1940. In an introduction to the 1956 reprint he wrote, 'Now I should not dare to write such a book at all. The capacity to make broad generalizations, to concentrate a number of ideas into a small compass in the hope that they will convey more of truth than of falsehood, is the result either of the rashness of youth or the wisdom of age.' It was far from the book he had intended to write. All his own original research into French art theory had been jettisoned. Instead he had produced an efficient textbook summary of the Italian Renaissance, much of it taken from German sources. It did its job, however, and over sixty years later is still in print.

The book came out as the Blitz began. In September, Wormwood Scrubs took a direct hit and the now homeless MI5 was split. A larger group went to Blenheim Palace in Woodstock, Oxfordshire, but Blunt joined the more senior group which moved to 58 St James's Street, ensuring that he would be well placed for promotion. A month or so later Tess Mayor and her friend Patricia Rawdon-Smith – the girl who had relieved Blunt of his virginity – came home to their flat in Gower Street and found 'the ceiling on the floor'. Victor Rothschild, with whom Tess now worked at MI5, offered them the lease of a flat at 5 Bentinck Street, next door to the house where Gibbon had written *The Decline and Fall of the Roman Empire*, where Rothschild had lived with his ex-wife, Barbara. It was large and luxurious and decorated with pink-tinted mirrors and rugs by Marion Dorn. They invited Blunt, who had given up his Palace Court flat to a Warburg secretary called Ida Herz* when he had left for France, to share the rent.

* Herz's devotion to Blunt was exceeded only by her adoration of Thomas Mann, whose archivist and chief and most exasperating fan she was.

Guy Burgess, who was a frequent visitor, moved in full-time in 1941. Tess later recalled that they needed another lodger to pay the rent. 'Anthony said Guy was looking for somewhere to live. We said, "As long as he doesn't bring pick-ups back." But of course he did.' The girls took the top floor; Blunt and Burgess slept in the bedrooms on the floor below. 'We'd take it in turns to do fire-watching on our roof. We had one meal together once a week.'

The flat at Bentinck Street has passed into espionage legend as a hotbed of spies and debauchery – 'a homosexual bordello serving as a viperous nest for Soviet Spies', as one author has described it. 'If one could capture who, and what, passed through Bentinck Street during those years,' the American writer Stephen Koch has written, a trifle overheatedly, 'it would be possible to reconstruct some grotesque but remarkably full secret history of the Second World War ... Bentinck Street became a kind of salon, in which Burgess gathered the homosexual underworld of London together with some of the most devious and despicable political operatives then at work.'

The myth derives from two descriptions of Bentinck Street, by Malcolm Muggeridge and by Goronwy Rees. In his memoirs, written in the 1970s, Muggeridge wrote of a wartime visit to Bentinck Street where he encountered a group that included John Strachey, J. D. Bernal, Blunt and Burgess:

> a whole revolutionary Who's Who. It was the only time I ever met Burgess;* and he gave me a feeling such as I have never had from anyone else, of being morally afflicted in some way ... [surrounded by] so distinguished a company – Cabinet Minister-to-be, honoured Guru of the Extreme Left-to-be, Connoisseur Extraordinary-to-be, and other notabilities, all in a sense grouped round Burgess ... hip

---

* Oddly, Muggeridge's edited diaries suggest that his memory of this occasion had lapsed in 1948, when he recorded meeting a 'character called Burgess': 'Lamentable character, very left-wing; obviously seeking to climb the Socialist bandwagon. Long tedious, rather acrimonious argument.'

before hipsters, Rolling before the Stones, acid-head before LSD ... There was not so much a conspiracy gathered round him as just decay and dissolution. It was the end of a class, of a way of life; something that would be written about in history books, like Gibbon on Heliogabalus, with wonder and perhaps hilarity, but still tinged with sadness, as all endings are.

The place's decadence was exemplified for him by the provision of rubber bones for people to bite on if they were terrified by the bombs.

In his memoirs, Goronwy Rees gave another, more lurid, account of Bentinck Street. He claimed the place was peopled with 'unconditional partisans of the Soviet Union', and was little more than a male brothel, 'a high-class disorderly house'. 'Guy brought home a series of boys, young men, soldiers, sailors, airmen', and either slept with them himself or set them up with civil servants, politicians, friends and colleagues. Politicians, Rees claimed, 'popped in and out of bed and then continued some absorbing discussion of political intrigue'.

Apropos these accounts, it is worth noting, that Muggeridge's invitation to Bentinck Street was actually due to Tess Mayor, whom he did not mention, and who was the cousin of his wife, Kitty. Mayor was fond of Muggeridge, but felt his disgust with Bentinck Street was entirely due to his irritation at the left-wing views of its occupants. Of the guests he described, John Strachey, who was by then fiercely anti-Soviet, and J. D. Bernal, who was a Communist, had actually been invited not by Burgess but by Patricia and Tess. As for Goronwy Rees, Tess recalled, 'I only remember Rees coming to stay once, and he was still drunk at breakfast.'

In fact Bentinck Street was very much of its time: it was a twenty-four-hour party, a place that exploited and defied the Blitz. 'One thing we went to all the time in the war', Noel Annan recalled, 'was parties. You met a staggering number of people that way. It was hysterical, certainly highly charged and rich in comedy.' Bentinck Street was also in constant chaos: ration books were mislaid, housekeepers disappeared, and there was a constant stream of visitors, many of whom slept on the floor in the blackout. Burgess wrote to Peter Pollock in the autumn of 1941: 'there seem to be even more people to breakfast than usual . . . 8 the other day (not counting someone who left at 5am)'.

It was Burgess's compulsive socializing that brought crowds to the flat. 'Would you like to meet Freddy Ashton?' he asked Pollock. 'I rather struck up with him – he is most civilised and sweet I think'. 'Nor does it, as things are,' he wrote after a tiff, 'look likely that you will meet [Laurence] Olivier who I am at last getting to know – at least not, I think through me. Miaow.' Blunt swam through this river of politicians, actors, writers, soldiers and chorus boys with an air of half-engaged bemused courtesy. 'Anthony appeared having been summoned to Jackie's [Hewit's] party,' Burgess wrote to Pollock, 'A. who has not much of a head for, or memory of, actresses, spent the evening being very polite and under the impression that Hermione [Baddeley, the actress] was Beatrix Lehmann.'

Among the house-guests over the years were John Strachey, who was thought to be conducting an affair, though with whom nobody could remember, and also the architect Richard Llewelyn Davies, who was after Patricia Rawdon-Smith. At least two MI5 officers – Desmond Vesey and Patrick Day – stayed there for a while. Among other regulars were Dennis Proctor, Brian Howard, Eric Kessler – a married, homosexual, Anglophilic, Swiss diplomat – and Andrew Revai – a homosexual Hungarian journalist friend of Blunt's. In public Howard squawked that Blunt was too stiff, too full of himself, too much a goody-goody; but in private, according to Hewit, they got on rather well. Kim Philby came occasionally to see Burgess, and Hewit remembered once meeting John Cairncross – whom Blunt thought was unaware of his involvement in his recruitment. 'He was a nobody; he was dull,' thought Hewit. Of Blunt's own friends, Ellis Waterhouse, Dadie Rylands, Peter Montgomery and occasionally MacNeice, with whom he spent Christmas 1942, came to visit.

It was certainly true that the love lives of the Bentinck Street inmates rivalled the tortuous complications even of Bloomsbury. The newly divorced Patricia Rawdon-Smith immediately embarked on a series of complicated affairs: 'She was always going to get married, but she never quite did', recalled Peter Pollock. In late 1940 Burgess wrote to him to tell him that Blunt was 'living with Patricia in singularly wedded bliss (tho' she's due to be married to somebody else in 3 months time and is having trouble with her past husband, whom she mothers and sisters, also with a parallel but militarily removed present lover, if you can work that out)'.*

When Burgess had first moved into the flat he had been accompanied by Peter Pollock, but the latter joined the army and was soon posted to Scotland. Then Jackie Hewit came to stay, but – infuriated by Burgess's endless pick-ups and nights out with Brian Howard – he moved out of Burgess's and 'into Blunt's room'. Burgess was still jealously in love with Pollock, to whom he wrote lively, needy, funny letters (which made no reference to his espionage secrets). His love life was additionally complicated by the fact that one of his best friends, the homosexual Swiss diplomat Eric Kessler, was also besotted with Pollock; and that the precocious young writer James Pope-Hennessy, brother to John, had 'totally and violently and very sweetly but also embarrassingly fallen for me', as Burgess reported to Pollock, hoping perhaps for a little jealousy. When none was forthcoming, he began to see James. 'James wrote to me asking me if I would give Guy up,' Pollock recalled, 'and he would love him for ever. He was besotted. Guy was rather pleased.'

* Patricia later married Richard Llewlyen Davies, a former Apostle, who became a well-known post-war architect and advocate of new towns. Made a life peer in 1967, she became the first woman chief whip in the Lords. In the 1980s, aged sixty-eight after her husband's death, she fell in love with Lord Alport, a strongly anti-Thatcherite Tory and founder of the One Nation group. She refused to marry him, because she thought it would damage him politically (and perhaps because she thought, old-fashioned and courtly as he was, he would make an old-fashioned husband). They kept their relationship secret until their deaths in the late 1990s.

Tess Mayor was described by Goronwy Rees as 'timid, gentle and genteel'. Efforts to find her a boyfriend always seemed to end in failure. She was in any case working at MI5 with the man she would marry after the war: Victor Rothschild. The years at Bentinck Street, however, cemented her friendship with Blunt. Peter Wright, Blunt's MI5 interrogator, later quoted her: ' "Anthony used to come back tight to Bentinck Street, sometimes so tight that I had to help him into bed," she used to say. "I would have known if he was a spy . . ." ' However, Wright left out, for libel reasons, his frequently voiced suspicion that they might have had an affair. This was probably Wright's fevered imagination – Hewit and Pollock were both insistent that they had not. What was true was that Tess became Blunt's closest female friend, and one of his most loyal: 'She was devoted to him,' Noel Annan later said. But she understood the limits of his ability to open himself up. 'He hardly ever talked about his private life, or childhood,' she said. 'He was good company, but always under control. He was kindly, but not really very interested in human relations – more interested in ideas.' John Golding – who became Blunt's pupil at the Courtauld in the early 1950s, and went on to become one of the few people whom Blunt allowed to see him across the spectrum of his social guises – recalled that years later 'Tess asked me, "Do you think Anthony was ever really in love with anybody?" I couldn't answer.'

In the autumn of 1940, as Blunt was sorting out his new domestic arrangements, the NKVD's Foreign Directorate finally reopened the London *rezidentura*, and once again installed Anatoli Gorsky as its chief. Gorsky had no idea what had happened to the Cambridge recruits, and showed little desire to find out. He seems to have rediscovered their whereabouts only after they asked Litzi Friedman and Edith Tudor Hart to put them back in touch with him in late 1940. He was amazed to discover that Philby and Blunt were now working for British Intelligence, and that Cairncross had become private secretary to Lord Hankey, the Cabinet's Minister without Portfolio, and had access to Cabinet papers.

Some NKVD officials in Moscow felt that the sudden reappearance of these young men in positions so extraordinarily advantageous to Soviet Intelligence might simply be too good to be true. Gorsky met Blunt on 28 December. It was three and a half years since Blunt had met with a Soviet control, and six months since he had joined MI5, where he was still languishing in 'D' Division. Gorsky, whom Blunt knew as 'Henry', reported that 'Tony' had 'made a good impression on him'. Blunt told him that he had access to Military Intelligence documents, including material on the Red Army, and could search MI5's registry for him. He passed his first documents in January 1941, including a copy of the debriefing of Walter Krivitsky. According to the Russian Intelligence Archives, he passed 1,771 documents to the NKVD between 1941 and 1945. By comparison Burgess supplied 4,605 between 1941 and 1945 – the great proportion after he joined the Foreign Office in June 1944, Maclean supplied 4,593 and Cairncross 5,832.

Blunt's journey towards submission to the Soviet intelligence machine was complete. He had moved from sceptical fellow-traveller to fully fledged Soviet agent. In 1937 he might have described himself as a talent scout for a coming post-apocalypse utopia; now he was handing over documents to a Russian he later told Peter Wright he found 'flat-footed and unsympathetic'. Gorsky was one of the new generation of obedient, unimaginative Soviet intelligence apparatchiks. As the last surviving member of the London *rezidentura*, he had been promoted almost by accident. He was the same age as Blunt, 'a short, fattish man in his mid-thirties, with blond hair brushed straight back and glasses that failed to mask a pair of shrewd, cold eyes'. Yuri Modin, who took over Gorsky's job as Blunt's contact seven years later, described him as 'domineering and bossy with his agents, belittling their work even when they produced excellent material'. Elisabeth Poretsky, whose husband, Ignace, had been assassinated by his former colleagues in the NKVD, wrote that the new generation of foreign NKVD officers were chosen 'primarily because they had roots in the Soviet Union and families who remained there. They were totally lacking in knowledge of the West: its languages, its culture . . . this background ensured their complete loyalty to Moscow, but deprived them of any initiative.'

Why Blunt went from talent spotter to Soviet agent, passing information to a foreign power – for there was no question in 1940 that he was working for anything other than the Soviet Union, now allied to Britain's enemy – was a question even he could never satisfactorily answer. After his exposure he was unwilling, even unable, to engage with the past. On the prompting of friends, he tried to write a memoir explaining himself, but he never finished it. Those who read it remarked on its pedestrian prose, and that it stopped just at the moment when it threatened to become interesting. On the rare occasions when visitors asked him why he'd done what he had, he came out with the phrases 'Cowboys and Indians' or 'Cops and Robbers', with a throwaway shrug. The words suggested that the sides to be taken seemed obvious, but also that Blunt viewed it all as a game or a show. Whether this was the older Blunt's resigned opinion of the frivolous futility of it, or how the younger Blunt had seen it, was never clear. Nor was it obvious which side was the cowboys and which the Indians, and which was supposed to be right.

In his 1974 novel *Tinker, Tailor, Soldier, Spy*, John Le Carré has his spycatcher George Smiley say of Bill Haydon, the Russian mole in British Intelligence:

> Moscow was Bill's discipline . . . He needed the symmetry of an historical and economic solution. This struck him [Smiley] as too sparse, so he added more of the man . . . Bill was a romantic and a snob. He wanted to join an élitist vanguard and lead the masses out of the darkness . . . he imagined Bill's Marxism making up for his inadequacy as an artist, and for his loveless childhood.

'Later of course,' Le Carré adds, 'it hardly mattered if the doctrine wore thin. Bill was set on the road and Karla [Smiley's opposite number and antagonist in Moscow] would know how to keep him there. Treason is very much a matter of habit.' Perhaps there were no great reasons why Blunt went from making notes on his training lectures to bringing out mounds of secret documents, just a fundamental banality, a habit, an almost dull inevitability – and Burgess, of course, living in his pockets, weaving round him a cocoon of political certainty and secrecy. It was not an unfamiliar trajectory: from innocent working for 'peace' to colluding spy. 'We made an independent psychological study once in the CIA,' Norman Mailer has a character say in his novel *Harlot's Ghost*, 'and learned to our dismay (it was really horror) that one third of the men and women who could pass our security clearance were divided enough, handled properly, to be turned into agents of a foreign power.'

It was, nevertheless, important to Blunt to feel that he was acting rationally, out of pure motives. This was a quality that others remarked upon. Victor Rothschild remembered that on meeting Blunt in 1929 he was 'immediately impressed by ... what, for want of a better phrase, I must call high moral ethical principals'. In the 1960s Michael Levey, director of the National Gallery, was struck by the way in which Blunt believed 'in his own high-mindedness', especially when he was in fixer mode – trying to get his nominee a job, or circumventing some tiresome committee. Burgess teased Blunt about his need of principles. Jackie Hewit recalled, 'We'd say that he was up for a knighthood. "Oh goodness no," Guy would say – "Anthony's holding out for canonization!" Anthony was rather pi. Guy would say, "The trouble with you, Anthony, is that you want to have your cake and eat it and give the impression that you're feeding it to the poor."'

And yet, according to the Russian Intelligence Archives, on at least two occasions Blunt accepted a gift of £100 from the Soviets, sent to him after Moscow deemed his contributions particularly useful. The other spies also accepted these very occasional sums. Though he and the others refused offers of pensions and incomes, these modest amounts destroyed any claims that he was acting out of pure principle. In June 1943, after receiving a note of thanks and £100 for information he had passed on German strategy on the eve of the Battle of Kursk, he wrote an almost embarrassingly effusive, awkward note in reply, so different from his usual reticence:

It is difficult to say how proud I feel to know that the work which I have been doing has been of value in the struggle against Fascism in which we are all engaged. Compared with the heroic tasks which our comrades in the Red Army are performing at home, the work which we are doing here seems trivial but this proof that it is worthwhile will, I hope, provide a stimulus to producing better results.

Observers in both his public and his secret worlds felt his commitment to the ideology was thin. 'I would have said Anthony wasn't interested in politics at all,' thought Stuart Hampshire; 'I doubt he bothered to read the papers at all. He was wholly intellectual – I might almost say academic. He was deeply interested in history . . . but he was never in the least bit interested in contemporary politics.' In 1943 Blunt's then control, Boris Kreshin, noted Blunt's limited interest in and lack of enthusiasm for politics. It was so important to Blunt to be right, and that the decision he had made be justifiable to himself on moral and rational grounds, that it became impossible for him to interrogate himself about what he was doing, to wonder what happened to those who wanted out. It was easier for a man with no liking for introspection to get further embedded – to please his control, to put his actions down to loyalty, friendship, and the cause – than to admit that it was all wrong.

There were also more 'impure' motives and satisfactions that Blunt would not excavate. His spying scratched the old itch of anger against the English bourgeois world. He had also discovered that he was congenitally suited to keeping parts of himself separate. 'In intelligence, we look to discover the compartmentalization of the heart,' says Mailer's hero in *Harlot's Ghost*. Blunt's heart was completely compartmentalized. The art critic John Richardson, who knew Blunt through his sometime partner Douglas Cooper, later wrote, 'I sometimes suspected him of suffering from some kind of multiple-personality syndrome.'

Then there was the kick. 'He liked running rings around people, he liked danger', said John Golding, Blunt's former pupil, friend and executor. Neil MacGregor, director of the National Gallery, and one of his last and favourite students, thought:

> He enjoyed the exercise of his skills in every area. He enjoyed knowing he could do something terribly well. I suspect he got a great deal of enjoyment out of keeping the two bits separate and not tripping up. You have to be very clever to carry it off, and he knew he was terribly clever. There was a delight in the game, in being able to do it so completely, and to live completely differently in the two worlds must have been quite exhilarating. My hunch would be that that was really what kept it going: the intoxication of playing this wonderfully complex game, like a dazzling piece of choreo-graphy.

Wilfrid bewilderedly recalled his brother turning to him after the exposure and saying almost proudly, 'You must admit I'm a very good actor.' He too believed that Blunt had got a kick out of the double game.

In *Tinker, Tailor, Soldier, Spy* George Smiley ultimately dismisses his attempts at explaining Haydon's motives and 'settle[s] instead for a picture of one of those wooden Russian dolls that opens up, revealing one person inside the other, and another inside of him'.

11. Spy

'a thorough, conscientious and efficient agent'

'B' Division was the heart of MI5. 'B' Division was where the Double-Cross system was run and where MI5's surveillance teams and agents were based. It was where Ultra – the summaries of the information translated by the Bletchley code-breakers from enemy coded messages, including those from the Germans' apparently unbreakable Enigma code – was delivered and analysed. In February 1941, a month after Blunt began to hand over secret documents to Anatoli Gorsky, Guy Liddell made him his personal assistant, moving him from his dull desk job in 'D' Division to the centre of things. Though the job did not work out – Liddell, Blunt told the NKVD, was 'not the kind of person who can have assistants since he always does all the work again himself'* – there were plenty of other tasks that needed to be done. Dick White began to use Blunt in his work in German counter-espionage. At the same time 'I was still nominally with Liddell, and I still have certain jobs which he gave me to do for him, such as the Directing of B6.' B6 was the surveillance section, which consisted of thirty-eight 'watchers' trained to follow suspects without being spotted, and which Blunt appears to have overseen for a time.

Eventually he found a niche monitoring foreign diplomatic missions, especially those of neutral countries – Portugal, Spain

---

* It has also been suggested that Blunt fell foul of Liddell's fearsome secretary Miss Huggins, who decided he was encroaching on her territory.

and Sweden, in particular – which MI5 suspected might be providing cover for German Intelligence. The job began when White asked him to assess what information MI5 had on foreign embassies and nationals. Blunt's coup was to discover that MI6 was collecting information from embassies which it was failing to share with MI5. 'After a lot of struggles which are not really interesting', he persuaded MI6 to hand over the material. The embassies project became a full-time job, and the task with which he was most closely identified at MI5. His next step was to develop methods of parting from their couriers the diplomatic bags the embassies sent home each week, so that MI5 could take a look at them. At ports, the couriers would be persuaded to hand their bags over to Port Security, who would put them into a safe. 'Blunt's people would open the back of the safe,' a colleague recalled, and take out the bags and examine them. At airports, flights would be 'delayed', and the couriers once again would be persuaded to hand over their bags for 'security', 'giving him time for his cronies to open the bags, open the envelopes, read everything in them, photograph some of them if need be, and put it all back so nobody would know a thing'. Blunt's department collaborated with the Post Office to develop special methods for opening the seals on the bags and repairing them without trace. As time went on, he was also given charge of monitoring the movement of diplomatic staff and foreign nationals, and enforcing regulations limiting their movement around the country.

How regularly Blunt saw his control at this time is not clear. The great mass of information he brought out for the Soviets dates from 1942, but there is no doubt he was giving the unlovely Gorsky MI5 documents in the months before June 1941, when Hitler broke the terms of the Nazi–Soviet Pact and invaded the Soviet Union – a move he had been planning since the fall of France the previous summer. The attack took Stalin by surprise – Molotov, his Foreign Minster, asked the German ambassador disbelievingly, 'What have we done to deserve this?' – even though NKVD intelligence sources had been warning for months that Hitler was planning to invade and that German troops were massing on the Russian border. The Russian Intelligence Archives have never revealed whether Blunt – who might have heard things through his links with German counter-espionage – was a warning voice. Even Churchill had tried to send warnings, but Stalin refused to hear them. He had a deal with Hitler. Beria, the head of the NKVD, asked leave to grind the offending sources 'into dust' for their 'systematic disinformation'. Such was the lamentable state of the Red Army, still recovering from the decimation of its officer ranks, that the Germans virtually walked into the USSR. Within days they had got as far as Minsk and millions of Soviet citizens had been taken prisoner (Soviet soldiers captured by the Germans were announced by Stalin to be 'malicious deserters'). The opening of the Eastern Front would cost the lives of an estimated 8 to 9 million Soviet soldiers and between 16 and 19 million Soviet civilians.

On 12 July, two and a half weeks after the invasion, the Soviet Union signed a Mutual Assistance Treaty with Britain in Moscow. Everyone seemed more than happy to forget that days before the USSR had been the enemy. Overnight, the CPGB became again fiercely anti-Nazi. The Artists International Association – on whose advisory committee Blunt now served – announced in its July bulletin, with tangible relief, 'we can now take as an association, a more positive attitude to the war on the result of which the whole future of European civilization and culture may depend'. Years later Dick White liked to describe Blunt, Philby and Burgess as 'double patriots' (a phrase which described Burgess's combination of disappointed imperialism and proselytizing Communism rather well), as if the era of the Pact had never existed. Blunt was himself relieved that the Soviet Union was again Germany's enemy. He later described the Pact as 'a tactical necessity to gain time', and insisted that before it broke up 'I had very little access to very little information.' (He also claimed that what he passed to the Soviets after the Pact had been broken was 'almost entirely about the German Intelligence Services. Largely intercepts.' This was by no means true.) Thus far the papers produced by the Russian Intelligence Archives suggest that Blunt was indeed not very prolific before the end of the Pact.

The new alliance with the Soviet Union stimulated a debate within the intelligence services. At Churchill's behest they stopped collecting Soviet intelligence and monitoring Soviet radio signals. At the same time, the decision was taken to keep secret from the Soviets the fact that Britain was gradually breaking the Enigma code. For the rest of the war, information relevant to the Soviets – particularly on German troop manoeuvres – that came from Ultra was disguised, or even withheld, so as not to alert the Soviets' suspicion that the British knew more than they were telling. There were those in British Intelligence, including Victor Rothschild, who felt that it was unjust to hold back such crucial information when Russians were dying in such terrible numbers. 'I remember it being argued in our service', Dick White later said, 'that we ought to be giving much more to the Russians than we were, during the German attack on Russia. And you could see that's an argument; that they were an ally. A lot of people thought we should have done more.' White himself felt it 'would be fatal to get involved with them to the point they could get inside our machinery'.

The belief that the Soviet Union deserved help was held by people well beyond British Intelligence. As Soviet casualties grew, sympathy throughout Britain grew too. By the middle of the war, Communist Party membership had risen to 50,000, its highest figure before or since. Douglas Hyde, a senior Party member, claimed that after June 1941 people from 'factories and forces, civil servants, scientists' were sending information about armaments and munitions to Party headquarters. Harry Hinsley, the official historian of twentieth-century British intelligence, confirms that British Intelligence knew that information was being passed to the CPGB, but decided for the moment to turn a blind eye. At her new job at Bush House, after the end of the Pact, a former MI5 secretary, Joan Miller, caught an army major passing messages about the Middle East to the Soviets. She was enraged when he wasn't punished.

*

It was in 1941 that Jackie Hewit moved into Blunt's bedroom at Bentinck Street and they began an affair. It continued on and off until after the war. Their friends were surprised. Hewit was ditzy, overtly camp, and tended towards the theatrical: 'Jackie's temperament is in full (purple) hue and cry (shrill),' Burgess once reported to Pollock. Hewit liked the frisson and comradeliness of the London gay clubs like Le Bœuf sur le Toit in Piccadilly – places to which Blunt was only occasionally and reluctantly dragged. Nevertheless, Blunt took on his familiar role: slightly distant, almost paternal. 'He educated me,' Hewit said later:

> he got me to read things and encouraged me. I remember him standing in front of the Van Gogh that hung on the staircase at the Courtauld, a self-portrait with his ear off, telling me the whole story. I never forgot it. I used to soak it up – knowledge. I left school at fourteen. If it hadn't been for him – for Burgess too – I would never have known anything.

What Blunt didn't do was preach politics. Like Pollock, Hewit found politics deathly dull.

There was, Hewit insisted, 'never any great romance between us. It was convenience for me and convenience for him – and great affection. He wasn't a passionate person – even at "the point of no return".' Peter Pollock agreed: 'I thought Jackie and Anthony was purely sexual and convenient. I didn't think Blunt was very interested in sex.' Blunt appears not to have exploited the Blitz's opportunities for easy sex. 'It's said in some books that he went with rough trade in public lavatories. That's absolute rubbish,' Hewit insisted. 'Blunt wasn't promiscuous,' said Tess Rothschild, 'but occasionally Burgess would pass a boyfriend on to him'. In contrast with his risky espionage world, Blunt wanted a quiet life: an early drink at the Reform, then a French film with Hewit – Blunt told him he looked like Fernandel – perhaps *Quai des Brumes* or *La Femme du Boulanger*, or a Marx brothers or even a western, to which he was partial. He took Hewit to *Fantasia* twice. 'Surprisingly enough,' Burgess told Pollock,

'Anthony enjoyed it very much indeed.' If anything, it was Hewit who strayed. 'Jackie is suffering rather seriously from Pollockitis, ie frustration,' Burgess wrote to Pollock. 'As A. points out the situation is getting *grave* (French) when not only I but also he are enlisted as Pimps. All (J's) swans turned out to be geese, and giggling geese at that.' It was widely acknowledged, even by those like Peter Pollock who regarded him as a cold fish, that Blunt's 'one and only true love' was Peter Montgomery, who occasionally came to stay on leave: 'I think Anthony really loved him.'

'If he is somehow to decompress an agent needs some kind of pastime,' Yuri Modin, Blunt's last control, wrote. Burgess's pastimes were sex and socializing. Even with his new affair, Blunt was most preoccupied by his academic work. During 1941, alongside his obligations to British Intelligence and his tasks for the NKVD, he continued with the second volume of Poussin drawings, lectured on Picasso at London University, organized a series of lectures on classicism with Fritz Saxl, mounted an exhibition of seventeenth-century English and Italian architectural drawings at the Courtauld with Wittkower, and edited the Warburg/Courtauld journal. He completed several academic articles. He spent a night a week at the Courtauld, and regularly visited the Warburg scholars, who, in accordance with Fritz Saxl's dream of setting up a self-sufficient scholastic community, and to avoid the bombs, had decamped to a big house in Buckinghamshire in May 1941. Blunt lent them his library and, when he came to stay, slept in a bath. 'Scholarly communal living drove people mad,' Margot Wittkower commented on this not altogether successful experiment.

The Warburg scholars had not done well in the war. The librarian, Meier, had died in a bomb blast, and two other scholars, Otto Demus and Ernst Kitzinger, had fallen victim to the government's clumsy internment policy and had been transported to camps in Canada and Australia. 'All our efforts to obtain Dr Demus's release have so far been unsuccessful', Fritz Saxl reported dolefully. Saxl himself had taken British citizenship before the war. Blunt tried to secure the release of a number of wrongly imprisoned internees, including the Austrian art historian Johannes Wilde and another German and the friend of a Warburg colleague, Reinhard Krauss, an industrial psychologist. He also wrote a reference for the Warburg scholar Hugo Buchtal in August 1940: 'He is a person who could be counted on to behave on all occasions with perfect loyalty to this country.' Perhaps Blunt enjoyed writing this: the irony – given that he himself was at his most energetically disloyal – is thick, though in some ways he was in a better position to judge Buchtal's likely riskiness to the war effort than anyone else.

He also published his second book that year. He had written it during the Blitz months of the autumn of 1940, 'with the bombs screaming in his ears', as he later told a student. It was a study of the French architect François Mansart, based on three lectures Blunt had given at the Warburg in August 1940. Mansart was part of the French seventeenth-century world in which Blunt now felt most intellectually at home. He was a neglected genius about whom even the French knew little, and, as the founder of French classical vernacular architecture, a figure arguably as important and influential as Poussin, his contemporary. Most of Mansart's work existed only on paper in the Archives Nationales in Paris, and little of what he had built was still standing, apart from the chateaux of Blois and Maisons-sur-Seine. Even there, what he had actually contributed was a subject of much debate.

The war threatened to destroy the last traces of Mansart's work, and Blunt felt it was up to him to rescue the architect from potentially irreversible obscurity. All he had were his pre-war notes, and the encouragement of Wittkower, whom he later thanked 'for spending so many hours discussing both the general and the particular points raised here'. 'My excuse for publishing [these lectures] in this imperfect form' – without being able to see anything in France – he wrote in his preface, 'is that almost nothing of value has been written on this architect, whose merits are yet so widely acknowledged, and that in the present circumstances one must publish what one can while one can.' The book was filled with descriptions of façades, interiors and staircases, and was aimed at a more specialized academic audience than *Artistic Theory*. But the circumstances of its creation captured the imaginations of the reviewers: that it had been 'written last summer in the scant leisure of an English soldier is a fact no less astonishing than it is gratifying', wrote Raymond Mortimer, who described it as 'exemplary in taste and erudition'. Nikolaus Pevsner called it 'scholarly yet readable', and commented, 'it is most gratifying to see that the war has not entirely stopped the publication of such books. Mr Blunt is in the Army, but he found the energy and the enthusiasm to publish last year his book on Italian art theory.' Blunt may not have been 'in the Army' in quite the way that Pevsner and Mortimer had in mind, but the Mansart book was nevertheless a considerable feat.

Anatoli Gorsky was never popular with his Cambridge charges, so Blunt, Burgess and Philby were not disappointed when he was replaced in the spring of 1942 by a new handler, Boris Kreshin, whom they knew initially as 'Bob' and later as 'Max'.* Kreshin – also known as Krotov or Krotenschild – was, according to his successor Yuri Modin, energetic, charming and Jewish. The latter fact appears to have blocked his rise in the NKVD. According to Modin, Kreshin's attitude to his agents was quite different to that of the brusque Gorsky: 'he just said, "Listen it would be marvellous if you could bring this off."' Kreshin approved of Blunt. He described him as a

> thorough, conscientious and efficient agent. He tries to fulfil all our tasks in time and as conscientiously as possible.

* There is, in fact, some confusion in the books from Soviet sources about who the Soviet *rezidents* and illegals were at this time. Kreshin was 'Max', but it is possible that Gorsky's successor with the spies was someone else. Pavel Sudaplatov says Gorsky's immediate successor as London chief was Konstantin Kukin. Philby's Russian biographer Genrikh Borovik rarely names the agents and chiefs of the London *rezidentura*, but says that after 1943 the *rezident* in London dealing with Blunt and the other spies was 'Igor', whom West and Tsarev gloss as Kukin. In the absence of further information, I assume that Kreshin was 'Bob' too.

Tony, by the way, is the opposite of Mädchen both in character and in his attitude to his duties to us. Tony is thoughtful, serious, will never promise if he knows about the difficulty or impossibility of giving an answer to this or that question.

From the documents so far published by the Russian Intelligence Archives, Blunt responded to what he described as Kreshin's 'patience and unfailing understanding', and between 1942 and 1944 produced far more information than he ever had before.

His latest task at MI5 had been to develop a network of informants in foreign embassies and among foreign communities. Hitherto the extent of MI5's Embassy surveillance had been limited to one agent in the Japanese embassy and one in a South American embassy. Blunt put in agents through a domestic staffing agency which used his people as cleaners or disposers of embassy rubbish. There was a secretary in the Spanish Embassy who brought him telegrams and private letters. There were several society ladies: a Susan Maxwell, wife of a British colonel killed in Libya, gave him titbits on the Swedish delegation, one of whom had been her boyfriend. Lady Dalrymple-Champneys, wife of the Permanent Under-Secretary at the Ministry of Health, knew the Egyptian ambassador and 'moves in a circle where she also meets a number of undesirable people'.

He also employed people closer to home – among them Jackie Hewit, Peter Pollock, the Swiss diplomat Eric Kessler and the Hungarian journalist Andrew Revai, who had become a good friend to Blunt and Burgess, and also happened to be Friedrich Antal's nephew. Kessler was supposed to pass on information on diplomatic circles, and Revai on Hungarians and foreign journalists, especially the Swedes. Both were frequent visitors to Bentinck Street, and Burgess numbered them among his best friends. The arrangements were incestuously, and typically, Burgessian – Hewit called Kessler and Revai 'Guy's spies'. Blunt told Moscow, and years later Nigel West, that he managed them 'through Burgess', who was once again – ostensibly at least – employed at the BBC. The idea that Burgess was actively involved in working for MI5 is controversial. Dick White insisted that Burgess had nothing to do with MI5 and that Guy Liddell had thought 'Burgess was a disgraceful figure ... He told everyone in MI5 that no one was to have anything to do with Burgess.' But Christopher Harmer, another 'B' Division officer, remembered that 'Burgess was always in and out of the office ... I don't think Liddell consciously gave him information but he was very indiscreet.' Stuart Hampshire remembered that the German anti-Nazi Gans zu Putlitz, who had passed German diplomatic documents to the British before the war, was also supposed to be involved. 'He was to be a double agent. He was gay and respectable and was on good relations with Anthony and Guy, and Anthony was going to use him. How it all ended I don't know. But it was typical of them – it bordered on the social, and was at the same time supposed to be in aid of the war effort.' It seems too that Brian Howard's brief sojourn in MI5 was a suggestion of Burgess's. Howard was employed to report on Nazi sympathizers in his set, but was sacked in 1942 after one too many noisy scenes in nightclubs. He would become overexcited and threaten unhelpful staff with MI5's mysterious powers.

The recently published *Mitrokhin Archive* claims that Burgess had previously recruited Kessler and Revai (or Revoi as he is sometimes known) for the NKVD as sources for information on Swiss–German relations and Hungarian attitudes in 1939.* If they were Soviet sources, it seems possible that Kessler at least, who was a raging Anglophile and appeared to think he was helping out the Foreign Office, was an unwitting one. After the war, Revai remained a friend of Blunt's and set up a company selling prints and reproductions through the *New Statesman*. 'Anthony was his idol of what an art historian should be', his post-war partner Robin Chancellor recalled. But many of Blunt's

---

* It should be noted that no other books from the Russian Intelligence Archives refer to Kessler and Revai as having been recruited by Burgess for the NKVD, and that those who knew them thought of them as keen Anglophiles.

friends felt there was something odd about Revai, though they
could not put their finger on quite what. He didn't fit. He seemed
to know Blunt from a world that they did not. There were even
rumours that he had had contacts with the French Communist
Party. Blunt's boyfriend of the late 1940s, Alan Baker,* felt Revai
was shifty, and that he and Blunt shared some secret. 'I remember
interrupting them once together, they started apart, guiltily. I
thought at first it was sex, but then no. He was a nice man, but
very unprepossessing.'

'Guy's spies' seemed to be madly unprofessional. Peter Pollock
believed his job was merely a ploy by Burgess 'to keep me in
London. I lived in the Savoy and the Dorchester, for which MI5
or 6 – I couldn't tell the difference – paid. I knew White and
Liddell from the Reform and Bentinck Street.' Burgess's habitual
combining of work and leisure and his closeness to Blunt are
illustrated in a letter to Pollock:

> I think we can say you have a more than 50% chance of the
> job. Touch wood cross fingers and don't believe it anyhow.
> Anyhow I've worked hard and so, for that matter has
> A[nthony]. I've assured A. that if you get it

> 1 you'll take it seriously and even tho' living in London not
>   get a worse reputation than necessary

> 2 that I think you are really just as keen as I to make a
>   success of us – which will be v necessary if we are to be
>   together, as we should if this came off.

Pollock felt he couldn't be giving value for money: 'I had a list of
people – all gay Hungarians, mostly nice people – I was supposed
to keep my eye on. I didn't really know what I was supposed to
do. I told Guy that when my unit was moved overseas I would
go, and I did. To Algeria.'

Jackie Hewit's job brought him back to London after he'd
enlisted. 'I had a chit which said I worked for A. F. Blunt at MI5.

* Not his real name.

All he asked me to do was to arrange meetings, like with the landlady of a pub near the Swedish Embassy where diplomats used to meet. He'd meet the landlady and she'd pass on bits.' On another occasion Hewit was sent by Blunt to a Catholic church in north London to track down a homosexual priest who was allegedly 'listening to Lord Haw Haw. I went to the pub instead.' Blunt told Moscow that the pub landlady was Mrs Newman of the Dover Castle in Portland Place, where the Swedish legation drank, and the priest was Father Clement Russell, who had been a member of the British Union of Fascists.

Despite the questionable effectiveness of Burgess's sub-agents, no one challenged Blunt's ability or commitment at MI5 – an indication perhaps that the place was not entirely the hive of efficiency that it has been claimed to be. If he was criticized, it was on the basis of his coolness or his homosexuality. A former MI5 secretary recalled, 'He was always said to be charming by the people who worked in his section, but the rest of us tended to regard him as an ice-cold bastard, knowing that anyone who was not important to him did not exist.' The young Hugh Trevor-Roper felt 'that he disliked me – that he looked down his nose at me and did not think me worth talking to. He was, after all, a Fellow of Trinity, and I was a nobody.' Stuart Hampshire also had reservations. 'I didn't really like him, though I liked being around him. I enjoyed his company. He was interesting, but there was no "warm glow".' Desmond Bristow, the MI6 man who worked with Blunt's friend Tomás Harris, found his homosexuality offensive: 'I'd met too many like that in my life – not my type of person by a long chalk, and one could see it a mile away. I just didn't like him, and a lot of other people in 5 and 6 didn't like him either.' Bristow was also insistent that Lt. Col. T. A. 'Tar' Robertson, the ex-Sandhurst officer who ran the Double-Cross section – 'a big haughty fellow with friendly eyes and an assertive way about him' – wouldn't have let any 'queers' near his department. Robertson himself said, 'I couldn't stick the man. One knew that he was queer and before the war one would not have countenanced letting him anywhere near the office . . . Let's face it, he kept some strange company – people like Burgess and other sods.' The Russian Intelligence Archives, however, suggest that Blunt considered Robertson a good and willing source of news, and show that in 1948, after Blunt left MI5, Robertson asked his opinions on some anti-Soviet projects. Blunt's best friend at 'the office', as it was known to its inmates, was Courtney Young, who before the war had briefly been a private tutor to the adopted daughter of Lord Leconfield of Petworth (to whom Blunt was distantly related). He and Blunt 'were inseparable at MI5. They would play schoolboy games [like leapfrog] in the canteen.'

From 1942, Blunt met Kreshin once a week, between nine and ten in the evening, in different parts of London. He would hand over the documents he had taken out of the office as 'homework'; they were photographed overnight – Blunt refused to do it himself; he claimed to be hopeless with all machinery, which was true – and early the next morning he would meet Kreshin again to collect the papers and return them. He said that he gave up taking out documents after he was stopped by a policeman one night when he had a caseful of ISOS papers. (These papers were very confidential non-Enigma coded messages from the German High Command, which Blunt offered to bring out in April 1942. They were decrypted by a section at Bletchley called 'Intelligence Service Oliver Strachey', named after its head, a member of the ubiquitous Strachey family.) The policeman had no idea what the papers were, but from that moment Blunt began to memorize texts, writing reports on them late into the night. In the eighteen months after he had first begun to pass documents, he had become an adept and assiduous gatherer of information. He later admitted to spending lunch hours searching colleague's desks, and looking up classified files from the registry, MI5's archive, at the Soviets' request. He gleaned gossip from White and Liddell. Liddell told Blunt so much that the NKVD eventually gave him his own code name.

Blunt went to great lengths to arrange for a huge range of secret information to come to his attention.

I get in the ordinary course of my job the deciphered diplomatic telegrams, the diplomatic telephone conversations, and the product of the various agents in the embassies . . . In addition, I have established a claim to see ISOS, although in fact it has nothing to do with my work and I have managed to get myself into a position where I can get a certain amount of operational information from Lennox's [head of MI5's Operations Department] section on the grounds that I have to watch for leakages in the diplomatic channels which I watch. I have also managed to get myself in touch with [Tar] Robertson who runs the double agents over the question of putting over false information through diplomatic channels. In this way I can usually get an idea of what is actually planned and what is being put across as cover. I have also made myself a sort of liaison officer for Shillito [who ran subversion against the Comintern and Soviet Intelligence, and was based at Blenheim Palace] in London and do all sorts of jobs for him which gives me the opportunity of talking to him about his work. In this way he is usually ready to tell me far more than is really necessary about his cases . . . he is well disposed and in fact tends to talk far too much. I have also got myself into a position of doing a good deal of liaison with other departments, particularly with the Foreign Office, the War Office, SIS, GC & CS [Bletchley] and Censorship.

He also met his old recruit Leo Long approximately once a fortnight, to collect information on the German order of battle. Long's fluent German had got him a job in MI14, where he worked on collating and analysing German strategic information, mostly from Ultra. Blunt came into Long's department on MI5 business one day in 1941 – after the end of the Pact, Long always insisted. (This is possible, as the first advances in breaking the Enigma code were made only in spring 1941, and army codes weren't broken until 1942.) He did not demand Long's cooperation, the younger man later remembered:

He said we were all on the same side. That the Russians would win the war. We weren't sure that the British were giving the Russians as much information as they should. Blunt said that he had this friend . . . I was slightly nervous [about agreeing to help]. The thought crossed my mind that Blunt was a genuine MI5 officer and that I was being led up the garden path.

They met at a pub in Portman Square or a snack bar in Jermyn Street. Long would pass a synopsis of his department's conclusions on the strength of the German army under the table. All his information was passed through Blunt, who wrote further reports on his meetings with Long.

In 1942 Kreshin made a summary of the papers that Blunt had recently passed to him. They included MI5 internal documents, personal files on people targeted for cultivation, wireless intercepts from Bletchley and weekly summaries of them, diplomatic telegrams, German Intelligence reports from the Eastern Front and elsewhere, papers MI5 had got from the diplomatic missions (including mail), military intelligence summaries, MI5 reports on immigrants, and surveillance information including telephone intercepts of various people suspected of Nazi sympathies. Blunt had also written personality profiles of key figures in MI5, including Liddell and White. What particularly fascinated the NKVD were his descriptions of the procedures and methods of MI5: how they inserted bugs, how they ran investigations, how they debriefed defectors.

Contrary to suggestions at the time of his exposure, there is no evidence that Blunt was the direct cause of any deaths.* As an MI5 officer, he worked only on operations within the British Isles.

---

* Peter Wright claimed that Blunt was responsible for the exposure of an MI6 spy, 'Gibby's spy', in the Kremlin. According to Nigel West, information about the Kremlin spy (by whom the Soviets were very exercised) appears not to have come from Blunt, and in any case the spy was never caught. A newspaper report in November 1979 that Blunt sent Dutch agents to their deaths in a disastrous operation to Holland confused Blunt with another officer of the same name.

Moreover, one of the NKVD's greatest reservations about him was the fact that his information was not thought to be sufficiently damaging to his own country. On the other hand, Blunt was quite willing to furnish the Soviets with whatever he could find, and the secrets he was able to impart to them – about the Double-Cross and the breaking of the Enigma code, which both came into their own after the end of the Pact; as well as the dates and place of the Allied landings in 1944 – would have been devastating, in every sense, if they had got into German hands. Nothing suggests that he would have held back had he been in a position to hand over more obviously destructive material.

The problem was that the NKVD could not cope with this manic industry. It now appears that much of the material the Cambridge spies worked so hard to bring out was never actually read by anybody. Yuri Modin, who went to work as an English translator in Moscow's Foreign Intelligence Directorate in 1943, said the seven translators who dealt with intelligence from England were so constantly drowned in paper that the material had 'barely a 50 per cent chance of being read'. Nigel West, who has seen some of the files, confirms that much of the material 'is in the original, in their handwriting – in manuscript or typed, as Blunt and the rest handed it to their Soviet contacts'.

The NKVD's problem was compounded by the fact that, in the face of the mountains of paper, analysers such as Modin were instructed to make a priority of finding confirmation of Stalin's paranoid preoccupation with Western conspiracies against him. It was called the Main Issue. According to Modin, this activity produced 'excellent results'. He claimed that intelligence from spies like Blunt, Burgess, Philby, Maclean and Cairncross 'proved' that in 1942 Churchill and the West deliberately put off opening a second front in order to bleed the Soviet Union. Modin's KGB contemporary Pavel Sudaplatov supported this belief in his memoirs, claiming that the Cambridge spies confirmed that the British were 'rationing information on German strategy' in 1943 (which was true). He also claimed that they had informed the NKVD that in 1944 and '45 Britain and the USA were secretly negotiating with Germany against the Soviet Union in Sweden and Switzerland.

The Russian Intelligence Archives make even stranger claims than Sudaplatov and Modin. They suggest that throughout the period that Blunt was at his most prolific as a spy, his NKVD masters were convinced that he and the other Cambridge spies were in fact British double agents. In 1942 – around the time that Kreshin took over as the London spies' control – there was another reshuffle among the staff at the Foreign Intelligence Directorate. The new regime was almost completely ignorant about its most valuable British agents. It began to put pressure on Kreshin to extract evidence from Blunt and Philby of British conspiracy and espionage against the Soviet Union. Blunt and Philby – who were beginning to produce a great deal of useful information on German strategy – kept telling Kreshin, as they had told Anatoli Gorsky before him, that there were no secret operations against the USSR, and the Soviet Embassy was not being watched. They explained that MI5 and MI6 had limited resources – MI5 could only tap a total of forty lines at a time, and had only thirty-eight watchers – and were directing all their efforts against Germany. But Blunt did inform the NKVD that there was an MI5 microphone hidden at CPGB headquarters.

This kind of information did not please Moscow. A combination of institutional paranoia and a total misconception about the Cambridge spies and their world – so far away from the narrow, brutal, carefully servile world of the NKVD – reignited old suspicions that they were not what they claimed to be. Kreshin himself had been a victim of this when he had worked in Moscow in 1940. Then he had concluded that Burgess was a British plant. In 1942 he wrote, 'Before I came here and before I came into contact with him I had a certain prejudice . . . Mädchen has produced a far better impression on me than that which I got from materials and characterizations at home.' The new regime's doubts were not calmed, however. To them Blunt, Philby, Burgess, Cairncross and even Maclean – who had not seen any of the others for years, and had only recently returned to England from a successful stint at the British Embassy in Paris – seemed too good to be true. They were also tainted by their links with the old disgraced illegals – Orlov, who had fled to America, and Maly, who had been shot as a German collaborator. The fact that Blunt and Burgess lived together and that Philby was in frequent touch with them violated basic Soviet intelligence protocols, and made Moscow additionally uneasy. That they claimed to be sincere, ideological converts made Moscow even more suspicious.

In August 1942 Kreshin was reprimanded for an 'insufficiently attentive and watchful attitude towards agents', and for not pushing them hard enough on the matter of counter-espionage against the Soviet Union. Kreshin's boss described Blunt's 'under-statement' of MI5's Soviet surveillance as 'suspicious'. Nor was he reassured by Burgess's latest characteristically wild suggestion – that he recruit an MI5 officer called Kemball Johnston. Kreshin was also admonished for informing Moscow that it would be impossible to split up Blunt and Burgess and to prevent Philby from seeing them. This, Kreshin's critic demanded, must be 'investigated immediately', and Kreshin was instructed to 'talk with each of these agents carefully and skilfully about the others, clarifying with each of them separately what their particular relations are, then comparing the received information, and to attempt to establish at whose initiative these meetings and conversations about contact with us take place'. Over the next eighteen months Blunt and Philby were set a series of tasks, including writing detailed memoirs about themselves and their colleagues, so that Moscow could examine their stories for inconsistencies. Blunt's 1943 memoir was written in response to this demand. He was also told to make a priority of searching for information not just about current British intelligence work against the USSR, but also about past cases. Thus it was that during the autumn and winter of 1942 – when the Battle of Stalingrad was beginning to claim huge numbers of Soviet casualties – the NKVD insisted that Blunt and Philby search for information on old espionage operations, rather than concentrate on German strategy and strength. Philby, at least, resented being asked to spend his time on such things. In March 1943 it was reported that 'in his opinion now is the time that attention should be paid primarily to getting information, and not writing various autobiographies'.

Despite Blunt and Philby's efforts, nothing seemed to defuse Moscow's distrust. In October 1942 Blunt reported that he was now 99 per cent certain that British Intelligence had no plans to spy on the Soviet Embassy. Along with this he sent a long description of the workings of MI5's watcher service, as well as a detailed account of MI5's handling of Soviet subversion in Britain in the 1920s and '30s, including how MI5 had got wind of the 1938 Woolwich Arsenal ring, even down to the names of the surveillance team that had been involved. The NKVD's response was a report which concluded that Philby's assertions 'about the Hotel's [MI6] weak activity against us and Tony's [Blunt] about the absence of Hut's [MI5] work against us on the Island [Britain] are suspicious. They do not mention being ill-informed, which proves the absurdity of it.'

The suspicions about the Cambridge spies seem to have been generated, and most strenuously promoted, by Elena Modrzhinskaya, a blonde, blue-eyed, congenitally suspicious NKVD officer, whom Philby's Russian biographer, Borovik, described as 'inclined to plumpness and the exposure of conspiracy theories'. According to one source, she ran the Third Department of the Foreign Directorate where British information was assessed; according to another, she held a less senior position in the 'Information Service', evaluating agent information. Whatever Modrzhinskaya's influence in the Directorate, it was gradually becoming impolitic to say that the Cambridge spies were genuine. Moreover, Modrzhinskaya's initial premise was not an absurd one: could British Intelligence really be so naive as to allow two former Communists to hold such senior positions in its two most important organizations, and to allow them to take out of the office such an extraordinary volume of secret material? In November 1942 she wrote a long report giving voice to Moscow's unease, insisting that all the Cambridge ring, even Maclean, were disinformation agents, planted on Soviet Intelligence just as the

British were using the Double-Cross against the Germans. She saw nothing odd in the fact that she knew about the Double-Cross system in such detail only because Blunt, Philby and the rest had told the NKVD about it in the first place. Despite these suspicions, it was decided that for the moment no further action would be taken because the material the spies were passing was actually extremely useful.

However, during the spring and summer of 1943 the officers in Moscow again became agitated. In April, Burgess, Blunt and Philby admitted to Kreshin that information that for two years they had been passing off as Burgess's had actually come from a man called Henri Smolka. Smollett, as he renamed himself in Britain, was an Austrian Marxist who worked at the Ministry of Information, where he was brilliantly successful at organizing pro-Soviet propaganda. Philby had recruited him in 1939, but Gorsky had insisted he terminate the connection in 1941, because he judged Smollett insufficiently useful. Philby had disobeyed Gorsky, and passed him on to Burgess. When Kreshin inquired about recontacting Smollett, the ruse was admitted. Gorsky, still *rezidentura* chief, was furious. Moscow decided that the spies' unreliability was now proven, but that Kreshin should continue to ask them for news of the German army – Blunt and Cairncross had recently been sent personal congratulations from a Red Army general for providing crucial information on German strategy. In a characteristic rationalization, Moscow ordered Burgess to stay in touch with Smollett. Then, in July, Burgess chose the worst possible moment to make another of his mad suggestions: he offered to murder Goronwy Rees, whom he said was 'hysterical and unbalanced', and who he feared might betray them all 'at any moment'. Moscow declined the offer, and concluded that it was deliberate provocation from MI5.

The NKVD always assumed that the spies knew nothing about its suspicions. This seems unlikely. In April 1943 Kreshin reported that Burgess had told him he was worried that the comrades did not trust them. Kreshin hurriedly brushed the suggestion aside; it was just Burgess's imagination, he said – though he admitted that

Moscow found it hard to believe that the British were not spying on them. Instead of letting the matter drop, Burgess launched into a long speech. There were three possibilities regarding British operations against the Soviet Union he began: (1) that there weren't any, as Blunt, Philby and Burgess said; (2) that the British knew that Blunt, Philby and Burgess were spying for the Soviets and were deliberately feeding them disinformation; (3) that he, Blunt, Philby and the rest were all double agents. He reasoned that if (2) or (3) was true, Blunt and Philby would never have reached the elevated positions they had, therefore it must be true that the British were not spying on the Soviets. Kreshin changed the subject.

Blunt was also aware of being scrutinized: it is clear from his NKVD memoir that he knew he was being asked to justify his entry into MI5 and his rise within it. And it seems unlikely that he did not spot the eight-man surveillance team that the NKVD sent to London that year to catch him, Burgess, Cairncross, Philby and Maclean meeting with their English controllers – the first time such an operation had been mounted. He had, after all, overseen the reorganization of MI5's surveillance section and knew many of its tricks. The NKVD group, moreover, were laughably bad at their jobs: far from blending into the crowd, they were ostentatiously Russian, visibly ill at ease, and equipped with not even the most basic English. What they hoped to accomplish, save to alarm their targets, is hard to imagine.

It was in 1943, and probably around this time, that Kreshin began to notice a torpor and unease in Blunt's manner which contrasted strangely with the diligence he still displayed in collecting information. This may have been the result of the realization of Moscow's distrust. It may also have been due to the strain of the constant fear of discovery, or even a response to an increasingly heavily suppressed sense of disenchantment.

He was still as zealous as he had ever been. As an agent he had never been more productive. The memoir he wrote for the NKVD in February 1943 had been earnest, supplicatory and full of precise information about the organization of MI5. The letter he wrote in June that year, after receiving a commendation for his information on German strategy just before the Battle of Kursk, was painfully gushing in its sincerity. 'That greater possibilities of useful work will develop I have no doubt, but this will give me redoubled energy for pursuing them . . . The encouragement and help which Max [Kreshin's new code name] and our other friends here have always given have been of inestimable value'. Nevertheless, Kreshin described his mood and appearance at meetings as 'very apathetic', and noted that his interest in politics seemed weaker and weaker:

> He comes very tired and forgetful. He speaks very little about his life and he strongly dislikes when this matter is touched on . . . Tony is very little interested in political matters, only seldom touches upon them, and only about current events at that. In this respect one has to urge him on sometimes but his answers are primitive, a very weak response to the simplest of political questions is perceptible. The only favourite topic of conversation is architecture. This is his favourite subject, which he gives all his time to. In spite of being busy in the Hut he continues to write articles on architecture, to lecture and so on. Partly this explains his weak interest in political life. Tony comes to meetings very punctually. He may be nervous but he has such a colourless, typical English face, that it is hard to notice it. When he is nervous, he drinks.

That year, in an article for the Warburg/Courtauld journal on William Blake, he wrote about the doomed hopes of an earlier generation of English would-be revolutionaries: the radicals around William Godwin – with whom Blake had been loosely connected – who dreamed in the early 1790s that the French Revolution would be exported to England. It was a revolution, he observed,

> which may have seemed near to realization in the fever created by events in France, but which England, with its

bourgeois revolution long passed and a solidly established commercial and land-owning oligarchy in power, would resist strongly and successfully. They were therefore doomed to sterility from the start, and the very remoteness and unreality of their themes is in itself a proof of this . . . to all the members of this circle, these ideas seemed intensely real and vitally important.

Blunt had nursed similarly naive hopes in 1937. By 1943 it was obvious that the Allies would win the war, that the apocalypse he had once predicted was not about to happen.

The article dwelt at some length on Blake's involvement in revolutionary politics, his excitement over the French Revolution, and his subsequent political disillusionment. According to Blunt, Blake had been a political innocent, his poems 'America' (1793) and 'Europe' (1794) revealing 'how far Blake was from understanding the true meaning of developments in France'. He had been horrified, Blunt added, by the excesses that had taken place in France in 1794, and this had brought about his subsequent retreat from revolutionary politics and a deep disenchantment with the world. He 'withdrew entirely into the field of the intellect. His anti-rationalism, which had separated him even in his most active days from the real revolutionaries, now becomes a dominant factor in his life.' Blake became, in Blunt's version, a semi-recluse, buried in his own mystical world, but with a 'bitter awareness of the evil of the world', and sympathies which 'remained with the oppressed against the oppressors'.

What is especially striking about the article is how Blunt made Blake's tangle with revolutionary politics, and his subsequent retreat from them, the central drama in the poet's life. What he most directly responded to in Blake was the natural opposition to authority of the one-time revolutionary. The poet's visionary mysticism and spirituality attracted – and repelled – him too, but he wrote very little about this overwhelmingly significant aspect of Blake. Few scholars today would agree that Blake's withdrawal from politics was as violent or as complete as Blunt suggested.

There were a number of personal and religious reasons why he ceased such activity, and he continued to be involved in politics – in various forms – throughout his life. It is hard not to draw the conclusion that Blunt's version of Blake, the political naif and the disappointed revolutionary, reflected his own situation and pre-occupations. His account of Blake's withdrawal from the world would also find an uncanny parallel in his own future.

Academic work was now becoming less of a pastime for Blunt and more a direct competitor with his espionage work for his time and energy. Alongside the long Blake article, in 1943 he began to write a series of academic pieces for the *Burlington Magazine* on neglected seventeenth-century French artists, companion studies to his work on Poussin. For the new volume of Poussin drawings on which he was working, he had begun to make regular visits to the large collection of Poussins in the Royal Library at Windsor Castle. In the course of his visits he caught the eye of the Royal Librarian, Owen Morshead, who was looking for someone conscientious to take on the task of cataloguing the Library's neglected collection of old-master drawings. Morshead was an old acquaintance of H. F. Stewart, Blunt's former tutor. Kenneth Clark, the Surveyor of the King's Pictures – who did not want the cataloguing job, which strictly lay within the realm of the Librarian – also knew Blunt from the Courtauld, where Clark occasionally lectured. (Blunt, in common with the rest of the Courtauld, regarded Clark as unbearably full of himself; Clark acknowledged Blunt's talents, but did not warm personally to him.) It was therefore perhaps not too surprising that Blunt was offered the job. He accepted, and during the next two years, in a series of extremely shrewd commissions, brought together a team of scholars which included established experts like A. E. Popham, *grand homme* of the British Museum's old-master drawings, and promising young men like Denis Mahon and John Pope-Hennessy. Mahon would later become a celebrated connoisseur and, in twenty years' time, Blunt's opponent in his most bitter professional feud. (Mahon's catalogue, on Guercino, did not come out until the early 1990s. Blunt had already finished his own volume, on seventeenth-century French drawings, by 1945.) His initiation of this series of great catalogues would be perhaps his greatest achievement in royal service. Pope-Hennessy, brother of Burgess's sometime lover James, increasingly regarded Blunt with a combination of envy, dislike and respect – feelings fully reciprocated by Blunt. Pope-Hennessy wrote of the project, 'He was supportive and helpful, but again and again one had the sense of coming up against a barred door in his personality.'

As the Allies began their northward push from the Mediterranean during the summer of 1943, Blunt became involved in the efforts to preserve artistic treasures caught in the conflict. When Rome was bombed by Allied planes in July, he planned a public protest with Pope-Hennessy. A month later he gave a talk on the BBC on the embryonic Monuments, Fine Arts and Archives (MFA&A), the organization charged initially with preserving art and culture from Allied pillaging in North Africa, and later with the retrieval of art stolen by the Nazis. Though he has never been credited with helping with the creation of MFA&A, it seems likely that Blunt did play some creative role. Burgess's commissioning note for the BBC talk mentioned that Blunt was 'connected with this scheme in an advisory, though not in an official capacity'. W. G. Constable had been campaigning for its creation from the USA, and Blunt knew the archaeologists Mortimer Wheeler and Leonard Woolley, who both took important roles in it, from the Courtauld.

On the surface all seemed well in the autumn of 1943. At MI5 his career was advancing. He had been promoted to major in the spring, and now he was made MI5's representative on various Whitehall committees involved in the deception plans for the coming Allied invasion of Europe. From the committees on which he sat he passed to the Soviets various documents on the Second Front – material they were also getting from Philby – as well as the date and place of the invasion of Italy – information which was confided to him by Liddell.

In Moscow, however, the NKVD finally persuaded itself that

the Cambridge spies were definitely British plants. In October, Philby passed a copy of a telegram sent to Tokyo by the Japanese ambassador in Berlin. The telegram had been intercepted and then decoded at Bletchley. It so happened that the last paragraph, which concerned Hitler's views on the Eastern Front, was missing from the text: Bletchley's radio-interception service had been unable to decipher it. The Soviets, however, had a copy of the whole of the same message from another source. They believed this discrepancy was proof that Philby was deliberately doctoring material. A letter dated 25 October 1943 was sent to the London *rezidentura* stating that, as Modrzhinskaya had insisted, Blunt, Burgess, Philby, Cairncross were disinformation agents and Maclean was their dupe. The Soviets finally had their conspiracy.

Modrzhinskaya's theory was that the Cambridge spies must have been working for British Intelligence since before their university days. (It is strange – or perhaps just a reflection of the nature of espionage paranoia – how forty years later Western conspiracy theorists came up with exactly the same kinds of theories about the ubiquity of Soviet Intelligence.) Blunt's political indifference and 'incomprehensible carelessness' in failing to photograph the documents he passed was brought up as evidence, as were Philby and Burgess's occasional 'politically incorrect judgements'. The pièce de résistance was the 'fact' – a perfect illustration of the prism of misinformation and paranoia through which Stalin's NKVD saw the world – that Philby and Burgess were the sons of British intelligence officers: Philby's father had worked for British Intelligence (he hadn't), and Burgess's stepfather – the hated navy stepfather – was also a spy (he wasn't). But all this took second place to the Soviets' principal evidence for the existence of a powerful British conspiracy against the Soviet Union, which was the fact that the Cambridge spies had brought them no evidence of a British conspiracy against the Soviet Union. Even by the convoluted, self-deceiving standards of the spy world, this was a masterpiece of irrational circular thinking.

Having finally convinced itself that its perfect agents were not so perfect, the heads of the NKVD Third Department decreed that no further action be taken. They reasoned that getting rid of the spies would alert British Intelligence, and it had to be admitted that some of their information was rather useful. The London *rezidentura* was ordered to sidetrack them from the 'Main Issue' and ask them to concentrate on German intelligence. It was a consummate piece of NKVD double-think. Should the spies somehow, at some point in the future, turn out to be genuine, no irrevocable steps had been taken, no heads would roll.

By Christmas, Blunt had fallen ill. Stress and exhaustion caused by overwork were the ostensible reasons. 'He worked very hard – bloody hard,' Hewit remembered. The quantities he was drinking did not help. 'Drink is the bugger of our age, type and generation,' Burgess wrote to Pollock a few years later. 'The mothers of even the best of us, such as Anthony or Dennis Proctor would be horrified, if they knew how much little Bobby really puts away.' Jackie Hewit believed that Blunt was 'verging on a breakdown. He was emaciated beyond belief – and he was skeletal to begin with.' He was sent, almost certainly by Victor Rothschild, to a Harley Street doctor called Emmanuel Herbert, an innovative practitioner who later set up one of the first company health schemes at Marks & Spencer. Herbert's notes of 14 January 1944 remark that Blunt had 'lost a great deal of weight'. By early spring there had been no improvement and Blunt was sent – again probably on the prompting of Rothschild – to Ruthin Castle, a nursing home in Wales. Despite his illness, he found it impossible to do nothing. He wrote to Wittkower in March, 'Poussin mythology [the next volume of the edited Poussin drawings] is going well, I think I can get it into order before I leave here, unless they decide to give me some frightful treatment.' He had still not fully recovered by mid-April, when he was unable to take his place at a Courtauld management-committee meeting – Boase had been sent to the Middle East, and Blunt was standing in for him. 'Major Blunt', a note informed Lord Lee, 'has been ill for some weeks.' The meeting finally took place, with Blunt, in May.

Blunt's illness may explain why Leonard Woolley, now head of MFA&A, thought he might be available in April 1944 to become

MFA&A's senior officer in Germany. 'The officer I would most prefer,' Woolley wrote to a colonel in the Twelfth Army, 'and could most strongly recommend as a capable man, a first rate German speaker and out of the top drawer as an art historian, is Major Anthony Blunt, now serving with MI5.' He asked his correspondent to do 'anything you can to help us get the services of this officer'. Blunt himself had not held out great hopes of being released from MI5. Nor was he.*

Instead, he was moved in May to what seems to have been a less stressful, and perhaps less influential, job – in a planning group putting the finishing touches to Fortitude, the deception plan for Operation Overlord, the Allied invasion of Europe. Blunt worked under Lt. Col. Noel Wild, who ran the deception scheme for the Supreme Headquarters Allied Expeditionary Force (SHAEF). Blunt's physical weakness after his illness may also explain why after D-Day, although he was a fluent speaker of French, German and Italian, he was not sent – as many senior MI5 officers such as White and Rothschild were – to Europe to follow the Allied advance and advise on intelligence matters. Blunt's job in the deception scheme seems to have been limited to the invention of a Canadian armoured division. According to the Russian Intelligence Archives, soon after he joined the scheme, on 26 May, he passed the details of the Allies' deception plan to Kreshin.

In the month before D-Day, when Blunt was moved to SHAEF, the NKVD made another attempt to bind its agents with money, offering them pensions in recognition of so 'many years of very valuable help', and softly assuring of them of its undying gratitude. Kreshin was instructed, 'At your usual meeting find out their opinion and wishes. Inform us of your ideas and opinions on the matter, find out what size pension would suit them, if they

---

* Blunt seems to have continued his informal links with MFA&A, because in September 1944 he asked Fritz Saxl for a list of important private art collections, objects of artistic interest, and museum personnel in Germany for the people 'in charge of the protection of monuments at the War Office'.

express the desire to receive one, and how the payments should be made and what the cover story will be to explain the presence of the money.' All the spies – Philby, Burgess, Blunt, Cairncross and Maclean – refused the offer. If principle contributed anything to their refusal, Kreshin did not pass this on: it was reported that they declined because they would not be able to pass off large sums legitimately as their own. The offer was evidence of a new wind in the Third Department of the Foreign Directorate. Elena Modrzhinskaya had recently left Soviet Intelligence, in the rank of colonel, and there were voices beginning to suggest that the Cambridge spies were bona fide.

Three days before D-Day, Blunt told Kreshin the details of a scheme to trick the Germans into thinking Field Marshal Montgomery was actually in the Mediterranean, by sending a *doppelgänger* to Gibraltar. Later that month he gave him a long account of 'B' Division's role in the Double-Cross and deception plans. And it was also in June that he and the other Cambridge spies were formally rehabilitated in Moscow. Kim Philby produced a group of documents on cooperation between the British and Soviet intelligence services which were completely corroborated by documents obtained by the NKVD through another source. Moscow wrote to the London *rezidentura*:

> This is a serious confirmation of S ['Söhnchen', Philby's code name]'s honesty in his work with us, which obliges us to review our attitude towards him and his entire group. Further contact with them should be based on the consideration of their great value to us, and any possibility of failure must be excluded ... On our behalf express much gratitude to S for his work, especially for passing to us the aforementioned file. If you find it convenient and possible, offer S in the most extremely tactful way a bonus of £100 or give him a gift of equal value.

The Foreign Directorate's eagerness to see Philby reinstated may also have been due to the news that he was tipped to become head of the anti-Soviet department of MI6. It accordingly wished to take some credit for this. In August, the deputy head of the NKVD, Vsevolod Merkulov, endorsed the Foreign Directorate's new-found trust in its agents and authorized prudent contact with the group. Perhaps as a symbol of the new dispensation, the Cambridge spies were given new code names, Blunt became 'Johnson', Philby became 'Stanley', and Burgess – freed at last from 'Mädchen' – became 'Hicks'. In some corners of the NKVD, however, old suspicions died hard. In 1951, when Burgess and Maclean defected to the Soviet Union, they were given months of harsh debriefings in what was virtually a labour camp. Even in 1992 Philby's biographer Anthony Cave Brown came across a KGB officer in Moscow who described the Cambridge spies as 'ideological shit'.

In September with the end of the war in sight, Blunt carefully told Kreshin that he wanted to return to civilian life and the art world after the war. 'Now that victory seems at last to be in sight,' he wrote in November 1944, after another commendation and gift of £100 from Moscow, 'I can only hope that I may be able to continue to be of use, though I fear that the opportunities will be less in the future.' He wanted out.

12. Success

*'Anthony like some great glacial avalanche is on the move ...
carrying everything desirable and otherwise in its broad path.'*

Post-war London was a drab and dreary place. Almost everything
was in short supply, including colour – all the major art collections had been evacuated to Wales, and a third of the commercial
galleries had closed down. Staying in a hotel in Half Moon Street
in Mayfair in late 1945, the American critic Edmund Wilson
wrote vividly – and with irritation – of the slovenliness of the
hotel waitresses, the miserable whores who crowded Piccadilly,
and the butchers' shops selling dead crows. 'These perhaps provide those slivers of "duck" which one finds in the restaurants
and which I noticed no one ordered but me.' Even the trees on
Tottenham Court Road seemed to bear the mutilations of war:
'gruesome ... with tufts of leaves at the end of the branches like
the necks and feet of plucked fowl ... peculiar desolation and
horror of this effect in the midst of an inhabited city'.

Like the city, Blunt seemed bled dry by the war. Boris Kreshin
regularly expressed concern to Moscow that Blunt might be about
to crack under the strain. What else could explain his extraordinary outburst, in the midst of a seemingly idle chat not long
before the end of the war, in which he announced to Tar
Robertson, 'It has given me great pleasure to have been able to
pass the names of every MI5 officer to the Russians.' Robertson
was taken aback, but couldn't imagine Blunt could be serious.
Pale and stick thin, Blunt's response to being overburdened, was,
as ever, to do more. From April 1945 he worked a couple of days

a week at MI5 and, now passing only occasional snippets of information to Kreshin, simultaneously took on the job of getting the battered and depleted Courtauld ready to open its doors again to students in October (the director, Tom Boase, was stuck in the Middle East). He finished his catalogue of French old-master drawings from the Royal Collection at Windsor; he worked on the forthcoming third volume of the Poussin drawings catalogue; he wrote three important articles on Poussin, Georges de la Tour and Mansart for the *Burlington Magazine*. It was also in April that he accepted the job of Surveyor of the King's Pictures, the first step in a seemingly inexorable rise that would take him in five years from gridlocked young academic to Establishment *grand homme*. By the autumn of 1945 he was back in hospital, once again exhausted.

The Surveyor of the King's Pictures was responsible for the maintenance of paintings in the Royal Collection, which was then probably the biggest private collection of art in the world. The job was regarded by many serious art historians as a poisoned chalice. With a few exceptions, the royal family were spectacularly uninterested in art. On a visit to the National Gallery in 1934 the late George V had announced, 'Turner was mad. My grandmother always said so,' and had tried to attack a Cézanne with his cane. For several decades the Windsors had shown little inclination to spend money and care on their own collection. The late King's appointee, Kenneth Clark, had resigned in early 1945, frustrated that his job had turned out mainly to involve answering queries about portraits of obscure aristocrats and royal pets, and turning up to Court functions – occasions which Clark found unutterably dreary, despite a close friendship with George VI's wife, Queen Elizabeth.

It was the Royal Librarian, Owen Morshead – who had encouraged Clark to take the job – who suggested Blunt as his replacement. In the two years that Blunt had spent working at the Royal Collection during the war, Morshead had noted his diligence, his habitual reticence and his perfect manners. (Even those who disliked Blunt acknowledged he had extremely good manners.) The two latter qualities were certainly prerequisites for a Royal Surveyor. The two men had also formed an unlikely friendship, and Blunt had become a regular visitor to Morshead's home in Windsor. A decade older than Blunt, Morshead – who had been a particular favourite of George V and Queen Mary – was cultured, serious, rather austere in his tastes and unquestionably forelock-tugging. His wife, Paquita, shared Blunt's love of Italy, where she had grown up, and was regarded as rather exotic in court circles. The Morshead children viewed Blunt as a kind of favourite uncle. After years of dilatory godfathering, he discovered that he was good with children. He treated them like grown-ups, discussing the finer points of westerns, while at the same time succumbing to their ragging and teasing. 'I think Anthony was happier there than many other places,' observed Sir Oliver Millar, Blunt's pupil and successor as Surveyor. 'They gave him what he wanted: friendship, work, fun.' When Erica O'Donnell, a former pupil of Blunt's, stayed with the Morsheads in the late 1940s, she found that the tutor she had once found so intimidating was in this setting a different man – someone she liked.

To many of Blunt's friends his acceptance of the Surveyor's job was puzzling to say the least. 'We all thought it was a joke for a Communist to become a courtier,' said Lillian Gurry, the Courtauld's librarian. It seemed highly ironic that the man who had preached the 'liberation' of private collections was now taking over the biggest one in the world – and, moreover, one which was largely inaccessible to the public. The Collection was also full of the kind of English art that Blunt found deeply dull. And it was, as he acknowledged to a post-war review of the visual arts sponsored by Nuffield College in 1946, badly run: 'inefficient, out of date, badly shown, understaffed and underpaid'. Indeed, Blunt's own post wasn't paid at all. Ellis Waterhouse, who liked to present himself as a socialist, and disapproved of the job, later claimed he always knew something was up – no art historian who didn't have an ulterior motive would have taken it on.

Blunt took on the Surveyorship as an act of self preservation –

who, after all, would suspect someone in his position of having been a Soviet spy? The new job might also have eased his withdrawal from MI5, since the Soviets, who habitually misunderstood the workings of British politics (they thought for a time that the homosexual journalist-turned-Labour MP Tom Driberg was head of the Labour Party), might have imagined their man standing behind the King as he signed top-secret documents. So far, however, no documents from the Russian Intelligence Archives mention anything about Blunt's work and relationships at Court. He must have enjoyed the sheer incongruity of his situation: a Soviet spy looking after the royal family's art collection. He was certainly amused by the camp unlikeliness of his Court life. He once told Wilfrid after a day at Buckingham Palace that it had been 'rather a strain; I was put between two Queens'. His acceptance was also, as Tom Boase – who pressed him to accept it – told him, an extremely good career move. Within weeks of his appointment Blunt was invited to join the executive committee of the NACF, the National Art Collections Fund, which raised money to buy works of art for public museums and galleries, and had an influence on what was bought for public view that was quite out of proportion to the sums it spent. Blunt spoke little at meetings – he preferred to have a quiet word in the right ear – but his influence was soon apparent in the sea change in British museum buying, as previously unfashionable and still cheap seventeenth-century paintings – Poussins, Vouets, le Sueurs – began to be bought by public galleries.

The Royal Collection did have other attractions, however. Most of it was in boxes in caves in Wales, where it had been evacuated for the war. This provided Blunt with the first opportunity in decades, or even centuries, to rehang and recatalogue it. Moreover, George VI, who was far more receptive to change than his father, had been persuaded by the Irish society painter and Royal Academician Gerald Kelly to lend 500 of the Collection's best works for an exhibition at the Royal Academy. (Kelly had spent much of the war at Windsor – where he met Blunt – painting the royal couple's portraits. He stayed so long he became known at Windsor as 'Kelly for keeps'.) This exhibition, planned for the winter of 1946–7, would be unprecedented, the rival of any of the great winter shows the Academy had put on before the war, and the new Surveyor would curate it. For all the pets and portraits, the Collection was extremely rich and varied: strong in particular in British, Dutch and Flemish painting, with several fine Italian early renaissance paintings and a famous set of Canalettos. In addition, Blunt wrote eagerly to Walter Friedlaender, 'the corridors and bedrooms in the various palaces contain endless things of interest, if not of first importance'. 'If you liked pictures, it was a job quite difficult to refuse,' Sir Oliver Millar observed. 'There was infinite scope for rearrangement, it was part-time, and, unlike the public galleries and museums, there were no interfering trustees or difficult staff.' There was also, conveniently, a full-time deputy, Blunt's art-historian friend Ben Nicolson, who before long was doing most of the practical work.

In the first five years, Blunt pursued his work on the Royal Collection with evident enthusiasm: 'He did the job with a sense of mission which I don't think Kenneth Clark ever brought to it,' Sir Oliver Millar said. He selected the pictures for the Royal Academy show and subsequently set up a programme of restoration and conservation using many of the leading restorers. To pay for this work he secured an annual allowance from the Lord Chamberlain's office. He planned 'a long term project for doing a complete catalogue of the whole collection' – though he never actually began it (that was the task of his successor, Oliver Millar), nor contributed to it. Sometimes it seemed as if the whole royal household was engaged in chasing after lost works, some of which had been missing since the previous century. Shortly after the end of the war, Jackie Hewit remembered a torn-out page from the *Burlington Magazine* arriving in the post. 'Anthony had written an article about some paintings last heard of at Kensington Palace. On the bottom of the page was scribbled, "Mr Blunt, I remember seeing this watercolour in the third maid's bedroom on the 15th floor" – or whatever – signed "Mary R".' The King's private secretary, Sir Alan 'Tommy' Lascelles, wrote to Blunt to let him know he'd had two pictures at home since 1938, and Queen Mary also informed him that a Sebastiano Ricci missing since the 1870s was now in the Queen's chapel in Marlborough House. He pressed – always in the most reasonable of tones, and never too hard – for more public access to paintings, more loans to exhibitions, more money for professional restoration. A major part of his strategy, his deputy observed, was to charm the household into taking the Collection more seriously. 'He was nice to them, and made them realize that the Royal Collection mattered, that it added lustre to the Crown.'

His early allies at Court were the small group regarded as arty and intellectual – among them Morshead, Tommy Lascelles, who was known at the Palace as a bit of an academic manqué, and Lord Cobbold, a courtier who eventually became Lord Chamberlain and was an enthusiastic private collector in his own right. But he went out of his way to be charming, and was in general liked at Court. 'We all liked him' recalled Sir Edward Ford, then the young Deputy Private Secretary to George VI. 'He had lovely manners, and treated everyone with respect – and was of course formidably intellectual.' The philistine opposition was represented by the civil and royal servants who did not really believe that 'the public' particularly wanted to see the pictures. When in 1947 Blunt suggested a new walkway round the Van Dyck Room and the Picture Gallery at Windsor – which had a unique collection of Italian and Flemish art – so that the public could actually see the paintings, the superintendent of the castle, Mr Williams, blustered, 'I think it would be a pity to spoil these arrangements for the very few people who are only interested in the pictures.' It would, he added, be dangerous for the public to be 'allowed as near to the works of art as Mr Blunt suggests'. These arguments continued throughout Blunt's time as Surveyor.

The day-to-day work of the Surveyor was done without any contact with the royal family. It was possible to go months without seeing them. Blunt was, however, very good at being a courtier. The royal family liked him: he was polite, effective and, above all, discreet. Over the years he divulged very little about his relations with the royal family – even to his friends, and even after his exposure. Only in his first few years did Burgess manage to worm out the occasional mildly revealing story. He seems to have got on with the Windsor women best. Queen Mary, famously shy and inarticulate (and famously pro-German – a view she was not shy about expressing), kept an eye on him in memory of her childhood friendship with his mother's family. She occasionally attended his lectures at the Courtauld, and invited him and his mother to tea at her rooms at Marlborough House. Blunt recalled that the place was filled with little three-legged tables covered with priceless objects, and it was like an obstacle race navigating round them. She took great pride in the Royal Collection – though it was said she had an unfortunate habit of going round and labelling paintings with the wrong artists. It was to her that Blunt brought new discoveries and newly cleaned pictures. Sir Edward Ford, who was himself new to Buckingham Palace, remembered that in 1946 he came across Blunt rushing to Queen Mary to show her a small painting he had just discovered by the fifteenth-century Italian painter Benozzo Gozzoli. Queen Mary in return sent him Christmas presents, though not always exactly appropriate ones. Jackie Hewit recalled that one Christmas she sent Blunt a reticule, a small woven purse, about the least appropriate present one could imagine.

Blunt had met the King and Queen at Windsor during the war, where they had lived a more than usually informal life, lunching each day with courtiers and visitors to the Castle in the Waterloo Chamber. Blunt had little regard for the awkward, unconfident King George VI, who had had the monarchy thrust upon him and struggled hard to measure up to it. In 1945 Burgess wrote to Pollock that Blunt had

had an hour alone with Queen Mary yesterday and, much more terrifying, an hour and ten minutes alone with the King last week. As A. said, 'I didn't know what to do. I'd been told that one isn't supposed to move until the King says

309

so. And he didn't tho' we'd finished our work in ten minutes. Fortunately I rather enjoy silences – do you know if he does?'

The King told Blunt that when he saw a portrait he never knew if the name on the bottom was the artist or the sitter, or so Blunt reported to his brother Wilfrid. Blunt also recalled George's response at seeing the British painter John Piper's wild grey and green semi-abstract paintings of Windsor Castle for the first time: 'Bad luck with the weather, what?!' Another favourite story of Wilfrid's went that during the war his brother had been given a lift to London by the King. As they had passed Runnymede, George VI had said, 'You know, Blunt, that's where all the trouble began!' In later years Blunt denied the story. Wilfrid did not entirely believe the denial.

Blunt did, however, like Queen Elizabeth. She belonged to a type of powerful, grand, aristocratic lady, couching an iron and imperious will in apparent sweetness, for which Blunt had a particular weakness. Of all the family, she showed most interest in art, liked a 'well-painted picture', and had even bought a Duncan Grant. Alan Baker, the young art student who became Blunt's boyfriend in the late 1940s, met her on his one visit to Buckingham Palace. Blunt was showing him a Van Dyck that was about to be cleaned.

We were both on the floor and he was pointing out where there might be overpainting, and a sweet little voice said, 'Oh Anthony, I hope that hasn't got to go. That's one of my favourite pictures.' It was the Queen Mother. I scrambled to my feet and was about to leave, and she said, 'Oh no, no, no', and we ended up having tea in her apartment. They were obviously very friendly. He liked her a lot.

But, although Blunt made a good courtier, he did not enjoy being one. In George VI's time he attended several 'excruciating weekends' at Windsor, about which he complained bitterly to Alan Baker. 'My God, I've had it,' he said after one of these. Along with some of the household and a few cabinet ministers, he had been forced to march up and down the corridors at Windsor, drilled by the King and Owen Morshead (who during the war had run the Castle's Home Guard), with a fire iron over his shoulder. 'He didn't really play a permanent part in the Court at all,' recalled Sir Edward Ford. 'One saw very little of him. He didn't come to household meals. In fact I can't remember Anthony ever appearing at Ascot, and I saw him very little at Buckingham Palace. But he had – reluctantly – to turn up to the full-dress diplomatic parties that were held every November.' After Ben Nicolson – who was even less inclined to attend royal occasions than Blunt was, and had a bad habit of making large cigarette holes in the Windsor carpets – resigned as deputy in 1947–8, Blunt appointed as his deputy his ex-pupil Oliver Millar, who had originally contacted him to ask 'rather cheekily' for a job at the Royal Collection. Millar, who enjoyed Court life, began to take over Blunt's social duties.

It was a measure of the trust that the royal family were already willing to place in Blunt that in August 1945 he was asked to accompany Owen Morshead on a confidential mission for George VI to the castle of Friedrichshof, the chief residence of the Landgraves of Hesse, near Frankfurt in Germany. The Royal Archives have an account of the trip, which gives as the reason for the mission Morshead's realization that 4,000 letters from Queen Victoria to her eldest daughter, the Empress Frederick of Germany, 'which were preserved with other important papers in Schloss Friedrichshof near Frankfurt, were exposed to risks owing to unsettled conditions after the war'. On the instructions of George VI, Morshead flew to Frankfurt on 3 August, taking with him Blunt, 'who', Morshead reported afterwards, 'was due to visit the British zone in Germany on business', and whose German 'made the task of examining the Empress Frederick's archives easy'.

The task was twofold: to find the relevant papers, and to get the permission of the seventy-three-year-old Princess Margaret of Hesse, 'who was eking out a sorrowful life in the house of her estate agent just outside the gates of Friedrichshof', to take the papers back to England. According to Morshead, the first task was easy. The next morning Blunt and Morshead locked themselves in the library, found their papers, and worked 'through till five'. Princess Margaret required more 'delicate handling'. She had lost three sons in two world wars and now felt 'rancorous hatred' towards England. Morshead nevertheless persuaded her that the letters would be safer at Windsor, and she signed an agreement. Morshead returned to England the next day; Blunt stayed on an additional day for his mysterious 'military business'. The letters were later returned in 1951.

In 1979 Blunt told the journalist Colin Simpson that it hadn't been quite as simple as that. While the Hesse family gave them permission to retrieve the papers, the American woman officer in charge of the castle, which had been turned into a rest and recreation club for senior American staff, was not so accommodating and refused them access. When she finally went to phone her headquarters, Blunt and Morshead grabbed the letters and left quickly. Another version of the story, told by the espionage writer Chapman Pincher, claims that, having been refused entry, Morshead and Blunt went off to see Princess Margaret of Hesse, who directed them to a back entrance. They broke in at night, found their treasure, and withdrew.

Elaborations on the story do not end there, however. It has also been suggested that, rather than retrieving a collection of nineteenth-century letters, Blunt and Morshead were actually in search of letters which the Duke of Windsor, the former Edward VIII, might have sent to his cousin, Philip, Landgrave of Hesse, who owned the Friedrichshof. Philip had been a prominent Nazi, and was now in an Allied prison. The letters were supposed to reveal the Duke's Nazi sympathies and possibly even that he had passed secrets to Hitler. What gives this story some credibility is that in October 1937, on a visit to Germany, the Duke of Windsor had met Hitler for a private audience, and that in Lisbon in 1940 he met a series of Nazi envoys, including Philip of Hesse. It is also true that George VI was extremely touchy about what the Allies might find out about his brother's political sympathies.

At Marburg in Germany a group of Allied historians of all nationalities were examining the official German archives and had already discovered a few documents relating to Edward VIII – telegrams from German officials recording meetings with him in Lisbon in 1940; a reference to Hitler's attempts in the 1930s to use the former Kaiser as an intermediary with the Windsors; and an account of a visit to England in 1936 by one of the Hesse family. Lord Cadogan confided to his diary at this time, 'King fussed about the Duke of Windsor's file and captured German documents.'

While it's possible that George VI did ask Blunt and Morshead to look out for any documents concerning the Duke of Windsor, it seems unlikely that they found any.*

Churchill had tried to suppress details of the few papers relating to Windsor in the German archives, but the international team already established for dealing with and publishing those archives made it impossible for documents already known to be suppressed.

The official version – that Blunt's mission was to recover 'the Vicky letters', as they were known (the Empress was christened 'Victoria' like her mother) is by far the most likely. Royal documents of any kind were subject to strict secrecy, and the Vicky letters, which were finally published in an edition by Blunt's former intelligence colleague Roger Fulford, turned out to be full of embarrassing and 'improper' comments about the awfulness of German politics and culture. Hugh Trevor-Roper vividly remembered going into MI5 one day in the autumn of 1945 to find Blunt amusedly recounting his adventures in Germany. He was sure that he made no mention of any correspondence between Edward VIII and his German relations. Blunt's task, he recalled, had been to secure the Vicky correspondence before the Ameri-

---

* Martin Allen's *Hidden Agenda* (London: Macmillan, 2000) repeats the story of Blunt's trip to Frankfurt (dating it wrongly to spring 1945), tying it to a letter the author claims shows Edward Windsor wittingly offering up Allied secrets to Hitler. Allen, however, suggests that Windsor's go-between with Hitler was not Philip of Hesse, but an American, Charles Bedaux, with no links to Friedrichshof at all. So what Allen thought Blunt was doing at Friedrichshof isn't clear.

cans found it and published it. The royal family had good reason to feel nervous for their family heirlooms. Among the Allied forces advancing into Germany, casual souvenir-hunting was not uncommon. When Blunt and Morshead arrived at Schloss Friedrichshof in August 1945, a convoy of trucks had already taken away desks, chairs and armoires to furnish Allied headquarters. Visiting GIs had walked off with bits of the family silver, porcelain and first editions. 'Pretty extensive looting had been in progress,' Morshead reported. Indeed the US authorities had been in 'consternation' that the 'King of England's representatives' would be shocked by the state of Friedrichshof, and had sent the local American MFA&A officer Captain Buchman, to tidy up the library – which had been 'in a condition of disarray' – for their arrival. For his work, Buchman confided to Blunt amusedly the next day, he had been issued with an official citation for 'tact and industry' for heading off an international incident. What no one knew was that the senior American officers in charge of the castle, Captain Kathleen Nash and Colonel Jack Durant, had broken into the Hesse family vault, and, while Blunt and Morshead searched for the letters, were in the midst of quietly shipping its contents – gold dinner services, emerald bracelets, diamond tiaras – back to America. They were caught and stood trial in America the following year, but only 70 per cent of the treasure was ever recovered.*

Another reason for the Crown's extreme caution was that fact that it didn't actually own any of the articles which Morshead and Blunt took out. As Morshead reported after a subsequent and similar trip to the Netherlands, 'The King expressly told me that we hold them on the same footing as we hold the things which I brought back from Frankfurt [the Hesse expedition], ie if the German family in the future want them back . . . well, we have no title to them; we only hold them in security for them, over

---

* Confusingly, among the items later recovered from America were nine volumes of letters from the Empress Frederick to *her* daughter Victoria, which were later returned to Germany.

here in England where things are less unsettled.' The Foreign Office was extremely worried that if it was discovered that the British Crown was engaged in 'evacuating' – if not actually smuggling – archives and objects from Germany, it would look extremely bad at a time when Britain was lecturing its Allies on the subject of war looting.

Blunt made three subsequent trips on behalf of the King during the next eighteen months. They were primarily to recover royal treasures to which the Crown did not have an automatic right. This seems to be confirmed by a letter Burgess wrote to Peter Pollock, probably in December 1945, when Blunt went on his second German mission – this time to Westphalia, to meet the Duke of Brunswick. Burgess wrote that Blunt was due to leave the next day for Germany

> in the King's private aeroplane to do some looting of historic Royal Family possessions (?ex-possessions) ... I really shouldn't repeat any of this but since I know you won't, you should hear this. The King: 'I tell you one thing, Blunt, I don't intend to pay for this stuff. Couldn't afford it.' And indeed he probably didn't since it's the silver furniture made for George I? II presented by the City of London and worth anything up to ½ a million.*

Blunt went to Westphalia on his own. By coincidence or not, his old source Leo Long, now a civilian working for the Control Commission in Germany as director of operations in Intelligence, had been posted to Bad Oeynhausen, the airfield to which Blunt flew. It was Long who drove him to meet the Duke of Brunswick, heir to the kings of Hanover, whose family had strong links to the Windsors. Long claimed that Blunt never revealed the purpose of his mission: Long just knew it was 'very hush hush'. Like the

---

* A pair of silver tables with matching mirrors were part of the Hanoverian possessions of the English Crown. Blunt did not bring them back to England, and they apparently remain in the hands of the Brunswicks. (They had previously been brought to England for safe-keeping during the Napoleonic wars.)

Frankfurt trip, it too inspired a series of fallacious speculations and rumours, this time among the local MFA&A staff, which by another coincidence included two of Blunt's former pupils, Olivier Bell and Cecil Gould. Bell heard that Blunt had come 'on behalf of Queen Mary to recover some documents of a private nature which she had sent her relatives the Brunswicks'. Privately, Bell wondered if Queen Mary, who was prone to declaring that the British had backed the wrong horse in the First World War, had been rather too tactless about the Second. Cecil Gould believed that the Duke of Brunswick was returning 'objects which had been borrowed from Windsor by his ancestor, Queen Victoria's uncle Cumberland and never returned . . . but nothing came of the affair in the end'. (Not that Brunswick was short of his own treasures. Blunt would later describe his tour of the castle: 'The Duke of Brunswick would open a drawer and sigh, "Oh no, not *another* golden fleece . . ." ')

Both were quite wrong. Blunt travelled back with a sealed packet which he instructed MFA&A must not be opened by Customs. The packet contained some of the treasures from the royal house of Hanover, including an extremely valuable twelfth-century illuminated manuscript and the diamond crown of Queen Charlotte, wife of George III. None of it actually belonged to George VI. It appears that the treasures were taken to protect them from seizure by occupying forces – this time the Soviets, who were about to occupy the area. Later, when Germany was split in two, the Brunswicks' estates were in the Communist zone.

As for Leo Long, he claimed his meeting with Blunt was entirely coincidental: 'I had got myself to Germany to get away from the spying business. Blunt didn't pressurize me. Nor did the Russians . . . I think Blunt sensed that I didn't want to know any more. We certainly didn't talk over old times.' According to the Russian Intelligence Archives, however, six months after Blunt had made a second trip to Westphalia, in March 1946,* he met

---

* Blunt's March 1946 visit was probably to reassure the Duke of Brunswick that his treasures were in safe hands. It appears that the Duke asked for his

Boris Kreshin and handed him information given to him by Leo Long, describing the organization of his intelligence division in Germany. Several months later, when Long applied for a job in the post-war MI5, Blunt recommended him to Dick White. White said he liked Long, but thought he would be better off in civilian life.

Eighteen months into his Surveyorship Blunt was able to render the royal family another service: 'The King's Pictures' opened at the Royal Academy. It was a huge success, drawing unprecedented numbers of art-starved visitors – 366,000 of them – and paying off the Academy's large debts. For a moment Blunt became an almost-celebrity, a position he avoided for ever after. Every newspaper pictured him showing the royal family round the exhibition, and he spoke enthusiastically about the exhibition on the BBC, claiming, slightly subversively, that the pictures were better hung and lit, and 'arranged more systematically', than they were in the royal residences. The exhibition brought him a new ally in the form of the sixty-year-old Gerald Kelly, who ran the Royal Academy's loan exhibitions and whose idea the exhibition had been. Kelly was a tremendous social climber with a propensity for being magnificently improper when drunk. In his mid-eighties, at an RA dinner, he announced to the Spanish ambassador of a Goya portrait of the Duchess of Alba, 'That's no duchess – that's a Goya fuck!' His saving graces were that he didn't take himself too seriously and he was extremely shrewd. He liked Blunt's combination of professionalism and sardonic humour. When he became president of the RA in 1949, he used Blunt as an informal adviser on the Academy's annual winter exhibitions – major events of the art-world calendar, in which Blunt now played a significant role. As governor of Dulwich Picture Gallery, which had been badly

---

treasures to be returned, and didn't get them: Olivier Bell took a message from the Duke asking to be informed 'if and when expected matter turned up'. The treasures were finally handed back in 1963, when the Duke's son requested them.

damaged in the war, Kelly also used Blunt as a consultant on its post-war restoration.

'The King's Pictures', planned in part as a gesture to show that the monarchy was in tune with the new post-war world, sparked a debate on the delicate subject of to whom the Royal Collection really belonged, and whether more of it should be on public view. Blunt, who exactly ten years before had preached state ownership of private collections, now advised that such questions should at all costs not be raised in public because it would 'involve unpleasantness from every point of view'. Instead he suggested that larger parts of Windsor should be opened to the public. 'I know that this would involve some expense . . . but I believe that the effect would be excellent.'

Blunt's last secret mission for the King took place in August 1947, when he accompanied Morshead to Haus Doorn in the Netherlands, the castle to which the Kaiser had been exiled after the First World War. They went to examine some objects that had once belonged to Queen Victoria, and to find anything that, as a letter from Owen Morshead to Alan Lascelles put it, was relevant to 'relations between the Courts of England and Germany during the past hundred years'. It was possible that George VI feared that the Kaiser's papers might contain embarrassing evidence of his approaches to the Windsors on behalf of Hitler. 'It will be seen', Morshead reported, 'that no documentary material was found – with the negligible exception of a pair of devotional books in which the ex-Kaiser was accustomed to make trivial annotations, of no interest whatsoever.' The objects that were eventually brought back – 'quietly secured by Sir Neville Bland, our Ambassador in the Hague', as Morshead reported – included a Cosway portrait of the Duke of Clarence, three diamante Garter badges, a few miniature gifts from Victoria to the Kaiser, 'none either beautiful or desirable', and one rosewater dish and ewer, 'very ugly indeed'.

When Blunt left MI5 in October 1945 – the month the Courtauld Institute reopened to students – he sent the NKVD a few parting gifts. He told them that MI5 knew about James Klugmann's espionage activities. On the microphone hidden at CPGB headquarters, Klugmann had been overheard saying he'd passed secret documents to Tito's Communist partisans in Yugoslavia, where he had been posted during the war. After a visit to Rome in September for MI5 to read the Italian Government Archives, Blunt was also able to report that the NKVD's pre-war source in the British Embassy in Rome, a servant called Francesco Constantini, had been in the pay of the Italians too, and that the British knew this.

Blunt always insisted that with the end of the war he stopped spying for the Soviet Union. For a year after he left MI5 this was true: he had no contact with the NKVD – and nor did Philby and Burgess. The main reason for this was the NKVD's anxiety over the defection in the autumn of 1945 of a Soviet military-intelligence clerk called Igor Gouzenko, whose testimony led to the arrest of twenty-two Canadian government officials and a British atom scientist called Allan Nunn May, who had passed information on the development of the atomic bomb to the Soviet Union during the war. Gouzenko's claims of Soviet penetration caused enormous panic in the West and became one of the defining moments in the beginning of the Cold War. It is also possible, however, that Blunt was left alone by the NKVD because it recognized that he was close to breaking point. A year later, in the midst of preparations for the King's Pictures exhibition, he began once again to meet the Soviets. In anticipation of new mountains of documents, the Soviets gave their British agents a new set of code names: Burgess became 'Paul', Blunt became 'Yan'. And Blunt continued to meet them on and off for the next five years. Before he had left MI5 he had promised Boris Kreshin that he would continue to gather what information he could, reporting that Guy Liddell wanted to continue using him as a consultant and still regarded him as a friend: 'With good contact with Liddell and [Tar] Robertson I think I will be able to get information about MI5 activity interesting enough for us.'

He was not, it must be said, very productive. He collected bits of gossip. In 1946 he passed on details he'd had from Liddell of MI5's post-war reorganization; in 1948, he reported that Tar Robertson had consulted him on ideas for anti-Soviet projects, and had complained that MI5 was getting nowhere in its attempts to root out Soviet espionage. That year he also passed on the news that the British were setting up a secret committee to supervise the development of bacteriological weapons. In 1949 he reported that a senior MI5 officer, Malcolm Cumming, had asked to use a room in the Courtauld Institute for meetings with agents recruited from Eastern bloc embassies. Blunt reported on only one such meeting, in September 1949 – after this the Russian Intelligence Archives seem to contain nothing further on the subject. It might, however, have been an occasion on which he put lives at risk. But his chief use to the Soviets during this period was as Burgess's proxy. From 1945 he passed on Burgess's documents and notes, and sometimes even photographed them – something he had refused to do during the war – with a Leica he kept at the Courtauld. In June 1944 Burgess had got a job in the press department of the Foreign Office, and he was producing the most extraordinary abundance of materials for the Soviets: 4,404 documents between mid-June 1944 and the end of the war, four times as many as Blunt passed during his whole time in MI5. In 1947 Burgess was made personal assistant to an old friend, Hector McNeil, the Labour Foreign Office Minister, and began to pass documents about the planned Western European Union and even on NATO. In late 1948 he got himself moved to the Far East Department, a job that was essentially a demotion, whence he supplied the Soviets with papers on the growing crisis in Korea.

The philosopher Stuart Hampshire, who continued to do some secret work after 1945, has suggested that some time after the war Blunt confessed his double past to someone in MI5 and was, from 1945, working for MI5 against the NKVD.

It's just a theory. I think there were at least one if not two British intelligence officers in whom he confided. He signed off as regards his commitment to the cause in 1945–6, but he was stuck with it. I'm sure he was disillusioned by the end. You had to be like Kim [Philby], your whole life in it, not to be. I believe people knew, and knew because he told them, and then said, 'OK, let it run, and we'll see what the Russians ask you to do. You needn't tell anyone else.' That is perfectly normal procedure. The only person who knows is Dick White, and he's dead. He could have easily satisfied himself that it was best to let Anthony run on his own.

What may give Hampshire's theory credibility is the fact that, though they knew Blunt had been extremely close to Burgess up to his defection in 1951, MI5 never challenged Blunt's assertion that he stopped working for the Soviets after the war. This was, publicly, at least, said to be a condition of his immunity. MI5 was well aware that, after the war, Blunt was being informally consulted by senior intelligence figures. It is possible that his tales to the Soviets of the willingness of MI5 to confide in him were part of a plan hatched by Liddell and White to feed them misinformation. In addition, the Russian Intelligence Archives show that after the war Blunt told the Soviets that Dick White and the fast-rising MI5 officer Roger Hollis, whom Blunt had known during the war, were 'almost hostile' towards him. The Russian Intelligence Archives appear to show, moreover, that Blunt was discretion itself on the subject of the Palace and his secret missions on its behalf. It is, however, extremely hard to square the scale of help and protection Blunt gave to Burgess during the late 1940s, with a confession to MI5.

Whether he confided in anyone else or not, Blunt was ambivalent about his continuing contacts with the NKVD. In the autumn of 1946, when he began to meet with the Soviets again, his friends observed that he was once more looking ill and wasted. 'I meet the pale and exhausted Blunt at the club,' wrote the Russian émigré Alexander Halpern* to Edgar Wind, the

* Halpern was a White Russian who had worked for Alexander Kerensky, the moderate socialist head of Russia's shortlived provisional government of 1917, and left Russia with him. He had spent the war in New York liaising with the

Warburg art historian. In December he wrote to Wind of 'the pale Anthony who occupies himself particularly with alcohol and young boys'. Blunt made no attempt to mask his lack of enthusiasm to his controls. When Yuri Modin first met him, in 1948, he found him nervous and strained, and obsessively vigilant about being followed. He was also deeply reluctant to discuss other parts of his life – except art. Modin, a newly promoted and ambitious young agent who had been an English translator at the Lubianka in Moscow, recalled that Blunt told him that, though he 'found our present policies ill-conceived, damaging to Communism, and every bit as imperialist as those of our predecessors in Russia', he would continue to work for the Soviet Union because 'he believed in one overriding truth, that the happiness of humanity would be accomplished only in the wake of a world-wide revolution'. Modin concluded he was 'anything but a convinced Marxist'. His suggestion that Blunt start talent spotting again was greeted with a stiff refusal, and Modin felt 'more and more that his work for us was irksome to him'.

What Blunt's feelings about the Soviet Union were was anyone's guess. Jackie Hewit remembered him cheering the Labour election victory with Victor Rothschild and his new bride, Tess Mayor. 'His politics were still socialist,' thought Alan Baker, 'but he rarely discussed them in front of me, and I didn't feel he was a political animal at all.' He was volubly critical of the Soviet

---

Americans for British Intelligence. With his wife, Salomea, a once-famous beauty and old friend of the poet Anna Akhmatova, he was part of a circle of sophisticated émigré Russians who included Isaiah Berlin, Anna or 'Niouta' Kallin (one of Blunt's regular producers at the BBC), the painter Oskar Kokoschka (whom Blunt invited to lecture at the Courtauld in the 1950s) and the legendary – and by this time rather large – Baroness Moura Budberg, lover of H. G. Wells, Robert Bruce Lockhart, Maxim Gorky and many others. She was charming and unscrupulous, and was rumoured to have spied for everyone, including the NKVD. Budberg was also a good friend of Douglas Cooper; Blunt occasionally attended her parties. His visits to Halpern's home at Chelsea Park Gardens may have given Blunt a frisson, but there is no evidence that he spied on the group for the NKVD.

plundering of eastern-European treasures. He said of his trips to
Germany, 'that there was so much good stuff and how horrifying
it was that so much had disappeared to Russia which would never
be got back. He didn't approve of what the Russians were doing
at all.' In other words he spoke only about art. It seems likely
that he chose never to assess consciously what he felt about
Communism. At his 1979 press conference he said that he had
come to reject it utterly, but

> This was a gradual process and I find it very difficult to
> analyse. It is, after all, more than 30 years ago. But it was
> the information that came out immediately after the war.
> During the war one was simply thinking of them as Allies
> etc., but then with the information about the camps . . . it
> was episodes of that kind. I have thought about this a great
> deal and I cannot say exactly at what time, but it was
> accumulative evidence.

He later told his family that a defining moment was, 'when the
White Russians were sent back to Yugoslavia', by which he
presumably meant the forced repatriation of Russians after Yalta
in 1945.

His old ties with Burgess still bound him, but not as strongly as
they once had. In 1945 he had moved into a room in Tom Boase's
flat at the Courtauld, and for the first time in eight years Burgess
was not living in his pockets. Burgess's ability to drag him into
the world no longer appealed to Blunt. It was felt among their
homosexual circle that he was withdrawing into himself; he had
given up on the possibility of happy homosexual love and had
made a deliberate decision to subordinate emotional fulfilment to
work. In 1945, after Peter Pollock made the first of several attempts
to break up with Burgess, Brian Howard wrote to him:

> We all of us – all five [Burgess, Blunt, Howard, Pollock and
> Eric Kessler] – share a certain emotional point of view about
> life that makes it not twice, but ten times more difficult for
> us to lead a happy and fruitful existence. We are haunted,

day and night, whether we realise it or not, and not only by immaterial fears and enemies. There are certain sensitive, prudent and strong-minded people of this kind – like K[essler] and B[lunt] – who come to find their position finally impossible. They forget that their life is only, say, ten times more difficult to arrange than other people's. They decide that it cannot be arranged at all. So what do they do? They take to their careers exactly as fugitives take to the hills, and if thence forward they consider themselves on a higher level, that level can be very barren, and very sad.

It was a perceptive letter which showed almost uncanny prescience about Blunt's future life.

'We tried', Burgess wrote in a valedictory letter to Pollock after their relationship limped painfully to a close in 1947, 'to do what in our world is one of the hardest things there is to do . . . look, Pete – how few have succeeded. Why shld [*sic*] I ever have thought we shld succeed when Eric and Ian failed, where Dadie never began to succeed, where Anthony has never really managed or attempted anything beyond Jackie (which is different anyhow, they won't "live together").'

By the late 1940s Burgess was increasingly unhappy, often drunk, and frequently filthy. The old wit was increasingly overlaid with bitterness. Even to his friends, as Cyril Connolly noted, 'he always seemed to hit upon the unforgivable thing to say'. His spying alone gave him a sense of achievement, and he brought to it a hungry enthusiasm, combined with increasing carelessness. On one occasion he spilled top-secret papers on the floor of a pub lavatory; on another he spent money given him to buy a car on a half-dead gold Rolls-Royce. Modin claimed that on their first meeting, Burgess insisted on meeting in his favourite pub in Soho. When Modin refused, he suggested they walk the streets and tell anyone who asked 'we're lovers and we're looking for a bed'.

In 1948 Burgess wrote of Blunt's inexorable rise, and obliquely of their increasing distance, 'Anthony like some great glacial avalanche is on the move scattering moraines and carrying everything desirable and otherwise in its *broad* path in all directions.' To Peter Pollock – who knew nothing about the papers Blunt continued to carry for his old friend – it was Jackie Hewit who increasingly provided the reason for the two men to go on seeing each other.

When Tom Boase resigned from the Courtauld in early 1947, to become President of Magdalen College, Oxford, everyone from Samuel Courtauld to Boase to Fritz Saxl could see that Blunt was the right person to succeed him. He was a home-grown rising star in art history, and had demonstrated his commitment to the Institute on many occasions. During the war, in Boase's absence, he had kept it alive with lectures and exhibitions; and he had supervised its resuscitation in 1945. Lord Lee, however, seems to have resisted Blunt's appointment. He had long been suspicious of Blunt's politics; he had seen his acceptance of the Surveyor's job as a sign of disloyalty, and as a punishment he had insisted that Blunt's Courtauld salary be reduced to compensate for the time he spent at the Palace. Now advancing ill health seemed to intensify Lee's underlying anxiety that Blunt the 'expert' and 'highbrow' (two of the worst words in his lexicon) would prise control of the Institute from his ailing fingers. Eventually the rest of the Institute's management committee had its way and Blunt was offered the job in June 1947, three months short of his fortieth birthday. 'I must say I am glad that the appointment has at last been made,' Fritz Saxl wrote to him, 'as the delay was beginning to get a little irritating.' In September, days before Blunt started the job, Lee tried to persuade Boase to change his mind. Boase was polite but firm: 'The committee nominated yourself, Mr Courtauld, [Lionel] Robbins and Kenneth Clark as representatives [to choose a successor] . . . I feel sad at leaving . . . but this is an unexpected opening which would have been hard to refuse.'

Blunt took over the whole of the Courtauld's spacious top-floor flat, where he would live for the next twenty-five years. The Institute was still underfunded, understaffed and relatively obscure, but Blunt had big plans for it: he wanted to create a

British school of art history that would rival, even surpass, the reputation and the exacting standards of the Germans. The attitudes of Courtauld and Lee, who still resisted the idea that the Courtauld should be primarily an academic and scholarly institution, promised to make this even harder to achieve than it might otherwise have been. But both Courtauld and Lee were in poor health, and they died within months of each other, in 1948. Blunt was immediately granted by default the kind of authority that his predecessors had been denied. The influence of the Institute's third founder, the irascible and arthritic Robert Witt, now wheelchair-bound in his house across Portman Square, was eclipsed by that of Blunt's new academic appointees. He made the august Viennese émigré art historian Johannes Wilde, the incarnation of German highbrow scholarship, his new deputy. He brought in an Oxford medievalist, Christopher Hohler – a brilliant and eccentric historian of bizarrely anachronistic right-wing views ('He would have liked to have been a medieval bishop; and failing that a robber baron,' reflected one of his most appreciative pupils), and obsessively high standards of accuracy. Burly Lionel Robbins, a professor at the London School of Economics and an anointed member of the great and good whose great cause was the expansion of higher education, became the new chairman of the Courtauld management committee and a new ally. It was very quickly clear that in Blunt's Courtauld the teachers, not the patrons, would be the dominant figures. Even Witt's promised gift to the Institute of his admirable collection of drawings was overshadowed by the offer in 1948 of the Gambier-Parry Collection, which included works by Simone Martini and Andrea Orcagna, Islamic metalwork, medieval carved ivories and Venetian glass. It was Blunt who got the credit for bringing the collection to the Institute – even though the offer had originally been made to London University, which passed it on. (On the other hand it was Blunt's years of coaxing and reassuring Mark Gambier-Parry, the then owner of the collection, which finally ensured its arrival in 1966.)*

---

* Gambier-Parry was a nineteenth-century musicologist who had built the

There was an appropriate synchronicity in the fact that, almost at the same time as Blunt became the Courtauld's director, his deputy Surveyor and friend Ben Nicolson left the Palace to become editor of the *Burlington Magazine*, which he turned into an internationally regarded learned journal. Nicolson was perceived to be one of Blunt's greatest admirers. According to the art historian Hugh Honour, he 'worshipped Anthony like the head prefect. Anthony's word was gospel. Ben would say, "Of course, *Anthony* says" . . . and that was it.' Blunt published almost exclusively in the *Burlington*, and as his best pupils came of age they too found their way into its pages. He persuaded Nicolson to set up an editorial board; Blunt's presence on it gave him considerable, though not unfailing, influence over the magazine's contents.

Nicolson's relationship with Blunt was, however, not quite as straightforwardly adulatory as some thought. Nicolson admired Blunt both for his work and almost romantically as, his friend Richard Wollheim thought, 'a perfect incarnation of Bloomsbury ideals'. But there was also a thread of envy and resentment in his feelings for Blunt, by whom he appears to have sometimes felt bullied, and whom he felt had never sufficiently acknowledged his work at the Royal Collection. After a lunch in November 1948 he wrote in his diary that Blunt

> treats me in rather too breezy, cavalier a fashion, telling me
> that when I had proposed in the summer resigning from the
> King's Pictures, he did his best to dissuade me, because he
> could not face a scene. Now he feels up to anything, can
> stand any racket, is prepared to see me go. Meaning, of
> course, "You are useless to me". Then he exhorts me to
> work harder. And all the Burlington business comes up

---

collection at his home, Highnam, near Cheltenham. It was offered by his grandson, Mark, who was unmarried and childless, desperately short of money, periodically depressive, and wrote regularly to Blunt over the next twenty years agonizing over whether he had made the right decision.

again: whether it wouldn't be better if a small inner cabinet decided what articles should be printed, and so forth.

In return, as Wollheim recalled, Nicolson could be 'quite malicious'. 'The enemies of scholarship are tact and urbanity,' Nicolson wrote. In the *Burlington* contributors took great bites out of each other and he was careful not to censor them. On occasion it was Blunt who got mauled.

From 1947, the invitations to join art committees, to become adviser to this or that institution, seemed to come almost automatically. Blunt had joined the small cabal of art-world movers and shakers, a combination of grand patrons and worthies who were invited to join, and run, everything. Busy as he was, he accepted everything offered. It was as if he couldn't say no. In 1947 he became 'London art representative' for the Toronto Art Gallery on the recommendation of Peter Brieger, a central European émigré who had found refuge at the Courtauld in the mid-1930s and was now professor of art history at the University of Ontario. In 1948 the National Gallery of Canada in Ottawa requested the same service,* and when, two years later, his friend Ellis Waterhouse became head of the Barber Institute he began to advise him on acquisitions too. In 1948 he also joined the British Council's Fine Arts Committee, which sent him abroad to lecture on British art – a subject which did not overly excite him, though his lectures incalculably raised his reputation overseas.

That same year, 1948, he also became the first picture adviser for the National Trust. Since the war the Trust had begun to accumulate an increasing number of stately homes, together with

* Between 1948 and 1955 Blunt bought Toronto a Poussin, a Reynolds, a Picasso sculpture, a Matisse maquette, and even a work by his pre-war *bête noire*, Ben Nicholson, all for what was described as 'a very modest budget'. He also bought Toronto's first Henry Moore – the gallery now has one of the largest collections of Moore's sculpture in the world – and fostered its embryonic relationship with the sculptor. In 1969 he even found the gallery its first Moore curator: Alan Wilkinson, a Canadian studying Moore at the Courtauld.

some extraordinary art collections which it was far from equipped to deal with. The invitation came from the grandest of Blunt's new friends among the art-world great and good, David Balniel, Lord Crawford, a former Conservative MP and a member of every arts panel in the land. He was the head of a very old aristocratic Scottish family, famous for its art collection at Balcarres Castle, which included a Duccio. Crawford was high-minded, intimidatingly serious, and possessed of a strong sense of duty and an old-fashioned austere puritanism which found an echo in Blunt. Even though the family had invested in electricity early in the century, Balcarres was one of the last places in Scotland to get electric lights.

It was the perfect moment for Blunt to join this world. Personal connections and networking still oiled the wheels, but power had begun to pass from wealthy private patrons to the institutions and to the committees that ran them. Blunt unthinkingly accepted the old world's underlying values: conscientious service for no financial reward, old-boy networking, personal connections, and the circumvention of red tape with an influential word here and there. At the same time he believed himself a supporter of the new post-war consensus, in which the state supported the arts, and the public had more access to them. The National Gallery and the Tate had just begun to get something approaching a decent government subsidy. Organizations such as the National Trust's Historic Buildings Committee, the British Council and the Arts Council were just coming into their own. The 1945 Labour government's taxation programme, which aimed at nothing less than fundamental income redistribution, seemed to be about to spell the end for the landed aristocracy – who well before the war had already found themselves unable to afford the upkeep of their grand houses and estates – and seemed to confirm that the day of the private patron was over. Perhaps almost more surprisingly, the rich seemed to bear the tax burden with a sense of resignation and inevitability. Thus Lord Crawford, a traditional Tory paternalist by birth and inclination, could be found in the mid-1950s, in an article he wrote for *Queen* magazine, stating calmly that the government and local authorities had 'collectively assumed the responsibility for preserving works of art formerly exercised by the great private collections of the past'. The article continued in classic dialectical terms:

This public conscience is the outcome of a long historical process by which this aspect of patronage has developed as a function, first of the individual, and gradually of the nation. In our day, the economic policies which have deprived private owners of the means to maintain their collections have meant an increase in state intervention to safeguard our inheritance . . .

Not every door was open to Blunt, however. There were still areas of the British art Establishment where he was sneered at for being a 'highbrow' (and tacitly no doubt for his homosexuality). In 1949 the outgoing president of the Royal Academy, Sir Alfred Munnings, a skilful painter of horseflesh who thought that even the Post-Impressionists were beyond the pale, attacked Blunt in his valedictory speech, which was broadcast on the BBC. Somewhat the worse for drink, he damned Blunt as a 'highbrow' and 'expert' exactly the same words, said in exactly the same derogatory tone, as Lord Lee had employed back in 1947, and for daring to claim that a 'Reynolds isn't as great as a Pee-cass-O'. Munnings also announced that Winston Churchill had once proposed that together they should kick Picasso's 'something something something' ('bony little arse' being a phrase unsuitable for the BBC in 1949), and railed additionally against Modigliani, Matisse and Henry Moore. When a huge fuss erupted in the art world the next day, Blunt – somehow characteristically – was absent. He had gone to Paris to give a lecture at the Louvre.

For all his involvement with his work, Blunt was not a monk. When Jackie Hewit came back after the war they resumed their ménage for a while. He also had other affairs. He may even have had an affair with a woman. In 1947, Pamela Tudor Craig, then a young Courtauld student, encountered on several occasions when she worked late in the Institute's library

a woman I have never forgotten. She was not tall, but she had great presence. She would say 'Good evening' in a sultry, musical but distinctly foreign accent. I noticed that although her clothes were very expensive, they appeared to be always the same, or nearly so. She wore a full fur coat, with a large collar, open at the neck to show fine jewels – I recall a choker or large pearls. Her hair was elaborately styled after a slightly old-fashioned mode. She wore much make-up, and was heralded by exotic scent. I imagine her to be something a little over thirty years old. Perhaps she was more. In any case she was among the most glamorous women I have ever seen. The clearest memory of all was the Director, standing at the top of that exquisite staircase, or on the half-landing, to greet her. Their faces were both radiant when they saw one another.

Blunt, Tudor Craig thought, was 'gaunt but totally attractive'. (It was a much-remarked-on fact that, while homosexual men tended not to find him especially sexy, some women found his ascetic looks – especially in his forties, when life had given his face an attractive mobility which photographs rarely captured – elusively desirable.) 'I thought at the time, as surely anyone would have thought, that I had observed an assignation of lovers.' The identity of this glamorous creature remains a mystery. Blunt knew several distinguished foreign women in their thirties and forties: the formidable Margot Wittkower, who was not especially glamorous; Dennis Proctor's first wife, Varda, a former Vogue model; Salomea Halpern, once a great beauty, now no longer young.

This mysterious liaison did not stop Blunt from falling for someone else. On 10 November 1948 Ben Nicolson reported in his diary that Blunt, 'on the top of the world', had 'just fallen in love with a boy called [Alan]'. Alan Baker* was a twenty-two-year-old art student whom Blunt met at a dinner party given by Sir Johnny Phillips, a rich bachelor whom he and Burgess had known for years. Phillips lived in Albany on Piccadilly, and endlessly complained that the young men he met were only after his money.

Two days later Blunt invited Baker to dinner *à deux* at the Courtauld, and 'One thing led to another.' Blunt's keenness took his friends, and Baker, by surprise. 'He was, dare I say it,' Baker reflected years later, 'besotted.' The younger man was darkly handsome with brawny film star looks, and bisexual. He was also a friend of Bunny Roger, an upper-class ex-army queen who gave the campest, glitziest fancy-dress parties in London. This was not Blunt's style at all – though he was extremely curious about Roger's set. Baker was bright, self-educated and eager to learn. 'I was mesmerized by Blunt. I liked older people. He wasn't beautiful, but I was impressed by his vision and knowledge.' As ever, Blunt fell into the role of the teacher and educator. 'In many ways I was a naive boy. I'd been in the Navy for four years. He was more my mentor than my lover, and he was such a good teacher. I would go to his lectures at the Courtauld. He gave ones on Picasso and Poussin which I thought were tremendous.' There was even, Baker mused, a frustrated paternal 'or maternal' streak in Blunt. They went to France and Italy, and Blunt took him to the stately homes he administered for the National Trust. In Paris, Baker noticed, Blunt already knew 'all the people at the Louvre, and had entrées to everywhere'. In Italy, Blunt went to Ischia to see W. H. Auden and Louis MacNeice, while Baker went to Capri and they met up in Naples 'with a Hollywood actress I had got to know called Ona Munson[†] and we all three went to Paestum'.

They never lived together, however. Nor did Blunt let his whole

---

* Not his real name.
† She had a large part in *Gone with the Wind*, and was married to the American painter Eugene Berman.

guard down. Their lives came together in the space between his work and Baker's energetic social life. 'He seemed very keen, but he wasn't possessive. That's the curious thing. I did have other lovers, and he never seemed to care – at least he never showed it.' Blunt set up a seven-year covenant to provide Baker with a small income of about £30 a month, 'so that I could be independent and wouldn't have to ask him to do the tipping when we were travelling, about which I used to get embarrassed, because I had little money. It wasn't a question of keeping me on a string, because he went on paying it after we split up.' Blunt was dominant, in control, but not controlling. Baker felt that Blunt had channelled a deep-seated romanticism away from the uncontrollability of sexual love into an idealized idea about 'the nobility of male friendship'.

By 1949 the juxtaposition of Blunt's various lives had achieved a kind of cosmic absurdity, and was inducing constant anxiety. On 19 January that year he was stopped by a policeman in Montagu Square in the middle of a meeting with the London *rezidentura*'s latest chief, Nikolai Rodin (aka Korovin). Blunt's bag, which was full of secret papers from Burgess, was searched, but the documents were wrapped in brown paper and the police did not realize what they were. Korovin reported that Blunt was extremely anxious and hard to calm. Yet Baker had no idea that anything was amiss. A few days later Blunt was in Lisbon being congratulated by the British ambassador for a British Council exhibition on 'British Painting 1740–1840' – 'the finest of its kind that has been seen in Lisbon for many years'.

Shortly after the Montagu Square meeting, Burgess, whose papers Blunt had been delivering, fell downstairs at Le Bœuf sur le Toit after a drunken tussle with his FO colleague and new drinking partner Fred Warner, and ended up in hospital. The fall left him with headaches and insomnia, and he began to take Nembutal and Benzedrine regularly. On his release from hospital, his mother sent him to Ireland to convalesce; there he had a car accident in March and was arrested for drunk driving. His old friends, among them Goronwy Rees, thought him 'profoundly unhappy'. Burgess did not welcome Blunt's new relationship, and made it clear he disliked Baker. 'Burgess was nasty. He could be very funny, but in a very vicious sort of way. He had decided that I was a stupid pretty face. It saved me a lot of bother. He never made a pass at me. He was just interested in rough trade by then.'

By 1949 the Labour government had severed friendly contacts with the Soviet Union. It was the year the Cold War froze. Communists took over in China, and America was consumed by the trial of the 'Red Queen' Elizabeth Bentley. Bentley's case was swiftly followed by that of Alger Hiss, the State Department official charged with passing documents to the Soviets in the 1930s. It was the year that J. Edgar Hoover described Communism as a 'worldwide conspiracy embracing a third of the world's population', its aim being 'the erasure of freedom, perhaps for ever, from the parchment of time'. President Truman announced in September that the Soviet Union now had the atom bomb. At the Apostles' annual dinner that year, Michael Straight, fresh from McCarthyite America, reminded Blunt of the various unpredictable avenues by which his secret might escape. Straight now owned and edited the liberal Washington-based magazine the *New Republic* and, though he was an opponent of McCarthy, was also loudly anti-Communist. At the end of the meal – during which he'd argued heatedly with the Marxist historian Eric Hobsbawm – Blunt and Burgess came up to talk, wanting to be reassured that he was not 'totally unfriendly' to them. Straight was reassuring. (In his memoirs he wrote that he wanted to tell the authorities what he knew, but he didn't have the courage. Or rather, 'It reflected my continuing inability to force an issue, to resolve a conflict, to make an enemy of another individual, and in this instance to break completely with my own past.')

In November, Burgess got himself into trouble again. On holiday in Gibraltar en route to Tangier, he got into a bitter argument about Franco with two British intelligence men in a bar and announced to the assembled company that his opponents were secret service men. A formal complaint was lodged against him, and a senior figure at MI6 demanded he be fired from the Foreign Office. He was saved by his ever infallible ability to make influential friends and patrons. Hector McNeil and Gladwyn Jebb, both extremely powerful in the Foreign Office, both persuaded of Burgess's talents, supported him.

When, in February 1950, Klaus Fuchs, head of theoretical physics at the Harwell atomic research centre, in Berkshire, was arrested for having passed atomic secrets to the Soviet Union while working at Los Alamos during the war, everyone was shocked: the Soviets and the spies. It turned out that Burgess could have warned Fuchs, but he had forgotten. Kim Philby, who had moved to Washington as MI6's liaison with the CIA the previous September, had told Burgess to pass on a story he had heard about a secret Anglo-American decryption project called 'Venona' which had begun to break Soviet wartime codes and was closing in on a Soviet spy – who would turn out to be Fuchs.

It was not until April that Burgess met up with his NKVD contact and told him what Philby had discovered about Venona. The Americans and the British had constructed a decryption machine which in one day did 'the work of a thousand people in a thousand years'. It was anticipated that the machine would be able to break all the Soviets' wartime codes within six to twelve months. (This turned out to be grossly optimistic.) The spies were, Korovin reported to Moscow, 'strongly alarmed'. Blunt was particularly worried that Fuchs might lead British Intelligence to Philby's first wife, Litzi Friedman, with whom he recalled having idly discussed the possibility of recruiting an atom scientist in 1940. A month later, in the course of telling Korovin that he had been cleared of misbehaviour in Gibraltar and been given a surprising (given his intense anti-Americanism) posting as Second Secretary to the British Embassy in Washington, Burgess asked for political asylum in the USSR for himself and Philby, should Venona expose them.

Blunt, however, did not want asylum. 'In Paul's [Burgess] opinion,' Korovin reported,

> if serious danger threatens, Yan [Blunt] will commit suicide. Paul said that Yan's moral qualities are not like Stanley [Philby]'s and Paul's . . . Paul considers Yan a good comrade, entirely devoted to our cause, but the spirit of an intellectual which is characteristic of Yan's profession is still firm in him, and this spirit makes him accept the inevitable and he doesn't mobilize for the struggle.

In fact they were, for the moment, safe. Venona produced no direct mention of Burgess, Philby and Blunt. Both MI5 and MI6 persisted in the belief that no one in their organizations could possibly have betrayed them to the Soviets. Even after Fuchs's confession, the head of the Foreign Office's security, George Carey Foster, believed it 'inconceivable that any senior member of the service could be a traitor'.

Blunt's morbid thoughts of suicide persisted, however. The day after Burgess left for the USA in July 1950, after a typically chaotic farewell party, Blunt met Yuri Modin, who reported, 'If danger of exposure arose he would try to flee to Paris or would commit suicide. The thought about suicide in the case of extreme necessity has appeared in his head because of his feelings towards his mother who, according to his words, will be able to get over his suicide but won't be able to get over his exposure and imprisonment.' Blunt apologized for his 'bourgeois individualism' but told Modin that he was a bourgeois to his fingertips and 'he would hardly be able to act differently and resolve to begin a new life'.

13. Accessory

'the act of a friend'

British Intelligence had been aware since 1948 that secret information was leaking out of the Foreign Office. However, it was another three years before they finally admitted to themselves that they had a problem and began to hunt for the spy in earnest. It was information from Venona that produced the codename of the Foreign Office agent, Homer, and the fact that he had worked in Washington. It was because of the Washington connection that Dick White told Kim Philby, MI6's man there, when he was briefly back from the USA in January 1951, that there was a spy in the FO and that he should keep an eye out at his end 'for someone who is unstable, living on his nerves. That will be our man.' Philby realized that it would only be a matter of time before Donald Maclean was apprehended.

Maclean had barely seen his fellow spies in seventeen years. In that time he had forged himself a very successful career in the Foreign Office, married an American girl, and passed to the NKVD a succession of extremely important documents, among them papers on the Anglo-American project to develop the atom bomb, and the details of the Marshall Plan for the post-war reconstruction of Europe. Having spent four years as First Secretary in Washington, he had in 1949 been sent to the Cairo Embassy as counsellor. There his life started to unravel. His implosion was oddly similar to Burgess's: it featured drunkenness and embarrassing public scenes. Eventually, having got blind drunk one night in Cairo, he broke into a colleague's flat and

smashed it up. He was sent home to England on six months'
leave. When he returned to work for the FO in London in
November 1950 he was still deeply depressed. 'In conversation a
kind of stutter would fall as if he had returned to some basic and
incommunicable anxiety,' Cyril Connolly later recalled. Friends
found him drunk and asleep in taxis, or unconscious in their
hallways. 'What would you do if I told you I was a Communist
agent . . . well I am, go on, report me,' he mumbled one night.
On another occasion he knocked down an acquaintance for
saying that Whittaker Chambers, the American ex-Communist
who had exposed Alger Hiss, was right. 'I am the English Hiss,'
he said.

It was not Maclean's behaviour that alerted the authorities that
he was their man. As his colleague Robert Cecil wrote of the FO,
'Adultery, alcoholism, bad behaviour were reprovable but ultimately acceptable, since nothing worse would be contemplated.'
Maclean was identified by a Venona message, cracked by an
English cryptographer on 30 March 1951. Once they knew,
however, neither the FO nor MI5 seemed inclined to corner their
quarry. They were hampered by the fact that it was felt to be so
important to keep Venona secret that it could not be used as
proof of Maclean's guilt, which would therefore have to be
provided by some other means. (Similar protocols had governed
the use of Ultra information during the war.) But the investigation
was conducted with extraordinary slowness. Instead of being
interrogated, Maclean was followed by MI5 and Special Branch –
though only in London, and in working hours, since both organizations claimed that overtime could not be justified. Maclean
was soon aware he was being followed. In addition MI5 decided
to delay a search of his home in Tatsfield, near Sevenoaks, for
two months until June, when his wife would be going into
hospital for a Caesarian.

At the beginning of April, Kim Philby, in his capacity as MI6's
liaison officer with US Intelligence, and no doubt helped by his
friendship with one of Venona's senior figures, Meredith Gardner,
got the news that the identity of the Foreign Office spy had been

discovered. Stuck in Washington he had no way of warning Maclean; he had been out of contact with the Soviets since he had moved to the USA. The solution came in the form of Guy Burgess. He had lived with Philby and his wife, who had been worried by his general decline, since he had arrived in Washington in 1950. His stay had involved one embarrassment after another. One of the worst was the occasion on which he had insulted the wife of a senior CIA officer at a party of Philby's; most of the time he had merely contented himself with publicly denouncing America and American foreign policy. The last straw came in April, when he was pulled up for drunk driving three times, in three separate states, in one day. The FO informed him that his nine lives were up, and he would be sent home and sacked. It has been suggested that Burgess deliberately engineered his own recall to England. Whatever the truth, his disgrace was entirely in character, and it gave Philby the opportunity to get his message through to Maclean. Before Burgess left, Philby impressed on him that, whatever happened, he must not escape with Maclean, for his departure would automatically cast suspicion on Philby.

It is possible that more than one message passed between Burgess, Philby and London at this time. Not long before Burgess left America, Alan Baker arrived in Washington. His relationship with Blunt had ended, and he had come over because he had fallen for an American boy he'd met in Italy. Blunt, in accordance with the Bloomsbury custom of regarding sexual jealousy as a great evil, had encouraged him, and had given him his latest book to deliver to Burgess – *The Nation's Pictures*, which he'd just completed with Margaret Whinney. It is possible that there was a message in the book. Yuri Modin – never a very accurate source – claimed that the NKVD knew that Maclean was under stress, and that Blunt had seen him in April. This seems unlikely. But Baker felt there was something odd about his errand:

Guy was to get in touch with me. I didn't know where he was, I didn't hear anything for a couple of days. Finally he telephoned me and said he couldn't get away, but 'Mr

Straight' would come and collect the book and take me to dinner. We had dinner, which was very nice. I have always assumed that this was Michael Straight. He didn't tell me much about Burgess. He gave me the impression that he disapproved of him.

Baker never saw the man again. Straight, who was also living in Washington at the time, says he never met Baker and met Burgess only once, towards the end of his time in Washington, when they had an acrimonious argument in front of the British Embassy on the subject of Korea.

Burgess arrived at Southampton on 7 May, with an American medical student called Bernard Miller in tow. Jackie Hewit, who had come to meet him, was extremely peeved, and even more so when Burgess then disappeared for two days. Hewit said that Burgess's first stop was Blunt. According to Yuri Modin – who provided the only published account of Blunt's involvement in the episode – Blunt became the go-between between himself and Burgess. Armed with the news of Maclean's imminent exposure, Modin contacted Moscow for permission to organize his defection.

Burgess's second stop was Goronwy Rees, who now lived with his wife and children by the Thames at Sonning. Rees was bursar of All Souls, Oxford, and had made a decent reputation for himself as a journalist. Since the dawn of the Cold War, he had also become a zealous anti-Communist. Communism, he now said, was 'perhaps an even greater danger than the Germany of Adolf Hitler'. But somehow he had not become quite what he had hoped to be. He drank too much. He nursed a chip about 'being victimized by a kind of "in-group" of *soi-disant* superior persons', as Stuart Hampshire put it. He was not pleased to see Burgess, whom he found cleaner and madder than he had ever seen him before, and who spent his visit haranguing his hosts about the awfulness of America. It seems likely that he was trying to gauge whether Rees would feel obliged to tell his secret if the Maclean story blew up. He was right to wonder. Rees was already twitchy. Only months before, Maclean had come up to him at the Gargoyle club and shouted, 'I know all about you. You used to be one of us, but you ratted.'

Finally Burgess went to see Maclean. They had not met in years. They lunched at the Royal Automobile Club, and Maclean immediately confided that he knew he was being followed. He baulked, however, at the thought of defection. His wife, Melinda, was due to give birth in three weeks' time. He asked that he might at least discuss the situation with her. Modin duly applied to Moscow for permission.

Having performed his errands, Burgess spent the next few days rushing round London visiting his old haunts. Quentin Bell remembered him drinking himself into swift oblivion at the Reform Club on gin and ginger, as he announced he was going to resign from the FO and complete the third volume of Lady Cecil's biography of Lord Salisbury. He asked his old schoolfriend Michael Berry – Lord Hartwell, proprietor of the *Daily Telegraph* and husband of the society hostess Pamela Berry – to give him a dinner party and a job. The dinner party was arranged; the job was not: when Berry asked for something of Burgess's to read, Burgess gave him a document marked 'Top Secret'. 'I was appalled when I read it. His writing had certainly gone to seed.'

When Melinda Maclean (who, Modin claimed, had briefly been her husband's go-between with the Soviets in the early 1940s) was finally told about her husband's predicament, she told him to go. Still he resisted. He now said he wanted a companion – Burgess – to travel with him. Burgess refused, arguing that if he went he would never return and Philby would be implicated. As if things weren't bad enough, ten days or so into his return Burgess received a telegram from Philby, apparently reminding him that he had left a car in the embassy car park, but bearing the postscript 'It's getting very hot here.' Modin, realizing that Maclean would not budge, began to put pressure on Burgess to go at least part of the way with him, reassuring him that he would be able to return home. He also quietly tried to persuade Blunt to defect. Blunt refused point-blank.

Finally, Burgess agreed in principle to accompany Maclean. The plan – thought up by Blunt – according to Modin, was to get the two men out of the country on one of the weekend cross-Channel cruise boats which made short stops in French seaside towns, and for which passports were not needed. Burgess bought two tickets for a cruise from Southampton leaving late on the night of the 25 May, and, warming to the game, spread the story at the Reform Club that he was going up to the north of England for a few days. With Hewit he seemed to change his mind and his mood every few minutes. 'Guy was vacillating all week,' Hewit remembered. 'He was maudlin one minute and then up the next. He was drinking an awful lot.' Burgess went to see Miriam Rothschild, who was renting an expensive flat near Piccadilly, and announced that he wanted to buy it for his mother. 'You couldn't possibly afford it,' said Rothschild. Burgess told her that money was not a problem. He told Hewit he would never go back to the FO, then that he would be going to Pamela Berry's dinner party the following Tuesday. He announced that he was taking his young American, Bernard Miller, to Saint-Malo for the weekend. Then that he was not. Then that 'A friend of mine is in a spot of bother. I'll use the tickets to get him away.' He might, he added, go on to Paris. Hewit also claimed – perhaps with a little poetic exaggeration – that the night before Burgess left he heard him arguing hysterically in a language he thought was French with someone whom he later believed to be his Soviet control.

Friday 25 May was Donald Maclean's thirty-eighth birthday. He left the office early, went on to his club, then took his usual train from Charing Cross to Sevenoaks. Burgess packed his collected edition of Jane Austen, his dinner jacket and Hewit's overcoat. Before he left, he called Goronwy Rees, who was out, and told Rees' wife he was about to do something which would amaze everybody. He also tried to call Wystan Auden, who was in England staying with Stephen Spender, to ask if he could come and stay at Ischia. He arrived at Maclean's after dinner, where, according to Melinda, he was introduced to her as 'Roger Styles'. Maclean told her they had to see a friend of his visitor's near Andover and would stay overnight. They made the Southampton boat, the *Falaise*, with minutes to spare, Burgess leaving his car askew on the quayside. At Saint-Malo they disembarked, took a taxi to Rennes, and that was the last that anyone in the West ever saw of them. The plan was to take a train from Rennes to Paris, and another on to Switzerland. According to Modin, they were to be issued with false passports at the Soviet Embassy in Berne, whence they would travel on to Zurich, where a flight to Prague would take them beyond the reach of Western Intelligence by Sunday evening. If no alarm had been raised by Monday morning, Modin would know that the escape had been successful.

When Burgess failed to come home on the Sunday evening, Jackie Hewit called Blunt. 'He told me he didn't know where Guy was. I said that I would call the Green Park Hotel to see if Bernard Miller was still staying there but Blunt told me not to do anything. I was used to taking orders from him so I didn't. I think that Anthony thought that Guy was coming back. Anyway, he said there was no point in upsetting people.' How much Hewit really knew about Burgess's trip we'll never know. It was never clear whether the attention the story brought him caused him to exaggerate and dramatize his role in it, or if he was obfuscating for his own preservation: probably a little of both.

Against Blunt's advice, Hewit called Goronwy Rees to tell him that Burgess had disappeared. As Hewit told him the news, Rees later wrote, 'I suddenly had an absolutely sure and certain, if irrational, intuition, that Guy had gone to the Soviet Union.' It wasn't an irrational intuition at all. Rees in turn called Burgess's old MI6 contact David Footman – whom he occasionally advised on Communist matters – and told him that he believed Burgess had defected. Then he called Blunt. Since the war they had had an awkward, phoney friendship. Rees had lived next door to Louis MacNeice, and he and Blunt had socialized in a rather desultory way which did nothing to quell their fundamental

343

dislike of each other: 'They were absolutely incompatible,' Stuart Hampshire observed. 'Anthony despised him, and he regarded Anthony as an awful fraud.'

Whether Blunt knew that Burgess was going for good is not clear. In his memoirs, Yuri Modin claimed he could never understand why Burgess didn't, as he'd planned, turn round and come back to England. But Kim Philby's Russian biographer, Genrikh Borovik, says Modin was well aware that Burgess would never be able to return, and the NKVD had no intention of letting him do so. Moscow had decided he was burnt out and too dangerous to leave behind. Thus he was effectively tricked into leaving, even though his departure would endanger Philby – as well as putting pressure on Blunt. Burgess must have realized, reluctantly, that it would be impossible to go back if he left. Modin, incidentally, was hailed in Moscow for his role in the extrication – it was one of the crowning moments of his career. Years later he was still lecturing on the case at the KGB training academy.

It is possible that Blunt thought, or hoped, that Burgess was coming back. He certainly expended a great deal of care in establishing that he was expecting to see him. He phoned Ellis Waterhouse to ask if Burgess was staying with him. Waterhouse remembered, 'He seemed worried and puzzled. I am sure that he didn't know where Guy had gone.' He dropped in on Bernard Miller, who later told the FBI that Blunt took him to see an old friend of Burgess's – probably Hewit. This old friend told Miller and Blunt about 'Burgess's plan for the weekend. Both Blunt and [Hewit] were disturbed because Burgess never went away without telling his mother . . . and Blunt seemed to think that Burgess was "going downhill mentally for a long time".' Miller said that 'Blunt told them that he was going to report Burgess's disappearance to some security agency connected with the British Foreign Office.'

The next day, Monday, Blunt went to see Goronwy Rees at Sonning. It was a beautiful summer day, and they sat in the garden by the Thames. Rees said that Blunt spent hours trying to dissuade him from telling what he knew. In his memoirs, he wrote

that he told Blunt – as ever unnamed, but described as 'a friend
... who had served in MI5 during the war ... the Cambridge
liberal conscience at its very best' – that he feared Burgess was a
Soviet agent, and that Blunt told him that there were no good
reasons for going to the authorities. After all, his suspicions were
based only on a chance remark from years before. In reality,
Rees's knowledge of Burgess's activities was rather more substan-
tial. It is more likely that Blunt tried to convince him not to talk
on other grounds: 'to make the kind of allegations I apparently
proposed to make about him [Burgess], was not ... the act of a
friend'.

It was too late. David Footman had already told Guy Liddell
about Rees's call. That very morning Melinda Maclean – having
waited the weekend – had called the FO to report Maclean
missing. Then Burgess's car was found on the quayside at Southampton. Witnesses described seeing them on the boat. The two
disappearances were put together. Dick White and Guy Liddell
couldn't believe it. Burgess had never been suspected of anything
except bad behaviour. 'It really was very challenging to anyone's
sanity to suppose that a man of Burgess's type could be a secret
agent of anybody's,' White said later. Indeed, MI5 and the FO
found it almost impossible to credit that anyone from the heart
of the English upper classes could be anything other than basically
loyal to the institutions which they had been raised to serve. The
escape, moreover, was a disaster which demonstrated incompetence, naivety and complacency at the highest levels in both organizations. Their immediate response was to find out what they
could and keep the story as quiet as possible.

On the Tuesday morning Blunt phoned Guy Liddell, who gave
him the extraordinary news. Blunt gave every indication of being
amazed. Liddell asked for – or Blunt offered to bring him – the
keys to Burgess's flat. This would circumvent the need for a
formal search warrant. Blunt collected the keys from Jackie
Hewit. 'Blunt was very uptight,' Hewit recalled. He advised
Hewit, rather sharply, to leave town for a while and said they
should keep out of each other's way. 'I said I might go to Italy.

He asked why I hadn't gone.' Blunt later said that he accompanied two MI5 men to Burgess's flat, where he managed to scoop up two incriminating letters, including Philby's telegram, while the others weren't looking. Other writers have speculated that Blunt searched the flat on his own first, before handing over the keys to Guy Liddell. (Rosamond Lehmann claimed that, shortly before he died, Blunt told her that Goronwy Rees had helped him. This could have been mischief on Blunt's part or a little imaginative elaboration on Lehmann's.) Either way, he did not do a thorough job. MI5 discovered a guitar case full of letters, including a postcard from Philby, papers from John Cairncross which so incriminated him that he resigned from his Civil Service job and left the country, and letters from Blunt. The letters also gave graphic accounts of Burgess's sexual liaisons since Cambridge.

That evening, Blunt attended the dinner that Pamela Berry had arranged for Burgess. Among the other guests were Sydney Butler, daughter of Samuel Courtauld and wife of the Conservative politician Rab, John Betjeman,* and Isaiah Berlin, who had not seen Blunt for several years. Blunt looked ill at ease, and waffled on to Berlin about the embarrassment of being found surrounded by Conservatives. 'I oughtn't to be at dinner here really ought I?' he said. 'Of course, she's all right,' he added, pointing out Sydney Butler, who was still very much involved with the Courtauld. 'She's high-minded.' 'I suppose', Berlin mused, 'he thought I knew he was a man of the Left. He felt I wasn't to think that he was really a friend of these terrible people.' When Burgess failed to arrive, Michael Berry, Lord Hartwell, called the Reform Club. Burgess hadn't been seen in several days. 'I did notice that Blunt went noticeably white. He spoke little at dinner and left directly after the coffee. It was said later, though I cannot remember by whom, that when news of the escape came out, a couple of days later, Blunt went to bed for a week.'

It almost seemed as if MI5 and the FO did not actually want

---

* It was at this dinner that Betjeman met and was smitten by Lady Elizabeth Cavendish, who became his lover until his death.

to know any more. Once again they dragged their feet. MI5 put off interviewing Melinda Maclean until 30 May, almost a week after Maclean's disappearance. By then the FO had advised her to say nothing – she protested her ignorance and innocence to MI5, and was pressed no further. The Maclean house was never searched – the reason given was Melinda's advancing pregnancy. Goronwy Rees later claimed to Andrew Boyle, whose book *The Climate of Treason* exposed Blunt, that when he met Guy Liddell for an informal chat about his views on Burgess that week, Liddell tried extremely hard to convince him not to take his accusations against Burgess any further. He also told Boyle – a fact which did not appear in either Boyle's book or Rees's memoirs – that, to his discomfort, Blunt was at the meeting too. Blunt's presence and Liddell's attempts to persuade him to keep quiet made Rees suspicious of Liddell.

Rees's subsequent interviews with MI5 went no better. He later claimed, 'they treated me as if I were a spy and a traitor with lots to hide. I held nothing back this time. I revealed the name of Blunt as the only other conspirator given to me by Burgess.' But, according to Dick White, Rees gave no clear answers to anything. White was incensed that Rees knew what Burgess had been doing all along:

> And he never said a single thing to us at that stage of the proceedings. That's what I made clear to him, and I thought he was a four-letter man. If he knew these things why didn't he come? Then he went on this spiel that he assumed we knew it all. So I said, 'You assumed we knew? Burgess was working for the Russians and we did nothing about it? What can you mean?' He was an arrogant intellectual of the worst kind. Really as slippery as an eel. He had a violent antipathy to Blunt. He said, 'Why don't you ask Blunt about these things?' He didn't say, repeat, DIDN'T SAY, 'Blunt's your man' or anything resembling that.

Rees, increasingly nervous, angry and paranoid, undermined his own credibility with cryptic answers and by flinging out a series of half-denunciations of other people of whom he had suddenly become suspicious – among them Guy Liddell, a Swiss family friend called Zaehner, and Stuart Hampshire, who the week before had advised the panicking Rees to keep his mouth shut and wait for MI5 to come to him. 'I thought that Jim Skardon, MI5's interrogator, was a real operator,' Hampshire later recalled. 'Goronwy wouldn't have lasted ten minutes with him. He'd start panicking and mumbling and get himself in more trouble. It was cynical advice, I know.' Rees seemed to suspect anyone who had tried to dissuade him from taking his story further. His feeling that Liddell wanted to keep him quiet was probably right: Liddell and White didn't trust him. Rees was a journalist and not noted for his ability to keep his mouth shut, and Blunt, whom both men took seriously, would have had little good to say about him. His other denunciations had no truth to them, but in the case of Liddell, in particular, they were very damaging – a fact which made Dick White even less inclined to take Rees's stories seriously.

Ten days after Melinda Maclean first reported her husband missing, on 7 June, the *Daily Express* splashed Burgess and Maclean's disappearance on its front page: 'Yard hunts two Britons'. The article speculated that they had gone to Russia. The story had apparently been leaked by the French security services, who had been asked to search for the two men. No arrangements had been made for dealing with press attention, and the Foreign Office reluctantly produced a statement disingenuous in its brevity: 'it is known they went to France a few days ago. Mr Maclean had a breakdown a year ago owing to over strain but was believed to fully have recovered.'

The Missing Diplomats, as they were dubbed, quickly became a huge news story. A little digging soon produced stories of Maclean's breakdown, their involvement with Communism, and, most juicy of all, Burgess's homosexuality. In America, where the story of two upper-class Englishmen with Communist pasts and links with Washington gripped the country, Burgess and Maclean were spotted everywhere. Another sighting had them in Buenos

Aires, with Maclean dressed up as a woman. In England, the *Daily Express* and the *Daily Mail* rivalled each other in offering larger and larger rewards for news of them. A babysitter the Macleans had used was offered £100 for any picture she could smuggle out of the house. Burgess's brother Nigel was offered £500 to collaborate with a water diviner to find his brother. In Asolo in Italy, Burgess's old friend Brian Howard was chased down a street by journalists; in Ischia Wystan Auden was door-stepped by hacks and watched by plain-clothes policemen. Stephen Spender gave an interview to the *Daily Express* quoting a letter in which John Lehmann said he regarded Burgess as a convinced Communist. Goronwy Rees wrote a piece for the 18 June *Daily Mail* in which he asserted that Burgess was 'one of the nicest men I ever knew ... To my knowledge he is not a Communist.' By 1962 the *Daily Express* had spent nearly £100,000 on the story.

The press coverage was a disaster for both the Foreign Office and MI5. Eager reporters got to potential sources before they did. Both organizations were made to look incompetent, and it became clear to the FBI and the American State Department, to whom they had played down the extent of the damage, that they had been actively misleading. The air of ineffectuality was compounded when Sir Percy Sillitoe, the head of MI5, flew to Washington on a secret mission to placate the head of the FBI, J. Edgar Hoover, and was photographed by the *Daily Express* actually getting on the plane. Hoover, far from impressed, immediately ordered his own investigation.

Nor was the press slow to make the link with the Surveyor of the King's Pictures. Blunt's friendship with the now notorious Burgess was soon common knowledge in Fleet Street. Within days of the story breaking there were 'millions and millions of journalists', as Stephen Rees Jones remembered, swarming round the Courtauld's Portman Square entrance. The phones were jammed with reporters hoping to trick someone into putting them through to Blunt. All his appointments were postponed. For several days he hid himself in his flat. It was rumoured that he was drinking from eleven o'clock in the morning. One of the few who managed to get in to see him was Alan Baker, recently back from Washington, where his new relationship had foundered. He found Blunt almost silent and 'in a terrible state. He wouldn't talk much, but he obviously was.' These periods of lethargy were punctuated by brisk activity, as Blunt set about ensuring his own survival. On one occasion he escaped through the Courtauld laboratory's back entrance, asking Stephen Rees Jones, who ran the laboratory, if he would accompany him up Baker Street. 'He asked me, "Could you be carrying something with you? Could it have a handle?" I picked up something from the lab. We walked out the back door and up Baker Street. Halfway up he said, "Thank you. You can go back now."'

Alan Baker found himself pursued by a Fleet Street journalist who hovered around the edges of London's homosexual social circles and made heavy hints about Blunt's sexuality. Baker knew that the man was homosexual himself. 'He hounded me, but he got no change out of me. I complained to Anthony about him – "He's driving me mad, can you do something?" Anthony asked me to dinner at the Reform Club.' When Baker arrived, Roger Hollis, the MI5 officer who had been in charge of Communist subversion during the war, was sitting with Blunt. 'I'd met him once before, at a Courtauld lecture, but I didn't know he was in MI5. Looking back on it, I think they were trying to find out how much I knew or suspected. It made me suspicious of Hollis's role in the spies' escape.' Blunt suggested that Baker leave London. He went to stay with relations, and then on to Capri.

Blunt also went to see Peter Pollock, who was now living as a gentleman farmer in Hertfordshire. Pollock had been utterly startled by the revelations: he had seen Burgess just two days before his disappearance, and had left his Rolls-Royce behind Burgess's flat.

The papers were full of Burgess and the mystery Rolls-Royce. Anthony had been sent by MI5 to find out what I knew about Guy. He told me later that MI5 searched my bank accounts. Anthony seemed very anxious. The best thing, he said, was to be quiet as quiet, not to make any statement. I thought he was telling me this out of kindness, but it was really because poor old Jackie Hewit was talking to anyone who'd listen. He was saying, 'You keep me out of it and I'll keep you out of it.' He kept his side of the bargain.

Blunt's closeness to Liddell and Hollis at this time has inspired suggestions that one of them may have been a Soviet mole. What seems rather to have been the case is that Blunt became an informal consultant to the whole investigation. From early on he had made himself indispensable to Liddell, White and their protégé Roger Hollis, on hand to explain to them both the complexities of the Cambridge Left in the 1930s and the web of Burgess's relationships. All three had known Blunt for ten years as reliable, discreet and professional. He had been a close friend of Burgess's; but Burgess had lot of close friends. For Blunt, being so close and so useful to the investigation helped to deflect, at least for a while, any emerging suspicions they may have had that he too had been working for the Soviets.

It is also possible, as Stuart Hampshire has tentatively suggested, that Blunt chose this moment to make an informal confession to White and Liddell, and offered himself as the key to Burgess's world. With Blunt to answer their questions, White and Liddell would have felt they could afford to put their efforts into keeping a lid on the story elsewhere – for example ensuring that Goronwy Rees did not make his suspicions public. It is curious, that, while White was very quickly convinced of Philby's guilt, lobbying energetically to get him dismissed from MI6 (Philby returned to London in July and resigned), he made no move to investigate Blunt, who had also been so closely linked with Burgess. It may be that White's suspicions about Philby were confirmed by Blunt. Blunt may even have been responsible for MI5's discovery that John Cairncross was a source of Burgess's and the Soviets. Their realization that Cairncross was part of Burgess's spy ring has usually been attributed to the discovery of letters by him in Burgess's flat. But Blunt could simply have told them; he would, at the very least, have been able to confirm Cairncross's involvement. A deal with MI5 might even explain the organization's apparent desultoriness over the years – particularly under the direction of Dick White and later Roger Hollis – in trying to extract a confession from Blunt. Of course, this is just another theory: there is no substantive evidence to support it.

According to Yuri Modin, it was at this time, after making a final attempt to persuade him to defect, that the NKVD formally ended its relationship with Blunt. The two men met in a square in west London. Blunt, who appeared extremely calm, immediately rejected Modin's offer. Modin has him say:

> No doubt you can also guarantee total access to the Château de Versailles, whenever I need to go there for my work . . . You have to understand . . . that I simply couldn't live in the Soviet Union under the conditions you are offering. I know perfectly well how your people live, and I can assure you it would be very hard, almost unbearable, for me to do likewise . . . I've worked for many years for the British counter-espionage services and I'm well aware of what's in store for me . . . I'm convinced that they can't bring me to confess if I don't feel like it and I don't in the least feel like it. If you want to know why I don't feel like it, I can tell you that, too. I have a deep respect and affection for Guy Burgess and I'd rather die than do anything that might place him in danger. He may have left the country, but still no proof exists that he is a Soviet agent. Therefore it's quite possible he'll come back here one day. As long as that possibility depends on me, there will be no proof against him, nor will I ever denounce him. That's why I categorically refuse to leave.

As they walked along, Blunt had a kind of fit. He choked, clawed at his chest, and broke out in a sweat. As he caught his breath, he admitted that this had happened before. 'Here's another good reason why I shouldn't scurry off to Russia. If I have to die of a heart attack, I'd rather do it here.' It was agreed instead that Soviet Intelligence would formally terminate its links with him. He was offered money, which he refused, and Modin noted that he 'seemed perfectly happy about Moscow's decision'.

It appears that Blunt managed to avoid suspicion for some time. It was a year or so before he became a formal suspect. Even then, his first interrogations were hardly tough. Dick White sent Blunt's old friend Courtney Young, who reported his 'vehement denials'. When William 'Jim' Skardon, the MI5 interrogator famous for his toughness – he had 'broken' Klaus Fuchs – went to see Blunt, it was 'to gain what info I could about the movements of Burgess and Maclean. I didn't make notes, he gave me no reason to think he was holding anything back. I wouldn't necessarily take notes. I would remember and put down notes afterwards. That was the Skardon method, if I may say so.' Blunt gave nothing away. They discussed a small Degas pastel which hung in his study.

Not everyone was so convinced of Blunt's innocence. Rosamond Lehmann tried several times to contact the security services to tell them what Goronwy Rees had told her years before about Burgess. She claimed that when she finally got to talk to Skardon he asked her about Rees and about Blunt. There were more questions about Blunt when she met more MI5 officers months later. Cyril Connolly was also deeply suspicious of Blunt. In 1952 he wrote a short book about Burgess and Maclean – he had known both of them – called *The Missing Diplomats*. In his notes for the book, Blunt's name is scribbled again and again in the margins. One of his sources was Goronwy Rees.

In 1951 Eddy Sackville-West, one of the archetypal bright young things of the 1920s, wrote of his youth:

> The individualism of the period was too extreme and intransigent: intellectual pride was erected into a faith, and had its result in an unhappy blend of cynicism and sentimentality. It was not ethics we lacked so much as religion, which, like

politics, was hardly considered a subject at all . . . we are paying for them now. To have been young in the 'twenties makes it difficult to be middle-aged in the 'fifties – just as people who were young during the Regency found it hard to breathe in the glum and puritanical atmosphere of England in the eighteen-fifties.

In the public mind the Burgess and Maclean case came to have an almost totemic significance. It seemed to draw a line between the pre-war world – its naivety, its social attitudes, its assumptions about the pre-ordained worthiness of the upper classes – and post-war Britain, with its democratic optimism combined with a new pursed-lipped morality and Cold War chilliness. What better illustrated the decadence and complacency of the pre-war upper-class Establishment than its promotion of Burgess, the chaotic drunken queer, and Maclean, the emotionally unstable red, to positions of trust? While it had been possible to sympathize with the atom scientist Klaus Fuchs, who had believed that science should have no boundaries and had been prepared to suffer for his beliefs, the fact that Burgess and Maclean were privileged sons of the Establishment rendered their actions less excusable, even to the liberal intelligentsia, and even though very little was known about what they had actually done.

There were a few public displays of sympathy, notably from homosexual Englishmen. E. M. Forster said that such actions were necessary 'as the only way finally to insult England'. Wystan Auden announced, 'It would be dishonourable of me to deny a friendship because the party in question has become publicly notorious.' Privately, however, Auden felt deeply uncomfortable about the whole affair. He wrote to Stephen Spender, 'the whole business makes me sick to my stomach. I still believe Guy to be a victim, but the horrible thing about our age is that one cannot be certain.' Among the literati, many of those who had once embraced Communism were now queuing up to repent their sins. In 1950 Spender, along with Arthur Koestler, André Gide and others, contributed to a book about their disillusionment with

Communism, *The God That Failed*. The idea that Burgess and Maclean might have acted out of sincere belief or misplaced idealism no longer seemed a legitimate argument in Cold War Britain. The Soviet Union was too frightening; the spies were too privileged. Though Cyril Connolly described the attraction of Communism to his generation in *The Missing Diplomats* – 'Communism made an intellectual appeal, standing for love, liberty and social justice or for a new approach to life and art' – he attributed Burgess and Maclean's actions to neurotic personalities and incipient schizophrenia.

One of the most damaging outcomes of the case was that it helped to fuel an upsurge of puritanism and homophobia in Britain far harsher than anything seen in the previous thirty years. Burgess became a symbol of the evils of homosexuality – predatoriness, blackmail, betrayal, mistrust – and conveniently tied them up with the other great evil of the day, Communism. Maclean was portrayed as an apparently respectable, successful yet weak man, entrapped and brought low by Burgess's machinations. Their story showed what happened when one turned a blind eye to such things – as during the 1930s and '40s, when homosexuality had been to some extent tolerated in institutions like the army and the security services. After 1951, prosecutions for homosexual activities grew sharply in Britain.* Some have seen this as a kind of sexual witchhunt, instituted by the famously homophobic Home Secretary of the time, Sir David Maxwell Fyfe. A campaign began to oust homosexuals from government service on the grounds that they were security risks. The Foreign Office's institution of 'positive vetting' – a direct result of Burgess and Maclean – made it virtually impossible for homosexuals to enter the FO without lying about their sexual orientation. In 1954 the Royal Navy instructed its officers to search sailors' underwear

---

* In 1938 in Britain there were 134 prosecutions for sodomy and bestiality, 822 for attempted sodomy, and 230 for gross indecency. In 1952 there were 670 for sodomy and bestiality, 3,087 for attempted sodomy and indecent assault, and 1,686 for gross indecency.

and even their bodies for signs of homosexual acts. The War Office also introduced new regulations against homosexuality.

As for Burgess and Maclean themselves, their Russian lives were a sad postscript to their English ones. When they arrived in the Soviet Union they were sent to Kuibyshev, a town Burgess later described as being permanently like 'Glasgow on a Saturday night in the nineteenth century', a prison in all but name. They were kept there for two years for 'debriefing', until Stalin's death; during this time Maclean became clinically depressed. In 1953 they were moved to Moscow, and Maclean's wife and children joined him. But Maclean was palpably disappointed by the realities of the Soviet Union and though he diligently wrote papers on international relations for the Communist Party, he found his closest friends among a small group of liberal intellectual dissidents, who included the poet Yevgeny Yevtushenko. In the 1960s his marriage fell apart, and eventually all his children emigrated to the West. When he died – alone – in 1983, his ashes were brought to England.

Burgess pined for England. He refused to learn Russian, and wrote plaintive letters to his friends at home, hoping against hope that he might be allowed to return. When Tom Driberg met him in Moscow in 1956, he found him 'guarded' by four secret police; his rooms were bugged, and he was desperately lonely and often drunk. Driberg claimed later that he had pointed the sex-starved Burgess in the direction of the local underground urinal behind the Metropole Hotel. It now appears that this act of generosity resulted in Driberg's being blackmailed into becoming a source for the KGB.

Within the security services the ripples of suspicion and distrust would reverberate for nearly thirty years. Kim Philby was forced to resign from MI6, but he was not charged with anything and friends in MI6, who refused to believe in his guilt, ensured he had a small pension and set up a job for him with the *Observer* in Beirut. Sir Percy Sillitoe, the head of MI5, retired in disgrace in 1953. Guy Liddell's brilliant career – he would almost certainly have become head of MI5 – was ruined by his connections with

Burgess. He left his post as deputy director in 1952, and died in the late 1950s. Dick White became head of MI5 and later MI6; Roger Hollis became his deputy and successor at MI5. Eventually even he was dogged by the case's long shadow.

At first it must have seemed to Blunt as if he had escaped relatively unscathed. He was at last free of Soviet Intelligence, and even, he might have admitted to himself, of his obligations to Guy Burgess. On 31 December 1951 he resigned from Burgess's old playground the Reform Club, and henceforward patronized the far more formal Travellers Club (haunt, nevertheless, according to one of its members, of 'spies, queers and Catholics'). But it was a temporary hiatus. Before long many people beyond MI5 – in the government, the Civil Service and the Foreign Office – knew that Blunt had been Burgess's great friend; that he had been the first person Burgess had seen on returning to England; that he had probably planned the two men's trip to France. In the USA the FBI's investigation several times turned up Blunt's name.

Then there was Goronwy Rees. After Burgess's flight, his daughter wrote, 'Nothing was ever to be the same again.' His history with Burgess plagued and obsessed him; to his children he became 'a kind of non-participating member of the family; our busy household revolved around him, but he seldom joined in'. His dislike of Blunt began to fester into full-blown hatred, and Blunt gradually became to him not just the symbol but somehow the source of his own guilt and troubles, while seeming to leap effortlessly from success to success. Within Rees, the germ of an idea began to grow that he would make Blunt pay.

14. Director

'a benevolent dictator'

In the ten years after Burgess's disappearance Blunt became the most powerful and influential figure in British art history, a kind of cattle baron in its new and developing territories. His influence derived from his ubiquity. Quite apart from the directorship of the Courtauld and his job at the Palace, his position as an increasingly highly regarded expert on seventeenth-century French and Italian art meant that his advice was sought internationally on purchases and attributions. As the National Trust's first picture adviser he dictated how stately homes were presented to the public for a generation. He was an energetic and peripatetic lecturer at home and abroad. His editorship of the Royal Collection catalogues and Zwemmers' Studies in Architecture series – which was intended, at a more specialized level, as a parallel series to Pevsner's Pelican History of Art – not only set precedents for style and thoroughness, and opened up new areas of study, but gave him patronage, as did the Surveyor's job in the world of picture restoration.

Of all Blunt's roles director of the Courtauld was the most important to him. The Courtauld was his base and his buttress against the world, and he worked hard to turn it into what he dreamed it might become. In the early 1950s, however, it was still far from evident that the Courtauld was in the process of becoming a centre of great learning. The art world continued to view it with suspicion – or, worse, dismissed it.

The place had a slightly chaotic, picturesque quality. Twenty

Portman Square's once-marbled walls had been painted dingy institutional green; but on them was hung Samuel Courtauld's art collection. The long and elegant windows of what was now the library were hidden by nasty metal bookcases, and the Oliver Messel-designed marble bathroom served as an office for the Institute's secretaries. In the library, Rhoda Welsford – never seen without her gloves – ran her empire like a Mayfair hostess, with fresh flowers every day and young society gels who sorted out the books. Upstairs in the Etruscan room, seated below Cézanne's cardplayers, Johannes Wilde – whose white hair, little round spectacles and ever-lit cigarette made him look like God emerging from clouds of smoke – communed with his great hero Michelangelo. In the basement, Mrs Winkle, the caretaker's wife, lived in near squalor, baked fresh cakes and buns for tea each day, and nursed her terrible feet, objects of amazement to all who beheld them: 'the excrescences were such that no carpet slipper could contain them. They were the sort of feet that Grünewald immortalised in his crucifixion.' Occasionally, poor, sad Phoebe Pool, one of Blunt's lady devotees, would be found in a crumpled pile, surrounded by plastic bags.

The students tended mostly to arrive by accident. Peter Kidson – who spent his whole career at the Institute, becoming in the process an internationally respected historian of medieval art – turned up on the Courtauld's doorstep in the early 1950s with a degree from Cambridge and no idea what he wanted to do with his life. The mild-mannered registrar, Charles Clare, told him there were no more places and suggested he waited a year. When Kidson declared 'with unwonted candour that if I didn't come then I would have to go out to work', Clare said hurriedly, 'In that case, dear boy, you'd better come at once.' Michael Kitson, a future expert on the seventeenth century, met John Pope-Hennessy and asked him how to become an art historian. 'Are you going to get a first?' Pope-Hennessy asked. 'No.' 'Do you have a private income?' 'No.' 'Oh well,' Pope-Hennessy said with a shrug, 'you'd better go to the Courtauld.'

Things were beginning to change, however. Blunt's generation of scholars, many of them influenced by the Warburg, was coming of age. John Pope-Hennessy, the connoisseur Denis Mahon, Douglas Cooper (who now styled himself 'lecturer at the Courtauld Institute'), Ernst Gombrich, the architectural historian John Summerson and others, along with Kenneth Clark and Nikolaus Pevsner, were turning art history from a pastime for rich dilettantes to an academic discipline, and were getting recognition from abroad for their efforts. In 1951 the *Times Literary Supplement* ran an article in praise of this rising generation. It began, 'During the last 20 years, in semi-obscurity, Britain's best brains have been quietly making an essential and indeed important contribution to the history of European culture.' At the same time, figures like Kenneth Clark and John Pope-Hennessy, both of whom had a taste for fashionable society, had, as Richard Wollheim recalled, 'a social visibility that was extraordinary'. Art history was becoming almost chic, and it had a distinctly unacademic relationship with the possessions of the rich which gave its new practitioners an additional social cachet.

The Courtauld's air of mild eccentricity, moreover, was deceptive. Behind the low-key chaotic facade, and the presence of the nice young ladies – a good proportion of whom were quite as bright and motivated as their male counterparts – the Institute was intensely high-powered. Peter Kidson discovered that the intellectual standards expected of him were far tougher than those he had encountered at Cambridge. 'Blunt, together with the Warburg Germans who were always on tap, operated at levels of scholarship and argument that I had never before encountered. It was a very bracing climate, exhilarating and dangerous, rather like academic mountaineering. You might be killed off, but once addicted, there was nowhere else to be. In my first two years I was often scared out of my wits, but I never wanted to leave.'

In those early years Blunt taught almost every student, and it was he who imbued them with a sense of the seriousness of the undertaking, conveying all the time his own intense feelings about the subject. 'There was a feeling that something very good was happening,' said John Golding, who later taught at the Courtauld and became one of Blunt's closest post-war friends,

> And I feel this was largely because of Anthony's presence and legacy. I felt it was a most brilliant moment at the Courtauld, both because of the quality of the pupils and because of Anthony's intellectual lustre. He turned it into an enclave of old-fashioned humanism. One was subliminally taught the value of learning as something noble in its own right.

'The atmosphere was fervid. It was like a religious seminary,' recalled the art critic Brian Sewell, who also arrived in the early 1950s. 'We were taught and we believed.' The commitment and passion that Blunt had once directed towards the quasi-religious theories of Clive Bell and then into Marxism were now invested in his belief that, as Michael Kitson put it, 'dedicating one's life to the pursuit and understanding of art was an eminently worthwhile thing to do', and the Courtauld should be the place to do it. 'There was a sense of adventure,' remarked the art historian and novelist Anita Brookner, another student of the early 1950s. 'It was a pioneering subject. Everyone was at the same stage of inexperience, and everything was a delight. It was a revelation. One never thought of cutting a lecture: one wanted to hear what was said. It was a golden age. We had the enthusiasm of neophytes. We all wanted to be like Blunt.'

Blunt's seriousness was evident in the almost touching – some felt almost comical – reverence he showed to his deputy, Johannes Wilde. 'Don't forget he's a very princely person,' he told Stephen Rees Jones, who was now the head of the Institute's laboratory – and himself making great advances in the use of X-rays to examine paintings. The admiration was mutual. Wilde, an expert on Michelangelo, was in his sixties, and grateful to Blunt for having given him the opportunity to do the teaching he loved. It was said that during the war Blunt had rescued him from internment, after he had been arrested as an enemy alien, having being caught in the blackout with a torch. To Blunt, Wilde represented

a tangible link with the great Viennese art historians of the past –
Alois Riegl, Franz Wickhoff and Max Dvořák, who had been
Wilde's great mentor. It was said that Wilde had such high
standards that he never published anything, because he felt one
never knew enough – in contrast to Blunt, who was obsessed with
getting things done, moving the subject into print and onwards.
Blunt presented Wilde as an infallible and omniscient authority
on the Renaissance, and ensured that every student who came to
the Institute was taught by him. What was not generally known,
however, was that Wilde had a radical past of which Blunt was
certainly aware. As a young man in Budapest he had worked with
Friedrich Antal at the Budapest Museum of Fine Art. Under Béla
Kun's shortlived Soviet Republic in 1919, he had shared with
Antal the job of 'liberating' privately owned works of art of
'national importance'. Like Antal, he had gone to Vienna after
the regime toppled. Unlike Antal, he had abandoned Marxism
almost immediately and become completely absorbed in the Viennese School.

Another reason why Blunt was comfortable with Wilde was
that he was no threat. Blunt's authority over the Institute was
absolute. After 7 p.m. on weekdays and at weekends the building
was closed to students and staff, much to their irritation, and
became his private house. He was the fount of all authority and
patronage – 'a benevolent dictator', as Michael Kitson described
him. With only two exceptions (Wilde and the medievalist Christopher Hohler), all members of staff for nearly twenty years were
graduates of the Institute – students whom Blunt had spotted and
encouraged, and who effectively owed their careers to him. 'There
was none of this business of advertising posts,' recalled Alan
Bowness, who studied and then taught at the Institute, before
becoming director of the Tate Gallery in 1980. 'Anthony hated
that. I was simply asked to do some teaching.' Like most of the
staff, Bowness never had a contract. 'We were all much younger
than him, and it seemed natural to look up to him,' Michael
Kitson recalled. 'It wasn't a university department,' observed
Stephen Rees Jones. 'It was like a court in which Anthony was

the prince and we were the courtiers. I didn't mind, because it worked.'

External interference was actively discouraged. Meetings of the Courtauld's management committee, which was populated by the great and the good, such as the Warburg's Ernst Gombrich, were carefully choreographed in advance by Blunt and his chairman, Lionel Robbins. Michael Levey, a future director of the National Gallery and member of the Courtauld's management committee – who did not study at the Institute but who, like much of the art world, observed Blunt with an amused fascination – recalled that he

rarely showed any impatience and was careful not to appear overbearing. Calm and logic marked his handling of any key item. He listened attentively to sometimes violently opposed points of view, and only gradually did his view emerge. It was not uncommon for those who found themselves ultimately concurring to feel vaguely aggrieved afterwards, aware that their objections had never been met ... I have known much older and indeed eminent people coming away from meetings both frustrated and angry even if ruefully admiring of what was virtually manipulation.

Michael Kitson, a staff member, was blunter: 'The actual meeting would go on for less than an hour. Robbins would say very little but somehow no one else managed to get a word in.'

Unsurprisingly this self-containedness, and the power Blunt exercised over his little empire, did not always make him popular outside it. In some parts of London University he was resented; his desire to keep the Institute separate was seen as a slight; the extent of his influence was envied. At the time of Blunt's exposure, a sociology don at the London School Economics, Donald McCrae, confided in a friend that one of the two men he most hated was Anthony Blunt, 'because of his superior attitude towards his professional colleagues at London University. Anthony made it clear he thought they were all second rate because they had not been appointed to a post either at Oxford or Cambridge – but Anthony did not think this applied to him.' There were those, also, who felt that the Institute's insularity was unhealthy. 'I thought the character of the Courtauld very inbred,' recalled John Steer, who was there in the later 1950s, 'and I think Anthony and his personality had lots to do with that. It wasn't secretive so much as it was a club. You were either of the elect or you were not. And as time went on there was a party line.' In some parts of the art world (especially the commercial art world, from which it particularly held itself aloof: Johannes Wilde insisted that dealers should not be allowed to enter the Courtauld) the Institute was criticized for being too academic and not practical enough. This, however, proved no bar to the future employment of Courtauld graduates.

Within the Institute, Blunt showed little inclination to display the extent of his control – sometimes almost the opposite seemed to be the case. He made few demands on his staff, letting them teach what and how they wanted. The Courtauld became, in the words of Peter Kidson, 'a federation of more or less independent specialists'. Kidson was incredibly happy there: 'it was a miniature paradise. It was a marvellous place, I loved it – it was informal; there was no stuffiness or protocol. It felt like Plato's academy where dedicated scholars were left to themselves to do what they could in their own time.' 'The real measure', said John White, who chose to leave the Institute,

> was that he built a team of people in their own fields as distinguished as he was in his. He was enormously proud of this. There was no sense in which he wanted to be surrounded by people less able than himself. And that's the most difficult thing to do: to build a team of scholars and hold that team. Scholars working individually, pursuing their own view of what is important, are the hardest possible kind of people to hold together in a consensus, because the whole point of scholarship is not to follow a consensus, but to pursue your own line. He held the Institute together, and with remarkably little *odium academicum*.

Nor did he show any desire to spawn a school of art history in the way that, say, Erwin Panofksy had. He was, on the contrary, now volubly anti-ideological. It was as if he had developed an active horror of theory. He would tell his young students, 'You are the person to do this piece of research because you don't go into it with prejudices,' a student of the early 1970s recalled. 'I was shorn of ideology. He believed that if you did research on a new subject, you had to see what you found and then become opinionated about it.'

This retreat from ideology was of a piece with his withdrawal from exerting control over all aspects of the Institute. It was one of a series of anomalies which suggested that Blunt was in flight from his past and had certainly not resolved his feelings about his past and his politics, either emotionally or intellectually. By the early 1950s art history in France, Germany and Italy was veering sharply in a Marxist direction, while the most senior academic art historian in Britain – Blunt – was moving speedily away from it; he himself embraced a kind of empiricism. His early appointments also suggest a sense of confusion and flight from the past. Despite Wilde's august background, and the devoted pupils he attracted, his appointment to deputy director was mildly surprising: truth be told, he was still in semi-shock from his wartime experiences and already an old man; and he was an ex-Marxist. Blunt's second big appointment – of Christopher Hohler as resident Medievalist, on the suggestion of Tom Boase – was also out of character. Hohler turned out to be a great asset to the Institute, his emphatically high standards in keeping with Blunt's own. Politically, however, he was virtually a proto-fascist, and the two men studiously avoided each other. It is also worth noting that when in the late 1940s a post for a lecturer in early Renaissance art history came up at the Institute, Blunt did not give it to the obvious candidate, Friedrich Antal, who was not only an early Renaissance expert, but the only truly distinguished Marxist art historian in England. Instead it went to a young Courtauld graduate, Peter Murray, a decision Blunt came enormously to regret, and which he undid only with a great deal of ill will on both sides. Strangely, over all, this peculiar vacuum of direction was a good thing for the Institute, it gave its constituent parts room to evolve, and combined with Blunt's appetite for definition and order, may also have made him a better, more receptive teacher than he had been before the war.

In a famous essay on Blunt, 'The Cleric of Treason', written shortly after his exposure, the academic George Steiner suggested that the great dichotomy in Blunt's character was the division between Blunt the attributer and Blunt the spy: on the one hand the ruthlessly honest, disinterested apostle of beauty and truth; on the other the liar, traitor and spy. Steiner's proposed dichotomy is suggestive, but one might more accurately say that the true division in Blunt was between the spy and the teacher. On the one hand, secrecy, concealment, obfuscation; on the other clarification, illumination, explanation. Maturity had made Blunt a great teacher. The tutorial arrangement did not merely suit him, it freed him and loosened him. Within its clear-cut framework he felt in control, and when he was in control he could afford to be generous, and even to allow his characteristic reserve to drop away. (However, as Ernst Gombrich observed, he dreaded excessive shows of emotion – like tears – in his students.) He liked the young: their curiosity and freshness and enthusiasm. 'He was very good with young people. He was conspicuously witty,' recalled one of his students of the 1960s, 'You felt he had a radical streak. He was very critical of pomposity. He was somehow fun to talk to if you were young.' He saw the young as allies in his grand project to advance art history (and of course the Courtauld).

He was not merely a quick and incisive critic, he also treated his students – by and large regardless of sex and class – with a formal courtesy and an unfaked seriousness that surprised and flattered them. He encouraged them to think for themselves and not to be limited by the textbooks. He allowed himself to be surprised by them, and receptive to them. 'If you said something new to him,' recalled a student of the 1970s – 'an idea or an image, no matter how badly expressed – he always listened intently. If one produced something he found engaging his enthusiasm was almost schoolboyish, almost fawning.' Brian Sewell remembered Blunt scrabbling round on the floor looking at architectural plans after a chance remark had set him thinking: 'It was a marvellous way to lead – the foremost man in the field prepared to take on an idea from a student.' One of his earliest star pupils, John White, caught his eye with an essay on Piero della Francesca in his first year. 'Instead of saying "Fine", Blunt said "Gracious!" and got me down to the Reform Club to discuss my theories. Later on I produced a theory about the development of pictorial space. As a result I had two articles in the Warburg journal when I was an undergraduate.'

Many Courtauld students who went on to work in art history dated the moment they picked their career to the occasion when the director made them feel that the subject was theirs.

He could be an equally compelling lecturer. In front of an audience he seemed more at ease than before a single person. 'He had this gift of speaking his lectures as if he was having a personal conversation with you,' said Dick Kingzett, of Agnew's:

He would talk about the most abstruse and difficult things, and it felt as if he was talking to me. In ordinary conversation you never got that close. I asked Anita Brookner if that was just my impression, and she said no. In personal conversation a blind came down, he kept you on the other side of the window. But in public you got the intimate man.

Another ex-pupil remembered being among an audience which Blunt reduced to tears in a lecture on William Blake and the conditions in which the new urban poor lived in the Industrial Revolution. 'He recited that Blake poem about miserable people pounding the streets. I discovered that tears were pouring down the faces of people around me, at the incredible pathos of the awful cruelty and social deprivation of the Industrial Revolution.' When Nancy Mitford heard Blunt lecture at the Louvre in January 1964 she wrote to an old friend, 'Diana and I went to a masterly lecture by somebody called Sir Anthony Blunt. It was at the Louvre in completely perfect and fluent French. Who is this Sir? I am in Love. I shall leave him something in my will.'

There was no doubt that the Courtauld was a hothouse. And that Blunt was talent spotting far more successfully than he had done for the Soviets. 'There was no pecking order,' Peter Kidson observed. 'There was, however, an elitism of a strictly academic kind, and with it went an undertow of unease. We were conscious of being constantly, though ever so discreetly, assessed.' Kidson, along with many of his peers, 'cherished the secret hope that we would turn out to be high flyers and be able to stay on, if not at the Courtauld, at least in the art history business.' Those who were chosen, whom Blunt and the Courtauld staff reckoned had the right stuff, could survive even disastrous exam results. Several Courtauld high flyers fluffed exams; Blunt would employ all his powers of persuasion to convince the obligatory external examiners that the paper might be better than they thought, or did not represent the best the student could produce. Failing that, if the final mark was felt to be wrong it was ignored and the student, who would have normally required a 2:1 or more to continue their studies, was quietly readmitted as a research student. Among the generation that came to the Institute in the early 1950s, when the place was still scrabbling for students, were Peter Kidson and Michael Kitson, and Michael Hirst, who became an expert on Michelangelo. These, John White remarked, were to become 'giants in their fields. He not only spotted them and appointed them, but let them grow, and in quite different ways.' The same generation also included John Shearman, who was to become professor of art history at Harvard, the architectural historian Rayner Banham, the future director of the Tate Gallery Alan Bowness, the Rubens expert and curator Michael Jaffe, the painter and art critic John Golding, the novelist-to-be Anita Brookner and the critic Brian Sewell.

Of course, there were those who were not happy there. 'He was a bit like a monarch,' thought Ernst Gombrich, who was now established at the Warburg. 'He had his favourites, and I'm sure he was very kind to them. But if he had a low opinion of a student, or if they rubbed him up the wrong way, he could be very dismissive.' There were those who felt ill-used, neglected, dismissed by the Courtauld regime. This was more apparent as Blunt got older, busier, more burdened with old anxieties. His chosen, however, were not easily categorizable, and, because the art world was expanding, there were many of them. 'The Courtauld had a great reputation for snobbery,' recalled Terry Measham, who arrived in the 1960s and went on to run the Powerhouse museum in Sydney. 'As a son of the working class I never encountered the slightest slight or put-down. On the contrary, all that mattered was what you said. I put this down to Blunt. He seemed to be genuinely curious about anybody's views – the secret of great teaching.' Sarah Whitfield, another 1960s graduate, remembered:

> Blunt persuaded me to go for a job at the Tate Gallery in 1964. I wasn't appointed. Afterwards he said, 'You should have got that job, but it's always going to be difficult for you because you're a woman.' He was the first person who ever acknowledged that it would be hard for me because of my gender, and was willing to back me.

Within the Institute especially, Blunt had a reputation for going out of his way to help students in trouble, to use his influence in helpful ways, to give time to anyone who showed a marked interest in his subject. He was notable within British academia for his promotion of women – though he was still capable of bouts of misogyny. The spouses of male colleagues still complained that he would often barely register them, and when at a lecture in the mid-1950s he was asked what role women had played in the art of the seventeenth century, he answered sharply, 'Women had very little influence on art. And the influence that they did have was perfectly wretched.'

During the 1950s, Blunt became an art-world fixer. In many ways it was the greatest manifestation of his influence. He created careers, made books happen, matched researchers to subjects, and found jobs for his students. 'I was to learn how tenacious he could be in matters of that kind,' Michael Levey recalled, 'but I think he had usually persuaded himself that his view was the right one (as doubtless it frequently was).' Levey was appointed to his first job at the National Gallery over one of Blunt's nominees. 'He felt the Courtauld should dominate everything,' the art historian Francis Haskell remembered. 'They had a missionary job. He felt this even about people he didn't want to give jobs to himself.' Haskell was appointed to a job at King's, Cambridge, in the early 1950s, to the cost of a candidate of Blunt's, Peter Murray, a former student he regretted having employed himself and was trying less than tactfully to offload. Noel Annan, the amiable provost of King's, who smarted over what he felt was Blunt's snooty dismissal of him, later recalled the appointment with some relish: 'Anthony was absolutely livid: he thought it was disgraceful. But we knew he was just trying to get rid of Murray.' Not that such jockeying for influence was unusual in the art world. 'He was mild compared to John Pope-Hennessy,' Haskell said. Both he and Michael Levey observed that Blunt did not hold their success against them; on the contrary, he was consistently encouraging and gracious. 'Of the 1950s grand figures, he was the most human,' thought Levey, 'the most aware of others.'

In the early 1960s Haskell was himself subjected to Blunt's habit of nudging people towards pieces of work or research he thought they ought to undertake, when Blunt heard that he had made a discovery complementary to some research by a student of his, Sheila Rinehart. Blunt persuaded Haskell to collaborate with Rinehart on an article which became something of a landmark in Poussin studies and benefited both authors. At the time, however, Haskell felt that his discovery had been wrested from him. 'It was true that we made it into a serious article on wider issues than the strict documentation I had discovered,' he reflected later, 'but I felt bullied, I was young. He would take people over and organize their lives. He said, "You must do it this way." It was done perfectly nicely, but in such a way that it was difficult to say no.'

Outside tutorials, Blunt was notable for his aura of elusiveness. As a student, Peter Kidson, who was never taught by him, thought him 'remote and distinctly Olympian, a rather unobtrusive figure unless you happened to be his student. He preferred to stand in the shadow of his eminence grise, Wilde.' He was, however, an Olympian in carpet slippers and a hole-ridden cardigan – his standard Courtauld uniform. These seemed to heighten rather than detract from the general effect. His tallness and slimness and surprising gracefulness were combined with perfect manners and a voice which was melodious and addicted to archaic pronunciations: 'Milan' to rhyme with 'Dylan'. 'He spoke in a charming upper-class drawl that was neither an affectation nor quite an Edwardian relic,' wrote Brigid Brophy, who met him through her husband, Michael Levey, 'and he seemed for ever on the verge of utter exhaustion. He was tall, slim and very nearly beautiful.'

To Michael Levey,

> The handsome, curved double staircase leading down into the hall, cool and restrained for all its elegance, symbolised an environment ideal for [Blunt's] personality. He may not exactly have sashayed down it to a chorus of murmured admiration from students and staff, but something of that possibility was in the atmosphere. To an outsider, at least, he seemed surrounded by devoted, chiefly female acolytes, whose references to 'Anthony' breathed deep respect.

Brigid Brophy found in Blunt the inspiration for her comic novella *The Finishing Touch* – about the exquisite, solipsistic, selfish headmistress of a French finishing school. Blunt accepted his devotees' attention, though he liked to pretend he didn't notice it.

Blunt's full-time devotees were an important aspect of life at the Courtauld. There was Margaret Whinney, the Institute's all-purpose teacher, administrator and dogsbody, whose dedication to the place was almost indistinguishable from her dedication to Blunt. She was even discovered on one occasion washing his floors. Another devotee was Else Scheerer, his doggedly loyal secretary. Scheerer was a hard-working, hard-smoking German who had come to England before the war. She was said to be a former Olympic athlete – unkind people mentioned the shot put, since she was a big woman. It was also murmured that she was an ex-Communist. What was certain was that there was nothing she wouldn't do for Blunt. 'She just worked and worked,' Stephen Rees Jones recalled. 'Anthony couldn't have achieved half the things he did but for Else typing everything. She was a chain-smoking machine, devoted to Anthony.' The last of the trio was Phoebe Pool, a former lover of William Coldstream who had transferred her emotions to Blunt. Phoebe was different from the others. She was more worldly and more desperate. Since her days at Oxford in the 1930s she had suffered debilitating bouts of depression. Her attempts to lead a normal life and exploit her evident intelligence were constantly disrupted by periods of hos-pitalizing melancholia. After her rejection by Coldstream she had flung herself on the Courtauld. Pool was a responsibility Blunt accepted from the time she became a postgraduate in 1954 until the day she died, seventeen years later – though he had been extremely reluctant to take her on, understanding from the start what her arrival at the Courtauld would mean. 'She would turn up every day in a heap, trailing bags with various green cardigans, and would hover on the stairs, Anthony's name on her lips,' remembered Anita Brookner. At times when she was particularly distraught she would appear at the Institute and Blunt would disappear to the library or his office and sit with her while she collapsed in exhausted misery. He showed no rancour or exasper-ation. Between her depressions, Pool began to teach, finished a thesis, and completed several short but well-received books.

All these women were in their own ways hopelessly in love with Blunt. All were spinsterish, slightly naive and plain. ('I can't bear being adored by ugly girls,' says the anti-heroine of *The Finishing Touch*, agonizedly.) All to varying degrees were aware of his homosexuality, which in some ways kept him safe for them. Blunt enjoyed their admiration, and often exploited it. Though there is no obvious Bluntian figure in her books, it is hard not to conclude that Anita Brookner, who knew all three, and who herself owed much to Blunt's encouragement and patronage, drew inspiration for her tales of female disappointment from this atmosphere of cloistered scholarship and frustrated love.

Beyond the Institute, and despite the influence he wielded, Blunt went out of his way to be inconspicuous. When in the late 1940s and the 1950s it seemed as if every art historian was up in arms over the National Gallery's restoration of certain oil paintings, which brought the pictures up to almost vulgar brightness, Blunt was almost the only prominent figure who didn't express himself publicly on the subject. 'I should be very much frightened of doing anything about it,' he told his BBC producer, Anna Kallin. When the art world split over accusations that John Rothenstein, the director of the Tate Gallery, was mishandling bequests and pocketing commissions, Blunt again absented himself from the debates, though his friend Douglas Cooper was among Rothenstein's most vituperative attackers.* It was Blunt, however, who brokered a peace between Cooper and Blunt's old friend Dennis Proctor, who was now chairman of the Tate trustees. Though he was in much demand as a speaker on radio, he was increasingly reluctant to broadcast. And while equivalent figures like Kenneth Clark, A. J. P. Taylor and John Betjeman became famous on television, Blunt shrank from the exposure (though a single appearance on *Animal, Vegetable or Mineral* with John Betjeman and John Summerson, in June 1956, received gushing reviews: 'Blunt both in looks and manner is a most attractive newcomer . . . A riveting programme').

In person, beyond a small group of friends, he was increasingly enigmatic. 'Even as we sat there,' Michael Levey later wrote, 'I might ponder on whether one would describe him as modest or

* The climax of the affair came at a black-tie opening at the Tate on 6 November 1954, when Rothenstein punched Cooper – who had been following him around crying, 'There's that *poor* little man who everybody keep *persecuting*. I do feel *so sorry* for him!' – in front of Ingrid Bergman, Dame Edith Evans and 400 guests. Cooper fell back crying, 'Help, help. I am bleeding from every corner.' Rothenstein was dubbed 'the Tiger of the Tate'.

vain, unworldly or intensely alive to the exercise of power, genuinely absorbed by our talk or privately aloof and barely engaged.' John Golding said, 'I felt I knew him well. But I was aware that there were certain aspects I didn't know. He was the most compartmentalized man I ever met.' It seems almost as if Blunt wished to excise personal traces of himself. His letters were never dated. Notes to his staff were written in pencil on tiny scraps of paper in unintelligible script. He seldom went out of his way to assert himself in company. From an entry in his diary for the 1960s, Roy Jenkins found that he had met Blunt at a dinner of Noel Annan's, but could remember nothing about him.

It was abroad, in Italy and France, that Blunt seemed most easily to unbend. In Rome in 1955 he wrote to Oliver Millar about the 'Sunshine which has restored my sanity.' Driving him round Bavaria in 1973 was for Peter Kidson, who had been at the Courtauld for twenty years, 'a revelation. He was charming, boyish, diffident, active in the way small boys are active. He had a curiosity and freshness that was irresistible.'

As he built up walls against the world, so his world view seemed to narrow. 'He seemed to shed, from an early date, real interests outside his own subject,' Michael Kitson observed. In 1951 Blunt wrote to Anna Kallin that he felt increasingly 'unable to express views on subjects outside my own'. Michael Hirst, one of the Courtauld's teachers and scholars, saw him as

a driven man and increasingly closed in. I think there was an element of expiation in the intensity of the work. I did speculate on this driven quality: it wasn't quite right. A lot of art historians worked very hard, but there was something peculiar about it, unrelenting. He was never a man who would have gone for a walk for the sake of it – a motiveless walk. There was no kind of relaxation. His partner John Gaskin told me he pretty much gave up listening to music, and he pretty well abandoned reading for fun. John Pope-Hennessy, for example, was a pianist and had this incredible social life. There was no relation between the sheer fame and celebrity and prestige of Anthony and the life he led, which was very undemonstrative and retiring. You never got the impression he was rushing off to the Royal Academy Dinner; he never appeared at these things. As far as I know he never went to any kind of gratuitous art-history Establishment events.

Blunt's life was deliberately austere. He owned one suit, for Palace occasions, hated eating at grand restaurants, and was famous for travelling as frugally as possible. 'If there had been a fourth class, Anthony would have travelled it,' recalled the art historian Hugh Honour. The harder and more uncomfortable the bed, the cheaper the hotel, the more he liked it. 'When he dined with Michael and me', Brigid Brophy recalled, 'he became the only person I have ever met to refuse Champagne.' Alan Baker recalled that, for all its beautiful pictures and handsome furniture, Blunt's flat was

> so spartan, so cold, with a very basic kitchen and bathroom, tired linoleum and threadbare carpets, and these wonderful pictures. I bought him a couple of chairs covered with great big, wide, candy-stripes, which he actually liked, but they stuck out like sore thumbs. The bedroom had two single beds. I remember from my bed I could see an etching of a man and a woman by Picasso – *Hunger*. I always thought the man looked liked Anthony. That long, drawn, haggard look.

Not that this picture of an ascetic recluse tells the whole story about Blunt's life in these years.

There was his life at Court. In 1956 he received a knighthood in recognition of his services to the Crown. (He claimed he accepted it only to please his mother.) By the 1950s he was known at Buckingham Palace as being, as Lord Charteris, the new Queen's deputy private secretary, noted, 'nice, but never there'. 'I was at one time proud to call him a friend,' Lord Charteris would add, rather dolefully, after Blunt's exposure. At home Blunt often complained about the philistinism and dreariness of court life: Alan Baker remembered Blunt commenting of the Court that 'playing golf with a piece of coal on the Aubusson carpets was their idea of a cultural evening'. By the time of the new Queen's coronation, in 1953, it was his deputy, Oliver Millar, who usually attended the supposedly obligatory social events at Court and did almost all the work. Since the end of the King's Pictures exhibition in 1947 and Blunt's accession to the Courtauld directorship, he had passed virtually all the day-to-day work to his deputy, while showing no inclination to retire. He remained Surveyor until 1972, and then took on the title of 'Adviser' to the Royal Collection until 1978. 'He was always available for discussion and friendly advice. He was always very encouraging of all that we did,' recalled Oliver Millar. The one area in which Blunt remained actively involved (apart from his supervision of the Royal Collection's drawings catalogues, a task actually outside the formal remit of the Surveyor) was the cleaning and restoration of major pictures, especially those undertaken by his protégé, John Brealey, a young restorer of acknowledged talent whom Blunt used a great deal, and whose career he did much to promote. (Brealey eventually became head of conservation at the Met in New York.) He also, almost against his better instincts, clearly enjoyed those odd moments in the limelight, when the press and television came to him for interviews and quotations about the Collection.

Relations with the new Queen were cordial. Blunt's social mode, polite but distant, was not unlike the Queen's polite unreadability, and he liked what he perceived as her practical good sense and dry humour – while being well aware that she was really more interested in horses than in paintings. One wonders what he thought of his job as official art cheerleader to the royal family. Queen Elizabeth, he told journalists in 1960 – announcing plans for a 'Queen's Gallery', which would show a revolving exhibition of paintings and objects from the Royal Collection, an idea of Prince Philip's – 'has developed a definite interest in art during the past few years. When she went to the Picasso exhibition at the Tate Gallery last month, she saw the whole show, then started all over again, for "perspective" she called it.' 'I remember him saying', one friend recalled, 'that he thought he was bringing the Queen round to take a some sort of intelligent interest, but I don't think it went very far. He was always trying to persuade her to buy Henry Moore drawings.'

That Blunt minded how he was regarded at Court can be seen in a rare moment of lost cool in 1960, when the American magazine *Newsweek* claimed that in an interview about the Royal Collection he had told a story about a series of Max Beerbohm drawings kept behind a panel in a drawing room of Windsor Castle. The drawings depicted England after a Bolshevik revolution, with the then Prince of Wales living in Lenin Avenue, Ealing. 'I would hardly expect them to be shown to the general public,' Blunt was reported as saying, 'although they are exhibited to friends.' Blunt was mortified. 'Thank you so much for letting me see this appalling document, I need hardly say that I made practically none of the statements which are attributed to me in it,' he bumbled. 'The only thing we discussed was the rumour that some Max Beerbohms of the Duke of Windsor were in the Royal Library, which I said was untrue.' Whether Blunt had been misquoted or found out in a moment of mischief was impossible to tell. Members of the household were asked to comment on what should be done. They advised inaction.

As the National Trust's first (unpaid) picture adviser, Blunt played his part in charming the aristocratic owners of the stately homes that the Trust had begun to acquire since the end of the war. By the mid-1950s it had over thirty houses, along with their art collections, which included Van Dycks and Gainsboroughs, Reynoldses and Lelys, Caravaggios and Poussins. 'Blunt had beautiful manners,' observed James Lees-Milne, who had been more or less singlehandedly responsible for bringing the houses to the Trust, 'but I thought he was an icicle.' Blunt found the Trust its second picture adviser, his pupil Bobby Gore, and its third, another pupil, Alastair Laing. One of his major contributions to

National Trust culture, however, was his insistence that the houses should feel like galleries, not monuments to the English aristocracy (which was precisely how Lees-Milne thought of them). 'We need only notice their existence as perhaps the latest symptom of the development of public ownership of paintings in this country,' Blunt wrote in *The Nation's Pictures* in 1950. At the same time, he developed an almost passionate attachment to Petworth House in Sussex, famous for its collection of Turners (which he disliked), its Lelys (which he called 'the dreary beauties') and its sculpture hall (which he claimed to find 'rather dull'). Between 1952 and 1956 he devoted months to rearranging and restoring Petworth, writing its guidebook and setting up an exhibition on it in London.

He also had a particular susceptibility to grand ladies of a certain age. The art critic John Richardson remembered him boasting about going to tea with Field Marshal Wavell's widow. On another occasion Blunt was spotted at a debutante's ball in the retinue of Princess Alice. His favourite was Dollie Rothschild, owner of Waddesdon Manor. Waddesdon was, and is, a huge pastiche eighteenth-century French chateau filled with a unique collection of French eighteenth-century furniture, English paintings and various other treasures, which had been left by Dollie's husband, James, to the National Trust on his death, in 1957. Dollie had married into the French side of the Rothschild family and was a second cousin to Victor Rothschild, who eventually inherited Waddesdon. 'She was very tough and ruled everyone at Waddesdon with a rod of iron,' one National Trust official recalled. 'She was the sweetest possible woman and cared desperately about the house,' insisted another. In 1958 Lord Crawford introduced her to Blunt, who was brought in to advise her on opening Waddesdon to the public. She had seen off the Trust's first adviser after he suggested one lunchtime that the ormolu needed cleaning. ('If he had got on with her,' said one of her National Trust advisers, 'he would have got strawberries in February like the rest of us.') But Dollie was generous to her favourites, and she was very fond of Blunt. There were invitations to tea at her house in St James's, weekends at her home at Eathrop, and a few bottles of Château Lafite each Christmas.

Blunt spent twenty-five years editing the Waddesdon catalogues, which noted every single item in the collection.* A nightmare they were too. Blunt spent seven years translating a French scholar's life's work on Savonneries. A Belgian expert with idiosyncratic English died halfway through his ground-breaking exposition on the study of illuminated manuscripts and Blunt had to oversee the book's completion. It was discovered that the house's collection of armour was mostly fake. All of this, however, was the sort of work Blunt enjoyed. The picture of his public life in these years is of an industrious, socially and academically unassailable intellectual who greatly enjoyed, and was never shy of using, his powers as a fixer and patron. If that had been the whole story of Blunt's life, he would have been a happy man.

---

* So expensive were the catalogues to produce that Dollie subsidized their production. They became models for future catalogues, such as those of the Thyssen collection.

15. Private Man

'the worst cook I think I have ever come across'

As Blunt ascended through the art world, the possibility of a ful-
filling long-term sexual relationship seemed to recede further and
further from his life. Shortly before Burgess had defected, Blunt's
affair with Alan Baker had ended when Baker left for America, to
live with his new boyfriend. When things did not work out and
Baker returned six weeks later, arriving unannounced at the Courtauld days before the Burgess debacle, 'It was obviously a terrific
shock to Anthony. He had expected me to be gone forever.' It
transpired, eventually, that Blunt had conceived a passion for one
of Baker's friends. He was 'hopelessly besottted', as he told John
Golding, with a tall and 'romantic-looking' Irish art student from
the Slade called Nicholas Biddulph. The painter John Craxton met
Blunt and Biddulph at a weekend house party of Robin and Mary
Campbell's in 1951. The Campbells bestrode London society from
the Gargoyle club to Bloomsbury: he was semi-bohemian, glamorous
and impoverished and worked at the new Arts Council; she had left
her husband, the millionaire Philip Dunn, for him (temporarily as
it turned out). 'Biddulph was very good-looking,' Craxton recalled.
'They went up to bed very early, and there was lots of tutting and
"He *is* rather a dish."' The next morning Blunt knocked on
Craxton's bedroom door. ' "Do you know where Nicholas is sleeping?" he asked. I was very surprised. I said jokingly, "No! I wish I
had . . ." He gave me a cold look and turned tail and went out.'*

* This may have been the same weekend at Easter 1951 which Frances Partridge

Biddulph was not homosexual and did not requite Blunt's feelings. 'It didn't go anywhere,' Baker said later. 'It was romantic and rather neurotic, I thought.' Biddulph and Blunt became friends, and Biddulph, who was enthusiastic to learn about art, became for a time a kind of protégé of Blunt's, going with him to exhibitions and lectures. The relationship would foreshadow the kind of romantic, slightly melancholic attachments that Blunt would for the rest of his life form with younger men who liked him, admired him, but did not love him. These relationships were transient, but also, because of their limitations, safe.

Blunt did not hide his homosexuality – at least not in the worlds of art history and literary London. 'Everyone knew,' said Ernst Gombrich, who musingly added, 'but then it was a sort of occupational disease among British art historians.' In fact Blunt could be very open indeed about his sexuality. Alan Baker recalled how impressed he was that Blunt 'was completely unthrown by the fact that people might wonder what we were doing together in public'. At the same time he hated the thought that he might be regarded as 'pansyish', and tried hard not to seem it. Baker thought he had a habit of brushing away his forelock and stroking the back of his head which was a 'dead giveaway'. 'Anthony would have been horrified if he had known.' The times were sufficiently innocent, and so little about homosexuality was pub- licly acknowledged, that despite the rise in prosecutions and public antipathy towards homosexuals in the early 1950s it was possible for a middle-class man to be more or less honest about his sexuality to those who understood, without giving offence to the uninitiated. Institutionalized ignorance helped: even well- meaning books characterized homosexuality as a deeply peculiar and hidden subculture. 'Very little is known about homosexuality

_____

recalls in her diaries, at which Blunt, Ben Nicolson, Blunt's former pupil Olivier Popham and Quentin Bell discussed 'vulgarity' and 'aesthetics', and Bell and Popham began a romance that ended in marriage. Partridge wrote of Blunt, 'I liked him; thought him very intelligent. Wrapped up in art history. We heard of him more than we saw him, probably mostly from Lawrence Gowing and Robin Campbell; both said he was a marvellous teacher.'

or about those who commit homosexual acts,' one 1960 study began, and went on to describe telltale signs such as a liking for the colour green and the wearing of dark-grey suits with a blue tie.

As Gombrich noted, the world of British art and art history was full of homosexual men. (The contemporary view of homosexual aesthetics is focused almost exclusively on the idea of camp. It is perhaps worth pointing out that this generation of scholars tended to specialize in spare, austere, intellectually demanding art: Blunt did definitive work on Poussin, John Pope-Hennessy on Piero della Francesca, Ben Nicolson on Georges de la Tour.) Some commentators have chosen to attribute the endemic feuding and preciousness of the subject to the prevalence of bitchy homosexuals. This argument doesn't really hold up, since straight art historians displayed no less of a taste for feuding – but it must be said that some of the rows between grand homosexuals in the field did have a particular edge. ('Queens are always at their worst about professional things,' one expert on the subject has averred.) Blunt liked to present himself as above the daily squabbles of art history. 'He gave the impression of shrinking from, or simply of being above, such things,' Michael Levey recalled. In fact he was nothing of the sort, and took pleasure in having *bêtes noires* such as, after the war, Edgar Wind (a spouter of 'incorrect nonsense') and, thoughout his career, John Pope-Hennessy. In the latter case the feeling was mutual. The relationship between 'the Pope' and Blunt was based on an intense but unstated competition, exacerbated by the fact that art history was still effectively *terra nullius*, open to powerful personalities keen to carve themselves kingdoms. Pope-Hennessy was openly and uncomplicatedly what Blunt was accused of being after his exposure: grand, snobbish, socially ambitious, and awful to those whom he considered his inferiors. Blunt, on the other hand, tended to reserve his rudeness for his peers. 'There was absolute antipathy,' Michael Hirst recalled. 'Pope-Hennessy was jealous of Blunt's educational role. He was a teacher *manqué*; he felt he'd missed out on having pupils – it gave a lot of power.' Blunt's one-time student Christopher Wright claimed he once heard Blunt say just before he went into an interview at the National Gallery, 'Michael Levey has become a bit of a prima donna. *Not*, I'm glad to say, a megalomaniac like the Pope.' He muttered into the air, '*That*, I gather, is a symptom of tertiary syphilis.'

Blunt had a public manifestation of homosexuality and a private one. This latter mode was reserved for a circle most of whom were not part of the highly competitive art world. In this company he was more relaxed and less the director than he was anywhere else. The group included Dadie Rylands and Arthur Marshall, and sometimes Howard Capes, a financial whizz with a taste for art, and Hugh Benham, an old Harrovian from a rich East Anglian family who had a disfiguring skin disease and spent much of his time in pyjamas. (Benham eventually died in Tangier, apparently so drunk he fell out of a hotel bedroom.) Other members of this group were 'Basil' Mackenzie, Lord Amulree, a doctor and one-time Liberal whip in the House of Lords and a devoted friend and former lover of Douglas Cooper; Paddy Barber, an Irish aristocrat who had a castle in Kinsale; and – when he could escape from his obligations at his estate at Blessingbourne in Northern Ireland, and as chairman of the Arts Council of Northern Ireland – Peter Montgomery.

Most summers during the early 1950s, Blunt would go to stay with Douglas Cooper and his then partner John Richardson at Cooper's chateau in the Vaucluse. When he felt comfortable a different man would emerge – a man with a 'sardonic sense of mischief', who 'drank far more and laughed far harder than most people realised'. Stuart Hampshire, who occasionally met him in all-male company, saw something more obviously camp. 'He would do a sort of gangling, limp-wristed kicking up his legs, especially with Dadie Rylands. I remember him bouncing about with Dadie to get the atmosphere going. They would play at pretending to be young, a kind of conception of *les boys*.' The writer Hugh Massingberd, Peter Montgomery's nephew, remembered meeting Blunt, very much 'off duty', with his uncle in 1965. 'It was a very hot day, and Blunt came in wearing virtually a G-string and a light sleeveless T shirt, and said, "Peter's over-dressed and I'm underdressed. How do you do?" It was a bit stagey.' His uncle also once took him to a party at Blunt's old stamping ground, Palace Court. 'There seemed to be a lot of oriental youths around, and Blunt and my uncle, one felt, had dropped their guards. It was full of opera queens and an odd mixture of seedy old faggots and oriental boys. It was very much a gay party.'

In 1953 Blunt began a relationship with a former guardsman, John Gaskin, who sold jewellery at a shop in Burlington Arcade called Armour & Winston, occasionally working as a courier for Thomas Cook's to feed his voracious appetite for travel. They had known each other for some years, for Alan Baker recalled having met Gaskin during his time with Blunt. No one knew quite how their relationship had begun. Blunt was said to have been very taken with Gaskin's dark, brawny good looks, which thickened over the years with drink. Gaskin, who was twelve years younger than Blunt, came from a working-class Irish back-ground. He had, however, acquired a little polish. He was a sharp dresser and liked Savile Row suits; he had worked on his elocu-tion, and now, like the working-class Newcastle-born Jackie Hewit, had a 'proper' accent. He was presentable, keen to be thought respectable, but extremely shy and completely intellectu-ally insecure. Blunt's friends and former colleagues constantly exclaimed at how 'completely uneducated' he was. Trying to put Gaskin at his ease, one colleague recalled, was 'a bit like patting a pet spaniel on the head'.

Gaskin never went to Courtauld parties, and when Blunt had students or staff or academics to the flat he would routinely disappear into the kitchen until they'd gone. No amount of cajoling would force him out. He often behaved in public more like a valet than a partner, walking a few steps behind Blunt. This, however, was the kind of behaviour which made such a relationship publicly acceptable. 'I took him to be his confidential manservant,' Blunt's former pupil Erica O'Donnell remembered of their first meeting, as Gaskin silently helped Blunt on with his coat. 'This is John,' Blunt said, proffering no more information. When Gaskin moved in with Blunt not long after their relationship started, Johannes Wilde told Stephen Rees Jones – and presumably others at the Institute whom Blunt felt would be 'confused' by the arrangement – that 'Anthony's doctor had said he must have someone to live with him to make sure he ate properly. They thought I'd be terribly shocked and wouldn't have a modern outlook on these things.' And indeed Gaskin did become Blunt's cook and housekeeper – a traditional wife in all but name. Blunt was virtually incapable of looking after himself. 'Practical matters he seemed to find gross,' Brigid Brophy wrote. 'To bend his attention on them he seemed to find impossible; the mere suggestion that he try seemed to drive him nearer than ever to the point of exhaustion.' Blunt's pupil Richard Verdi remembered, 'Anthony once tried to cook me a meal. It wasn't quite a disaster. Let us just say it was very, very simple.' The French scholar Pierre Rosenberg was more explicit: 'He was a terrible cook. The worst cook I think I have ever come across. But then English male art historians . . .'

From the start, Blunt's friends and colleagues found the relationship with Gaskin a puzzle. The relationship seemed so baldly functional, and Gaskin was so ignorant about Blunt's intellectual life. Barbara Proctor, the second wife of Blunt's old friend Dennis, remembered that the first time they came to supper Gaskin didn't know which side Blunt had supported in the Spanish Civil War. 'It can't last!' she thought. It did, and twice a year or so, as Blunt and Dennis Proctor swapped art world gossip, she would steel herself to draw out the awkward Gaskin, who was so shy with women he could barely speak. 'I used to think Anthony rather exploited John,' Michael Kitson said. 'He seemed to be just the cook, and when I came to see Anthony in the flat he would nearly always withdraw. He would take it for granted that Anthony and I would want to talk about things that were above his head, and I was always a bit embarrassed by this. He was very difficult to talk to.'

Gaskin's appeal to Blunt lay in his presentability and his

invisibility, but most of all in his differentness. He was a respite from the rest of Blunt's relentlessly cerebral life, and from the other unspoken burdens. When the academics weren't around, Gaskin was a different person: 'He was a terribly uninhibited character, a good mimic, and made Anthony laugh. Anthony liked cutting off from higher concerns,' observed John Golding, one of the members of the Courtauld whom Blunt admitted into parts of his other life. Blunt liked Gaskin's campery and frivolity and dirty jokes, and Gaskin was also someone with whom Blunt could drink – which he was doing a great deal. 'Gaskin was a nice boy, good company,' thought John Craxton, who occasionally went to supper at the Courtauld flat – 'the kind of boy Anthony liked because he could relax with him. He was a decent cook, and they liked nice wine. He must have been a perfect antidote to Anthony's world.' Gaskin was also streetwise in a way which did not easily translate to the world of academic drinks parties. It was rumoured that early in their relationship Blunt was being blackmailed and Gaskin sorted it out. And he had one more quality that contributed to the relationship's longevity: according to Howard Capes, whose partner Clive Hislop was an old friend of Gaskin's, 'He didn't like to know anything that would upset him.'

Blunt was not the only one who needed looking after. There was something vulnerable about Gaskin, who had his own demons. During the war he had been captured – as Blunt nearly was – when the British Expeditionary Force retreated from northern France in 1940. It was known that he had had 'bad experiences' as a prisoner of war. In his autobiography, Graham Smith, who first met Blunt in the early 1960s as partner of the art forger Eric Hebborn, described an account Gaskin, one drunken evening, gave of his wartime experiences. Gaskin insisted that he had been heterosexual until he had been in the German POW camp, where he'd been forced to become an older man's 'bum boy', loaned out for cigarettes and little luxuries. Manipulated by the older man, he had, he said, become emotionally dependent on his abuser and they had made plans for the future. When Gaskin found the man after the war, it transpired that he was married and he spat at Gaskin in the street.

As if to confirm the convenient nature of the relationship, the sexual side of it seems to have cooled within a short time. Gaskin moved into a separate room and began to have affairs. 'Gaskin came to Crete once in the late 1960s,' John Craxton said, 'and took a boy from a friend of mine. He wasn't a paragon of good behaviour.' With Blunt's approval, he brought young men back to the flat – usually working-class pick-ups, often from the forces. 'He had a gift for picking up sailors,' Craxton recalled. He took the risks and enjoyed them, and Blunt too had affairs – often with men Gaskin had picked up for him. Gaskin had been in the Irish Guards, and the lower ranks of guardsmen had the reputation of being 'the high-class courtesans of the gay world'. They were big strapping boys, appallingly paid, who wore splendid bright uniforms. Those who chose to make themselves 'available' were to be found in certain pubs round Buckingham Palace and the West End, including the Bag o' Nails near the Wellington Barracks and Buckingham Palace, and the Joseph Paxton in Knightsbridge. The latter pub was, apparently patronized by middle-class men with a penchant for Horse Guards, who were more expensive, allegedly more virile and more sophisticated than the sailors to be found at Marble Arch. 'It was less squalid than going to public lavatories,' recalled Noel Annan, who shared a flat for several years with Blunt's homosexual friend Arthur Marshall. 'There were endless jokes about how frightfully stupid they were, and how awful the evening would be. On the other hand there were people like Roger Senhouse [one of Lytton Strachey's friends] who positively enjoyed their company. Artie Marshall adored the guards. What he wanted was to be sitting on the knee of a moustachioed guardsman.' There were discreet rituals attached to picking one up. The pursuer might wrap a ten-shilling note round his calling card and slip it into the guardsman's boot. If the guardsman followed he'd get the other ten shillings. Sailors, who were equally badly paid, were said to be happy with an evening out and a good breakfast.

Despite the apparently equable arrangements betwen Gaskin and Blunt, there were tensions within the relationship. Gaskin seemed far more emotionally dependent on Blunt than Blunt was on Gaskin. He lived vicariously through Blunt's status and its reflected glory. Blunt's involvement in his work meant that Gaskin often had time on his hands and got bored. If he felt his position was threatened by a young man on whom Blunt had formed a particularly strong crush he would become intensely jealous and bitter. On one such occasion Gaskin ended up fighting his rival. There were more plaintive feelings too, as remembered by Eric Hebborn: 'He said to me, "I was very upset the other day by Anthony. He's very affectionate to me, and he puts his hand on my shoulder when I'm sitting at the breakfast table as he passes me, in a certain way. The other day I saw him do it to somebody else. I thought it was just for me." ' Notwithstanding that glimpse of a soft side to Gaskin, Hebborn and his partner Graham Smith did not like him. Smith thought him 'camp, bitter and sarcastic', as well as rude, demanding and obsessed with money. They felt he deliberately stirred up arguments with Blunt, usually when drunk. Blunt accepted his scenes with a pained powerlessness and tried, ineffectually, to offer comfort. Hebborn claimed that if the night before had been particularly drunk, or he felt that Blunt had mistreated him in some way, Gaskin would exact little penalties – for example he would claim one of Blunt's old-master drawings and sell it.* Perhaps aware that Gaskin felt more strongly than he did, or even that he was holding back so much of himself from Gaskin, Blunt accepted his games and encouraged him to take an interest in art. Gaskin would go to the salerooms and indulged in a little picture-dealing.

---

* Blunt's salary as director and the smallish sums from his books made him reasonably affluent. He had few outgoings apart from his and Gaskin's clothes and upkeep, and in this he was famously frugal, apart from having a liking for good wine. He himself had begun to collect pictures and prints in the 1930s, when he had developed a nose for a bargain. By the 1960s he was a keen, though occasional, buyer and seller of old master drawings and prints, careful with his money and usually offsetting a purchase with a sale.

Though Blunt kept this part of his life largely separate from his professional one, the young men Gaskin brought back were noticed by those who understood such things. 'I heard from other sources, some of them in the Institute,' wrote John Pope-Hennessy, 'of the homosexual parties he gave in his official flat (there was no objection to his giving homosexual parties, but there were strong objections to his giving them in the building in which he was in charge).' Michael Kitson remembered that

> In the 1950s and early 1960s he used to have quite rowdy parties in the flat. I remember going up to the library about six. One could hear them going on. He didn't disguise them he made wry jokes. He'd get into the lift clutching a boxful of bottles of gin looking rather coy, but in no way shamefaced. I never went to a party given by him. I occasionally went up for a drink in the evening or for a gossip. The party side was completely separate. Not secret, just separate.

There were stories about young men turning up on the doorstep and announcing, 'Tony told us to come', and disappearing up in the lift that was off-limits to the students. From time to time young men employed to do a bit of painting and redecorating or dusting would be seen emerging from Blunt's flat. John White remembered, 'You'd suddenly meet an Australian whom Gaskin had allegedly picked up in a public lavatory, who was moderately handsome but not *that* handsome – the latest boyfriend, and thick as two short planks.'

Before Gaskin, Blunt had been, at the very least, extremely discreet about casual sex, and several former lovers have insisted that sex had simply not been very important to him. Now, however, he seemed to become actively promiscuous. Sex seems to have become a valve for the release of the pressures he was increasingly feeling, and Gaskin's encouragement, and willingness to do what effectively amounted to procuring, made it easy. In the mid-1950s Gaskin's friend Clive Hislop spent a night at the Courtauld while Gaskin was away. Blunt seemed restless, and announced he was going out. Hislop decided to accompany him.

They went to Piccadilly Circus, the centre of gay pick-ups and rough trade, to a bar famous for its roughness – famous for being the place where one went to pick up large Irish labourers. 'I hid in the corner – I was terrified. Anthony came out with this great big sailor. We went back to the flat. I was in the spare room, and suddenly he came running in shouting, "Come and help me, he's going to bash me."' Eventually they managed to calm the sailor down.

Blunt's ménage, with its visiting sailors and manual labourers, was regarded by some as being rather domestic and tame, however. 'All those hairdressers!' scoffed David Carritt, another homosexual art historian whose preference was apparently for the 'virile' Horse Guards (and who felt an intense and fully reciprocated dislike for Blunt). Brigid Brophy recalled that

> Whenever we went there the evening was shattered by brief incursions of young men introduced by first name only, who might have been sailors or might have been students of Poussin and were very likely both. [They were almost certainly the former.] They would put to him practical domestic problems ('The mustard you said would be in the cupboard on the left isn't') and he would wave a hand, dismissing not the person but the problem.

Sex was not the only reason for the frequent presence of the young men at the flat. They were, as Gaskin had been, a respite. 'He liked the contrast of simple, good-natured, good-looking young men to relate to. It was a totally different side of his life,' said John Golding. 'He enjoyed helping them with handouts. Many of them were straight, and some were tarts.' And working class. That middle-class homosexuals were attracted to the working classes was practically a cliché. It came, according to Francis King, from 'a feeling that working class men were tough and simple and direct and there was some kind of enervation of the middle classes – partly because the classes were so segregated, and you only met people of your class. There was a feeling of mystery, and you wanted to explore them.' Blunt had retained a deeply romantic view of the working class, left over from his Cambridge days. The art historian Hugh Honour remembered finding him one evening in the 1950s at the Polidor, an old, cheap, working-class Paris bistro.

> Much to my surprise, there was Anthony. He still had this genuine romantic 1920s and 1930s thing of wanting to be among the working classes. He wanted to eat among what he thought was the real McCoy. Of course he stuck out like a sore thumb. We went on to a rough-looking bar, which he loved, where we had a camomile tisane – a normal thing to order. Anthony looked at us and said, 'Good heavens! I wouldn't dare order something so sissy in a place like this!'

Over the years Blunt developed several romantic attachments to the young men who came to the flat. There was Mike, a good-looking bisexual former guardsman who did odd jobs for Blunt and dreamed of becoming a singer. He gave a few concerts at the Wigmore Hall singing lieder, but, despite a small following (mostly of dewy-eyed men of a certain age), he was not a huge success. 'He had a loud voice but very little musicality,' recalled John Golding. Blunt left him £200 in his will. 'I don't think Anthony was in love with him, but he found him pleasant and nice to have around. He was a sweet man.' Blunt was fond of Mike's wife too, and became godfather to their child. Another passion of Blunt's was a young burglar called Ray. Blunt bought him a small boat. Gaskin became jealous and there was a fight. Ray was eventually caught and went to prison. (As with Auden and J. R. Ackerley, among others, a number of Blunt's pick-ups were petty criminals.) And there was Spud Murphy, another blue-eyed Irish ex-guardsman, who became a photographer – apparently to assuage his voyeuristic compulsions. He was dashing and funny, and said to be completely honest and utterly amoral. He thought nothing of sleeping with anyone. It was said he kept his memoirs, which were outrageous, in Blunt's safe. Murphy acted as Blunt's unofficial chauffeur – Blunt had stopped driving in the late 1940s after, he claimed, he had driven the battered old

Railton, given to him by Burgess's old boyfriend Peter Pollock, to Rome with the handbrake on. He had been so exasperated by its overheating that he abandoned it on the via del Corso, grabbed his luggage and never saw it again. Murphy drove Blunt all the way to Rome with the handbrake on. He drove him to his mother's once a week, and round Italy one summer, in 1958. When he died young, in the late 1960s, Blunt and Murphy's wife were the chief mourners at the funeral.

Eric Hebborn was rather different. He and Blunt had met in 1959 – over a long, drunken discussion on the decline of painting – at the British School in Rome, where Hebborn was studying painting. Blunt, with his nose for dangerous people, was fascinated by Hebborn. The younger man was a homosexual ex-Borstal boy from the East End, whose previous misdemeanours included burning down his school. He had had little formal education, but was widely read, extremely intelligent, and blessed with an 'eye' – a natural talent for reading pictures and understanding an artist's technique. He is said, in youth, to have looked like a tough Botticelli angel. (In later life he looked like a short boxer who'd had too much to drink.) Hebborn in turn was impressed by Blunt – especially his manners. 'Anthony was endlessly patient with me, never once gave me the impression he was talking down.' They never had an affair. Hebborn's preference, as his sometime boyfriend Graham Smith observed, was for 'beautiful boys'. Hebborn claimed that his one potential sexual encounter with Blunt ended in blind drunkenness, and they both passed out on Blunt's bed. The next morning Blunt brought tea and aspirin. (Smith also noted that Blunt 'never attacked me or showed any of the signs of jealousy I was used to receiving'.) Blunt and Hebborn settled on friendship, though Hebborn noticed, and minded, Blunt's compulsive compartmentalization. 'He was a mystery to me in many ways,' he said later. 'I knew John Craxton, and so did he, but he never spoke of him to me; and he rarely talked about the Courtauld. I never met John Golding, for example.'

In 1963 Hebborn and Smith moved to Rome, where Hebborn

began to deal in art. Blunt's attitude to dealers was ambivalent. He made a point of telling his students to have nothing to do with the trade, and would not allow dealers in the Institute. However, he bought and sold pictures himself in a low key-way (encouraging his students to do the same), and had allowed Gaskin to take up a little dealing on the side. He constantly gave advice to dealers, auctioneers and would-be buyers on the likely authenticity of seventeenth-century paintings and drawings, and he had a small group of dealers with whom he was closely associated – among them Tomás Harris, from whom he was only too happy to take advice on pictures and valuations, and Colnaghi's, the most respectable dealer in London.

In his relations with Hebborn, however, Blunt's ambivalence was most vividly acted out. What Hebborn was selling were his own extremely skilful forgeries, mainly of old-master drawings. Not only did Hebborn frequently stay with Blunt when he came to London – the favour was reciprocated: when in Rome, Blunt occasionally stayed at Hebborn's flat in the Piazza Paganica – Blunt even helped Hebborn to establish himself as a dealer. When the link between the two men was made public in 1980, a London dealer told the *Daily Telegraph* that when Hebborn had first approached him the head of his firm had told him that Blunt had called to ask that they should be 'nice' to Hebborn. Hebborn denied this, but admitted that he would drop the fact that he was staying with the august director of the Courtauld. It also emerged that Blunt had been among a number of experts who had authenticated a 'Castiglione' and a 'Pontormo', both by Hebborn, which Christie's had sold in 1968. Even more damagingly, Hebborn had occasionally used John Gaskin as an agent in London: 'Dealers and buyers', Hebborn reasoned, 'liked buying from a fresh face.' Gaskin, he later claimed, had on one occasion cheated him.

Hebborn and his partner Graham Smith always insisted that Blunt had been duped. He was in good company. Hebborn had some claim to having been the best forger of the twentieth century, and he fooled the best – including Philip Pouncey of the British Museum, widely regarded as the finest connoisseur of his day. He also went out of his way to cultivate a number of older admirers in the art world – among them Tony Clarke, director of the Minneapolis Institute of Arts, John Maxton, director of the Chicago Institute, and Ellis Waterhouse, who, according to Hebborn, had authenticated a 'Gainsborough' of his. He took great delight in tricking his little band of experts. According to Graham Smith, Hebborn would say that 'art experts were fools and knew nothing about art, though he did, so serve them right. If their attributions proved wrong, they had only themselves to blame.' While admiring Blunt and going to great lengths to entertain him graciously when he came to Italy, Hebborn also described him as a 'file clerk who knew all the names, dates and places', but nothing else. He claimed that Blunt had inadvertently taught him everything he knew about Castiglione.

It may be that, while Blunt was not directly implicated in the forgeries, he realized what Hebborn was doing, and quietly enjoying seeing the art Establishment bamboozled.* Graham Smith claimed that Hebborn told him that, when he had first met Blunt, the older man had admired some copies he had made of Poussin drawings and had remarked that if they had been on old paper they might have passed as originals. Smith also described an episode in Rome in the early 1960s when Blunt suggested he 'rescue' – or rather steal – a carved marble Roman fragment they had come across on a trip to an archaeological excavation. He declined to, but asked Blunt later how seriously he had intended his words. Blunt replied, 'I was interested in what you might do.' In the mid-1970s John Golding had come across a couple of bronze statues and a portfolio of eighteenth-century drawings belonging to Hebborn in Blunt's rooms. 'I saw exactly the same leg in the bronze as in the drawings. There was something uncomfortable about the way the upper leg and the lower leg met. I said nothing to Anthony. After all, he had such a shrewd eye. It would have been characteristic of him to have known and strung Hebborn

* Blunt's former pupil Brian Sewell, who worked at Christie's in the 1960s, is credited with being one of the first to realize that Hebborn's pictures were fakes.

along.' It was about this time, moreover, that Blunt and Hebborn stopped meeting. Hebborn said the break came about because John Gaskin had been rude to his latest boyfriend.

The word about Blunt in the art world and among dealers was not that he was dishonest, but that he wasn't as good a connoisseur as he liked to think, that he did not really have 'an eye', and that he was easily swayed. 'Anthony could be very persuadable about a picture. If you persisted, he often didn't stick to his guns. In the end he almost always admitted one was right,' recalled Dick Kingzett of Agnew's. If his closeness with Tomás Harris was questioned, for example, it was because he was felt to be too easily impressed by Harris's persuasive manner. 'I'm quite unaware of anyone in the art world ever having questioned Anthony's honesty, I got the feeling that the story was that Anthony was attracted to Hebborn sexually,' remarked Jack Baer, one of the dealers whom Blunt regarded as 'respectable'. 'There are some stories', Michael Kitson observed, 'in which some dealer may have persuaded him against his better judgement to think such and such. What is much more true is that he made mistakes and wouldn't always admit them.'

Whatever the truth, what may be said is that in the art world and his private life, as in his political affiliations, Blunt did not always choose his friends well.

Precisely when Blunt became an acknowledged suspect in the Burgess and Maclean case is not clear. Rosamond Lehmann claimed that two months or so after Burgess and Maclean defected she spent a whole day answering questions from a couple of MI5 officers who kept returning to the subject of Blunt and Goronwy Rees. According to Chapman Pincher, whose major source was Peter Wright, who became his chief MI5 interrogator in the 1960s, Blunt was not formally interviewed until 1952. What is certain is that by September 1953, when Melinda Maclean disappeared from her new home in Switzerland and went to join her husband in Russia, Blunt was being questioned. Jackie Hewit was also called in for questioning by MI5 at this time. Hewit recalled he was asked repeatedly about Blunt. 'They wanted to know if I had been to bed with him.' By his own account he admitted nothing.

By the autumn of 1953, MI5 had not only its own research on the case, but also the conclusions of the FBI and the CIA. These were brought back to England by a young, ambitious and hard-working MI5 officer called Arthur Martin, who had been sent to Washington to research Burgess's time in America. FBI interviews suggested damning links between Burgess and Philby, and made several references to Blunt. The FBI was keeping tabs on Blunt and was aware that he was planning his first trip to America – an obligatory pilgrimage for any art historian with an international reputation. A letter from July 1953 in the FBI's Burgess and Maclean files reads, 'After we learn from the State Department the reason given on Blunt's visa for his trip to the United States and after we have heard from our Legal Attaché, we will give consideration to the advisability of interviewing Blunt if he actually arrives in this country.' Either his visa was refused or Blunt realized he was under observation, for the autumn trip was cancelled, even though he had been granted a term's sabbatical to make it.* The FBI's suspicions were shared by MI5. Pamela Wyndham, Lady Egremont – whose husband was Private Secretary to Harold Macmillan as well as the heir to Petworth House, which his uncle had given to the National Trust – met Blunt in 1953, when he came to advise on the house's art collection for the Trust. He was, she felt, infinitely conscientious and generous with his time over Petworth; at the same time she guessed that Blunt was being questioned by MI5 – and that Macmillan suspected he was guilty.

The newspapers added to the tension by regularly publishing

---

* Blunt finally went to America in the spring of 1956, for a three-month lecture tour of thirty-five cities. The FBI was watching. A dispatch dated 16 March 1956 from Louisville, Kentucky, to J. Edgar Hoover reminded him that Blunt had been the first person Jackie Hewit had called after Burgess's defection, and reported that Blunt was due to give a lecture there on the 27th.

pieces about the Missing Diplomats. Calm, if unreadable, though Blunt seemed, the strain of the investigations took their toll. Pamela Wyndham could see the symptoms. 'I know that 1952–3 was a very difficult time: he was under severe pressure. Some days he was very twitchy.' In August 1953, on a train in France, Blunt had a sudden attack of Bell's palsy. The right side of his face spasmed, completely paralysed, as if he had had a stroke. He told Pamela Wyndham that it had happened because he'd been sitting in a draught on a train, 'but I suspected he was being grilled'. The palsy particularly upset him – 'Professor Blunt is so anxious about himself', his medical notes recorded. At the Courtauld his staff could see he was extremely aware of his affliction, and very embarrassed by it. Bell's palsy was a highly public betrayal of his inner trials, turning his face into something resembling the mask he had been metaphorically wearing for many years.

In November that year Blunt went on a British Council lecture tour to Athens, where he was chaperoned by the writer Francis King. Blunt's dead cheek was still obvious.

> He kept laying the palm of his hand on the frozen area, not so much to conceal it, it seemed to me, as to check as if any sensation were returning. Eventually, he said to me, 'You must be wondering what has happened to my face? . . . It's something called Bell's palsy. It tends to afflict one after some shock or strain. I've been through a lot of shock and strain recently.'

Within a few hours of their meeting Blunt asked King, who was himself homosexual, about 'queer' life in Athens. Was it easy to find sex? What was the going rate? His specification was 'big, butch, good teeth'. Rather embarrassedly – 'I was surprised by his lack of discretion' – King found him a young man, discovering in the process that picking up a young man in Athens was 'far easier than finding a taxi'. Afterwards Blunt seemed happy and relaxed. 'Oh, I am grateful to you. That was just what I needed. I feel much, *much* better now.' That night King was woken by Blunt screaming. He had had a nightmare.

King was very taken by Blunt. 'He was very good company. Very amusing and entertaining. I felt there was a genuine warmth between us.' Blunt was also very indiscreet. In the tavernas he would lean over to whisper, 'That one's rather jolly' or 'I like that one over there.' On his departure he told King, 'You really made my visit.' A few months later, King bumped into Blunt at the Travellers Club. Blunt cut him. 'I realized that he felt I belonged to the world of Athens, where he had enjoyed himself and let himself go. I met him again later, and he was in a cool way friendly, but never as he had been in Greece.'

It wasn't until the following year that movement began to return to Blunt's face. Ten years later his upper lip was still half-frozen. When he was very angry it was the involuntary twitching of that upper lip that let one know that he was struggling with his self-control.

Some of Blunt's friends, and a number of his staff, realized that something was preying on his mind, but its actual nature eluded them. The Wittkowers, for example, knew he was being inter-viewed about something. John Golding was aware that Blunt had been in MI5 during the war and could see that he was under pressure: 'I knew about the spy side, but one also knew it was something he would never talk about. We knew about the interrogations very early on – one heard odd rumours'. After Blunt's exposure, Rosamond Lehmann used to recount a story about sharing a cab home with him in the mid-1950s, after a party given by an American art collector called Arthur Jeffries. Blunt suddenly burst into tears and gasped out between sobs, 'I'm very, very sorry, Rosamond. Can you ever forgive me?' He gave no further explanation, and on reaching her destination she left him sobbing in the cab. As for Gaskin, he saw what he wanted to see, and chose to read the occasional visits from mysterious civil servants as manifestations of his partner's importance. Eric Heb-born remembered that on one visit to Blunt's flat 'John Gaskin said to me, "Eric we must go into the kitchen, because Anthony has got some very important visitors", and he sat in the kitchen and told me the important visitors were from MI5, because

The Adam staircase at 21 Portman Square, home of the Courtauld Institute: Michael Levey wrote that Blunt 'may not exactly have sashayed down it to a chorus of murmured admiration from students and staff, but something of that possibility was in the atmosphere.'

Blunt the Director, c. 1962.

Blake's *Glad Day*. Blunt saw Blake as a revolutionary turned recluse, and was drawn to his personality: 'His passionate sincerity, his uncompromising integrity, his hundred per cent quality command respect and admiration,' he wrote. But as he got older he came to feel that Blake's art did not really measure up to the man or the poetry.

Blunt on holiday with the Hollywood actress Ona Munson at Paestum, c. 1949.

Blunt as Surveyor, escorting the Queen around the Courtauld Institute in 1959.

Poussin's *Death of Germanicus*, c. 1627. For Blunt this was a watershed painting in which his beloved Poussin began to show his mature style and the *peintre-philosophe* he would become.

Poussin's late version of *Rebecca and Eliezer at the Well*, the painting Blunt bought for £100, which was given to him by Victor Rothschild in 1933.

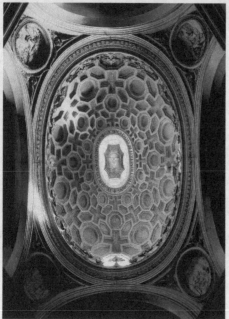

The interior of the cupola of San Carlo alle Quattro Fontane in Rome, built by Borromini in the 1660s. Blunt loved Borromini's virtuosity and his fascination with mathematics; but he also deeply identified with Borromini's tortured misanthropy.

Margaret Whinney (left), one of the Courtauld's longest-serving teachers, and Else Scheerer, Blunt's long-suffering secretary. Both were in their quiet ways hopelessly devoted to him.

Blunt in his study at the Courtauld, c. 1952. Behind him is a Renoir nude.

Blunt's kitchen and bedroom at the Courtauld: the juxtaposition of the fine furniture (much of it not owned by Blunt) and pictures with the curling lino made an impression on many visitors. One boyfriend recalled it as 'so spartan, so cold, with a very basic kitchen and bathroom, tired linoleum and threadbare carpets and these wonderful pictures . . . I remember from my bed I could see an etching of a man and a woman by Picasso, *Hunger*. I always thought the man looked liked Anthony. That long, drawn haggard look.'

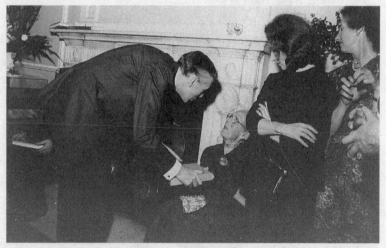

Blunt with his mother at the party in 1967 celebrating his thirty years at the Courtauld and his sixtieth birthday.

Sir Denis Mahon, the art historian who challenged Blunt's dating of Poussin's work, and ultimately his whole concept of Poussin.

Blunt at a summer school in Germany in 1973. Left to right: John Heward, David Thompson, Pauline Plummer, Blunt, Geoff Ashton.

Blunt in Italy c. 1967. Abroad, Blunt was a different person, noticeably far more relaxed than he was in London: 'He was charming, boyish, diffident, active in the way small boys are active. He had a curiosity and freshness that was irresistible'.

Blunt answering questions at his press conference at *The Times*, on 20 November 1979. After it was broadcast on the national news the *Daily Mail* said he showed 'supreme insolence' and 'contempt', and *Now!* magazine described his performance as 'one of the most outrageous exercises in disinformation yet attempted'. In the *New Yorker* the academic George Steiner wrote of his 'cold sophistries', his 'self-satisfaction', and his eyes 'flat and chill as glass'.

Blunt reading his statement at the same press conference.

Anthony had once been a very important figure in MI5 in the war.' Among the Courtauld students of the 1950s Blunt's colourful past as a friend of Burgess's seemed highly exotic. 'We used to say, "I expect he's a spy", but we didn't really think it. We said, "What a lark if he was!"'

According to MI5, Blunt was formally interrogated eleven times between 1951 and 1964. There may well have been many more 'informal' questionings. Peter Wright scornfully described even the formal sessions as 'comfortable conversations', in which Blunt was interviewed by old friends like Courtney Young and was never pressed too hard. He admitted nothing.

MI5's failure to extract a confession, and to find any real evidence of Blunt's guilt, has been attributed to, among other things, its post-war decline. Even its members agreed it was no longer the organization it had been during the war. Most of its clever wartime recruits had left after 1945, and during the 1950s it made a consistently poor impression on ministers and civil servants: 'Too many MI5 officers they met', writes Tom Bower, 'were of questionable quality, puzzling specimens whose origins and outbursts suggested fuzzy misunderstanding about the distinction between an aggressive leftist and a subversive.' In 1961 the Radcliffe report on the security services called MI5 and MI6 'the natural home of the incompetent'. But there were other reasons why the case was not pursued as intensely as it might have been. MI5 had an almost insurmountable problem with Blunt in that it had only circumstantial evidence of his guilt, and no credible witnesses. Despite the fact that, according to Peter Wright, MI5 'bugged and burgled [its] way across London', in the 1950s, in a public prosecution, MI5 needed either an admission of guilt or proof that had been come by legally. However skilled or brilliant the MI5 interrogators were, if Blunt admitted nothing there was little that could be done to bring him to book. In addition, the government and the upper ranks of MI5 were far from certain how much more they really wanted to investigate the penetration of the organization, since such news would almost inevitably bring interference, resignations and questions about its future.

In 1954 Yuri Modin contacted Blunt once more. Moscow wished to get money to Philby, who was still suspended from MI6, under surveillance, and in financial need. Blunt, it was decided, was the answer. According to Modin, however, it took three months to track Blunt down, since he failed to respond to any of the old agreed methods for making contact. Finally Modin turned up at one of Blunt's lectures at the Courtauld and sat in the front row. 'But strange to relate, he didn't recognize me.' Afterwards, Modin hung around until the cluster of admiring women students subsided, then handed Blunt a postcard specifying that they should meet at a pub in Ruislip the following evening, at 8 p.m. Blunt gave him a long stare and agreed. When they met the next day, Modin told Blunt about the errand. Blunt was obviously unwilling to help, and asked why Modin could not do the job himself. But eventually he caved in. They met again in a small square off Caledonian Road in Islington. Modin gave Blunt £5,000. Then – in what may be one of his not infrequent embroideries on the truth – Modin claimed he realized they were being watched. Blunt looked sheepish. He said that the figure in the shadows was Kim Philby himself, who had hoped to speak to Modin alone. Modin, tempted, refused, and the figure never showed himself.

Even when his past was not actually returning to haunt him, Blunt seemed unable to avoid its shadow. On 2 May 1955 Blunt went to his doctor with a new condition to add to his frozen face: his right eye would not stop weeping. He was diagnosed with epiphora, and told to stop smoking. He protested that this was impossible until the summer holidays, 'because of work which causes him to smoke heavily'.

The pressure was building. A few months later, in September 1955, the newspaper *The People* published a well-informed story which claimed that Burgess and Maclean had been recruited as Communist spies at Cambridge; that their escape had been planned by the Soviets; and, most explosively, that they had escaped as a result of help from a third man. The article's source was a former KGB agent called Vladimir Petrov, who had recently defected to Australia and was shortly to publish his own potboiling account of life under Stalin, *Empire of Fear*. The government and the security services found the newspaper's claims about Soviet penetration of British Intelligence deeply discomfiting. Harold Macmillan decided that it was time for an official response to the Burgess and Maclean story. That response – a White Paper on Burgess and Maclean published in October – was a pitiful thing, little short of dishonest. According to Dick White, who wrote the first draft, it had been bowdlerized by Cabinet Office and Foreign Office officials. The White Paper outrageously claimed that Burgess had been a 'satisfactory' career diplomat and that Maclean had not had access to sensitive information. It suggested that the security services had been tracking both men from the start, and that their escape had been a virtual miracle. No one was impressed. *The Times* dismissed it as 'too little, too late'. The *News Chronicle* said it was 'laughable'.

J. Edgar Hoover was so irritated by the White Paper's obfuscation and so sure that Kim Philby was guilty that on 23 October he planted a story naming him as Burgess's accomplice in the New York *Sunday News*. The British papers went to town, speculating that Philby was the 'third man'. But the leak had the opposite effect to the one Hoover had expected. The ever cautious Harold Macmillan, always wary of 'muckraking and innuendo' (especially if it might have consequences for his career and his party), decided it was more important to kill the story than to allow a public inquiry – especially as an inquiry would almost certainly reveal the extent of the messy half-lies that had been told. He publicly exonerated Philby in Parliament on 7 November. The next day Philby called a press conference and announced, 'I have never been a Communist.' Dick White, who had done everything he could to force a serious investigation of Philby and was convinced of his guilt, was livid. Yet the following year, when he became director of MI6, White seems to have made a volte-face and allowed Philby to be put on a retainer to pass information to the MI6 officer in Beirut, where he was still working for the *Observer*. From 1960, with White's knowledge,

Philby began to submit regular reports on Arab politics to MI6. British Intelligence's failure to pursue Philby, and by extension Blunt, owed quite as much to its own determination to keep its activities (and mistakes) beyond public scrutiny as it did to the lack of real evidence and the two men's slipperiness.

Still the story would not go away. Three months after Philby's press conference, in February 1956, Burgess and Maclean sensationally reappeared in a room at the National Hotel in Moscow. It was five years since they had disappeared. They read a prepared statement to the correspondents of Reuters, Tass, *Pravda* and the *Sunday Times*. They had, they admitted, been life-long Marxists, but they insisted, 'We neither of us have ever been Communist agents.' They claimed they had left Britain after realizing that their attempts to 'put Marxist ideas into practical effect' would come to nothing while Britain and America were not serious about 'upholding world peace'; they had come to the USSR to 'better understanding between the Soviet Union and the West'.

A few days after the press conference, Burgess called Peter Pollock, who was now living on his farm outside Hemel Hempstead. 'I was terrified,' Pollock said later. 'I thought the whole of MI5 would be listening in.' Burgess also wrote to Pollock's sister Sheila, of whom he had been very fond, apologizing for having caused them embarrassment, and claiming he was drinking less: 'This is rather an achievement here, drink being both cheap, very strong and popular.' He added that 'Socialism really does produce a good sort of person among ordinary people . . . I mention this not for propaganda reasons but to explain why in spite of obvious difficulties I find life here very satisfactory and have been pulled together by it.' Pollock called Blunt, whom he had not seen for several years, to ask if there was any way to stop Burgess from contacting him. Blunt invited him to meet Dick White at the Travellers Club. White told Pollock that nothing could be done, and that he should simply tell MI6 each time that Burgess called. 'He called every week for years,' Pollock said. 'He wanted gossip, and I sent him books from Hatchard's.'

Blunt's own feelings for Burgess were deeply contradictory. He retained the acknowledgement to Burgess in *Artistic Theory in Italy* for the world to see. He had stored some of Burgess's possessions at the Courtauld – an act several of his staff felt unwise. He remained in contact with Burgess's mother, Mrs Bassett, to whom he inscribed a copy of his 1959 book on William Blake which found its way into Burgess's library in Moscow. She in turn left him a little money in her will. He always spoke loyally of Burgess. Even Peter Wright wrote that, throughout the years of their interrogations, Blunt was sentimental and admiring of Burgess. Yet Burgess's reappearance made Blunt extremely uncomfortable. He appears to have refused to keep up a correspondence with him, concerned no doubt that Burgess might let slip something incriminating. Burgess's other friends, like Harold Nicolson and Roy Harrod, wrote to him regularly. Blunt became convinced that Burgess would try to find some clumsy way of getting in contact with him. On one occasion he asked George Zarnecki, the Polish medievalist at the Courtauld, to translate an article on works of art behind the Iron Curtain. 'Why don't you go and look at them yourself?' Zarnecki asked. 'I wouldn't dream of going there,' Blunt replied. 'Guy would try to come and meet me.' Blunt dreaded the possibility that the lonely and homesick Burgess might return to England. In 1960 he told Harold Nicolson at a party at the French Embassy that MI5 had informed him that Burgess would be immediately arrested if he ever came back; there would be a trial, and Blunt would be forced to be chief witness and would lose his job.

Blunt was not the only person to be unnerved by Burgess's reappearance. Within days Goronwy Rees had approached a tabloid newspaper, *The People* – which had run the Petrov article the year before – and offered his story on Guy Burgess for 2,000 guineas, on condition that he see the proofs. On 11 March 1956 *The People* blazed the piece across its front pages: 'Guy BURGESS stripped bare! HIS CLOSEST FRIEND SPEAKS AT LAST!' Rees was not named in the article, which had been recast in full tabloid style, but the article was written in the first person. Burgess was described as a promiscuous homosexual blackmailer, and it was implied that he and Maclean had been lovers. (Burgess was utterly disgusted by this: 'It would have been like going to bed with a great white *woman*!'). The Rothschilds and Guy Liddell were mentioned in the piece, and there was a lubricious account of life at Bentinck Street. Blunt was not named, but it was suggested that Burgess had been protected by homosexual friends at MI5, and that he had had the help of a fellow spy – 'One of Burgess's boon sex companions and he holds a high position in public life today'. This person was now one of the country's 'most celebrated academic figures'. Four more weeks of revelations were promised.

The story caused a furore. To those who knew Burgess it was quite clear who the author was, and that the unnamed 'agent' was meant to be Blunt. The following week the *Daily Telegraph* named Rees, and the whole episode began to backfire horribly on him. Rees's friends were shocked. Stuart Hampshire – who did not know that Rees had also denounced him to MI5 – was furious with him for causing great and witting damage to his friends. 'Victor Rothschild was a great friend of mine and so I wrote a very angry letter, which I have regretted ever since, and told Rees that I really could have no more relations with him and we all sat around speculating about why he'd done it.' But Rees was also humiliatingly sacked from his position as principal of the University College of Wales at Aberystwyth, a job he had held for two years, during which time he had made many enemies, the result of a series of impolitic attacks he had made on Welsh nationalism, his failure to pay his bills, and resentment at his close links with bohemian London. The story provided a perfect opportunity for the university to get rid of him.

The People article was an act of tremendous self-destruction. Many of Rees's acquaintances attributed it to his chronic money problems. Isaiah Berlin thought that Rees was terrified – just as Blunt was – that Burgess might start blabbing. 'I think he did it because he was afraid. He was afraid of Burgess spreading disinformation and telling terrible stories about him, and he had to get in first . . . I think he thought that anything could happen, and he panicked. Goronwy was easily panickable.' Perhaps almost as strong as his fear, however, was his desire to bring down Blunt. Instead, he only damaged himself. Now he was truly in disgrace, his academic career ruined; those who realized who his target was felt that Blunt had been maligned. The two men never spoke again. Rees himself described the article as his horrified response to the discovery that his suspicions about Burgess were true. In fact he'd known the truth about Burgess long before. At some level he obviously needed to confess and to punish himself. The choice of *The People* was part of this self-immolation. As Isaiah Berlin said later, if he had published the story in *Encounter* the outcome would have been very different.

Blunt performed his own act of denial at the end of 1956, when on behalf of Andrew Revai, who was deeply upset by the Soviets' crushing of the Hungarian uprising, he wrote to Isaiah Berlin – and almost certainly other academics – asking if he would be willing to sign a petition condemning the invasion 'in order to stir up opinion in the US'. Berlin's biographer calls this 'breath-taking in its bad faith'. It may have been that, but it was also entirely in keeping with Blunt's belated attempts to remake himself through fine deeds, while at the same time trying to deny even to himself that the past had happened.

Rees's kiss-and-tell piece was by no means the last publication which threatened Blunt's peace of mind. Throughout the 1950s and the early 1960s, books and articles threatened to do what MI5 had failed to do and expose him. Within weeks of *The People* article came the news that Tom Driberg had gone to Moscow to interview Burgess and write a book about him. A few months later there was the publication of Vladimir and Evgenia Petrov's *Empire of Fear*, which maintained that there had been a systematic Soviet conspiracy to recruit agents at Cambridge in the 1930s, and described Burgess 'bringing out briefcases full of Foreign Office documents'. Petrov's key source had been a KGB agent called Kislitsin, who had worked in London. In the event none of the books unmasked Blunt, but they served to make him ever more withdrawn, careful to reveal less and less of himself, and on occasion nervously defensive. When George Zarnecki, who became Blunt's deputy after Wilde retired, was contacted by Professor Lorentz, the director of the National Museum in Warsaw in 1959 – his first official contact with his homeland since the war – he asked Blunt for advice. 'Anthony said, "You must *not* meet him. I'll give you four or five days off. Take your family away from London, Don't speak to him." Lorentz wrote to me later saying, "All I wanted to do was to invite you to the centenary celebration of the National Museum in Warsaw. Why did you avoid me?" '

A number of people who encountered Blunt during the post-war years and found him unusually difficult, erratic or even actively unfriendly, and who had been involved with Communism, or the Security Services, or thought they might have inadvertently stumbled upon something which touched uneasily on his secret past, later wondered whether his response to them was due to his constant fear of discovery. Among these was Lesley Lewis, a Courtauld student of the 1930s, whose 1960 book *Connoisseurs and Secret Agents* contained a vivid portrait of two prominent figures in eighteenth-century Roman scholarship and art collecting, an amoral homosexual German scholar and a beautiful and successful young Cardinal. Their dual involvement in spying and scholarship provided a peculiarly apposite parallel with Burgess and Blunt. Lewis always felt that Blunt had 'sunk' her book, and prevented it from getting the attention it deserved, because it was too close to the bone. He was certainly on one occasion rude about it in her company. The eminent Australian scholar Bernard Smith also wondered whether Blunt's treatment of him might have been influenced by Blunt's own anxieties. When Smith arrived at the Courtauld after the war, all set to work under Blunt, he was dispatched – sidelined, he felt – to the Warburg. Blunt gave as his reason the fact that there was no one at the Courtauld who could cater to Smith's postgraduate needs so well as they could at the Warburg, and indeed the Courtauld's records on Smith show that Blunt was very complimentary about him. Smith, however, found his treatment rather peremptory,

Private Man

putting it down to English froideur and superiority. After Blunt's exposure he wondered if it was because, before the war, he had been an active Communist in Australia. He knew that Australian Intelligence had been aware of this, and wondered whether Blunt had been informed by his contacts in MI5.

Blunt's health continued to betray the constant strain. He was capable of great bursts of energy, but often seemed on the edge of total exhaustion. In 1959 he was treated for severe rectal bleeding and piles, and in the autumn of the following year he fell ill again, with a stomach ulcer, and was confined to bed for several months. He did not return to work until April 1961, and then resigned from several committees.* It was reported at the Courtauld that 'he would need considerable rest before he was fit enough to resume his work'. As ever, however, Blunt could not be idle, and he filled the days with work on the fifth volume of Poussin drawings.

* The Courtauld's annual report announced that as a result of his indisposition, Blunt had resigned from the National Buildings Record, the board of studies in archaeology, and Cambridge University's board of the Faculty of Arts.

16. Writer

*'My nature compels me to seek and love things which are
well ordered, fleeing confusion, which are as contrary and inimical
to me as is day to the deepest night'*

NICOLAS POUSSIN, C.1642

In 1953, the year that his MI5 interrogations began in earnest, Blunt published *Art and Architecture in France: 1500–1700*, his survey of French classicism and baroque art, part of Nikolaus Pevsner's famous Pelican History of Art series. Blunt had, by 1953, made himself a reputation with a series of important articles published in the *Burlington Magazine* on major artists of the period: Philippe de Champaigne, Jean Lemaire, Charles Lebrun, Simon Vouet, Georges de la Tour; and, of course, there was his book on Mansart. But it was *Art and Architecture in France* that made his reputation, not just in Britain, but internationally. 'French art historians still revere Blunt for this book,' its French translator, the art historian Monique Chatenet, has said. 'It was original; it gave importance in particular to buildings that no one had studied. It was a landmark. It laid the foundations for others to go further.' It reappraised the French mannerists, like Jacques Bellange and Jacques Callot, and it provided a comprehensive rethink of the invention of French classical architecture – which would find its apotheosis in Versailles – giving new interpretations not only of the contribution of François Mansart, but also of the sixteenth-century architect Philibert de l'Orme (aka Delorme). What was most impressive, however, and what summed up Blunt as an art historian was not so much any

408

innovations of research, but the great lucidity of the exposition, and his ability to bring together all the different existing threads of research into one clear whole. André Chastel, Blunt's contemporary and the dominant figure in French art history at the time, aptly described the book as a 'masterpiece of pedagogical clarity'. Its elegant summary of Poussin was a perfect encapsulation of Blunt's conception of the artist and his achievements.

Blunt's writing was – as reviewers would endlessly repeat – clear, cool, thorough and not infrequently very, very dry. On the page, as elsewhere in his life, it was as if he sought to absent himself. Nothing personal about him, beyond a calm authoritativeness, could be divined from his writing. 'Though Professor Blunt becomes at times incandescent he never really catches fire,' one reviewer remarked of *Art and Architecture in France*, accidentally pinpointing the essence of Blunt's deliberate dispassion. But while his clarity made his scholarly meanings transparent, in other ways it was a blind. Every writer's opus is an intellectual autobiography, but there was also a kind of personal and emotional revelation in Blunt's writing that manifested itself in his choice of artists and the intense personal engagement he seemed to have with them. Through this and his concentration on certain recurring themes he revealed how he thought of himself. The style was the encryption.

The kind of art that attracted Blunt was deliberately intellectual, intended to appeal not merely to the senses but to the mind too: art that might even be deliberately visually unappealing – like the impassive stone-like figures in Poussin's chilly later paintings. Blunt liked to have a puzzle to solve, iconography to elucidate, meanings to find, esoteric influences to track down, and, as he grew older and drier, stylistic motifs to trace. He enjoyed art that demonstrated a pleasure in mathematics – in the 1950s he wrote short essays on Seurat, the modern master of mathematical composition, and on Cézanne, whose dictum that nature should be viewed in terms of spheres, cylinders and cones had become almost a cliché. He was drawn to art which showed an extreme control and manipulation on the part of the artist –

art that was cool but intense at the same time. Picasso rather than Matisse; Poussin rather than Titian.

The artists who caught his attention tended to be thinkers, theorizers or technical innovators, and difficult – in all senses. Blunt's portraits of the architects Philibert de l'Orme and François Mansart in *Art and Architecture in France* were perfect illustrations of this. De l'Orme was a thinker and doer: an engineer who had studied Roman antiquities in Italy. A friend of Rabelais, he wrote two influential and semi-autobiographical books on architecture, in which he advocated the need for a theoretical knowledge of mathematics – which he loved. His work was characterized by its brilliant practical innovativeness, and also its 'love of ingenious structure . . . with great inventiveness in plans and architectural forms'. Mansart, whom Blunt described as 'an architect of almost unparalleled subtlety and ingenuity', was also well versed in mathematics, and was inspired by ancient Greek and Roman building. Both architects had been neglected – not least because almost everything they had designed had been destroyed or never built at all, and existed only in plans and drawings. The significance of their most innovatory ideas had been forgotten or misunderstood. The task of reconstructing their works and reputations did not bring the instant gratification of studying a painting: it required the painstaking study of bits of buildings and plans.

The two architects were also difficult in another sense. Philibert de l'Orme had been explosive, badly behaved and quick to make enemies. According to Blunt, Mansart was 'arrogant, obstinate, intolerant, difficult and probably dishonest', but, he added, 'these qualities were only the unattractive reverse of his high feeling for his own calling and his justifiable confidence in his ability as an architect. He made many enemies, who attacked him during his lifetime on all scores, charging him with incompetence as well as corruption.' Their personalities could not have presented a starker contrast with the calmness of the French classicism they practised: the pursuit, as Blunt described it, 'of certain qualities of clarity and simplicity . . . a static and monumental style'. 'Blunt had a clear intellectual and emotional engagement with Philibert de l'Orme and Mansart,' David Thomson, one of his later architectural students, believed. 'He couldn't resist knowing about his research quarry from a personal point of view. It was as if in part he needed to explain works of art by saying, "The people who painted them were like this." '

Alongside his attraction to hard intellectual art, Blunt nursed a deeply romantic attraction to artists whom he felt had been at odds with the established order: misanthropes, recluses, revolutionaries; men – they were always men – of turbulent emotions, who controlled and transformed those feelings by channelling them into their work. Their work was always described as intense, violent struggle. This characterization occurred again and again in Blunt's writing. Perhaps the starkest example was Borromini, the great overlooked genius of Roman baroque architecture and another contemporary of Poussin's, who seemed to channel his near-madness into controlled yet fluid buildings; could hardly bear the company of other people; all but destroyed his career with his neuroses; and took his own life.

Another artist profoundly at odds with the established order was William Blake, on whom Blunt published a long article in 1943 and, in 1959, a book: *The Art of William Blake*. At first sight, Blake was not Blunt's type at all: he was a romantic, an anti-rationalist who believed that science and Reason were evil things which crushed man's potential, curbed his imagination, and held him back from expressing his deepest impulses. 'Passions and Expression is beauty itself,' he wrote. But, though Blunt believed himself a devotee of classicism and saw himself in essence as a rational man, he was deeply attracted by Blake's Dionysian wildness, his public spurning of organized religion and social hypocrisy, his belief that man's impulses should not be restrained 'whether by law, religion, or moral code'. He admired Blake the man too: 'His passionate sincerity, his uncompromising integrity, his hundred-percent quality command respect and admiration,' he wrote. 'His complete individualism and his bold defence of personal liberty have clear topical significance today, and his bold assertion of spiritual values has a direct appeal to those who are themselves trying to escape from the dominance of materialism.' He saw Blake as a man fundamentally at odds with his time: a natural opponent of authority, a revolutionary-turned-recluse.

Blunt felt that Blake – traditionally portrayed as mad and uneducated, an isolated visionary – had been much misunderstood. His engravings and drawings had attracted little serious study. Blunt established that he had actually been part of a group of radical artists, and had been well read, and well versed in classical and Christian iconography through his work as an engraver. He tracked down the sources of Blake's obscure iconography.* Ironically, Blunt's desire to root Blake in a tradition, and to see him as a revolutionary rather than an intensely spiritual half-mad genius, to pin down his influences, in some senses missed the point of him. His most significant contribution to Blake studies was to show how inextricably the art and the poems were bound together.

As Blunt got older he increasingly recognized that it was Blake's personal qualities, rather than his art, that appealed to him. He felt that Blake was not really good enough as an artist: his drawings had the force of bad art. He increasingly distrusted his attraction to Blake, writing of the poet's 'magnetic power' which 'sometimes even hypnotises . . . those who study him today'. He told one student, 'I think anyone who works on Blake must be half-crazy', and another that he had written the 1959 book as 'an exorcism' to get Blake 'out of his system'.

According to Neil MacGregor,

> There was an ardent side to Blunt's nature which I think is
> very clearly expressed in the books. If you look at the artists

---

* Blunt showed, for example, that the godlike, bearded figure in the famous relief etching of *The Ancient of Days* was no benevolent deity but Urizen, the villain in Blake's prophetic books, who sought to reduce the infinite to the finite by stretching compasses (in Western art, a familiar symbol for science and mathematics) across the world.

he worked on, in every case what Blunt managed to achieve was a mythic, poetic recreation of the artist, which reflected his own preoccupations at the time of writing. You could actually divide Anthony's biography into Blake, Poussin and Borromini – a wonderfully un-Marxist, profoundly romantic projection of self and poetic creation – and it is why the books are so powerful. Blake, Poussin, Borromini – it's an extraordinary sequence. All have the great ambivalence of the gifted individual towards the established order. Blake and Borromini don't make the compromises, whereas Poussin does. Poussin has to be the one in the middle, Blake is the young man's artist, and Borromini is the old man's. It's impossible to think of it otherwise.

A similar attraction influenced Blunt's taste for Delacroix, on whom he began to lecture in the early 1950s, even though it was his contemporary Ingres who was usually seen as the heir of French classicism. However, Ingres was the purveyor of a delicious but essentially sensuous and comfortable art, whereas Delacroix's journals, like his paintings, reveal him as an intensely intellectually curious artist, and as a man in constant schism – something Blunt knew all about – torn intellectually between classicism and romanticism, and emotionally between control and passion. The conflict between these oppositions, Blunt told his audience, 'seems to have tortured him all through his career'. Delacroix, in Blunt's eyes, was by nature and preference a classicist, but could not quench in himself an attraction to romanticism. He thought Racine better than Shakespeare but, Blunt said, 'he cannot altogether get Shakespeare out of his system'. He was torn by a desire to paint 'with fire and energy' and the need to work slowly and calmly. 'When I feel myself sweating and my blood getting heated, I know I must take care,' he wrote. 'He was', Blunt told his audience, 'violently attacked as an innovator and a revolutionary . . . but he was mostly a hater of novelty and a believer in tradition.' In his early career, Delacroix – like Blunt – had tied art to politics, but he had been disillusioned by the revolution of 1830. According to Blunt, he assumed a deliberate coldness both in his art and in his personal dealings, for the good of his work: 'personally he was shy, haughty, and almost affectedly aristocratic – only to very old family friends did he show a warmth and affection which those who knew him slightly could not believe that he possessed'. He aimed for 'a perfect balance between enthusiasm and coldness' or, in Delacroix's phrase, '*le sang-froid animé*'. It is hard to imagine a better description of Blunt. Hard too not to feel that Blunt himself must have undergone a pretty devastating political disillusionment, however unwilling he was to describe it.

That this was the case seems to be confirmed by Blunt's creeping horror, during the years after the war, of anything smacking of theory and ideology. It also seems apparent in the way he wrote about Picasso, whom he once again admitted was his favourite living artist. Picasso entirely fitted Blunt's tastes. His Cubist monochrome paintings, especially, had a cool neoclassicism, and Blunt described his work as the result of 'the struggle between violent character and intellectual control.' 'He tears apart his forms, he throws aside all the sensuous attractions of painting; he bullies his medium into doing things for which it seems totally unsuited.' Such phrases excited and inspired his young audience at the Courtauld. In his post-war writing on Picasso, Blunt now put *Guernica*, the painting that he had spurned so violently in 1937, at the centre of his whole conception of the artist.

Blunt returned to *Guernica* in 1951, fourteen years after his original denunciation of the artist for failing to keep the personal separate from the political, and a few months before Burgess's defection. In the painting, he wrote, Picasso had 'attempted once again to treat a theme that was human, tragic and even political'. It was 'a manifestation of Picasso's sensitivity to human problems, which has never deserted him'. In 1953 he called Picasso 'the most intense exponent of the tragedy of the twentieth century', and compared him to Michelangelo. In 1961 he described *Guernica* as the climax of the artist's whole œuvre, 'in which, for me at any rate, all his prowess both of imagination and of intellectual control are manifest'. He called it 'the last great painting in the European tradition'. Almost, one feels, as an act of expiation, he set himself the task of unravelling the process of the painting's creation – Picasso had famously completed it in six days – and its meanings. He produced a series of six lectures on it, out of which came a book, *Guernica*, published in 1969 (and dedicated to the mysterious Andrew Revai). Of the symbols which Picasso had originally created to describe his personal pain, he now wrote that 'under the impulse of the Spanish Civil War Picasso was able to raise them to an altogether higher plane and use them to express his reaction to a cosmic tragedy'. It was the closest he ever came to admitting he had been wrong about all of it – the art, the aesthetics, the politics.

Blunt's other book on Picasso, written with Phoebe Pool, *Picasso: The Formative Years* (1962), had set out to show that Picasso had been 'a great traditionalist as a well as a great revolutionary', by exploring his early influences. It inadvertently revealed Blunt's weaknesses as a Picasso critic: it was somehow creaky and old-masterish, and stood aloof from the overtly sexual and emotional nature of much of Picasso's work.

By now, as the Picasso work implied, Blunt was looking back at his old writings with distaste. When his student Alan Bowness, who was himself a pacifist with 'left-wing' views, asked him about them, Blunt told him, 'Let me give you a word of advice. Don't ever think of reprinting your early work.' 'I said,' Bowness recalled, ' "You wrote some interesting articles." He completely dismissed them.' Blunt seems, however, never to have entirely escaped the Marxist way of seeing the world as a set of permanent contradictions. Dialectics of some description continued to appear in his writing. 'We appreciate a struggle between opposites,' he wrote of Borromini in 1979, 'not, as the Romantics did, in the expectation of defeat, but in the hope that a synthesis will be achieved. To us the struggle in Borromini between imaginative energy and intellectual control can be more attractive than the easy achievement of Bernini's rhetoric.' The traces of Marxism which still appeared in his writing – an emphasis on historical and social context in particular – were now common to pretty much all history and art-history writing. Several of his students of the 1950s, however, felt they could detect a lurking radicalism. Every year he gave a lecture on *Guernica* and its political context. He refused to go to Spain while Franco was alive. He was known to be a Labour voter. To those who expressed an interest in Marxism, he would recommend Friedrich Antal's articles in the *Burlington Magazine*. Alan Bowness felt 'the political commitment hadn't gone away: it was just more obvious when he spoke about modern art and in personal conversation'. But, as the 1950s progressed, he spoke less and less about modern art, and less and less about politics. He still had a taste for the paintings of William Coldstream and the sculptures of Henry Moore, but increasingly he found contemporary art 'plumb in the middle of my blind spot'.

Of all the artists he wrote about, it was Poussin, as Blunt admitted in his 1967 monograph on the artist, who was 'my first love'. Poussin was the artist about whom he felt most strongly, and was the centre of his intellectual world. He would also become the subject of Blunt's most bitter professional feud. Somehow it was appropriate that it should be so. It would be hard to think of a more difficult, recondite, mysterious artist. It seems apt that like Blunt, Poussin has proved a magnet for conspiracy theorists and fantasists.* For Blunt, however, there were genuine mysteries surrounding Poussin. There was no consensus about what precisely his corpus of work consisted of; many paintings were missing, many attributions confused. Blunt set out to rectify this. Poussin also had a reputation primarily as a chilly master of formal composition, unemotional and forbidding. Blunt believed he was a great deal more than that. His paintings had used erudite

---

* The best known of the Poussin conspiracy theories is set out in *Holy Blood, Holy Grail* by Baigent, Lincoln and Leigh (London: Cape, 1982). Blunt thought it hilarious, and read it at least twice. 'If you believe this,' he told one of his students, 'you'll believe God's coming to dinner next Saturday!'

symbolism to convey meaning. After his death Poussin had been called a '*peintre-philosophe*', a painter-philosopher, and was famous for his learning. In his *Lives of the Painters*, Poussin's biographer and contemporary, Giovanni Pietro Bellori, had praised him for his 'fine mind and his wide reading, not only, I say, of history and tables and the branches of learning in which he excelled, but in the other liberal arts and in philosophy'. Blunt's other task, therefore, was to rediscover Poussin's intentions and the significance of his iconography. Walter Friedlaender had begun to work on both these problems, and now Blunt followed in his footsteps, sorting out Poussin's corpus, and explaining his meanings: a combination of traditional connoisseurship and Warburgian art history. Out of the connoisseurship came the five-volume catalogue of Poussin's drawings, on which he collaborated with Friedlaender; a series of articles in the *Burlington Magazine*, which were called collectively 'Poussin Studies'; and a 1966 critical catalogue, *The Paintings of Nicolas Poussin*, as well as a host of other pieces on Poussin's followers and copyists. From Blunt's attempts to understand Poussin's intentions and meanings came, along with a cluster of articles, his 1967 book *Nicolas Poussin*.

Blunt's personal feeling for, even identification with, Poussin was remarked upon by almost everyone he taught. There were certainly echoes of his own life in the way he wrote about the artist. Poussin was born in northern France in 1594, and he moved at the age of thirty to Rome. As a young man he had been wild, given over to hedonism and the artistic debates of the time, and might even have dabbled in political subversion. 'Poussin seems to have been a man of rather strong temperament and violent passions,' Blunt stated. A contemporary had described him as 'a young man who is like one possessed'. His early paintings were sensuous and used warm vibrant colours, but he seems to have veered from one artistic style to another as he got caught up in contemporary artistic debates in Rome on the superiority of *colore*, colour, versus *disegno*, line. At the age of thirty-six he appeared to have suffered some kind of crisis –

perhaps a breakdown, possibly an attack of syphilis. As a result he gave up his rackety life, his painting matured, and he began to develop the static monumental allegorical style and cool palette for which he became best known. He also made a deliberate decision to withdraw from public life and art-world politics. He gave up the opportunity to become a a wealthy court painter in Paris, devoted himself to his work and to a small circle of true friends and patrons (mostly bourgeois merchants and civil servants), and lived a life of great simplicity. He was, Blunt believed, a recluse, but managed, nevertheless, to accommodate himself to the demands of artistic life in Rome and international fame. 'This picture of the grave, deliberate, and serious artist, living apart from the world and contemplating it with detachment and even a certain scorn, was something of a rarity in the Baroque period,' Blunt wrote. 'Although he must have had friends who could have brought him into regular contact with the great, his name never appears in gossip, and his paintings never adorned the altars of the great churches.'

Blunt had come to believe that from 1630 and his 'crisis' Poussin had adopted the precepts of neo-Stoicism, which in seventeenth-century Europe was arguably the most influential philosophy after Christianity. Neo-Stoicism was based on the principle that emotional investment in transient things such as human beauty, wealth and office was bound to end in disappointment. The ideal was not to compete for office or wealth, but to divest oneself of possessions and worldly ambitions and live a simple, austere life in line with the dictates of Reason. In its seventeenth-century meaning, Reason governed the harmony of all of nature, it was a manifestation of the divine, it kept chaos at bay, and it was the fount not merely of beauty, but of creativity.

Blunt saw the influence of neo-Stoicism in Poussin's letters. 'One must attain virtue and wisdom in order to stand firm and remain unmoved before the assaults of mad, blind fortune,' the painter wrote to his friend and patron Paul Fréart de Chantelou. 'Whatever happens to me, I am resolved to accept the good and bear the evil. Miseries and disasters are things so common with men that I am surprised that men of sense would get angry at them.' Blunt also believed that from the 1630s to his death in 1665, Poussin had tried to give visible expression to his Stoic beliefs in his paintings, through the use of allegory. These beliefs were what the paintings were about. Among the consequences of Poussin's attempts to make his meanings as clear as words was a decision deliberately to set aside naturalistic figures and the jewel-like colours of his early work in favour of statues stuck in frozen poses with grey, mask-like faces. Their poses, which followed the formal language of classical rhetoric, had very specific meanings. 'Just as the twenty-four letters of the alphabet are used to form our words and to express our thought, so the forms of the human body are used to express the various passions of the soul and make visible what is in the mind.'

'It would be wrong to conclude that, because Poussin relied principally upon reason, his works were cold or unimaginative,' Blunt wrote. His ardour for the artist was apparent in every phrase as he continued:

> His pursuit of a rational form of art was so passionate that it led him in his later years to a beauty beyond reason; his desire to contain emotion within its strictest limits caused him to express it in its most concentrated form . . . led him to create paintings which, though impersonal, are also deeply emotional and, though rational in their principles, are almost mystical in the impression they convey.

Towards the end of his life Poussin had become even more detached from the world than in his middle years: 'he lived only for his art and for the company of a very restricted circle of friends who really understood it . . . In his old age he cared nothing for what the world thought.' His final landscapes illustrated the overwhelming power of nature and the inevitability of the cycle of life with a pantheistic calm. Blunt admired Poussin's approach to life. He saw in Poussin the Stoical qualities he wished for himself: rationality, scepticism, the subordination of emotion to reason, pleasure in friendship, the valuing of private life over public office. He aspired to Poussin's equanimity in the face of the world's vicissitudes and to his rejection of the blandishments of public life. Poussin's semi-reclusiveness and reliance on a small circle of true friends also struck a chord. 'Blunt's book on Poussin', Neil MacGregor has said,

> has a huge number of questions it fails to address. It's a difficult book, but the poetic achievement is so high you feel you're in a world that is completely coherent, which is why it will live as one of the great art-history books. Poussin is the intellectual who is on good terms with the court and academic world, and can map and navigate these waters, but nonetheless chooses to live slightly on the sidelines and on his own terms. Blunt could write that without anyone imagining that it was autobiographical – nobody else at the time would have thought of him in those terms.

Yet, although he admired Poussin's Stoic values, Blunt could not quite live by them. He could do without the grand and comfortable life, he could push the world away, but he couldn't resist his own ambition – the itch to be part of the very world he wanted to reject. 'Contrary to what you'd suppose in just talking to him,' Stuart Hampshire observed,

> I thought he was rather, if not very, ambitious. There was a mask that suggested he always tried to appear above things, that he was wholly absorbed in thinking about Poussin or trying to appear as a Stoic. He wanted to achieve those posts which he did achieve: the Surveyor of the Royal Collection and all that – his public status. He wanted to be a dominant figure in the art world.

It was yet another instance in which Blunt set himself the highest standards of conduct and then seemed to go out of his way to fail to live up to them.

Perhaps the crowning moment of Blunt's academic career was his curatorship in 1960 of the first exhibition of Poussin's work at the Louvre in Paris. It confirmed his position as the world expert on Poussin, demonstrated the very considerable extent of his standing outside England, and effectively turned Poussin from an unfashionable, difficult artist into a first-rank, mainstream old master.

The exhibition was a great success. For the French Poussin expert and future director of the Louvre Pierre Rosenberg, it was 'the explosion in my heart for Poussin. I went to the exhibition and I came out drunk.' (Blunt's former student John Shearman recalled that the only criticism was that the giant fake palm trees that had been placed throughout the exhibition were tremendously ugly.) Blunt – relaxed, enthusiastic and excited – proudly showed round friends, old pupils and acquaintances. His mother, now nearly eighty, came to the opening in May 1960. He lectured – in perfect French – at the École du Louvre. There was a grand dinner at which he was toasted by the grandees of the French art Establishment – though to his old pupil Rosalys Coope, who was working in Paris and had watched him hang the exhibition, he grumbled about having to attend it.

There had been the usual art-world bitcheries. The director of the Louvre, Germain Bazin, jealous of the fuss the exhibition was attracting, had insisted that the Louvre's head of painting, Charles Sterling, who was hanging the exhibition with Blunt, should not be present at the opening. Sterling was terribly upset. When congratulating Blunt on his excellent French after his lecture, Bazin could not resist observing patronizingly that he had heard only one mistake. A potential Poussiniste dispute with the great German art historian Erwin Panofsky had been headed off through diplomatic discussion. Panofsky wrote to thank Blunt 'cordially for the extremely kind way in which you have expressed whatever disagreement still exists between us and for the leniency with which you have treated what is indeed an inexcusable slip of the pen'.

One person did not think the exhibition had been a success, however. Denis Mahon was not a Poussin scholar. His area was Bolognese seventeenth-century painting – in particular the artist

Guercino, whose reputation he had more or less single-handedly resurrected. Mahon, like Blunt, was one of the generation of English art historians who had been inspired by the arrival of the Warburg in the 1930s. Five years younger than Blunt, he was from a wealthy Anglo-Irish family, had never had a job, and lived a life of almost monastic devotion to his study at home with his mother. His outlook was very different from Blunt's. He was recognized as a skilled connoisseur, and for him poring over a painter's style and brushwork would always reveal more about a painting than studying the documentary evidence and the artist's background.

Mahon said later:

I went to the exhibition hoping that Poussin would become clearer as an artistic personality. Instead of which I saw chaos. I realized Blunt didn't have an eye. I was appalled by the way that the exhibition was hung. Blunt knew a great deal about many aspects, but he didn't care about, or didn't see, this. I felt that if this hotchpotch of an order took root – it was fundamentally off course – it would become the canon and it wasn't right.

At its simplest, the problem as Mahon saw it was that the order of the paintings attributed to Poussin's early period, between 1624 and 1633, was completely wrong and showed that Blunt had misunderstood Poussin's artistic development. Mahon decided it was up to him to come up with the right chronology using his skills as a connoisseur: his 'eye', 'looking and feeling', and his understanding of Poussin's 'artistic handwriting'. Mahon travelled back and forth between Paris and London – looking and writing, looking and writing. 'I had to get the article out while the exhibition was still on, so people could see the exhibition and see if they agreed with me.'

The article was to be published in the *Burlington Magazine*'s July issue, which was to be devoted to Poussin. Before it came out, Mahon wrote to Blunt to let him know it was coming.

I felt frightfully upset to find that my reading of the whole early development was so very different from yours; and I felt the more upset in that I feel sure that I would never even have got to the stage of achieving much of an opinion on these matters if it were not for your work in bringing all the issues out in connection with the show ... I want to emphasise that the whole business of differing from you in this way, and on this subject, has been a bloody awful nightmare to me. Inevitably you will regard me as misguided, but I hope you will realise that I would have enormously preferred to have seen these things your way if I could possibly have brought myself to do so.

The article struck a different tone: 'One is virtually compelled to take up a position as soon as one enters the exhibition ... I simply cannot bring myself to swallow the disparities which emerge, or the series of fundamental volte-faces which their arrangement in this sequence entails,' Mahon wrote. Blunt's conclusions on the paintings were challenged one after another: 'I cannot agree ... I cannot agree ... I simply cannot conceive ... I cannot myself visualise a rich sombre Baroque picture of this type between the Sacchiesque elegance of ...'

Blunt was at first flexible. In a brief note that followed Mahon's article, he admitted that the chronology for the exhibition had always been provisional: only twelve of the forty-eight pictures Mahon dated to the period 1624-33 had any external evidence to date them at all, and the paintings had never before been seen together. He had hoped the exhibition would help to make Poussin's development clearer. 'On many points', he added in a longer answer published in the *Burlington* two months later, 'I entirely agree with Mr Mahon's conclusions; on some indeed I have expressed similar views.' It wasn't unusual for Blunt to be so amenable. He had a reputation for being willing to admit if he had got something wrong. 'It was almost what was nicest about Anthony,' thought John Richardson. 'Blunt was always ready to accept he was wrong, he was always changing his mind about dates,' observed Pierre Rosenberg. 'This wasn't because he was not sure of his eye. It was an attitude to do with his belief that art history was constantly in progress, that things must be constantly evaluated.' This surprised many French art historians, who were used to the haughty infallibility of their own grand professors.

Blunt could not conceal, however, that he was mightily irritated by Mahon's article. 'I should point out', he wrote in a footnote in September, 'that Mr Mahon has misinterpreted what I suggested, made no reference at all to my general thesis, and ignored almost all my arguments.' He was particularly exasperated by Mahon's insistence that, without any documentary evidence, he could date the paintings not just to particular years, but to actual months. This, he wrote, was the fundamental issue on which 'I cannot follow Mr Mahon.' He pointed out that Mahon's chronology was of necessity guesswork, and that 'great caution and great humility are necessary'. Blunt in turn infuriated Mahon by avoiding him. 'I would have thought he would have asked me to discuss it, to explain it,' Mahon said later – 'that's what I would have done. He didn't. I think he'd been very possessive of Poussin; he thought he owned him.'

Mahon was far from finished. Seven months later, Blunt claimed to be 'contemplating renewing relations with Mahon', or so he wrote to Rudi Wittkower, who was now teaching art history at Columbia University (and was very proud of the fact that he was the best-paid art historian in the USA), 'because I want to ask him about a Bolognese painting. My intention may be frustrated however, because I suspect he will have a piece in the April *Gazette des Beaux-Arts*, which I believe is being devoted to Poussin.' Mahon's choice of publication was unfortunate. Georges Wildenstein, its owner, and perhaps the most successful art dealer in the world, was regarded with suspicion by many academics. He employed art historians to compile learned catalogues of a particular artist's work, which would just happen to include items owned by Wildenstein's. It was said he used the catalogues to sell his stock. He had recently published a catalogue of engravings after Poussin which Blunt believed was seriously flawed. 'In view of my relations with M. Wildenstein,' Blunt wrote, 'I do not suppose it will be very friendly.' He added, in response to an enquiry by Wittkower after his health, 'I did have an ulcer, but am now completely mended, and I should hate to think that I was so feeble as to be made ill (as distinct from sick) by Denis Mahon.' Mahon's article, 'Poussiniana', which in fact came out in 1962, was not very friendly. It made it quite clear that there was more to the disagreement than the dating of a few pictures: Mahon produced a completely new chronology for the whole of Poussin's career. This was a direct challenge to Blunt's interpretation of Poussin's development – to his whole conception of the artist – as well as to his skills as a connoisseur. Of these, Mahon wrote that Blunt's criteria for dating the pictures were 'so wide, so capricious, and so ungraduated as to rule out by implication the recognition of any sequence of development . . . if it be argued then, that unlike can be associated with unlike, it follows that almost any sequence remains possible and none becomes probable'.

Once again, however, he kept urging Blunt to meet him. 'I should of course, be quite willing to have a talk, or talks, about Poussin problems,' Blunt replied at the end of 1962, 'but I think I ought to say straight away that I am not very sanguine about their producing useful results. I fear that, as you have yourself said, we approach things from totally different points of view, so much so that we now seem actually to see different things.' He did attempt a rapprochment, by suggesting that he might send Mahon some entries from his forthcoming catalogue raisonné of Poussin's paintings. 'I do not expect that you will agree with them, but if we can iron out some of our differences in private before we have another set-to in public, it would obviously be all to the good.'

However, Mahon's next article, 'A Plea for Poussin as a Painter', published in 1965, showed that those differences were as deep as they had ever been. It argued persuasively that the aesthetics of the paintings had been neglected, and that Poussin had been, certainly in his early paintings, a sensual painter. It also implied, none too subtly, that Poussin was not Blunt's austere *peintre-philosophe*: Blunt had misread the artist, idealized and over-intellectualized him, and fatally ignored his painterly qualities. To Mahon, Poussin's main preoccupations were not intellectual, but to do with wanting to paint beautiful pictures. The meanings of his paintings, his intentions – which Blunt had tried to excavate for thirty years – were merely the 'backstage elements', and Mahon obliquely referred to Blunt's work as 'a rather unconvincing blind alley'.

Beyond the rights and wrong of the arguments, there was a conflict of personalities and approaches. The two men were antipathetic. Mahon was famous for his persistence, his passion for detail, the fact that he was always completely convinced by his own arguments, and his tenacity in attempting to persuade others to his view. He often exhausted his opponents into submission. As Blunt's great fan Cecil Gould put it:

> In essentials he was almost a caricature of a professional. His obsession with detail and to leaving no loophole in his arguments had left him to develop a style of writing compared to which the later manner of Henry James would appear almost concise. Though no trouble, and no expense, was too great when he was checking his facts his passion for precision was apt to get the better of him. In particular, his wish to establish the exact date of the pictures he was studying caused him to propose a degree of chronological inflexibility more characteristic of the bureaucratic mentality than of the artistic temperament.*

---

* Here is an example of Mahon's style, his criticism, and also his rising exasperation: 'When criticising this footnote from the point of view of method, I drew attention to the fact that it was phrased in such a way as to convey an insufficiently precise indication of Sir Anthony Blunt's opinion. He, however, seemed to have jumped to the conclusion that the real essence of my criticism was a complaint that he had accused me of maintaining that all the pictures in question were contemporary. This misses the point, which was of course that

Mahon was demanding that Blunt throw away thirty years' work, and could not see that anything Blunt had done himself had any relevance. Nor could he understand why Blunt didn't see things his way. 'One was flummoxed', he said later, 'that he didn't see what one was doing.' This, it was said by the Blunt camp, was the result of Mahon's never having had to accommodate himself to others – he had, for instance, never had a job – of never having had to learn that the truth never lies just with one person. 'I thought this was a tremendous advantage,' Mahon commented. 'I could say exactly what I thought.' He also had an unerring knack for riling Blunt: 'I must own that I am getting more and more into a fog as to how you "read" a picture stylistically,' he wrote.

The fact was, however, that Mahon's claims could not be completely ignored. He was generally acknowledged to be an exceptionally good connoisseur – a better one, many in the art world believed, than Blunt – and many people felt that his dating, certainly of the early years, was very convincing. He had also shown up Blunt's relative neglect of Poussin's painterly qualities. Ironically, one of the main reasons for this neglect had been the fact that when Blunt had first come to the subject, thirty years before, almost everything written about Poussin concentrated on the look of the paintings: their stiff formal qualities. It had seemed to Blunt then that the task was to revive the meanings of Poussin's pictures to show that he had not been a dry, cold, dull painter. There was another irony in the fact that it was his success in doing so that had brought Mahon into the fray.

By early 1965 it was clear that the two men would never come to an agreement. Then the feud was racheted up to another level of bitterness. In 1964, at a sale at Sotheby's, a painting had caught Mahon's eye. 'This picture was dirty and hung high. I

---

the footnote (op. cit. p. 396) was so expressed that it could have no exact meaning unless I had maintained the contemporaneity of the picture; and this, as I have explained, I had not in fact done. To say one of Sir Anthony Blunt's own expressions, heaven only knows what a careful reader was expected to make of his footnote.'

realized at once that it was probably a Poussin. I didn't dare ask for a ladder – that would put the price up – so I got a dealer to bid for it.' The picture had been attributed to a contemporary of Poussin's, Pietro Testa. Once he had bought it, Mahon was sure it was a Poussin, and when the canvas was cleaned and relined an inscription was found which proved that it had belonged to Poussin's great patron Cassiano dal Pozzo. By an uneasy coincidence, the subject was the biblical story of how Eliezer, servant of Jacob, saw his master's future wife, Rebecca, at the well; exactly the same as the Poussin which Blunt owned. Blunt believed that his picture was one that was known to have belonged to Cassiano dal Pozzo. But now Mahon became convinced that *his* picture was this *Rebecca*, and Blunt's was a very late painting from around 1660 after Pozzo's death – a claim which cut right back to their differences over Poussin's chronology, and could not have made Blunt feel more threatened. Mahon resolved to publish his *Rebecca* in the art magazine *Apollo*, along with an article explaining why it was the dal Pozzo commission.

Not surprisingly, Blunt was far from receptive to this idea. He had also just read Mahon's highly critical 'A Plea for Poussin as a Painter'. 'I think it extremely ingenious,' he wrote to the editor of *Apollo*, Denys Sutton, who sent him a proof of the Rebecca piece in early February 1965, 'but necessarily remain unconvinced, because I simply cannot believe from looking at the picture that it is by Poussin.' He had, he claimed,

> had the painting here for some time, and a number of people saw it in my room and not a single person agreed with the suggestion of the then-owner that it is by Poussin . . . I am, as you can imagine, very unhappy at finding myself in disagreement with Denis over a picture that he has acquired; my opinion, however, was not formed lightly but as a result of careful examination of the picture over a relatively long period.

Blunt wielded a great deal of power when it came to attributions. If he said something was or was not a Poussin, people from auctioneers to the curators at the national museums usually felt obliged to follow him. But Mahon had, as he knew, an equivalent reputation as a connoisseur. Blunt had other reasons apart from personal vendetta for rejecting the picture. He did not think it was a very good painting, and one of Blunt's faults as a Poussin connoisseur was that he found it hard to accept that Poussin could have painted what he felt was a mediocre picture – a problem which had led to confusions over other attributions. And, though he was loath to admit it to himself, his eyesight was beginning to deteriorate. By 1968 his optician reported that he was myopic and astigmatic, adding, 'He is quite adamant that he manages very well with regard to distant vision without assistance, and that being the case there is no point in pressing the need upon him to wear distance correction; which in fact would make him see so much better.'

When Sutton told him about the letter, Mahon was predictably furious. He decided to track down the painting's previous owners to find out when exactly Blunt had seen the painting. His discovered that his immediate predecessor, a Mr Jerdein, had sent Blunt a black-and-white photograph of it but had never taken the painting itself to the Courtauld. Making attributions from photographs was not unusual among connoisseurs – Mahon had done it himself. The photograph of the unrestored painting is still in Blunt's files at the Institute, together with a letter dated March 1964 from Mr Jerdein giving the painting's dimensions. Mahon set a trap for Blunt. He sent him a series of polite, niggling letters, guaranteed to irritate him, asking exactly when Blunt had seen the painting, and whether he remembered its frame: 'I mean in which year, e.g. "during 1963", "early last year", and so on . . . perhaps if this occurred in the presence of others, you could let me have their names.' Blunt said that he had no memory of the frame. To Mahon this was a virtual confession that he had never seen the picture, since the frame with which Jerdein had bought it was extremely conspicuous and unusually strikingly carved. When Denys Sutton then asked Blunt to come and see the picture and explain himself, he procrastinated. 'I was depressed at the prospect of what would obviously be a very painful interview.' Ten days later Mahon sent a solicitor to the Courtauld with a demand that Blunt sign a document stating that he had never seen the picture. Mahon claimed that he just wanted to ensure that, when Blunt published his long-awaited catalogue of Poussin's paintings – which would aim to establish not merely the order they had been painted in, but also which were genuine and which were not – he should not be able to deny the authenticity of the painting if he had not seen it.

Now Blunt was furious. He refused to sign the document. Others were sympathetic. Bringing in solicitors was not the way in which academic squabbles were conducted. 'He [Mahon] really is the most awful, devious, and malicious man,' one letter of commiseration went. 'I am horrified that you should suffer for the vendetta of this ignoble creature,' wrote Lord Crawford, 'and that he should give you this odious trouble and anxiety.' But Crawford also advised Blunt to admit quickly that he had not seen the picture at the Courtauld, thus removing the keystone of Mahon's case. Blunt refused. 'There were many ways of approaching the matter,' he sputtered in a deposition to his solicitors at the end of February in reply to Mahon's solicitor's letter,

> of which the simplest would have been to write to me asking me whether I was really quite sure that I had seen it in the Courtauld Institute. Instead he pressed me with a series of questions about the frame which can only have been designed to trap me into, some further statement . . . I am naturally not prepared to sign any statement to the effect that I have not seen the picture in the original, because I am confident that I have, though it is possible that my memory is overlaying two separate incidents.

He added, trying to show that Mahon had himself failed to follow art-world protocols, that it was not done to publish articles on a picture which you owned. In the proof copy he had read Mahon's ownership had not been declared – though it was when the article was published in the following month, March. 'If Mr Mahon had approached me with any frankness, the whole of this problem could have been cleared up quickly and amicably.'

'The only fact that shakes me', he finished, demonstrating his own uncertainty, 'is that two people whose judgement I trust . . . have seen the picture in the original and believe, in one case firmly and in the other hesitatingly, the picture to be an original.' Among those who were coming round to the idea was the Courtauld's other seventeenth-century specialist, Blunt's former pupil Michael Kitson. Mahon asked him to look at the painting, and took him to lunch. 'I'm glad to report it was a pretentious and tasteless lunch at the Knightsbridge grill', Kitson later reported to Blunt, before coming to the bad news. 'The awful thing is that, after seeing the original, I'm afraid it has a better chance of being by Poussin than I thought from either the black and white photograph or the *Apollo* reproduction.'

In April, after having tried to prove the unprovable, Blunt seemed to admit in an article in the *Sunday Times* that he had seen only a photograph of the picture. Mahon's solicitors demanded a formal withdrawal and an apology. Blunt made a formal request through his solicitors to see the painting. Mahon refused, as Blunt had assumed he would. He had told his solicitors that, if Mahon refused, he would have an excuse to leave it out of his catalogue altogether. There was no victory on either side, but each could claim that he had got his own way. 'I have omitted in this catalogue all reference to the *Rebecca* recently published by Denis Mahon,' Blunt wrote in the catalogue, 'as I have been unable to examine the original in its cleaned state.' 'This', he told his solicitors, rather optimistically, 'will make it perfectly clear to the reader what I think of it.' The irony was Blunt *had* seen the picture. In the early 1960s his former pupil Brian Sewell had taken him to see it at the Pimlico shop of the interior decorator Geoffrey Bennison, who had briefly owned it. It is a measure of the extent to which Mahon – and other pressures – had upset him, that Blunt was unable to dredge up this fact.

Neither man's anger with the other ever abated. Blunt refused to attend events where they might meet. John Pope-Hennessy claimed that Blunt tried to stop him nominating Mahon to the British Academy, as it would make his own position at meetings very difficult. When one of his students, Sheila Somers, took Mahon's line, he fell out irretrievably with her. Another, Richard Verdi, was not allowed to meet Mahon. 'One of the few times I ever actually saw him lose his temper', remembered John Golding, 'was when Mahon had been in the building. It was the only time I ever saw Anthony in a real rage.' One night, on a trip to southern Italy, after a great deal of alcohol and at his most unbuttoned, Blunt was heard to say, 'Lady Mahon should have dropped Denis off in the Borghese gardens when he was sixteen. Then he would have finally lost his virginity.'

Mahon was still angry thirty years later. 'This really was monstrous – a lapse of professional ethics,' he said. 'He tried to sink my publication. He was being economical with the truth. But then, he was so experienced in lying. I think if you make a profession of spying that's what you do – lie. It was going to spill over.'

The question of why Blunt was *so* affected by Mahon remains. Since his exposure as a spy, some of the hostility directed towards Blunt's wartime actions has been deflected on to his career as an art historian. In the case of the Mahon feud, it has been suggested that Mahon completely eclipsed Blunt's work. Blunt's former pupil Brian Sewell has claimed that Blunt knew that Mahon was right and he was wrong, and couldn't bear to admit it. Well before Mahon published, Sewell averred, Blunt was already full of doubts about his work on Poussin. Sewell stated that on the eve of the opening of the 1960 exhibition he had driven Blunt to the Louvre and escorted him round. 'The moment we were in the first room', Sewell told a television interviewer in 1995,

he muttered, 'I was wrong', and he went on muttering, 'I was wrong, I was wrong.' It was immediately clear to him as to others . . . that the majority of his conclusions were in error. He really saw all this material together for the first time in 1960. I'm really convinced that had it been possible to close the exhibition before it had been opened I'm sure he would have done it. He was in a state of great distress, and at a rather formal dinner that night, when he was being lauded by French academics and scholars, he was very ill at ease – almost sheepish – when they praised him, because he knew that a deluge of arguments was about to break and he wished to join it, he wished to revise it himself.

Sewell's memory may have betrayed him. Blunt supervised the hanging of the exhibition himself, and had been at the Louvre for several weeks before it opened. Many, many other friends and pupils have commented on the intensity of Blunt's pleasure at its success. But there is some truth in Sewell's story. Mahon had stumbled upon the aspect on which Blunt felt most vulnerable in his Poussin work. There was a degree of provisionality and uncertainty about his view of Poussin's artistic development, an uncertainty that never left him. In 1973 he wrote to Pierre Rosenberg, after seeing a new exhibition the younger man had curated, 'I got back last night and after looking at more of the pictures allotted to Poussin's early period I am increasingly worried . . . In fact I wonder if I have not confused the whole of the early phase by including in it things which have no business to be there and are not by Poussin at all.' He was constantly changing his mind over the dating of the pictures. It was, perhaps, the manifestation a peculiar kernel of uncertainty that seemed to lie at the heart of Blunt himself. It was true that he had hoped that seeing the pictures all together at the exhibition would provide him with an opportunity to rethink the chronology.

Mahon's new suggestions threw into confusion the conclusions that Blunt had worked so long towards, raising all kinds of questions that he increasingly did not have the energy to resolve. The Poussin catalogue which came out in 1966 (he had first delivered it in 1961, but then spent another five years worrying over it) was not the clear and definitive work he had hoped it would be. And with the *Rebecca*, Mahon had publicly questioned, and damaged, Blunt's reputation as a connoisseur, showing he was capable of making big mistakes. Mahon's challenges gave dealers and museum curators the opportunity to repeat the old saws about academic art historians in general and Blunt in particular: they didn't live in the real world, they looked at photographs, not at the originals. Blunt, it was even said by some, had no 'eye' for a painting.* In later decades Blunt seems to have quietly come broadly to accept Mahon's chronology of the early years, as most art historians currently do – though he never publicly admitted it, just as he never acknowledged that Mahon was right about the *Rebecca*, which is now accepted as the Cassiano dal Pozzo picture of around 1627.

Perhaps Mahon also made Blunt realize that he had divided his favourite painter in two, just as he had divided himself. He had separated Poussin's meaning and iconography from the way the pictures had actually been painted: the iconography from the style, the thinking from the feeling – a division which recurs in Poussin studies today, as scholars still tend to concentrate on either the style or the references. In Blunt's 1967 book on Poussin he wrote that he hoped that 'at some time I shall write a book – a much shorter book – in which . . . Poussin's supreme merits as a painter can be made the principal theme'. He never did.

Yet Blunt had undeniably done a great deal of work in rediscovering Poussin's work. 'There is a great deal of difference', Pierre Rosenberg has said, 'between the man reconstructing the ground and the man who arrives on the reconstructed ground.' Whatever Mahon believed about Blunt's work on Poussin, his own work on the artist had been limited to one aspect: connoisseurship. He did nothing to challenge the validity of Blunt's work on Poussin's intentions and his artistic personality. Though both

---

* It has recently been established that Blunt, without realizing it, actually owned another early Poussin, an *Agony in the Garden* which he had attributed to a follower of the artist. In 2001 the painting was confirmed, after restoration, cleaning and the discovery of an autograph on the back of the canvas, to be by Poussin himself. Once again, it seems Blunt had convinced himself that the painting wasn't good enough to be by his favourite painter.

would have hated the fact, to the generations that succeeded them Mahon and Blunt's work on Poussin was complementary. Mahon's Poussin was the young painter of sensual pictures, the fine colourist searching for a style; Blunt's Poussin was the cooler, darker, more thoughtful man of middle and old age. 'In England,' Pierre Rosenberg observed, 'people think too much about Blunt versus Mahon. Mahon arrived at a good moment, he stimulated a lot of thinking. That was good for the subject.' Blunt's art-historical feuds never again reached the same pitch.

When it came out in 1967, *Nicolas Poussin* was hailed by many as a masterpiece. Although many aspects of it have been challenged over the years, it is still the most complete and confident evocation of Poussin's artistic personality. Debates still rage over Poussin's various influences; whether he can truly be seen as an intellectual; whether he was really a Stoic, or whether he might have been influenced by the Jesuits instead, or even by the *libertins*, a small group of semi-heretical, possibly even atheist, radical thinkers who worked in the heart of Rome – an idea Blunt played with but dismissed, fuelling constant speculation that he might have done so for other than scholarly reasons. And the number of paintings included in Poussin's accepted œuvre waxes and wanes, giving the lie to the idea that any attributor is ever infallible. (Currently the Poussin œuvre stands at approximately sixty paintings more than Blunt allowed in his catalogue *raisonné*. It is highly likely that this number will decline during the next twenty years.)

There was something about the kerfuffle with Mahon, combined with new strains that the 1960s had brought, that made Blunt turn away from writing about painting and about iconography. It was as if ideas per se had come to seem too intangible, too unreliable. After 1967, with the exception of his book on *Guernica* and a short monograph on Poussin's drawings, he turned his attention to the austere monochrome solidity of architecture, and the dry factualities of architectural style analysis. 'It was as if', Michael Kitson observed, 'all he could trust to was the art itself.'

17. Penitent Impenitent

'It is true'

The early 1960s were the apotheosis of Blunt's career. The Poussin exhibition of 1960 had been a huge success, and, as art-history courses sprang up all over the country, Blunt's talents as patron and fixer were given free rein. He was asked to advise on almost every new course and every new appointment. Above all, the Courtauld had suddenly made the transition from little-known, though increasingly respected, study centre to full-blown academic success story: applicants were being turned away in droves, the original building was unable to accommodate the existing students, and by 1961 the Institute had colonized the two houses on either side of it in Portman Square.

Blunt's relationship with the Institute had changed. Between 1960 and 1962, Johannes Wilde, Margaret Whinney and Else Scheerer had all retired, and Blunt seemed less and less present at the Institute. He taught only those who studied his particular specialisms. Among his own students, Blunt still inspired intense feelings, though the immediate warmth that his students of the 1950s had witnessed seemed less present. Beyond this circle he was increasingly viewed as an intimidating, distant, slightly mysterious figure, inviting respect and curiosity rather than affection. 'To go to his room to see him was always a little frightening because he was so cold and aloof,' one student of the early 1960s recalled. 'There was not the slightest touch of geniality, no hint of warmth. He seemed to me to be like a man on the run with his guard always up . . . I wouldn't say Blunt was popular at all (he was too distant for that). But we much admired him. We were proud of him.' Some found him actively unfriendly and felt alienated by the Institute's hothouse atmosphere. Others found him almost shy. He would occasionally attempt to engage them in polite conversation after lectures, but eventually he would flee up the stairs to the sanctuary of his office, his black lecture gown and skinny arms and legs making him look like a great black bird.

He seemed more distant and distracted to the staff too – oblivious of the extra hours of teaching that the Institute's sudden success had put on them, and negligent about arranging for salary increases and promotions. Eventually, John Shearman, by then one of Blunt's most senior teachers, took their grievances to him. Mildly embarrassed to be making such demands, Shearman began to describe how little time he had for his young family. To his bewilderment Blunt burst into tears. He bowed to the need for change, and, from 1965, staff vacancies were advertised ('Anthony was horrified') and there were even staff meetings ('Anthony didn't want them. Anthony hated meetings'). Sometimes, indeed, 'it seemed as if he was almost too willing to agree with others and delegate', Alan Bowness, another senior staff member, observed. There were contracts and salaries, and an efficient new bursar, Ron Davies, a former Foreign Office Africa hand with a military bearing and a neat moustache – very un-Courtauld. In hindsight, he was suspected by some former students of being an MI5 plant. He was certainly a symptom of London University's attempts to draw the Courtauld finally into the fold – attempts usually foiled not just by Blunt, but by his staff, who liked the independence they enjoyed.

Among the students, Blunt's withdrawal and inscrutability generated a series of myths and speculations about him – a mystique powerfully fuelled by strange little details that kept coming to light: the acknowledgement to Guy Burgess in *Artistic Theory in Italy*; the oddly confessional annual lecture he gave every year about Communism and the 1930s; the rumours that he held wild homosexual parties. 'We had an intimation that there was more to him than we knew. There was a feeling around that he had trodden on a lot of toes,' recalled one post-graduate of the early 1960s. An American student, Laurie Harwood, became curious about Blunt when a friend of her parents, whom she later realized was 'latently gay', told her he was concerned about her. He had gone to a party of Blunt's at which, he said, there were 'unusual people'. There were more whispers among the students in the late 1960s when a picture of Blunt dressed up as 'Christina Rossetti' did the rounds of the ladies' lavatories. (It was the 1929 photo of Blunt in drag for the *Granta* spoof of *Orlando*.) Other students of the early 1960s had more specific suspicions. Sibylla Jane Flower was sure that Blunt had a secret, 'but we didn't know it had anything to do with espionage ... we had very good antennae but we didn't know'. She was curious about Else Scheerer – 'she was East German and such an incredibly unlikely person to be at the Courtauld' – and about the mild-mannered registrar, Charles Clare: 'under the guise of being stupid he was much brighter. We felt he knew things, but he didn't quite fit. We heard he was sacked for having his hand in the till. We thought there was an antipathy between him and the Blunt/Scheerer camp. We were very, very curious about the Burgess dedication.' There was a story about a feud with the director of the National Gallery, Philip Hendy, that was supposed to date back to differences 'during the war'. There were rumours that Blunt's old friend Ellis Waterhouse was mixed up in something. One of the girls on the Courtauld's switchboard remarked that, whenever Blunt travelled abroad to Italy, packages from abroad followed his return. It was also said that during the war he had been para-chuted into Germany behind enemy lines, which was the reason for his high standing with the royal family.

Among the many rumours was one which had it that Blunt had been a Soviet spy. 'I knew for certain that Blunt was a spy in the Burgess, Philby, Maclean group,' recalled Michael Taylor, who was an undergraduate at the Courtauld in the early 1960s.

I knew MI5 had offered him immunity if he would confess, that he had got up, walked over and poured himself a drink and gone and gazed out of the window for a while before turning around and admitting he was a spy. I knew he had been questioned a number of times over the years and had proved too clever to be trapped. And I knew that the car of the last of the three had been finally located in the car park of the Courtauld Institute galleries ... To me this was common knowledge and it was told to me by a fellow under-graduate in 1961 (or perhaps 1962).

Taylor's recollections betray the problems of hindsight. Blunt would not confess until 1964, and the car story seems to have been a red herring. Taylor did, however, tell many of his fellow students that he had heard that Blunt was a Soviet spy – among them Eric Fernie, who thirty years later became director of the Courtauld himself. Their contemporary Laurie Harwood remembered working in the slide library when a batch of slides were sent off to Russia: '"Oh that just confirms it," we said.' The information seemed exotic rather than sinister. 'If I, who was no one, knew (I took it absolutely for granted)', said Michael Taylor, 'everyone else knew as well.'

How precisely the story came into the Institute is a mystery, but it was probably via a relative or a family friend of some well-connected student of the early 1960s, by which time Blunt's guilt was canteen gossip at MI5. This was how Barbara Murek, who arrived at the Courtauld in 1969, found out. The daughter of a Polish Embassy official, she dined on Friday nights with an old wartime friend of her father's from MI5. 'One night he remarked to me that there is a spy in my school. Who did I think it was. Without even reflecting, I answered, "Sir Anthony." He responded – "Clever Girl!"' Murek already knew the story. 'I no longer remember where I heard it, or which fellow student told me that Sir Anthony was a Russian spy; it did, however, seem to be common knowledge.' In 1970 the art critic Richard Dorment was shown round the Courtauld by a friend. As Blunt shuffled past in his usual uniform of holey old jumper and carpet slippers, Dorment's friend told him, 'That is the great Anthony Blunt. And he's the Fourth Man.'

Not everyone knew. 'I think the information was more common in the upper section [of the undergraduates],' recalled Michael Taylor, 'the undergraduates' common room was very fragmented and cliquish.' Lindsay Stainton, who arrived in 1971 had no idea, 'though we all knew he'd been a left-winger, a fellow-traveller, and that at the time of Burgess and Maclean there'd been police and security people. It seemed rather romantic.' The story appears never to have reached the staff room either, even though the teachers enjoyed speculating about their director's past, and his links with the infamous Guy Burgess.

The year 1963 was a frenetic one for Blunt. He was made Slade Professor of Art History at Oxford. He was awarded an honorary D.Lit. from Durham University. He joined the Treasury committee reviewing the sale of art works by public bodies. He travelled to Jerusalem, Beirut and Athens to advise and speak on art history, made a lecture tour of the Low Countries, taught a summer school at Pennsylvania State University, and sat on a committee selecting contemporary art for an exhibition in Barcelona. And he was dogged by shadows of the past and forebodings of the future.

Early in 1963 he had been confronted at the Travellers Club by a journalist called Douglas Sutherland, who was writing a book about Burgess. Sutherland accused Blunt of being the 'Third Man'. His source was Goronwy Rees, who was recovering from a nervous breakdown which had seen him admitted to a psychiatric hospital. Rees's recovery had done nothing to cool his obsession with Blunt – it seemed to his family to have got worse. Blunt was palpably shaken by Sutherland's accusation. He was speechless for a moment, then stammered a denial, insisting that Burgess's defection had been a complete surprise to him. After several minutes, however, he managed to stop shaking and mumbling and 'told me in a comparatively firm voice that I would hear from his solicitors immediately if his name appeared any more in connection with the case, and beat a hasty retreat'. On 19 April 1963 it was reported in the *Daily Mirror* that Burgess and Maclean were rumoured to be planning to return to England, and that a warrant had been issued for their arrest for breaking the Official Secrets Act. The story was a hoax, possibly instigated by the security services themselves to discourage Burgess from contemplating a return. When the Sutherland book was published, in May, it contained no mention of Blunt, though it did claim that Burgess had been tipped off about Maclean's imminent arrest by an unnamed homosexual former MI5 officer.

On 19 August, while Blunt was in America teaching a summer school at Pennsylvania State University, Burgess died in Moscow at the age of fifty-three. A combination of drink-related disorders – angina, hardening of the arteries, and liver disease – had killed him. His last years had been pitiful. He was often drunk and desperately homesick. The art historian Francis Haskell encountered him shortly before his death. Haskell was in Moscow trying to get his future wife – who was an art historian at the Hermitage – out of the country. He was invited by a friend to a party to celebrate Burgess's birthday. Burgess reminisced about England all night, getting progressively drunker and drunker, until finally he said loudly, apropos of nothing, 'Of course we're bugged in here.' Haskell shrank into a corner, wishing he was somewhere else. 'I know where it is,' shouted Burgess, and he pointed, 'It's up in that corner', and shook his fist at the invisible bug. 'I *hate* Russia, I simply *loathe* Russia. I'm a Communist, of course, but I'm a British Communist, and I *hate* Russia!'

Then on 3 September, barely two weeks later, Louis MacNeice died unexpectedly after a bout of flu turned into pneumonia. Like Burgess, alcohol had played its part in weakening his constitution. Blunt was deeply upset.

Over the winter, he cheered himself with a trip to Rome, where he stayed briefly with Eric Hebborn, who was by now dealing in 'old-master drawings' of his own manufacture. Italy had its magic effect on Blunt. 'He was easy to talk to and very different from the worried, unhappy man Eric and I stayed with in London a few years later,' wrote Hebborn's partner Graham Smith. He admired young men in the street, wandered idiotically around their apartment for a whole day in a fur hat, and planned an opera buffa based on James Thurber's *The Night the Bed Fell*, casting himself as the Father. One evening he held forth for hours on the fantasy of becoming a Roman street singer in a black cloak, giving his renditions of Edith Piaf and Josephine Baker numbers. 'He thought the idea had great potential but wondered if he would have the necessary energy or stamina. "Nevertheless," he said, "I shall mark it down as a possibility for my retirement." ' He was also impressed by a Castiglione drawing Hebborn owned, and offered to buy it. Hebborn refused. It was, according to Graham Smith, a forgery which Hebborn later sold at Christie's.

Blunt's spirits were also lifted that autumn by the rediscovery of a long-lost Poussin. A Courtauld student, Sarah Oppenheim (later, under her married name, Whitfield, to become a distinguished art historian in her own right), had spotted it on a trip to Charleston farmhouse to meet Duncan Grant and study his paintings. Grant and Clive Bell – both now rather doddery – still lived at Charleston, and showed her a painting hanging over the mantelpiece. The picture, which Grant had bought in Paris for £40 forty years before, was a landscape with a man pursued by a snake. Roger Fry had told Grant it was probably by an artist close to Poussin. Oppenheim asked Bell if Blunt had ever seen it. Bell thought not. Would Blunt be interested in seeing it, he wondered. Oppenheim resolved to ask Blunt on her return to London. A few weeks later, she accompanied Blunt to Charleston – his first visit in thirty-five years. Blunt immediately recognized the painting as a Poussin. 'We all just stood there looking at the painting in silence. After a while, he turned to me, put a hand on my shoulder and said, "Thank you, Miss Oppenheim." That was his way of saying that the painting was "the real thing".' He took the picture to London to have it X-rayed, and wrote to Grant, 'I can only say that it is giving me indescribable pleasure, as I have it propped up facing my desk, and it has been universally acclaimed by everyone who has seen it as obviously by Poussin.' Grant said he would need to sell the painting – Charleston was extremely damp and in need of renovation – but he wanted it to go 'to someone who loves it'. Blunt had it valued by Colnaghi's, Christie's, the National Gallery and Tomás Harris. It was Col-naghi's, the most reputable dealer in Bond Street, which came up with the highest figure, of £12,000.

It was obvious that Blunt longed to have it, and in early January 1964 he asked to buy it, pleading that he might be allowed to pay for it in three annual instalments – and keeping studiedly reticent about the fact that Colnaghi's Roddy Thesiger had put in his letter of valuation that the painting might easily get £15,000. Grant agreed. In the midst of the negotiations, a Courtauld student with journalistic ambitions took the story of the rediscovered Poussin to the newspapers. Blunt incorrectly assumed that Oppenheim was the culprit. Stopping her on the stairs one day he said severely, 'I wish you wouldn't talk to journalists.' Though Oppenheim denied the charge, she never felt he quite believed her.

At the end of January, Blunt sent his first cheque for £4,000 to Duncan Grant – telling him that he had never written one for so large an amount – and delightedly took possession of his Poussin. But even this acquisition would not be without its consequences. After his exposure, he would be accused of having cheated Grant out of his picture.

It was in January 1964 that MI5 finally got hold of real evidence that Blunt had been a Soviet spy. The information came from Michael Straight in the USA. In June 1963 the Kennedy adminis-tration had offered him a job as chairman of the National Endowment for the Arts. Straight accepted the job, but began to worry about what an FBI check on his past might turn up. Moreover, McCarthyism had had its day and there was a more liberal atmosphere in Washington. Straight decided it was time to unburden himself.* The FBI, for its own reasons, waited for six months before telling Arthur Martin, the MI5 officer who had worked with the Bureau in the 1950s over the Burgess and Maclean investigation. He was in America to interview John Cairncross, who was in America lecturing on French literature, and whom Martin believed had done a great deal more for the Soviets than the evidence then suggested. The FBI set up a meeting between Straight and Martin. Straight told his story – adding that he would be willing to 'go public and stand up in a British court'.

Blunt's guilt had been common gossip at MI5 for years, ever since a report compiled by the service's counter-intelligence department had concluded that he had almost certainly been involved in Burgess's ring, but there was not enough evidence to try him. Even so, the new evidence was not altogether welcome, for the MI5 Arthur Martin returned to was in the throes of debilitating internal wrangles, the responsibility for which lay in no small part with Martin himself. During the 1950s, with a junior officer called Peter Wright, Martin had become convinced that there were still Soviet moles at large in all areas of British life, that MI5 was being infiltrated at the highest levels, and that a serious investigation was needed. Their views were opposed by many other officers, who felt that the two men were peddling unproven conspiracy theories which would harm the service in the long run. Martin, however, had some support from Dick White, who was now director of MI6. To make matters more complicated, Martin and Wright were beginning to think that Roger Hollis, now MI5's director, might be their prime suspect.

The divisions were all the more bitter because Martin and Wright were perceived, and perceived themselves, as outsiders in the public-school-dominated world of MI5. Martin was a

---

* In his autobiography, Straight claimed that he had made three previous attempts to confess. Several times, he said, he had walked into the British Embassy in Washington DC, but he always weakened at the last minute. In 1948, he had even got his wife to give Blunt and Burgess's names to her analyst, who was married to a British Embassy official. The information was never passed on.

grammar-school boy, Wright's family had been ruined in the Depression and he had got into MI5 as a technician, not an agent. Both felt they were fighting complacency and snobbery as well as Soviet infiltrators. Their opponents believed they had been promoted because of their relentless keenness, and well beyond their limited abilities. The stand off was aggravated by the support Martin and Wright received from the CIA's manipulative counter-intelligence chief, the paranoid Cold War warrior par excellence, James Jesus Angleton. Angleton was convinced that there was a giant and incredibly successful Soviet conspiracy to penetrate Western intelligence at the highest levels. He encouraged Martin's suspicions that there was a senior mole at MI5. He also wanted, according to Wright, to 'swallow MI5 up whole and use it as an Agency outstation'. Unsurprisingly, Angleton's support did not endear Wright and Martin to senior figures at MI5.

Matters were not helped by the fact that by early 1964, thanks to a series of operational cock-ups, British Intelligence's public reputation had taken a terrible drubbing, largely because of a series of high-profile trials involving Soviet spies. In 1961 Gordon Lonsdale, a Russian-born Canadian Soviet agent, was arrested and convicted of espionage. Later the same year George Blake, a member of MI6, was found guilty of spying for the Soviets since the early 1950s, and in 1962, John Vassall, who had been blackmailed by the Soviets into handing over Admiralty secrets, was arrested and convicted. Things were not improved when Kim Philby defected in January 1963. Armed with new evidence that he had been a Soviet spy, Dick White had sent Philby's friend the MI6 agent Nicholas Elliott to Beirut to offer him immunity in return for a confession. Philby confessed, Elliott returned to England, MI6 carelessly failed to contact Philby for another two weeks, and Philby defected. It is distinctly possible that MI6 wanted Philby to leave; the embarrassment of his defection, though great, would nevertheless not be as bad as that caused by arrest and a trial. When he did flee, they were in no hurry to reveal the fact: they kept his disappearance secret until July 1963, when the American press broke the story. Philby's first remark to

Elliott – 'I rather thought it would be you', the words of a man always desperate to prove that he was three steps ahead of everyone else – further fuelled Martin and Wright's suspicions: they concluded that he must have been tipped off.

There was plenty more embarrassment to come. In July 1963 the trial of Giuseppe Martelli, who had been charged with 'preparing' to give the Soviets atom secrets – he had been apprehended before he had managed to do so – collapsed for lack of proof. In August the Profumo affair blew up. John Profumo, a Cabinet Minister, was discovered to be having an affair with a girl called Christine Keeler, who was also sleeping with the Soviet naval attaché – who was a KGB officer. Keeler's 'protector', Stephen Ward, committed suicide the morning he was to due to be sentenced. Profumo, having denied sleeping with Keeler in Parliament, admitted his affair and resigned in ignominy. It transpired that Ward had been encouraged by MI5 to use Keeler as bait for the naval attaché, and that MI6 had known Profumo was involved with her all along.

The information about Blunt, Peter Wright later wrote, was a 'dreadful embarrassment' to MI5. Hollis almost wished it would just go away. Blunt was, after all, no longer a threat, just a potential scandal. That MI5 had suspected him for thirteen years – during which time he had ascended to the top of his profession, accepted a knighthood, and worked for the Queen – simply provided yet another example of the incompetence of British intelligence and another messy scandal for the government. Such a scandal might easily result in the resignations of a whole generation of intelligence bigwigs – including White and Hollis. There was, moreover, no evidence against Blunt apart from Straight's word, which would make a criminal prosecution hard to secure. In America, similar cases where one man's word had been pitted against another's had resulted in the McCarthy witch-hunts. The recent failure to convict Martelli also made the idea of putting Blunt on trial seem particularly unappealing.

Roger Hollis and Dick White were increasingly of the opinion that making British intelligence's misfortunes public just made everyone look bad. This view had been heavily promoted by the former Prime Minister Harold Macmillan, whose own career had been ended by the Profumo scandal. When MI6 had caught George Blake in 1961, Macmillan had suggested that, rather than having a public trial, the story should be be kept quiet and Blake be offered immunity from prosecution in return for a full confession. 'The government could fall on this,' he told Dick White. White refused to cooperate. When John Vassall had been arrested by MI5, Macmillan told Roger Hollis:

I am not at all pleased. When my gamekeeper shoots a fox, he doesn't go and hang it up outside the Master of Foxhounds' drawing room: he buries it out of sight. But you can't shoot a spy as you did in the war. You have to try him ... better to discover him, and then control him, but never catch him.

By the time Philby's guilt had been established, Macmillan was telling White to 'keep a lid on things', and by now White had come to agree with him. He offered Philby immunity in return for total cooperation. White's response on hearing of Philby's defection was 'What a shame we reopened it all, just trouble.'

Hollis, much encouraged by Dick White, decided that Blunt should be offered immunity from prosecution and confidentiality, in return for a confession – as MI6 had tried to arrange with Philby. This would prevent another scandal, not only for MI5, but for the government and Buckingham Palace. MI5 would at last have someone who could tell them about Burgess, Maclean and Philby and the extent of Soviet penetration; the nagging questions plaguing the organization might be laid to rest. Hollis and White persuaded the Home Secretary, Henry Brooke, and the Attorney General, John Hobson, to authorize an offer of immunity to Blunt if he confessed and agreed to cooperate in their investigations.* When Blunt was exposed fifteen years later, the

---

* Brooke did not, however, tell Alec Douglas-Home when the latter became Prime Minister in November 1963. It has been suggested that this was because

juxtaposition of his immunity next to long sentences meted out to George Blake and John Vassall – Blake was given forty-two years – made the decision look like cronyism or worse. The fact was that the offer of immunity suited MI5 and the government quite as much as it suited Blunt. The Americans agreed to it too: their one proviso, Blunt confided to a friend years later, was that he never set foot in the USA again.

The Queen was also informed, according to her one-time private secretary Lord Charteris and to Roy Jenkins, Home Secretary in the Labour government whose victory in the 1964 general election was a direct consequence of the Profumo affair. It is reported that she afterwards never referred to the subject. Sir Michael Adeane, her private secretary, asked what action should be taken against Blunt, and was advised that he should be left where he was. 'Any action', Margaret Thatcher said later, in the speech which finally exposed Blunt in 1979, 'could, of course, have alerted Blunt's former Russian controllers and others who were already under suspicion to the fact that he had confessed.' In the long run, Adeane was given bad advice. Blunt could perfectly well have resigned from the Surveyor's job. Kenneth Clark had left it after ten years, and Blunt could easily have justified his departure on the grounds of his many other obligations – he had not been involved in the Royal Collection's day-to-day running for years. According to Peter Wright, Adeane also told MI5, 'From time to time . . . you may find Blunt referring to an assignment he undertook on behalf of the Palace – a visit to Germany at the end of the war. Please do not pursue this matter. Strictly speaking, it is not relevant to considerations of national security.'

Lord Charteris, who was Adeane's deputy and became the

Douglas-Home had announced that he would set up an Independent Security Commission in January 1964 to review in breaches in intelligence. If he had been told he would have felt obliged to inform the new commission, among whom there were opposition MPs only too keen to maximize the government's embarrassment.

Queen's private secretary in 1968, insisted in later interviews that, with the discovery of his guilt, Buckingham Palace closed its doors to Blunt. This was not entirely true. Blunt continued to meet the Queen at official events. She came to the opening of the Courtauld's new galleries in 1968, and in 1972 she personally congratulated Blunt on his retirement, when the Lord Chamberlain, knowing nothing of his disgrace, offered him the honorary post of Adviser on the Queen's pictures – inadvertently continuing his association with the Palace for another six years. 'I nearly fell off my chair,' remembered Charteris.

> I scuttled round to Cabinet Office – lots of apologies – 'Oh, we'd better leave it.' So he went on being a member of the household, which I think was very wrong. I *was* able to stop him being made a GCVO [Knight Grand Cross of the Royal Victorian Order, a reward for personal service to the monarchy]. I saw Anthony's name at the top of the list and I said, 'We can't do this.'

Away from official events, however, Blunt avoided the Queen. The Louvre's former director, Michel Laclotte, remembered that when Blunt escorted him round Buckingham Palace in the early 1970s he crept round on tiptoe, obviously desperate not to encounter her.

One member of the royal family who continued to be on good terms with Blunt was the Queen Mother. In 1968, for example, after Blunt had shown her round the recently rehung Courtauld Institute Galleries, her private secretary wrote to thank Blunt profusely for the tour – it had been, he told Blunt, 'a great treat'. A week later one of the Queen Mother's ladies-in-waiting wrote asking that she might visit again when the galleries' newest bequest, the Spooner collection of English watercolours, went on show. Very occasionally Blunt would share a box with the Queen Mother at the opera.

It seems that Blunt also continued to perform the odd tricky diplomatic mission on behalf of the Palace. In the summer of 1963, only a few months before his confession, he had apparently quietly acted on behalf of the royal family to purchase a series of drawings that Stephen Ward – then a key witness in the Profumo affair – had made of the Duke of Edinburgh. In the late 1960s the journalist Barrie Penrose uncovered a story about the discovery, in the basement of a Cork Street gallery, of a sheaf of old-master drawings which had the stamp of the Royal Collection on them. Penrose called the Surveyor's office and got through to Blunt, who recognized the drawings immediately and said that they had been sold in the 1920s. Could the Palace have them back? Rex Nankevell, the gallery's owner, was understood to be happy to leave them to the Palace in his will, but had always fancied a knighthood. Penrose passed the information on to Blunt, who was entirely calm about the request. 'He made a note of it,' Penrose recalled. 'And the interesting thing is, Rex Nankevell was knighted.'

One of the many conspiracy theories surrounding Blunt is that he obtained his immunity from prosecution by threatening to expose his knowledge – and perhaps even provide documentary proof – that the Duke of Windsor had been plotting with the Nazis during the Second World War, information that (according to this theory) he acquired on his mission to Germany for the Palace in 1945. The arguments for this hardly bear scrutiny. First, the Duke's German sympathies were hardly a secret. Second, if Blunt had been exposed and publicly disgraced as a spy, it is hard to imagine that anything he could have said that was meant to be damaging to the royal family would have stood up against the word of the Palace, especially in the forelock-tugging days of the 1960s. Finally, if Blunt was in possession of such overwhelming proof of the Duke of Windsor's guilt, and it was regarded as such powerful leverage, how was it that he was ever exposed at all?

When Blunt eventually was exposed, MI5 and the government did nothing to discourage these fantastic rumours. The idea that Blunt had extracted his immunity by threat played to their advantage. It helped distract attention from the fact that they had offered Blunt immunity because doing so was convenient.

*

On 23 April 1964 Arthur Martin went to see Blunt to offer him MI5's deal. It was an encounter he never forgot. He sat down in the living room of Blunt's flat and asked if he might use a tape recorder. Blunt, mystified, agreed. Martin took a deep breath and announced that he had unequivocal evidence that Blunt had been a Soviet agent during the war. Blunt denied it, as he always had before. Martin suggested he might change his mind. 'I think I said something like: I saw Mr Straight the other day and he told me about his relations with you and the Russians.' Blunt seemed quite unmoved, and Martin began to lose heart. He told Blunt that he had been authorized by the Attorney General to give him immunity from prosecution. Blunt, blank and unreadable, walked to the window, poured himself a large drink, paused long and dramatically, turned round and said, 'It is true.'

Thus began eight years of interviews. Once a month or more, Blunt met up with his interrogators, first Arthur Martin, then Peter Wright, who taped hours of recordings, first at MI5 safe houses, later at Blunt's flat. 'He was a very likeable man,' Martin said later. 'But I never felt that he really came clean with me . . . I had the feeling that he felt he had done the right thing by becoming a Communist.' Martin also believed, as did Peter Wright, that, however relieved Blunt might have been by Burgess's death, he had been genuinely upset by his decline and end. 'Philby had been embarrassed by Burgess, I don't think Blunt was. He was sorry to see a friend disintegrate like that.'

Far from being a release for Blunt, the confession seemed to take a harsh toll on his health. Two weeks after he met Martin he went to his doctor, anxious, eczematic and peeing blood. 'He is a thin man who has had considerable tension, and has been drinking half a bottle of whisky a day. I understand that he does not eat an adequate amount of fruit and vegetables. He tells me that he has had some blood, presumably from the genital tract, which is to be investigated.' Martin could see that Blunt was not as calm as he liked to seem. 'Sometimes he would look ghastly when we met and would say that he had had a ghastly night. He had obviously been drinking a good deal.'

According to Martin, by the end of 1964 Blunt had identified his NKVD case officers from photographs. He had confirmed that he had given details of MI5's internal structure and operations to the Soviets, including how the 'watcher' service worked, that he had handed over what he could of German radio intercepts, and that he had told them that the CPGB headquarters was being bugged. He admitted that he had known before the war that Philby and Maclean had been recruited as Soviet agents, that he had recruited Leo Long and that he knew about John Cairncross. He volunteered that he had met Yuri Modin in 1954 and acted as his courier to Philby. According to Peter Wright, both Long and Cairncross were brought in for questioning, and – confident that they, like Blunt, must be safe from prosecution – confessed their involvement. Then Blunt ran out of things to say.

For Arthur Martin and Peter Wright the interrogations had only just begun. Martin was convinced that Blunt had been allowed to extricate himself from MI5 because the Soviets had another agent in place. Blunt had no answer to this. There was also the question of how Maclean had known about his arrest – which Blunt could answer – and whether Philby too had been tipped off, which he could not and did not. As it happens, the most likely explanation is that Philby was tipped off by MI6. Most of all, Martin and Wright wanted evidence of the big conspiracy and more names. They were constantly disappointed. 'When we threw new information at him,' Martin remembered, 'he would say that he had forgotten about it. The information didn't flow from him at all.' Blunt had told him on that first meeting, when he had agreed to confess, that he would find it very difficult to betray his friends, adding, 'I suppose most of my friends have drifted away now.' It seemed to Martin and Wright that Blunt never informed on anyone about whom they did not already have suspicions or who, for that matter, was not already safely dead.

In order to try to stimulate Blunt's memory, Martin arranged for Michael Straight to come to London to meet him in the September after he had confessed. In Straight's account, far from being bitter or hostile at his betrayal, Blunt actually thanked him. 'I just wanted to tell you: Thank God you did what you did! . . . When they said that you had told them your story, it lifted a heavy burden from my shoulders. I was immensely relieved.' He asked Straight what had made him go to the authorities. Straight wrote, ' "Because of the arts," I said. "Because our government finally decided to support the arts. Kennedy was going to make me the head of his new arts agency," I added. "That forced the question." ' In an interview in 1980, some years before Straight's book came out, Blunt gave a different version of the meeting. He said that Straight completely avoided the subject of his FBI statement and talked about a seventeenth-century painting he had recently acquired. In Blunt's annotated copy of Straight's autobiography (Straight sent Blunt a copy inscribed, 'Anthony from Michael 1983. Too bad – that we had only one life to live'; Blunt subbed the book's spelling mistakes) he marked Straight's account of their meeting with a 'NO!', and with question marks all the way down the page. At the bottom Blunt wrote, 'We actually talked about a painting by Bellaye that he'd bought.' Arthur Martin was equally dismissive of the meeting. 'It was a total flop. The two men were completely incompatible. They must have had something in common when they were undergraduates. But that had gone by 1964.' They never met again.

Towards the end of 1964 the divisions in MI5 grew worse and Martin was finally suspended for being a disruptive influence and contradicting a senior officer. He was seconded to Dick White's MI6. Hollis retired under a cloud the following year and Peter Wright was made Blunt's chief interrogator. Apart from Arthur Martin's recollections, Wright's book *Spycatcher*, his memoir of his career in MI5 from the 1950s to the 1970s, provides the only account of Blunt's interrogation. Before it came out, in 1987, the British government tried, disastrously, to prevent its publication in Australia on the grounds that it contravened the Official Secrets Act. This gave the book a notoriety that guaranteed huge sales, as well as a rather spurious credibility. In fact, while much of it was broadly true, plenty of details and dates were not, and its interpretations were wide open to dispute. Wright, an inveterate conspiracy-theorist, believed that Hugh Gaitskell had been poisoned by the KGB, that Harold Wilson had been a KGB plant, and that Hollis was a double agent. He also believed there was a massive conspiracy to infiltrate university-educated Soviet moles into government and the intelligence services. This, for him, explained Britain's post-colonial, post-war decline. That his theories were overblown, to say the least, was confirmed by the publication of Andrew and Mitrokhin's *The Mitrokhin Archive* in 1999, which showed that the greatest undiscovered threats to post-war British security were a bearded academic from Hull and a grandmother from south London. Wright also felt he had been ill-treated by MI5, which had failed to pay him a proper retirement pension – a fact about which he was very bitter. Over the years, he had become convinced not only that Blunt had never been totally honest with him, but that he had found proof of his conspiracy, and that his findings had been ignored. For several years before he wrote *Spycatcher* Wright had been giving off-the-record briefings to Fleet Street journalists such as the espionage writer Chapman Pincher. He was not averse to changing details in order to sound more convincing. In *Spycatcher* he distorted events and muddled sources in order to beef up his story.

Blunt's debriefing by Wright was in once sense almost comically similar to his dealings with the NKVD. Just as he had been unable to provide the Soviets with evidence of Western plots against them of whose existence they were a priori convinced, so he would not – and almost certainly could not – give Wright his giant conspiracy. He told Wright that his chief suspects, Tomás Harris, and Blunt's old Cambridge contemporaries Alister Watson and Dennis Proctor – had not been involved. Wright, in response, began a mass interrogation of Blunt's old acquaintances and contemporaries, among them Victor Rothschild, John Hilton, Charles Madge, Isaiah Berlin, Arthur Marshall, Stuart Hampshire, as well as Watson and Proctor themselves.

He was too late to talk to Tomás Harris, who had died in a car crash in Majorca in early 1964. The timing of his death – a year after Philby absconded; a few months before Blunt confessed – has led to suggestions that he might have been assassinated, though no good reason for an assassination has ever been suggested: if him, why not Blunt? Whether foul play was involved has never been proved. What seems most likely is that Harris was drunk. In semi-retirement in Majorca he had been increasing his already prodigious intake. In contrast to his charming and very controlled sobriety, he became aggressive and out of control when inebriated, and in the years before his death his friend and Intelligence colleague Desmond Bristow had witnessed a drunken Harris start several bitter agruments, and a violent fight, with his wife, Hilda. Bristow later reported Hilda's account of the accident. On the way home from Palma, Majorca's main town, after 'a couple of drinks' and a quarrel, Harris had driven 'like hell' along the notoriously twisting coast road, and when she had asked him to slow down he had just driven faster. Eventually he had skidded into a tree. Hilda, thrown out of the car by the collision, had survived. Harris had died at once.* Blunt honoured his dead friend on several occasions. In 1965 he tried to get the BBC to commission him to give a talk on Harris's posthumously published study of Goya's etchings: 'It is an astonishing piece of work, and he was a very remarkable person,' he told his producer. He wrote a fulsome entry on Harris for the *Dictionary of National Biography*, and in 1975 he even put on a exhibition of Harris' own paintings at the Courtauld, prompting certain Courtauld wits to say that Blunt must have been very deeply in Harris's debt to exhibit so many awful pictures.

For seven years MI5 pored over the careers of Oxbridge students of the 1930s.† Through the thin walls of 21 Portman

---

* In other versions of the story it has been suggested that Harris collided with a mysterious other car – the presence of another car on Majorca's quiet roads in the early 1960s being sufficiently out of the ordinary to suggest that something sinister had been afoot.

† In 1971 MI5 contacted Charles Rycroft, who had gone to Russia with Blunt in 1935, after he published 'Memoirs of an Old Bolshevik' in *New Society*. 'A friend in MI6 rang me up and asked if I would be prepared to be quizzed by

Square, which had recently been leased by the ever-expanding Courtauld, Wright installed microphones in the chimney of the room Blunt used for entertaining and working. (The microphones resurfaced in the late 1990s, when No. 20 was renovated and turned into a club.) He also condemned Blunt to seven years of monthly meetings.

Wright wrote later:

We had to adopt a subtle approach, in an attempt to play on his character. I could tell that Blunt wanted to be thought helpful, even where it was clear that he was not. Moreover, he disliked intensely being caught in a lie. We had to extract intelligence from him by a slow process of cumulative pressure ... Often we drank, he gin and I Scotch; always we talked, about the 1930s, about the KGB, about espionage and friendship, love and betrayal. They remain for me among the most vivid encounters of my life.

Writing of *Spycatcher*, Anita Brookner described 'the semi-amorous and symbiotic relationship between spycatcher and victim'. Wright certainly seems to have been fascinated by his quarry:

Blunt was one of the most elegant, charming, and cultivated men I have met ... the most striking thing about Blunt was the contradiction between his evident strength of character and his curious vulnerability. It was this contradiction which caused people of both sexes to fall in love with him ... Blunt was capable of slipping from art historian and scholar one minute, to intelligence bureaucrat the next, to spy, to waspish homosexual, to languid establishmentarian. But the roles took their toll on him as a man. I realized soon after

MI5. They wanted me to identify a lot of photographs of people. I knew quite a lot of them actually. They asked me who as a psychologist I thought could possibly be the Fourth Man. I remember going to great pains to say it couldn't be Anthony Blunt – they made a bit of a fool of me. I thought they were rather nice, lonely people these spies. One man took me out for dinner three or four times for no good reason other than to chat.'

we began meeting that Blunt, far from being liberated by the immunity offer, continued to carry a heavy burden. It was not a burden of guilt, for he felt none ... His burden was the weight of obligation placed on him by those friends, accomplices, and lovers whose secrets he knew, and which he felt himself bound to keep.

We'll never know whether Blunt was equally impressed by Wright. In an interview in 1980 he insisted that, having decided to cooperate with MI5, he had done so wholeheartedly, and that he had been on good terms with Wright, to the point of exchanging Christmas cards. In *Spycatcher* Wright recounted bits of gossip which suggested that intimacies had been imparted. There was a story about Burgess planning to woo and marry Clarissa Churchill, the niece of Winston Churchill, during the war – she later married Burgess's acquaintance Anthony Eden. Wright claimed that Blunt had told him he had had two affairs with women. He believed that one of these had been Tess Rothschild, before she married Victor; she had always refused to believe the rumours of Blunt's guilt. The Rothschilds were told that he had confessed because they had known Blunt had been in MI5 during the war. 'Tess did not cry; she just went terribly pale, and sat hunched up and frozen, her eyes staring at me as she listened ... "All those years," she whispered, "And I never suspected a thing."' Victor described the knowledge as 'devastating, crushing and beyond belief'. Secretly Wright added the Rothschilds to his list of suspects. This was to prove horribly ironic, as it was Victor Rothschild who paid for Wright's trips from his retirement in Australia to London in the 1980s, to speak to journalists. Rothschild misguidedly hoped that Wright would clear him of the suspicions that had clung to him since Blunt had been exposed. Wright nobly repaid the assistance by being careful to express his own suspicions about the Rothschilds only when speaking off the record.

Among his other assertions in *Spycatcher*, Wright claimed that Blunt had had an affair with the German aristocrat and anti-Nazi

Gans zu Putlitz – for which there is no evidence – and stated that
Putlitz had definitely been a Soviet spy. He implied that Blunt had
confirmed that Burgess's Foreign Office friend Tom Wylie had
been a Soviet spy. He said Blunt had accepted responsibility for
telling the NKVD the identity of 'Gibby's spy', an agent in the
Kremlin who had given Politburo documents to MI6 before the
war. It now appears that during the period that Blunt was passing
information to the Soviets there was no spy in Moscow for him
to betray. Wright also claimed that he had extracted 'partial
confessions' from both Alister Watson and Dennis Proctor. He
reported that Blunt had unwillingly acknowledged that Watson
must have been an NKVD plant too: ' "I suppose you're right,"
. . . his eyes gleaming with emotion. "I suppose he must be one of
us, but I never recruited him, and Guy never told me he had." '
He had Blunt say, damningly, of Proctor, 'All I can say is he must
have been the best source Guy ever had. But I didn't know what
role he was playing.' Wright ensured that Watson, who worked
in a secret department at the Admiralty, was demoted and lost his
security clearance. In the early 1980s he told journalists that
Watson had definitely been a spy. After *Spycatcher* was published,
Watson and Proctor denied utterly that they had confessed anything to Wright. While it seems possible that Watson was
approached by the Soviets in the 1930s – perhaps at Kim Philby's
suggestion – no evidence has come to light which proves that he
actually did become a source. The Russian Intelligence Archives
suggest that Burgess used Dennis Proctor as an unwitting source,
just as he used Harold Nicolson and Tom Wylie.

It's impossible to know the extent to which Blunt was lying
and playing with Wright; whether he succumbed, as Anita Brookner speculated, to the peculiar closeness of the interrogation
process, or whether he just saw Wright as an interminable pest.
Arthur Martin observed that Blunt often seemed mildly amused
by his interrogations. He liked playing games. It must have been
a great temptation to play with Wright, the man obsessed with a
conspiracy which didn't exist, who barely seemed to understand
the difference between a fellow-traveller and a spy, and who

prided himself on his ability to play mind games as well as anyone. Blunt certainly lied when he claimed, as Wright reported, that he had stopped working for the Soviets after 1945. It may also be significant that, while Wright was certain that the German Gans zu Putlitz had been an agent for the Soviets, there is no mention in *Spycatcher* of Burgess's much closer relationships with Andrew Revai or Eric Kessler, whom he apparently recruited in 1939.

Perhaps the most unlikely person whom Wright pulled into his web was Phoebe Pool – still besotted with Blunt, but increasingly deaf and subject to ever more acute depressive periods. Wright convinced himself she was the link between Blunt and what he described as the Oxford Ring, a group he believed must have existed in tandem with the one at Cambridge, though he never found solid evidence of this. In *Spycatcher* he wrote that 'the first hard source on the Oxford Ring came from a colleague of Blunt's at the Courtauld Institute, Phoebe Pool. Blunt admitted that she had been his courier during the 1930s.'

This was not true. For one thing, Blunt had nothing to pass to the Soviets in the 1930s; moreover, he had barely known Pool at the time. It was only after she began her affair with William Coldstream in the late 1940s that Pool got to know Blunt well. Also, Wright's 'hard evidence' of Oxford Communists actually came from Jenifer Hart, née Williams, an Oxford historian who had married an MI5 colleague of Blunt's, the Oxford law professor Herbert Hart. At a party in the mid-1960s she had talked a little too volubly about Communism in the 1930s. MI5 had contacted her and asked if she would tell them what she knew. 'I felt I had nothing to hide. I spoke very frankly. They were fascinated,' Hart remembered. She had joined the Communist party after she had left Oxford in 1935, and had been told by a senior Party member, Bernard Floud, that if she wanted to follow her ambition and join the Civil Service she should become a secret member, which meant apart from keeping her political views to herself, cutting herself off from her friends in the Party. Later on she had been introduced via a trade unionist, Arthur Wynn, to an eastern European called 'Otto' – almost certainly Arnold Deutsch – whom she met a couple of times in London parks. Isolated from the very thing that had drawn her into politics to begin with, Hart had felt increasingly uncomfortable with the arrangement, and found 'Otto' distinctly creepy. She severed the connection and left the Party. Once they had heard her story, Hart said, MI5

> tried to follow up everyone I'd ever known at Somerville. I tried to tell them that just because someone knew me at Somerville didn't mean they were a dangerous spy. Peter Wright wouldn't believe that I hadn't given anything away to the Russians. I had occasionally been on the Civil Service selection board. Wright got me taken off. I didn't like him. He put the most sinister turn on everything.

Phoebe Pool had been one of Jenifer Hart's best friends at Oxford – Hart had saved her from a suicide attempt in 1934. Now Pool was at the Courtauld. Wright drew his conclusions. Hart was a Communist, therefore Pool was a Communist – even though all Pool's friends knew that she had never taken any interest in politics, at Oxford or later. Her passion was for literature and art, her energy channelled into managing her depressions. In *Spycatcher*, Wright claimed that he had wanted to question her but that Blunt had said 'she was a neurotic, and already in the process of a nervous breakdown. He said that she would clam up, or worse, if I spoke to her directly.' Wright claimed that Blunt arranged for Anita Brookner to relay his questions to her, and that Pool 'told Anita Brookner that she used to run messages for Otto to two brothers, Peter and Bernard Floud ... Pool also said a young woman, Jennifer [*sic*] Fisher Williams, was involved, and urged Brookner to ensure that "Andy Cohen", the senior diplomat Sir Andrew Cohen [another of Wright's targets], was warned too, as he was also at risk.'* When

---

* Wright also gave a slightly different version of this story to Chapman Pincher. See Pincher's *Too Secret, Too Long*, p. 38.

Spycatcher was published and Anita Brookner heard this story, she felt that Blunt had used her badly. But her memory of the one occasion when she visited Pool on Blunt's behalf was very different from Wright's account. Pool was in a psychiatric ward.

> Various people from the Courtauld were detailed to go and see her. Alan Bowness went. I think Blunt went to see her once. It was very distressing and frightening. Phoebe was incoherent, incapable of speaking above a rambling whisper. There was no doubt that she had deteriorated from the distracted creature she habitually seemed to her friends. Accurate reporting was so far out of the question as to be irrelevant. She knew who I was, but that was all. When I got back to the Institute Blunt said, 'What's she talking about, is she mentioning any names?' I couldn't remember any names – Gabriel, maybe – but I may have misheard that.

As for 'Bernard Floud', Brookner was sure she had heard nothing so coherent.

According to Wright, Bernard Floud was soon afterwards interviewed by MI5, and then committed suicide.

> Not long after, Blunt telephoned me with more bad news.
> 'Phoebe's dead,' he said.
> 'Good God, how?' I gasped.
> 'She threw herself under a tube . . .'

Wright concluded, 'Three deaths [Andrew Cohen also died, of a heart attack, in the mid-1960s], two of which were suicides, in a small group of people, at a time when we were actively investigating them, seemed far more than bad luck. MI5 were terrified that it would be linked publicly with the deaths, and all further work was suspended.'

In fact the synchronicity was not nearly as neat as Wright suggested. Brookner dated her visit to the asylum to about 1965. Floud committed suicide in 1967. According to many of his friends, he had been plunged into a depression by his wife's recent death, and had decided to kill himself well before his interrogation. It was four years later that Phoebe Pool committed suicide, in November 1971. As the 1960s progressed, her black periods had become more and more frequent, she was harder and harder to be with, and she spent more and more time in hospital. Chapman Pincher, Wright's one-time confidant wrote, 'Whether Blunt felt any responsibility for her suicide will never be known but his interrogators did not notice any sign of remorse.' At the Courtauld his distress at her death was no secret. She left him a small painting by Coldstream.

It is possible that Pool did know something about Blunt's past. Her old friends like Jenifer Hart always felt she could not have been a witting spy, but that she would have done anything for Blunt. In hindsight, some of Pool's Courtauld colleagues remembered that in her good periods, after a few drinks, she would start to hint about big secrets in Blunt's past. 'She would often be on the point of telling you something. It was like someone pushing a titbit across the table at you and then snatching it away,' remembered Michael Kitson. In 1961 she had contributed a small ad pointedly aimed at Blunt, to a spoof issue of the *Burlington Magazine* – 'something along the lines of "Art historian, having to leave the country in a hurry, wishes to dispose of complete set of the Warburg and Courtauld journals." This was shown to Anthony and he was very, very unamused.'

Whether or not Blunt was playing with Wright, the confessions were a constant strain upon him. From 1963 he was regularly prescribed Seconal, a tranquillizer sometimes used as a sleeping tablet, and occasionally Equanil, another used to treat anxiety disorders, which he continued to take into the 1980s. He continued to drink heavily though he only rarely showed any ill-effects; only a very few people had ever seen him falling down drunk, Barbara Proctor was one, Hugh Honour another, and they were memorably unusual and infrequent occasions. There were sudden unexpected bouts of tears. He cried when John Shearman asked him for a reduction in teaching hours. He cried when John Golding told him Phoebe Pool had committed suicide. He burst into tears in front of Graham Smith while showing him a photograph of John Gaskin as the handsome young man he no longer was. (Smith wrote, cruelly, 'There was no connection between the face of that young, beautiful man and the stooping, shrunken, drink-bloated face of Anthony's John, mincing spite-fully about the flat, complaining and bitching.') Hebborn and Smith felt that Blunt's unhappiness and strain – ever more evident as the 1960s progressed – were largely due to Gaskin, whom they found increasingly difficult. This did not prevent Hebborn from using Gaskin from time to time to sell pictures and sculptures to London dealers. In his autobiography, Smith recounted a horrible scene from the late 1960s when a drunken, hysterical Gaskin, shrugging off Blunt's attempts to calm him, started to talk about a French former boyfriend of Blunt's:

'All big eyes and butter wouldn't melt in her mouth. I could see what was going on and I soon put an end to her. I wasn't having any bloody French bitch putting on airs around here! ... Giving him ideas she was, Miss French. Making him think he was a man. He tried to bugger me. *Look* at him. Trying it on with *me*. Can you imagine *him* doing *me*?' He stared at Anthony with undisguised hatred.

Throughout the years of interrogation, Blunt's public life continued to bear fruit. In 1967 he celebrated his sixtieth birthday, and his twentieth year as director of the Courtauld. There was a party and a Festschrift volume of essays: *Studies in Renaissance and Baroque Art Presented to Anthony Blunt on his 60th Birthday*. The Courtauld galleries reopened to show the new Gambier-Parry bequest – 'One of the best things to have happened in London since the war,' the *Sunday Times* announced. The Poussin monograph was published to admiring reviews. But 1967 was also the year in which, from Moscow, Kim Philby published his autobiography, *My Silent War*, a deadpan portrait of MI6 as a club of upper-class idiots, with an enthusiastic preface by his old friend Graham Greene. Its criticism of both British intelligence and the upper echelons of the Establishment chimed with the rise of what was being called the counter-culture, growing opposition to the Vietnam War, student demonstrations. (The closest the Courtauld students came to taking to the streets was to protest at the possible sale abroad of Titian's *Diana and Actaeon*. Direct action took the form of a mass exodus to Florence to help after the 1966 floods; the students were put up by Violet Trefusis, the now rather elderly one-time amour of Vita Sackville-West.) The following year, John Le Carré's foreword to the book *Philby: The Spy Who Betrayed a Generation*, by the *Sunday Times*'s Insight team, argued that in Philby the fossilized, smug British Establishment got the spy it deserved. 'I do not much believe in the political motive of Kim Philby; but I am sure that the British secret service kept it alive as no other environment could have done . . . Behind the sealed doors, puzzled men could take refuge from the swiftly changing world.' Philby threatened to become a cult figure. In response to this unexpected turn of events, 'Whitehall' decided that it must override its usual reticence on intelligence matters and act to squash any claims to virtue or principle on Philby's part. Media briefers began to push the line that Philby had caused real damage to the security of the state and had put lives in danger. When Blunt's turn in the spotlight came, the briefers would be ready to quash any murmurings of sympathy.

18. Traitor

'the spy with no shame'

In 1972 Blunt's health problems took their most serious form to date. He was diagnosed with bowel cancer, and was not expected to survive. MI5 made plans in preparation for his death, when his story would be made public. A former Cabinet secretary, Burke Trend, reviewed the evidence about Blunt. A file called 'When Blunt Dies', recounting the story, and including allegations against other people linked to Blunt, was compiled. According to Lord Hunt, the Cabinet Secretary of the time, it made pretty dull reading, and concluded that there was no way of knowing if Blunt had told all he knew. But Blunt didn't die. In August he had major abdominal surgery to remove the cancer. The day after the operation he was found dictating letters in bed.

No amount of convalescence could cure his other physical ailment: the deterioration of his eyesight – something he did his utmost to hide. By 1975 cataracts rendered him almost unable to distinguish colours and to see anything clearly except at very close range. Rather than admit his disability, he described buildings and pictures from memory. On a trip to Rome in 1976 with the Courtauld's summer school, the trip's organizer, Barbara Robertson, whispered Latin inscriptions that he could no longer see, so no one would realize, and he translated them. On another occasion, to his acute embarrassment, he mistook a student for a visiting lecturer. It was not until 1977 that the first of the cataracts was removed. After the operation Blunt went straight to see the

Poussins at Dulwich Picture Gallery. He told John Golding, 'You cannot imagine what it's like to see blue again.'

A series of deaths left him increasingly isolated. In 1969, at the age of ninety, Hilda had finally died in Kingston hospital announcing to her sons in her final delirium that she was in Russia, the food was 'simply disgusting', and the royal family were in attendance. Johannes Wilde died in 1970, Phoebe Pool in 1971, and Rudi Wittkower in 1972 – not long before Blunt's discovery of his cancer. In an attempt to express his distress, Blunt wrote an inarticulate letter to Margot: 'I find it almost impossible – One can never express what one feels, everything one says seems inadequate and can't possibly – one feels – develop in any way which is at all . . .' He couldn't finish the sentence. He was barely speaking to Ellis Waterhouse. There had been an argument the cause of which the two men never admitted. It was probably about Blunt's dissatisfaction with Waterhouse's work on the Waddesdon painting catalogue he had entrusted to him. Not was he speaking to Eric Hebborn. It was noticed at the Courtauld that the homosexual parties had stopped some years before and young men no longer turned up on the doorstep.

Perhaps it was as a result of these intimations of mortality that in the early 1970s Blunt began to lecture on his last great artistic passion, Francesco Borromini, the brilliant, depressive architect of seventeenth-century baroque Rome. Blunt still made a remarkable figure, one of his audience remarked. He was like a thin, graceful seahorse: 'his posture was exactly like that; and he was slim and slightly horny, crustacea-like. He would wear grey suits that gave him a sort of silvery-grey submarine appearance.' But what struck his audience most forcibly about the lectures was the extent to which they were self-revelatory.

'It was the most highly charged lecture I ever heard him deliver,' Peter Kidson later observed. 'At the time I thought it was the anguish of letting go after thirty years; but I later realized that it was as near as he ever came to revealing the existence of deeper secrets.' Such feelings could only be touched on vicariously, through his identification with a seventeenth-century kindred spirit.

Blunt identified with Borromini's passion for mathematics and revelled in his ingenuity with form, describing his architecture as one 'in which the essentially Baroque feature of movement is given its most brilliant expression, undisturbed by the distractions of colour, richness of materials or drama. One looks at Bernini's buildings with the eyes; one feels Borromini's with the whole body.' But he also identified with Borromini's 'melancholy, nervous and uncompromising' temperament, the 'maniacal concentration' he required to create, and the creeping neurotic misanthropy that came to dominate him until, embittered and maddened by failure, at the of sixty-eight he tried to fall on his sword. But the attempt was botched, and as he bled slowly to death Borromini dictated an almost frighteningly clear-headed account of his suicide. In death he had been excoriated as the destroyer and corrupter of the natural laws of architecture: 'the great anarchist of architecture, the man who overthrew all the laws of the Ancients and replaced them with disorder'; a genius who had destroyed his talent by breaking all the rules. In the lectures Blunt dwelt particularly on Borromini's decline and death. 'It was as if', one listener observed, 'he anticipated dying at the same age.'

In the book he wrote about Borromini, which was published in 1979, however, this intensity was excised. What was left was an admirable synthesis of current research on the architect with a few interesting ideas about him that were yet to be proved. (Blunt's theories that Borromini was influenced by Galileo would be established by subsequent researchers.) His previous book, *Neapolitan Baroque and Rococo Architecture*, published in 1975, was heavy, encyclopedic, useful, and dull for any but the most committed academic rococophile. *Borromini* was comparably uninspired. This, according to Neil MacGregor, was to be expected. 'To write about Borromini in the terms he spoke about him would have been revealing more than he chose to, firstly because of questions of decorum, which he felt strongly about, but also questions of sheer discomfort. It would have been too painful to write.'

Blunt retired from the Courtauld in 1974, aged sixty-seven. In the *Burlington Magazine*, Ben Nicolson devoted an admiring editorial to him: 'Blunt above all turned [the Courtauld] into what it now represents . . . his contribution to British art history has surely been greater than that of another single person, in ways that are not easy to define because he has never been a demonstrative man who laid down hard and fast rules, but silently set an example to be silently followed.' With unconscious irony he praised Blunt's 'passionate addiction to the truth about the past'. The Courtauld staff and favourite students gave Blunt a party and bought him a television set. 'We are going to watch *Match of the Day*,' he told his incredulous audience, and seemed profusely grateful, though it was noted afterwards that he had failed to thank Margaret Whinney and Else Scheerer, both present and dressed in their best.

Retirement meant leaving the Courtauld flat, Blunt's home for over twenty-five years (though more or less every visitor now commented on the appalling spartanness of the kitchen and the frightening primitiveness of the lavatory). Blunt and Gaskin moved into a flat in a dreary 1930s block in Bayswater called Portsea Hall, equidistant between the Courtauld and Blunt's childhood home in Paddington. To pay for it and to supplement his pension, which was around a seventh of his Courtauld salary, Blunt had to sell one of his Poussins. After much hesitation and deliberation, he chose to part with the painting he had bought from Duncan Grant nearly ten years before. Inflation and rising art prices had driven the value of the painting, bought for £12,000, to over £100,000. Grant viewed this with 'philosophic forbearance', which led some to feel that he had been cheated.

In the end Goronwy Rees had his revenge. Over the years, he had never lost his obsession with Blunt and had tried several times to force the spotlight on to him, but he was always hampered by an inability to be direct about his accusations. His 1972 memoir *A Chapter of Accidents* – dominated by his portrait of Burgess as a vivid, manipulative, chaotic succubus – failed to name Blunt, but featured him as a number of different unnamed individuals. In 1977 Rees told *The Times* that the Fourth Man in Burgess and Maclean's ring had taught French at Cambridge and that his name had five letters and began with 'B'. (Or at least it was 'that twister Rees' whom Dadie Rylands held responsible when *The Times* claimed that Donald Beves, a blameless elderly language don from King's, was the Fourth Man.) What changed things was Rees's diagnosis in 1978 with terminal cancer, which, following on the death of his wife in 1976, made him feel he no longer had anything to lose. In 1978 he met Andrew Boyle, a radio journalist who had been commissioned to write a book about the Cambridge spies. Boyle had heard rumours about Blunt, and Rees was now ready to pour out his story. Unbeknown to Rees, Boyle had also persuaded several retired intelligence officers who had known about Blunt, including Dick White, to answer his questions.

Blunt first heard the rumours that a story was brewing about him in late 1978. He was told by a former pupil, Alistair Laing, who had had it from the art historian Hugh Honour, who in turn had heard it from the society hostess Pamela Berry – wife of the proprietor of the *Daily Telegraph*. Other events conspired for a time to distract him. Ben Nicolson died of a heart attack in the street, and Blunt's elderly mentor Andrew Gow – now so curmudgeonly that Blunt was almost his only regular visitor – died in Cambridge. Peter Montgomery had begun to sink into senile dementia, and was visited by terrible fits of anxiety. Eventually Blunt called Dennis Proctor and asked him for advice – admitting in the process that he had been involved in Burgess's schemes, though he gave no details. Proctor recommended a solicitor familiar with high profile cases, Michael Rubinstein. In November, Blunt gave his notice as Adviser to the Royal Collection. The Royal Librarian, Robin Mackworth-Young, thanked him for all he had done to professionalize the running of the Collection and the old-master drawings in the Royal Library: 'We can now face any criticism from the press or indeed anyone else with equanimity,' he wrote with an ill-placed optimism. For the next few months Blunt busied himself with his various committees, the publication of the Borromini book, working on the catalogues of Waddesdon Manor, and writing the introduction to a catalogue for a forthcoming exhibition on the 'Treasures of Chatsworth' – going out of his way, however, to avoid occasions which might bring him to the attention of the press. In anticipation of what might happen if he was seen walking into the theatre, he cancelled a trip with Alistair Laing to see *Another Country*, a fictionalized account of Guy Burgess's time at Eton then playing in the West End.

In September 1979, unable to restrain himself any longer, Blunt told Michael Rubinstein that he must see the typescript of Boyle's book, which was to be published by Hutchinson in November. Boyle, however, had decided to give Blunt a pseudonym – the not terribly subtle 'Maurice', after the homosexual hero of an E.M Forster novel – so technically there was no defamation and Boyle's editor, Harold Harris, refused to cooperate. The story of Rubinstein's request to Hutchinson was promptly leaked to *Private Eye*. On 28 September an account of it ran in the magazine, naming Blunt as the interested party and explaining that Boyle's book would describe the career of 'Maurice', the 'so-called Fourth Man' and one-time 'head of the MI5 secretariat', who had confessed to MI5 'in 1957'. Blunt asked whether he could sue for libel, but Rubinstein advised against it.

Blunt realized it was time to prepare his friends and family for what was to come, but he could not bring himself to tell the whole truth, suggesting to his brothers Wilfrid and Christopher and a handful of friends that his involvement with the NKVD had been quite limited. Even so, Wilfrid was completely bewildered. 'I had always considered us to be a fairly close-knit family; it was inconceivable that Christopher and I could have known *nothing*.' Ellis Waterhouse set aside his exasperation with Blunt and had him to stay, noting how anxious he was and how unwilling to discuss his problems.

In early November extracts of Boyle's book, *The Climate of Treason*, appeared in the *Observer*. *Private Eye* took its cue, and three days later, on 8 November, named Blunt as 'Maurice'. The day the story came out, Blunt left London for Oxford, arriving at seven o'clock in the morning at the house of a rather surprised Francis Haskell, who now held the university chair in art history. Blunt was due to give a lecture on bourgeois life in seventeenth-century art, and had arranged to lunch with Haskell. He apologized profusely for his early arrival, explained nothing, and spent the morning calmly correcting the proofs of Haskell's latest book. Haskell knew that some scandal about Blunt was about to come out, but assumed it concerned his homosexuality. As the hour of the lecture approached, Blunt confided that he was worried there might be journalists in the audience. There were none; instead the loyal Tess Rothschild had rallied a number of bemused Oxford grandees, among them Stuart Hampshire and Isaiah Berlin, to turn up in solidarity. 'The lecture was astounding,' Haskell recalled. 'He must have known that his world was collapsing around him. It was an impeccable performance: cool, polished, no notes, interesting, well-delivered. He was calm, and there was no hint of crisis. It was very impressive indeed. Then he came back to our house and asked for an enormous tumbler of whisky. But then he always did that.' He was equally calm that night, at a disastrous dinner with the university vice-chancellor at Merton College, where the boilers broke down and there was no food for hours.

The *Private Eye* story, which Haskell saw the next day, set out the similarities between the careers of 'Maurice' and Blunt, suggesting that it was Blunt's royal connections that had secured him immunity from prosecution. The *Eye* also outed Blunt as a homosexual, saying he lived with 'a Belfast-born former bandboy called John. John it was who persuaded Anthony to accept the knighthood. Friends of Sir Anthony teasingly refer to his companion as "Lady John".'

In the interviews that Andrew Boyle now began to give to publicize his book, however, he refused to confirm that Blunt was

'Maurice'. That, he said, was the government's responsibility. The Prime Minister, Margaret Thatcher, personally affronted by Blunt's immunity, took the bait. She had no time for liberal interpretations of his motives: a traitor was a traitor, and she found the whole episode thoroughly reprehensible, and reeking of Establishment collusion. Though the head of the Security Service, Michael Hanley, asked her not to intervene, she took the advice of her Attorney General, Sir Michael Havers, instead. Havers suggested that if Blunt were not named he would be free to sue for libel over something which was true. Downing Street contacted a backbench Labour MP, Ted Leadbitter, who had been thinking about asking a question about security at Prime Minister's Question Time on 15 November, and asked him to turn it into a question about Blunt. Leadbitter agreed. It was decided that Blunt did at least deserve to be informed of his forthcoming exposure. The Cabinet secretary, Sir Robert Armstrong, invited Michael Rubinstein to meet him.

> He told me that Mrs Thatcher was going to make this announcement. He was very courteous and very helpful, but said he had no control over what Mrs Thatcher said. She took a certain line that Blunt was a traitor, that the book had led to press interest, and this had given rise to parliamentary questions. He indicated to me that as far as Cabinet Office was concerned they didn't want to make it any more difficult for Anthony than it already was.

On the afternoon of Thursday 15 November, in response to Leadbitter's question, Thatcher stood up in the House of Commons and read a statement. She announced that in 1964, in return for immunity from prosecution, Sir Anthony Blunt, former Surveyor of the Queen's Pictures, had confessed to having been recruited by the Soviet Union as a talent spotter and to having subsequently passed information to the NKVD when he became a member of British Intelligence during the war; that he had first come under suspicion after Burgess and Maclean's disappearance; and that he had subsequently been interviewed by MI5 eleven times. In the lobby Leadbitter met Thatcher. She said, 'And it damn well serves him right.' Minutes later a Buckingham Palace spokesman announced that Blunt would be stripped of his knighthood.

From his bed in Charing Cross Hospital, where he was in the last stages of his illness, Goronwy Rees watched Blunt's disgrace on television. 'Got you, you swine,' he said. That night he fell into a coma.

The story was the lead item on every television news bulletin and front page that day and for days after. It completely eclipsed the other big story of the day: that the bank rate was to rise to 17 per cent – a record high, and one more in a series of bad economic news stories that were damaging the government. This, as the Conservative MP Alan Clark confided to his diary, was a 'lucky break' for the government: Blunt's disgrace 'diverted attention from the really alarming manner in which our economy seems to be conducted'. It also made the news in America and all over Europe. It had everything: spies, class, homosexuality, off-the-peg outrage, and a villain who had not only betrayed his country, but had embarrassed the Queen. The front page of Friday's *Daily Mail* said it all: 'Traitor at the Queen's Right Hand'.

Within minutes of the announcement Portsea Hall had been surrounded by journalists, but Blunt had disappeared. The evening news reported that he was 'said to be abroad'. In an effort to locate its quarry, the press began a frantic hunt. Journalists turned up at John Craxton's house in Hampstead, where a group of musicians from the London Sinfonietta were rehearsing. 'We've come for Anthony Blunt,' they said. 'Anyone here called Anthony Blunt?' asked the confused conductor. Stephen Rees Jones, now retired as the Courtauld's technical expert, was called by *Daily Express* reporters who announced they were about to arrive for Blunt. He persuaded them that their quarry was not with him, adding that he happened to be 'in bed with my wife'. For several days the press beseiged Francis Haskell's home in Oxford. The fact that he had a Russian wife seems to have prompted several journalists to imagine that Blunt was hiding there in preparation for an escape to the Soviet Union. They rang up throughout the night, claiming to be friends of 'Anthony's'. 'I could have got rid of them all if I'd let them in the house. But my repulsion was so strong that I felt I wanted to stick it out. I didn't want my house sullied. The "high-minded" press were as bad as the rest.' In Tuscany, a couple of reporters turned up on the doorstep of the art historians Hugh Honour and John Fleming. In Rome, Eric Hebborn teased the hacks clustered in the street by shouting, 'It's them, Anthony, get upstairs!'

The media's muddle and excitement were particularly evident in the fuss that suddenly surrounded the declining Goronwy Rees. A tabloid reporter was found wandering round Charing Cross Hospital, having confused Rees with Blunt. One of Rees's doctors panicked and suggested that Rees's coma might have been induced. Two men had been seen near his room. Perhaps they had been Russians. Perhaps they had injected him with insulin. His bed was placed under police guard. When Rees woke from his coma a few days later, the doctors agreed that it had been his illness that had brought it on; but the story of the police guard had already taken a hysterical and stubborn hold on the press's imagination.

When the former prime ministers Alec Douglas-Home and Harold Wilson insisted that they had known nothing of the immunity – Wilson had been told, but had forgotten – the air of conspiracy that surrounded the story seemed to become even thicker. Andrew Boyle suggested that there might be as many as twenty-three to thirty more agents in high places, though he admitted that 'their usefulness is long since over'.*

The problem for the newspapers was that no one seemed to know very much about Blunt. His years of careful withdrawal had done their work. Apart from the spare details of Thatcher's announcement, there was little to go on. British Intelligence maintained its usual silence. The papers filled their pages with

---

* Boyle's theory, also described in *The Climate of Treason*, that atom scientist Basil Mann had also been a spy turned out to be entirely misplaced.

speculation. Why had Blunt been given immunity? How did he fit in with Burgess, Philby and Maclean? Had he tipped off Burgess and Maclean? What had he done in MI5, or was it MI6? Did the Queen know? (The Palace insisted that she did not.) Who was Blunt and what was he like?

In the absence of Blunt himself, the papers were only too keen to pick up any damaging stories about him, no matter how inaccurate. Over the next few days the characterization that would become his enduring media image was swiftly constructed. In the *Evening Standard* Malcolm Muggeridge, who had barely known him, described him as a 'pansy aesthete'. In the *Daily Express* John Junor described him as a 'treacherous Communist poof'. In the *Daily Telegraph* a soldier who had served with him in the British Expeditionary Force in 1940 said Blunt had been 'a hopeless officer' and the article hinted at cowardice. Another story recounted how he'd changed his mind about a putative Poussin owned by the Gimpel brothers, whom he had looked after on a holiday to the Italian lakes in the late 1920s. Jean Gimpel speculated that Blunt had changed his mind about the attribution of the painting to Poussin out of spite. (He hoped that the publicity might prompt its reattribution to Poussin. It didn't.) Another series of newspaper articles suggested that Tomás Harris had been paymaster to the Cambridge spies – a theory whose source appeared to be Muggeridge – and that he and Blunt might have conspired to misauthenticate the *Augustus and Cleopatra*, which Harris had owned and Blunt had attributed to Poussin in *Apollo* in 1938. (Harris had sold the painting fifteen years later to the National Gallery of Canada. By the 1960s it was generally agreed that it was not a Poussin.)

Several stories about Blunt's private life came from a Northern Irish writer called Robin Bryans, who wrote under the pseudonym Robert Harbinson, and who told many imaginative stories about a relationship with Blunt and Burgess which he claimed dated back to the 1940s. Bryans/Harbinson had first turned up regularly in London literary circles in the 1960s, when he was commissioned to edit a collection of short stories for Faber and Faber.

It turned out, after publication, that he had written all the stories himself. There was a row over royalties, which ended with Harbinson chaining himself to the railings outside Faber, a bout of fisticuffs with a Faber employee and a brief prison sentence. After the exposure Harbinson found an eager audience for anecdotes about Blunt's sex life. ('If Anthony was with a young man he wouldn't be with him for more than ten minutes without trying to take the trousers off him.') According to Harbinson, it was he who had furnished *Private Eye* with the details of Blunt's homosexuality. He latterly kept reporters enthralled by his claims that he had known about Blunt's spying all along, and that Blunt's old friend Peter Montgomery, who knew Harbinson from Northern Ireland, had also been involved.*

Another source was Christopher Wright, a disaffected former student who felt that Blunt had stalled his career. On the television news he was described as Blunt's 'long-time friend'. He told an interviewer that 'Blunt tended to inspire awe – people seemed almost to be frightened of him'. In the *Daily Mail* 'an acquaintance' told a reporter 'he was . . . quite openly a snob . . . both socially and intellectually. He was certainly able to frighten people and make them feel inferior.' The article added that Blunt had enjoyed

> a lifestyle of faultless discretion and taste. His home, a sixth-floor apartment at Portsea Hall – an expensive block of flats near Marble Arch – is worth at least £125,000. It has spacious rooms and is rich in furnishings [almost all the furniture was in fact on loan from the Courtauld] and, of course, paintings. Blunt lived in this block for more than 20 years, recently sharing his apartment with a young man.

* By the 1990s Harbinson was claiming that along with Louis Mountbatten, Blunt had been involved in 'an old boy network which held gay orgies in country houses on both sides of the Irish border'. He even suggested that Blunt might have had links through Montgomery with Kincora, the children's home in Northern Ireland where young boys were systematically and violently sexually abused. No evidence exists to support any of these claims.

Most seriously, the *Sunday Telegraph* printed an extraordinary story claiming that Blunt had been head of the Dutch section of the Special Operations Executive and accusing him of having sent forty-nine Dutch secret agents to their deaths after the Germans were tipped off. It was suggested that the goal was to 'weaken moderate, Right-wing Resistance to the benefit of the communists and other Left-wing groups'. The story was not true: there had been a confusion with another Blunt. But, despite Rubinstein's requests, the paper refused to print a retraction. Rubinstein explained to Blunt that there was very little that could be done. He had lost his good name and he had no reputation to defend. If he sued for libel 'he would have made a very unsuccessful plaintiff before a judge: as a traitor and a homosexual. The chances of his winning, whatever the facts, were very poor.' It was now possible to say and publish almost anything about him. Within the press the attitude appeared to be that, since he had escaped formal punishment, a little rough-housing in the papers was the least he deserved. He was a villain who had done the indefensible. Everyone who attacked him was in the right.

Alternative views on the significance of the affair seemed remarkable by their absence. One of the very few who sounded a questioning note was the writer Francis King, in a letter to *The Times*: 'Can anyone hear, through the din made round the Blunt affair by those seeming to exploit it for personal or political advantage, a small voice asking what public good has been served by the indiscretions of some and the relentless ferreting of others resolved to reanimate a spy scare whose lesson those concerned must have digested years ago?'

Blunt had not left the country. He and Gaskin were in hiding with John Golding and his partner, James Joll, a professor at the London School of Economics, at their home in Hammersmith. Another old pupil and friend, Brian Sewell, had picked them up in his car and driven them to Golding's as soon as Thatcher's announcement had been made. For four days they sat in Golding's house and never stirred, Blunt displaying an almost eerie calm.

He spent much time composing a statement. In the evening he discussed military strategy with James Joll. It was Gaskin, who was drinking heavily, who was obviously shell-shocked.

Two days after the exposure, on 17 November, three letters in support of Blunt from former students were published in *The Times*. The letters suggested that Blunt's contribution to British cultural life and as a teacher should not be forgotten in all the fuss. All three were instantly held up as examples of Blunt's 'pernicious influence' over his students. In *The Times*, Bernard Levin lambasted the authors for being 'victims' of 'moral blindness', and quoted George Orwell: 'You have to be an intellectual to believe that – no ordinary man could be so stupid.' The author of one letter, Michael Jacobs, one of Blunt's last graduate students, who had referred to Blunt's spying as 'a minor and ultimately irrelevant aspect of his life', subsequently received death threats and abusive mail. Another would-be public supporter, Rosalys Coope, had her letter sent back by the letters editor of *The Times* with a note telling her 'not to be so silly'.

The most interesting and strident of the three letters came from Brian Sewell, then not yet famous as a critic and pundit. It robustly attacked the government for having reneged on its deal, described the withdrawal of Blunt's knighthood as petty, and hinted at inside knowledge: the letter ended, 'And the fifth man is dead.' Sewell's address was printed at the bottom. Within hours journalists had turned up on his doorstep hoping for a scoop. They were not disappointed. Sewell, who was described as an art dealer, was a small, neat man with an extraordinarily grand speaking voice – every vowel definitively strangled – and a confident tone which fully matched his bold words. In the absence of Blunt, interviews with him appeared all over the Sunday and Monday papers.

'My function is to play the fool,' he told *The Times*, 'and I've been doing that very effectively for 48 hours to help give Anthony peace of mind and time to consider. I shall continue to tell you what he had for breakfast, but nothing more.' In fact, he said a great deal more. He told the *Observer*, 'the root and branch of the operation is now dead' and that Blunt felt 'the Government had failed to keep its side of the bargain'. He told the *Daily Mail* that Blunt thought the security services had helped Boyle in order deliberately to break his cover; to the *Daily Telegraph* he reported that Blunt was 'furious with Mrs Thatcher. He believes that her action in exposing him will ensure that future promises of immunity from prosecution will fail to persuade Russian agents to own up.' When asked if he knew that Blunt had been the Fourth Man, 'Mr Sewell smiled enigmatically and answered with equal vagueness, "It's a difficult question to answer. There are things you know without knowing them, like knowing the facts of life."' He added that he had drawn his own conclusions about the identity of a Fifth Man, and that he had been told his phone was being tapped.

Sewell had been at the Courtauld in the early days of the 1950s, along with Anita Brookner, John Golding and Michael Kitson. Even then he had had a talent for outraging, infuriating and amusing, and a reputation for hating all art that could possibly be described as modern. Blunt, with his attraction to extreme characters, had enjoyed Sewell's arrogance and his evident intelligence. He had helped Sewell to get one of his first jobs – at the Royal Collection, working on a catalogue of drawings by Carlo Fontana, and his next one, at Christie's. When Sewell left Christie's, in the late 1960s, Blunt had recommended him as an adviser on European purchases for the Toronto Art Gallery, and as a drawings expert to Colnaghi's, 'Though as I say he is extremely outspoken and has very definite opinions. I think I forgot to mention that he was for a time at Christie's where he was unhappy.' In return, Sewell had become what he described as 'a practical, dogsbody-kind of friend', running errands for Blunt, checking provenances, now and again consulting him on attributions, and on occasion entertaining him: he had given a dinner for Blunt's seventieth birthday two years before. One point of conflict was the fact that he did not get on with Gaskin.

Sewell's defence of Blunt was in several ways more damaging than helpful to him. His interviews produced headlines like 'Blunt

Furious'. The newspapers interpreted Sewell's comments as evidence of Blunt's arrogance and brazenness, and the excitement they generated overshadowed the statement Blunt made through Rubinstein on the Monday, which in a characteristically low-key manner expressed the hope that he might be able to resume his work and said that he would welcome an inquiry into the case. Sewell's role, moreover, appears to have been a self-appointed one. Neither Golding nor Rubinstein knew he was planning to speak to the papers, and Blunt, in a press conference the next day, contradicted both Sewell's main claims: 'Quite frankly it has been said that I am furious with Mrs Thatcher for breaking her part of the bargain. I have never said any such thing and do not feel it.' He added, 'This story of a Fifth Man is a complete mystery. You are referring to Brian Sewell's statement. I don't know what he means, I haven't had the opportunity of talking to him about it, I have absolutely no idea of what he means or who he is referring to, or what his evidence is.'

On the Monday, Blunt's hiding place was discovered. It was later reported that a journalist had spotted Brian Sewell dialling Golding's telephone number in a phone box. What is certainly true is that a journalist who was a former pupil of Golding's partner, James Joll, had recognized Joll's voice when he anonymously called a radio news programme to say that Blunt was safe. Joll agreed to give his old student a statement if he would go away. Golding rushed Blunt and Gaskin back to Portsea Hall, running three red lights. By the time he got home his house was surrounded. The reporters stood on the front garden wall and rang the bell so constantly that Golding disconnected it. He discovered that Blunt had left his address book behind. 'It was extraordinary. It had the address of every influential person you can imagine in it.'

On the Tuesday Blunt gave his press conference. It had been Rubinstein's idea – an attempt to 'clear the air' – and it would be Blunt's only public appearance after his exposure.

Rubinstein decided to hold the occasion at *The Times*, and to invite only journalists from *The Times*, the *Guardian*, and the

BBC and ITN news. Transcripts were handed to the Press Association afterwards. Blunt arrived alone and was bundled in through the back entrance, since the front of the building was choked with photographers and reporters. In the corridors on the way to the press-conference room, Blunt and his *Times* minders encountered the former Prime Minister, Ted Heath, on his way out of a meeting. The minders pushed Blunt into a side room; Heath either did not, or pretended not to have, noticed.

Blunt read a statement and answered questions for an hour. He seemed, as ever, composed and calm. He said he 'bitterly regretted' what he had done – but repeated several times that he had 'acted according to my conscience', though he now realized he had been 'totally wrong'. He denied having had a sexual relationship with Burgess, and insisted that he had not 'accepted' his knighthood but, in line with Palace practice, had not known about it until it was announced in *The Times*; he said he had offered to relinquish it, but had had no answer from the Palace.

The papers were savage, many of them additionally irritated by their exclusion from the press conference. Blunt's calm particularly riled them. The *Daily Mail* called him 'the spy with no shame', and said he had shown 'supreme insolence' and 'contempt'. *Now!*, a short-lived magazine owned by the right-wing entrepreneur James Goldsmith, described the press conference as 'one of the most outrageous exercises in disinformation yet attempted' and Blunt as 'this evil arrogant poseur'. Andrew Boyle called Blunt's performance 'totally obnoxious'. When it was reported that Blunt had been given a lunch of smoked trout, fruit salad, wine, coffee and cigars at *The Times*, the *Daily Express* wrote, 'Professor Blunt would not have been offered so much as a stale kipper in the Express offices ... because he is such a phoney old humbug.' The other stories of the day – the no less extraordinary news that 120,000 men had gone on strike at British Leyland, and that the entire NEC had resigned – were completely eclipsed.

It was true that Blunt gave no sense in the interview that he was grappling with his conscience or engaging with his past.

When asked if he had worried that his actions might embarrass the Queen, he answered that he had 'believed wrongly that the matter was dead'. He especially exasperated his interviewers by refusing to answer certain questions on the grounds that he was bound by the Official Secrets Act. In fact Rubinstein had been to see Sir Robert Armstrong the previous day and had promised that Blunt would say 'nothing prejudicial to national security'. He didn't. His answers drew fire to himself, away from MI5, the government and the Palace. He insisted that no one at the Palace had known he had been a spy, that he had hardly ever been at Court; he said that he had barely known Dick White, that he could not name his MI5 interrogators, and that Guy Liddell had not been involved. By his own lights he was honourable. By his audience's he was evasive.

In a parliamentary debate the next day, MPs queued up to pour out their disgust for Blunt. The motion itself, however – that there should be a public inquiry into Soviet penetration of public services – was defeated. The fact that the immunity had been granted by a tottering government and an intelligence service both desperate to protect themselves from public scrutiny was barely discussed. Larger questions about the way in which the government and British Intelligence were run, and about the need for more open government, receded. The Establishment which had been accused of covering for Blunt turned on him too, leaving him the focus of outrage and largely escaping any opprobrium itself. Thatcher's announcement – hailed as the start of a new era of open politics – turned out to be quite the opposite, an exercise in damage limitation and deflection. In 1964 Blunt's immunity had served the government's purposes; it is hard to escape the conclusion that his exposure in 1979 did the same thing.

In the immediate aftermath of the press conference, Blunt and Gaskin returned to a kind of house arrest in Portsea Hall. For several months there were always journalists outside and it was virtually impossible to leave the flat without being mobbed. They stayed indoors, kept away from the windows, and pulled the curtains. When the phone's persistent ringing became too much it was placed under a cushion and was answered only if the caller used the correct code – three rings, then off, then ringing again. There was little to do but work and drink.

In the following weeks the world polarized. There were many letters of sympathy from grateful old students, letters of commiseration from long-lost acquaintances, covert letters of sympathy from people who felt that their positions made it impossible to be supportive in public. Outside, the world felt hostile. Blunt would make jokes about being insulted in the street and when he finally began to go outside again he cut his hair and disguised himself with a hat – a homburg or a deerstalker – and sometimes dark glasses. There were occasional incidents which frightened him. In February 1980 he was booed and slow-clapped out of a showing of *La Cage aux Folles* at the Gate cinema in Notting Hill. On a trip to York to stay with his old pupil Richard Verdi a barman refused to serve him. Now and again, he told his friends, a stranger would come up to him in the street, and he would fear the worst, but they would shake his hand. The incidents were small and occasional, but enough to keep him always on his guard. When, in late 1980, the Royal Academy decided he should be permitted to see the 'Treasures of Chatsworth' exhibition on which he had worked, and invited him in early one morning before the public arrived, he accepted with alacrity; but, as public opening approached, his apparent calm left him and he became wild-eyed and nervous. He was all too grateful when it was suggested that he leave by a back entrance.

A cluster of old friends – the Proctors in particular, and former students and staff – brought in food, books and bottles of whisky. 'I've been like Elijah fed by ravens', said Blunt. There were, of course, personal rejections too. George Zarnecki, who had succeeded Johannes Wilde as Blunt's deputy at the Courtauld, and who had fled fascism and Communism, was horrified by Blunt's exposure and could not bring himself to speak to him. Alan Bowness, who was about to become director of the Tate Gallery, stood aloof. An early protégé, John White, who had fought in the Second World War, could not reconcile himself to Blunt's actions. Ellis Waterhouse at first refused to speak to him, furious that Blunt had not come clean with him when he might have. Blunt was visibly shaken by his rejection. Waterhouse later relented and visited him to discuss art-history matters, but never truly thawed. Moore Crossthwaite, whom Blunt had met through MacNeice nearly fifty years before, and who had been the ambassador to Beirut when Blunt had visited on two occasions in the early 1960s, was furious at the thought that Blunt might have used him as an excuse to see Philby, who had been living in the Lebanon. He said he wished him dead. Pamela Wyndham, who had long known about MI5's suspicions, received a letter from Blunt she never answered. Oliver Millar, still working at the Royal Collection, was informed he must avoid Blunt. 'I knew he desperately needed friends, and he did call. It was ghastly – embarrassing all round.' Tess Rothschild continued to visit him, but Victor could not forgive him – not least for casting suspicion over him. Other friends felt that, despite their dismay at the revelations, they could not turn their backs on him. Among these was Dadie Rylands, who could, however, never recapture his old feelings for Blunt. One thing both friends and enemies reflected upon later was their surprise at how strangely unsurprised they felt by the revelation.

Throughout it all, Blunt was remarkably uncomplaining. He seemed almost relaxed. It was as if he had been in training for these very circumstances all his life. He worked on his latest project, a guide to baroque Rome, and said he was cheered by the letters of commiseration he'd received. He was in some senses relieved that everything had finally come out. Some of his friends saw in Blunt's apparent equanimity a kind of denial, an almost naive inability to understand what he had done. 'Anthony refused to recognize the spot he was in, which was characteristic,' thought Howard Capes, who had been shocked by the revelations and was angry with Blunt, but felt he could not abandon him and

Gaskin when they were so evidently in need. The two would spend weekends at Capes's home in Esher. They were, he recalled, awful guests. Gaskin expected to be waited on, Blunt buried himself in a chair and a book, and both started drinking at 11 a.m.

In the end it was Gaskin, not Blunt, who buckled under the strain. He was overwhelmed by the hostility of the press, and horrified by being outed – in the papers he was called 'Lady John', which he hated. With Blunt's disgrace, his own position in the world had collapsed. The fact that for years he had ignored any hint of Blunt's past sins made the truth additionally unbearable. In the weeks after the exposure he would harangue Blunt over and over: 'You betrayed me. How could you have betrayed me? How *could* you? How *could* you?' Blunt would look at him, apologetic, pleading, but mute. Cooped up all day for months after the revelation, Gaskin brooded on his misfortunes and grew daily more depressed and paranoid. He began to crawl around on the floor so that the journalists outside couldn't see him. Once outside he cowered behind cars, convinced that hostile eyes were watching him.

In the weeks before Christmas the newspapers disclosed the story of Blunt's royal mission to Germany. The fact that no one quite knew what he had brought back merely inspired ever more imaginative speculation. The royal family maintained their customary silence, even in Court circles. The Queen apparently never spoke of him. As for the Queen Mother, just after Blunt's exposure there was a lunch at Lady Perth's to which she had been invited. Before her arrival, the conversation was riveted on the subject of Blunt and whether anyone dared ask her about it. As she swept into the room, the by then rather elderly former bright young thing Harold Acton leaped forward and boldly asked her what she thought. 'Lovely day, isn't it?' she said, deadpanning. She would not be drawn. After Blunt's death she spoke to Isaiah Berlin about him. Berlin remembered that she was 'rather kindly about him. She liked all homosexuals. She liked pansies – queers as such. She said about him, "Oh well, one can't blame them all. A lot of people made terrible mistakes – one shouldn't really go on persecuting them."'

Old friends and enemies began to be named as possible fellow conspirators. *The Times* speculated that Blunt might have converted Wittgenstein. Victor Rothschild was mentioned, along with one of Blunt's least favourite people, the former head of Sotheby's, Peter Wilson. The reason seemed to be that Wilson had been viewed as a machiavellian figure in the art world, was homosexual, and had been in MI5 – never mind that he had been extremely right-wing and Blunt had disliked him. Before Christmas the *Sunday Times* investigative journalists Barrie Penrose and Simon Freeman, working on a tip-off, tracked down John Cairncross in Rome, where he admitted that he had passed bits of information to Burgess. In early December, shortly before he died, Goronwy Rees gave a final interview to Andrew Boyle, which was published by the *Observer* in January of the new year. He said that Blunt had cast 'a long shadow' over his life, added that Blunt had had a passionate affair with Burgess, and suggested that Guy Liddell had been an MI5 mole.

Within days of Margaret Thatcher's announcement, Blunt's academic titles, honorary doctorates, fellowships, memberships, editorships began to disappear, hastily and often embarrassedly withdrawn. In December the fellows of Trinity College, Cambridge, voted to relieve him of his fellowship if he did not resign it voluntarily. He did. Alan Hodgkin, the master of the college, who had known Blunt in the 1930s and argued that he should be allowed to keep the fellowship, was taken aback by the vehemence of the attack. He later felt he was punished for his support of Blunt by being removed early from his post. Once Blunt realized how things were, he began to offer his resignation in advance. He was informed that the Courtauld's management committee had decided it would be preferable for him to avoid the Institute for the foreseeable future. No senior art figures came forward to defend him publicly – and would not until after his death. A much-mooted letter to be signed by a number of internationally renowned art luminaries – including the most powerful and eminent art historian in France, André Chastel, with whom Blunt had enjoyed an extremely warm professional friendship – never materialized. Courtauld staff had been asked not to speak publicly on the matter. Some academics were too nervous to make public statements; some were covertly pleased to see such a grand figure brought low. When he heard the revelations, John Pope-Hennessy rubbed his hands and ushered a bemused John Craxton into his red velvet office at the Metropolitan Museum of Art in New York, where he was now director. 'The Pope' whispered a story he'd heard that Blunt had authenticated as a Poussin a painting owned by Tomás Harris which had been sold to raise money for the Communist Party.

There was one show of support. Towards the end of January 1980, London University's convocation, which consisted of any graduate who paid a small membership fee, voted on a motion proposing that Blunt should be stripped of his emeritus professorship. It was argued by the proposers – two science professors – that the university should show the world that academia understood its duty. The meeting, on 9 February, had a record attendance – large numbers of former Courtauld students turned out, including Anita Brookner and Brian Sewell – and the motion was defeated by 246 votes to 147.

Three days later, at five o'clock in the morning, Gaskin fell eighty feet off the balcony of the flat. He was found lying on the ground, and claimed he'd been 'out for a breath of air'. Miraculously, his injuries were not fatal. He was taken to hospital, and the story made the front page of the London *Evening Standard*: 'Traitor's flatmate plunges six floors'. It was even rumoured that a Soviet assassin had mistaken him for Blunt. It was also said that journalists were dressing up as little old ladies and claiming to be Gaskin's auntie in order to try to see him. There was no question among Blunt's friends that it had been anything other than a suicide attempt. The evening before the two men had drunk even more than usual, then squabbled. Blunt had gone to bed. Gaskin had jumped.

Blunt was dazed and upset, not least by the fact that he was not allowed to visit Gaskin, and was given short shrift when he phoned the hospital to see how he was. According to John Richardson, he eventually managed to smuggle himself into the hospital without the press knowing. On his discharge, Gaskin went on to a convalescent home to be treated for his depression, and Blunt lived alone for several months, forced to look after himself for the first time in years. Once again his old students pulled together, drawing up a rota to help with shopping and food and company. One night, after the Proctors had spent the evening with him and Dennis had decided to stay over, he escorted Barbara down to her car. Slightly tearfully and drunkenly, as she had never seen him before, he put his arms around her, hugged her, and whispered, 'God bless you, God bless you, God bless you.' When Gaskin came home, fragile and shaken, as he would be for ever after, Blunt became carer, cook, comforter.

He made a point of never complaining about his predicament. It was almost as if the exposure had given him a last opportunity to live according to those Stoic ideals he had failed to live up to, to achieve the kind of calm detachment that he had attributed to Poussin's last years: to accept his disgrace uncomplainingly, to trust only to a small group of friends, to devote himself to his work, to not pine for his lost honours and position, to accept the damaging and often inaccurate stories with resignation. He might have easily taken refuge abroad, in Italy. 'I'd kill myself first,' he told John Golding. It was perhaps a way of recovering some shreds of integrity. The anger he clearly felt was displaced into concern for friends whom he felt had been maligned, and a generalized scorn of the press. When the *Observer* printed Rees's accusation against Guy Liddell, Blunt wrote angrily to deny it, pointing out that Rees had told conflicting versions of the story on different occasions. It didn't seem to occur to him that his word no longer had any force. Nor could he resist a final swipe at his nemesis. 'I think', he told Rosamond Lehmann after Rees died, 'you should know that Goronwy was up to his neck in it all.'

Barbara Proctor, who before had always felt that she had come a poor second to her husband in Blunt's eyes, found herself coming to like and even admire him, 'for the stoical pride and dignity with which he held the remains of his life together and his ability to enjoy his work, his friends and what remained of pleasure – viz. painting and drink.' It was a liking that not even Peter Wright's later claims that Blunt had implicated Dennis could strip away. Others felt similarly: Richard Verdi, who as a post-graduate student of Blunt's had enjoyed a bumpy and sometimes difficult relationship with him, felt, 'I only really got to know him after 1979. He began to ring me more regularly. He was far more communicative, and warmer towards me.' In the summer of 1982 Quentin and Olivier Bell went, somewhat reluctantly, to a lunch organized by the Proctors for Blunt. Quentin was surprised by what he found.

He was old and worn but he did not look like the total wreck I was expecting to see. In fact I was amazed at his resilience. He could sit with us and crack jokes about his fall from grace. Never for a moment was he bitter, angry or sorry for himself. It was a most successful lunch party and if he was anxious, downcast and down-hearted he never let us see it. Whatever else he may have lacked, he did not lack courage.

Not everyone who met him was so impressed. In 1980 the espionage writer Nigel West managed to persuade Blunt to meet him, telling him he was researching a wartime history of MI5 that would be incomplete if it did not deal with Soviet penetration. West was compiling his own very unofficial history of MI5, with the help of a number of former officers, including Tar Robertson. He met Blunt three times.

Blunt was very candid in my judgement, not remotely remorseful, and gave the impression that he was really just a highly professional intelligence officer. At one point he hap-pened to work for the Russians with enthusiasm, and since

Anthony Blunt: *His Lives*

his confession he had worked with equal enthusiasm with the British Security Service. I found this quite grotesque. I was quite repelled by what he told me. He was completely cold blooded about everything. I went home and I couldn't eat my dinner, which is very unusual for me. I was absolutely repulsed.

As a rule, however, Blunt almost never brought up the subject of his disgrace. 'We never spoke about anything but art gossip,' Francis Haskell remembered of his occasional visits. 'He seemed extraordinarily resilient, and he never showed anything, never talked about it. Anthony was steel hard.' 'He knew I wouldn't ask awkward questions,' said Michael Kitson. 'I knew I wouldn't have got a straight answer. The basis of our friendship was totally about other things – academic gossip, who was in, who was out, university things; a new book.'

In the later spring of 1980 Blunt went to the Hertziana Institute in Rome to continue work on his guide to baroque Rome. He had been invited by the Institute's director, Wolfgang Lotz, and his deputy, Richard Krautheimer. Krautheimer recalled, 'We felt it must have been awful for him. We both knew the 1930s – we'd gone through them. I left in 1933, Lotz stayed in Germany under Hitler, and we both understood those years and how a liberal young man would have been pulled into that.' Krautheimer remembered an occasion when Blunt, looking out over the panoramic view of Rome from the window of his study, gestured vaguely towards the steeple of St George's, the English church, which stuck out like a sore thumb in the midst of the Roman cupolas. 'I do apologize for all this,' he said. Krautheimer never knew whether he meant the vulgar spire of St George's or the trouble he'd caused.

It was as if Blunt had so deliberately cut off the memories of his spying that he could not now recover them. At the prompting of Rubinstein and Tess Rothschild, he tried to write a memoir explaining himself. He abandoned it unfinished. In odd letters he expressed contrition: 'Now that there is a lull – only temporary, I

490

fear – in the storm I must write to thank you for [your letter]. I got particular consolation from letters written by people like yourself who knew what the 'thirties were like. How wrong we all were – but much of the essential evidence about Russia didn't really get through to us until too late.' John Gaskin told Michael Kitson that Blunt had no answer to why he had done it. He'd said, 'For the hell of it I suppose.'

Margot Wittkower asked him *how* he'd managed it. For her, as for many others, staying in touch was not an easy decision, but she could not break off forty years of friendship.

We met, we sat together, we talked about colleagues, what he was working on, what I was doing, and once the talk came to this very difficult question. I said, 'Anthony, do you mind if I ask you a question? If you do I won't ask it.' He said, 'I don't mind any questions. You can ask me what you like.' I said, 'How did you live though all that? You had lunch with the Queen, you were the conservator of her paintings, you knew the whole royal family, you accepted invitations for weekends, you travelled with people of a class that you wanted to destroy. And on the other hand you were an art historian without any interference of your other life. How did you live through that?' Blunt lifted the glass of whisky in his hand, and said, 'With this, and more work and more work.'

Then came the news that the Cambridge historian J. H. Plumb was campaigning for Blunt's expulsion from the British Academy. Plumb, Isaiah Berlin later said, 'had been a Communist in the 1930s and he had become a terrific snob, though he was a good historian. Plumb said, "We're a public organization, we get money from the state. This man is a traitor, he has betrayed the state." He really foamed at the mouth.' Berlin had been shocked by Blunt's actions, but he did not approve of the proposed expulsion, believing – with some justification – that it was the sort of thing they did in the Soviet Union. Others felt more strongly. A. J. P. Taylor wrote to *The Times* to announce that he would resign if Blunt was expelled. Few in the Academy saw this as an admirable gesture. A letter sent to *The Times* under the forged name of Lord Beloff suggested that this would be as good a reason as any for ousting Blunt. It was decided that Blunt's fate should be settled at the Academy's annual general meeting in July 1980.

By the time of the meeting the issue had taken on a life of its own, drawing out old enmities and angers. On the day, an alternative motion, that the Academy deplored Blunt's behaviour but would not proceed further, drafted by Berlin, was proposed by Blunt's old ally Lionel Robbins. There were hours of fractious debate, at the end of which an exhausted member suggested that they vote merely to pass on to the next item on the agenda – the implication being that no further action would be taken against Blunt. A motion to that effect was passed by 120 votes to 42, with 25 abstentions. The *Daily Mail* jeered at 'Britain's Academy of Cowards'. A. J. P. Taylor and another eminent academican, Ralf Dahrendorf, were quoted as saying it was a just outcome and that the Academy should not judge its members beyond the area of scholarship.

This was far from the end of the story. A vocal minority of members refused to accept the situation. Three or four resigned, and Plumb and two more historians, Ian Christie and Norman Gash, threatened to leave by the end of the year if Blunt was still a member. Berlin recalled, 'Plumb began to write letters. He went on and on and on: "He must be removed!" He was very vicious about it. I was shocked by the fact that he was so nasty. This wasn't *odium academicum*: it was *odium personali*.' Christie wrote to the papers to resurrect the story, later suggesting that *The Times* did not print his letter because it had made a secret deal with Blunt. Eventually Blunt wrote to the Academy's president, Kenneth Dover, apologizing for the way in which the papers had used him to attack the organization. Dover asked him to resign, as a way of 'healing the wounds of the Academy'. Blunt took two days to decide, then agreed. A. J. P. Taylor resigned immediately, later describing Blunt as 'always a soft character', and saying he'd taken the easy way out. A *Daily Express* reporter phoned Dover to ask if Taylor and Blunt enjoyed a 'special relationship'.* Another Academician – probably Richard Cobb – was persuaded by Blunt not to resign. Kenneth Dover later admitted that he'd found the whole affair 'absorbingly interesting and therefore intensely enjoyable'. He also noted that no member of the public to whom he had spoken had been in favour of expulsion or any other punitive action against Blunt, and added, 'those whom I knew as the fiercest enemies of Blunt were all academics'.

There was a peculiar element of self-flagellation in some of the academics' responses to Blunt. Some British academics set about accusing themselves and their kind of various sins: of elitism and arrogance, of 'moral cowardice' and lax, relativistic, overliberal morals; of poisoning themselves in the labyrinth of esoteric study. 'Less intellectual people have simpler ideas and more direct instincts,' wrote Gash. The evils of academia were a theme of perhaps the most sophisticated piece of journalism that came out of Blunt's exposure, George Steiner's *New Yorker* article, 'The Cleric of Treason'. Steiner characterized Blunt as an incarnation of 'the scholar absolute', a creature cancerous with the dark nastiness of academia with its blind and obsessive addiction to the 'holiness of the minute particular'. Such self-criticism would become almost a frequent pastime for a certain type of academic and intellectual during the the next ten years, bespeaking a kind of unease, almost an embarrassment, at their status in the chilly world of Thatcherism. At the same time academics would become less and less publicly valued, more and more financially squeezed. Ten years later it would be hard to imagine any academic dispute making front-page news, except as a joke.

By the autumn of 1980 Blunt's life began to approach some semblance of normality. Outside Portsea Hall the journalists were

---

* Taylor had actually been looking for a reason to storm out for years, but later enquired of the secretary of the Academy if he might come back.

no longer in evidence. Blunt began to make regular trips to the local supermarket himself, disguised in his deerstalker. So regular were his visits that Arthur Martin, now in retirement, and longing for 'one last crack at him', planned to 'accidentally' bump into him there. But every so often the story would return. An article by Blunt in some reputable publication – the *Times Literary Supplement* or the *Literary Review* – or a sighting at a public lecture would be greeted by warnings that the traitor might be gaining acceptance in public life. When the Royal Academy's 'Treasures of Chatsworth' exhibition opened in October, Blunt's name appeared in the catalogue – he had written the introduction. There were demands in the press that his name be removed. Brian Sewell, now making a name for himself as an art critic, having been signed up for *Tatler* by its smart young editor, Tina Brown, could now be relied on for a quotation about Blunt: 'The cost of altering the catalogue would be astronomical,' he commented. But there was no rehabilitation. For all the letters of sympathy and support, Blunt was quite isolated.

Brian Sewell weighed in again on the subject of Blunt several months later, in 1981, when Blunt's former pupil Christopher Wright began to claim publicly that a painting in the Met in New York, *The Fortune Teller* by Georges de la Tour, was in fact a fake, and that Blunt had been involved in efforts to pass it off as genuine. His main evidence of Blunt's involvement appeared to be that Blunt had disagreed with his doubts about the painting. The story created such a buzz that Sewell became involved in attempts to research the authenticity of the painting, and a television documentary was commissioned to examine the claims. Its writer and presenter, Edwin Mullins, quickly proved beyond doubt the picture's authenticity – not least by finding a document confirming its existence in the nineteenth century when de la Tour had been a completely forgotten artist. In 1984, Wright neverthe-less published a book, *The Art of the Forger*, reiterating his claims that the picture was a fake, to which *Private Eye* gave space over several issues, alongside suggestions that Blunt had been in cahoots with the dealer who had sold the painting to the Met,

Georges Wildenstein, and had salted away a fortune abroad. As for Sewell, so vivid was the impression he made, and so great his forthrightness on Blunt's behalf, that the ever absent Blunt would be for ever associated in the public mind with him and his unforgettable accent. Reporters, unable to speak to the man himself, began to go to Sewell whenever there was a new angle on Blunt's case. To many he almost seemed to be Blunt's official spokesman. The extent to which Blunt became viewed as an older version of Sewell – sharp, arrogant, opinionated, but without Sewell's mitigation, that he was funny and innocent – would be demonstrated when the actor James Fox played Blunt in the television adaptation of the Alan Bennett's play, *A Question of Attribution*. He sounded not like Blunt, but like Sewell.

As time passed, however, Sewell's appreciative and sympathetic comments about Blunt were gradually punctuated by oddly critical and negative notes. By the 1990s, for example, he was claiming that Blunt's work on Poussin had been 'inconclusive, even disorderly' and his conclusions about the artist fundamentally wrong – a fact he claimed that Blunt had come to realize painfully at the 1960 Poussin exhibition, an event which had caused him tremendous 'anguish'. He even claimed on a television programme in 1995 that Blunt's *Rebecca* had been a terrible disappointment to him: 'The painting turned out to be extensively damaged,' Sewell said, 'and had to be extensively repainted. And he lived with this painting until the end and one might almost say was reproached by it . . . It's a wry thing to say, but it is the truth, that the picture which he regarded as the key turned out to be overpainted and not by Poussin at all.' This was a strange thing to say. The painting was certainly known to be damaged, but was also acknowledged as an important example of Poussin's late work. It is claimed by some that, after the exposure, Sewell actually fell out with Blunt over his eagerness to talk to the press. When Blunt wrote his will in 1982, he ask Howard Capes and John Golding to be his executors. Capes believed that he was taking Sewell's place because Sewell had set himself up as Blunt's self-appointed representative, which Anthony hated. He told Sewell to shut up and mind his own business, but of course he wouldn't. He never, never, never, never stayed with Sewell after the exposure. Anthony loathed his indiscretion. He was vehement about that and I was asked many times to get him off his back and to make it fairly plain to people who had any influence at all, to make it quite clear that Sewell was non grata.

By the New Year of 1981, Blunt had aged terribly. Tess Rothschild felt he was 'worn out and flattened by the exposure'. He complained to his doctor of spreading chest pains, and said he woke in the small hours with palpitations and short of breath. He began to walk with a stick. 'Emotional upset yesterday,' his doctor put in his notes in the autumn of that year. Blunt's *Guide to Baroque Rome* was published, and mostly ignored by the British press – though it was well received in the scholarly community. He started work on a new book on Pietro da Cortona – architect, sculptor, painter contemporary of Borromini – and on a couple of occasions, at the behest of old pupils, he gave lectures at Reading and Manchester universities. But his angina was worse and his heartbeat irregular, and he also almost certainly knew that his cancer had returned.

In early 1983 he began to give away his Poussin papers and some of his architectural volumes. He invited a young German scholar, Jorg Merz, whom he had met at the Hertziana, if he would like to collaborate on his almost completed book on Pietro da Cortona and gave him the manuscript. Merz, like so many others before him, was overwhelmed by the confidence of the grand professor, and gratefully accepted. A week or so later Blunt scribbled a list of little bequests from his collection: Phoebe Pool's Coldstream to John Golding, a Dalou sculpture of a head to the Proctors, drawings and objects to eight or so others.

After breakfast on 26 March 1983, sitting at his desk, about to make a phone call, Blunt had a heart attack and died immediately.

'Blunt the high-class spy dies in disgrace at 75' was the *Sunday*

Times's headline. In among a spate of new allegations against him came a surprisingly generous testimony from John Pope-Hennessy and a kind remark from his former interrogator Arthur Martin: 'I am sorry for him. He had a ghastly life. I liked the man but I cannot excuse what he did though I dimly understand his motives. I have never felt indignation. I never despised him. I always had time for him. I have always thought . . . there but for the grace of God.' In the *Daily Telegraph*, however, the journalist Godfrey Barker attacked the 'myth' of Blunt's art-historical reputation, claiming his scholarship had been 'inflated' and that the art-history world was still in 'academic servility' to him. He cited the *Spectator* articles of the 1930s as evidence of Blunt's inferiority as a scholar, along with the 'botched chronology' of the Poussin, and described Blunt's work as an 'extraordinary failure of visual perception', characterized by 'limp condescensions and bitchiness'. Among academics, it was left largely to foreigners to review Blunt's art career. André Chastel wrote a fulsome obituary in the *Burlington Magazine*. In Italy the architectural historian Cesare da Seta, with whom Blunt had researched baroque architecture in Naples, published another generous piece.

Blunt was cremated at Putney Vale in south-west London on a grey spring day. The press outnumbered the mourners. Three months later Christopher Blunt scattered his brother's ashes on Martinsell Hill overlooking Marlborough, where he had walked as a schoolboy.

Even in death, Blunt could not stay out of the press. The newspapers announced that his estate was worth £800,000 – a considerable amount of money for an academic art historian in 1983. This was principally made up of the Poussin *Rebecca*, along with the flat, other pictures he had bought over the years, drawings and rare books. (*Private Eye* printed a story which claimed that Blunt had actually owned a secret flat in Rome next door to the Hassler Hotel and had millions of pounds invested abroad.) Blunt left his library, architectural drawings and copyrights to the Courtauld, made a few small bequests to family and friends – including Druce, the porter at Portsea Hall, who had defended him from the press – and left everything else, except the Poussin, to Gaskin.

Material prosperity and security did not bring John Gaskin any comfort. After Blunt's death he descended once again into depression. Without Blunt he seemed lost. Howard Capes would catch him looking at himself in the mirror for hours, examining himself almost as if checking to see if he still existed. He hated growing old. A few of Blunt's friends continued to see him, but he became harder and harder to be with. He would fall into panics. He called John Golding one day, half-hysterical, insisting that Blunt's unfinished memoir be removed from the flat, but refused to touch it himself. Golding and James Joll took the manuscript to the British Library and donated it anonymously, with the proviso that it should not be read for twenty-five years. Towards the end of 1987, feeling there was nothing left for him in London and having sold off most of Blunt's pictures, Gaskin moved to Dundee, to be near his niece. He bought a flat overlooking the Tay. On a warm July day in 1988 he walked out to a railway line nearby and threw himself under a train. Cause of death was given as 'multiple injuries' and 'blunt force trauma'.

As for Blunt's best-loved possession, Poussin's *Rebecca and Eliezer at the Well*, that too was shadowed by its association with him. Blunt had wanted to leave the painting to the nation, and his executors hoped it would be accepted in lieu of death duties. The usual criterion for acceptance was whether a picture was sufficiently pre-eminent. The *Sunday Telegraph* reported that the *Rebecca* might be refused on the grounds that it had come from Blunt. 'This possibility is, however, discounted in heritage circles.' The government hemmed and hawed over the offer for over a year before the Arts Minister, the Earl of Gowrie, rejected it. (There was a certain irony to this, as in 1976, as a consultant for Thomas Gibson Fine Art, Gowrie had approached Blunt offering to buy the *Rebecca* on behalf of another party who, he said, was willing to pay around a quarter of a million pounds for a painting 'of the character and quality of yours'.) This left Blunt's executors with a problem: they needed a large and available sum to pay

Blunt's upcoming death duties. If they could not sell the Poussin, something else would have to go, Blunt's flat most probably, leaving Gaskin homeless. For a moment they considered the unpalatable possibility of selling Blunt's unfinished memoir to whoever would pay the most for it, and for several days various interested parties scrabbled to try and buy it.

In the end, an old enemy of Blunt's, Michael Jaffe, director of the Fitzwilliam in Cambridge, who had long wanted a Poussin for his museum, bought the painting for £192,000 – a good price, as it had at one point been valued at £350,000 – scraping together the money from a bequest left by Blunt's old mentor Andrew Gow and a grant from the Pilgrim Trust. *Rebecca and Eliezer at the Well* hangs in the Fitzwilliam today. Visitors to the museum have no way of knowing to whom the painting once belonged.

References

Note *(i) All quotations attributed within the text but not directly credited in these notes come from interviews with the individuals quoted conducted by the author on the dates given in the Bibliography and Sources. (ii) Interviews not credited to anyone else were conducted by the author. (iii) Titles of most books quoted from in the text have been abbreviated in the notes. Where the full title is not cited, it can be found in the Bibliography. (iv) The following abbreviations are used in the references:*

AB	Anthony Blunt
AFB	Anthony Frederick Blunt (the name used in the Courtauld Institute's archives)
CCCS	Colonial and Continental Church Society
CI	Courtauld Institute
GLMS	Guildhall Library, Manuscripts Department, Corporation of London
GRI	Getty Research Institute, Los Angeles, California
KCL	The Archive Centre, King's College Library, Cambridge
LM	Louis MacNeice
MFA&A	Monuments, Fine Arts and Archives
RA/RCD/ PIC	Royal Archives, Royal Collections Department, Surveyor of Pictures
WA	Warburg Archives

Prologue

xiii   **the spy with no shame:** *Daily Mail*, 21 Nov. 1979.

      arrogant evil poseur: *Now!*, 23 Nov. 1979.

      treacherous Communist poof: J. Junor, *Daily Express*, 19 Nov. 1979.

      blackmailed impressionable undergraduates: see Koch, *Double Lives*, p. 184–6, and Costello, *Mask*, pp. 188–94.

the deaths of forty-nine: *Sunday Telegraph*, 18 Nov. 1979.

conspiracies with Louis Mountbatten: see Richard Deacon, *The Greatest Treason* (London: Century, 1989).

a fortune abroad: 'Merde Most Foul', *Private Eye*, 27 Sept. 1984.

responsible for the suicide: ibid.

even a paedophile: see Moore, *Kincora*, p. 90.

a fake George de la Tour: see Christopher Wright, *The Art of the Forger* (London: Gordon Fraser, 1984).

stolen the credit: F. Haskell interview.

borrowed money: The Rt Hon. Lord Waldegrave of North Hill, letter to the author, 4 July 2000.

cheated the elderly Duncan Grant: see *Charleston Newsletter*, no. 17, 1986.

xiv   relegate British art: Al Weil, 'The Somerset House Conspiracy', Douglas Cooper papers, GRI (sent to Cooper by Alan Bowness, 1984).

Less intellectual people: Norman Gash, *Policy Review*, winter 1981.

xv   Pampered with an upper class education: 'Anthony Blunt', NBCi, accessed 17.12.2000.

moral blindness: B. Levin, *The Times*, 20 Nov. 1979.

xviii   he only ever had one ambition: Wright, *Spycatcher*, p. 229.

He lived only for his art: A. Blunt, *Poussin*, p. 312.

1. Son

The main source for this chapter is Wilfrid Blunt's Married to a Single Life, *pp. 1–47, 81–100, 123–9, 274–83. All quotations in the chapter are from this book unless otherwise specified.*

1   I have been in this quiet place: Edwards, *Bournemouth*, p. 141.

2   Archbishop of Melbourne: A. S. V. (Stanley) Blunt, *R. F. L. Blunt*, p. 120.

scrimped and saved: ibid., p. 122.

saw but little of him: ibid., pp. 76–7.

was acknowledged: ibid., p. 184.

He always seemed: Walter Blunt to Oscar Browning, Dec. 1890, Oscar Browning letters, KCL.

6   Wilfrid Scawen Blunt: see Longford, *Pilgrimage of Passion*.

7   vicars' earnings: see Haig, *Victorian Clergy*; Russell, *Clerical Profession*.

£150 a year: *Crockfords Clerical Directory*, 1909.

8   with some hesitancy: CCCS minute book 1912, p. 14, GLMS.

References

Up to the present: CCCS annual report 1912–3, GLMS.

9 Lord Bertie of Thame: see Gladwyn, *Paris Embassy*, pp. 160–76.
an event which I think: A. Blunt, 'From Bloomsbury'.

10 my earliest recollection: ibid.
as though admitting: Sir Michael Levey, unpublished memoir.

11 small feats of gallantry: Lillian Gurry interviewed by B. Penrose and S. Freeman, 1985.
My mother was very close: Penrose and Freeman, *Conspiracy*, p. 1.

12 a tremendous success: Adams, *Paris Sees it Through*, p. 136.

13 The CCCS sent him: CCCS annual report 1914–15, GLMS.
did little but: Penrose and Freeman, *Conspiracy*, p. 10.

14 Anthony's 'silent father': John Hilton, quoted in O. Millar interview.

15 I was brought up: A. Blunt, 'From Bloomsbury'.

17 Anthony and his brothers: C. Gould, unpublished memoir.

2. Schoolboy

The main source for this chapter is Louis MacNeice's The Strings Are False, *pp. 80–101, 228–30 and 239–50, which includes John Hilton's recollections of Marlborough. Any quotations not attributed elsewhere come from this.*

18 the people I came: A. Blunt, 'From Bloomsbury'.

19 Deserted by the coaches: Betjeman, *Summoned*, chapter 7.
hostile, friendless: Worsley, *Flannelled Fool*, p. 38.
a double row: Hinde, *Paths of Progress*, p. 135.
I have been beaten: L. MacNeice to his stepmother, Georgina MacNeice, 2 Oct. 1921, Bodleian Library.

20 very poor: T. D. F. Money interview.
sneering contempt: Worsley, *Flannelled Fool*, p. 40.

21 Wilfrid Blunt received a beating: W. Blunt, *Married*, p. 50.
hated compulsory Games: 'Conversation Piece, an interview with Anthony Blunt', *The Marlburian*, Lent term, 1966.
the Taper: Tom Mynors believed that it was Christopher, Anthony's brother, who was originally called 'the Taper'. T. D. F. Money, who was in the same year and house as Anthony and Mynors, insists that Anthony carried the name for a while.
I did not mind 'A' House: 'Conversation Piece'.

22 as though it were not merely: Nichols, *The Unforgiving Minute*, p. 1.
My first year: 'Conversation Piece'. In *Mask of Treachery*, p. 68, John Costello claims that Blunt stopped the bullying with 'sexual blackmail'.

References

His 'source' was Robert Cecil, a contemporary of Blunt's at Cambridge, whom Costello claimed suggested this in an interview. There is no evidence that this was the case, nor has it ever been suggested by any of Blunt's Marlborough contemporaries.

You might find: Worsley, *Flannelled Fool*, p. 47.

23 **It was a perfectly bestial place:** 'Conversation Piece'.
They surrounded him: Betjeman, *Summoned*, chapter 7.
If I were a captain: L. MacNeice, *Return to a School*, BBC radio play, 1954, transcript in Marlborough College Archives.

24 **a much more luscious life:** LM to Georgina MacNeice, 16 Oct. 1923, Bodleian Library.
What really dominated: A. Blunt, 'From Bloomsbury'.

25 **The generation before mine:** ibid.

26 **when the toughs:** quoted in Hillier, *Young Betjeman*, p. 99.
We went out of our way: A. Blunt, 'From Bloomsbury'.
believed that all art stopped: 'Conversation Piece'.
I remember Betjeman: T. D. F. Money interview.

27 **very learned and Olympian:** A. Blunt, 'From Bloomsbury'.
a man full of enthusiasm: 'Conversation Piece'.
What the Louvre: John Betjeman, *Ghastly Good Taste* (new edn. Antony Blond, 1970), p. xx.
Botticelli? Leonardo?: MacNeice, *Return to a School*.

28 **Modern art in 1923:** A. Blunt, 'From Bloomsbury'.

29 **the most difficult:** O. Millar interview.
It 'was planned': A. Blunt, 'From Bloomsbury'.
It is rather dangerous: A. Blunt, 'Some Aspects of Modern Art', *Heretick*, no. 1, Mar. 1924.

30 **It wasn't very good:** A. Blunt, 'From Bloomsbury'.
There is no such thing: A. Blunt, 'Art and Morality', *Heretick*, no. 2, June 1924.
provoked by a row: A. Blunt, 'From Bloomsbury'.

31 **The second issue:** 'Conversation Piece'.
We were inspired: A. Blunt, 'From Bloomsbury'.
a room with walls: W. Blunt, *Married*, p. 122.

n. **I discovered that Oscar Wilde:** Hillier, *Young Betjeman*, p. 116.

32 **teetotallers, anti-gamblers:** Clive Bell, *Art* (all subsequent Clive Bell quotes are also from *Art*).
He considered it very: L. MacNeice, *Strings*, p. 95.

33 **certainly didn't prevent:** J. Hilton interviewed by B. Penrose and S. Freeman, 1985.
he would be president: 'Conversation Piece'.
astonishingly dull: ibid.

References

n. **highly respectable:** ibid.

34 **the logical end:** 'Picasso and Cubism', a paper delivered to the Anonymous Society, Oct. 1924, in the possession of John Golding. (Copies also now in AFB papers, Courtauld Institute.)
   the greatest innovator: ibid.

35 **there would almost certainly:** A. Blunt, 'From Bloomsbury'.
   possessed, rather surprisingly: ibid.
   so many human contacts: L. MacNeice, 'When I was 21', *The Selected Prose of Louis MacNeice*, ed. Alan Heuser (Oxford: Clarendon Press, 1990), p. 223.

36 **As Blunt says:** LM to Georgina MacNeice, 10 May 1926, Bodleian Library.
   by far my closest friend: A. Blunt, 'From Bloomsbury'.
   astonishing visual sensibility: ibid.

37 **all slate blues:** LM to AB, 15 Oct. 1926, KCL.

38 **Parents he already rejected:** J. Hilton interviewed by B. Penrose and S. Freeman, 1985.
   He always makes me: John Betjeman, *Letters*, vol. 2, ed. Candida Lycett-Green (London: Methuen, 1995), p. 349.
   prostitute his talents: W. Blunt, 'Slow on the Feather', p. 256.

39 **colossal bore:** J. Bowle interviewed by B. Penrose and S. Freeman, 1985.
   I wish you: LM to AB, 15 Oct. 1926, KCL.
   I expect he was shocked: ibid.
   There was not much: Hillier, *Young Betjeman*, p. 115.

40 **Yes, beautiful, beautiful:** Gathorne-Hardy, *Public School*, p. 301.
   the vice was sensational: ibid., p. 164.
   the convention of the crush: Lehmann, *In the Purely*, p. 22.
   a cup and saucer: W. Blunt, *Married*, p. 79.
   enchanting, highly intellectual: AB interviewed by Jon Stallworthy, 1982.

41 **beautiful Basil:** LM to AB, 4 May 1928, KCL.
   Marlborough is not: LM to Georgina MacNeice, 26 Jan. 1926, Bodleian Library.
   worthy of a pavement artist: ibid., 6 Nov. 1925, Bodleian Library.
   We are afraid: ibid.

42 **With tears in his eyes:** 'Conversation Piece'.
   If the artist: A. Blunt, 'Art and Morality', *Heretick*, no. 2, June 1924.
   The harsh green outline: *Marlburian*, 20 Mar. 1926.
   One sometimes got the impression: J. Hilton in L. MacNeice, *Strings*, p. 243.

43 **curious mixture:** A. Blunt, 'From Bloomsbury'.
   I am indeed wicked: LM to Georgina MacNeice, 1 Sept. 1925, Bodleian Library.

References

I believe there was: 'Conversation Piece'.

'beautiful', but 'irredeemably heterosexual': AB interviewed by Jon Stallworthy, 1982.

We lived in this: A. Blunt, 'From Bloomsbury'.

44 **persistent efforts:** 'The Master's Speech', *Marlburian*, 26 July 1926.

Guillebaud was enraged: LM to Georgina MacNeice, 20 May 1926, Bodleian Library.

3. Undergraduate

45 **There was in general:** V. G. Kiernan, 'On Treason', *London Review of Books*, 25 June 1987.

I'm sure you'll bear: LM to AB, 25 Sept. 1926, KCL.

46 **You must not:** ibid., 23 Oct. 1926, KCL.

If one keeps: ibid., 1 Jan. 1928, KCL.

He was always: John Hilton to Barrie Penrose, 1985.

was very worried about: LM to AB, 6 Dec. 1926, KCL.

I'm sorry to have been: ibid., 3 Nov. 1926, KCL.

47 **Marlborough Musketeers:** A. MacDonald interview.

Just because you: LM to AB, 5 Jan. 1927, KCL.

48 **I had tea:** John Hilton in MacNeice, *Strings*, p. 262.

As I had no religion: ibid., p. 119.

Shepard has got hold: LM to AB, 6 Dec. 1926, KCL.

I don't believe: LM to AB, 25 Sept. 1926.

I shall give you: ibid., 4 June 1928, KCL.

Get yr hair: ibid., LM to AB 11 June 1928, KCL.

49 **the logical explanation:** 'Picasso and Cubism', a paper delivered to the Anonymous Society, Oct. 1924, in the possession of John Golding.

50 **very distasteful:** A. Blunt, 'From Bloomsbury'.

We were, I think: ibid.

What fun selling: LM to AB, 9 Jan. 1927, KCL.

Italian purgatory: LM to AB, 7 Nov. 1927, KCL.

51 **said to have fallen wildly:** K. Raine interview.

52 **one of the bright:** Prince Chula Chakrabongse, *Brought up in England* (London: Foulis, 1942), p. 127. John Costello has suggested that, through Chula, Blunt may have met the bisexual Duke of Kent and the circle around Viscount Mountbatten. My research has found no evidence of this, and Mountbatten's biographer, Philip Ziegler, says, 'I cannot recollect coming across a single reference to Blunt except in passing after

his detection. I would be very surprised if Blunt ever had anything much to do with the Duke of Kent' (letter to the author, 1 Dec. 1995).

53 **The people who taught me:** E. Playfair interview.
sweet canary Don: Holroyd, *Lytton Strachey*, p. 643.
dominant force: A. Blunt, *From Bloomsbury*.

54 **of easy intercourse:** E. M. Forster, *Listener*, 11 Oct. 1956.
it was not sufficient glory: E. M. Forster, *The Longest Journey* (Edinburgh: Blackwoods, 1907).
For the halcyon period: L. P. Wilkinson, *A Century of King's* (Cambridge: Cambridge University Press, 1980), pp. 77–8.
to an extraordinary extent: A. Blunt, 'From Bloomsbury'.
at the same time: Powell, *Journal 1982–86*, p. 204.

55 **one of the most:** Julian Trevelyan, *Indigo Days* (London: MacGibbon & Kee), p. 15.
rather hard work: Skidelsky, *Keynes: The Economist as Saviour*, p. 293.
I think he was a bit shy: F. Partridge, letter to the author, 13 July 1996.

56 **the higher sodomy:** Skidelsky, *Keynes: Hopes Betrayed*, p. 129.
the constant topic: L. P. Wilkinson, *Kingsmen of a Century* (Cambridge: Cambridge University Press, 1980), p. 92.
Our conversation: Lehmann, *In the Purely*, p. 29.

57 **Physically we lacked:** ibid., p. 28.
The homosexual temperament: G. Lowes Dickinson, *The Autobiography of Goldie Lowes Dickinson*, ed. D. Proctor (London: Duckworth, 1973), p. 11.
like being blind: W. Blunt, *Married*, p. 210.
did not know for certain: W. Blunt, *Slow*, p. 245.

58 **Please don't:** LM to AB, 18 Apr. 1928, KCL.
My love to: ibid., 29 Feb. 1928, KCL.
a strong girlish streak: private information.
no one was quite certain: 'Verandah, a biography', *Granta*, 7 June 1929.
Julian Bell, John Lehmann: John Hilton in MacNeice, *Strings*, pp. 258–9.

59 **an own goal:** ibid., p. 251.
His rooms were: AB letter, *The Times*, 11 Feb. 1978.
kept tears: 'A. E. Housman', *The English Auden*, p. 238.
He had an unwelcoming manner: Hodgkin, *Chance and Design*, p. 53.
'He is', Hodgkin wrote: ibid.
If I have any standards: A. Blunt, 'From Bloomsbury'.

60 **Blunt always mentioned:** John Hilton to Barrie Penrose, 1985.
viewed him with some mistrust: W. Blunt, *Slow*, p. 43.
I was wound: Penrose and Freeman, *Conspiracy*, p. 52.

61 **I couldn't have:** John Hilton to Barrie Penrose, 1985.
the two most recent recruits: records of the Apostles Society, private

References

source. In *Mask of Treachery* (p. 141), John Costello suggests that Blunt's election at the end of his second year was late by Apostolic standards, and claimed that Blunt, having been initially rejected by the society had subsequently 'conspired to get himself in'. There's no evidence to support this and many Apostles – Dennis Proctor and Alan Hodgkin, for example – were elected in their third years. Costello also claims (p. 194) that Blunt and Alister Watson 'set about restructuring the Apostles ... They enlisted the support of Julian Bell to seize control of the society through the traditional authority of the junior Apostle to vet embryos.' He cites no evidence to support this, and nothing the author has discovered suggests that this is true.

n.   **I learnt my Marxist theory:** Wright, *Spycatcher*, p. 253.
62   **It was a principle:** Holroyd, *Lytton Strachey*, p. 82.
       I think that: A. Blunt, 'From Bloomsbury'.
       the most important event: Stansky and Abrahams, *Journey*, p. 47.
63   **one must be:** Straight, *After Long Silence*, p. 93.
       their view of life: A. Blunt, 'From Bloomsbury'.
       We repudiated entirely: Skidelsky, *Keynes: Hopes Betrayed*, pp. 142–3.
       doing whatever they liked: Holroyd, *Lytton Strachey*, p. 92, and see Alasdair Macintyre, *After Virtue* (London: Duckworth, 1981), pp. 14–17.
       Bloomsbury un peu passé: Stansky and Abrahams, *Journey*, p. 48.
64   **Among the votes:** records of the Apostles Society, private source.
       States of mind: A. Blunt, 'From Bloomsbury'.
       In the Cambridge: J. Bell letter, *New Statesman*, 8 Dec. 1933.
       the supremely civilising pursuit: quoted in Terry Eagleton, *Literary Theory* (Oxford: Blackwells, 1985), p. 45.
       The Apostles were never: A. Blunt, 'From Bloomsbury'.
65   **who was already:** Lehmann, *Whispering*, p. 150.
n.   **a young post-graduate:** Michael Redgrave, *In My Mind's Eye* (London: Weidenfeld & Nicolson, 1983), pp. 62–3.
n.   **mercenaries:** Lehmann, *Whispering*, p. 150.
66   **the extreme left:** ibid.
       Theories are dangerous: V. Woolf, *Roger Fry* (London: Hogarth Press, 1940), p. 241.
       obscurity of modern poetry: J. Bell, *Venture*, Feb. 1930.
       much the more positive: A. Blunt, 'From Bloomsbury'.
67   **the first article in English:** A. Blunt, 'Johann Michael Fischer and the Bavarian Rococo', *Venture*, June 1929.
       set up a meeting: LM to AB, undated, *c.* autumn 1928, KCL.
       loved and admired Bloomsbury: Stansky and Abrahams, *Journey*, p. 4.
       I sent Blunt: Julian Bell to Vanessa Bell, undated, *c.* autumn 1928, Charleston papers, KCL.

508

References

Well, God has arrived: Ray Monk, *Wittgenstein* (Cape, 1980), p. 255.
Blunt's first paper: records of the Apostles Society, private source.
upset by what you think happened: J. M. Keynes to AB, 17 Mar. 1929,
Keynes letters, KCL.
not rare, *bêtes noires*: J. Hilton in MacNeice, *Strings*, p. 259.
the Julian Bells: Monk, *Wittgenstein*, p. 257.

69 But who, on any issue: J. Bell, *Venture*, Feb. 1930.
put to shame: H. Jennings in *Experiment* 2.
the same person: G. Rossetti, letter, *Cambridge Review*, 26 Apr. 1929.
Bad temper: AB, letter, *Cambridge Review*, 3 May 1929. (The original
letter by Blunt was published in *Cambridge Review*, 19 Apr. 1929).
fairly complete examples: A. Blunt, letter, *Cambridge Review*, 19 April
1929 (Goodison's article was published in *Cambridge Review*, 1 March
1929).
May I assure you: J. Bell, letter, *Cambridge Review*, 3 May 1929.

70 He was a great, untidy, sprawling figure: Lehmann, *Whispering*, p. 141.
I shan't dare: J. Bell to Q. Bell, 7 Mar. 1929, Bell letters, KCL.
I have had: J. Bell to Q. Bell, 28 Mar. 1929, Bell letters, KCL.
I hope Anthony: J. Bell to Q. Bell, Saturday before easter 1929, KCL.
Yes, Mary Ezra: LM to AB, 27 Mar. 1929, KCL.

71 I have so much: J. Bell to V. Bell, 14 May 1929, Charleston papers, KCL.
Lytton (who is . . .): J. M. Keynes to V. Bell, 24 May 1929, Charleston
papers, KCL.

72 I had a charming: R. Fry to V. Bell, 21 May 1929, Charleston papers,
KCL.
He would always listen: A. Blunt, *Seurat*, introduction p. 8; see also A.
Blunt, 'Professor Roger Fry (Obituary)': *Cambridge Review*, 19 Oct.
1934.

n. Bell and Blunt had talked: J. Bell to V. Bell, 4 May 1929, Bell papers,
KCL.

73 convivial male college occasion: Dadie Rylands interview.
Lytton and Anthony Blunt: 21 Sept. 1929, V. Woolf, *Diaries, Vol. 3:
1925–30*, ed. A. O. Bell (London: Hogarth Press, 1980), p. 255.
It was characteristically: W. Blunt, *Married*, pp. 207–9.
What a loss: ibid.

74 at present in rather a gloomy position: J. Bell to V. Bell, Nov. 1929, Bell
letters, KCL.
intense involvement: Stansky and Abrahams, *Journey*, p. 58.
dirty little Jew: Derek Wilson, *Rothschild: A Story of Wealth and Power*
(London: André Deutsch, 1988), p. 361.
putting people at their ease: Rt. Hon. William Waldegrave, address at
Victor Rothschild's memorial service.

509

References

75 **Like many others:** Rothschild, *Random Variables*, p. 203.
   remarks endlessly: Althea Graham, 'Summer with two Julians', *Charleston Magazine*, summer 1992.
   the falseness of considering: 'R.P.' (Roy Pascal), *Cambridge Review*, 13 June 1930.
76 **I hear you were much pained:** LM to AB, 13 July 1930, KCL.

4. Angry Young Man

77 **He was marvellously irreverent:** Lord Annan interview.
   missed hardly one issue: Driberg, *Guy Burgess*, p. 14.
   a professional gambler: Boyle, *Climate of Treason*, p. 92.
78 **He was immensely:** Connolly, *Missing Diplomats*, p. 18.
   how many serious people: N. Annan, *New York Review of Books*, 22 Oct. 1987.
   I always rather liked: S. Runciman interviewed by B. Penrose and S. Freeman, 1985.
   Our sheltered existence: A. Blunt, 'From Bloomsbury'.
   smuggling Mary St-Clare Erskine: Penrose and Freeman, *Conspiracy*, p. 74.
79 **at this time:** A. Blunt, 'From Bloomsbury'.
80 **father confessor and pimp:** G. Rees, *Chapter*, p. 113.
   gross and even brutal: ibid.
   with coat hangers: confidential source.
81 **He was the most persistent:** G. Rees, *Chapter*, p. 113.
   He was secretly: private information.
82 **he was amusing:** Penrose and Freeman, *Conspiracy*, p. 240.
   I don't think: Nigel Burgess interviewed by B. Penrose and S. Freeman, 1985.
   Blunt's findings: see Paul Alfassa, 'L'origine de la lettre de Poussin sur les modes d'après un travail récent': *Bulletin de la Société de l'Histoire de l'Art Français*, 1933, pp. 125–43.
83 **He is an extremely serious student:** H. F. Stewart to O. Morshead, 27 July 1932, RA/RCD/Librarian, Royal Archives, Windsor.
   This is a remarkable piece: W. G. Constable, report on A. Blunt's thesis, 2 Oct. 1932, AFB papers, CI, Appendix ii.
   artistic theory in France and Italy: Jonathan Smith, manuscripts cataloguer, Trinity College Library, letter to author, 18 Oct. 1994.
   which Blunt reviewed: see *Cambridge Review*, 4 Mar. 1932.

References

84 **Friedlaender loved him:** Margot Wittkower interview transcript,
   Interviews with Art Historians, GRI, Research Library 94109.
   freely admitted: see A. Blunt, *Nicolas Poussin*, p. x.
   take wings: records of the Apostles, private source.
   'secured' Burgess's election: Boyle, *Climate of Treason*, p. 71.
   There can be no question: Deacon, *The Cambridge Apostles*, p. 107.

85 **Anthony Blunt, whom I had met:** Hodgkin, *Chance and Design*, p. 88.
   Arthur Lee: see Lee, *A Good Innings*.

86 **the most detested figure:** K. Clark, *Another Part*, p. 178.
   a full-time staff of three: Courtauld Institute prospectus, 1932–3.
   the pyramids to Picasso: S. Rees Jones interview.
   I was absolutely terrified: A. Blunt, CI tapes, 1980.

87 **Probably our:** Ruth Harwood, *Newsletter of the Courtauld Association of
   Former Students*, Sept. 1995.
   £46 in 1929: see AB to Duit's, 16 Dec. 1961, AFB papers, CI.
   impeccable eye: LM to AB, 17 Nov. 1934, KCL.
   My father told me: Rothschild, *Random Variables*, p. 204.

88 **presented Dadie:** D. Rylands interview.
   criticized Matisse: *Spectator*, 25 Nov. 1932.
   when you have seen one: ibid.
   It denies to reason: A. Blunt, 'Paris Exhibitions', *Sir Galahad*, 14 May
   1929, MacNeice papers, KCL; for Blunt on Surrealism see also *Spectator*,
   11 Nov. 1932 and 2 Feb. 1934.

89 **the greatest living:** *Listener*, 26 July 1933. See also *Spectator*, 14 July
   1933.
   curious and captivating: *Spectator*, 12 May 1933.
   the best achievement: ibid., 7 Dec. 1934.
   positively shocking: quoted in Madge Garland, *The Indecisive Decade*
   (London: Macdonald, 1968), p. 214.
   a sculptor of genius: *Spectator*, 1 Feb. 1935.
   I found almost: ibid., 5 May 1933.
   the disastrous result: ibid., 7 July 1933.
   inventiveness . . . and perhaps life: ibid., 15 Oct. 1932.

90 **the outcome of impressionism:** ibid.
   Purely scholarly analysis: *Cambridge Review*, 4 Mar. 1932.
   You always were: LM to AB, 24 May 1936, KCL.
   I cannot remember: unsigned letter, *Spectator*, 10 Jan. 1934, AFB papers,
   vol. 489, CI.

91 **Mr Wilenski has clearly:** *Cambridge Review*, 13 June 1930.
   owing to the recent: *Spectator*, 29 Oct. 1932.
   This is to say to you: R. H. Wilenski to AB, 31 Oct. 1932, AFB papers,
   vol. 489, CI.

References

He is not a great: George Oglethorpe (AB), *Venture*, Nov. 1929.
a long critical piece: A. Blunt, *Cambridge Review*, 5 Feb. and 12 Feb. 1932.
I receive practically no: S. Sitwell to AB, 20 Feb. 1932, AFB papers, vol. 489, CI.

92   **an admirable introduction**: *Spectator*, 14 July 1933.
petulance: see apology for piece on Mark Gertler, ibid., 19 Oct. 1934.
Consider this and in: March 1930, Auden, *The English Auden*, pp. 46–7.
It is time for the destruction: October 1929, ibid., p. 40.

93   **the Eton cricket eleven**: J. Strachey, *Left Review*, Dec. 1934.
I honestly believe: MacNeice, *Strings*, p. 233.
silted harbours: Auden, 'Consider this and in our time', *The English Auden*, pp. 46–7.
Everybody is so weak: C. Connolly, 'England My England' (1928) in *The Condemned Playground* (London: Routledge, 1945), p. 196.
I joined: MacNeice, *Strings*, p. 146.

94   **probably met**: Enriqueta Frankfort, letter to the author, 9 Dec. 1995: 'I met him at the CI and it was probably through me that he met my brother.'
immaculately turned out: D. Kingzett and J. Baer interviews.
The first thing: A. Blunt, 'Tomás Harris, 27 Feb. – 31 March 1975', CI; see also A. Blunt, 'Tomás Harris' in *Dictionary of National Biography 1961–70*, ed. E. T. Williams and C. S. Nicholls (Oxford: Oxford University Press, 1981).

95   **not one of the great**: *Spectator*, 4 Aug. 1933.

96   **embarrassingly unpredictable**: Pope-Hennessy, *Learning to Look*, p. 137.
An unholy alliance: B. Robertson, *Sunday Telegraph*, 14 Nov. 1999; see also Richardson, *Sorcerer's Apprentice*.
ghastly English philistinism: Richardson, *Sorcerer's Apprentice*, p. 24.
egged Blunt on: A. Bowness interview, Mar. 1996.
palpably academic: MacNeice, *Strings*, p. 133.
quite the nicest: LM to AB, 7 May 1936, KCL.
A charade: MacNeice, *Strings*, p. 143.
clearer memories: J. Stallworthy interview.

97   **Even his close friends**: J. Hilton, letter to J. Stallworthy, 1973, possession of Baroness Hilton.
basically dishonest: MacNeice, *Strings*, p. 143.
cold blue eyes: MacNeice (as Louis Malone), *Roundabout Way* (Putnam, 1932).
spiced up: LM to AB, Oct. 1932, KCL.
head poised like a Cobra: *Roundabout Way*, p. 72.

98   **Herewith my unhappy novel**: LM to AB, Oct. 1932, KCL.

a novel about public school: ibid., 21 Jan. 1932, KCL.

invited Blunt to Birmingham: ibid., 15 Nov. 1932, KCL.

If one keeps: ibid., 1 Jan. 1928, KCL.

When Blunt had an affair: private information.

99 never frightfully liked: Penrose and Freeman, *Conspiracy*, p. 45.

Youngish dons: G. Ewart interview.

a women friend a teaching job: see LM to AB, 11 May 1931, KCL: 'I broached your girlfriend today but he [E. R. Dodds] said that the French professor is all for having a man.' John Costello (*Mask*, p. 213) suggests this was Jean Stewart, but she was already engaged to be married at this time and had given up teaching.

5. Don

101 Auden turned up: LM to AB, 19 Jan. 1933, KCL.

I do not think anything: Russian Intelligence Archives TONY file no. 83895, vol. 1, p. 240, quoted in West and Tsarev, *Crown Jewels*, p. 129.

102 Blunt praised Fry: *Spectator*, 10 Feb. 1933.

divorced 'art from life': ibid., 28 July 1933.

even though illness: Driberg, *Guy Burgess*, pp. 15–16.

Guy thought: M. Grant interview.

103 British School: British School in Rome, annual report, 1933–4.

the 'cleverest' member of staff: Clark, *Another Part*, p. 224.

I came to Rome: A. Blunt, *Borromini*, p. 9.

Anyone living in Italy: Arthur Trendall, letter to the author, 21 Oct. 1994.

104 picnics out to the Campagna: D. Kingzett interview.

Blunterhouse: Waterhouse, 'Preface', p. ix.

Being a Goddamn Britson: Ezra Pound to AB, 2 Nov. 1933, AFB papers, vol. 489, CI.

Complimenti: ibid., 22 Nov. 1933, AFB papers, vol. 489, CI.

bikes of excruciating form: Waterhouse, 'Preface', p. ix.

the sillier passages: ibid., p. ix.

105 Then the rooks: *Spectator*, 9 Feb. 1934.

He used to tell us: Penrose and Freeman, *Conspiracy*, p. 106.

a 'socialist' at school: Driberg, *Guy Burgess*, p. 12.

found Marxist books: Boyle, *Climate of Treason*, p. 84.

He didn't approve: C. Madge interview.

Marxism hit Cambridge: A. Blunt, 'From Bloomsbury'.

References

106 **By the end of 1933:** J. Bell, letter, *New Statesman*, 9 Dec. 1933.
   n. **Several unconvincing attempts:** for example Cave Brown, *Treason in the Blood*, p. 145, and Costello, *Mask*, pp. 191 and 197.
107 **which we felt bore:** G. de Freitas in Cradock, *Recollections*, pp. 139–40.
   politics and religion: 'Letter from Cambridge', *Spectator*, 3 Mar. 1933.
108 **seemed so simple:** James Klugmann in J. Clark, *Culture and Crisis*, p. 14.
   It had become evident: Harold Macmillan, *The Winds of Change* (London: Macmillan, 1966), p. 283.
109 **In opposing:** A. J. P. Taylor, *A Personal History* (London: Hamish Hamilton, 1983), p. 125.
   Quite a decent amount: J. Bell to Q. Bell, undated, *c.* late 1933, Bell papers, KCL.
110 **The demonstration:** Sloan, *John Cornford*, pp. 99–101. See also T. E. B. Howarth, *Cambridge*, p. 212.
   like a tank: J. Bell to Q. Bell, undated, *c.* late 1933, Bell papers, KCL.
   The hunger marchers: Penrose and Freeman, *Conspiracy*, p. 98.
   hounded by external events: S. Spender, *World Within World*, p. 137.
111 **The strongest appeal:** MacNeice, *Strings*, p. 146.
   self-fulfilment through self-abnegation: ibid., p. 169.
   the only organization: M. Straight interview.
   after a marathon: Rycroft, 'Memoirs', p. 209.
112 **I like your visualisation:** D. Proctor to J. Bell, 31 Dec. 1933, Bell papers, KCL.
   It is not so much: J. Bell, letter, *New Statesman*, 9 Dec. 1933.
   There is a general feeling: J. Bell, ibid.
113 **found that the intellectuals:** A. Blunt, quoted in West and Tsarev, *Crown Jewels*, p. 129.
   a stalwart of the Trinity Communist cell: V. G. Kiernan, letter to the author, 11 July 1994.
   nothing but a means: *Spectator*, 5 Jan. 1934.
   perhaps the only painter: ibid., 2 Mar. 1934.
114 **There are quite a lot:** LM to AB, 31 May 1934, KCL.
   Events which took place: A. Blunt, quoted in West and Tsarev, *Crown Jewels*, p. 129.
   I would quote: *Spectator*, 5 Oct. 1934.
   found himself making detours: W. Blunt, *Married*, p. 235.
   Here what seemed a nightmare: J. Rees, *Looking*, p. 67.
115 **the 'sexually bold' Moore Crossthwaite:** see Stallworthy, *Louis MacNeice*; see also MacNeice letters Dec. 1928 and 10 Oct. 1929, KCL.
   This person: J. Hilton interviewed by B. Penrose and S. Freeman, 1985.
   Write and tell us: LM to AB, 31 May 1934, KCL.
116 **the keenness of my interest:** Lehmann, *In the Purely*, p. 75. Lehmann

writes of a Viennese boy who gets involved in 'the shadier side of international diplomacy, extremely dangerous at that time' and comes to London (pp. 48–9).

whom he visited in Freiberg: AB to Margot Wittkower, 1 Oct. 1976, Wittkower papers, Columbia University Library: 'I happened to stay with W.F. a month or two after it [the Festschrift] was published (and a week or so after he'd been dismissed)'. See also LM to AB (sent c/o Friedlaender), June 1933, KCL.

Blunt later remembered: AB to W. Friedlaender, 5 March 1953, AFB Papers, vol. 347, CI. 'It was actually in the summer of 1934 that I came to see you in Freiberg . . .'

About your quandaries: LM to AB, 30 Sept. 1934, KCL.

Cambridge seems a little: AB to D. Rylands, 4 Oct. 1934, Rylands papers, KCL.

117 **exhibit your personal charm:** LM to AB, 10 Oct. 1934, KCL.

I feel that my knowledge: AB to I. Berlin, undated, *c.* Oct. 1934, Isaiah Berlin papers, Bodleian Library.

The bloody old sots: LM to AB, 10 Nov. 1934, KCL.

coquettishly chaste: MacNeice, *Strings*, p. 156.

118 **another student remembered:** C. Rycroft interview.

Spender would claim: see entry for 28 March 1983, S. Spender, *Journals 1939–83* (London: Random House, 1983), p. 442.

Blunt met Tess Mayor: T. Rothschild interview.

119 **He was different from:** confidential information.

the most romantic scenes: *Spectator*, 14 May 1937.

I happened to be present: C. Rycroft interview.

120 **The undergraduates:** A. Blunt, 'From Bloomsbury'.

I found myself: West and Tsarev, *Crown Jewels*, p. 129.

121 **a glamorous figure:** A. Blunt, 'From Bloomsbury'.

strange and, I thought: S. Runciman interviewed by B. Penrose and S. Freeman, 1985; see also V. G. Kiernan, 'Recollections' in Sloan, *John Cornford*, pp. 116–24.

who had been: A. Blunt, 'From Bloomsbury'.

122 **the pure intellectual:** ibid.

that Communism was: Rycroft, 'Memoirs', p. 210.

124 **Burgess claimed:** G. Rees, *Chapter*, p. 112.

later said recruited: ibid.

found dead drunk: ibid.

At first I could see: West and Tsarev, *Crown Jewels*, p. 130.

held that culture: Rycroft, 'Memoirs', p. 210.

Painting being as important: *Spectator*, 10 Apr. 1936.

They were against: J. Klugmann in J. Clark, *Culture and Crisis*, p. 31.

References

125 **The intellectual is no longer:** *Spectator*, 11 Oct. 1935.

Marxism made everything rich: J. Klugmann in J. Clark, *Culture and Crisis*, p. 34.

reduces [painting] to: A. Blunt, 'Art under Capitalism and Socialism', p. 107.

made out of materials found: 'The Beaver and the Silk Worm', *Spectator*, 2 Nov. 1934.

Social realism had been adopted: Ades, *Art and Power*, pp. 186–8.

126 **Art belongs to the people:** F. Klingender quoted in Rycroft, 'Memoirs', p. 210.

127 **In Budapest:** Ann Wesselly, 'Antal and Lukács: A Marxist Approach to Art History', *The New Hungarian Quarterly*, no. 73 (1979), pp. 114–25.

'captivated' by the Hungarian: Pope-Hennessy, *Learning*, p. 305.

128 **an art 'of escape:** *Spectator*, 17 Jan. 1936.

a member of an anti-fascist committee: Virginia Woolf, *Diaries, Vol. 4: 1931–35*, ed. A. O. Bell (London: Hogarth Press, 1982), p. 280 (20 Feb. 1935).

n. **the banker against the aristocrat:** 'Letters by Balzac', *Spectator*, 12 Nov. 1937.

n. **article on Balzac's villains:** 'The Criminal King in a 19th Century Novel', *Journal of the Warburg Institute*, 1937–8.

n. **Peter Kidson has ventured:** Peter Kidson, Morley College, special guest lecture in honour of Andrew Martindale, 10 Nov. 1995.

129 **the first piece in Britain:** 'Time and Place in the Arts II', *Listener*, 2 Jan. 1935.

Rivera's frescoes: ibid.

to play . . . their own: *Spectator*, 25 Jan. 1935.

As a critic: ibid., 1 Feb. 1935.

130 **almost the only:** ibid., 11 Oct. 1935.

put him on a retainer: M. Rothschild interview.

n. **Blunt wrote a piece:** 'De la Tour', *Spectator*, 1 Mar. 1935.

6. Fellow-Traveller

131 **was terra incognita:** Cecil, *Divided Life*, p. 5.

Anthony and I: W. Blunt, *Married*, p. 295.

132 **in moderate discomfort:** ibid.

a Chinese who: ibid.

the kind of thing: Mayhew, *Time*, p. 24.

Freedom at last: W. Blunt, *Married*, p. 295.

References

133 **a new and higher phase**: quoted in Ades, *Art and Power*, p. 191.
     to which so much: *Spectator*, 27 Sept. 1935.
     false statistics: see Conquest, *Stalin*, p. 190.
     Some things we saw: Mayhew, *Time*, pp. 25–6.
134 **buildings heroic**: *Spectator*, 20 Sept. 1935.
     For our part: C. Mayhew, *Time*, p. 25.
     I believe nobody: Maurice Dobb, *Soviet Russia To-day and To-morrow*
     (London: Hogarth Press, 1930), p. 10.
135 **accepted censorship**: John Lehmann, *Left Review*, Feb. 1937.
     I feel: Mayhew, *Time*, p. 25.
     estimated 15 million: Conquest, *The Great Terror*, pp. 19–20; see also
     Robert Conquest, *Harvest of Sorrow: Soviet Collectivisation and the
     Terror Famine* (London: Hutchinson, 1986).
     years later he remembered: Michael Kitson interview.
     getting Blunt to hold: Mayhew, *Time*, p. 26.
136 **Wilfred later wrote**: W. Blunt, *Married*, p. 296.
     I have never: W. Blunt, *Married*, pp. 295–6.
     conscientiously shabby: W. Blunt, *Married*, p. 296.
137 **'scientific' arrangement**: *Spectator*, 6 Sept. 1935.
     the uninteresting use: ibid., 27 Sept. 1935.
     the circle round Malevich: see Ades, *Art and Power*, p. 196.
138 **bedful of dreamers**: *Spectator*, 11 Oct. 1935.
     When his experiments: ibid.
     the function of abstract art: ibid., 22 Nov. 1935.
  n. **vamped up**: K. Clark, 'Ben Nicholson and the Future of Painting',
     Listener, 9 Oct. 1935.
139 **Naturally when**: West and Tsarev, *Crown Jewels*, p. 130.
     I was . . . commonly: ibid.; also B. Simon interview.
140 **The child of evangelicism**: James Wood, *London Review of Books*, 3 Oct.
     1996.
     got on very well: Margot Wittkower interview transcript, Interviews with
     Art Historians, GRI, Research Library 94109.
141 **Klibansky, abandoned**: R. Klibanksy interview.
     Kurz had been hit: E. Gombrich interview.
     Gombrich and Kurz lived: E. Gombrich, 'Otto Kurz' in *Tributes* (London:
     Phaidon, 1984), p. 241.
142 **Pope-Hennessy saw**: Pope-Hennessy, *Learning*, p. 71.
     We found ourselves: Edgar Wind's papers.
     I am delighted: AB to F. Saxl, 25 Feb. 1935, Blunt correspondence, WA.
143 **At that time everyone**: M. Wittkower interview transcript, Interviews with
     Art Historians, GRI, Research Library 94109.
     It was said at the Institute: E. Gombrich interview.

References

This was not Friedlaender's cup of tea: A. Blunt, CI tapes, 1980.
144 It became perfectly clear: ibid.
    Friedlaender has a habit: AB to Fleischer, 30 July 1936, Blunt correspondence, WA.
    [This] is contrary: AB to W. Friedlaender, 29 Sept. 1949, AFB papers, vol. 347, CI.
145 M. is not here: LM to AB, 9 Dec. 1935, KCL.
    great big Rugger-playing: G. Shepard to J. Hilton, 14 Feb. 1936, in the possession of Baroness Hilton (Hilton's daughter).
    You needn't come: LM to AB, 11 June 1935, KCL.
    I must stop: ibid., undated, early 1936, KCL.
    going to Spain: G. Shepard to J. Hilton, 14 Feb. 1936, in the possession of Baroness Hilton.
    Clearly you: J. Stallworthy interview.
146 ripe as an egg: MacNeice, *Autumn Journal*, VI.
    And a vulture: ibid.
    a favourite occupation: J. Stallworthy interview.
    with an air: MacNeice, *Autumn Journal*, VI.
147 the three great: MacNeice, *Strings*, p. 159.
    The Hammer and Sickle: MacNeice, ibid., p. 161.
    We saw the mob: MacNeice, *Autumn Journal*, VI.
    looking, Anthony said: MacNeice, *Strings*, p. 162. Ernst Toller was a left-wing German expressionist playwright; he committed suicide in the late 1930s.
    slightly stoned: AB interviewed by Jon Stallworthy, 1982.
    If Spain goes: MacNeice, *Strings*, p. 161.
    And the next day: MacNeice, *Autumn Journal*, VI.
148 Cambridge was still full: MacNeice, *Strings*, p. 156. In *The Strings are False* this quote seems to refer to occasions before the trip to Spain, and the visit to Cambridge is also placed before Spain, but in fact letters and MacNeice's biography show that it actually took place after. MacNeice changed the order in *Strings*.
    You see, I am really: LM to AB, 7 May 1936, KCL.
    Couldn't you get: ibid.
    I really must: ibid.
    the chief criticism: Julian Symons, *The Thirties and the Nineties* (Manchester: Carcanet, 1990), p. 66.
149 Is Art Propaganda?: A. Blunt, 'Rationalist and Anti-Rationalist Art', *Left Review*, July 1936.
    the dead end: *Spectator*, 10 June 1938.
    ordinary life of: A. Blunt, introduction to *The New Realism in Sculpture: L. Peri*, Gordon Fraser Gallery, Cambridge, Apr.–May 1937. Blunt's first

References

piece on Peri was in the *Spectator* of 5 June 1936. He reviewed a
Cambridge exhibition by Peri in *Cambridge Review*, 23 Apr. 1937, and
Granta, 21 Apr. 1937.

n. **who had been instrumental:** *Arts Review*, 25 May 1968.

150 **Take Blake's:** *Spectator*, 19 June 1936.

Blunt spoke against: Blunt's speech was written up in *Left Review*, July
1936.

Surrealism's supporters: see Harrison, *English Art and Modernism*,
pp. 313–15. See also F. Klingender on David Gascoyne's *A History of
Surrealism*, *Left Review*, May 1936.

reality transformed by the imagination: Harrison, *English Art and
Modernism*, p. 313.

the suspicions which: *Spectator*, 19 July 1936.

151 **more than a little:** Pope-Hennessy, *Learning*, p. 137.

I did not accept: A. Blunt, quoted in West and Tsarev, *Crown Jewels*,
p. 130.

n. **to the repressive education:** *Spectator*, 19 July 1936.

7. Recruit

153 **Arnold Deutsch:** Andrew and Gordievsky, *KGB*, pp. 159–69; see also
Andrew and Mitrokhin, *Mitrokhin Archive*, pp. 73–5.

a very serious: Borovik, *Philby Files*, p. 46.

You are a bourgeois: Tsarev and Costello, *Deadly Illusions*, p. 136.

154 **not of confusion:** Andrew and Gordievsky, *KGB*, p. 31.

a triumph: ibid., p. 40.

the English bourgeoisie: ibid., p. 84.

attack his rival Trotsky: ibid., p. 85.

155 **distinguished by its:** Nadezhda Mandelstam, *Hope Against Hope*
(London: Collins, 1971), p. 79.

Theo Maly: Andrew and Gordievsky, *KGB*, p. 158. See also West and
Tsarev, *Crown Jewels*, pp. 113–22 (West and Tsarev question Maly's
claim that he had been a priest), and Poretsky, *Our Own People*, p. 42.

Born in 1904: see West and Tsarev, *Crown Jewels*, pp. 103–4.

156 **a plaque:** Andrew and Gordievsky, *KGB*, p. 601, n. 181.

157 **was dominated by Burgess:** A. Care Brown, *Treason in the Blood* (Robet
Hale, 1995), p. 140.

158 **the Austrian Committee:** Borovik, *Philby Files*, p. 14.

I've got six: Andrew and Gordievsky, *KGB*, p. 158.

Edith Tudor Hart: Borovik, *Philby Files*, p. 31.

References

The KGB took on: P. Knightley in Borovik, *Philby Files*, p. x.

159 I have decided: Tsarev and Costello, *Deadly Illusions*, p. 137.
The result: Borovik, *Philby Files*, p. 39.
It turns out: ibid., p. 40.
taught me the rules: ibid., p. 33.
Blunt's wasn't on it: Borovik, *Philby Files*, p. 42. See also Tsarev and Costello, *Deadly Illusions*, p. 185.
The Swede: Borovik, *Philby Files*, p. 44.
Donald Maclean first: Tsarev and Costello, *Deadly Illusions*, p. 187.

160 He must have been: Brown, *Treason in the Blood*, p. 171.
the majority: West and Tsarev, *Crown Jewels*, p. 128.
While we were talking: Brown, *Treason in the Blood*, p. 171.

161 his ability to get to know: Tsarev and Costello, *Deadly Illusions*, p. 187.
the party work was something: quoted in Tsarev and Costello, *Deadly Illusions*, pp. 225–7; see also West and Tsarev, *Crown Jewels*, p. 128.

162 Captain Jack Macnamara: G. Rees, *Chapter*, p. 124.
Édouard Pfeiffer: ibid., p. 124
There was: ibid., p. 117.

163 late 1935, early 1936: AB interview with *The Times*, 21 Nov. 1979.
It used to amuse me: G. Rees, *Chapter*, p. 133.

164 the nucleus of a cloud: J. Hilton interviewed by B. Penrose and S. Freeman in 1985.
in January 1937: West and Tsarev, *Crown Jewels*, p. 245.
To us the issue: Worsley, *Fellow Travellers*, p. 113.
Never since: Weintraub, *Last Great Cause*, p. 2.

165 The Tory press: Worsley, *Fellow Travellers*, p. 113.
It was common knowledge: ibid., p. 121.
Stalin sent 648 aircraft: Conquest, *Stalin*, p. 219.
I was persuaded: AB interview with *The Times*, 21 Nov. 1979.

166 he began to talk about Spain: B. Simon interview, Mar. 1995.
It is hard: A. Blunt, *Guernica*, p. 8.
a polished and public statement: Caroline Tisdall, *Guardian*, 28 Mar. 1983.
it gave me the chills: Barbara Murek, letter to the author, 23 June 1997.

167 Wystan is very pleased: LM to AB, 24 May 1936, KCL.
The only hope: *Spectator*, 8 May 1936.
a pseudonymous article: 'Honest Doubt' in *New Verse*, June 1936, under the initials J.B.
Pity you didn't: LM to AB, postcard, 21 Aug. 1936, KCL.

168 I am for anything: Cecil Day-Lewis quoted in Davenport-Hines, *Auden*, pp. 127–8.

References

the most likeable: *Spectator*, 26 June 1936.
169 though they once spent: ibid., 30 Apr. 1937.
As long as art remains a parasite: For Blunt's version see 'Academies',
ibid., 9 and 16 Aug. 1935.
damn great artists: see 'Matisse', ibid., 1 Jan. 1937; 'Seurat', ibid., 29 Jan.
1937.
Lord Hastings: *Left Review*, Feb. 1937.
the small, smothered morality: Davenport-Hines, *Auden*, p. 54, re Auden
and Isherwood.
170 I know exactly why: ibid., p. 179.
Auden came to stay: W. H. Auden to AB, postcard, 11 Nov. 1936, KCL.
Mr Coldstream is: *Spectator*, 27 Nov. 1936.
171 Dear Blunt: W. H. Auden to AB, 22 Nov. 1936, KCL (I am indebted to
Professor Edward Mendelson for identification of the *Hamlet* quotation).
Carpenter has speculated: Carpenter, *W. H. Auden*, p. 207n.
I have decided: W. H. Auden to E. R. Dodds, 8 Dec. 1936, Bodleian
Library.
didn't think it was: R. Lehmann in Penrose and Freeman, *Conspiracy*,
p. 199.
It is perhaps: G. Rees, *Chapter*, p. 138.
172 What attracted me: Day-Lewis, *Buried Day*, p. 21.
The final test: Weintraub, *Last Great Cause*, pp. 9–10.
lost contact with life: A. Blunt, 'Art under Capitalism and Socialism',
p. 111.
The new ills: *Spectator*, 8 Oct. 1937.
I could believe: Day-Lewis, *Buried Day*, p. 212.
The forces of evil: *Spectator*, 10 Dec. 1937.
173 Nobody I know: Davenport-Hines, *Auden*, p. 104.
174 Bernard Pares: Caute, *Fellow Travellers*, p. 118.
We were uneasy: J. Hart interview.
I used to say to Blunt: M. Grant interview.
I did not accept: A. Blunt, quoted in West and Tsarev, *Crown Jewels*,
p. 130.
175 as one critic: Jon Stallworthy in *Louis MacNeice*.
you keep to: 'Hetty to Nancy', in Auden and MacNeice, *Letters from
Iceland*, p. 150.
the Marxist: MacNeice, *Strings*, p. 161.
Not that personally: 'Hetty to Nancy', in Auden and MacNeice, *Letters
From Iceland*, p. 168.
176 Synthesis is a bloody word: LM to AB, 3 Aug. 1936, KCL.
the only possible scientific basis: *Spectator*, 9 Sept. 1938.
We entirely repudiated: Skidelsky, *Keynes: Hopes Betrayed*, pp. 142–3.

177 **blindly furious**: Christopher Isherwood, *Christopher and His Kind* (London: Methuen, 1985), p. 17.

178 **Every criminal act**: Davenport-Hines, *Auden*, p. 111.
the type of: A. Blunt, 'The Criminal King in a 19th century Novel', *Journal of the Warburg Institute*, 1937–8.
Love and loyalty: E. M. Forster, 'What I Believe' (1939) in *Two Cheers for Democracy* (Harmondsworth: Penguin, 1965), pp. 76–7.
he used the same words: G. Rees, *Chapter*, p. 208.

179 **In early January 1937**: Tsarev and Costello, *Deadly Illusions*, p. 245. See also West and Tsarev, *Crown Jewels*, p. 128. Both refer to Deutsch's 'History of the Cambridge Group' in the 'History of the London Residentura', 89113, vol. 1, and Burgess's file, no. 83792, vol. 1, p. 75, in the Russian Intelligence Archives.
We did not think: Cecil, *Divided Life*, p. 33.
Cornford is: S. Spender reviewing Sloan, *John Cornford*, in *New Statesman*, 12 Nov. 1938.
The conflict was: A. Blunt, *Guernica*, p. 8.

180 **he doubted he would ever**: Wright, *Spycatcher*, pp. 227–8.
Burgess was always insistent: Lord Annan interview.
combine the difficult task: West and Tsarev, *Crown Jewels*, p. 130.
Tony is: ibid., p. 133.

8. Talent Spotter

181 **It is of course**: AB to F. Saxl, undated, *c*. early 1937, Blunt correspondence, WA.
We simply *knew*: quoted in Boyle, *Climate of Treason*, p. 72.
What a field day: *Spectator*, 8 Jan. 1937.

182 **I can say that**: West and Tsarev, *Crown Jewels*, p. 133.
had their dreams analysed: Straight, *After Long Silence*, p. 38.
of the ten pupils: M. Straight interview.
John said, 'This: ibid.

183 **a student of unearthly beauty**: Straight, *After Long Silence*, p. 81.
It was was no use: ibid.
emotionally dependent: M. Straight interview.

184 **I would say**: ibid.
We never spoke: Straight, *After Long Silence*, p. 105.
Some of your friends: ibid., pp. 101–3

185 **my response was shaped**: ibid., p. 105.
Why didn't I: ibid., p. 104.

References

self-centred: M. Straight interview.

I had no resistance: ibid.

would be considered: Straight, *After Long Silence*, p. 104.

Stalin, of course: M. Straight interview.

I cited every: Straight, *After Long Silence*, pp. 109–10.

If so the letter: Blunt's copy of *After Long Silence* is in the possession of his nephew, Simon Blunt.

My name became: Straight, *After Long Silence*, p. 110.

186 a job in the Roosevelt administration: L. Miall interview.

At times he denied: In Stansky and Abrahams's 1966 book on Julian Bell and John Cornford, *Journey to the Frontier*, p. 24, Straight claimed not to have been a member of the Party.

You never showed: D. Worcester interview.

for having converted: see Frank Singleton in Cradock, *Recollections*, p. 153.

187 stroked one of the mantelpieces: ibid., pp. 152–3.

Sing me a song: ibid.

And a lot of other things: ibid., p. 523.

188 I needed to sacrifice: Straight, *After Long Silence*, p. 105.

those who are privileged: M. Straight interview.

He was on the contrary: Straight, *After Long Silence*, p. 105.

he was a serious, conflicted: M. Straight interview.

Blunt never taught him: Alex Cairncross (brother), letter to the author, 20 Feb. 1996. 'The idea that Blunt taught John . . . is ludicrous.' See also J. Cairncross, *The Enigma Spy*, p. 37.

One could not: West and Tsarev, *Crown Jewels*, p. 204.

189 lively and warmhearted: ibid., p. 211.

secretly stage managed: Cairncross, *Enigma Spy*, p. 61.

the moving spirit: ibid., p. 37.

a powerful position: Cairncross, *Enigma Spy*, p. 37.

190 Thereafter, Blunt reported: West and Tsarev, *Crown Jewels*, pp. 130–1.

He was very glad: ibid., p. 208.

191 I had a deep sense: L. Long in Penrose and Freeman, *Conspiracy*, pp. 118–20.

Blunt never tried: Costello, *Mask*, p. 408.

in order to remake contact: West and Tsarev, *Crown Jewels*, p. 131.

192 *If Anthony has taken Leo*: Straight, *After Long Silence*, p. 143.

But, according to Long: Penrose and Freeman, *Conspiracy*, p. 121.

It was all a bit of a racket: ibid.

193 could be called lifelong: Noel Annan, *Our Age*, p. 319.

I think the bitterest: Stansky and Abrahams, *Journey*, p. 49.

We're going to kill it: M. Straight interview.

References

I responded with the names: ibid.

To my *great* sorrow: A. Blunt, CI tapes, 1980.

194   **a mind of great:** H. F. Stewart reference, A. Blunt's application for a
Harris scholarship, autumn 1936, KCL. John Costello (*Mask*, p. 260)
claims that Keynes dismissed Blunt's application as 'a lot of Marxist
nonsense'; he fails, however, to cite a source for this, and no report is
attached to the application in King's College Archives. Nor are there
minutes of meetings on fellowship elections.

  in that marvellous way: A. Blunt, CI tapes, 1980.

  Moreover, Lord Lee: West and Tsarev, *Crown Jewels*, p. 136.

  much more than half: AB to G. Bing, undated, *c.* late Mar. 1937, Blunt
correspondence, WA.

  I am trying: ibid., mid Apr. 1937, Blunt correspondence, WA.

195   **I don't think:** AB to F. Saxl, 3 May 1937, Blunt correspondence, WA.

  perhaps a word: ibid., 11 May 1937, Blunt correspondence, WA.

  I still think: ibid., *c.* early June 1937, Blunt correspondence, WA.

  to my old friend: 'Last Will and Testament' in Auden and MacNeice,
Letters from Iceland, p. 248. See Blunt on Holman Hunt's *The Scapegoat*,
Spectator, 19 Jan. 1934.

196   **It is far too amateur:** AB to G. Bing, undated, *c.* Apr. 1937, Blunt
correspondence, WA.

  a year's work in America: AB to F. Saxl, 5 June 1937, Blunt
correspondence, WA.

  [The] collaboration between us: F. Saxl to AB, 7 June 1937, Blunt
correspondence, WA.

197   **a raffia bower:** L. Miall interview.

198   **a stocky, dark-haired Russian:** Straight, *After Long Silence*, p. 121.

  a plea to the Soviet government: ibid., p. 144.

199   **We are international:** Poretsky, *Our Own People*, p. 219.

  He was found dead: Verne Newton, *The Cambridge Spies* (New York:
Madison Books, 1991), pp. 25–30.

  I should have written: Poretsky, *Our Own People*, pp. 1–3.

  n. **We were not sorry:** Sudaplatov, *Special Tasks*, p. 49.

200   **writing directly to Stalin:** ibid., pp. 45–6.

  They will kill me: Poretsky, *Our Own People*, p. 214.

  I have decided: Orlov, *Secret History*, pp. 235–7.

  Theo Maly appears: Borovik, *Philby Files*, p. 92.

201   **I hardly like:** AB to V. Bell, undated, *c.* 1938, Charleston papers, KCL.

  n. **Blunt and his people:** Koch, *Double Lives*, p. 181.

  n. **There was no question:** Frances Spalding, *Vanessa Bell* (London:
Macmillan, 1983), p. 293.

202   **reaching the public:** *Spectator*, 19 Nov. 1937.

In the present state of capitalism: A. Blunt, 'Art under Capitalism and Socialism', p. 108.
Now that . . . bad art: ibid., pp. 105–22.
203 the typically English band: C. Connolly, *New Statesman*, 16 Jan. 1937.
It is still an effort: AB to F. Saxl, undated, *c.* late Aug. 1938, Blunt correspondence, WA.
to those whose minds: *Spectator*, 9 Apr. 1937.
204 Now I had better: 'How I look at a Modern painting', July 1938, BBC Written Archives.
205 I was very much moved: 'From Bloomsbury'.
The painting is disillusioning: *Spectator*, 6 Aug. 1937.
There is something: 'Picasso Unfrocked', ibid., 8 Oct. 1937.
206 modern Calvary: Herbert Read letter, ibid., 15 Oct. 1937.
207 use art for some end: ibid., 22 Oct. 1937.
a revitalisation of: in 'Specialists', ibid., 22 Oct. 1937.
I can only suspect: Herbert Read letter, ibid., 5 Nov. 1937.
merely an awareness: A. Blunt letter, ibid., 5 Nov. 1937.
it would be of little use: Roland Penrose letter, ibid., 29 Oct. 1937.
208 though I think: A. Blunt letter, ibid., 5 Nov. 1937.
was all carried out: A. Blunt, 'From Bloomsbury'.
joined the Reform Club: R. A. M. Forrest (secretary of the Reform Club), letter to the author, 10 Aug. 1995.
We used frequently: A. Blunt, 'From Bloomsbury'.
egged Blunt on: A. Bowness interview, May 1996.
He regretted the damning: B. Simon interview, Mar. 1995.

9. Art Historian

209 a large front room: O. Bell interview.
Anthony had: Margot Wittkower interview transcript, Interviews with Art Historians, GRI, Research Library 94109.
Edgar Wind, reported: M. Wind interview.
210 I'd never had: A. Blunt, CI tapes, 1980.
transformed Anthony: Pope-Hennessy, *Learning*, p. 71.
his book: see Blunt correspondence, WA – e.g. AB to Wittkower, undated, *c.* mid-1937.
I am most grateful: AB to F. Saxl, undated, *c.* end Aug. 1938, Blunt correspondence, WA.
n. Sorry to encroach: editorial dept to AB, 24 Aug. 1938, Blunt correspondence, WA.

References

211 **You know how much:** AB to M. Wittkower, 23 July 1972, Wittkower papers, Columbia University Library.
The first issue: Margot Wittkower interview transcript, Interviews with Art Historians, GRI, Research Library 94109.

212 **I have absolutely no:** AB to R. Wittkower, undated, *c.* June 1937, and undated summer 1937, Journal Contributors file, WA.
the results, incomplete: ibid., undated, c. June 1937, Journal Contributors file, WA.
his first article on Poussin: 'Poussin's Notes on Painting', *Journal of the Warburg Institute*, 1937–8.
familiarity with Greek philosophy: 'Poussin's *Et in Arcadia Ego*', *Art Bulletin*, 1938, pp. 96–100.
his first published attribution: 'A newly discovered Poussin', *Apollo*, XXVII, 1938, p. 197.

n. **There have been suggestions:** *National Post*, Canada, 14 Dec. 2000.

213 **the province of pedantry:** *Architectural Review*, Dec. 1930, p. 235.

214 **alarmingly primitive:** Alla Weaver, letter to the author, May 1997; see also Renée Marcousse, CI tapes, 1980.
questions to Kenneth Clark: Lillian Gurry quoting Joan Evans, in conversation with Mary Woodall and Cecil Farthing, CI tapes, 1980. The National Gallery archives show that exam and course papers were submitted to Clark for approval.
they didn't understand Spanish: Francis Watson, CI tapes, 1980.
Lovely picture: Margot Wittkower interview transcript, Interviews with Art Historians, GRI, Research Library 94109.
a smattering: H. Read, editorial, *Burlington Magazine*, Mar. 1937.
You do *close*: S. Rees Jones interview.
the massage king: Mrs Constable, CI tapes, 1980.

215 **The teaching staff complain:** Witt minority report, Lee papers, Box 2, CI.
consumed by personal ambition: Lee, *A Good Innings*, p. 321.
hounding out Constable: see D. S. McColl, *The Nineteenth Century*, Mar. 1936.
Lord Lee was: Mrs Constable, CI tapes, 1980.

n. **wholeheartedly backed:** W. G. Constable to Lord Lee, 29 Apr. 1929, Lee papers, Box 1, CI.

216 **I believe I shall:** AB to G. Bing, 15 Oct. 1937, Blunt correspondence, WA; see also AB to F. Saxl, 23 Sept. 1937, Blunt correspondence, WA.
Margaret was devoted: O. Bell interview.
She adored him: E. O'Donnell interview.

217 **glamour personified:** W. Blunt, *Slow*, p. 259.
Though I was still: C. Gould, unpublished memoir.
Cecil was naive: K. Garlick interview.

References

Very often my tutorials: C. Gould, unpublished memoir.

218   **to make little bombs**: S. Rees Jones, CI tapes, 1980.

two Marxist students: Cecil Farthing, CI tapes, 1980.

219   **she 'made him retreat**: Lesley Lewis, unpublished memoir, p. 20.

a copy of Marx: A. Blunt, CI tapes, 1980.

Though the international situation: C. Gould, unpublished memoir.

to an anti-fascist meeting: Anne Marie Meyer interview.

as Herbert Read: Editorial, *Burlington Magazine*, Sept. 1937.

perfectly bland: I. Berlin interview.

220   **He was encouraging**: Christl Bergson, CI tapes, 1980.

reputable art critic: G. Burgess, note on arrangements for A. Blunt's talk on 'The Winter Exhibition at the Academy', 20 Jan. 1938, Blunt file, BBC Written Archives.

the 'technician' class: W. J. West, *Truth Betrayed* (London: Duckworth, 1987), p. 50.

certainly the first talk: ibid.

The many housewives: 'The Winter Exhibition at the Academy', BBC radio, 27 Jan. 1938, BBC Written Archives.

221   **It is the most complete**: 'Michelangelo paints the Sistine Chapel', *Forgotten Anniversaries*, BBC radio, 21 Apr. 1938, BBC Written Archives.

In the heaven of painting: *Spectator*, 25 Mar. 1938.

his old teacher Clifford Canning: see AB to Canford 1936, and 8922.4.113 Canning, 12 Apr. 1937, Coldstream papers, Tate Gallery Archives.

got Coldstream to fill in: AB to W. Coldstream, 11 June 1937, Coldstream papers, Tate Gallery Archives.

222   **The slump made me**: W. Coldstream, 'How I Paint', *Spectator*, 15 Sept. 1937.

ordinary realistic painting: in 'A Plan for Artists', Coldstream papers, Tate Gallery Archives.

most striking ordinary painting: *Spectator*, 5 Nov. 1937.

the Picasso debacle: W. Coldstream, letter, ibid., 22 Oct. 1937.

very feeble: G. Grigson, 'Remarks on painting and Mr Auden', *New Verse*, Jan. 1939.

A Coldstream exhibition: ibid.

holding back: 'Coldstream' in David Sylvester *About Modern Art: Critical Essays 1948–1997* (Pimlico, 1997), p. 160.

223   **an element of snobbism**: ibid.

Our English Realists: *London Bulletin*, 1938, p. 20.

pseudo-philosophical: Edgell Rickward, *Left Review*, Apr. 1938.

224   **no artist comparable**: A. Blunt, *Spectator*, 25 Mar. 1938; see also Harrison, *English Art and Modernism*, p. 333, and James King, *The Last*

Modern: A Life of Herbert Read (London: Weidenfeld & Nicolson, 1990), pp. 163–4.

In art, as in morals: *Spectator*, 25 March 1938.

In the present state: A. Blunt, 'Art under Capitalism and Socialism', p. 108.

225 **made many listeners furious:** see letter from Dion Murray, *Listener*, 30 Sept. 1938, and unsigned letter, *Listener*, 29 July 1938.

It's no good: William Coldstream, 'A Modern Artist Answers Questions', BBC radio, 25 July 1938, BBC Written Archives.

Standards: 9 Sept., 16 Sept., 23 Sept. 1938.

n. **saw his new idiom:** Laughton, *Euston Road School*, p. 184.

n. **Art now has so little relation to society:** G. Bell, quoted in Laughton, ibid., pp. 186–7.

n. **little thatched cottages:** letter to *Spectator*, 1 Sept 1938.

226 **would impede his acceptance:** Pope-Hennessy, *Learning*, p. 138.

Blunt wrote perceptively: 'Rodin', *Spectator*, 26 Mar. 1937; 'de Chirico', ibid., 25 June 1937; 'Contemporary German art', ibid., 8 July 1938; 'Walter Gropius', ibid., 15 Jan. 1937.

I had become more: A. Blunt, 'From Bloomsbury'.

I'd scarcely seen him: J. Hilton, letter to to B. Penrose, 1985.

227 **round Coldstream:** Laughton, *Euston Road School*, p. 169.

I must, I think: AB to F. Saxl, undated, *c.* Mar. 1938, Blunt correspondence, WA.

228 **It was very good:** AB to I. Berlin, undated, *c.* spring 1937, Isaiah Berlin papers, Bodleian Library.

I rather think I'm: AB to D. Rylands, undated, *c.* Oct. 1939, Rylands papers, KCL.

submerged in: G. Rees, *Chapter*, p. 127.

a very large, very heavy iron saucepan: ibid.

He was fascinating: L. Long interviewed by B. Penrose and S. Freeman, 1985.

229 **I was steeped in sin:** Penrose and Freeman, *Conspiracy*, p. 201.

given by Tom Wylie: Brown, *Treason in the Blood*, p. 172.

said to be so beautiful: P. Pollock interview.

231 **I was afraid that he:** West and Tsarev, *Crown Jewels*, p. 209.

n. **Grigori Grapfen:** West and Tsarev, *Crown Jewels*, p. 210.

232 **I played at conspiracy:** G. Rees, *Chapter*, p. 118.

must not think for themselves: MacNeice, *Strings*, p. 168.

I want to tell you: G. Rees, *Chapter*, pp. 135–6. See also J. Rees, *Looking*, p. 275.

233 **who could not have carried:** G. Rees, *Chapter*, p. 136.

I have always felt: J. Rees, *Looking*, p. 275.

References

234 **when Guy Burgess thought:** West and Tsarev, *Crown Jewels*, p. 131.
　　He used his BBC work: Tsarev and Costello, *Deadly Illusions*, pp. 232–3.
　　Konrad Heinlein: G. Rees, *Chapter*, p. 147.

235 **Goronwy Rees claimed:** G. Rees, *Chapter*, p. 147.
　　a vague effort: B. Simon interview, Mar. 1995.
　　filthy homosexuality: Borovik, *Philby Files*, p. 128.

 n. **my visit to Beziers:** AB to F. Saxl, 8 Sept. 1938, Blunt correspondence, WA.

236 **offered to courier:** West and Tsarev, *Crown Jewels*, p. 209.
　　The curtain lines: Waterhouse, 'Preface', p. x.

237 **Of course this is all:** A. Blunt, CI tapes, 1980.
　　I am very glad: Lord Lee to registrar, 10 Mar. 1939, Lee papers, Box 1, CI.

238 **I couldn't do very much:** A. Blunt, CI tapes, 1980.
　　told the Polish ambassador: Andrew and Gordievsky, *KGB*, p. 196.
　　There are KGB men: Sudaplatov, *Special Tasks*, pp. 95–6.

239 **It was clear:** A. Weaver, letter to the author, 27 May 1997.
　　a request from Blunt for advice: West and Tsarev, *Crown Jewels*, p. 134.
　　When he disclosed this: N. West interview.

10. Soldier

241 **Guy said instantly:** Penrose and Freeman, *Conspiracy*, p. 213.
　　Guy and I: R. Cecil, quoted in Costello, *Mask*, p. 336.
　　We argued: *The Times*, 21 Nov. 1979.
　　shattered: R. Lehmann interviewed by B. Penrose and S. Freeman, 1985.
　　I never want to have anything: G. Rees, *Chapter*, p. 150.

242 **Goronwy thinks that I:** West and Tsarev, *Crown Jewels*, p. 131.
　　puzzled questions: Borovik, *Philby Files*, pp. 146–7.
　　I am fighting for a better Britain: Hyde, *I Believed*, pp. 67–8.

243 **much more cheerful:** C. Gould unpublished memoir.
　　an *enchanting* girl: A. Blunt, CI tapes, 1980.
　　report on 16 September: MOD departmental records show that Blunt was made second lieutenant on 16 Sept. 1939; see also West and Tsarev, *Crown Jewels*, pp. 134–5.
　　advertising on the BBC: Alan Berends, unpublished memoir.

244 **renegade illegal Walter Krivitsky:** see Boyle, *Climate of Treason*, p. 199.
　　a long and difficult conversation: West and Tsarev, *Crown Jewels*, p. 135.
　　I am sure: ibid., p. 136.
　　All decent people have: ibid., p. 137.

References

quite nice: Anthony Powell, *To Keep the Ball Rolling* (London: Penguin, 1983), p. 168 (4 Oct. 1939).

245 **On each he made notes:** see West and Tsarev, *Crown Jewels*, p. 144.
an earlier posting at General Headquarters: 'the cancelled orders were for a post at G.H.Q.': T. Boase to Lord Lee, 26 Nov. 1939, Lee papers, Box 1, CI.
We were all very curious: G. Curry, letter to the author.

246 **standing on the quayside:** Alan Berends, unpublished memoir.
a pleasant, cultured, rather aloof man: ibid.
getting to know the French: AB to F. Saxl, 3 Feb. 1940, Blunt correspondence, WA.

247 **how little I mind my:** AB to D. Rylands, undated, *c*. Feb. 1940, Rylands papers, KCL.
It is only tiresome: AB to F. Saxl, 3 Feb. 1940, Blunt correspondence, WA.
There have been moments: ibid.
its revolvers were confiscated: Alan Berends, unpublished memoir.

248 **Kim Philby met Blunt:** West and Tsarev, *Crown Jewels*, p. 144.
apparently content to await: Alan Berends, unpublished memoir.
I do not know what part: G. Curry, letter to the author.

249 **some commentators have suggested:** See Costello, *Mask*; R. Deacon, *The Greatest Treason* (London: Century, 1990).
Wilfrid remembered: see W. Blunt, *Slow*, p. 261.
he joined MI5: West and Tsarev, *Crown Jewels*, p. 129.

250 **Diplomats and intelligence agents:** West, *MI5*, p. 13.
the following account: West, *Seven Spies*, p. 99. West interviewed Victor Rothschild in 1987. MOD records state that Blunt was made 'available to MI IX on 18 June', then 'lent from Intelligence Pool for duty with MI5 on 1 July', less than two weeks later.

251 **on the purely military side:** West and Tsarev, *Crown Jewels*, p. 131.
for only two months: West, *MI5*, p. 333.
claimed that Blunt: see Pincher, *Their Trade is Treachery*, p. 112.
The way Blunt came into MI5: D. White interviewed by B. Penrose and S. Freeman, 1985.

252 **had been since February:** see West and Tsarev, *Crown Jewels*, p. 144.
Marjorie Maxse: Andrew and Gordievsky, *KGB*, pp. 237–8; see also Philby, *My Silent War*, pp. 39–40.

253 **came from the aristocracy:** Wright, *Spycatcher*, p. 39.
young men who had never worked: Miller, *One Girl's War*, p. 14.
extremely conspicuous: West, *MI5*, p. 40.
talk to the working classes: T. Bower, *Perfect English Spy*, p. 41.

254 **talk to working-class people without fuss:** see Mark Urban, *UK Eyes Alpha: Inside British Intelligence* (London: Faber, 1996), p. 44.

more efficient: Trevor-Roper (Lord Dacre), letter to the author, 24 Sept. 1996.

Neither class: Trevor-Roper, *Philby Affair*, p. 71; see also Bower, *Perfect English Spy*, p. 30.

A large part of the suspicion: Trevor-Roper, letter to the author, 24 Sept. 1996.

255 **The essential difference in attitude:** ibid.

256 **Blunt definitely cultivated Liddell:** D. White interviewed by B. Penrose and S. Freeman, 1985.

I saw quite a lot of him: ibid.

I must say: ibid.

257 **open house for their friends:** D. Bristow interview; see also Bristow, *A Game of Moles*, p. 41.

258 **Dick White told his biographer:** Bower, *Perfect English Spy*, p. 47.

It was quite well known: Penrose and Freeman, *Conspiracy*, p. 274.

the precaution to mention: West and Tsarev, *Crown Jewels*, p. 138.

Oh yes, we know: confidential information, Nov. 1995.

259 **monumental threat and:** Bower, *Perfect English Spy*, p. 24.

It was an orthodox position: D. White interviewed by B. Penrose and S. Freeman, 1985.

Our more conservative colleagues: Trevor-Roper, *Philby Affair*, p. 31.

I thought he was homosexual: D. White interviewed by B. Penrose and S. Freeman, 1985.

at least a quarter of a million homosexuals: 'Homosexuality and War', *Timewatch*, 29 Sept. 1998, BBC2.

260 **They wanted me:** confidential source.

All too obviously: King, *Yesterday*, p. 252.

latterly claimed: Francis King interview.

'A.'s book is out: G. Burgess to P. Pollock, undated, *c.* late 1940, Pollock letters.

the stimulus of constant discussion: A. Blunt, *Artistic Theory*, preface.

261 **there's a lot about his poetry:** G. Burgess to P. Pollock, undated, *c.* late 1940, Pollock letters.

and it markedly cooled: quoted by Anne Wesselly in a letter to the author, 18 Nov. 1996; see Wesselly's articles on Antal in *Kritische Berichte*, vol. 4 (1979), nos. 2–3, pp. 16–37.

thoroughness . . . clarity: Francis King interview.

milk-and-water Marxism: J. Pope-Hennessy, *Horizon*, Jan. 1941; see also reviews in *Apollo*, Dec. 1940, *Listener*, 17 Apr. 1941.

262 **I now hate the sight:** AB to F. Saxl, 3 Feb. 1940, Blunt correspondence, WA.

the ceiling on the floor: Tess Rothschild interview.

References

263 a homosexual bordello: Costello, *Mask*, p. 390.
     If one could capture: Koch, *Double Lives*, p. 200.
     a whole revolutionary Who's Who: Malcolm Muggeridge, *The Infernal Grove* (London: Collins, 1973), p. 107.
  n. character called Burgess: Malcolm Muggeridge, *Like it Was*, ed. John Bright Holmes (London: Collins, 1981), p. 242.
264 unconditional partisans of the Soviet Union: G. Rees, *Chapter*, pp. 155–9.
265 there seem to be even more people: G. Burgess to P. Pollock, 1 Sept, 1941, Pollock letters. The letter starts, 'N3, My dearest dear'.
     Would you like to meet: ibid.
     Nor does it: ibid., undated, *c.* 1945, Pollock letters. The letter starts, 'The fact that my attitude towards you'.
     Anthony appeared: ibid., Apr. 1941, Pollock letters.
     spent Christmas: J. Hilton interviewed by B. Penrose and S. Freeman, 1985.
266 living with Patricia in: G. Burgess to P. Pollock, undated, *c.* late 1940, Pollock letters.
     totally and violently: G. Burgess to P. Pollock, undated, *c.* 1941, Pollock letters.
  n. Patricia later married: *Guardian*, 8 Mar. 1999.
267 timid, gentle and genteel: Rees, *Chapter*, p. 154.
     Anthony used to come back tight: Wright, *Spycatcher*, p. 215.
     they asked Litzi Friedman: ibid., p. 228.
268 too good to be true: N. West interview.
     Gorsky met Blunt: Borovik, *Philby Files*, p. 153.
     made a good impression: West and Tsarev, *Crown Jewels*, p. 145.
     passed 1,771 documents: ibid., p. 70.
     flat-footed and unsympathetic: Cecil, *Divided Life*, p. 66.
     a short, fattish man: Elizabeth Bentley, *Out of Bondage* (London: Hart-Davis, 1952), pp. 173–7.
     domineering and bossy: Modin, *Cambridge Friends*, p. 103.
     primarily because: Poretsky, *Our Own People*, p. 82.
269 Cowboys and Indians: M. Kitson, interview.
     Moscow was Bill's discipline: John Le Carré, *Tinker, Tailor, Soldier, Spy* (1974) (London: Coronet, 1994), pp. 364–5.
270 We made an independent: Norman Mailer, *Harlot's Ghost* (New York: Random House, 1991), p. 11.
     immediately impressed: Rothschild, *Random Variables*, p. 203.
     in his own high-mindedness: M. Levey, unpublished memoir.
     Blunt accepted a gift of £100: West and Tsarev, *Crown Jewels*, p. 156.
271 It is difficult to say: ibid., p. 156.
     Blunt's limited interest: ibid., p. 153.

532

References

In intelligence: Mailer, *Harlot's Ghost*, p. 11.
272 I sometimes suspected: Richardson, *Sorcerer's Apprentice*, p. 152.
You must admit: W. Blunt, *Slow*, p. 246.
settle[s] instead: Le Carré, *Tinker, Tailor*, p. 365.

11. Spy

273 made him his personal assistant: see West, *MI5*, p. 426; West interviewed
Blunt in 1980.
not the kind of person: West and Tsarev, *Crown Jewels*, p. 139.
n. Miss Huggins: see West, *MI5*, p. 426.
274 After a lot of struggles: ibid., p. 140.
Blunt's people would open: D. Bristow interview.
275 into dust: Conquest, *Stalin*, p. 234.
we can now take as an association: *AIA Bulletin*, July 1941.
double patriots: D. White interviewed by Penrose and Freeman, 1985. See
also Boyle, *Climate of Treason*.
a tactical necessity: *The Times*, 25 Nov. 1979.
276 monitoring Soviet radio signals: see F. H. Hinsley, *British Intelligence in
the Second World War*, (abridged volume) (London: HMSO, 1993),
p. 115.
I remember it being argued: D. White interviewed by B. Penrose and S.
Freeman, 1985.
factories and forces: Hyde, *I Believed*, p. 145.
turn a blind eye: Hinsley, *British Intelligence*, vol. 4, p. 284.
he wasn't punished: see Miller, *One Girl's War*, p. 133.
277 Jackie's temperament: G. Burgess to P. Pollock, undated, *c.* 1941, Pollock
letters. The letter starts, 'Dearest, literally just a few lines'.
Surprisingly enough: ibid.
278 Jackie is suffering: G. Burgess to P. Pollock, undated, *c.* 1941, Pollock
letters. The letter starts, 'Light of two worlds'.
If he is somehow: Modin, *Cambridge Friends*, p. 24.
lectured on Picasso: 'Aspects of Classicism since the Renaissance',
reported in *Cork Examiner*, 7 Feb. 1941, AFB papers, vol. 491, CI.
classicism with Fritz Saxl: Warburg Institute, *Annual Report*, 1940–1.
Scholarly communal living: Margot Wittkower interview transcript,
Interviews with Art Historians, GRI, Research Library 94109.
All our efforts: Warburg Institute, *Annual Report*, 1940–1.
279 He is a person: Reference for Hugo Buchtal by A. Blunt, Edgar Wind
papers.

533

References

with the bombs: P. Smith interview.
for spending so many hours: A. Blunt, *François Mansart*, preface, p. 5.
My excuse for publishing: ibid.
280 written last summer: R. Mortimer, *Architectural Review*, Mar. 1942.
scholarly yet readable: N. Pevsner, *Spectator*, 26 Dec. 1941.
he just said: Modin, *Cambridge Friends*, p. 104.
thorough, conscientious and efficient: West and Tsarev, *Crown Jewels*, p. 146.
281 patience and unfailing understanding: AB to Moscow, 2 Nov. 1944, TONY, file no. 83895, Russian Intelligence Archives, Moscow. This letter can also be seen on the flyleaf of the hardcover edition of West and Tsarev, *Crown Jewels*.
several society ladies: see West and Tsarev, *Crown Jewels*, pp. 151-2.
moves in a circle: West and Tsarev, ibid., p. 151.
Both were frequent visitors: P. Pollock interview.
through Burgess: West and Tsarev, *Crown Jewels*, p. 152.
282 Burgess was a disgraceful figure: Penrose and Freeman, *Conspiracy*, p. 249.
Burgess was always: C. Harmer interviewed by B. Penrose and S. Freeman, 1985.
Brian Howard's brief sojourn: see Humphrey Carpenter, *The Brideshead Generation* (New York: Houghton Mifflin, 1990), p. 341.
previously recruited Kessler: see Andrew and Mitrokhin, *Mitrokhin Archive*, p. 110.
283 I think we can say: G. Burgess to P. Pollock, undated, *c.* 1942, Pollock letters.
284 Blunt told Moscow: West and Tsarev, *Crown Jewels*, p. 152.
He was always said: Glees, *Secrets of the Service*, p. 372.
a big haughty fellow: Bristow, *Game of Moles*, pp. 43-4.
wouldn't have let any 'queers': D. Bristow, letter to the author, 17 July 1996.
I couldn't stick: Penrose and Freeman, *Conspiracy*, pp. 252-3.
285 Robertson asked his opinions: West and Tsarev, *Crown Jewels*, p. 176.
were inseparable at MI5: C. Elwell interview.
He said that he gave up: N. West interview.
He later admitted: N. West interview.
286 I get in the ordinary course: West and Tsarev, *Crown Jewels*, pp. 142-3.
287 He said we were all: Penrose and Freeman, *Conspiracy*, p. 279.
strength of the German army: Andrew and Gordievsky, *KGB*, p. 244.
under the table: Penrose and Freeman, *Conspiracy*, p. 281.
n. Peter Wright claimed: Wright, *Spycatcher*, p. 220.
288 barely a 50 per cent chance: Modin, *Cambridge Friends*, p. 39.

References

excellent results: Modin, *Cambridge Friends*, p. 115.

rationing information: Sudaplatov, *Special Tasks*, p. 142.

289 **a total of forty lines:** West and Tsarev, *Crown Jewels*, p. 150.

did not please Moscow: Borovik, *Philby Files*, pp. 204–5.

Before I came here: West and Tsarev, *Crown Jewels*, p. 163.

290 **insufficiently attentive and watchful:** Borovik, *Philby Files*, p. 200.

291 **in his opinion:** ibid., p. 206.

about the Hotel's: West and Tsarev, *Crown Jewels*, pp. 148–9; see also Borovik, *Philby Files*, pp. 200–1.

inclined to plumpness: Borovik, *Philby Files*, p. 212.

ran the Third Department: West and Tsarev, *Crown Jewels*, p. 147.

a less senior position: Borovik, *Philby Files*, p. 212.

292 **the ruse was admittted:** West and Tsarev, *Crown Jewels*, p. 157.

hysterical and unbalanced: West and Tsarev, *Crown Jewels*, p. 162.

293 **Burgess launched into a long speech:** West and Tsarev, *Crown Jewels*, p. 164.

eight-man surveillance team: Andrew and Mitrokhin, *Mitrokhin Archive*, p. 160.

294 **That greater possibilities:** West and Tsarev, *Crown Jewels*, p. 156.

He comes very tired: ibid., p. 153.

which may have seemed: A. Blunt, 'Blake's Pictorial Imagination', *Journal of the Warburg and Courtauld Institutes*, 1943.

296 **regular visits to . . . the Royal Library:** Owen Morshead's diaries (in the Windsor archives) note that Blunt came regularly to Windsor from 1943.

297 **He was supportive:** Pope-Hennessy, *Learning*, p. 138.

public protest with Pope-Hennessy: James Lees-Milne, *Ancestral Voices* (London: Chatto & Windus, 1975), p. 209 (19 July 1943).

connected with this scheme: G. Burgess commissioning note, 12 Aug. 1943, Blunt file, BBC Written Archives. For more on MFA&A see Lynn H. Nicholas, *The Rape of Europa* (London: Macmillan, 1994).

298 **Philby passed a copy:** West and Tsarev, *Crown Jewels*, p. 168.

A letter dated 25 October 1943: Borovik, *Philby Files*, p. 216; see also West and Tsarev, *Crown Jewels*, p. 166.

299 **The London *rezidentura* was ordered:** Borovik, *Philby Files* p. 218.

Drink is the bugger: G. Burgess to P. Pollock, undated, *c.* 1946/7, Pollock letters. The letter starts, 'Dear Pete, I tore up my vitriolic letter'.

lost a great deal of weight: E. Herbert medical notes, 14 and 26 Jan. 1944, in the possession of the author.

Poussin mythology: AB to R. Wittkower, 20 Mar. 1944, Blunt correspondence, WA.

Major Blunt: letter to Lord Lee, 10 Apr. 1944, management-committee notes, Lee papers, Box 1, CI. The meeting was delayed until 9 May

References

(Courtauld management-committee minutes, 9 May 1944, Registry papers, CI).

300 **The officer I would:** L. Woolley to C. E. D. Bridge, German Section, Twelfth Army Group, 17 Apr. 1944, quoted in Costello, *Mask*, p. 443.
Blunt's job in the deception scheme: Michael Howard, letter to the author, 12 Aug. 1996.
many years of very valuable help: Borovik, *Philby Files*, pp. 241–2; see also Modin, *Cambridge Friends*, p. 45, and West and Tsarev, *Crown Jewels*, p. 171.
At your usual meeting: Borovik, *Philby Files*, pp. 241–2.
n. **in charge of the protection of monuments:** AB to F. Saxl, 15 Sept. 1944 and undated, *c.* Oct. 1944, Blunt correspondence, WA.
301 **the rank of colonel:** Borovik, *Philby Files*, p. 234.
Three days before D-Day: West and Tsarev, *Crown Jewels*, p. 168.
completely corroborated: ibid., p. 166.
This is a serious confirmation: Borovik, *Philby Files*, pp. 232–4.
302 **ideological shit:** Brown, *Treason in the Blood*, p. 351.
Now that victory: AB to Moscow, 2 Nov. 1944. (This letter can be seen on the flyleaf of the hardcover edition of West and Tsarev, *Crown Jewels*.)

12. Success

303 **These perhaps provide:** Edmund Wilson, *The Forties*, ed. Leon Edel (New York: Farrar, Straus & Giroux, 1983), pp. 111–12.
Kreshin regularly expressed: Andrew and Mitrokhin, *Mitrokhin Archive*, pp. 183–4.
It has given me: Penrose and Freeman, *Conspiracy*, p. 287.
304 **three important articles:** 'The Joueur de Vielle of G. de la Tour', *Burlington Magazine*, LXXXVI/LXXXVII, 1945; 'Two newly discovered landscapes by Nicholas Poussin', ibid.; 'The Chateau de Balleroy', ibid.
back in hospital: G. Burgess to P. Pollock, undated, *c.* Aug. 1945, Pollock letters.
Turner was mad: Clark, *Another Part*, p. 237.
305 **We all thought:** L. Gurry interviewed by B. Penrose and S. Freeman.
inefficient, out of date: AB to Mr Cox, Dartington Hall, The Arts Enquiry, 13 May 1946, RA/RCD/PIC Publications.
306 **rather a strain:** W. Blunt, *Slow*, p. 262.
307 **Kelly for keeps:** Sir Oliver Millar interview.
the corridors and bedrooms: AB to W. Friedlaender, Nov. 1945, AFB papers, vol. 347, CI.

a long term project: AB to Royal Comptroller, 11 Nov. 1946, RA/RCD/
PIC Publications.

308 **two pictures at home:** Sir A. Lascelles to AB, 8 Nov. 1947, RA/RCD/PIC
Movements and Rearrangements.

a Sebastiano Ricci: Ben Nicolson to Gosling (Minstry of Works): 'until the
other day when Queen Mary informed Mr Blunt that it was moved to the
Queen's chapel': 7 Nov. 1946, RA/RCD/PIC Movements and
Rearrangements.

the most reasonable of tones: see for example AB to Ulick Alexander, 31
Jan. 1947, RA/RCD/PIC Movements and Rearrangements.

I think it would be a pity: Mr Williams, superintendent, Windsor, memo,
4 Nov. 1947, RA/RCD/PIC Access.

309 **little three-legged tables:** A. Baker interview.

had an hour alone: G. Burgess to P. Pollock, undated, *c.* 1945, Pollock
letters.

310 **George's response:** Alan Baker, letter to author, 13 August 2001.

You know, Blunt: W. Blunt, *Slow*, p. 262.

well-painted picture: O. Millar interview.

311 **which were preserved:** Unsigned, undated account of Owen Morshead's
trip to Friedrichshof in Aug. 1945, RA RCD/Librarian.

was due to visit: Owen Morshead's account of the trip to Friedrichshof, 7
Aug. 1945, RA VIC/ADD AI/10.

312 **told the journalist Colin Simpson:** *Sunday Times*, 25 Nov. 1979.

Another version of the story: see Pincher, *Their Trade is Treachery*, p. 350.

313 **King fussed about the Duke:** see Sarah Bradford, *George VI* (London:
Weidenfeld & Nicolson, 1989), pp. 425–6.

314 **Pretty extensive looting:** Morshead's account of the trip to Friedrichshof,
7 Aug. 1945, RA VIC/ADD AI/10.

The King expressly told me: Owen Morshead, pendant to the Doorn
memorandum, 23 Oct. 1948, Public Record Office FO/370/1698.

315 **in the King's private aeroplane:** G. Burgess to P. Pollock, undated, *c.*
1945, Pollock letters.

very hush hush: Penrose and Freeman, *Conspiracy*, p. 301.

316 **objects which had been borrowed:** C. Gould, unpublished memoir.

The Duke of Brunswick would open: N. MacGregor interview.

with a sealed packet: Wednesday 19 Dec. 1945, Olivier Bell's records,
MFA&A, Imperial War Museum; see also *Art Newspaper*, no. 42, Nov.
1994.

I had got myself: Penrose and Freeman, *Conspiracy*, p. 301.

he met Boris Kreshin: West and Tsarev, *Crown Jewels*, p. 174.

317 **when Long applied:** L. Long interviewed by B. Penrose and S. Freeman,
Conspiracy, 1985.

References

arranged more systematically: *Listener*, 7 Nov. 1946.

That's no duchess: Sidney Hutchinson interview.

318 involve unpleasantness: AB to Ulick Alexander, 31 Jan. 1947, RA/RCD/PIC Movements and Rearrangements.

relations between the Courts: O. Morshead to Sir A. Lascelles, 28 Sept. 1947, Public Record Office FO/370/1698.

319 Klugmann had been overheard: Andrew and Mitrokhin, *Mitrokhin Archive*, p. 167.

the NKVD's pre-war source: West and Tsarev, *Crown Jewels*, p. 170.

close to breaking point: Andrew and Gordievsky, *KGB*, p. 303.

With good contact: West and Tsarev, *Crown Jewels*, p. 176.

320 4,404 documents: ibid., pp. 172–3.

321 almost hostile: West and Tsarev, *Crown Jewels*, p. 176.

I meet the pale: A. Halpern to Edgar Wind, 30 Sept. 1946, Edgar Wind papers.

n. Halpern was a: M. Wind interview; see also Amanda Haight, *Anna Akhmatova* (London: Oxford University Press, 1976).

322 the pale Anthony: ibid., 11 Dec. 1946, Edgar Wind papers.

found him nervous: Modin, *Cambridge Friends*, pp. 160–1.

found our present policies ill-conceived: ibid., pp. 178–9.

more and more that his work: ibid., p. 180.

323 This was a gradual process: *The Times*, 21 Nov. 1979.

We all of us – all five: B. Howard to P. Pollock, 21 Oct. 1945, Pollock letters.

324 We tried: G. Burgess to P. Pollock, undated, c. 1947, Pollock letters.

he always seemed to hit: Connolly, *Missing Diplomats*, p. 25.

we're lovers and we're: Modin, *Cambridge Friends*, p. 152.

Anthony like some great: G. Burgess to P. Pollock, Sept. 1948, Pollock letters.

325 everyone from Samuel Courtauld: see T. Boase to K. Clark, 16 Apr. 1947: 'The issue is whether to advertise or simply put forward Blunt's name. Sam, I gather, favours the latter procedure' (Clark-Courtauld file, Tate Gallery Archives).

I must say I am glad: F. Saxl to AB, 22 June 1947, Blunt correspondence, WA.

The committee nominated: T. Boase to Lord Lee, 16 Sept. 1947, Box 1, Lee papers, CI.

326 He would have liked to have been: Kidson, 'The Recent Transformation'.

327 treats me in rather too breezy: Ben Nicolson, 10 Nov. 1948, unpublished diaries.

328 The enemies of scholarship: Peter Vansittart, *In the Fifties* (London: John Murray, 1995), p. 132.

n. **a very modest budget:** Martha Kelleher, letter to the author, 27 Sept. 1995.

330 **collectively assumed the responsibility:** Lord Crawford, unpublished manuscript of 'Serving our Artistic Heritage', for *Queen* magazine, NACF records, Tate Gallery Archives.
Reynolds isn't as great: Alfred Munnings, BBC radio broadcast, 28 April 1949.
to Paris to give a lecture: *Arts*, reviewing Blunt's speech at the Louvre, 30 Apr. 1949, AFB papers, vol. 493, CI.

331 **a woman I have never forgotten:** Pamela Tudor Craig, letter to the author, 1998.
on the top of the world: Ben Nicolson, 10 Nov. 1948, unpublished diaries.

333 **stopped by a policeman:** West and Tsarev, *Crown Jewels*, pp. 176–7.
the finest of its kind: Public Record Office BW/78/2, confidential report, Jan. 1949.

334 **profoundly unhappy:** J. Rees, *Looking*, p. 153.
Burgess was nasty: A. Baker interview.
worldwide conspiracy: Peter Allen, *The Fifties* (London: Heinemann, 1978), p. 80.
totally unfriendly: Straight, *After Long Silence*, p. 231.
It reflected: ibid., pp. 230–1.

335 **Burgess could have warned:** West and Tsarev, *Crown Jewels*, p. 180.
the work of a thousand: ibid., p. 182.

336 **In Paul's [Burgess] opinion:** ibid., p. 184.
inconceivable that any senior member: Bower, *Perfect English Spy*, p. 91.
If danger of exposure arose: West and Tsarev, *Crown Jewels*, p. 181.

13. Accessory

337 **secret information was leaking:** see West, *Venona*, p. 135.
for someone who is unstable: Bower, *Perfect English Spy*, p. 102.
among them papers on: see Sudaplatov, *Special Tasks*, pp. 173, 231; Modin, *Cambridge Friends*, pp. 117–18.

338 **In conversation:** Connolly, *Missing Diplomats*, p. 29.
What would you do if: ibid., p. 31.
I am the English Hiss: ibid., p. 33.
Adultery, alcoholism: Cecil, *Divided Life*, p. 147.
on 30 March 1951: West, *Venona*, p. 135; see also Cecil, *Divided Life* p. 117.

References

339 **no way of warning:** Modin, *Cambridge Friends*, pp. 199–200; see also Borovik, *Philby Files*, p. 277.

insulted the wife: Robert Lamphere, *The FBI–KGB War* (New York: Random House, 1986), p. 230.

must not escape with Maclean: Cecil, *Divided Life*, p. 131.

Modin . . . claimed that the NKVD: Modin, *Cambridge Friends*, p. 200.

340 **Straight . . . says he never met Baker:** M. Straight interview; see also Straight, *After Long Silence*, p. 251.

arrived at Southampton: Cecil, *Divided Life*, p. 133.

Hewit, who had come: J. Hewit interview.

the only published account: Modin, *Cambridge Friends*, p. 200.

perhaps an even greater danger: J. Rees, *Looking*, p. 152.

cleaner and madder: G. Rees, *Chapter*, p. 197.

341 **I know all about you:** ibid., p. 191.

He asked that he might at least: Modin, *Cambridge Friends*, p. 203.

Lady Cecil's biography: Connolly, *Missing Diplomats*, p. 26.

I was appalled: J. Rees, *Looking*, p. 186.

briefly been her husband's go-between: Modin, *Cambridge Friends*, p. 203.

she told him to go: see Borovik, *Philby Files*, p. 281.

It's getting very hot: A. Blunt in Cecil, *Divided Life*, p. 137.

342 **thought up by Blunt:** Modin, *Cambridge Friends*, pp. 205–6.

Guy was vacillating: Penrose and Freeman, *Conspiracy*, p. 348.

He left the office early: Cecil, *Divided Life*, p. 140.

Burgess packed his collected edition: Driberg, *Guy Burgess*, p. 95.

Hewit's overcoat: J. Hewit interview.

he called Goronwy Rees: G. Rees, *Chapter*, p. 204.

He arrived at Maclean's: Cecil, *Divided Life*, p. 143.

343 **According to Modin:** Modin, *Cambridge Friends*, p. 209.

He told me he didn't know: Penrose and Freeman, *Conspiracy*, p. 357.

Against Blunt's advice, Hewit: J. Hewit interview.

I suddenly had an absolutely sure: G. Rees, *Chapter*, pp. 206–7.

344 **Modin claimed he could never:** Modin, *Cambridge Friends*, p. 209.

Borovik, says Modin: Borovik, *Philby Files*, pp. 282–4.

He seemed worried and puzzled: Penrose and Freeman, *Conspiracy*, p. 354.

Burgess's plan for the weekend: FBI Burgess and Maclean file 71-10-51, interviewee probably Bernard Miller.

to see Goronwy Rees: G. Rees, *Chapter*, pp. 207–8.

345 **It really was very challenging:** D. White in Bower, *Perfect English Spy*, p. 113.

346 **Blunt later said that he accompanied:** West, *MI5*, p. 334; see also Cecil, *Divided Life*, p. 137.

540

References

Rosamond Lehmann claimed: R. Lehmann interviewed by Penrose and Freeman, 1985.

he did not do a thorough job: George Carey Foster, head of Foreign Office security, told Barrie Penrose in 1985 that Blunt came to his notice when Burgess's flat was searched and revealed letters from him to Burgess.

I oughtn't to be at dinner here: I. Berlin interview.

I did notice that: Lord Hartwell, letter to the author, 5 June 1996.

347   **she protested her ignorance**: Cecil, *Divided Life*, p. 156.

Rees later claimed: Penrose and Freeman, *Conspiracy*, p. 356.

they treated me: J. Rees, *Looking*, p. 165.

And he never said a single thing: D. White interviewed by B. Penrose and S. Freeman, 1985.

348   **it is known**: Cecil, *Divided Life*, p. 148.

349   **A babysitter**: ibid., pp. 150–2.

Burgess's brother: N. Burgess interviewed by B. Penrose and S. Freeman, 1985.

Stephen Spender gave an interview: Cecil, *Divided Life*, p. 150.

a secret mission to placate: Bower, *Perfect English Spy*, p. 120.

ordered his own investigation: see FBI Burgess and Maclean files.

It was rumoured that he was drinking: G. Zarnecki, quoted in Penrose and Freeman, *Conspiracy*, p. 362.

351   **very quickly convinced of Philby's guilt**: see Bower, *Perfect English Spy*, pp. 122–3.

352   **No doubt you**: Modin, *Cambridge Friends*, pp. 222–4.

353   **Dick White sent**: Bower, *Perfect English Spy*, p. 132.

to gain what info I could: W. Skardon interviewed by B. Penrose and S. Freeman, 1985.

Rosamond Lehmann tried several times: Penrose and Freeman, *Conspiracy*, pp. 362–3.

Cyril Connolly was also: Jeremy Lewis (biographer of Connolly), letter to the author, 14 June 1996. Connolly's notes are in the Connolly papers, McFarlin Library, University of Tulsa, Oklahoma.

The individualism of the period: Eddie Sackville-West, *Listener*, 22 Feb. 1951.

354   **as the only way finally**: Peter Vansittart, *In the Fifties* (London: John Murray, 1995), p. 150.

It would be dishonourable: Carpenter, *W. H. Auden*, p. 368.

the whole business makes me sick: Davenport-Hines, *Auden*, pp. 275–6.

355   **The God That Failed**: Arthur Koestler and R. H. S. Crossman, eds., *The God That Failed* (London: Hamish Hamilton, 1950).

Communism made an intellectual appeal: Connolly, *Missing Diplomats*, pp. 16–17.

a kind of sexual witchhunt: For a more detailed description of this see

References

Richard Davenport-Hines, *Sex, Death and Punishment* (London: Fontana, 1991), pp. 299–302.

n. **In 1938 in Britain:** ibid., p. 299.

356 **Glasgow on a Saturday night:** Tom Driberg, *Guy Burgess*, p. 100.
When Tom Driberg met him: Tom Driberg, *Ruling Passions* (London: Cape, 1977), pp. 231–8.
Driberg's being blackmailed: Andrew and Mitrokhin, *Mitrokhin Archive*, p. 523.

357 **On 31 December 1951 he resigned:** R. A. M. Forrest (secretary of the Reform Club), letter to the author, 10 Aug. 1995.
turned up Blunt's name: see FBI Burgess and Maclean file 100-374183-556 2. One FBI document (in which the name of the interviewee is blacked out) goes, 'Burgess asked —— to assist him in carrying out his work and stated that one of his other sources of information was ANTHONY BLUNT.' Blunt was also named as one of Burgess's closest friends by Christopher Isherwood.
Nothing was ever: J. Rees, *Looking*, p. 8.

14. Director

359 **the excrescences were such:** Peter Kidson, 'The Recent Transformation'.
with unwonted candour: ibid.
Are you going to get a first?: M. Kitson interview.

360 **During the last 20 years:** *Times Literary Supplement*, 24 Aug. 1951.

361 **The atmosphere was fervid:** B. Sewell, *The Late Show*, 23 Jan. 1995, BBC2.

363 **rarely showed any impatience:** M. Levey, unpublished memoir.
because of his superior attitude: Charles Elwell, letter to the author, Oct. 1996, transcribed from his diaries.

364 **a federation:** Kidson, 'The Recent Transformation'.

365 **You are the person:** D. Thomson interview.

366 **The Cleric of Treason:** Steiner, 'The Cleric of Treason', *New Yorker*, 8 Dec. 1980.
He was very good with: D. Bindman interview.
If you said something new: D. Thomson interview.

367 **It was a marvellous way to lead:** B. Sewell, *Desert Island Discs*, 19 June 1994, BBC Radio 4.
He recited that Blake poem: R. Coope interview.
Diana and I . . .: Nancy Mitford to Violet Hammersley, 12 Jan. 1964, in *Love From Nancy: The Letters of Nancy Mitford*, ed. Charlotte Mosley (London: Hodder & Stoughton, 1993), p. 423.

368 There was no pecking order: Kidson, 'The Recent Transformation'.
369 The Courtauld had: T. Measham, letter to the author, 16 Nov. 1998.
Women had very little influence: *Daily Telegraph*, Feb. 1955.
I was to learn how tenacious: M. Levey, unpublished memoir.
371 remote and distinctly Olympian: Kidson, 'The Recent Transformation'.
He spoke in a charming: Brophy, *Finishing Touch*, introduction.
The handsome, curved double staircase: M. Levey, unpublished memoir.
372 I can't bear: Brophy, *Finishing Touch*, p. 10.
373 I should be: AB to Anna Kallin, 10 Dec. 1951, Blunt file, BBC Written
Archives.
Blunt both in looks and manner: *Evening Standard*, 15 June 1956.
Even as we sat there: M. Levey, unpublished memoir.
n. There's that *poor* little man: Brian Robertson, *Sunday Telegraph*, 14 Nov.
1999.
374 Roy Jenkins found: Jenkins, *A Life at the Centre*, p. 189.
Sunshine which has restored: AB to Oliver Millar, Nov. 1955, RA/RCD/
PIC Correspondence Millar 1950–60.
unable to express: AB to Anna Kallin, 13 Feb. 1951, Blunt file, BBC
Written Archives.
375 When he dined with: Brophy, *Finishing Touch*, introduction.
376 has developed a definite interest: Irwin Goodman, *Newsweek*, 20 Sept.
1960.
377 I remember him saying: F. Haskell interview.
I would hardly expect: *Newsweek*, 20 Sept. 1960.
Thank you so much for letting me see: AB to Oliver Miller, 20 Sept.
1960, RA/RCD/PIC/Surveyor Personel.
378 We need only notice: A. Blunt, *The Nation's Pictures*, p. xxiii.
an almost passionate attachment to Petworth: National Trust
correspondence, 1952–56, re: Petworth House, National Trust Archives.
She was very tough: confidential source.
She was the sweetest possible: confidential source.
If he had got on with her: confidential source.

15. Private Man

380n. This may have been: F. Partridge, letter to the author, 16 July 1996; see
also Frances Partridge, *Everything to Lose: Diaries 1945–1960* (London:
Gollancz, 1985).
381 Very little is known: Gordon Westwood, *A Minority: A Report on the
Life of the Male Homosexual* (London: Longman, 1960), p. 73.

382 He gave the impression: M. Levey, unpublished memoir.

383 sardonic sense of mischief: Richardson, *Sorcerer's Apprentice*, p. 152.

385 Practical matters he seemed: Brophy, *Finishing Touch*, introduction.

386 Gaskin insisted that he had: Smith, *Celebration*, p. 193.

387 the high-class courtesans: Lord Annan interview.

388 camp, bitter and sarcastic: Smith, *Celebration*, p. 185.

  n. Blunt's salary as director: see Blunt records, Registry papers, CI.

389 I heard from other sources: Pope-Hennessy, *Learning*, p. 139.
     Tony told us to come: G. Zarnecki interview.

390 I hid in the corner: C. Hislop interview.
     All those hairdressers!: from interview with M. Honour and J. Fleming.
     Whenever we went there: Brophy, *Finishing Touch*, introduction.

391 He had been so: Brian Sewell, London *Evening Standard*, 5 November
     2001 and letter to author, 1 December 2001.

392 When he died young: E. Hebborn interview.
     Anthony was endlessly patient: Hebborn, *Drawn to Trouble*, p. 198.

393 'nice' to Hebborn: *Daily Telegraph*, 2 Mar. 1980.

394 art experts were fools: Smith, *Celebration*, p. 182.
     file clerk who knew: ibid., p. 160.
     might have passed as originals: ibid., p. 122.
     I was interested in what: ibid., p. 155.

395 According to Chapman: Pincher, *Too Secret, Too Long*, p. 355.

396 After we learn: A. H. Belmont to D. M. Ladd, 31 July 1953, FBI Burgess
     and Maclean file 100-374183399.

  n. Blunt finally went to America: 'Louisville to Director', 16 Mar. 1956, FBI
     Burgess and Maclean file 100–374183399.

397 a sudden attack of Bell's palsy: Dr Denis Williams to Dr E. Herbert, 4
     Nov. 1953, Blunt medical records, in the possession of the author: 'he
     seems to have had a simple but severe Bell's palsy on the 20th August, and
     there is now naturally enough still no movement. Recovery will be delayed
     until about 5 months after the event, and as he has waited so long I see no
     purpose in interfering in the meantime.'
     Professor Blunt is so anxious: ibid.
     At the Courtauld his staff: J. Shearman interview.
     He kept laying the palm of his hand: King, *Yesterday*, pp. 129–30.

398 I realized that he felt: F. King interview.
     When he was very angry: Hebborn, *Drawn to Trouble*, pp. 287–9.
     Rosamond Lehmann used to recount: R. Lehmann interviewed by B.
     Penrose and S. Freeman, *Conspiracy*, 1985.
     We used to say: M. Whiteley interview.

399 comfortable conversations: Pincher, *Too Secret, Too Long*, p. 355.
     Too many MI5 officers: Bower, *Perfect English Spy*, p. 88.

bugged and burgled: Wright, *Spycatcher*, p. 54.

400 **But strange to relate:** Modin, *Cambridge Friends*, p. 230.
When they met: ibid., p. 232; see also Borovik, *Philby Files*, p. 309.
because of work: Dr Marcelli Shaw to Dr E. Herbert, 2 May 1955, Blunt
medical records, in the possession of the author.

401 **a White Paper on Burgess and Maclean:** White Paper, Oct. 1955.
According to Dick White: Bower, *Perfect English Spy*, p. 154.
I have never been: Bower, *Perfect English Spy*, p. 158.
Dick White, who had done everything: see ibid., pp. 153–8.

402 **We neither of us:** Driberg, *Guy Burgess*, pp. 121–4.
This is rather an achievement: G. Burgess to Sheila Pollock, 20 May 1956,
Pollock letters.
He had stored: G. Zarnecki interview.

403 **left him a little money:** A. Lownie (biographer of Burgess) interview.
Even Peter Wright wrote: Wright, *Spycatcher*, p. 226.
he told Harold Nicolson: James Lees-Milne, *Harold Nicolson: A
Biography* (London: Chatto & Windus, 1980), p. 324.
It would have been like: Francis Wheen, *Tom Driberg: His Life and
Indiscretions* (London: Pan, 1992), p. 313.

404 **Rees was also humiliatingly sacked:** J. Rees, *Looking*, p. 186.
I think he did it: ibid., p. 187.

405 **Rees himself described:** G. Rees, *Chapter*, p. 256–60.
breathtaking in its bad faith: M. Ignatieff, *Isaiah Berlin: A Life* (London:
Cape, 1998).
bringing out briefcases: Vladimir and Evgenia Petrov, *Empire of Fear*
(London: André Deutsch, 1956), p. 271.

406 **contained a vivid portrait:** Lesley Lewis interview.
Australian scholar: Bernard Smith, letter to the author, 1998.

407 **severe rectal bleeding:** Mr O.V. Lloyd-Davies to Dr E. Herbert, 19 Mar.
1959, Blunt medical records, in the possession of the author.
he would need considerable rest: Courtauld management-committee
minutes, 1 Nov. 1960, Registry papers, CI.
Poussin drawings: AB to W. Friedlaender, 14 Dec. 1960, Friedlaender
correspondence, AFB papers, vol. 347, CI.

16. Writer

408 **made himself a reputation:** for reviews of *Art and Architecture in France:
1500–1700* see *Listener*, 7 Jan. 1954, and *Burlington Magazine*, July 1954.

409 **Though Professor Blunt:** *Art News and Reviews*, 26 Dec. 1953.

References

410 **love of ingenious structure:** A. Blunt, *Art and Architecture in France*,
p. 78.
an architect of almost unparalleled: ibid., p. 132.
arrogant, obstinate, intolerant: ibid., p. 202.
of certain qualities: ibid., p. 12.

411 **Passions and Expression:** A. Blunt, *The Art of William Blake*, p. 28; see
also A. Blunt, 'Blake's Pictorial Imagination', *Journal of the Warburg and
Courtauld Institutes*, 1943, p. 192.
whether by law: A. Blunt, 'Blake's Pictorial Imagination', *Journal of the
Warburg Institute*, 1943, p. 192.
His passionate sincerity: A. Blunt, *The Art of William Blake*, p. 95.

412 **magnetic power:** ibid.
I think anyone: D. Bindman interview.
an exorcism: J. Golding interview, Aug. 1994.

n. **Blunt showed, for example:** A. Blunt, 'Blake's Ancient of Days', *Journal of
the Warburg Institute*, 1938.

413 **seems to have tortured him:** Alan Bowness, notes on Blunt's 1954-5
lectures, in the possession of the author.
he cannot altogether get Shakespeare: ibid.
When I feel myself sweating: A. Blunt, 'Delacroix', BBC radio, 7 July
1952, BBC Written Archives.

414 **personally he was shy:** ibid..
the struggle between: Alan Bowness, notes on Blunt's 1954-5 lectures, in
the possession of the author.
He tears apart: BBC radio debate with Richard Wollheim, Andrew Forge,
Basil Taylor, 20 Oct. 1961, BBC Written Archives.
attempted once again: A. Blunt 'The École de Paris in Retrospect',
Listener, 22 Feb. 1951.
the most intense exponent: A. Blunt, 'Picasso in Rome', *Listener*, 9 July
1953.
in which, for me: BBC radio debate, 20 Oct. 1961.

415 **the last great painting:** Blunt lecture reported in *Eastern Evening News*,
23 Mar. 1957.
under the impulse: A. Blunt, *Guernica*, p. 26.
a great traditionalist: Edith Hoffman, review of *Picasso: The Formative
Years*, *Burlington Magazine*, Jan. 1966, pp. 97-8.
We appreciate a struggle: A. Blunt, *Borromini*, p. 222.

416 **plumb in the middle of my blind spot:** AB to Martin Baldwin, curator, Art
Gallery of Ontario, 26 Feb. 1959, AGO Archives.
who was 'my first love: A. Blunt, *Nicolas Poussin*, p. ix.

n. **If you believe this:** D. Thomson interview.

417 **fine mind and his wide reading:** ibid., p. 172.

References

417 **a cluster of articles:** for example a 1938 essay, 'Poussin's Notes on Painting', *Journal of the Warburg Institute*, on the painter's literary sources; and the 1944 essay 'The Heroic and the Ideal Landscapes of Nicolas Poussin', *Journal of the Warburg and Courtauld Institutes*, on how Poussin's landscapes of the 1640s showed the influence of neo-Stoicism.
Poussin seems to have been: A. Blunt, 'Poussin's Letters': BBC radio talk, 20 June 1955, BBC Written Archives.
a young man who: ibid.

418 **This picture of the grave:** A. Blunt, *Nicolas Poussin*, pp. 172–5.
One must attain virtue: ibid., p. 167.
Whatever happens: ibid., p. 168.

419 **Just as the twenty-four letters:** ibid., p. 222.
It would be wrong to conclude: ibid., p. 7.
he lived only for his art: ibid., p. 312.

421 **the explosion in my heart:** P. Rosenberg, *The Late Show*, 23 Jan. 1995, BBC2.
proudly showed round: among those who recalled him showing them round the exhibition were John Richardson, Rosalys Coope, Dick Kingzett, Derek Hill, John Shearman and Michael Levey.
only one mistake: R. Coope interview.
cordially for the extremely kind way: E. Panofsky to AB, 26 Sept. 1960, AFB papers, vol. 347, CI.

422 **looking and feeling:** Mahon, 'Poussin's Early Development'.

423 **I felt frightfully upset:** D. Mahon to AB, 15 June 1960, AFB papers, vol. 347, CI.
One is virtually compelled: Mahon, 'Poussin's Early Development'.
In a brief note: A. Blunt, *Burlington Magazine*, July 1960.
On many points: A. Blunt, 'Poussin Studies XI', *Burlington Magazine*, Sept. 1960.

424 **contemplating renewing relations:** AB to R. Wittkower, 24 Apr. 1961, Wittkower papers, Columbia University Library.
the best-paid: Joseph Connors interview.

425 **so wide, so capricious:** D. Mahon 'Poussiniana', *Gazette des Beaux-Arts*, July–Aug. 1962, pp. 1–138.
I should of course: AB to D. Mahon, 5 Dec. 1962, AFB papers, vol. 347, CI.
A Plea: D. Mahon, 'A Plea for Poussin as a Painter', in *Walter Friedlaender zum 90* (Berlin: Walter de Gruyler and Co., 1965), pp. 113–42.

426 **In essentials:** C. Gould, unpublished memoir.
  n. **When criticising this footnote:** footnote 56, 'Poussiniana', *Gazette des Beaux-Arts*, July–Aug. 1962.

427 **I must own:** D. Mahon to AB, 15 Dec. 1962, AFB papers, vol. 347, CI.

428 **I think it extremely ingenious:** AB to D. Sutton, quoted in Blunt's deposition, 25 Feb. 1965, AFB papers, vol. 317, CI.

429 **He is quite adamant:** Dr Marcelli Shaw to Dr E. Herbert, 17 June 1968, Blunt medical records, in the possession of the author.
   together with a letter: Mr Jerdein to AB, 13 Mar. 1964, AFB papers, vol. 317, CI.
   I mean in which year: Blunt's deposition, 25 Feb. 1965, AFB papers, vol. 317, CI.
   I was depressed: ibid.

430 **He [Mahon] really is the most:** note from 'Michael' (no surname, probably Kitson), 28 Feb. 1965, AFB papers, vol. 317, CI.
   I am horrified: Lord Crawford to AB, 23 Feb. 1965, AFB papers, vol. 317, CI.
   There were many ways: Blunt's deposition, 25 Feb. 1965, AFB papers, vol. 317, CI.

431 **I'm glad to report:** M. Kitson to AB, 7 Apr. 1965, AFB papers, vol. 317, CI.
   I have omitted: A. Blunt, *The Paintings of Nicolas Poussin*, p. 3.
   'This', he told his solicitors: AB notes to solicitors, 17 June 1965, AFB papers, vol. 317, CI.
   Blunt had seen the picture: Brian Sewell, London *Evening Standard*, 5 November 2001 and letter to author, 1 December 2001.
   John Pope-Hennessy claimed: Pope-Hennessy, *Learning*, p. 138–9.

432 **Lady Mahon should have:** confidential source, May 1995.
   The moment we were in the first room: B. Sewell, *The Late Show*, 23 Jan. 1995, BBC2.

433 **I got back last night:** AB to P. Rosenberg, 3 and 6 June 1973, AFB papers, vol. 182, CI.

434 **at some time I shall write:** A. Blunt, *Nicolas Poussin*, p. x.
n. **Blunt . . . owned another early Poussin:** M. Simpson, Hazlitt, Gooden and Fox, letter to the author, 7 Mar. 2001.

17. Penitent Impenitent

436 **To go to his room:** Michael Taylor, letter to the author, 8 Feb. 1996.

437 **Anthony was horrified:** A. Bowness interview, May 1996.
   an MI5 plant: Tim Hilton, *Guardian*, 11 Apr. 1992.
   We had an intimation: D. Bindman interview.

438 **unusual people:** L. Harwood, letter to the author, 25 Sept. 1996.

did the rounds of the ladies' lavatories: Barbara Murek, letter to the author, summer 1997.

but we didn't know: S. J. Flower, letter to the author, 17 June 1996.

parachuted into Germany: F. Whitford interview.

I knew for certain: M. Taylor, letter to the author, 8 Feb. 1996.

439 **Oh that just confirms it:** L. Harwood, letter to the author, 25 Sept. 1996.

One night he remarked: B. Murek, letter to the author, summer 1997.

440 **Slade Professor of Art History:** Courtauld annual report, 1963.

told me in a comparatively firm voice: Sutherland and Purdy, *The Fourth Man*, p. 18.

441 **Of course we're bugged:** H. Honour interview.

He was easy to talk to: Smith, *Celebration*, p. 160.

442 **He thought the idea:** ibid., p. 159.

sold at Christie's: ibid., p. 182.

We all just stood there: S. Whitfield interview.

I can only say: AB to Duncan Grant, 13 Nov. 1963, AFB papers, vol. 272, CI.

443 **to someone who loves it:** Duncan Grant to AB, 16 Nov. 1963, AFB papers, vol. 272, CI.

Blunt had it valued: AB to Duncan Grant, 3 Jan. 1964, AFB papers, vol. 272, CI.

the highest figure: Roddy Thesiger, Colnaghi's, to AB, 11 Dec. 1963, AFB papers, vol. 272, CI.

three annual instalments: AB to Duncan Grant, 3 Jan. 1964, AFB papers, vol. 272, CI; see also *Charleston Magazine*, no. 17, Dec. 1986.

so large an amount: AB to Duncan Grant, 27 Jan. 1964, AFB papers, vol. 272, CI.

Straight decided it was time: see Straight, *After Long Silence*, pp. 318–19.

444 **to interview John Cairncross:** see Penrose and Freeman, *Conspiracy*, p. 400.

go public: M. Straight interview.

common gossip at MI5: see Bower, *Perfect English Spy*, pp. 323–4.

might be their prime suspect: see Wright, *Spycatcher*, p. 213.

n. **three previous attempts:** M. Straight, *After Long Silence* and interview.

445 **swallow MI5 up whole:** Wright, *Spycatcher*, p. 275.

446 **I rather thought:** Bower, *Perfect English Spy*, p. 297.

the trial of Giuseppe Martelli: Wright, *Spycatcher*, p. 271.

dreadful embarassment: ibid., p. 213.

just made everyone look: Bower, *Perfect English Spy*, p. 258.

447 **The government could fall:** ibid., p. 267.

I am not at all pleased: Alistair Horne, *Macmillan*, vol. 2 (London: Macmillan, 1989), p. 461.

References

keep a lid on things: Bower, *Perfect English Spy*, pp. 295–6.

What a shame: ibid., p. 304.

encouraged by Dick White: ibid., p. 325.

persuaded the Home Secretary: *Hansard*, 21 Nov. 1979, col. 408.

n.   It has been suggested: Pincher, *Too Secret, Too Long*, p. 373.

448   their one proviso: A. Ciechanowiecki interview.

The Queen was also: Lord Charteris interview; see also Jenkins, *A Life at the Centre*, p. 189.

never referred to the subject: Sarah Bradford, *Elizabeth: A Biography of Her Majesty the Queen* (London: Heinemann, 1996), p. 317.

Sir Michael Adeane . . . asked: *Hansard*, 21 Nov. 1979.

Any action: ibid.

From time to time: Wright, *Spycatcher*, p. 223.

449   a great treat: Malcolm Gilliat, private secretary to the Queen Mother, to AB, 28 Feb. 1968, Courtauld Institute Galleries files, CI.

A week later: Ruth Fermoy to AB, 4 Mar. 1968, Courtauld Institute Galleries files, CI.

share a box: see *Private Eye*, 25 Feb. 1980.

450   acted on behalf of the royal family: Bradford, *Elizabeth*, p. 307.

He made a note of it: B. Penrose interview.

451   I think I said: Penrose and Freeman, *Conspiracy*, p. 416.

He was a very likeable man: ibid., p. 418; see also Wright, *Spycatcher*, p. 226.

He is a thin man: Dr L. Forman to Dr E. Herbert, 7 May 1964, Blunt medical records, in the possession of the author.

Sometimes he would look ghastly: Penrose and Freeman, *Conspiracy*, p. 419.

452   According to Peter Wright: Wright, *Spycatcher*, pp. 221–2.

When we threw: Penrose and Freeman, *Conspiracy*, p. 419.

I suppose most of my friends: ibid., p. 417.

453   I just wanted to tell you: Straight, *After Long Silence*, p. 326.

In an interview in 1980: N. West interview.

In Blunt's annotated copy: this copy is currently in the possession of his nephew, Simon Blunt.

It was a total flop: Penrose and Freeman, *Conspiracy*, p. 424.

455   a couple of drinks: Bristow, *A Game of Moles*, p. 279.

It is an astonishing piece of work: AB to Anna Kallin, 17 June 1995, Blunt file, BBC Written Archives.

456   We had to adopt: Wright, *Spycatcher*, p. 224.

the semi-amorous and symbiotic: Anita Brookner, *Spectator*, 25 July 1987.

Blunt was one of the most: Wright, *Spycatcher*, pp. 224–5.

457   exchanging Christmas cards: N. West interview.

Tess did not cry: Wright, *Spycatcher*, p. 216.

devastating, crushing: Rothschild, *Random Variables*, pp. 203–5.

458 **Putlitz had definitely been:** Wright, *Spycatcher*, p. 257.

Tom Wylie had been: ibid., p. 251.

Gibby's spy: ibid., p. 220.

I suppose you're right: ibid., p. 259.

All I can say: ibid., p. 264.

Arthur Martin observed: Arthur Martin interviewed by Penrose and Freeman, 1985.

459 **the first hard source:** Wright, *Spycatcher*, p. 264.

460 **she was a neurotic:** ibid.

told Anita Brookner: ibid.

461 **Not long after:** ibid., p. 266.

462 **Whether Blunt felt:** Pincher, *Too Secret, Too Long*, p. 383.

she would have done anything for Blunt: J. Hart, letter to the author, 27 May 1999.

something along the lines of: M. Hirst interview.

463 **There was no connection:** Smith, *Celebration*, p. 192.

All big eyes: ibid., p. 194.

One of the best things: *Sunday Times*, 19 Mar. 1967.

464 **I do not much believe:** John Le Carré, introduction to David Leitch et al., *Philby: The Spy Who Betrayed a Generation* (London: André Deutsch, 1968), p. 36.

Media briefers began: see Brown, *Treason in the Blood*, p. 573.

18. Traitor

465 **major abdominal surgery:** Operation, 15 Aug. 1972, Blunt medical records, in the possession of the author.

whispered Latin inscriptions: Barbara Robertson interview.

On another occasion: S. J. Flower interview.

466 **simply disgusting:** W. Blunt, *Married*, p. 283.

I find it almost impossible: AB to M. Wittkower, 23 July 1972, Wittkower papers, Columbia University Library.

his posture was exactly like that: N. Penny interview.

467 **in which the essentially Baroque:** A. Blunt, *Borromini*, p. 24.

melancholy, nervous and uncompromising: ibid., p. 21.

the great anarchist of architecture: ibid., pp. 219–20.

It was as if: L. Stainton interview.

468 **Blunt above all turned:** editorial, *Burlington Magazine*, Sept. 1974.

References

We are going to watch: O. Millar interview.

had failed to thank: ibid.

to supplement his pension: Blunt's pension reduced his annual income from £7,600 to a little under £1,000. See Blunt personal file, Registry papers, CI.

philosophic forbearance: *Charleston Newsletter*, no. 17, Dec. 1986.

469   **Proctor recommended:** B. Proctor interview.

      We can now face: R. Mackworth-Young, to AB, 28 Nov. 1978, RA/LIB.

470   **Rubinstein advised against it:** M. Rubinstein interview.

      I had always considered: W. Blunt, *Slow*, p. 243.

      Ellis Waterhouse set aside: Lady Waterhouse, letter to the author, 23 Apr. 1995.

472   **He told me that Mrs Thatcher:** M. Rubinstein interview.

473   **And it damn well:** Penrose and Freeman, *Conspiracy*, p. 506.

      Got you, you swine: J. Rees, *Looking*, p. 253.

      a 'lucky break': Alan Clark, *Diaries: Into Politics* (London: Weidenfeld & Nicolson, 2000), p. 136.

      Anyone here called: J. Craxton interview.

474   **In Tuscany:** J. Fleming interview.

      In Rome, Eric Hebborn: E. Hebborn interview.

      His bed was placed under police guard: J. Rees, *Looking*, p. 254.

      their usefulness is long since over: A. Boyle, *News at Ten*, 15 Nov. 1979, ITV.

475   **pansy aesthete:** M. Muggeridge, *Evening Standard* (London), 19 Nov. 1979.

      treacherous Communist poof: J. Junor, *Daily Express*, 19 Nov. 1979.

      a hopeless officer: *Daily Telegraph*, 17 Nov. 1979.

      Jean Gimpel speculated: *The Times*, 29 Nov. 1979.

      Another series: see, for example, *Daily Telegraph*, 17 Nov. 1979 and *Now!* 23 Nov. 1979.

      which he claimed dated back: Penrose and Freeman, *Conspiracy*, pp. 310–11.

476   **If Anthony wash:** ibid.

      Private Eye: ibid., p. 485.

      old friend Peter Montgomery: ibid., p. 414

      tended to inspire awe: C. Wright, *News at Ten*, 15 Nov. 1979, ITV.

      he was ... quite openly: *Daily Mail*, 19 Nov. 1979.

  n.   **an old boy network:** *Now* magazine, Dublin, Apr. 1990.

  n.   **links through Montgomery with Kincora:** Moore, *Kincora*, p. 90.

477   **weaken moderate Right-wing Resistance:** *Sunday Telegraph*, 18 Nov. 1979.

      Can anyone hear: F. King, letter, *The Times*, 20 Nov. 1979.

References

He and Gaskin were in hiding: J. Golding interview, July 1994.

478 moral blindness: B. Levin, *The Times*, 20 Nov. 1979.
not [to] be so silly: R. Coope interview.
My function: *The Times*, 19 Nov. 1979.
the root and branch: *Observer*, 18 Nov. 1979.

479 to break his cover: *Daily Mail*, 19 Nov. 1979.
furious with Mrs Thatcher: *Daily Telegraph*, 19 Nov. 1979.
Though as I say: AB to Jacob Rothschild, Colnaghi's, 3 Aug. 1971, AFB papers, vol. 500, CI.
a practical, dogsbody-kind of friend: *Sunday Express*, 18 Nov. 1979.

480 Quite frankly: *The Times*, 21 Nov. 1979.
recognized Joll's voice: J. Golding interview, July 1994.

481 Heath either: M. Rubinstein interview.
the spy with no shame: *Daily Mail*, 21 Nov. 1979.
one of the most outrageous: *Now!*, 23 Nov. 1979.
talking of his 'condescension': Steiner, 'The Cleric of Treason'.
Professor Blunt would not have been offered: *Daily Express*, 21 Nov. 1979.

482 nothing prejudicial to national security: *Hansard*, 15 Nov. 1979, col. 320.
In a parliamentary debate: ibid., 21 Nov. 1979, cols. 402–520.

483 Blunt would make jokes: E. Hasloch interview.
booed and slow-clapped: *Private Eye*, 29 Feb. 1980.
a barman refused to serve him: R. Verdi interview.
Now and again: E. Hasloch, R. Verdi interviews.
his apparent calm left him: Sidney Hutchinson (former secretary of the Royal Academy) interview.
I've been like Elijah: D. Bindman interview.

484 Ellis Waterhouse at first refused: reaction to Blunt from Waterhouse and Crossthwaite: H. Capes, M. Kitson and J. Golding interviews.

485 You betrayed me: R. Verdi interview.
royal mission to Germany: *Sunday Times*, 25 Nov. 1979.
Lovely day, isn't it?: confidential source.

486 a long shadow: *Observer*, Jan. 1980.
taken aback by the vehemence: Marni Hodgkin, Oct. 1994.
to avoid the Institute: M. Kitson interview.
A much-mooted letter: J. Shearman interview.

487 Courtauld staff had been asked: P. Lasko memo, 16 Nov. 1979, Registry papers, CI: 'The Chairman of the Management Committee and I feel most strongly that it would be inappropriate, and not in the best interests of our Institute, for any member of staff to speak to the press or television for the time being.'
Blunt had authenticated as a Poussin: J. Craxton interview.

References

emeritus professorship: *Guardian*, 22 Jan. 1980.
out for a breath of air: *Evening Standard* (London), 12 Feb. 1980.
Traitor's flatmate: ibid.
The evening before: H. Capes interview.

488 managed to smuggle himself: Richardson, *Sorcerer's Apprentice*, p. 154.
Blunt wrote angrily to deny it: AB letter to *Observer*, 20 Jan. 1980.
'I think', he told Rosamond Lehmann: Penrose and Freeman, *Conspiracy*, p. 523.

489 for the stoical pride: B. Proctor, unpublished memoir.
Peter Wright's later claims: Wright, *Spycatcher*, p. 264.
He was old and worn: Quentin Bell, *Elders and Betters* (London: John Murray, 1995), p. 211.

490 Now that there is a lull: AB to E. Penning Rowsell, 3 May 1980, in the possession of Penning-Rowsell.

491 We met, we sat together: Margot Wittkower interview transcript, Interviews with Art Historians, GRI, Research Library 94109.

492 A. J. P. Taylor wrote: Dover, *Marginal Comment*, p. 215.
A letter sent: ibid.
Britain's Academy of Cowards: *Daily Mail*, 8 Aug. 1980.
a secret deal with Blunt: Prof. I. Christie to Adam Sisman (biographer of A. J. P. Taylor), Nov. 1992.
healing the wounds: Dover, *Marginal Comment*, pp. 216–17.
Blunt took two days: statement in *The Times*, 19 Aug. 1980.

493 always a soft character: A. J. P. Taylor, *A Personal History* (London: Hamish Hamilton, 1983), pp. 270–1.
special relationship: Adam Sisman, *A. J. P. Taylor: A Biography* (London: Sinclair-Stevenson, 1994), p. 392.
absorbingly interesting: Dover, *Marginal Comment*, pp. 212–20.
set about accusing themselves: see Ian Christie, 'A Confusion of Fellows': *Encounter*, Oct. 1980.
Less intellectual people: Norman Gash, *Policy Review*, winter 1981.
the scholar absolute: Steiner, 'The Cleric of Treason'.

 n. later enquired of the secretary: A. Sisman, *A. J. P. Taylor: A Biography* (London: Sinclair-Stevenson, 1994), p. 393.

494 one last crack at him: B. Penrose interview.
The cost of altering: *Daily Express*, 27 Oct. 1980.
reiterating his claims: Christopher Wright, *The Art of the Forger* (Gordon Fraser, 1984).
Private Eye gave space: see for instance 'Merde Most Foul', *Private Eye*, 27 Sept. 1984.

495 inconclusive, even disorderly: B. Sewell, foreword to Anthony Blunt, *Nicolas Poussin* (London: Pallas Athene reprint, 1995), p. xiii.

References

The painting turned out: B. Sewell, *The Late Show*, 23 Jan. 1995, BBC2.

496 **spreading chest pains:** Blunt medical records, 9 Dec. 1980, in the possession of the author.

Emotional upset yesterday: ibid., 5 Oct. 1981, in the possession of the author.

gave him the manuscript: J. Merz, letters to the author, 29 Oct. and 19 Nov. 1994.

a list of little bequests: J. Golding interview, Sept. 1994.

about to make a phone call: ibid.

Blunt the high-class spy: *Sunday Times*, 27 Mar. 1983.

497 **surprisingly generous testimony:** ibid.

I am sorry: Penrose and Freeman, *Conspiracy*, p. 534.

Godfrey Barker attacked the 'myth': G. Barker, *Daily Telegraph*, 4 Apr. 1983.

***Private Eye* printed a story:** 'Merde Most Foul', *Private Eye*, 27 Sept. 1984.

498 **On a warm July day in 1988:** 27 July 1988.

This possibility: *Sunday Telegraph*, 25 Oct. 1983.

of the character and quality of yours: The Earl of Gowrie, Thomas Gibson Fine Art Ltd, to AB, 18 Oct. 1976, AFB papers, vol. 497, CI.

Bibliography and Sources

Books and Articles

Listed here are books and articles referred to in the notes which have not been fully cited there, plus a number of useful books not directly quoted from. I have made no attempt to give a full bibliography of Blunt's works, but have listed those which have been most useful in the writing of this biography. A full bibliography to 1967 can be found in Michael Kitson and John Shearman, eds., Studies in Renaissance and Baroque Art presented to Anthony Blunt on his 60th Birthday *(London: Phaidon, 1967).*

Adams, H. Pearl, *Paris Sees it Through 1914–1918* (London: Hodder & Stoughton, 1929)

Ades, Dawn, et al., *Art and Power: Europe under the Dictators 1930–45* (London: Hayward Gallery, 1995)

Andrew, Christopher M., *Secret Service: The Making of the British Intelligence Community* (London: Heinemann, 1985)

Andrew, Christopher M., and Gordievsky, Oleg, *KGB: The Inside Story* (London: Hodder & Stoughton, 1990)

Andrew, Christopher M., and Mitrokhin, Vasili, *The Mitrokhin Archive* (London: Allen Lane, 1999)

Annan, Noel, 'Et Tu Anthony', *New York Review of Books*, 22 Oct. 1987
– *Our Age* (London: Weidenfeld and Nicolson, 1990)
– 'The Fabulous Five', *New York Review of Books*, 12 Jan. 1995.

Auden, W. H., *The English Auden*, ed. Edward Mendelson (London: Faber, 1977)

Auden, W. H., and MacNeice, Louis, *Letters from Iceland* (London: Faber, 1937)

Bell, Clive, *Art* (London: Chatto & Windus, 1914)

Betjeman, John, *Summoned by Bells* (London: John Murray, 1960)

Blunt, A. S. V., *R. F. L. Blunt: Bishop of Hull* (London: Macmillan, 1913)

Bibliography and Sources

Blunt, Anthony, *Art and Architecture in France: 1500–1700* (London: Pelican, 1953)

– 'Art under Capitalism and Socialism' in C. Day-Lewis, ed., *The Mind in Chains* (London: Frederick Muller, 1937)

– 'Art and Morality', *The Heretick*, June 1924

– *The Art of William Blake* (New York: Columbia University Press, 1959)

– *Artistic Theory in Italy, 1450–1600* (Oxford: Clarendon Press, 1940)

– 'Blake's Pictorial Imagination', *Journal of the Warburg and Courtauld Institutes*, 1943

– 'From Bloomsbury to Marxism', *Studio International*, Nov. 1973

– *Borromini* (London: Allen Lane, 1979)

– 'De Cubismo', *The Marlburian*, 23 Apr. 1926

– *François Mansart* (London: Warburg Institute, 1941)

– *Guernica* (London: Oxford University Press, 1969)

– 'The Heroic and the Ideal Landscapes of Nicolas Poussin,' *Journal of the Warburg and Courtauld Institutes*, 1944

– *The Nation's Pictures* (with Margaret Whinney) (London: Chatto & Windus, 1950)

– *Neapolitan Baroque and Rococo Architecture* (London: Zwemmer, 1975)

– *Nicolas Poussin* (London: Phaidon, 1967)

– *The Paintings of Nicolas Poussin: A Critical Catalogue* (London: Phaidon, 1966)

– *Philibert de l'Orme* (London: Zwemmer, 1958)

– *Picasso: The Formative Years* (with Phoebe Pool) (London: Studio Books, 1962)

– 'Poussin Studies XI', *Burlington Magazine*, Sept. 1960

– 'Poussin's Development: Questions of Method', *Burlington Magazine*, July 1960

– 'Poussin's Notes on Painting,' *Journal of the Warburg Institute*, 1938

– 'Rationalist and Anti-Rationalist Art', *Left Review*, July 1936

– 'The "Realism" Quarrel', *Left Review*, Apr. 1937

– *Seurat* (London: Phaidon, 1965)

– 'Some Aspects of Modern Art,' *The Heretick*, Mar. 1924

(See also Blunt's art reviews in *The Spectator*, 1932–8.)

Blunt, Wilfrid, *Married to a Single Life* (Wilton, Wilts.: Michael Russell, 1983)

– *Slow on the Feather* (Wilton, Wilts.: Michael Russell, 1987)

Borovik, Genrikh, *The Philby Files* (London: Little, Brown, 1994)

Bower, Tom, *The Perfect English Spy* (London: Heinemann, 1995)

Boyle, Andrew, *The Climate of Treason* (London: Hutchinson, 1979)

Brendon, Piers, *The Dark Valley: A Panorama of the 1930s* (London: Cape, 2000)

Brentall, H. C., and Kempson, E. G. H., *Marlborough College: The First One*

Bibliography and Sources

Hundred Years, 1843–1943 (privately printed by W. A. Lewis at Cambridge University Press, 1943)

Bristow, Desmond, *A Game of Moles* (London: Little, Brown, 1993)

Brophy, Brigid, *The Finishing Touch* (London: Gay Men's Press, 1987)

Brown, Anthony Cave, *Treason in the Blood: St John Philby, Kim Philby and the Spy Case of the Century* (London: Robert Hale, 1995)

Cairncross, John, *The Enigma Spy* (London: Century, 1997)

Carpenter, Humphrey, *W. H. Auden: A Biography* (London: Allen & Unwin, 1981)

Caute, David, *The Fellow Travellers* (London: Weidenfeld & Nicolson, 1973)

Cecil, Robert, *A Divided Life: A Biography of Donald Maclean* (London: Bodley Head, 1988)

Clark, Jon, et al., eds., *Culture and Crisis in Britain in the Thirties* (London: Lawrence & Wishart, 1979)

Clark, Kenneth, *Another Part of the Wood* (London: John Murray, 1974)

Connolly, Cyril, *The Missing Diplomats* (London: Queen Anne Press, 1952)

Conquest, Robert, *The Great Terror; A Reassessment* (London: Pimlico, 1990)
 – *Stalin, Breaker of Nations* (London: Viking, 1991)

'Conversation Piece: An Interview with Anthony Blunt', *The Marlburian*, Lent Term, 1966

Costello, John, *Mask of Treachery* (London: Collins, 1987)

Costello, John, and Tsarev, Oleg, *Deadly Illusions* (London: Century, 1993)

Cradock, Percy, ed., *Recollections of the Cambridge Union 1815–1939* (Cambridge: Bowes & Bowes, 1953)

Cunningham, Valentine, ed., *Spanish Front: Writers on the Civil War* (Oxford: Oxford University Press, 1986)

Davenport-Hines, Richard, *Auden* (London: Heinemann, 1995)

Day-Lewis, C., *The Buried Day* (London: Chatto & Windus, 1960)

Deacon, Richard, *The Cambridge Apostles* (London: Robert Royce, 1985)

Dover, Kenneth, *Marginal Comment: A Memoir* (London: Duckworth, 1994)

Driberg, Tom, *Guy Burgess: A Portrait with Background* (London: Weidenfeld & Nicolson, 1956)

Edwards, Elizabeth, *A History of Bournemouth* (Chichester: Phillimore, 1981)

Ferns, H. S., *Reading from Right to Left* (Toronto: University of Toronto Press, 1983)

Gathorne-Hardy, Jonathan, *The Public School Phenomenon* (London: Hodder & Stoughton, 1977)

Bibliography and Sources

Gladwyn, Cynthia, *The Paris Embassy* (London: Collins, 1976)

Glees, Anthony, *The Secrets of the Service* (London: Cape, 1987)

Haig, Alan, *The Victorian Clergy* (London: Croom Helm, 1984)

Harrison, Charles, *English Art and Modernism* (London: Allen Lane, 1981)

Hebborn, Eric, *Drawn to Trouble* (Edinburgh: Mainstream, 1991)

Hewison, Robert, *Under Seige: Literary Life 1939–45* (London: Weidenfeld & Nicolson, 1977)

Hillier, Bevis, *Young Betjeman* (London: John Murray, 1988)

Hinde, Thomas, *Paths of Progress: A History of Marlborough College* (London: James & James, 1992)

Hodgkin, Alan, *Chance and Design* (Cambridge: Cambridge University Press, 1992)

Holroyd, Michael, *Lytton Strachey* (London: Chatto & Windus, rev. edn 1994)

Howarth, T. E. B., *Cambridge Between the Wars* (London: Collins, 1978)

Hyde, Douglas, *I Believed* (London: Heinemann, 1951)

Jenkins, Roy, *A Life at the Centre* (London: Macmillan, 1991)

Kidson, Peter, 'The Recent Transformation of Art History', Morley College special guest lecture in honour of Andrew Martindale, 10 Nov. 1995, Courtauld Institute

Kiernan, V. G., 'On Treason', *London Review of Books*, 25 June 1987

King, Francis, *Yesterday Came Suddenly* (London: Constable, 1993)

Koch, Stephen, *Double Lives* (London: HarperCollins, 1995)

Laughton, Bruce, *The Euston Road School* (Aldershot: Scolar Press, 1986)

Lee, Arthur, *A Good Innings*, ed. Alan Clark (London: John Murray, 1974)

Lehmann, John, *In the Purely Pagan Sense* (London: Blond & Briggs, 1976)

– *The Whispering Gallery* (London: Longman, 1955)

Longford, Elizabeth, *Pilgrimage of Passion: The Life of Wilfrid Scawen Blunt* (London: Weidenfeld & Nicolson, 1979)

MacNeice, Louis, *Autumn Journal* (London: Faber, 1939)

– *Roundabout Way* (by 'Louis Malone') (London: Putnam, 1932)

– *The Strings are False* (London: Faber, 1965)

Mahon, Denis, 'A Plea for Poussin as a Painter', *Walter Friedlaender zum 90* (Berlin: Walter de Gruyler and Co., 1965)

– 'Poussin's Early Development: An Alternative Hypothesis', *Burlington Magazine*, July 1960

– 'Poussiniana', *Gazette des Beaux-Arts*, July–Aug. 1962

Mayhew, Christopher, *Time to Explain* (London: Hutchinson, 1987)

Bibliography and Sources

Millar, Oliver, *The Queen's Pictures* (London: Chancellor Press, 1984)

Miller, Joan, *One Girl's War* (Dingle, Co. Kerry: Brandon, 1986)

Modin, Yuri, *My Five Cambridge Friends* (London: Headline, 1994)

Moore, Chris, *The Kincora Scandal* (Dublin: Marino Books, 1996)

Nichols, Beverley, *The Unforgiving Minute* (London: W. H. Allen, 1978)

Orlov, Alexander, *The Secret History of Stalin's Crimes* (New York: Random House, 1953)

Penrose, Barrie, and Freeman, Simon, *Conspiracy of Silence* (London: Grafton, 1986)

Philby, Kim, *My Silent War* (London: Grafton, new edn 1989)

Pincher, H. Chapman, *Their Trade is Treachery* (London: Sidgwick & Jackson, 1981)

– *Too Secret, Too Long* (London: Sidgwick & Jackson, 1984)

Pope-Hennessy, John, *Learning to Look* (London: Heinemann, 1991)

Poretsky, Elisabeth, *Our Own People* (London: Oxford University Press, 1969)

Powell, Anthony, *Journals 1982–86* (London: Heinemann, 1997)

Rees, Goronwy, *A Chapter of Accidents* (London: Chatto & Windus, 1972)

Rees, Jenny, *Looking for Mr Nobody* (London: Weidenfeld & Nicolson, 1994)

Richardson, John, *The Sorcerer's Apprentice* (London: Cape, 1999)

Rothschild, Victor, *Random Variables* (London: Collins, 1984)

Russell, Anthony, *The Clerical Profession* (London: SPCK, 1980)

Rycroft, Charles, 'Memoirs of an Old Bolshevik' in *Psychoanalysis and Beyond* (London: Hogarth Press, 1985)

Secrest, Meryle, *Kenneth Clark* (London: Weidenfeld & Nicolson, 1984)

Skidelsky, Robert, *John Maynard Keynes: The Economist as Saviour, 1920–1937* (London: Macmillan, 1992)

– *John Maynard Keynes: Hopes Betrayed, 1883–1920* (London: Macmillan, 1983)

Sloan, Pat, ed., *John Cornford: A Memoir* (London: Cape, 1938)

Smith, Graham, *Celebration* (London: Mainstream, 1996)

Spender, Stephen, *World Within World* (London: Faber, 1977)

Stallworthy, Jon, *Louis MacNeice* (London: Faber, 1995)

Stansky, Peter, and Abrahams, William, *Journey to the Frontier* (London: Constable, 1966)

Steiner, George, 'The Cleric of Treason,' *The New Yorker*, 8 Dec. 1980, reprinted in *George Steiner: A Reader* (London: Penguin, 1984)

Bibliography and Sources

Steiner, Wendy, 'Scholarship and its Afflictions', *London Review of Books*, 30 Mar. 1989

Straight, Michael, *After Long Silence* (London: Collins, 1983)

Sudaplatov, Pavel, *Special Tasks* (London: Little, Brown, 1994)

Sutherland, Douglas, and Purdy, Anthony, *The Fourth Man* (London: Arrow, 1980)

Symons, Julian, *The Thirties: A Dream Revolved* (London: Cresset Press, 1960)

Trevor-Roper, Hugh, *The Philby Affair* (London: William Kimber, 1968)

Tsarev, Oleg, and Costello, John, *Deadly Illusions* (London: Century, 1993)

Waterhouse, Ellis, 'Preface' in Michael Kitson and John Shearman, eds., *Studies in Renaissance and Baroque Art presented to Anthony Blunt on his 60th Birthday* (London: Phaidon, 1967)

Weintraub, Stanley, *The Last Great Cause: Writers and the Spanish Civil War* (London: W. H. Allen, 1968)

West, Nigel, *MI5: British Security Service Operations: 1906–45* (London: Bodley Head, 1981)

 – *Seven Spies Who Changed the World* (London: Secker & Warburg, 1991)

 – *Venona: The Greatest Secret of the Cold War* (London: HarperCollins, 1999)

West, Nigel, and Tsarev, Oleg, *The Crown Jewels* (London: HarperCollins, 1998)

Wood, Neil, *Communism and British Intellectuals* (London: Gollancz, 1959)

Worsley, T. C., *Fellow Travellers* (London: London Magazine Editions, 1971)

 – *Flannelled Fool* (London: Alan Ross, 1965)

Wright, Peter, *Spycatcher* (Victoria: Heinemann Australia, 1987)

Papers and Collections

Anthony Blunt's correspondence in the archives of the Warburg Institute, London

Anthony Blunt's file at the BBC Written Archives, Caversham

Anthony Blunt's reviews and articles in *The Spectator*, 1932–8

Courtauld Institute/Anthony Frederick Blunt papers at the Courtauld Institute, London

Courtauld Institute tapes: interviews recorded in 1980 by Lillian Gurry, librarian of the Courtauld Institute, on the early days of the Institute

Bibliography and Sources

Edgar Wind papers at the Bodleian Library, Oxford

Getty Research Institute, Los Angeles, CA
Guy Burgess's letters to Peter Pollock, in the possession of Peter Pollock

'Interviews with Art Historians' recorded and transcribed by the Getty Research
Institute, Los Angeles

King's College literary archive, Cambridge, including Louis MacNeice's letters
to Anthony Blunt, and the Charleston and Bell papers

Louis MacNeice's papers at the Bodleian Library, Oxford

Royal Archives, Windsor Castle

Tate Gallery Archives, including Kenneth Clark papers and William Coldstream
papers, London

Interviews

Professor Christopher Andrew (Sept. 1996), Lord Annan (Oct. 1994), Jack Baer
(July 1996), Olivier and Quentin Bell (July 1994), Sir Isaiah Berlin (Aug. 1994),
David Bindman (Jan. 1996), John Blamey (Feb. 1996), Tom Bower (Sept. 1996),
Sir Alan Bowness (Mar. and May 1996), Helen Braham (June 1995), Desmond
Bristow (Aug. 1996), Anita Brookner (July 1995), Howard Capes (July 1994),
Robin Chancellor (Mar. 1995), Lord Charteris (June 1995), Monique Chatenet
(May 1997), Professor Andrew Ciechanowiecki (Mar. 2000), Thomas Cocke
(Dec. 1995), Rosalys Coope (Aug. 1995), Professor Joseph Connors (Jan. 1996),
John Craxton (Sept. 1995), Norah David (Feb. 1995), His Grace the Duke of
Devonshire (Oct. 1995), The Dowager Lady Egremont (Nov. 1995), Caroline
Elam (Sept. 1995), Charles Elwell (Oct. 1996), Gavin Ewart (May 1995), Denis
Farr (June 1995), Eric Fernie (Jan. 1996), John Fleming (Sept. 1994), Sibylla
Jane Flower (June 1995), Sir Edward Ford (June 1995), Kenneth Garlick (July
1995), John Golding (July, Aug. and Sept. 1994), Sir Ernst Gombrich (July
1994), St John Gore (July 1995), Michael Grant (May 1995), Rosamund Griffin
(Nov. 1995), Sir Stuart Hampshire (Aug. 1994), Jenifer Hart (May 1999),
Francis Haskell (Nov. 1994), Elizabeth Hasloch (May 1995), Alethea Hayter
(Sept. 1996), Eric Hebborn (Sept. 1994), Jackie Hewit (Nov. 1995), Derek Hill
(July 1995), Baronness Hilton (Nov. 1994), Michael Hirst (May 1995), Clive
Hislop (July 1994), Hugh Honour (Sept. 1994), Lord Hunt (Jan. 1999), Sidney

Bibliography and Sources

Hutchinson (Oct. 1995), Michael Jaffe (June 1995), Stephen Rees Jones (Dec. 1994), Martha Kelleher (Jan. 1996), Peter Kidson (May 1995), Francis King (Feb. 1995), Dick Kingzett (Feb. 1995), Michael Kitson (Aug. 1994), Raymond Klibanksy (Mar. 1995), Richard Krautheimer (Sept. 1994), Michel Laclotte (May 1997), Alistair Laing (Feb. 1996), James Lees-Milne (Mar. 1995), Sir Michael Levey (July 1994), Lesley Lewis (July 1996), Andrew Lownie (Mar. 1999), Alastair MacDonald (Oct. 1994), Neil MacGregor (Feb. 1996), Polly Maguire (Jan. 1995), Charles Madge (Mar. 1995), Sir Denis Mahon (July 1995), Hugh Massingberd (Jan. 1995), Anne Marie Meyer (July 1995), Leonard Miall (Feb. 1996), Sir Oliver Millar (May 1995), T. D. F. Money (Oct. 1994), Edwin Mullins (July 1995), Tom Mynors (Oct. 1994), Erica O'Donnell (May 1995), Edward Penning-Rowsell (Mar. 1995), Nicholas Penny (Mar. 1995), Barrie Penrose (July 1996), Sir Edward Playfair (June 1995), Peter Pollock (Oct. 1999), Barbara Proctor (Aug. 1994), Kathleen Raine (Feb. 1995), John Richardson (June 1995), Barbara Robertson (June 1995), Pierre Rosenberg (May 1997), Mark Roskill (Jan. 1988), Miriam Rothschild (Aug. 1995), Tess Rothschild (Oct. 1994), Michael Rubinstein (Mar. 1995), John Russell (Nov. 1997), Charles Rycroft (July 1995), Dadie Rylands (Aug. 1994), Aydua Scott-Elliot (Oct. 1995), John Shearman (Jan. 1996), Brian Simon (Mar. and July 1995), Peter Smith (May 1997), Lindsay Stainton (July 1996), Jon Stallworthy (Nov. 1994), John Steer (May 1995), Julian Stock (Sept. 1994), Michael Straight (Apr. 1996), Michael Parke Taylor (Jan. 1996), Roddy Thesiger (July 1996), David Thomson (Nov. 1995), Richard Verdi (June 1995), Giles Waterfield (Mar. 1995), Nigel West (Oct. 1996), John White (Mar. 1995), Mary Whiteley (Nov. 1995), Sarah Whitfield (Mar. 2000), Frank Whitford (June 1996), Simon Wilson (July 1995), Margaret Wind (July 1995), Christopher Wright (Oct. 1995), Richard Wollheim (Aug. 1994), Dikker Worcester (Nov. 1995), George Zarnecki (Mar. 1995)

Index

Index

Index

Index

Index

Index

Boulogne 248
Bournemouth 1, 7
Bowen, Elizabeth 232
  The Death of the Heart 232
Bower, Tom 256, 399
Bowle, John 26, 38–9
Bowness, Alan 363, 368, 415, 416, 437, 461, 483–4
Bowra, Maurice 52, 87, 232
Boyle, Andrew 84, 469, 474, 479, 481, 486
  The Climate of Treason 84, 347, 470–1, 474*n*
Braithwaite, Richard 85
Brancusi, Constantine 138
Braque, Georges 89
Brealey, John 376
Brickendonbury Hall 252
Brieger, Peter 328
Briggs, M. S., *In the Heel of Italy* 104
Bristow, Desmond 255–6, 257, 284, 455
British Academy 432, 491–3
British Council 329, 333, 397
  Fine Arts Committee 328
British Expeditionary Force 242, 245, 386, 475
British Intelligence xv, 154, 298, 337, 445, 463, 474
  see also MI5; MI6
British Leyland 482
British Library, London 498
British Museum, London 296, 393, 428
'British Painting 1740–1840' (exhibition) 333
British Union of Fascists 260, 284
Britten, Benjamin 122, 237
Brocklebank, Tom 186
Brodsky, Izaak 137
Bronowski, Jacob 65, 75
Brooke, Henry 447
Brooke, Rupert 1
Brookner, Anita 361, 367, 368, 372–3, 456, 458, 460–1, 479, 487
Brophy, Brigid 371, 375, 385, 390
  The Finishing Touch xviii, 371, 372
Brown, Tina 494
Browning, Oscar 2
Browning, Robert 3
Bruce Lockhart, Robert 153–4, 158, 322*n*
Die Brücke 226
Brueghel, Pieter 34, 39, 41, 67, 69
  Hunters in the Snow 39
Brunswick, Duke of 315–16
Bryans, Robin (alias Robert Harbinson) 475–6
Buchman, Frank 107

Buchtal, Hugo 279
Buckingham, George Villiers 1st Duke of 221
Buckingham Palace, London 306, 310–11, 321, 358, 387
Budapest 127
  Museum of Fine Art 362
Budberg, Baroness Moura 322*n*
Buenos Aires 348–9
Bukharin, Nikolai 124
Burgess, Guy
  on AB 324, 335–6
  and AB's *Artistic Theory in Italy* 260–1, 402, 437, 438
  AB's gossip about 457
  and AB's work for BBC 220, 297
  and Apostles 192–3
  on Julian Bell 201
  book by Douglas Sutherland about 440
  and Cairncross 188–90, 486
  code names 161, 180, 302, 319
  and Deutsch 156*n*, 161
  dislike of 'Baker' 334
  disturbing public behaviour 337, 441
  on drink 299
  drunkenness 102, 441
  and FBI 444
  on Jackie Hewit 277, 324
  homosexuality 77, 80, 148, 161, 180, 348
  letters to Pollock 309–10, 315, 324
  MacNeice on 96, 148
  and Marxism/Communism 105, 110, 112–13, 120–1, 123–4, 161–2
  and Modin 288
  and Nazi–Soviet Pact 241–2
  and Philby 157, 159, 160, 235, 252, 265
  portrayed in novel 406
  Powell on 244
  and Proctor 244
  and Rees 114, 124, 231–4, 236, 241–2, 292, 340–1, 403–5, 469
  relationship with Pollock 324
  Soviet distrust of 289–94, 297–8
  in Soviet Union 124
  and Straight 183
  White on 275
  and White Paper (1955) 401
  Forgotten Anniversaries (BBC series) 220

Life
  at Cambridge 77–82, 102–3
  leaves Cambridge 130
  approaches AB 160–5
  at BBC 163, 164, 252
  and Modin 250

570

Index

Index

Index

Index

Index

Index

Index

Index

Index

Index

Index

MI5 (*cont.*)
  and defection of Burgess and Maclean
    349, 403–4
  directors 356–7
  'Double-Cross' system 254, 257, 273,
    284, 288, 292, 301
  embarrassed by information on moles
    445–8
  and embassies 281
  'F' Division 260
  gossip about AB at 439, 444
  and Jenifer Hart 459–60
  Howard at 282
  information about AB supplied by Straight
    443–4
  interrogation of AB 451–63, 482
  and Klugmann 318–19
  lack of suspicion of AB and other agents
    336, 345
  and Maclean 338
  offer of immunity to AB 439, 451–4
  post-war reorganization 319
  and Profumo affair 446
  and Radcliffe report 399
  and Straight 192
  suspected of plant at Courtauld 437
  sympathy for Soviet Union at 276
  Ultra 273, 276, 286, 338
  and John Vassall 447
  and Wright 453–4
  see also Blunt, Anthony Frederick, Life,
    work for MI5; interrogation by MI5
MI6 (SIS, Special Intelligence Service)
  251–60
  AB and 274, 289, 357
  George Blake and 445, 447
  Burgess and 236, 252, 335
  Footman and 234, 236
  Philby and 338, 445, 463
  and Profumo affair 446
  and Radcliffe report 399
  Section D (Joint Broadcasting Committee)
    236, 252
  Special Operations Executive (SOE) 252
  White and 251, 256
MI14 286
Miall, Leonard 197
Michelangelo 210, 220, 261, 359, 361, 368,
  414
'Mike' (ex-guardsman) 391
Military Intelligence 239, 242, 245
Millar, Sir Oliver 305, 307, 311, 374, 376,
  484
Miller, Bernard 340, 342, 343, 344
Miller, Joan 253, 276

Milton, John 48
Minley Manor, Hampshire 243–5
Minneapolis Institute of Arts 393
Minsk 275
Miró, Joan 95–6, 150, 204, 224
Mitchell, Julian, *Another Country* 470
Mitford (later Mosley), Diana 367
Mitford, Nancy 367–8
Mitrokhin archive 160
Modigliani, Amedeo 330
Modin, Yuri
  on AB 322, 336, 340, 352–3, 400
  as AB's contact 268, 278, 452
  and Burgess 324
  and conspiracy theory 288–9
  on Gorsky 268
  on Kreshin 280
  on Maclean 339–44
  My Five Cambridge Friends 250
Modrzhinskaya, Elena 291–2, 298, 301
Moholy-Nagy, László 94
Molotov, Vyacheslav 274
Money, T. D. F. 24, 27, 503*n*
Monte Carlo 102
Montgomery, Field Marshal Bernard 301
Montgomery, Peter 51–2, 58, 99, 265, 278,
  383–4, 469, 476
Montgomery Massingberd, Field Marshal Sir
  Archibald 51
Montgomery Massingberd, Hugh 52, 383–4
Monuments, Fine Arts and Archives
  (MFA&A) 297, 299–300, 316
Moore, Decima 12
Moore, G. E. 53, 62, 63
  Principia Ethica 53, 63
Moore, Henry 89, 129–30, 225*n*, 328*n*,
  330, 377, 416
Moral Rearmament 107
Morisot, Berthe 89
Morris, William 6
Morrison, Ian 82
Morshead, Owen 83, 296, 304–5, 308, 311,
  311–14, 318
Morshead, Paquita 305
Mortimer, Raymond 280
Moscow 126, 133–4, 135, 137, 153–4,
  186–7, 200, 356, 405
  Academy of Sciences 128*n*
  British Embassy 136
  First All-Union Congress of Soviet Writers
    126
  Hermitage 132, 136–7, 441
  Kremlin 135
  Lubianka 322
  Metro 133

Index

Index

Index

584

Index

Index

romanticism 128

Rome 114, 177, 297, 337, 374, 392, 393, 394, 418, 441, 465, 466, 474
  British Embassy 319
  British School 103, 104
  government archives 319
  Hassler Hotel 497
  Hertziana Institute 490, 496
  Poussin in 435
  St George's English church 490
  Sistine Chapel 220–1

Ronda 146

Roosevelt, F. D. 109, 186

Roosevelt, Theodore 85

Rose, Millicent 218–19

Rosenberg, Paul, gallery, Paris 35

Rosenberg, Pierre 385, 421, 424, 433, 434, 435

Rossetti, Geoffrey 69

Rothenstein, John 373

Rothschild, Dollie 378–9

Rothschild, James 378

Rothschild, Miriam 79, 99, 255, 342

Rothschild, Mrs 130, 162, 229

Rothschild, Tess see Mayor, Tess

Rothschild, Victor
  on AB 75, 270
  AB and xiii
  and AB's illness 299, 300
  Annan on 74
  and Apostles 63, 84–5
  and Bentinck Street flat 262–3
  buys Poussin *Rebecca* for AB 87–8
  at Cambridge 74–5, 78
  generosity 87–8
  gives party for AB 196–7
  and Barbara Hutchinson (first wife) 183, 253
  in Italy with AB 102
  left-wing views 130
  MacNeice and 148
  at MI5 253
  questioned by Wright 454
  recruits AB for MI5 250–1, 254
  and Rees newspaper article 404
  at Reform Club 257
  shocked by AB's exposure 457, 484
  and Soviet Union 276
  and Tess 118, 267, 322, 457
    see also Mayor, Tess
  under suspicion 457, 484, 486
  and Waddesdon Manor 378
  and Wright 454
  Random Variables 74

Rouault, Georges 30, 113–14

Royal Academy of Art, London 83, 89, 90, 125, 220, 306–7, 317, 375, 483, 494

Royal Albert Hall, London 219

Royal Automobile Club, London 341

Royal Collection 306–8, 327, 358, 376–7, 448, 450, 469–70, 479, 484

Royal Library, Windsor Castle 296, 469

Rubens, Peter Paul 221, 368

Rubinstein, Michael xiv, 469, 470, 472, 477, 480–2, 490

Runciman, Steven 78, 99, 121

Runnymede 310

Ruskin, John 15, 16, 92

Russell, Bertrand 62, 85, 182

Russell, Father Clement 284

Rutherford, Ernest 49

Ruthin Castle, Wales 299

Rutter, Frank 213

Rycroft, Charles 81, 111–12, 114, 118, 122, 124, 130, 132, 135, 139, 139–40, 186–7, 455–6n
  'Memoirs of an Old Bolshevik' 455n
    Rylands, George ('Dadie')
  on AB 53, 58
  and AB 383, 484
  AB writes to 116, 228, 247
  and Apostles 61
  at Bentinck Street 265
  on Burgess 79, 81
  Burgess and 78–9
  Burgess on 324
  circle at Cambridge 52–9, 73n, 105, 188
  on Barbara Hutchinson 183
  in Italy 102
  and Rosamond Lehmann 233
  and MacNeice 67
  and Peter Montgomery 51
  political apathy 130
  production of *Julius Caesar* 118
  and Rees 469
  on Victor Rothschild 75, 88
  and Lytton Strachey 71
  and Virginia Woolf 73

Ryle, Gilbert 253

Sackville-West, Edward 353–4

Sackville-West, Vita 228, 464

St Peter's school, Seaford, Sussex 14

Saint-Malo 342, 343

Salisbury, Lord 341

Sassoon, Sir Philip 34

Savernake Forest 40

Savoy Hotel, London 283

Saxl, Fritz

Index

Index

Index

Index